Self and Social Identity

Perspectives on Social Psychology

The four volumes in this series collect readings from the *Blackwell Handbooks of Social Psychology* and present them thematically. The results are course-friendly texts in key areas of social psychology – *Social Cognition, Self and Social Identity, Emotion and Motivation*, and *Applied Social Psychology*. Each volume provides a representative sample of exciting research and theory that is both comprehensive and current and cross-cuts the levels of analysis from intrapersonal to intergroup.

Social Cognition, edited by Marilynn B. Brewer and Miles Hewstone
Self and Social Identity, edited by Marilynn B. Brewer and Miles Hewstone
Applied Social Psychology, edited by Marilynn B. Brewer and Miles Hewstone
Emotion and Motivation, edited by Marilynn B. Brewer and Miles Hewstone

Preface

When the *Blackwell Handbooks of Social Psychology* project was conceived, we sought to go beyond a simple topical structure for the content of the volumes in order to reflect more closely the complex pattern of cross-cutting theoretical perspectives and research agendas that comprise social psychology as a dynamic enterprise. The idea we developed was to represent the discipline in a kind of matrix structure, crossing levels of analysis with topics, processes, and functions that recur at all of these levels in social psychological theory and research. Taking inspiration from Willem Doise's 1986 book, *Levels of Explanation in Social Psychology*, four levels of analysis – intrapersonal, interpersonal, intragroup, and intergroup – provided the basis for organizing the Handbook series into four volumes. The two co-editors responsible for developing each of these volumes selected content chapters on the basis of cross-cutting themes represented by basic social psychological processes of social cognition, attribution, social motivation, affect and emotion, social influence, social comparison, and self and identity.

The four-volume handbook that resulted from this organizational framework represents the collective efforts of two series editors, eight volume editors, and 191 contributing authors. The *Intraindividual Processes* volume, edited by Abraham Tesser and Norbert Schwarz, provides a comprehensive selection of work on social cognition, affect, and motivation which focuses on the individual as the unit of analysis. The *Interpersonal Processes* volume, edited by Garth Fletcher and Margaret Clark, also covers the cognition, affect, and motivation themes as they are played out in the context of close interpersonal relationships and dyadic exchanges. Again, in the volume on *Group Processes*, edited by Michael Hogg and Scott Tindale, the themes of cognition, affect, and motivation are well represented in work on collective behavior in small groups and social organizations. Finally, the volume on *Intergroup Processes*, edited by Rupert Brown and Samuel Gaertner, covers work that links cognitive, affective, and motivational processes to relationships between social groups and large collectives.

Across all four volumes and levels of analysis, the concepts of *self* and *identity* occupy a central position in social psychological theory and research. Because of the matrix structure of the handbooks, it is possible to draw from all four volumes to create a selection of readings on the social self that cross-cuts the levels of analysis from intrapersonal to intergroup. This book contains a set of such readings which we have selected for the purpose of providing a representative sampling of exciting research and theory in this area that is both comprehensive and current.

Marilynn Brewer and Miles Hewstone

Acknowledgments

The editor and publishers gratefully acknowledge the following for permission to reproduce copyright material:

Brown, Rupert & Gaertner, Sam (Eds.) (2001). *Blackwell Handbook of Social Psychology: Intergroup Processes*. Oxford: Blackwell Publishing (reprinted with permission.)

Fletcher, Garth J. O. & Clark, Margaret S. (Eds.) (2001). *Blackwell Handbook of Social Psychology: Interpersonal Processes*. Oxford: Blackwell Publishing (reprinted with permission.)

Hogg, Michael A. & Tindale, Scott (Eds.) (2001). *Blackwell Handbook of Social Psychology: Group Processes*. Oxford: Blackwell Publishing (reprinted with permission.)

Tesser, Abraham & Schwarz, Norbert (Eds.) (2001). *Blackwell Handbook of Social Psychology: Intraindividual Processes*. Oxford: Blackwell Publishing (reprinted with permission.)

The publishers apologize for any errors or omissions in the above list and would be grateful to be notified of any corrections that should be incorporated in the next edition or reprint of this book.

Introduction to this Volume

Within social psychology, the nature of "the self" has been studied from many different angles, including research on the nature of self-awareness and self-consciousness, knowledge about the self and the structure of the self-concept, the executive functions of the self as an agent of motivation and action, the origins and consequences of self-esteem, and the self as a product of interpersonal and cultural processes (Baumeister, 1998). A bit more circumscribed, the study of "identity" refers to the content of self-knowledge as it is represented to and by others. Identity represents the conceptual link between the individual and the society as a whole (Tajfel, 1981).

As the bridge between the psychology of the individual and the structure of social groups within which the self is embedded, the meaning of social identity has two faces (Brewer, 2001). On the one hand, social identity refers to those aspects of self-knowledge that are derived from membership in specific social groups, meaning identity that is located *within* the individual self-concept. In this usage, social identities are aspects of the self that have been particularly influenced by the fact of membership in specific social groups or categories and the shared socialization experiences that such membership implies. The emphasis here is on the *content* of identity, the acquisition of psychological traits, expectations, customs, beliefs, and ideologies that are associated with belonging to a particular social group or category. Identification refers to the centrality of a particular social group membership to the individual's sense of self and the meaning that is derived from that identity.

On the other side, social identity refers to the perception of self as an integral or interchangeable part of a larger group or social unit. This meaning of social identity is best captured by self-categorization theory, in which social identity is defined as a "depersonalized" sense of self entailing "a shift towards the perception of self as an interchangeable exemplar of some social category and away from the perception of self as a unique person" (Turner et al., 1987, p. 50). Thus, the two meanings of social identity are essentially the inverse of each other, reversing the nature of the part–whole relation. From one perspective, social identity is the group within the self; from the other perspective, it is the self within the group.

Although a great deal has been written on the structure and content of the self-concept at the individual level (for a review, see Baumeister, 1998), our focus in the present volume is on the *social self*, that is, the study of self and identity as these are embedded in interpersonal relationships and social group memberships. The readings reflect both meanings of social identity – how group memberships shape the content of the individual's self-concept, and how the sense of self is expanded as a consequence of identification with other individuals and the group as a whole. As these readings suggest, the study of the interplay between the individual self and collective selves is an arena of rich theory and research in social psychology.

We have organized the readings in this volume around two themes. The first is "self and identity," exploring the self as a product of interpersonal and group processes. The second theme is "group identities," and illustrates some of the phenomena associated with representing a group or a social category as a collective.

REFERENCES

Baumeister, R. F. (1998). The self. In D. Gilbert, S. Fiske, & G. Lindzey (Eds.), *Handbook of social psychology. 4th edition*, (Vol. 2, pp. 680–740). New York: McGraw-Hill.

Brewer, M. B. (2001). The many faces of social identity: Implications for political psychology. *Political Psychology, 22*, 115–125.

Tajfel, H. (1981). *Human groups and social categories: Studies in social psychology.* Cambridge, UK: Cambridge University Press.

Turner, J. C., Hogg, M. A., Oakes, P. J., Reicher, S. D., & Wetherell, M. S. (1987). *Rediscovering the social group: A self-categorization theory.* Oxford, UK:. Blackwell.

PART I

Self and Identity

Introduction

The theme running through all of the readings in this section is understanding the self as a product of interpersonal and social group processes. This theme is well represented in Oyserman's conceptualization of identity as answering the questions "Who am I?", "Where do I belong?", and "How do I fit?" Although the focus of these questions is on the "I" – the individual self-concept – the self is meaningful only in the context of one's relationship to others and one's position in social groups. In this view, the self is a cognitive construction, developed in the course of social interaction and experiences as a group member. Further, the self has a temporal dimension, incorporating representations of the past (personal history) and the future (possible selves), as well as the present (Ross & Buehler). Parallel to this extension of the self through time is the idea of extension of self across persons. Through the development of close relationships and identification with social groups, the self is expanded by inclusion of others into the self-concept (Aron, Aron, & Norman). Aron and his colleagues argue that such self-expansion serves to enhance identity resources beyond the capabilities and experiences of a single individual.

An important debate in the literature on the self revolves around explaining the nature and function of self-esteem, the extent to which one sees oneself as worthwhile and of positive value. Consistent with the theme of the socially embedded self, the "sociometer" theory of self-esteem views the adaptive function of self-esteem as a regulator of inclusion and belonging (Kirkpatrick & Ellis). High self-esteem reflects positive regard from others and sufficient inclusion in social networks. Low self-esteem signals deficiencies in interpersonal relationships and motivates corrective actions to restore belonging. For a highly socially interdependent species, then, the need for positive self-esteem serves an important regulatory function. When functioning adaptively, there is an intimate connection between self-esteem and close personal relationships (Kirkpatrick & Ellis; Campbell & Baumeister). But self-esteem enhancement can also become maladaptive for interpersonal relationships if it takes the form of unrealistic self-regard and narcissism (Campbell & Baumeister).

If the construction and evaluation of the self is closely linked to the quality of social relationships and inclusion in social groups, then the issue of how individuals develop and maintain a positive self-image in the face of devaluation by others is one of central importance to the social psychological understanding of the self. Crocker and Quinn define social stigma as negative identities derived from membership in socially devalued groups. Stigma is the product of socially shared beliefs, values, and prejudices. When an individual is identified with a stigmatized group or social category, he or she also takes on the collectively shared negative evaluations associated with that group. At the same time, however, group identification also serves to buffer the individual from the negative consequences of devalued identity for personal self-esteem (Crocker & Quinn). Thus, understanding the mechanisms by which members of stigmatized groups preserve and maintain positive self-esteem provides important clues to a general understanding of the interrelationships between personal and collective identities.

CHAPTER ONE

Self-concept and Identity

Daphna Oyserman

In its widest possible sense . . . a man's Self is the sum total of all that he can call his, not only his body and his psychic powers, but his clothes and his house, his wife and children, his ancestors and friends, his reputation and works. . . . If they wax and prosper, he feels triumphant, if they dwindle and die away, he feels cast down.

James, 1890/1950, pp. 291–292

Self-concept and *identity* provide answers to the basic questions "Who am I?", "Where do I belong?", and "How do I fit (or fit in)?" In our society, each self-concept is assumed to be unique, different from any other self, and private – fully knowable only to the self (Fiske, Kitayama, Markus, & Nisbett, 1998). Improving oneself, knowing oneself, discovering oneself, creating oneself anew, expressing oneself, taking charge of one's self, being happy with oneself, being ashamed of oneself, are all essential self-projects, central to our understanding of what self-concept and identity *are* and how they *work*. Our images of the self we might be, expect to be, are afraid we might be, motivate current behavior and color understanding. *Self-concept* and *identity* are what come to mind when we think of ourselves (Neisser, 1993), including both personal and social identities (Stryker, 1980; Tajfel, 1981). They are our theory of our personality (Markus & Cross, 1990), what we know or can know about ourselves.

Being human means being conscious of having a self and the nature of the self is central to what it means to be human (Lewis, 1990). The self has been correlated with an array of life situations and life outcomes and is considered a psychological resource – self-concepts differ not only in content but also in their effectiveness (for reviews of assessment and context issues see Byrne, 1996; Harris, 1995; Wylie, 1989). Self-concepts differ in complexity (Linville, 1987), organization of positive and negative self-relevant information (Showers, Abramson, & Hogan, 1998), and the extent that they promote persistent striving versus disengagement, sense of general contentment or incipient despair. Variously conceptualized as a dependent, independent, mediator, and moderator construct, the self-concept has emerged

Partial funding for this chapter comes from a W. T. Grant Faculty Scholar Award.

as one of the most studied areas of psychology. *Psychological Abstracts* shows 23,943 publications from applied and basic science journals (including almost 150 from this year's *Journal of Personality and Social Psychology* alone) with the key word "self-concept" and standard textbooks on social psychology almost invariably contain chapters on self-concept and related concepts such as self-esteem. Recent reviews of self-concept and identity from a social psychological perspective include Banaji & Prentice (1994), Baumeister (1998), Brown (1998), Kihlstrom & Klein (1994), and Markus & Wurf (1987). The focus of this chapter will be to integrate the main themes highlighted in self-concept research within a broader cultural and contextual perspective. In order to do so, I will briefly highlight themes in the social development of self-concept – its content, structure, and organization – and then turn to the ways that a sociocultural frame illuminates new issues and guides hypotheses testing.

Defining the Self-concept

The self-system is both an array of self-relevant knowledge, the tool we use to make sense of our experiences, and the processes that construct, defend, and maintain this knowledge (Epstein, 1973; Higgins, 1996; Markus, 1977). The self-concept functions as a repository of autobiographical memories, as an organizer of experience, and as an emotional buffer and motivational resource (Markus & Wurf, 1987). The notion that each of us has a self-concept, an idea or set of ideas of who we are, and that this conceptualization is relatively constant over time, is intuitively appealing. Not surprisingly, some aspect of the self-concept has been studied within all branches of psychology. Yet what is actually meant by self-concept seems variable across disciplines and research methodologies, as does the self's assumed and documented stability versus malleability. Most dramatically, clinical field trials suggest that it is hard to change one's self-concept, while experimental researchers routinely document that the self is extremely variable and easily changed by even minor experimental manipulations (Markus & Kunda, 1986).

While clearly there is a self-concept that provides an answer to the "Who am I?" question quite simply by anchoring reality and providing the response "*I am me*," what is meant by the self-concept in research and theorizing is often quite ambiguous. The best summary of what is normally meant in experimental research is likely to be the working self-concept – the part of the self-concept that is relevant or made salient in a particular situation (Markus & Kunda, 1986). Even here there is some ambiguity as to whether what is meant is the content that is temporarily accessible or the self-relevant cognitive processing mechanisms that are made temporarily salient. For example, a number of lines of research suggest that observing an other's successes or failures influences both the content of one's on-line or working self-concept and also the cognitive process that is salient – particularly the extent that one focuses on self-enhancement (selectively processing in a self-enhancing manner). Conversely, in quasi-experimental and correlational research, what is meant by the self-concept are the chronically salient aspects of the self-concept, most likely to be repeatedly brought to mind given the everyday contexts in which the individual is embedded.

That the self is both stable and mutable is in fact necessary to our theories of change and self-improvement. The self is seen as an active agent, seeking competence, resolution of life phase conflicts, and mastery in real world terms (see Brown, 1998), yet it is also viewed as importantly molded and shaped by early experiences and relationships (e.g. Aber, Allen, Carlson, & Cicchetti, 1989; Mikulincer, 1998; Rogers, 1954). What the self-concept does is mutually constructed by developmental shifts in cognitive abilities and the requirements of particular life tasks embedded in particular times and spaces (e.g. Maddux, 1991; Moretti, Higgins, & Simon, 1990). Yet in a particular situation, the self-concept is a centrally import-ant cognitive concept and memory structure (Andersen, Glassman, & Gold, 1998). Rel-evance to the self is basic to such cognitive processes as similarity judgments (Catrambone, Beike, & Niedenthal, 1996) and increases processing speed and facilitates inferences (Catrambone & Markus, 1987; Markus, 1977; see Kihlstrom & Klein, 1994, for a review). What we remember, how we remember it, and the sense we make of our experience are each importantly shaped by our self-concepts.

Assessing the Self-concept

In spite of or perhaps because of its centrality for cognition and memory, assessing the content of self-concept continues to be an elusive goal. First, the self-concept contains a dizzying array of content, such a rich array of episodic, experiential, and abstracted informa-tion about the self that not all of it can be salient at any given point in time. Therefore, when asked to report on the self, individuals can only report on that subset of all the self-relevant information that is salient and therefore seems important or central at that point in time. Importantly, saliency-eliciting cues are likely to go unnoticed by the research participant. For example, a researcher interested in shyness is likely to find that average ratings of shyness are higher when instructions request a specific instance of shyness (easily brought to mind) and lower when instructions request a specific instance of extroversion (also easily brought to mind) (Fazio, Effrein, & Falender, 1981). This influence of accessible content, however, is influenced by the ease with which it comes to mind. Information that comes to mind easily is assumed to be more self-defining, more "true" of the self, than are self-descriptions that require effortful search in memory, so that in response to questions about the self-concept, we rely on what comes to mind easily to report on the self. Yet using this "ease of retrieval" heuristic in deciding what is true about the self-concept means that all self-concept measures are open to a variety of confounds (Schwarz, 1998; Schwarz, Bless, Strack, Klumpp, Rittenauer-Schatka, & Simons, 1991). Following the same example, researchers obtaining a longer list of instances of shyness (or extroversion) are likely to find lower ratings of these social characteristics because difficulty of bringing to mind the requested number of examples is used as a judgment cue in the research context. This means that paradoxically, bringing to mind twenty examples of shyness may convince the respondent that he is less shy than bringing to mind three or four examples.

Second, subtle contextual cues including features of the interview schedule can make salient particular aspects of the self, for example personal or social characteristics of the self (Trafimow & Smith, 1998). Because these contextual influences go unnoticed, the instru-ment and immediate setting may well create the context. For example Norenzayan, Schwarz, & Rothman (1996) found that the letterhead on which the questionnaire was printed influenced content of self-concept in open-ended descriptions. Participants used more social roles in describing themselves when the questionnaire was printed on a letterhead from the department of political science and more personal traits to describe themselves if they thought the study was taking place in a psychology department. Though the self-concepts of these participants could hardly be said to change as a result of the letterhead, what they reported about themselves did. It seems unlikely that this was a conscious act, therefore leading to the conclusion that the self-concept, though vital in guiding motivation, behavior, and understanding, is highly susceptible to social and situational structuring.

Operating a Self-concept: The Self-concept in Action

In spite of these difficulties in assessment, it seems clear that the self-concept is a social force: it influences what is perceived, felt, and reacted to and the behavior, perceptions, and reactions of others (Harris, 1995; Kihlstrom & Klein, 1994). It can be thought of as an information processor, functioning to reconfigure social contexts, diffuse otherwise negative circumstances, and promote positive outcomes for the self. The self-concept is inferred to be at work when making one's self momentarily salient results in behavioral change: when seeing oneself in the mirror (for a review, see Banaji & Prentice, 1994), bringing to mind one's group membership (Steele, 1997), or even when wearing a bathing suit (Fredrickson, et al., 1998). More directly, the self-concept is inferred to be at work when it moderates outcomes – among youth, positive racial–ethnic minority identity mediates risk of declining academic performance (Oyserman & Harrison, 1997), while positive self-views reduce risk of bullying (Egan & Perry, 1998). Self-relevant thinking, emotion regulation, and motivation (Banaji & Prentice, 1994; Greenwald & Pratkanis, 1984; Kihlstrom & Cantor, 1984; Markus & Wurf, 1987) are all examples of the self-in-action. For example, controlling for ability, persistence on a math task drops when minority status is made salient, but not for youth who self-define as both members of their minority group and also members of larger society (Oyserman, Kemmelmeier, & Brosh, 1999). For these dual identity youth, the self-concept responses to the "Who am I?", "Where do I belong?", and "How do I fit (in)?" questions bolster motivation and facilitate persistence as opposed to the stereotype threat experienced by their peers (Steele, 1997).

Because the self-concept frames experience and motivates action, the self-concept has been described as a "theory" about oneself that represents and organizes current self-knowledge and guides how new self-knowledge is perceived (Epstein, 1973). As a theory, the self-concept is made of the current state of knowledge about the self and is assumed to be veridical enough to help organize experience, focus motivation, regulate emotion, and guide social interaction. It is not assumed to reflect some absolute truth about one's skills, abilities, competencies, or worth. More than simply a theory about the self, some researchers have posited that the self-concept is the seat of basic effectance and competency drives, reflecting an innate need to become effective, more competent over time (Maslow, 1954), and a desire to improve the self. Models based in this premise, termed *self-assessment, learning, efficacy*, and *self-improvement* models (Maddux, 1991; Trope, 1986), have received some support. These models suggest that individuals are motivated to seek out accurate information about the self in order to be able to improve the self (Wurf & Markus, 1991). Two other basic functions of the self-concept have been outlined: the promotion of positive self-views, termed *self-evaluation maintenance* or *self-affirmation* (Steele, 1988), and the provision of a consistent anchor for information processing, termed *self-consistency* or *self-verification* (Swann, 1997).

Since the early writings of James (1890/1950), feeling good about oneself, evaluating oneself positively, feeling that one is a person of worth, have been described as a basic goal of the self-concept, a basic human need, akin with the pleasure principle. Numerous studies have shown a robust tendency to maintain and enhance a positive image of the self (Greenwald, 1980). The notion that positive self-esteem is a fundamental human need is the basis for an array of self-concept theories, including group-based theories such as social identity theories (Haslam, Oakes, Turner, & McGarty, 1996; Tajfel, 1981; Turner, Hogg, Oakes, Reicher, & Wetherell, 1987) and collective self-esteem theory (Crocker, Luhtanen, Blaine, & Broadnax, 1994). According to self-esteem maintenance assumptions, all else being equal, individuals prefer to feel good about themselves and so will self-define in such a way as to maintain positive self-feelings. In this view, the self is a positivity-seeking information processor. It seeks out domains in which positive self-definitions are possible (e.g. Steele, 1988), disengages from domains in which positive self-definitions are not possible (James, 1890/1950), and compares the self to others in ways that reflect favorably on the self (e.g. Beauregard & Dunning, 1998). While tending toward somewhat rosy self-descriptions (Taylor & Brown, 1988), individuals differ in the extent that they bias their self-evaluations upward. The upward trend is most pronounced when evaluating the self on a dimension that is clearly valenced (Asendorpf & Ostendorf, 1998) and high self-esteem individuals may be better able to shift self-definitional focus to create a positive identity in the face of setback (Murray, Holmes, MacDonald, & Ellsworth, 1998).

In addition to its self-promotive functions, the self-concept also provides and maintains a cognitive anchor, a consistent yardstick, or way of making sense of who one is and therefore what to expect of the self and others. According to Swann's self-verification theory, individuals are motivated to preserve self-definitions and will do so by creating a social reality that conforms to their self-view (see Banaji & Prentice, 1994; Baumeister, 1998; Swann, 1997, for reviews of this perspective). The assumption is that we prefer a consistent sense of self in order to be able to use the self-concept to make predictions about the world (Greenwald, 1980), and to maintain relationships with those others with whom these self-definitions were created (see Higgins, 1996). This means that the self-concept is a conservative information processor. Important self-relevant information, even if negative, is maintained in the face of contradictory information if it is in a domain central to one's self-definition and one is given a chance to process it.

Building a Self-concept: The Self-concept as Structure

Clearly, the self-concept requires memory and in some basic way it is all of those things that we can remember about ourselves. However, it is not simply a collection of autobiographical memories, it is also a cognitive structure. We remember information better if it is linked to the self-concept (Kihlstrom & Klein, 1994) and currently salient self-concept content influences ongoing information processing, meaning-making and behavioral, motivational, and affective responses (Kemmelmeier & Oyserman, in press; Trafimow & Smith, 1998). A common conceptualization of the self-concept is that it is a multifaceted set of self-relevant schemas containing self-knowledge, guiding and directing action and providing future-oriented goals (Carver & Scheier, 1981; Epstein, 1973; Fiske & Taylor, 1994; Greenwald, 1982; Holland & Quinn, 1987; Markus, 1977). As a cognitive concept, self-concept is based in experience and as a cognitive structure, it shapes experience by guiding both what we pay attention to and the meaning we make of it.

By conceptualizing the self-concept as a set of self-schemas, researchers imply that the self-concept is not necessarily hierarchically organized. In fact, different models have been suggested (for a review, see Kihlstrom & Klein, 1994). First, abstract traits may cue specific exemplars, which are stored as situated memories, or specific exemplars. For example, thinking of one's self as shy may bring to mind the times one was too tongue-tied to volunteer one's opinion in a classroom debate. Second, specific exemplars may cue trait descriptors. For example, remembering a time one was tongue-tied may make salient the feeling that one is shy. Third, exemplars and trait descriptors may be independently stored in memory. In this case, bringing to mind a memory of one's self as shy would cue other such memories and these would be separate from memories of the self as tongue-tied and so on. Although the first model is often assumed to be correct, this assumption is not well supported (Marsh & Yeung, 1998) and current evidence suggests most support for the latter model type, termed *independent storage models.* These models do not assume that specific exemplars and abstracted traits are hierarchically arranged. Rather, when context or other cues make abstract trait information salient, specific examples are not elicited and similarly, when specific examples are elicited, this does not reliably cue general trait information. It is this independence that makes possible the ease of retrieval errors described above.

Developing a Self-concept: The Self-concept as Cognitive Product

How does this cognitive construct and memory structure, so central to our understanding of personhood, emerge? Developmental research suggests that the self-concept is both a *basic tool* of cognitive and social development and an important *consequence* of this development (see excellent reviews by Bretherton, 1992; Damon & Hart, 1988; Lewis, 1990). Sense of self initially involves simply sensing that one's body is separate from others, so that identity begins with a physical sense of the boundaries of one's body and where it is in space (Lewis, 1990). Yet because infants cannot engage their environment directly, this insight must occur within the context of interactions with others. Thus, the infant's emerging relationality scaffolds and supports its emerging identity. Adult caregivers frame and carry the interaction in the social space between infant and adult so that in some basic way, infants learn who they are through the sense their caretaker provides of who they are. These initial interactions, termed synchronized exchanges, involve caretaker and infant in linked interactions that take into account the responses of the other. Caretaker–infant synchrony develops rapidly in the first few months of life (Tronick & Gianino, 1986). The quality of this synchrony has been related to later child self-characteristics such as self-control (Feldman, Greenbaum,

& Yirmiya, 1999) and affect regulation (Weinberg, Tronick, & Cohn, 1999). It is posited that these interchanges are the basis of attachment style or working model of relationality (Bretherton, 1992), that sets up a basic sense of worth, esteem, and efficacy (for a review, see Hammen, 1991).

Basic sense of efficacy in turn provides an impetus to explore the world, stimulating cognitive and language development – highlighting the influence of self-concept development on cognitive development. As the capacity for memory develops in the first year of life, infants begin to develop a more nuanced sense of identity because they can engage in and store differential interaction with different others. At two years of age, self-consciousness begins to emerge, solidifying by the end of the fourth year of life. Early self-consciousness involves being able to distinguish unexpected changes in the self. By age two, but not reliably before, toddlers touch their forehead when they look in the mirror and see a red paint smear (Lewis & Brooks-Gunn, 1979). A temporal sense of self follows by age four; at this age, toddlers reliably touch their forehead when viewing their paint-smeared forehead on a video monitor only when it is a "live tape" and not an image from a previously videotaped play session (Povinelli & Simon, 1998). This emerging self-concept is linked to self-conscious emotions such as embarrassment at recognizing the self, fear when the mother leaves, and pride in the self's accomplishments (for a review, see Hammen, 1991).

In the years from two to eight, as language develops, children begin to make self-descriptive statements, with content shifting from age two to eight from physical to psychological terms (Damon & Hart, 1988). In early adolescence, both past and future orientation to the self evolves and youth begin to use more abstract descriptions, shifting from descriptions of what they usually do to comparative assessments, to interpersonal concerns, to systematic beliefs and plans. Utilizing James's basic framework of dimensions of the self, Damon & Hart (1988) suggest a developmental progression from material, to social, to psychological perspectives on the self, with each new level integrating and transforming the previous one. As the psychological self evolves, youth grapple to integrate various perspectives on the self – how they present themselves to the world, who they aspire to become, who they were, and who they are now (Harter, 1990; Harter, Marold, Whitesell, & Cobbs, 1996; Ruble, Eisenberg, & Higgins, 1994). Development of a sense of the adult one will become has been viewed as a main task of adolescence, yet who one is and where one belongs continues to be central across adulthood (Erikson, 1968).

Constructing the Self: The Self-concept as Social Product

This multifaceted self-concept that takes on and grapples with the life phase-appropriate versions of the basic questions "Who am I?", "Where do I belong?", and "How do I fit (in)?" is clearly social in nature (see Higgins, 1996; Lewis, 1990; Markus & Cross, 1990). From the beginning, theorists have conceptualized the self-concept as a *social product* that develops through relationships with others and what they see in one's self. In this way, social reality can be more potent than behavioral or observed reality. For example, while related to their actual school performance, middle schoolers' academic self-concepts are more influenced by their parents' perceptions of their abilities than by their actual school grades (Frome &

Eccles, 1998). William James (1890/1950) described this as the social aspect of the self-concept and *social selves* were described as the unique version of the self reflected in each human interaction. Other early conceptualizations of the self-concept also highlighted the ways others' views of us, or at least our perceptions of these appraisals, influence how we conceive of ourselves (Cooley, 1902). Others were seen as vital to the production and experience of being a self: "the self can exist for the individual only if he assumes the roles of the others" (Mead, 1921–1925/1964, p. 284). The self is thus experienced "indirectly, from the particular standpoints of other individual members of the same social group, or from the generalized standpoint of the social group" (Mead, 1934/1964, p. 138).

Selves are created within contexts and take into account the values, norms, and mores of the others likely to participate in that context. By adolescence, individuals are able to distinguish between the selves they would like to be and become and the selves others want them to be (Moretti, Higgins, & Simon, 1990). Students given a say in their social contexts are more likely to report expressing their "true" selves, the selves they want to be, rather than feeling compelled to present situation-appropriate "false" selves, the selves they know others want them to be (Harter, Waters, Whitesell, & Kastelic, 1998). Others are clearly present in the self-concept, they are standards of comparison – we feel good when we outperform others, bask in the success of close others if there is little chance we will be compared negatively to them. We feel less likely to succeed if similar others fail (Kemmelmeier & Oyserman, in press). In this way, the accomplishments and failures of close others help define the self. By 11 years of age if not sooner, children see the actions of close others as self-relevant, feeling pride in a close other's accomplishments and shame in their failings (Bennett, Yuill, Banerjee, & Thomson, 1998). More generally, others are arbitrators of personal worth and self-esteem drops in the face of public devaluation such as bullying or teasing (Egan & Perry, 1998; Graham & Juvonen, 1998), and is strengthened by peer acceptance (Roffey, Majors, & Tarrant, 1997).

But the influence of social contexts is not limited to self-relevant information gleaned from interactions with particular others. Who one *is* in a particular situation is importantly framed by the social context. Being a "solo," the only one of one's gender, racial–ethnic or other social category in a particular context makes these categories salient in self-definition (e.g. McGuire & Padawer-Singer, 1976). Moreover, solo status can intensify negative effects of stereotypes about members of one's social group on self-regard (e.g. Frable, Platt, & Hoey, 1998). At the same time, we are loath to be too similar to others in our social groups, striving instead for an optimal level of both uniqueness and similarity (Brewer, 1991). In this way, self-concepts emerge through interactions, making one's most basic identities part and parcel of and specific to the particular groups within which one is embedded (Raeff, 1997).

By taking into account the influence of social statuses more generally, social psychological research has begun to explore more systematically areas previously left to fields such as cultural, race–ethnicity, and gender studies. Building on these earlier insights, the current generation of social psychological theorizing about the self is taking a new look at what constitutes a social context and the implications of social context for self-concept development, content, and structure, and the behavioral, motivational, and affective consequences of self-concept. For example, Croizet & Claire (1998) show that making one's working-class status salient impairs academic performance, while Shih, Pittinsky, & Ambady (1999) show that making one's Asian-ness salient improves or impedes performance depending on the content of the local social stereotype about being Asian.

These examples make clear that social contexts enable, elicit, and scaffold certain selves while dis-enabling, suppressing, and dismantling others even in the face of what might appear to be objective evidence of these self-dimensions. It is also becoming increasingly clear that the social construction of the self depends not only on particular relationships or immediate situations but also on larger sociocultural and historical factors. Being Serb or Albanian in Kosovor matters and is likely to establish ways of being in the world, open certain possible selves, and close off others. Feeling Serbian or Albanian in Kosovor sets up patterns of action, ways of making sense of the world in ways that are quite different from feeling Serbian or Albanian in the United States or Switzerland. The way that this matters for self-concept is not rooted in the influence of a particular other's view of the self but rather in a more global, societal stance as to whether the self can be fundamentally separate from group memberships.

Having and Being a Self: The Self-concept in Sociocultural Context

Societies and cultures differ in the way that they make sense of what it means to be an individual, the aspects of human experience that are centralized, and the resolutions to basic human dilemmas that they endorse or value (Hofstede, 1980). These basic dilemmas include how to deal with human inequality, the premium placed on reducing or avoiding uncertainty about the future, the nature of the valued or normative relationship between individuals and groups, and the value assigned to enhancing versus attenuating differences between the sexes (Hofstede, 1980). It seems reasonable to suppose that the self-concepts created in differing cultural milieux will take on these culture-specific ways of being (e.g. Weigert, Teige, & Teige, 1990). Yet, perhaps because it is so broadly encompassing as to be transparent, unnoticed, culture has not typically informed social psychological research on the self-concept (Bond & Smith, 1997; Oyserman & Markus, 1993, 1998; Oyserman, Coon, & Kemmelmeier, 1999). While the self-concept has long been viewed as a social product and the implications of contextual salience are mainstream research foci, the field is just beginning to explore the ways larger social structures such as culture may set up the nature of both the social interactions and immediate contexts. At issue for self-concept theorizing and research is whether self-concept development and processes studied in one cultural context can be generalized to others.

The bulk of the research described in this chapter focuses on North American participants and assumes a North American cultural context, so it is particularly important to understand how this cultural frame may influence how the self has been conceptualized and studied. Broadly speaking, North American and Western European cultures have been described as individualistic. That is, they socialize members to believe in individual rights and personal freedoms, the centrality of personal pleasure and autonomy, and the personal, private, and unique self. These cultures are viewed as not highly accepting of human difference, prefer-ring models of equality to one's assuming hierarchy. Yet, though highly accessible and part of popular representations in these countries, this democratic, individualistic frame is also transparent, that which goes without saying so that its influence on the way the self is studied, the research questions asked, and the theories developed, is only recently being questioned.

Thus, current theories about personality (DeNeve & Cooper, 1998) and well-being (Ryff & Keyes, 1995) imply a bounded, autonomous goal-oriented self focused on attainment of personal happiness-making goals, able to make friends and develop helpful social networks with relative strangers – all characteristics of democratic individualism. Given the relative size of North American publication impact (Bond & Smith, 1997), it seems reasonable to propose that North American individualism is the standard prism through which psychological phenomena are construed, whether or not culture is an explicit unit of analysis (Fiske, Kitayama, Markus, & Nisbett, 1998; Oyserman & Markus, 1993). Yet by not making explicit a cultural frame, researchers have limited their opportunity to investigate the way culture may influence all aspects of the self-concept – its definition and assessment, its structure and functions. Having and being a self may not be a fully generalizable experience. In the remaining portion of this chapter, I review what we currently know about the generalizability of the North American and Western European self-concept presented until now.

Societies that emphasize individualism are said to value individual rights, not duties or obligations, to emphasize personal autonomy and self-fulfillment, and believe that the self is created through personal achievements and accomplishments, not group memberships (Kim, 1994; Triandis, 1995). Within this cultural frame, the self is viewed as bounded, distinct, and stable, with attitudes and behavior ensuing derived from this stable self rather than being a social and situational product (Bellah, Madsen, Sullivan, Swidler, & Tipton, 1985; Kagitcibasi, 1999; Markus & Kitayama, 1991; Sampson, 1977; Triandis, 1989). Within this worldview, creating and maintaining a positive sense of self is assumed to be a basic human endeavor. Feeling good about oneself and having many unique or distinctive personal attitudes and opinions is valued (Oyserman & Markus, 1993; Markus, 1998; Triandis, 1995), as is positive self-esteem (Kitayama, Markus, Matsumoto, & Norasakkunkit, 1997). Concerns about the possibility that individualism is not a universal socialization goal are echoed in gender studies and racial–ethnic studies research as well (Frable, 1997).

Although societies differ in many ways, most commonly societies that emphasize individualism have been contrasted with societies that emphasize collectivism, summarized as a focus on the group membership or social aspects of the self (Schwartz, 1990). These societies emphasize somewhat different resolutions to basic human dilemmas. Rather than placing emphasis on the individual and his or her unique attributes, emphasis is on the individual's place within a group and the group's unique attributes (Triandis, 1995). In this way, the interdependence between the individual and ingroup is emphasized; because individuals are parts, not stand alone wholes, others are represented within the self-concept (Hofstede, 1980; Kim, 1994). Moreover, rather than striving to become valued due to unique individual abilities and independence, individuals strive to become valued due to their ability to maintain relationships and interpersonal harmony (Markus & Kitayama, 1991). The social, not the personal self is emphasized through cultural practices such as dropping use of personal pronouns, co-producing sentences (Kashima & Kashima, 1997), and using enigmatic similes in which the speaker provides half the simile so that meaning becomes clear only upon joint completion (Rohsenow, 1991).

Empirical support is accruing for the notion that when collectivism is salient ingroup membership is seen as a fixed, meaningful part of identity (Kim, 1994), personal goals and group needs are viewed as congruent (Oyserman, Sakamoto, & Lauffer, 1998), even when the group is faring poorly (Chen, Brockner, & Katz, 1998). Similarly, individuals who rate themselves as focused on collectivist values are lower in personal need for uniqueness, higher in self–other affiliation, and are also more sensitive to the other's rejection (Yamaguchi, Kuhlman, & Sugimori, 1995). Also, students from those societies which emphasized individualism more, viewed personal success as a particularly important basis of self-esteem, while participants from countries that emphasized individualism less viewed family life as a particularly important basis of self-esteem (Watkins, et al., 1998).

Cross-cultural research suggests the cultures place differential emphases on abstract versus episodic, experiential aspects of the self-concept, self-esteem maintenance versus self-improvement, and active versus quiescent self-related emotions. Rather than the self-enhancement or self-esteem maintenance goal central in cultures emphasizing individualism, cultures that emphasize collectivism make central self-goals such as fitting in and being a good group member, becoming more competent, and avoiding embarrassing oneself or others (for a review, see Oyserman, Coon, & Kemmelmeier, 1999). For example, preliminary support for the notion that societies differ in the extent that they emphasize self-esteem maintenance comes from research comparing Japanese and North American students. After receiving failure feedback, North American students are more likely to attempt to compensate or buffer self-feelings by working on easier problems or choosing another task, while Japanese students are more likely to choose the self-improvement strategy of working more on the failed task (Kitayama, Markus, Matsumoto, & Norasakkunkit, 1997).

To the extent that the self-concept is defined, studied, and theorized about within individualistic assumptions, self-concept research is likely to focus on the domains valued by individualism as a cultural frame. This appears to be the case. For example, since knowing and positively evaluating the self – self-concept and self-esteem – are intimately linked in Western tradition and common language, they are used interchangeably in much of the literature (Blascovich & Tomaka, 1991). Since being happy, outgoing, and sociable are valued characteristics within an individualistic cultural frame it is likely that these characteristics will be seen as normative. In fact, the ability to "bounce back" and focus on the positive rather than dwelling on the negative after failure is both culturally valued and – in North America – a characteristic of high rather than low self-esteem individuals (Dodgson & Wood, 1998). Further, the high cultural value placed on positive self-evaluation has resulted in a shift in the meaning of self-esteem from the notion that self-esteem means defining oneself as an adequate person, of equal value as others, toward implicitly assuming that positive self-regard means extremely positive identity (Baumeister, 1998).

In the West, particularly the US, source of much psychological theorizing on the self-concept (Bond & Smith, 1997), it is clear that people tend to have positive views of themselves, at least as assessed by our measures of self-esteem. While a focus on self-esteem seems less useful if researchers are to understand other functions of the self-concept, self-esteem is often used as a key individual difference variable and fluctuations in self-esteem are used to show the influence of social situations on the self. Yet in contexts other than the US, feeling good may be less of a cultural imperative.

Individualistic contexts highlight the importance of a positive self-view and focus attention on the self-concept as an array of traits. North American and European student based research evidence supports these assumptions about the nature of the self: individuals attempt to set up interactions in ways that protect positive self-views, and anticipating negative social feedback is disturbing (Leary, Haupt, Strausser, & Chokel, 1998). American children as young as kindergarteners learn to assess themselves and others in terms of stable and fixed traits (Heyman & Gelman, 1998). North Americans believe that self-interest is a prime motivating factor (Miller & Ratner, 1998) and view relationships with ambivalence, correctly assuming that close others may inhibit self-enhancing tendencies (Sedikides, Campbell, Reeder, & Elliot, 1998).

Yet we may be finding individualistically oriented selves and self-processes because our models focus on these and utilize mostly research participants from countries where individualism is likely to be chronically salient. Within a country, though individualism and collectivism could be separately primed to study the generalizability of findings about self-concept processes, this is typically not done. Further, self-concept and self-esteem are typically assessed, manipulated, or made salient in psychological research paradigms focusing on interactions with strangers, achievement situations, or situations in which attainment of personal goals is centralized, the very situations likely to make an individualistic worldview most prominent (Oyserman, Coon, & Kemmelmeier, 1999). North American and Western European research paradigms rarely study situations likely to evoke a collectivist worldview such as interactions with family members or situations where a sense of common fate with ingroup members has been elicited. Thus, they are unlikely to find evidence of these collective self-processes. Thus, the situations and participants that form the bulk of mainstream social psychological research on the self-concept are heavily weighted toward finding evidence of individualistic self-concept content and processes. This is not to say that evidence for collectivist processes and content would not be found if these were the focus of research attention.

Clearly, however, even within the US, not all contexts promote individualism; behaving individualistically may require power and resources not available across gender and ethnic boundaries (e.g. Kerber, 1991). American collective structures and created spaces afford and sustain the individual focus of American society, particularly the middle class white niche of that society that forms the bulk of our researchers and research participants. These contexts afford and bolster the centralization of the individual in construing cause and effect, and make personal choice, free will, and personal happiness plausible constructs. Clearly, one's place within the social structure influences whether and how individualism is expressed. Broadening the frame of self-concept research will facilitate research dealing with these context-bound aspects of the self. Thus, studying self-concept more broadly, by taking into account both the situations likely to be experienced and the goals likely to be pursued in contexts that make collectivism salient, would do much to deepen understanding of what the self-concept is and how it functions.

Cultural psychological theorizing has made the omission of culture as the broader context in standard self-concept research more obvious and has highlighted the congruence between theories of self-esteem maintenance and individualistic values. Only by broadening the focus of our research attention can we begin to learn the extent to which other goals – such as intimacy and relational goals – motivate the self. In addition, while people often focus on positive aspects of the self, it is also the case that people are interested in seeking accurate information about themselves and in preserving a sense of consistency, even if the consistent information reflects badly on one's self. By taking a broader perspective on the self-concept, the workings of these other self-goals can be more successfully pursued. Using a cultural perspective also highlights the potential for mismatches between the goals assumed by the larger culture and personal goals. For example, an individual may be focused on relationality or self-improvement in contexts that reward autonomy and self-enhancement.

Some research has taken into account issues emerging in this new look at the self. In particular, European literature on social identities (e.g. Tajfel, 1981; Tajfel & Turner, 1986; Turner, Hogg, Oakes, Reicher, & Wetherell, 1987) posits that group membership is an important component of one's identity and that individuals are motivated to view their groups as positive, distinct from other groups. In addition, a new look at social contexts is emerging from a convergence of evidence that contexts matter not only because they influence the situational content elicited by self-concept probes, but importantly because they influence the structure and function of self-concept. These converging lines of research include efforts to explore the effects of social stigma on self-esteem (Crocker, Luhtanen, Blaine, & Broadnax, 1994), the effects of race and racial identity on self-concept (Oyserman & Harrison, 1998), and the effects of gender on self-schemas (Cross & Madson, 1997; Markus & Oyserman, 1989). Together, these perspectives suggest ways that insights about the self-concept gained from studies of primarily white middle-class European American undergraduates are in fact culture-bound and could vary systematically by cultural frame. These insights, combined with the work on racial and ethnic aspects of identity and social identity more generally, provide insight into new directions in self-concept research.

While there is preliminary evidence suggesting that Euro-Americans and Western Europeans generally may be more likely to have the kinds of selves assumed by self-concept researchers, evidence is as yet preliminary and is often based on correlational methodologies (Oyserman, Coon, & Kemmelmeier, 1999). The strength of cultural perspectives lies in their challenge to the assumed universality of psychological theories of self-concept, but the perspective is hampered by a reliance on cross-national studies that assume that participants hold mutually exclusive, stable, and uniform individualistic or collectivistic views. By bringing cultural constructs to the study of self-concept, this paradigm has made clear that there are multiple self-goals – to be part of and connect with others and to be unique from and distinct from others. While cultural psychologists have not emphasized group boundaries *per se*, social identity theories highlight the need to take into account not only group membership but also the way that the group is constituted in relation to other groups. This research has utilized laboratory settings to manipulate group size, salience, permeability of boundaries, and other potentially relevant cues, showing that individuals who are committed to an identity respond differently to threats to this identity than noncommitted individuals (Jetten, Spears, & Manstead, 1998; Spears, Oakes, Ellemers, & Haslam, 1998). Cultural research, exploring cultural context, specific goals, constructs and contexts, including the influences of migration and other acculturation processes, is likely to provide rich material for future research on the generalizability of self-processes.

REFERENCES

Aber, J., Allen, J., Carlson, V., & Cicchetti, D. (1989). The effects of maltreatment on development during early childhood: Recent studies and their theoretical, clinical, and policy implications. In D. Cicchetti (Ed.), *Child maltreatment: Theory and research on the causes and consequences of child abuse and neglect* (pp. 579–619). New York: Cambridge University Press.

Andersen, S., Glassman, N., & Gold, D. (1998). Mental representations of the self, significant others, and nonsignificant others: Structure and processing of private and public aspects. *Journal of Personality and Social Psychology, 75*, 845–861.

Asendorpf, J., & Ostendorf, F. (1998). Is self-enhancement healthy? Conceptual, psychometric, and empirical analysis. *Journal of Personality and Social Psychology, 74*, 955–966.

Banaji, M., & Prentice, D. (1994). The self in social contexts. *Annual Review of Psychology, 45*, 297–332.

Baumeister, R. (1998). The self. In D. Gilbert, S. Fiske, & G. Lindzey (Eds.), *Handbook of social psychology* (Vol. 2, pp. 680–740). New York: Oxford University Press.

Beauregard, K. S., & Dunning, D. (1998). Turning up the contrast: Self-enhancement motives prompt egocentric contrast effects in social judgments. *Journal of Personality and Social Psychology, 74*, 606–621.

Bellah, R., Madsen, R., Sullivan, W., Swidler, A., & Tipton, S. (1985). *Habits of the heart: Individualism and commitment in American life.* Berkeley: University of California Press.

Bennett, M., Lyons, E., Sani, F., & Barrett, M. (1998). Children's subjective identification with the group and in-group favoritism. *Developmental Psychology, 34*, 902–909.

Bennett, M., Yuill, N., Banerjee, R., & Thomson, S. (1998). Children's understanding of extended identity. *Developmental Psychology, 34*, 322–331.

Blascovich, J., & Tomaka, J. (1991). Measures of self-esteem. In J. Robinson, P. Shaver, & L. Wrightsman (Eds.), *Measures of personality and social psychological attitudes* (pp. 115–160). New York: Academic Press.

Bond, M., & Smith, P. (1997). Cross-cultural social and organizational psychology. *Annual Review of Psychology, 47*, 205–235.

Bretherton, I. (1992). Attachment and bonding. In V. Van Hasselt & M. Hersen (Eds.), *Handbook of social development* (pp. 133–155). New York: Plenum Press.

Brewer, M. (1991). The social self: On being the same and different at the same time. *Personality and Social Psychology Bulletin, 17*, 475–82.

Bronfenbrenner, U. (1995). The bioecological model from a life course perspective: Reflections of a participant observer. In P. Moen, H. Elder, Jr., & K. Luscher (Eds.), *Examining lives in context: Perspectives on the ecology of human development* (pp. 599–618). Washington, DC: American Psychological Association.

Brown, J. (1998). *The self.* Boston, MA: McGraw-Hill.

Byrne, B. (1996). *Measuring self-concept across the life span.* Washington, DC: APA Press.

Carver, C., & Scheier, M. (1981). *Attention and self-regulation: A control theory approach to human behavior.* New York: Springer-Verlag.

Catrambone, R., & Markus, H. (1987). The role of self-schemas in going beyond the information given. *Social Cognition, 5*, 349–368.

Catrambone, R., Beike, D., & Niedenthal, P. (1996). Is the self-concept a habitual referent in judgments of similarity? *Psychological Science, 7*, 158–163.

Chen, Y., Brockner, J., & Katz, T. (1998). Toward an explanation of cultural differences in in-group favoritism: The role of individual versus collective primacy. *Journal of Personality and Social Psychology, 75*, 1490–1502.

Cooley, D. (1902). *Human nature and the social order*. New York: Scribners.

Cooper, C., & Denner, J. (1998). Theories linking culture and psychology: Universal and community-specific processes. *Annual Review of Psychology, 49*, 559–584.

Crocker, J., Luhtanen, R., Blaine, B., & Broadnax, S. (1994). Collective self-esteem and psychological well-being among white, black, and Asian college students. *Personality and Social Psychology Bulletin, 20*, 503–13.

Croizet, J., & Claire, T. (1998). Extending the concept of stereotype threat to social class: The intellectual underperformance of students from low socioeconomic backgrounds. *Personality and Social Psychology Bulletin, 24*, 588–594.

Cross, S. E., & Madson, L. (1997). Models of the self: Self-construals and gender. *Psychological Bulletin, 122*, 5–37.

Crystal, D., Watanabe, H., Weinfurt, K., & Wu, C. (1998). Concepts of human differences: A comparison of American, Japanese, and Chinese children and adolescents. *Developmental Psychology, 34*, 714–722.

Damon, W., & Hart, D. (1988). *Self-understanding in childhood and adolescence*. New York: Cambridge University Press.

DeNeve, K. M., & Cooper, H. (1998). The happy personality: A meta-analysis of 137 personality traits and subjective well-being. *Psychological Bulletin, 124*, 197–229.

Dodgson, P., & Wood, J. (1998). Self-esteem and the cognitive accessibility of strengths and weaknesses after failure. *Journal of Personality and Social Psychology, 75*, 78–197.

Egan, S. K., & Perry, D. G. (1998). Does low self-regard invite victimization? *Developmental Psychology, 34*, 299–309.

Epstein, S. (1973). The self-concept revisited or a theory of a theory. *American Psychologist, 28*, 405–416.

Erikson, E. (1968). *Identity: Youth and crisis*. New York: Norton.

Exline, J., & Lobel, M. (1999). The perils of outperformance sensitivity about being the target of a threatening upward comparison. *Psychological Bulletin, 125*, 307–337.

Fazio, R., Effrein, E., & Falender, V. (1981). Self-perceptions following social interactions. *Journal of Personality and Social Psychology, 41*, 232–242.

Feldman, R., Greenbaum, C., & Yirmiya, N. (1999). Mother–infant affect synchrony as an antecedent of the emergence of self-control. *Developmental Psychology, 35*, 223–231.

Fiske, S., & Taylor, S. (1994). *Social cognition*. 2nd. edn. Reading, MA: Addison-Wessley.

Fiske, A., Kitayama, S., Markus, H., & Nisbett, R. (1998). The cultural matrix of social psychology. In D. Gilbert, S. Fiske, & G. Lindzey (Eds.), *Handbook of social psychology*. New York: McGraw-Hill.

Frable, D. (1997). Gender, racial, ethnic, sexual, and class identities. *Annual Review of Psychology, 48*, 139–162.

Frable, D., Platt, L., & Hoey, S. (1998). Concealable stigmas and positive self-perceptions: Feeling better around similar others. *Journal of Personality and Social Psychology, 74*, 909–922.

Frederickson, B. L., Roberts, T.-A., Noll, S. M., Quinn, D. M., & Twenge, J. M. (1998). That swimsuit becomes you. Sex differences in self-objectification, restrained eating, and math performance. *Journal of Personality and Social Psychology, 75*, 269–284.

Frome, P., & Eccles, J. (1998). Parents' influence on children's achievement-related perceptions. *Journal of Personality and Social Psychology, 74*, 435–452.

Graham, S., & Juvonen, J. (1998). Self-blame and peer victimization in middle school: An attributional analysis. *Developmental Psychology, 34*, 587–599.

Greenwald, A. (1980). The totalitarian ego: Fabrication and revision of personal history. *American Psychologist, 35*, 603–618.

Greenwald, A. (1982). Ego task analysis: An integration of research on ego-involvement and self-awareness. In A. Hastorf and A. Isen (Eds.), *Cognitive social psychology* (pp. 109–148). New York: Elsevier.

Greenwald, A., & Pratkanis, A. (1984). The self. In K. S. Wyer & T. Srull (Eds.), *Handbook of social cognition*, Vol. 3 (pp. 129–178). Hillsdale, NJ: Erlbaum.

Hammen, C. (1991). *Depression runs in families: The social context of risk and resilience in children of depressed mothers.* New York: Springer-Verlag.

Harris, J. (1995). Where is the child's environment? *Psychological Review, 102,* 458–489.

Harter, S. (1990). Adolescent self and identity. In S. S. Feldman & G. Elliot (Eds.), *At the threshold: The developing adolescent* (pp. 352–387). Cambridge, MA: Harvard University Press.

Harter, S., Marold, D., Whitesell, N., & Cobbs, G. (1996). A model of the effects of parent and peer support on adolescent false self behavior. *Child Development, 67,* 160–174.

Harter, S., Waters, P., Whitesell, N., & Kastelic, D. (1998). Level of voice among female and male high school students: Relational context, support, and gender orientation. *Developmental Psychology, 34,* 892–901.

Haslam, S. A., Oakes, P., Turner, J. C., & McGarty, C. (1996). Social identity, self-categorization, and the perceived homogeneity of ingroups and outgroups: The interaction between social motivation and cognition. In R. Sorrentino & E. T. Higgins (Eds.), *Handbook of motivation and cognition: The interpersonal context* (pp. 182–222). New York: Guilford Press.

Heyman, G. D., & Gelman, S. A. (1998). Young children use motive information to make trait inferences. *Developmental Psychology, 34,* 310–321.

Higgins, E. T. (1989). Continuities and discontinuities in self-regulatory and self-evaluative processes: A developmental theory relating self and affect. *Journal of Personality: Special Issue: Long-term stability and change in personality, 57,* 407–444.

Higgins, E. T. (1996). Shared reality in the self-system: The social nature of self-regulation. In W. Stroebe & M. Hewstone (Eds.), *European review of social psychology*, Vol. 7 (pp. 1–30). Chichester, UK: Wiley.

Hofstede, G. (1980). *Culture's consequences.* Beverly Hills, CA: Sage.

Holland, D., & Quinn, N. (1987). *Cultural models in language and thought.* Cambridge, UK: Cambridge University Press.

James, W. (1890/1950). *The principles of psychology.* New York: Dover.

Jetten, J., Spears, R., & Manstead, A. (1998). Defining dimensions of distinctiveness: Group variability makes a difference to differentiation. *Journal of Personality and Social Psychology, 74,* 1481–1492.

Kagitcibasi, C. (1996). *Family and human development across cultures.* Mahwah, NJ: Erlbaum.

Kashima, E., & Kashima, Y. (1997). Practice of self in conversations: Pronoun drop, sentence co-production and contextualization of the self. In K. Leung, U. Kim, S. Yamaguchi, & Y. Kashima (Eds.), *Progress in Asian social psychology* (pp. 164–179). Singapore: John Wiley & Sons.

Kemmelmeier, M., & Oyserman, D. (in press). When similar others fail: The gendered impact of downward social comparisons. *Journal of Social Issues,* forthcoming special issue, *Stigma: An Insider's View.*

Kerber, L. (1991). Can a woman be an individual? The discourse of self-reliance. In R. W. Curry and L. B. Goodheart (Eds.), *American chameleon: Individualism in trans-national context.* Kent, Ohio: Kent State University Press.

Kihlstrom, J., & Cantor, N. (1984). Mental representations of the self. *Advances in Experimental Social Psychology, 17,* 1–47.

Kihlstrom, J., & Klein, S. (1994). The self as a knowledge structure. In R. Wyer, Jr., & T. Srull (Eds.), *Handbook of social cognition, Vol. 1: Basic processes* (pp. 153–208). Hillsdale, NJ: Lawrence Erlbaum Associates.

Kim, U. (1994). Individualism and collectivism: Conceptual clarification and elaboration. In U. Kim, H. C. Triandis, C. Kagitcibasi, S. Choi, & G. Yoon (Eds.), *Individualism and collectivism: Theory, method, and applications* (pp. 000–000). Thousand Oaks, CA: Sage.

Kitayama, S., Markus, H. R., Matsumoto, H., & Norasakkunkit, V. (1997). Individual and collective process in the construction of the self: Self-enhancement in the United States and self-criticism in Japan. *Journal of Personality and Social Psychology, 72*, 1245–1267.

Klaczynski, P., & Narasimham, G. (1998). Development of scientific reasoning biases: Cognitive versus ego-protective explanations. *Developmental Psychology, 34*, 175–187.

Leary, M., Haupt, A., Strausser, K., & Chokel, J. (1998). Calibrating the sociometer: The relationship between interpersonal appraisals and state self-esteem. *Journal of Personality and Social Psychology, 74*, 1290–1299.

Lewis, M. (1990). Self-knowledge and social development in early life. In L. Pervin (Ed.), *Handbook of personality: Theory and research* (pp. 277–300). New York: Guilford Press.

Lewis, M., & Brooks-Gunn, J. (1979). *Social cognition and the acquisition of self.* New York: Plenum Press.

Linville, P. (1987). Self-complexity as a cognitive buffer against stress-related illness and depression. *Journal of Personality and Social Psychology, 52*, 663–676.

McGuire, W., & Padawer-Singer, A. (1976). Trait salience in the spontaneous self-concept. *Journal of Personality and Social Psychology, 33*, 743–754.

Maddux, J. (1991). Self-efficacy. In C. R. Snyder (Ed.), *Handbook of social and clinical psychology: The health perspective* (pp. 57–78). Pergamon general psychology series, Vol. 162. New York: Pergamon Press.

Marcia, J. (1980). Identity in adolescence. In J. Adelson (Ed.), *Handbook of adolescent psychology* (pp. 159–187). New York: Wiley.

Markus, H. (1977). Self-schemata and processing information about the self. *Journal of Personality & Social Psychology, 35*, 63–78.

Markus, H., & Cross, S. (1990). The interpersonal self. In L. Pervin (Ed.), *Handbook of personality: Theory and research* (pp. 576–608). New York: Guilford Press.

Markus, H., & Kitayama, S. (1991). Culture and the self: Implications for cognition, emotion, and motivation. *Psychological Review, 20*, 568–579.

Markus, H., & Kunda, Z. (1986). Stability and malleability of the self-concept. *Journal of Personality and Social Psychology, 51*, 858–866.

Markus, H., & Oyserman, D. (1989). Gender and thought. The role of the self-concept. In M. Crawford & M. Gentry (Eds.), *Gender and Thought: Psychological perspectives* (pp. 1000–127)

Markus, H., & Wurf, E. (1987). The dynamic self-concept. *Annual Review of Psychology, 38*, 299–337.

Marsh, H., & Yeung, A. (1998). Top-down, bottom-up, and horizontal models: The direction of causality in multidimensional, hierarchical self-concept models. *Journal of Personality and Social Psychology, 75*, 509–527.

Maslow, A. (1954). *Motivation and personality.* New York: Harper.

Mead, H. (1921–1925/1964). *The genesis of the self and social control.* Indianapolis, In: Bobbs-Merrill.

Mead, H. (1934/1964). *Mind, self, and society: From the standpoint of a social behaviorist.* Chicago: University of Chicago Press.

Mikulincer, M. (1998). Adult attachment style and affect regulation: Strategic variations in self-appraisals. *Journal of Personality and Social Psychology, 75*, 420–435.

Miller, D., & Ratner, R. (1998). The disparity between the actual and assumed power of self-interest. *Journal of Personality and Social Psychology, 74*, 53–62.

Moretti, M., Higgins, E. T., & Simon, F. (1990). The development of self-system vulnerabilities: Social and cognitive factors in developmental psychopathology. In R. Sternberg (Ed.), *Competence considered* (pp. 286–314). New Haven, CT: Yale University Press.

Murray, S., Holmes, J., MacDonald, G., & Ellsworth, P. (1998). Through the looking glass darkly? When self-doubts turn into relationship insecurities. *Journal of Personality and Social Psychology, 75,* 1459–1480.

Neisser, U. (1988). Five kinds of self-knowledge. *Philosophical Psychology, 1,* 35–59.

Neisser, U. (1993). *The perceived self: Ecological and interpersonal sources of self-knowledge.* New York: Cambridge University Press.

Neisser, U. (1995). Criteria for an ecological self. In P. Rochat (Ed.), *The self in infancy: Theory and research* (pp. 17–34). Amsterdam, Netherlands: North-Holland/Elsevier Science Publishers.

Norenzayan, A., Schwarz, N., & Rothman, A. (1996). Conversational relevance in the presentation of the self. *International Journal of Psychology, 31,* 184–194.

Oyserman, D. (1993). The lens of personhood: Viewing the self and others in a multicultural society. *Journal of Personality and Social Psychology, 125,* 307–337.

Oyserman, D., & Harrison, K. (1998). Implications of ethnic identity: African American identity and possible selves. In J. K. Swim & C. Stangor (Eds.), *Prejudice: The target's perspective* (pp. 281–300). San Diego: Academic Press.

Oyserman, D., & Markus, H. (1990). Possible selves and delinquency. *Journal of Personality and Social Psychology, 59,* 111–125.

Oyserman, D., & Markus, H. (1993). The sociocultural self. In J. Suls (Ed.), *Psychological perspectives on the self,* Vol. 4 (pp. 187–220). Hillsdale, NJ: Erlbaum.

Oyserman, D., & Markus, H. (1998). Self as social representation. In U. Flick (Ed.), *The psychology of the social* (pp. 107–125). New York: Cambridge University Press.

Oyserman, D., Coon, H., & Kemmelmeier, M. (1999). How American is individualism? Lessons from cultural and cross-cultural research. Under revision, *Psychological Bulletin.* Ann Arbor: University of Michigan.

Oyserman, D., Kemmelmeier, M., & Brosh, H. (1999). Racial–ethnic minority identity schemas. Manuscript submitted for publication. Ann Arbor: University of Michigan.

Oyserman, D., Sakamoto, I., & Lauffer, A. (1998). Cultural accommodation: Hybridity and the framing of social obligation. *Journal of Personality and Social Psychology, 74,* 1606–1618.

Povinelli, D. J., & Simon, B. B. (1988). Young children's understanding of briefly versus extremely delayed images of the self: Emergence of the autobiographical stance. *Developmental Psychology, 34,* 188–194.

Raeff, C. (1997). Individuals in relationships: Cultural values, children's social interactions, and the development of an American individualistic self. *Developmental Review, 17,* 204–238.

Roffey, S., Majors, K., & Tarrant, T. (1997). Friends – who needs them? What do we know and what can we do? *Educational and Child Psychology, 14,* 51–56.

Rogers, C. (1954). *Becoming a person.* Oberlin, Ohio: Oberlin College.

Rohsenow, J. (1991). *A Chinese–English dictionary of enigmatic folk similes.* Tucson: University of Arizona Press.

Ruble, D., Eisenberg, R., & Higgins, E. T. (1994). Developmental changes in achievement evaluation: Motivational implications of self–other differences. *Child Development, 65,* 1095–1110.

Ryff, C., & Keyes, C. (1995). The structure of psychological well-being revisited. *Journal of Personality and Social Psychology, 69,* 719–727.

Sampson, E. E. (1977). Psychology and the American ideal. *Journal of Personality and Social Psychology, 35,* 767–782.

Schwarz, N. (1998). Accessible content and accessibility experiences: The interplay of declarative and experiential information in judgment. *Personality and Social Psychology Review, 2,* 87–99.

Schwarz, N., Bless, H., Strack, F., Klumpp, G., Rittenauer-Schatka, H., & Simons, A. (1991). Ease of retrieval as information: Another look at the availability heuristic. *Journal of Personality and Social Psychology, 61*, 195–202.

Schwartz, S. H. (1990). Individualism–collectivism: Critique and proposed refinements. *Journal of Cross-Cultural Psychology, 21*, 139–157.

Sedikides, C., Campbell, W., Reeder, G., & Elliot, A. (1998). The self-serving bias in relational context. *Journal of Personality and Social Psychology, 74*, 378–386.

Shih, M., Pittinsky, T., & Ambady, N. (1999). Stereotype susceptibility: Identity salience and shifts in quantitative performance. *Psychological Science, 10*, 80–83.

Showers, C., Abramson, L., & Hogan, M. (1998). The dynamic self: How the content and structure of the self-concept change with mood. *Journal of Personality and Social Psychology, 75*, 478–493.

Shweder, R. (1990). Cultural psychology: What is it? In J. Stigler, R. Shweder, & G. Herdt (Eds.), *Cultural psychology: Essays in comparative human development* (pp. 1–46). New York: Cambridge University Press.

Spears, R., Oakes, P., Ellemers, N., & Haslam, S. (Eds.) (1998). *The social psychology of stereotyping and group life.* Cambridge, Mass.: Blackwell.

Steele, C. M. (1988). The psychology of self-affirmation: Sustaining integrity of the self. In L. Berkowitz (Ed.), *Advances in experimental social psychology,* Vol. 21 (pp. 261–302). New York: Academic Press.

Steele, C. M. (1997). A threat in the air: How stereotypes shape intellectual identity and performance. *American Psychologist, 52*, 613–629.

Stryker, S. (1980). *Symbolic interactionism: A social structural version.* Palo Alto, CA: Benjamin/Cummings.

Stryker, S. (1987). Identity theory: Developments and extensions. In K. Yardley & T. Honess (Eds.), *Self and identity: Psychosocial perspectives* (pp. 83–103). New York: Wiley.

Swann, W. (1997). The trouble with change: Self-verification and allegiance to the self. *Psychological Science, 8*, 177–180.

Tajfel, H. (1981). *Human groups and social categories: Studies in social psychology.* Cambridge, UK: Cambridge University Press.

Tajfel, H., & Turner, J. (1986). The social identity theory of intergroup behavior. In S. Worchel & W. Austin (Eds.), *Psychology of intergroup relations,* 2nd. edn. (pp. 7–24). Chicago: Nelson-Hall.

Taylor, S., & Brown, J. (1988). Illusion and well-being: A social psychological perspective on mental health. *Psychological Bulletin, 103*, 193–210.

Trafimow, D., & Smith, M. (1998). An extension of the "two-baskets" theory to Native Americans. *European Journal of Social Psychology, 28*, 1015–1019.

Triandis, H. C. (1989). The self and social behavior in differing cultural context. *Psychological Review, 93* (3), 506–520.

Triandis, H. C. (1995). *Individualism and collectivism.* Boulder, CO: Westview Press.

Tronick, E. Z., & Gianino, A. (1986). Interactive mismatch and repair: Challenges to the coping infant. *Zero to Three, 6*, 1–6.

Trope, Y. (1986). Self-enhancement and self-assessment in achievement behavior. In R. Sorrentino (Ed.), *Handbook of motivation and cognition: Foundations of social behavior* (pp. 350–378). New York: Guilford Press.

Turner, J. C., Hogg, M. A., Oakes, P. J., Reicher, S. D., & Wetherell, S. M. (1987). *Rediscovering the social group: A self-categorization theory.* Oxford: Blackwell Publishers.

Watkins, D., Akande, A., Fleming, J., Ismail, M., Lefner, K., Regmi, M., Watson, S., Yu, J., Adair, J., Cheng, C., Gerong, A., McInerney, D., Mpofu, E., Singh-Sengupta, S., & Wondimu, H. (1998). Cultural dimensions, gender, and the nature of self-concept: A fourteen-country study. *International Journal of Psychology, 33*, 17–31.

Weigert, A., Teige, J., & Teige, D. (1990). *Society and identity: Toward a sociological psychology*. Cambridge, UK: Cambridge University Press.

Weinberg, M., Tronick, E., & Cohn, J. (1999). Gender differences in emotional expressivity and self-regulation during early infancy. *Developmental Psychology, 35*, 175–188.

Wurf, E., & Markus, H. (1991). Possible selves and the psychology of personal growth. In D. Ozer (Ed.), *Perspectives in personality*, Vol. 3 (pp. 39–62). London: Jessica Kingsley Publishers.

Wylie, R. (1989). *Measures of self-concept*. Lincoln: University of Nebraska Press.

Yamaguchi, S., Kuhlman, D., & Sugimori, S. (1995). Personality correlates of allocentric tendencies in individualist and collectivist cultures. *Journal of Cross-Cultural Psychology, 26*, 658–672.

CHAPTER TWO

Identity Through Time: Constructing Personal Pasts and Futures

Michael Ross and Roger Buehler

People's sense of identity often includes a perception of who they were, who they are, and who they will be. While thinking about her sociability, a woman may remember being shyer as a teenager and anticipate becoming more outgoing as she ages. While evaluating her job performance, she may remember her previous positions and envision future promotions. In this chapter, we describe and contrast people's thoughts about their personal pasts and futures. We begin by discussing reasons that social psychologists should be concerned with these topics. Why not leave the study of autobiographical memory to cognitive psychologists and the study of the future to prophets or economists?

The Social Psychological Importance of Personal Pasts and Futures

The past matters

Social psychologists are interested in memory because it plays a key role in many of the phenomena of concern to them. Individuals or social groups in conflict often dispute their shared histories (Rouhana & Bar-Tal, 1998). They argue about who did what to whom, and when and why. Such quarrels can serve to maintain and exacerbate conflict, whether it be between nations or spouses. When a feud is longstanding, as in the Middle East, clashing views of events that transpired hundreds, even thousands of years ago, can arouse outrage today. These arguments about ancient history represent more than intellectual debates; the acceptance of some assertions over others can have important consequences. A group's claim to land and property is legitimized, legally and morally, by its accounts of the past. A major function of religious and national groups is to perpetuate their preferred versions of history. From an early age, children are taught history from the perspective of their group and to disregard opposing views. Along the same lines, contestants in a divorce base their claims to property and custody of children on their competing memories of the history of their marriage. Spouses are also likely to convey their own versions of the marriage to their friends and children.

People's personal histories are important to them, even in the absence of disputes. Individuals' assessments of their abilities, personalities, and self-worth are grounded in their memories of their pasts (e.g. Singer & Salovey, 1993). People form summary judgments of themselves such as: I am good at chess, poor at singing, and shy in groups of strangers but boisterous with close friends. These evaluations reflect individuals' recollections of their past experiences in the different domains. People who lose their autobiographical memories following a head injury lose their sense of self as well (Schacter, 1996).

People's memories also influence their current well-being and behavior. When individuals recall happy episodes their mood tends to improve and when they remember distressing episodes it tends to worsen. Researchers studying negative or positive emotions often temporarily create these feelings by prompting participants in experiments to recall unpleasant or pleasant personal experiences (e.g. Martin, 1990; Salovey, 1992). In everyday life, distressful events sometimes produce repetitive and intrusive memories that influence people's behavior and well-being (Davis, Lehman, Wortman, Silver, & Thompson, 1995; Holman & Cohen-Silver, 1998; Loftus, 1993; Pennebaker, 1990). For example, Nolen-Hoeksema & Morrow (1991) reported that frequency of rumination about an earthquake ten days after its occurrence predicted depression and symptoms of post-traumatic stress disorder seven weeks after the quake.

As authors of their own histories, people sometimes reinterpret past experiences and change their emotional impact (McFarland, Ross, & Giltrow, 1992; Strack, Schwarz, & Gschneidinger, 1985; Watson & McFarland, 1995). Remembering events that were initially unpleasant actually improves mood when people focus on beneficial, longer-term consequences of the episodes, such as personal growth and change (Watson & McFarland, 1995). There is other evidence for the therapeutic value of reinterpreting unpleasant experiences. Psychoanalysts often encourage patients to adopt explanations for past events that enhance their views of themselves (Spence, 1982). Likewise, social psychologists use attributional retraining techniques to influence people's beliefs about their experiences (e.g. Wilson & Linville, 1982). When successful, these attributional procedures shift people's explanations of previous failures from stable, uncontrollable causes (I am terrible at mathematics) to more unstable, controllable causes (I haven't tried hard enough). If people perceive failure as stable and uncontrollable, they are inclined to give up. If individuals perceive the cause of failure as controllable, then they are more likely to persist. They hope and expect to bring about success through their own efforts (Dweck, 1975, 1990). The trick is to distinguish outcomes that are possibly affected by one's own actions from outcomes that are not, and to adjust one's behavior accordingly.

The future matters

People's conceptions of the future often include their goals (e.g. marriage or job advancement) and their plans for attaining them. Such scenarios of the future influence people's current decisions and behavior; people act in ways that they believe will help them to obtain their objectives (Karniol & Ross, 1996). In addition to forming scenarios of how the future might unfold, people sometimes create images of possible selves, representations of how they might behave, look, or feel in the future (Cantor, Markus, Niedenthal, & Nurius, 1986;

Markus & Nurius, 1986; Markus & Ruvolo, 1989). People imagine selves that they would like to achieve as well as those that they would prefer to avoid, and these images can motivate behavior. For example, a thin person who fears becoming obese may choose to nibble crackers instead of cheesecake.

People's thoughts about the future influence how they process information. Individuals pay increased attention to aspects of themselves and their surroundings that promote attainment of their objectives (Baumeister & Newman, 1994; Dweck, 1990; Gollwitzer, 1996; Kruglanski, 1989; Kunda, 1990). Gollwitzer's analysis of the different phases of goal pursuit illustrates how people's thoughts become attuned to the information that is most relevant for their present purposes. While deciding whether to pursue a goal, people impartially evaluate information related to the feasibility and desirability of various alternatives. After deciding on a particular goal, however, people ignore information about its desirability and focus instead on their plans for achieving it (Gollwitzer, Heckhausen, & Steller, 1990).

People also exaggerate the goal relevance of ambiguous behavior in their eagerness to obtain information about their likelihood of attaining their objectives (Vorauer & Ross, 1993, 1996). For instance, a friend of the authors was anxiously awaiting a response from a journal editor regarding whether he had accepted her manuscript for publication. Meanwhile, she exchanged several email messages with this editor. In his first two notes, the editor simply launched into his message without any salutation. In a third message, the editor greeted her by her first name (Dear –), closed with his own first name, and promised that he would make a decision soon. Our friend took his friendlier style as a good omen.[1] People are often reduced to the equivalent of reading tea leaves when they are desperate for information about how the future will unfold.

People's images of the future also influence their reactions to current circumstances (Frijda, 1986; Karniol & Ross, 1996; Markus & Nurius, 1986; Showers, 1992). Goals provide a basis for evaluating self-relevant events. A student who aspires to be a professional athlete is likely to be more devastated by failing to make the varsity team, than a student who lacks such ambitions. Individuals are sometimes willing to tolerate inferior outcomes in the present (e.g. work at demeaning jobs, maintain calorie-reduced diets) in order to achieve long-term goals. At times, people will refuse immediate rewards, if they believe doing so will help them to avoid trouble or to attain superior results in the future (Mischel, 1974, 1996).

We don't want to exaggerate the power of the future, however. All too often, people give into temptation and suffer the long-term consequences of their desire for immediate gratification (Platt, 1973), as numerous dieters and some US presidents are painfully aware. Many self-help books describe procedures that supposedly help individuals to pursue long-term objectives (e.g. wonder diets). As evidence of the difficulty of achieving this end, each year welcomes a new series of self-help books that attack exactly the same problems as the previous year's tomes.

Generating Memories and Forecasts

We have argued that the future and past matter because they influence people's present emotions, decisions, and behavior. We next consider how people create their pasts and imaginary futures. Both memories and forecasts occur in the present and typically in response to people's ongoing concerns. If people think about earlier relationship failures or future shopping trips, it is usually because some present event or idea leads them to consider these things. The means by which people generate memories or forecasts are quite similar. Autobiographical memories and forecasts are creative constructions of the human mind. The suggestion that memory is a creative act may seem surprising. Words such as remembering, recalling, recollecting, and reminiscing all imply thinking of something again, bringing forth earlier thoughts from memory into current consciousness. From this perspective, remembering is more similar to reproduction than to invention. Many psychologists and philosophers have suggested, however, that the past is often partly constructed or inferred, rather than simply retrieved from memory (e.g. Bartlett, 1932; Greenwald, 1980; McAdams, 1993; Mead, 1934, 1964; Neisser, 1967; Ross, 1989; Schacter, 1996). Neisser argues that only fragments of an episode are stored in memory. He suggests that people reconstruct an event from these bits of memory, just as a paleontologist reconstructs a dinosaur from a few bones.

Constructing memories

To examine the role of construction and inference, we consider a simplified depiction of the recollection process that includes three main components: an external event, an internal representation of that event in long-term memory, and a current recollection of the event. How are these components related to each other?

Although the internal representation resembles the external event, it is typically not a precise copy for several reasons:

1 People are unlikely to notice all of the aspects of a situation. In most everyday contexts, there is simply too much going on for a person to take it all in. Also, what perceivers detect depends, in part, on their vantage point, current concerns, and emotional and physical states (a sleepy person is likely to notice less than an alert individual).
2 People's current knowledge affects their perception and interpretation of events (Bransford & Franks, 1971; Bruner & Goodman, 1947; Mead, 1964; Spiro, 1977). Consider, for example, how a game of ice hockey or cricket would appear to an expert, as opposed to a person who views it for the first time.
3 People do not transfer everything that they observe from working memory to longer-term memory. Information that is not transferred cannot be recalled later.

Just as internal representations are not exact copies of external events, recollections are not necessarily precise reproductions of the original, internal representations stored in long-term memory. Both encoding and retrieval processes contribute to differences between recollections and initial representations. People's original representations of events vary in strength and quality (depending, for example, on the importance and distinctiveness of the event), with the result that individuals forget some episodes more rapidly than others (Brewer, 1988; Johnson, Hashtroudi, & Lindsay, 1993). Also, repeated experiences of similar events may become confused with each other and combined into a generic memory (Carlston & Smith,

1996; Neisser, 1981). The details of specific events are difficult to extract from these general memories (Brewer, 1988; Linton, 1982).

During memory retrieval, people's current knowledge and beliefs influence their recollections. Memories consistent with people's present knowledge are often more accessible than memories containing contradictory information; as well, people tend to interpret ambiguous memories as congruent with their current knowledge (Anderson & Pichert, 1978; Bahrick, Hall, & Berger, 1996; Bartlett, 1932; Hastie, 1981; Hirt, 1990; Markus, 1977; Ross, 1989; Taylor & Crocker, 1981). Furthermore, when remembering an episode individuals often explain or justify their own and other people's behavior. These explanations may be inferred or revised while the episode is being reconstructed and may not have been part of the rememberer's original encoding of the event.

Ross (1989) examined the impact of a particular type of current knowledge on people's autobiographical recall. He proposed that when individuals try to recall what they were like in the past on some characteristic or trait (e.g. their attitude toward abortion five years ago or how shy they used to be) they construct the answer using two sources of information. The first is their present standing on the attribute (e.g. how shy they are now); the second is an implicit theory of how the trait is likely to have changed with time. Implicit theories incorporate specific beliefs regarding the inherent stability of an attribute, as well as general principles concerning the conditions likely to promote change. A theory of this sort is implicit in that people typically do not learn it through formal education and they may rarely discuss it.

People's implicit theories may often be quite accurate and yield recollections that correspond well with their original views. At other times, people's theories may lead them astray. Ross (1989) reported numerous examples of biases in recall that he attributed to misleading assumptions of personal stability. For example, several researchers demonstrated that people who had changed their attitudes exaggerated the consistency between their earlier and new opinions. In one of these studies, participants described how they had recalled their earlier attitudes. Many individuals reported that they assumed that their beliefs were stable over time and that they inferred their previous opinions from their current attitudes.

More recently, Levine (1997) asked supporters of Ross Perot to report their emotional reactions to his abrupt withdrawal from the US presidential race in July of 1992. Perot reentered the race during the following October and eventually received nearly a fifth of the popular vote. After the elections in November, Levine asked supporters to recall their earlier emotional reactions to Perot's withdrawal and to describe their current feelings toward Perot. People's memories of their earlier emotions were biased in the direction of their current appraisals of Perot. McFarland & Ross (1987) found a similar effect for people's recollections of their earlier evaluations of their dating partners. People who fell more in love after their initial evaluations exaggerated, and those who fell less in love underestimated, the degree to which they had previously reported caring for their partner. The findings from these two studies suggest that people suppose that their emotional reactions to individuals are fairly stable over time and that they use their current assessments as a basis for inferring their earlier feelings.

Feldman Barrett (1997) studied the relation of people's enduring self-concepts to their recollections of their emotional reactions. Respondents kept diary ratings of their emotional experiences and subsequently recalled the emotions they had reported. Those who scored high on a neuroticism scale remembered experiencing more negative emotion than they had reported; conversely, respondents who scored high on extroversion remembered feeling more positive emotion than they had reported earlier.

Just as individuals sometimes exaggerate their stability, they may also overestimate the degree to which they have changed. Retrospective overestimation of change is likely when people experience a circumstance that they expect to produce change, but that in reality has minimal impact. Self-help programs are a context in which people's expectancies and hopes of change are likely to be disappointed. Although such programs often have considerable face validity, they tend to be remarkably unsuccessful (Ross & Conway, 1986). Conway & Ross (1984) studied the relation between memory and expectations for change in the context of a study skills program. They asked university students to evaluate their study skills and then randomly assigned half of them to a study skills program that lasted several weeks and the remaining half to a control condition. Although participants in the treatment program expected to improve their grades, their program, like most other study skills courses, was ineffective. At the conclusion of the course, participants in the treatment and control conditions were asked to recall their original ratings of their study skills. They were reminded that the researcher had their initial ratings and would assess the accuracy of their recall. Participants who took the course remembered their pre-program ratings as being worse than they had initially reported. In contrast, control participants, who had not received the program, exhibited no systematic bias in recall. The biased recollections of participants in the study skills course would support their theory that the program had improved their skills. More generally, a tendency to revise the past in order to claim personal improvement may explain why many individuals report that they benefit from ineffective pop therapies and self-improvement programs (Conway & Ross, 1984).

The research on autobiographical recall does not indicate that biased recollections are more common than accurate recollections, or that people's implicit theories of personal change or stability are generally false. Indeed, some researchers have reported impressive degrees of accuracy, as well as evidence of biased recall (e.g. Bahrick, Hall, & Berger, 1996; Feldman Barrett, 1997; Levine, 1997). Also, research conducted on autobiographical memory in other contexts has revealed that people's recollections can be fairly accurate, at least for the gist of past experiences (e.g. Neisser, 1981). The studies we have described do suggest, however, that individuals' self-concepts, beliefs, and implicit theories influence their memories.

Now, let's return to the scheme of the recollection process and subtract a couple of elements. Suppose that there was no external event, and therefore no internal representation of that event in long-term memory. Imagine, however, that people think about an event and discuss it with others. They may subsequently mistake the source of their recollection, believing that the thoughts stem from an external event that occurred to them (Johnson, Hashtroudi, & Lindsay, 1993; Johnson & Raye, 1981). Indeed the more often they think or talk about it, the more likely they are to believe that it is a genuine memory (Schacter, 1996). Researchers have also shown that leading questions and misleading information can cause people to confess to crimes they apparently didn't commit (Ofshe, 1992) and to report experiencing events that they only imagined (Ceci, Ross, & Toglia, 1987; Hyman & Pentland, 1996; Loftus, 1993).

People remember what they want to

There is another reason that people's recollections may differ from their original encoding of an episode. Recall is selective and goal driven. People don't necessarily retrieve everything they have stored; they recover details that suit their current purposes (e.g. Anderson & Pichert, 1978; Ross & Buehler, 1994). To demonstrate the impact of motivation on reconstructive memory, researchers have altered people's beliefs about the desirability of specific behaviors and then assessed people's memories of their past actions (e.g. Klein & Kunda, 1993; McDonald & Hirt, 1997; Murray & Holmes, 1993; Ross, McFarland, & Fletcher, 1981; Sanitioso, Kunda, & Fong, 1990). Murray and Holmes asked undergraduates in dating relationships to report the amount of conflict they had with their partner while deciding on joint activities. Participants in the experimental condition then read a bogus psychological article that argued that the development of intimacy in a relationship depended on people's willingness to express disagreement. Thus, experimental participants who had earlier reported that they and their partner experienced little conflict now found out, much to their surprise, that this was actually bad news for their relationship. A control condition contained participants who had also reported low conflict with their partners, but who did not read the bogus article.

How did experimental participants cope with their new understanding that conflict was desirable? One thing they did was alter their views of their partner's past behaviors. When asked to assess their relationships on a number of dimensions, experimental participants were more likely than controls to endorse items such as "My partner clearly expresses his/her needs even when he/she knows that these needs conflict with my needs." In short, they "discovered" that their relationship was appropriately conflict-ridden. The precise mechanism underlying this finding is unclear. It seems likely, however, that participants selectively recalled and interpreted behaviors in accordance with their preferences.

There is a small research literature on memory for conflicts that provides intriguing evidence of the impact of motivation on recall. Baumeister and his colleagues (Baumeister, Stillwell, & Wotman, 1990; Baumeister, Wotman, & Stillwell, 1993; Stillwell & Baumeister, 1997) have studied how people who anger someone else (perpetrators) remember a dispute as compared to individuals who are provoked (victims). Provoking behavior is generally seen as less harmful and more justifiable by perpetrators than by victims. Along the same lines, young children recall disputes with their siblings in a manner that tends to absolve themselves of blame. They remember more harmful actions by their siblings than by themselves, as well as portray their own actions as justifiable, and their siblings' behavior as arbitrary and incomprehensible (Ross, Ross, Wilson, & Smith, in press). People seem to be more willing to accept responsibility for harmful actions in conflicts that happened a long time ago than in recent disputes (Wilson, Celnar, & Ross, 1997).

Recent studies of mood regulation provide further evidence of motivated remembering. Several theorists have suggested that individuals who are feeling blue may attempt to improve their moods by selectively retrieving pleasant memories (Clark & Isen, 1982; Isen, 1987; Singer & Salovey, 1988). In the first demonstration of this effect, Parrott & Sabini (1990) found that participants experiencing negative moods were more likely to recall pleasant events from their lives than were participants experiencing positive moods. Subsequent researchers suggested that certain personality traits may predispose individuals to alleviate negative affect by engaging in mood-incongruent recall (Boden & Baumeister, 1997; McFarland & Buehler, 1997; Smith & Petty, 1995). For example, McFarland and Buehler found that only individuals who are especially inclined to focus on their feelings recruited more pleasant memories after a negative mood induction than after a neutral mood induction.

In addition, the precise manner in which people focus on their moods moderates the impact of moods on memory (McFarland & Buehler, in press). When people adopt a reflective orientation to their moods (characterized by a willingness to attend openly to their feelings and an inclination to improve their feelings), they respond to negative moods by recalling pleasant past experiences. In contrast, when people assume a ruminative orientation to their moods (characterized by a sense that their feelings are threatening, confusing, and inescapable), they react to negative moods by remembering unpleasant past experiences.

When memories don't fit people's needs

The claim that recall is selective implies that people can retrieve memories that satisfy their current concerns. Sometimes, however, there is a mismatch between the information the person requires and the past that is represented in his or her memory. As a result, rememberers must reconstruct the past to suit their needs. One of us was recently invited to complete a survey on diet, life style, and health. The questions asked middle-aged respondents how many hours per week, on average, they spent on various activities in the past year (e.g. sitting, standing, or walking in the home), how frequently, on average, they consumed various beverages and foods (per day, per week, per month), and how often each year they engaged in recreational pursuits at different points in their life (e.g. swam at an outdoor pool, sunbathed, hiked, played baseball, soccer and football, or climbed a glacier between the ages 0–9, 10–19, 20–29, 30–39, 40–49, 50–59, 60+). Respondents were also asked to describe themselves now and in the past on specific dimensions (e.g. current weight and weight at 20 years of age).

One difficulty with many of these questions is that they cannot be answered simply by accessing relevant recollections. Few people have noted and stored in memory how many hours per week they sit at home, or how frequently they sunbathed per year between the ages of 20–29. Answers to such questions have to be constructed from memories (e.g. how many hours people remember sitting at home yesterday), arithmetic calculations (to derive averages), and people's intuitions about how they have changed or remained the same over time (e.g. how much weight have I gained since the age of 20?). Not surprisingly, perhaps, people's answers to such questions sometimes shift dramatically in response to changes in the framing of the items or response scales (Schwarz, Groves, & Schuman, 1998). When individuals make up answers on the spot, they tend to use whatever cues are available in a rather frantic attempt to respond to difficult queries.

We don't present this example as an indictment of surveys. Instead, we suggest that a disparity between current needs and stored information is a ubiquitous feature of everyday recall. Information is often not stored in a format that matches exactly what people need at the time of recall, as students writing examinations know only too well. Moreover the disparity may exist even when people pose questions to themselves. When individuals attempt to evaluate their friendliness or honesty, they may discover pertinent episodes stored in memory, but they will need to weigh, integrate, and interpret the information in a manner that allows them to answer the question at hand. How friendly am I if I am outgoing with my friends but shy and awkward with strangers? How honest am I if I return a wallet I find on the street to its rightful owner, but I cheat on my income tax? People's current goals and beliefs are likely to have a strong impact on the integration and interpretation process.

It has probably not escaped the reader's notice that there is a circularity to our description of the relation between recall and present beliefs. Just as people's current views are influenced by their memories, so too their prevailing beliefs affect their recollections. The process doesn't end here, however. When people revise the past on the basis of their current knowledge, their recollections can then serve the function of justifying and thereby strengthening their present beliefs. In a demonstration of the reciprocal relation between beliefs and recall, researchers first changed participants' attitudes using a persuasive communication (Ross, McFarland, Conway, & Zanna, 1983). Next, they prompted participants to recall behavior that was relevant or irrelevant to their new attitudes. Participants in the relevant-recall condition selectively recalled acting in a manner that was consistent with their new beliefs. Importantly, the recall of relevant behavior then served to bolster the new attitudes. Participants in the relevant-recall condition were more resistant to attacks on their new attitudes and more likely to state an intention to act on their new beliefs. These studies indicate that attitudes affect recall of past actions which, in turn, influences people's commitment to their attitudes.

Finally, note that people seem to underestimate the malleability of their own recollections and, as a result, have too much faith in the accuracy of their memories (e.g. Neisser & Harsch, 1992; Ross, 1997; Trope, 1978). Even when confronted with evidence that their own memory conflicts with someone else's, individuals tend to believe their own recollections (Ross, Buchler, & Karr, 1998). People appear to view themselves as relatively immune to the biases and errors in recall that afflict other individuals.

Constructing forecasts

In contrast to remembering, forecasting is obviously a creative act. People infer the future – it doesn't exist in the present. Forecasts are constructions based partly on imagination and partly on other relevant sources of information. For example, our expectations for how long it would take us to write this chapter reflected our beliefs about how busy we would be with work and family in the coming months, our memories of our earlier collaborative efforts, and our knowledge of the deadline for its submission.

That the future is clearly a construction does not mean that forecasters simply give their imagination free reign. Except in rare flights of runaway fantasy, people imagine futures that are consistent with their self-knowledge and theories about how the world works (Armor & Taylor, 1998; Johnson & Sherman, 1990). Having settled long ago into academic positions, the authors of this chapter are as unlikely to predict becoming starting pitchers for the New York Yankees as they are to recall having assumed this role in the past. Just as people construct pasts that are plausible to them in light of their current beliefs and theories, so too they imagine futures on the basis of their present knowledge (Johnson & Sherman, 1990; Loewenstein & Schkade, in press; Mead, 1934, 1964). As Loewenstein and Schkade observed, if beliefs and theories are important to remembering when people have past experiences to retrieve, then beliefs and theories likely play an even more important role in forecasting, especially of novel experiences.

People's depictions of the future often take the form of scenarios (Buehler, Griffin, & Ross, 1994; Dawes, 1988; Johnson & Sherman, 1990; Kahneman & Tversky, 1982a; Rehm & Gadenne, 1990; Zukier, 1986). Based on their beliefs about themselves and the circum-stances they are likely to confront, people develop scenarios that describe, in a narrative representation, the progression of the present to the future. These scenarios frequently con-sist of concrete, causally linked sequences of events (e.g. I'll get to my office by nine a.m., work exclusively on the Gleber contract, and have it ready for signing by 12 noon). When people base predictions on such imagined scenarios do they appreciate the tentativeness of their forecasts, recognizing that the future could actually unfold in a variety of ways? Apparently not. People tend to construct a single, or very small number of scenarios, for any given judgment situation, and to assume the validity of their scenario representation (Griffin, Dunning, & Ross, 1990).

Memory researchers have shown that when people repeatedly imagine a past experience that did not occur, they become increasingly confident that it actually happened (Schacter, 1996). Along the same lines, when individuals imagine the occurrence of a future event, they become more convinced that it will come to pass (Johnson & Sherman, 1990; Koehler, 1991; Olson, Roese, & Zanna, 1996). Individuals instructed to imagine particular outcomes for events ranging from football games to presidential elections subsequently estimate those results as more likely (Carroll, 1978). People who are asked to explain why they might excel on upcoming tasks predict that they will perform better than do individuals who are asked to describe why they might fail (Campbell & Fairey, 1985; Sherman, Skov, Hervitz, & Stock, 1981). Apparently the construction of a scenario for a particular outcome focuses people's attention on that sequence of events and interferes with their ability to generate scenarios that would yield alternative outcomes (Hoch, 1984; Koehler, 1991). As a result of this differential focus, the hypothesized scenario and outcome seem more probable.

Unfortunately, the hypothesized scenario is less likely to occur than people typically think (Kahneman & Tversky 1979, 1982b; Kahneman & Lovallo, 1993). Even when a particular scenario is relatively probable, the likelihood that a somewhat different sequence of events will occur is often greater. Consider a woman who plans to finish many complex projects on the weekend. Her careful detailed scenario for completing the projects may be more prob-able, in advance, than any other single scenario. Nevertheless, the chances of some event occurring that would prevent her from completing all of the projects may be greater, simply because of the vast number of potential impediments (power failures, illness, unexpected visits from friends, computer crashes, writing block, and so forth). Although each of these obstacles may have a relatively low likelihood of occurrence, the probabilities are additive; the likelihood that *some* unexpected event will arise is high.

In addition to promoting overconfidence, the scenario approach to prediction results in the neglect of other kinds of information that could help people to form more accurate forecasts. In discussing plan based predictions, Kahneman & Tversky (1979, 1982b) distinguished between two modes of judgment, which they labeled the inside and the outside views. The inside view corresponds to the focus on plan based scenarios that we have described: people derive their predictions from specific scenarios and impressions of the particular case at hand. The outside view treats the current case as an instance of a broader set of similar cases. For instance, people might base their forecasts of how long they will take to finish an upcoming project on a set of their own past experiences (personal base rates) or others' experiences (population base rates) with a set of similar projects. People could often make more realistic predictions if they adopted an outside view and considered relevant base rates (Dunning & Story, 1991; Osberg & Shrauger, 1986; Shrauger, Mariano, & Walter, 1998; Vallone, Griffin, Lin, & Ross, 1990).

The scenario approach to prediction tends to yield overly optimistic, as well as overly confident predictions. Theoretically, people could be too confident about either pessimistic or optimistic predictions, and scenario based thinking should not always produce optimistic forecasts. However, there is reason to suppose that people will typically construct scenarios that depict pleasant outcomes. When thinking about the future, people often focus on their goals (Karniol & Ross, 1996). They consider how events will transpire so as to produce their preferred outcomes. They often neglect to think about the possibility of setbacks or failures and how they might deal with such difficulties. As Armor & Taylor (1998) have noted, people rarely plan to fail. Thus scenario thinking is a cognitive mechanism that can help us to understand why people's forecasts often look suspiciously similar to their desires.

Finally, note that people do not always generate scenarios when contemplating their futures. The emphasis on scenarios may reflect the nature of events and plans that researchers have typically examined. Investigators have focused on the prediction and planning of single events that are relatively specific and discrete. In everyday life, people may sometimes contemplate their futures at a more general level. Rawls (1971) proposed that people develop an overarching life scheme that provides a framework for more specific and immediate plans. When people engage in life planning, they contemplate the possible purpose, content, and general course of their lives. Relative to everyday plans, life plans have a longer time frame, and involve goals that are more complex, abstract, vague, and open-ended (Smith, 1996). Whereas everyday plans are likely to include a scenario depicting a concrete sequence of decisions and actions, life plans are more likely to be at the level of a vague intention.

Predictions as wish fulfillment

Scenario thinking provides a cognitive explanation of optimistic forecasts. Motivation also plays an important role, in part by guiding the types of scenarios people generate. Across many domains, individuals' predictions of what will happen appear to reflect what they would like to see happen (Armor & Taylor, 1998; Kunda, 1990; Taylor & Brown, 1988). Lehman & Taylor (1988) studied California students who were assigned, on the basis of a lottery, to live in dormitories rated either seismically sound or unsound. When asked to predict the likelihood and severity of a future earthquake, students who were living in the unsafe dorms tended to downplay the threat.

People's rosy view of the future extends beyond their personal lives. Granberg & Brent (1983) examined data from national surveys conducted prior to eight US presidential elections and found that people tended to expect their preferred candidate to win by a ratio of about 4 : 1. Although very robust, this "preference–expectation link" was strongest in years in which the outcome was relatively unclear in advance, and among respondents who were highly involved but poorly informed. Analyses of panel data indicated that people's preferences were more stable than their expectations; they were more likely to bend their expectations to match their preferences than vice versa.

A more recent study examined the interplay between motivation and cognition in producing overly optimistic task completion estimates (Buehler, Griffin, & MacDonald, 1997). Individuals with incentives to finish tasks early showed more unrealistic optimism than those without such incentives. Canadians who expected an income tax refund predicted they would file their tax returns much earlier than those who did not expect a refund. In actual fact, the two groups mailed their forms at about the same time and later than either group predicted. A subsequent study identified mediating cognitive mechanisms by examining participants' thoughts as they generated task predictions. Monetary incentives for early completion led people to focus on plan based scenarios for the future and to ignore relevant past experiences. In other words, the motivation to finish early appeared to prompt the very pattern of cognitive processes that produces unrealistic optimism.

Imagined futures can be self-fulfilling

An additional consequence of scenario based predictions should tend to counteract unrealistic optimism: people's thoughts and forecasts sometimes influence what actually transpires. Asking people to imagine or predict specific future actions increases the likelihood of occurrence of the predicted actions (e.g. Greenwald, Carnot, Beach, & Young, 1987; Gregory, Cialdini, & Carpenter, 1982; Sherman, 1980; Sherman & Anderson, 1987). In an early demonstration of the self-fulfilling nature of predictions, Sherman (1980) asked one group of people whether they would agree to collect donations for the American Cancer Society if they were asked to do so; 48 percent said they would. By comparison, only 4 percent of a control group of respondents, who had not made predictions, agreed to help collect donations when asked to do so. As a result of making their predictions, however, the first group was much more helpful than controls: 31 percent of these participants agreed to collect donations when contacted several days later, thus bringing their behavior more in line with their forecasts.

Even in the absence of explicit predictions, the act of imagining future events may help to bring them about. Taylor & Schneider (1989) proposed that "mental simulations" of future episodes can facilitate goal achievement by increasing people's expectations of success, increasing their motivation, and suggesting concrete plans. Recent research suggests that mental simulations focused on precisely *how* the individual will attain the desired outcome, rather than on the outcome itself, can be particularly effective (Pham & Taylor, in press; Taylor, Pham, Rivkin, & Armor, 1998). For example, students who were instructed to simulate the process of studying for a midterm exam subsequently studied longer and received higher grades than students who did not mentally rehearse their exam preparation.

Similarly, Gollwitzer (1993, 1996) has argued that the process of forming clear, specific, future plans helps individuals to achieve their objectives. Gollwitzer notes that plans assist people to overcome problems with initiating and successfully executing goal-directed actions. Plans serve to connect an anticipated situational context (opportunity) with a specific, goal-directed behavior (action). Thus a man might plan: "As soon as my child falls asleep, I will go downstairs to my office, turn on the computer, and begin working on that Gleber contract." As a result of planning, people become more likely to detect the opportunities for achieving their goals (child is asleep) and to seize those opportunities when they arise (head straight to the office).

Mental simulations may be most effective if they lead people to vividly imagine the future. Memory researchers have shown that when people are asked to visualize past events that never happened, they are more likely to believe afterward that the episodes actually occurred (Hyman & Pentland, 1996; Johnson, Raye, Wang, & Taylor, 1979). For example, people who are asked to visualize childhood events that didn't occur are later more likely to report that these events transpired (Hyman & Pentland, 1996). By the same token, vividly imagining future events may increase people's belief in the occurrence of these episodes. Such increases in confidence may, in turn, prompt people to behave in ways that will cause the events to materialize.

The evidence that mental simulation and concrete planning can spur desired behavior might seem inconsistent with the finding that detailed, plan based future scenarios produce overly confident and optimistic forecasts. The answer is that scenario thinking and planning have dual effects, rendering predictions more optimistic and actions more likely to occur. Whether these mental processes produce overly optimistic forecasts depends on their relative impact on prediction and behavior. We suspect that mental simulations will often exert a stronger impact on people's predictions than on their behavior. Whether people's plans are self-fulfilling likely depends on such factors as the length of time between the plan and its execution (which may be associated with the probability that people's priorities will change) and the extent to which its implementation is affected by factors outside the control of the individual (e.g. Buehler & Griffin, 1996; Hoch, 1985; Wilson & LaFleur, 1995). All too often, external events conspire to prevent even the best-intentioned and most committed individuals from fully accomplishing their objectives.

Improving predictions

Attempting to counteract overconfidence and unrealistic optimism, researchers have explored a number of possible interventions. One general approach, evident in the research just described, involves prompting people to bring their behavior in line with their forecasts. Where possible (such as when the events are relatively immediate and controllable) this may be the preferable approach (Armor & Taylor, 1998; Taylor, Pham, Rivkin, & Armor, 1998). An alternative tactic is to try to bring forecasts in line with likely behavior. In this regard, techniques based on prompting people to generate scenarios that differ from their initial scenario would appear promising (Dougherty, Gettys, & Thomas, 1997; Griffin, Dunning, & Ross, 1990; Hirt & Markman, 1995; Hoch, 1985). Such techniques directly target people's natural inclination to become committed to a single scenario for the future. Forecasters are not allowed to dwell exclusively on the scenarios they prefer or can readily generate.

In many business and organizational contexts, where uncertain and uncontrollable events present serious difficulties for long-term planning, techniques involving multiple scenarios have become popular forecasting tools (Bunn & Salo, 1993; Kuhn & Sniezek, 1996; Schnaars & Topol, 1987; Schoemaker, 1993). By the 1980s, more than half of the "Fortune 500" industrial companies were using such "scenario-analysis" techniques (Linneman & Klein, 1983). Despite the growing popularity of this approach in business contexts, the few relevant studies that evaluate its effects yield conflicting results.

Advocates of multiple scenario analysis claim that the approach prompts people to appreciate the unpredictability of the future, thus countering overconfidence in any one specific prediction and promoting contingency planning. Several studies indicate that asking people to contemplate more than one possible future outcome does serve to lower their confidence in the predictions they subsequently generate (Dougherty, Gettys, & Thomas, 1997; Griffin, Dunning, & Ross, 1990; Hoch, 1985; Schoemaker, 1993). Other researchers have found that considering alternative scenarios can actually increase people's confidence in an initially favored forecast (Kuhn & Sniezek, 1996; Schnaars & Topol, 1987). Rather than instilling a sense of cautious uncertainty, then, the alternative scenarios seemed to embolden forecasters. Researchers who found that alternative scenarios increase people's confidence in their forecasts presented scenarios to participants. In contrast, researchers who demonstrated a reduction of confidence required participants to generate their own scenarios. To be effective, alternative scenarios must seem credible to forecasters (Hirt & Markman, 1995; Kahneman & Tversky, 1982a). Conceivably, people find alternative scenarios that they generate themselves to be more plausible and relevant to their individual concerns than those provided by a researcher.

There is even less research assessing the impact of multiple scenario generation on accuracy than there is on confidence. Hoch (1985) reported that the generation of multiple scenarios increased the accuracy of predictions. In contrast, Wilson & LaFleur (1995) found that thinking about the reasons favoring and opposing one's predictions reduced the accuracy of forecasts. Finally, Schoemaker (1993) found no impact of multiple scenario generation on accuracy. At this point, there is little evidence that multiple scenario generation increases the accuracy of predictions.

Finally, people sometimes try to increase the accuracy of their forecasts by seeking advice from others, including experts and friends. Over the centuries, humans have consulted such "experts" as oracles, psychics, and, in more recent times, economists and financial consultants. In ancient Greece, the temple of Delphi was operated as a forecasting service (Makridakis, 1990). The oracles tended to offer equivocal predictions that were difficult to invalidate. In his history of the Ancient World recorded in the fifth century BC, Herodotus (1996) presented the tale of Croesus who asked the Delphi oracles whether he should attack the Persians. The oracles replied that if Croesus attacked the Persians, "he would destroy a mighty empire" (ibid., p. 23). So Croesus attacked the Persians and did destroy a great empire – his own. The Delphi oracles stayed in business for more than 500 years and became the wealthiest institution in Greece, even though the predictive power of their prophecies was low (Makridakis, 1990).

It is not clear that professionals in the forecasting business tend to perform much better today (Makridakis, 1990; Yates, 1990). For example, Makridakis reports that forecasts offered by financial experts are of little or no value. Statistical analyses reveal that, because changes in stock market prices are essentially random, forecasting future prices (either as a whole or for any individual stock) cannot be done any better by experts than by using "today's" closing price as the forecast. If stock market experts could forecast accurately, then professionally managed portfolios and mutual funds would outperform the market average. There is no strong indication that this is true. Although by chance some experts might outperform the market average for a certain period of time, there is little evidence that they can do so consistently.

In everyday life, people often consult family members or friends when pondering their personal futures. MacDonald & Ross (in press) compared students' predictions about the longevity of their own dating relationships, to predictions reported by their parents and roommates. The young lovers focused predominantly on the positive aspects of their relationships while generating their predictions and were too optimistic. Interestingly, the roommates and parents offered both less optimistic and more accurate predictions.

Observers are often less motivated than concerned individuals to focus on a biased subset of the available information. Thus, a knowledgeable, detached observer may be able to offer more realistic appraisals of your chances of sticking to a new diet or having your home renovations completed according to schedule. In contrast, observers who share your desires, may also share your overly optimistic views of the future. Buehler & Griffin (1998) found that when offered a cash incentive based on another person's achievements, observers' predictions for the performers were as optimistically biased as those of the performers themselves.

Optimism and temporal proximity of future events

People's pervasive optimism about the future declines as an event gets closer in time. For example, students anticipate a stronger performance on a midterm exam when asked on the first day of class than on the day of the examination itself (Gilovich, Kerr, & Medvec, 1993). One explanation of such effects is that different information becomes salient as the event approaches (for alternative interpretations see Gilovich, Kerr, & Medvec, 1993 and Savitsky, Medvec, Charlton, & Gilovich, 1998). Well before an exam, students may have exaggerated expectations about the amount of studying they will do. On the day of the examination, they know all too well how much they have studied. Along the same lines, Liberman & Trope (1998) noted that people's thoughts about events change as the events approach. They suggested that distant future events are assessed in terms of their desirability, whereas more immediate events are evaluated in terms of their feasibility. For example, when we contemplate a vacation six months from now, we think of "rest and relaxation"; when the same vacation is about to happen we focus on last-minute work arrangements, packing suitcases, and crowded airports. In their research, Liberman and Trope found that desirable events often appear better from a distant vantage point.

Sheppard, Ouellette, & Fernandez (1996) studied the impact of temporal proximity on people's expectations about test results. Students who were initially optimistic about their scores on an examination became overly pessimistic (relative to their actual performance) just before receiving their grades. Likewise, people undergoing tests for serious medical conditions, who are optimistic about their results weeks before they are known, abandon their optimistic outlook moments before learning the results (Taylor & Sheppard, 1998). Sheppard and his colleagues suggested that this shift from optimism to pessimism as feedback approaches is motivated, in part, by a desire to avoid feelings of disappointment. People lower their hopes to "brace themselves" for bad news.

This research on temporal proximity appears to indicate that people readily entertain quite different scenarios about the future. One day they anticipate glorious futures in which they achieve their desired goals; sometime later they are more pessimistic. These shifts reflect the changing information that is salient to people as they make their predictions and their shifting motivational concerns. We don't mean to imply, however, that people are quite willing to alter their predictions. As noted earlier, at any given point in time, individuals seem to be wedded to their current scenario of the future and assume that alternative scenarios are implausible.

Assessing the Accuracy of Forecasts

If people's long-term predictions tend to be as misguided as we imply, why do individuals continue to exhibit high confidence in their forecasting ability? One answer is that people process outcomes that confirm forecasts differently than those that disconfirm predictions. For example, even when an outcome is unambiguously different from the one they predicted, people may minimize the degree of their error. In one line of research (Gilovich, 1983; Gilovich & Douglas, 1986), gamblers who forecasted, and bet on, professional football games were later asked to think aloud about the outcomes of their bets. Individuals who made incorrect forecasts tended to convince themselves that they were almost right (and hence that their prediction was not really in error), whereas those who were correct were not inclined to consider that they were almost wrong. Tetlock (1998) obtained similar results in the realm of political prediction.

A second problem is that people do not precisely specify the evidence that will count as support for their predictions, and thus can end up "detecting" too much support (Gilovich, 1991). People's vaguely stated predictions can often be confirmed by various outcomes after the fact, many of which would not have been deemed acceptable criteria *a priori* (remember the Delphi oracles). This problem is exacerbated when the target of the prediction is inherently fuzzy or hard to define. Consider a worker who predicts that her newly appointed supervisor will create havoc. What exactly is havoc and how is it to be assessed? Because of the vagueness of the target outcome, this person may be overly impressed by any number of events with only tenuous connections to the prediction.

A third explanation for people's confidence in the accuracy of their predictions is that they misremember their forecasts. Once people know an outcome, they often claim to have predicted that very result, even though they didn't (Fischhoff, 1975; Fischhoff & Beyth, 1975). This hindsight bias may occur because individuals integrate the outcome information with their other relevant knowledge, creating a scenario in which the known outcome is the most plausible result (Fischhoff & Beyth, 1975). When a man's proposal of marriage is rejected, he may conclude: "Of course she'd say no. Why would a beautiful woman want to marry a loser like me?" When asked to retrieve an earlier prediction individuals are influenced by their current belief that the known outcome is highly likely. Having concluded that rejection was almost certain, our swain is likely to recall being more pessimistic than he actually was before he popped the question.

There may be another reason that this hindsight bias occurs. As noted earlier, individuals may generate not just one prediction, but a series of different predictions as an event approaches. Some days a lover might imagine that his proposal of marriage will be accepted and other days (probably closer in time to the proposal) that it will be rejected. The outcome that eventually occurs may then bring to mind whichever prediction matches it. When the lover then claims that he "knew" that he would be rejected, he is right – sort of. However, he also "knew" that the opposite outcome would happen.

Forecasting Future Feelings

Recently, researchers have begun to examine people's predictions of their future feelings. This area of research has important practical implications because people often base their decisions on how they think they will feel about different outcomes (Kahneman, 1994; Kahneman & Snell, 1992).

At a gross level, people are quite accurate in making such predictions. For example, most people probably think correctly that they would prefer a massage to an electric shock. People's predictions about the magnitude and duration of their emotional reactions to events are often wrong, however. In summarizing the rapidly growing literature on affective forecasting, Loewenstein & Schkade (in press) identified three separate, but interrelated, mechanisms that may produce errors in predicting feelings: people may hold incorrect implicit theories about the determinants of their feelings, they may focus on different considerations when predicting their reactions to events than when actually experiencing those events, and when in a "cold" state (e.g. when calm) they may have difficulty predicting how they will feel or behave in a "hot" state (e.g. when angry or sexually aroused).

First consider the problem of inaccurate intuitive theories. Gilbert, Pinel, Wilson, Blumberg, & Wheatley (1998) proposed that people underestimate their ability to cope with unpleasant events. In several studies, participants predicted they would be more devastated by such outcomes as a relationship break-up, a failed election bid by their favored candidate, negative test feedback, and the failure to obtain a job, than they in fact were. An anecdotal example may resonate with the reader. Think of someone who has endured a personal tragedy that you have not suffered yourself (e.g. loss of a spouse or a serious illness), and consider how well that person has coped with the problem. You may find yourself thinking that the person has managed surprisingly well, far better than you would under similar circumstances. We suggest that such feelings of surprise reflect the erroneous theories people have about human resilience. Individuals are able to transform, invent, and ignore information in ways that enable them to mitigate the impact of unpleasant events.

Lowenstein and Schkade discussed an additional obstacle to accurate affective forecasting. People may exaggerate the emotional impact of a future event because they focus on that event alone and fail to consider the effects of the many other factors that influence their well-being at any given time. Wilson (1997) termed this the "focalism" problem and described a study in which college students overestimated the emotional impact of an upcoming event, such as a win or loss by their school football team, unless they were prompted to consider the other events in their lives that would occur at that time.

A third source of prediction errors involves the "empathy gap" that exists between different hedonic states (Loewenstein, 1996; Loewenstein & Schkade, in press). People often have difficulty imagining how they will feel or behave when they encounter temptation, high arousal, or duress. Christensen-Szalanski (1984) found that a majority of expectant women who anticipated that they would not want to use anesthesia during childbirth, reversed their decision when they went into labor. Similarly, people with a full stomach may underestimate the difficulty of dieting when hungry; people who are not sexually aroused may underestimate their likelihood of failing to use condoms during intercourse; and people who are not in shopping malls may misjudge their urge to spend money when they get there.

Collective Remembering and Forecasting

Although we have portrayed remembering and forecasting as solitary acts, pasts and futures are shared as well as individual constructions. People's memories of their personal histories are affected by what others tell them about themselves. Thus, researchers studying people's earliest recollections cannot be certain whether individuals recall their own experiences or whether they inadvertently include information that other people have provided about an event (Ross, 1997; Usher & Neisser, 1993). Similarly, individuals' expectations for the future reflect information they obtain from their social environments.

Memories and futures are shared in other ways. People who work or live together often distribute information to be remembered among each other so that another person's mind can serve as an external memory repository (Hollingshead, 1998; Moreland, Argote, & Krishman, 1996; Wegner, 1987; Wegner, Erber, & Raymond, 1991). A married couple might distribute memory tasks as follows: "You remember the phone numbers of your family and I'll remember those of mine; you remember our doctor's appointments and I'll remember when the car needs an oil change; you remember the dates of our children's birthdays and I'll remember which baseball teams won the World Series over the last decade." Of course, memory tasks are typically not assigned as explicitly as these examples imply. The allocation often occurs naturally over time as a result of people's differing experiences, interests, and expertise. Dixon & Gould (1996) have proposed that cognitive collaboration increases with age, and may help older adults to compensate for age-related declines in individual memories.

Even more than remembering, planning for the future is likely to be a social rather than personal activity (Smith, 1996). In a social relationship, the plans and goals of one individual will greatly influence the plans and goals of others. Something as mundane as preparing a family meal often involves harmonization of the schedules and preferences of several people. Individuals may alter or delay their goals to satisfy those of significant others in their lives. In addition, individuals sometimes construct plans for others. For instance, parents and teachers design children's futures, and spouses choose meals or entertainment for each other. Often planning for another person involves trying to predict his or her likes and dislikes (e.g. regarding gifts, meals, and entertainment), a social form of affective forecasting that might be fraught with error.

Thus individuals can serve as external planners just as they serve as external memory reservoirs. Although psychologists have shown great interest in investigating people's forecasts, they have paid little attention to the social-interactive aspects of goal selection and planning, and to the fact that individuals typically synchronize their goals with the desires and plans of others. Such accommodations are likely to involve negotiation and compromise, to evoke happiness, disappointment, or anger, and to have long-term implications for individuals as well as their relationships. The study of the social aspects of goal setting would appear to be fertile ground for investigation.

Conclusions

Describing her vigil over her critically ill daughter, the novelist Isabel Allende (1995) wrote, "I am trampled by memories, all happening in one instant, as if my entire life were a single, unfathomable image. The child and girl I was, the woman I am, the old woman I shall be, are all water in the same rushing torrent. My memory is like a Mexican mural in which all times are simultaneous" (ibid., p. 23). The mind can serve as time machine (Tulving, 1983) that indeed renders all times simultaneous. However, the mind is an imperfect time machine. It transports people to the past, but individuals are unable to recapture completely their original experiences. It also transports individuals to the future, but the future that finally arrives may bear little resemblance to people's imaginings.

While traveling to the past, people sometimes rewrite history, altering details of previous episodes. Consequently, individuals need to be cautious about the judgments they form about themselves, other individuals, and social groups on the basis of evidence culled solely from memory. Mental time travel to the future has its own problems. Evolution has provided us with a brain that allows us to anticipate possible futures and thus to act to control our life course. That's the good news. The bad news is that people are often too optimistic and confident about their futures and fail to plan sufficiently for alternative possibilities. The bad news is tempered by the finding that predictions are sometimes self-fulfilling. When this is true, people are in a position to shape their own destinies. In everyday life, individuals sometimes specify the scope of their possibilities, as when they state that they can't imagine committing adultery or that they can imagine taking parachute lessons. Conceivably, a want of imagination can prevent people from striving for attainable objectives, but it might also keep them out of trouble. An implication of the research on the self-fulfilling nature of predictions is that people should be careful about what they wish for.

Like any voyage, mental time travel has both its risks and rewards. We have stressed the risks, in part because people are inclined to overlook them. Individuals tend to be too confident about the validity of both their memories and their forecasts. People need to remind themselves more often of two simple psychological principles. Memory is more malleable and the future is more uncertain than they typically imagine.

NOTE

1   The editor eventually rejected the manuscript.

REFERENCES

Allende, I. (1995). *Paula*. New York: HarperCollins.

Anderson, R. C., & Pichert, J. W. (1978). Recall of previously unrecallable information following a shift in perspective. *Journal of Verbal Learning and Verbal Behavior, 17*, 1–12.

Armor, D. A., & Taylor, S. E. (1998). Situated optimism: Specific outcome expectancies and self-regulation. In M. P. Zanna (Ed.), *Advances in experimental social psychology*, Vol. 30 (pp. 309–379). New York: Academic Press.

Bahrick, H. P., Hall, L. K., & Berger, S. A. (1996). Accuracy and distortion in memory for high school grades. *Psychological Science, 7*, 265–271.

Bartlett, F. C. (1932). *Remembering: A study in experimental and social psychology*. Cambridge, UK: Cambridge University Press.

Baumeister, R. F., & Newman, L. S. (1994). How stories make sense of personal experiences: Motives that shape autobiographical narratives. *Personality and Social Psychology Bulletin, 20* (6), 676–690.

Baumeister, R. F., Stillwell, A. M., & Wotman, S. R. (1990). Victim and perpetrator accounts of interpersonal conflict: Autobiographical narratives about anger. *Journal of Personality and Social Psychology, 59*, 994–1005.

Baumeister, R. F., Wotman, S. R., & Stillwell, A. M. (1993). Unrequited love: On heartbreak, anger, guilt, scriptlessness and humiliation. *Journal of Personality and Social Psychology, 64*, 377–394.

Boden, J. M., & Baumeister, R. F. (1997). Repressive coping: Distraction using pleasant thoughts and memories. *Journal of Personality and Social Psychology, 73*, 45–62.

Bransford, J. D., & Franks, J. J. (1971). The abstraction of linguistic ideas. *Cognitive Psychology, 2*, 331–350.

Brewer, W. F. (1988). Memory for randomly sampled autobiographical events. In U. Neisser & E. Winograd (Eds.), *Remembering reconsidered: Ecological and traditional approaches to the study of memory* (pp. 21–90). New York: Cambridge University Press.

Bruner, J. S., & Goodman, C. C. (1947). Value and need as organizing factors in perception. *Journal of Abnormal and Social Psychology, 42*, 33–44.

Buehler, R., & Griffin, D. (1996). Getting things done: The impact of predictions on task completion. Paper presented at the annual meeting of the American Psychological Association, Toronto, Canada.

Buehler, R., & Griffin, D. (1998). Motivated prediction for self and others. Unpublished manuscript, Wilfrid Laurier University.

Buehler, R., Griffin, D., & MacDonald, H. (1997). The role of motivated reasoning in optimistic time predictions. *Personality and Social Psychology Bulletin, 23*, 238–247.

Buehler, R., Griffin, D., & Ross, M. (1994). Exploring the "planning fallacy:" Why people under-estimate their task completion times. *Journal of Personality and Social Psychology, 67*, 366–381.

Bunn, D. W., & Salo, A. A. (1993). Forecasting with scenarios. *European Journal of Operational Research, 68*, 291–303.

Campbell, J. D., & Fairey, P. J. (1985). Effects of self-esteem, hypothetical explanations, and verbaliza-tion of expectancies on future performance. *Journal of Personality and Social Psychology, 48*, 1097–1111.

Cantor, N., Markus, H. R., Niedenthal, P., & Nurius, P. (1986). On motivation and the self concept. In R. M. Sorrentino & E. T. Higgins (Eds.), *Handbook of motivation and cognition: Foundations of social behavior* (pp. 96–121). New York: Guilford Press.

Carlston, D. E., & Smith, E. R. (1996). Principles of mental representation. In E. T. Higgins & A. Kruglanski (Eds.), *Social psychology: Handbook of basic principles* (pp. 184–210). New York: Guilford Press.

Carroll, J. S. (1978). The effect of imagining an event on expectations for the event: An interpretation in terms of the availability heuristic. *Journal of Experimental Social Psychology, 14*, 88–96.

Ceci, S. J., Ross, D. F., & Toglia, M. P. (1987). Suggestibility of children's memory: Psycholegal implications. *Journal of Experimental Psychology: General, 116*, 38–49.

Christensen-Szalanski, J. J. (1984). Discount functions and the measurement of patients' values: Women's decisions during childbirth. *Medical Decision Making, 4*, 47–58.

Clark, M. S., & Isen, A. M. (1982). Toward understanding the relationship between feeling states and social behavior. In A. H. Hastorf & A. M. Isen (Eds.), *Cognitive social psychology* (pp. 73–108). New York: Elsevier/North Holland.

Conway, M., & Ross, M. (1984). Getting what you want by revising what you had. *Journal of Personality and Social Psychology, 47*, 738–748.

Davis, C. G., Lehman, D. R., Wortman, C. B., Silver, R. C., & Thompson, S. C. (1995). The undoing of traumatic life events. *Personality and Social Psychology Bulletin, 21*, 109–124.

Dawes, R. M. (1988). *Rational choice in an uncertain world.* Orlando, FL: Harcourt Brace Jovanovich.

Dixon, R. A., & Gould, O. N. (1996). Adults telling and retelling stories collaboratively. In P. B. Baltes & U. M. Staudinger (Eds.), *Interactive minds: Life-span perspectives on the social foundation of cognition* (pp. 221–241). New York: Cambridge University Press.

Dougherty, M. R. P., Gettys, C. F., & Thomas, R. P. (1997). The role of mental simulation in judgments of likelihood. *Organizational Behavior and Human Decision Processes, 70*, 135–148.

Dunning, D., & Story, A. L. (1991). Depression, realism, and the overconfidence effect: Are the sadder wiser when predicting future action and events? *Journal of Personality and Social Psychology, 61*, 521–532.

Dweck, C. S. (1975). The role of expectations and attributions in the alleviation of learned helplessness. *Journal of Personality and Social Psychology, 31*, 674–685.

Dweck, C. S. (1990). Self-theories and goals: Their role in motivation, personality, and development. In R. A. Dienstbier (Ed.), *Nebraska Symposium on Motivation: Perspectives on motivation*, Vol. 38 (pp. 199–235). Lincoln: University of Nebraska Press.

Feldman Barrett, L. (1997). The relationship among momentary emotional experiences, personality descriptions, and retrospective ratings of emotion. *Personality and Social Psychology Bulletin, 23*, 1100–1110.

Fischhoff, B. (1975). Hindsight is not equal to foresight: The effects of outcome knowledge on judgment under uncertainty. *Journal of Experimental Psychology: Human Perception and Performance, 1*, 288–299.

Fischhoff, B., & Beyth, R. (1975). "I knew it would happen:" Remembered probabilities of once-future things. *Organizational Behavior and Human Performance, 13*, 1–16.

Frijda, N. H. (1986). *The emotions.* Cambridge: Cambridge University Press.

Gilbert, D. T., Pinel, E. J., Wilson, T. D., Blumberg, S. J., & Wheatley, T. A. (1998). Immune neglect: A source of durability bias in affective forecasting. *Journal of Personality and Social Psychology, 75*, 617–638.

Gilovich, T. (1983). Biased evaluation and persistence in gambling. *Journal of Personality and Social Psychology, 44*, 1110–1126.

Gilovich, T. (1991). *How we know what isn't so: The fallibility of reason in everyday life*. New York: Free Press.

Gilovich, T., & Douglas, C. (1986). Biased evaluations of randomly determined gambling outcomes. *Journal of Experimental Social Psychology, 22*, 228–241.

Gilovich, T., Kerr, M., & Medvec, V. H. (1993). Effect of temporal perspective on subjective confidence. *Journal of Personality and Social Psychology, 64*, 552–560.

Gollwitzer, P. M. (1993). Goal achievement: The role of intentions. In W. Stroebe & M. Hewstone (Eds.), *European review of psychology*, Vol. 4 (pp. 141–185). Chichester UK: Wiley.

Gollwitzer, P. M. (1996). The volitional benefits of planning. In P. M. Gollwitzer & J. A. Bargh (Eds.), *The psychology of action: Linking cognition and motivation to behavior* (pp. 287–312). New York: Guilford Press.

Gollwitzer, P. M., Heckhausen, H., & Steller, B. (1990). Deliberative and implemental mind-sets: Cognitive tuning toward congruous thoughts and information. *Journal of Personality and Social Psychology, 59*, 1119–1127.

Granberg, D., & Brent, E. (1983). When prophecy bends: The preference–expectation link in US presidential elections, 1952–1980. *Journal of Personality and Social Psychology, 45* (3), 477–491.

Greenwald, A. G. (1980). The totalitarian ego: Fabrication and revision of personal history. *American Psychologist, 35*, 603–618.

Greenwald, A. G., Carnot, C. G., Beach, R., & Young, B. (1987). Increasing voting behavior by asking people if they expect to vote. *Journal of Applied Psychology, 72*, 315–318.

Gregory, W. L., Cialdini, R. B., & Carpenter, K. M. (1982). Self-relevant scenarios as mediators of likelihood estimates and compliance: Does imagining make it so? *Journal of Personality and Social Psychology, 43*, 89–99.

Griffin, D. W., Dunning, D., & Ross, L. (1990). The role of construal processes in overconfident predictions about the self and others. *Journal of Personality and Social Psychology, 59*, 1128–1139.

Hastie, R. (1981). Schematic principles in human memory. In E. T. Higgins, C. P. Herman, & M. P. Zanna (Eds.), *Social cognition: The Ontario symposium*, Vol. 1 (pp. 39–88). Hillsdale, NJ: Erlbaum.

Herodotus (1996). *Histories*. Ware, UK: Wordsworth.

Hirt, E. R. (1990). Do I see only what I expect? Evidence for an expectancy-guided retrieval model. *Journal of Personality and Social Psychology, 58*, 937–951.

Hirt, E. R., & Markman, K. D. (1995). Multiple explanation: A consider-an-alternative strategy for debiasing judgments. *Journal of Personality and Social Psychology, 69*, 1069–1086.

Hoch, S. J. (1984). Availability and interference in predictive judgment. *Journal of Experimental Psychology: Learning, Memory, and Cognition, 10*, 649–662.

Hoch, S. J. (1985). Counterfactual reasoning and accuracy in predicting personal events. *Journal of Experimental Psychology: Learning, Memory, and Cognition, 11*, 719–731.

Hollingshead, A. B. (1998). Retrieval processes in transactive memory systems. *Journal of Personality and Social Psychology, 74*, 659–671.

Holman, E. A., & Cohen-Silver, R. (1998). Getting "stuck" in the past: Temporal orientation and coping with trauma. *Journal of Personality and Social Psychology, 74*, 1146–1163.

Hyman, I. E., Jr., & Pentland, J. (1996). The role of mental imagery in the creation of false childhood memories. *Journal of Memory and Language, 35*, 101–117.

Isen, A. M. (1987). Affect, cognition, and social behavior. In L. Berkowitz (Ed.), *Advances in experimental social psychology*, Vol. 20 (pp. 203–253). San Diego, CA: Academic Press.

Johnson, M. K., & Raye, C. L. (1981). Reality monitoring. *Psychological Review, 88*, 67–85.

Johnson, M. K., & Sherman, S. J. (1990). Constructing and reconstructing the past and the future in the present. In E. T. Higgins & R. M. Sorrentino (Eds.), *Handbook of motivation and social cognition: Foundations of social behavior*, Vol. 2 (pp. 482–526). New York: Guilford Press.

Johnson, M. K., Hashtroudi, S., & Lindsay, D. S. (1993). Source monitoring. *Psychological Bulletin, 114*, 3–28.

Johnson, M. K., Raye, C. L., Wang, A. Y., & Taylor, T. H. (1979). Fact and fantasy: The roles of accuracy and variability in confusing imaginations with perceptual experiences. *Journal of Experimental Psychology: Human Learning and Memory, 5*, 229–240.

Kahneman, D. (1994). New challenges to the rationality assumption. *Journal of Institutional and Theoretical Economics, 150*, 18–36.

Kahneman, D., & Lovallo, D. (1993). Timid choices and bold forecasts: A cognitive perspective on risk taking. *Management Science, 39*, 17–31.

Kahneman, D., & Snell, J. (1992). Predicting a changing taste: Do people know what they will like? *Journal of Behavioral Decision Making, 5*, 187–200.

Kahneman, D., & Tversky, A. (1979). Intuitive prediction: Biases and corrective procedures. *TIMS Studies in Management Science, 12*, 313–327.

Kahneman, D., & Tversky, A. (1982a). The simulation heuristic. In D. Kahneman, P. Slovic, & A. Tversky (Eds.), *Judgment under uncertainty: Heuristics and biases* (pp. 201–208). Cambridge, UK: Cambridge University Press.

Kahneman, D., & Tversky, A. (1982b). Variants of uncertainty. *Cognition, 11*, 143–157.

Karniol, R., & Ross, M. (1996). The motivational impact of temporal focus: Thinking about the future and the past. *Annual Review of Psychology, 47*, 593–620.

Klein, W. M., & Kunda, Z. (1993). Maintaining self-serving social comparisons: Biased reconstruction of one's past behaviors. *Personality and Social Psychology Bulletin, 19*, 732–739.

Koehler, D. J. (1991). Explanation, imagination, and confidence in judgment. *Psychological Bulletin, 110*, 499–519.

Kruglanski, A. (1989). *Lay epistemics and human knowledge: Cognitive and motivational biases.* New York: Plenum.

Kuhn, K. M., & Sniezek, J. A. (1996). Confidence and uncertainty in judgmental forecasting: Differential effects of scenario presentation. *Journal of Behavioral Decision Making, 9*, 231–247.

Kunda, Z. (1990). The case for motivated reasoning. *Psychological Bulletin, 108*, 480–490.

Lehman, D. R., & Taylor, S. E. (1988). Date with an earthquake: Coping with a probable, unpredictable disaster. *Personality and Social Psychology Bulletin, 13*, 546–555.

Levi, A. S., & Pryor, J. B. (1987). Use of the availability heuristic in probability estimates of future events: The effects of imagining outcomes versus imagining reasons. *Organizational Behavior and Human Decision Processes, 40*, 219–234.

Levine, L. J. (1997). Reconstructing memory for emotion. *Journal of Experimental Psychology: General, 126*, 165–177.

Liberman, N., & Trope, Y. (1998). The role of feasibility and desirability considerations in near and distant future decisions: A test of temporal construal theory. *Journal of Personality and Social Psychology, 75*, 5–18.

Linneman, R. E., & Klein, H. E. (1983). The use of multiple scenarios by US industrial companies: A comparison study, 1977–1981. *Long Range Planning, 16*, 94–101.

Linton, M. (1982). Transformations of memory in everyday life. In U. Neisser (Ed.), *Memory observed* (pp. 77–91). San Francisco: Freeman.

Loewenstein, G. (1996). Out of control: Visceral influences on behavior. *Organizational Behavior and Human Decision Processes, 65*, 272–292.

Loewenstein, G., & Schkade, D. (in press). Wouldn't it be nice? Predicting future feelings. In E. Diener, N. Schwarz, & D. Kahneman (Eds.), *Foundations of hedonic psychology: Scientific perspectives on enjoyment and suffering.* New York: Russell Sage Foundation Press.

Loftus, E. F. (1993). The reality of repressed memories. *American Psychologist, 48*, 518–537.

Lyubomirsky, S., Caldwell, N. D., & Nolen-Hoeksema, S. (1998). Effects of ruminative and distract-ing responses to depressed mood on retrieval of autobiographical memories. *Journal of Personality and Social Psychology, 75,* 166–177.

McAdams, D. P. (1993). *The stories we live by: Personal myths and the making of the self.* New York: Morrow.

MacDonald, T. K., & Ross, M. (in press). Assessing the accuracy of prediction about dating relation-ship: How and why do lovers' predictions differ from those made by observers? *Journal of Personality and Social Psychology.*

McDonald, H. E., & Hirt, E. R. (1997). When expectancy meets desire: Motivational effects in reconstructive memory. *Journal of Personality and Social Psychology, 72,* 5–23.

McFarland, C., & Buehler, R. (1997). Negative affective states and the motivated retrieval of posit-ive life events: The role of affect acknowledgment. *Journal of Personality and Social Psychology, 73,* 200–214.

McFarland, C., & Buehler, R. (in press). The impact of negative affect on autobiographical memory: The role of self-focused attention to moods. *Journal of Personality and Social Psychology.*

McFarland, C., & Ross, M. (1987). The relation between current impressions and memories of self and dating partners. *Personality and Social Psychology Bulletin, 13,* 228–238.

McFarland, C., Ross, M., & Giltrow, M. (1992). Biased recollections in older adults: The role of implicit theories of aging. *Journal of Personality and Social Psychology, 62,* 837–850.

Makridakis, S. G. (1990). *Forecasting, planning, and strategy for the 21st century.* New York: Free Press.

Markus, H. (1977). Self-schemata and processing information about the self. *Journal of Personality and Social Psychology, 35,* 63–78.

Markus, H., & Nurius, P. (1986). Possible selves. *American Psychologist, 41,* 954–969.

Markus, H., & Ruvolo, A. (1989). Possible selves: Personalized representations of goals. In L. A. Pervin (Ed.), *Goal concepts in personality and social psychology* (pp. 211–241). Hillsdale, NJ: Erlbaum.

Martin, M. (1990). On the induction of mood. *Clinical Psychology Review, 10,* 669–697.

Mead, G. H. (1934). *Mind, self and society.* Chicago: University of Chicago Press.

Mead, G. H. (1964). *Selected writings.* Ed. A. J. Reck. Chicago: University of Chicago Press.

Mischel, W. (1974). Processes in delay of gratification. In L. Berkowitz (Ed.), *Advances in experimental social psychology,* Vol. 7 (pp. 249–292). New York: Academic Press.

Mischel, W. (1996). Principles of self-regulation: The nature of willpower and self-control. In E. T. Higgins & A. Kruglanski (Eds.), *Social psychology: Handbook of basic principles* (pp. 329–360). New York: Guilford Press.

Moreland, R. L., Argote, L., & Krishman, R. (1996). Socially shared cognition at work: Transactive and group performance. In J. L. Nye & A. M. Brower (Eds.), *What's social about social cognition? Research on socially shared cognition in small groups* (pp. 57–84). London: Sage.

Murray, S. L., & Holmes, J. G. (1993). Seeing virtues in faults: Negativity and the transformation of interpersonal narrative in close relationships. *Journal of Personality and Social Psychology, 65,* 707–722.

Neisser, U. (1967). *Cognitive psychology.* New York: Appleton–Century–Crofts.

Neisser, U. (1981). John Dean's memory: A case study. *Cognition, 9,* 1–22.

Neisser, U., & Harsch, N. (1992). Phantom flashbulbs: False recollections of hearing the news about Challenger. In E. Winograd & U. Neisser (Eds.), *Affect and accuracy in recall: Studies of "flashbulb" memories* (pp. 9–31). New York: Cambridge University Press.

Nolen-Hoeksema, S., & Morrow, J. (1991). A prospective study of depression and posttraumatic stress symptoms after a natural disaster: The 1989 Loma Prieta earthquake. *Journal of Personality and Social Psychology, 61,* 115–121.

Ofshe, R. J. (1992). Inadvertent hypnosis during interrogation: False confession due to dissociative state; misidentified multiple personality, and the satanic cult hypothesis. *International Journal of Clinical and Experimental Hypnosis, 40*, 125–156.

Olson, J. M., Roese, N. J., & Zanna, M. P. (1996). Expectancies. In E. T. Higgins & A. Kruglanski (Eds.), *Social psychology: Handbook of basic principles* (pp. 211–238). New York: Guilford Press.

Osberg, T. M., & Shrauger, J. S. (1986). Self-prediction: Exploring the parameters of accuracy. *Journal of Personality and Social Psychology, 51*, 1044–1057.

Parrott, W. G., & Sabini, J. (1990). Mood and memory under natural conditions: Evidence for mood incongruent recall. *Journal of Personality and Social Psychology, 59*, 321–336.

Pennebaker, J. W. (1990). *Opening up: The healing power of confiding in others.* New York: William Morrow.

Pham, L. B., & Taylor, S. E. (in press). From thought to action: Effects of process-versus outcome-based mental simulations on performance. *Personality and Social Psychology Bulletin.*

Platt, J. (1973). Social traps. *American Psychologist, 28*, 641–651.

Rawls, J. (1971). *A theory of justice.* Cambridge, UK: Cambridge University Press.

Rehm, J. T., & Gadenne, V. (1990). *Intuitive predictions and professional forecasts: Cognitive processes and social consequences.* Oxford, UK: Pergamon Press.

Ross, H., Ross, M., Wilson, A., & Smith, M. (in press). The dandelion war. In S. R. Goldman, A. C. Graesser, and P. Van den Broek (Eds.), *The Tom Trabasso Festschrift Volume.* Hillsdale, NJ: Erlbaum.

Ross, M. (1989). The relation of implicit theories to the construction of personal histories. *Psychological Review, 96*, 341–357.

Ross, M. (1997). Validating memories. In N. L. Stein, P. A. Ornstein, B. Tversky, & C. Brainerd (Eds.), *Memory for everyday and emotional events* (pp. 49–82). Hillsdale, NJ: Erlbaum.

Ross, M., & Buehler, R. (1994). Creative remembering. In U. Neisser & R. Fivush (Eds.), *The remembering self* (pp. 205–235). New York: Cambridge University Press.

Ross, M., & Conway, M. (1986). Remembering one's own past: The construction of personal histories. In R. M. Sorrentino & E. T. Higgins (Eds.), *Handbook of motivation and cognition: Foundations of social behavior,* Vol. 1 (pp. 122–144). New York: Guilford Press.

Ross, M., Buehler, R., & Karr, J. W. (1998). Assessing the accuracy of conflicting autobiographical memories. *Memory and Cognition, 26*, 1233–1244.

Ross, M., McFarland, C., & Fletcher, G. J. O. (1981). The effect of attitude on the recall of personal histories. *Journal of Personality and Social Psychology, 40*, 627–634.

Ross, M., McFarland, C., Conway, M., & Zanna, M. P. (1983). Reciprocal relation between attitudes and behavior recall: Committing people to newly formed attitudes. *Journal of Personality and Social Psychology, 45*, 257–267.

Rouhana, N. N., & Bar-Tal, D. (1998). Psychological dynamics of intractable ethnonational conflicts. *American Psychologist, 53*, 761–770.

Salovey, P. (1992). Mood-induced self-focused attention. *Journal of Personality and Social Psychology, 62*, 699–707.

Sanitioso, R., Kunda, Z., & Fong, G. T. (1990). Motivated recruitment of autobiographical memories. *Journal of Personality and Social Psychology, 59*, 229–241.

Savitsky, K., Medvec, V. H., Charlton, A. E., & Gilovich, T. (1998). "What, me worry?": Arousal, misattribution, and the effect of temporal distance on confidence. *Personality and Social Psychology Bulletin, 24*, 529–536.

Schacter, D. L. (1996). *Searching for memory.* New York: Basic Books.

Schnaars, S. P., & Topol, M. T. (1987). The use of multiple scenarios in sales forecasting: An empirical test. *International Journal of Forecasting, 3*, 405–419.

Schoemaker, P. J. H. (1993). Multiple scenario development: Its conceptual and behavioral foundation. *Strategic Management Journal*, *14*, 193–213.

Schwarz, N., Groves, R. M., & Schuman, H. (1998). Survey methods. In D. T. Gilbert, S. T. Fiske, & G. Lindzey (Eds.), *The handbook of social psychology*. 4th. edn. Boston: McGraw-Hill.

Sedikides, C. (1992). Changes in the valence of the self as a function of mood. In M. S. Clark (Ed.), *Review of personality and social psychology*, Vol. 14 (pp. 271–311). Newbury Park, CA: Sage.

Shepperd, J. A., Ouellette, J. A., & Fernandez, J. K. (1996). Abandoning unrealistic optimism: Performance estimates and the temporal proximity of self-relevant feedback. *Journal of Personality and Social Psychology*, *70*, 844–855.

Sherman, R. T., & Anderson, C. A. (1987). Decreasing premature termination from psychotherapy. *Journal of Social and Clinical Psychology*, *5*, 298–312.

Sherman, S. J. (1980). On the self-erasing nature of errors of prediction. *Journal of Personality and Social Psychology*, *39*, 211–221.

Sherman, S. J., Skov, R. B., Hervitz, E. F., & Stock, C. B. (1981). The effects of explaining hypothetical future events: From possibility to actuality and beyond. *Journal of Experimental Social Psychology*, *17*, 142–158.

Showers, C. (1992). The motivational and emotional consequences of considering positive or negative possibilities for an upcoming event. *Journal of Personality and Social Psychology*, *63*, 474–484.

Shrauger, J. S., Mariano, E., & Walter, T. J. (1998). Depressive symptoms and accuracy in the prediction of future events. *Personality and Social Psychology Bulletin*, *24*, 880–892.

Singer, J. L., & Salovey, P. (1988). Mood and memory: Evaluating the network theory of affect. *Clinical Psychology Review*, *8*, 211–251.

Singer, J. L., & Salovey, P. (1993). *The remembered self: Emotion and memory in personality*. New York: Free Press.

Smith, J. (1996). Planning about life: Toward a social-interactive perspective. In P. B. Baltes & U. M. Staudinger (Eds.), *Interactive minds: Life-span perspectives on the social foundation of cognition* (pp. 242–275). New York: Cambridge University Press.

Smith, S. M., & Petty, R. E. (1995). Personality moderators of mood congruency effects on cognition. *Journal of Personality and Social Psychology*, *68*, 1092–1107.

Spence, D. P. (1982). *Narrative truth and historical truth: Meaning and interpretation in psychoanalysis*. New York: Norton.

Spiro, R. J. (1977). Remembering information from text: Theoretical and empirical issues concerning the "state of schema" reconstruction hypothesis. In R. C. Anderson, R. J. Spiro, & W. E. Montague (Eds.), *Schooling and the acquisition of knowledge* (pp. 137–165). Hillsdale, NJ: Erlbaum.

Stillwell, A. M., & Baumeister, R. F. (1997). The construction of victim and perpetrator memories: Accuracy and distortion in role-based accounts. *Personality and Social Psychology Bulletin*, *23*, 1157–1172.

Strack, F., Schwarz, N., & Gschneidinger, E. (1985). Happiness and reminiscing: The role of time perspective, affect, and mode of thinking. *Journal of Personality and Social Psychology*, *49*, 1460–1469.

Taylor, K. M., & Sheppard, J. A. (1998). Bracing for the worst: Severity, testing, and feedback timing as moderators of the optimistic bias. *Personality and Social Psychology Bulletin*, *24*, 915–926.

Taylor, S. E., & Brown, J. D. (1988). Illusion and well-being: A social psychological perspective on mental health. *Psychological Bulletin*, *103*, 193–210.

Taylor, S. E., & Crocker, J. (1981). Schematic biases of social information processing. In E. T. Higgins, C. P. Herman, & M. P. Zanna (Eds.), *Social cognition: The Ontario symposium*, Vol. 1 (pp. 89–134). Hillsdale, NJ: Erlbaum.

Taylor, S. E., & Schneider, S. K. (1989). Coping and the simulation of events. *Social Cognition*, *7*, 174–194.

Taylor, S. E., Pham, L. B., Rivkin, I. D., & Armor, D. A. (1998). Harnessing the imagination: Mental simulation, self-regulation, and coping. *American Psychologist, 53*, 429–439.

Tetlock, P. E. (1998). Close-call counterfactuals and belief system defenses: I was not almost wrong but I was almost right. *Journal of Personality and Social Psychology, 75*, 639–652.

Trope, Y. (1978). Inferences of personal characteristics on the basis of information retrieved from one's memory. *Journal of Personality and Social Psychology, 36*, 93–106.

Tulving, E. (1983). *Elements of episodic memory.* Oxford, UK: Clarendon Press.

Usher, J. A., & Neisser, U. (1993). Childhood amnesia and the beginnings of memory for four early life events. *Journal of Experimental Psychology: General, 122*, 155–165.

Vallone, R., Griffin, D. W., Lin, S., & Ross, L. (1990). Overconfident prediction of future actions and outcomes by self and others. *Journal of Personality and Social Psychology, 58*, 582–592.

Vorauer, J., & Ross, M. (1993). Making mountains out of molehills: A diagnosticity bias in social perception. *Personality and Social Psychology Bulletin, 19*, 620–632.

Vorauer, J., & Ross, M. (1996). The pursuit of knowledge within close relationships: An informational goals analysis. In G. Fletcher and J. Fitness (Eds.), *Knowledge structures in close relationships: A social psychological approach* (pp. 369–398). Hillsdale, NJ: Erlbaum.

Watson, J., & McFarland, C. (1995). *The impact of recalling life events on mood: The role of current interpretation.* Paper presented at the meeting of the Canadian Psychological Association, Charlottetown, Prince Edward Island.

Wegner, D. M. (1987). Transactive memory: A contemporary analysis of the group mind. In B. Mullen & G. R. Goethals (Eds.), *Theories of group behavior* (pp. 185–208). New York: Springer-Verlag.

Wegner, D. M., Erber, R., & Raymond, P. (1991). Transactive memory in close relationships. *Journal of Personality and Social Psychology, 61*, 923–929.

Wilson, A. E., Celnar, C., & Ross, M. (1997). Siblings' self and other perceptions of past and present conflict. Poster presented at the annual meeting of the American Psychological Association, Chicago.

Wilson, T. D. (1997). Affective forecasting and the durability bias: The problem of focalism. In D. T. Gilbert (Chair), *Affective forecasting.* Symposium conducted at the annual meeting of the Society of Experimental Social Psychology, Toronto, Ontario, Canada.

Wilson, T. D., & LaFleur, S. J. (1995). Knowing what you'll do: Effects analyzing reasons on self-prediction. *Journal of Personality and Social Psychology, 68* (1), 21–35.

Wilson, T. D., & Linville, P. W. (1982). Improving the academic performance of college freshmen: Attribution theory revisited. *Journal of Personality and Social Psychology, 42*, 367–376.

Yates, J. F. (1990). *Judgment and decision making.* Englewood Cliffs, NJ: Prentice-Hall.

Zukier, H. (1986). The paradigmatic and narrative modes in goal-guided inference. In R. M. Sorrentino & E. T. Higgins (Eds.), *Handbook of motivation and cognition: Foundations of social behavior*, Vol. 1 (pp. 465–502). New York: Guilford Press.

CHAPTER THREE

An Evolutionary-Psychological Approach to Self-esteem: Multiple Domains and Multiple Functions

Lee A. Kirkpatrick and Bruce J. Ellis

Evolutionary Perspectives on Self-evaluation and Self-esteem

Perhaps more ink has been devoted to the issue of *self-esteem* – loosely, the degree to which we evaluate ourselves positively or negatively – than to any other single topic in psychology. Self-esteem has been defined in a variety of ways and been analyzed into any number of constellations of dimensions, types, and subtypes. It has been recurrently implicated in phenomena of considerable psychological and social importance, from prejudice, aggression, and criminality to mood disorders, eating disorders, and other serious mental health problems. Much research focuses on perceived abilities and competence, while other research focuses on interpersonal relations, physical attractiveness, or perceived control over outcomes. Some scholars focus on defense and maintenance of self-esteem; others on its enhancement. Virtually every major psychological theory touches on the issue in some way, and the need to maintain and enhance self-esteem is widely assumed to be a fundamental human motive (Leary & Downs, 1995).

What is sorely needed is a deeper, overarching theoretical framework to bring order to this fragmented literature, to organize future research, and to provide a solid basis for applications of this knowledge in the real world. In this chapter we endeavor to show that the emerging paradigm of evolutionary psychology (Buss, 1995, 1999; Symons, 1987; Tooby & Cosmides, 1992) offers a powerful metatheoretical framework for doing so. We do not aspire, in this brief chapter, to develop a comprehensive theory of self-esteem. Our more modest goal is merely to illustrate some ways in which an evolutionary-psychological perspective is valuable in illuminating a variety of issues surrounding the topics of self-evaluation and self-esteem.

We wish to thank David Buss, Michael Kernis, and Mark Leary for their very helpful comments on an earlier version of this chapter.

Our point of departure is sociometer theory, as developed by Leary and his colleagues (Leary & Baumeister, in press; Leary & Downs, 1995; Leary, Tambor, Terdal, & Downs, 1995), which we review briefly in the next section. We then introduce two general sets of issues raised by an evolutionary-psychological perspective – adaptive function and domain-specificity – and suggest some extensions and refinements of sociometer theory in light of these issues. In the final major section of the chapter, we address a sampling of prominent topics and problems in the social-psychological literature on self-esteem, and suggest some ways in which our framework may provide some unique insights, and a basis for generating testable hypotheses for empirical research, concerning these topics.

Sociometer Theory and Evolutionary Psychology

We believe that sociometer theory represents a significant advance over previous theories about the nature and origins of self-esteem. Leary and colleagues offer several important arguments that illustrate the application and utility of evolutionary-psychological thinking to social-psychological topics, and provide a general conceptualization of self-esteem that differs fundamentally from previous conceptualizations and provides a strong foundation upon which we will build in this chapter.

Leary et al. (1995) begin by noting that while theorists have long taken for granted the importance of self-esteem, and many researchers have investigated numerous causes and consequences of low and high self-esteem, few have asked the fundamental questions: (1) What exactly *is* self-esteem?, and (2) what is its *function*? (for a notable exception see Greenberg, Solomon, & Pyszczynski, 1986; Solomon, Greenberg, & Pyszczynski, 1991.) Their answer is that self-esteem is not a free-floating goal state that people are motivated to enhance and protect. Rather, it is an internal index or gauge – a "sociometer" – designed to monitor our success with respect to other adaptive goals. Leary et al. offer as an analogy the fuel gauge in an automobile, which is designed to alert the driver to refill the tank when the fuel level becomes dangerously low.

Leary et al. (1995) argue persuasively that the domain monitored by the sociometer is that of interpersonal relationships. Consistent with many other theorists such as Cooley (1902) and Rosenberg (1979), they suggest that self-esteem reflects in large part people's perceptions of how others feel about them. More specifically, they argue that the sociometer is designed to monitor one's level of *social inclusion* or *acceptance* versus *social exclusion* or *rejection*. They argue further that this sociometer represents an adaptation designed by natural selection for this purpose. A crucial adaptive problem faced by our ancestors, they maintain, was to be accepted by others as part of "the group," as rejection by the group would pose a significant threat to survival and a loss of the many well-documented benefits of group living. The sociometer is thus designed to alert one when one's level of social inclusion is dangerously low, so as to motivate corrective action to restore inclusion/acceptance to a favorable level.

We cannot overemphasize the degree to which this perspective represents a radical (and long overdue) shift from the prevailing framework underlying much past and current research on self-esteem. As summarized by Harter (1993, p. 87), "It is commonly asserted in the literature that the self-concept is a theory, a cognitive construction, and that its architecture – by evolutionary design – is extremely functional. . . . One such widely touted function is to maintain high self-esteem." From an evolutionary perspective, however, the idea that a self-system has been crafted by natural selection with the function of "maintaining high self-esteem" is dubious. It is not clear why having high self-esteem per se would have been adaptive – in the evolutionary currency of inclusive fitness – for our ancestors. Simply feeling good, for example, does not directly translate into viable offspring.[1] More-over, there are costs to be considered as well: the effects of high self-esteem on and inter-personal functioning and mental health are by no means uniformly positive (Baumeister, Smart, & Boden, 1996; Colum, Block, & Funder, 1995; Tennen & Affleck, 1995). If perpetually high self-esteem per se were in fact universally adaptive, natural selection would have designed us simply to have it.

Another consequence of the prevailing conceptualization is that it entails the supposition that *low* self-esteem reflects some kind of maladaptation or malfunction. Harter (1993, p. 88), for example, is led to ask: "Given this functional scenario, why should the system falter, leading certain individuals to experience . . . low self-esteem?" The subtitle of the book in which her chapter appears, "The puzzle of low self-esteem," clearly illustrates this underlying assumption. From an evolutionary point of view, however, low self-esteem is no more a puzzle than is high self-esteem, and it surely does not necessarily reflect malfunctioning of an adaptive system. If you take a swig of spoiled milk and experience an unpleasant taste, has your evolved taste system malfunctioned? If you later enjoy a delicious culinary feast in a fine restaurant, is the system now working better? In both cases the system is functioning exactly as it was designed, alerting you as to which foods to avoid and which to ingest with gusto. In ancestral environments, individuals who were capable of such discriminations and differential affect died of fewer diseases and had healthier offspring; those who could not did not become our ancestors. We are not designed to enjoy the taste of all foods, or there would be no point in having a capacity to discriminate flavors.

According to Leary and colleagues, self-esteem works in a similar (though more complex) way: It is designed to monitor something about our success and failure in solving one or more adaptive problems (cf. avoiding disease-laden foods and seeking nutritious, healthful ones). The evolutionary approach then leads directly to the next questions: What adaptive problem(s) are these?, and how do self-evaluations and self-esteem help us to solve them?

Multiple Domains of Self-esteem[2]

A central premise of evolutionary psychology is that the brain/mind comprises numerous, domain-specific mechanisms (much as the remainder of the body comprises numerous, functionally distinct organs) representing evolved solutions to recurrent adaptive problems in ancestral human environments. Stated simply, qualitatively different adaptive problems require qualitatively different solutions: The brain/mind cannot be designed entirely as a general problem-solving device "because there is no such thing as a general problem," just as there are no all-purpose kitchen devices that perform all possible food-processing tasks (Symons, 1992, p. 142; also see Tooby & Cosmides, 1992, for a detailed discussion). Numerous domain-specific mechanisms are required to solve the diverse adaptive problems faced by our ancestors, from procuring food to finding suitable habitats, negotiating status hierarchies, and avoiding predators.

Likewise, interpersonal relationships of various types differ qualitatively with respect to the particular adaptive problems they pose and the solutions required to negotiate them success-fully (Daly, Salmon, & Wilson, 1997). Attachment and caregiving systems guide parent–infant interactions but not sibling interactions; mechanisms of reciprocity and cheater-detection underlie social exchange relationships but not nepotistic relationships; mechanisms of sexual attraction guide mateships but not friendships. To paraphrase Symons, there can be no such thing as an all-purpose set of decision rules for guiding behavior in social relationships because there is no such thing as an all-purpose social relationship.

We therefore suggest that natural selection is likely to have fashioned numerous psycho-logical mechanisms for monitoring functioning in distinct types of relationships. A general social-inclusion gauge alone seems unlikely to provide sufficiently detailed information about the nature of the adaptive problem to be solved, or to be very useful in guiding appropriate behavior to solve that problem. For example, a sociometer that monitors levels of inclusion and exclusion from professional work coalitions may be useful in guiding job search strat-egies, but not very useful in deciding whether to challenge or submit to competitors in agonistic encounters. Similarly, a sociometer that monitors levels of acceptance and rejection from romantic partners may be useful for guiding one's mate-selection strategy but not for guiding one's job-search strategy.

To return to Leary's dashboard analogy, a global sociometer designed to monitor success across all kinds of social relationships seems akin to a single, all-purpose gauge designed to monitor the engine's overall functioning. Cars do not (typically) possess such an all-purpose gauge, however; instead, they come equipped with a fuel gauge for monitoring levels of gasoline, a tachometer for monitoring engine speed in rpm, a thermometer for monitoring engine temperature, and so on. This is the case for at least two reasons. First, it is not clear how one would design an all-purpose gauge. What part of the car would it hook up to as a source of input? The only way to design such a gauge would be to first construct more specific mechanisms to tap into particular aspects of the car's functioning (engine tempera-ture, fuel level, etc.), and then send output from these mechanisms to the global gauge. Second, and perhaps more important, a global automotive-functioning gauge would not be very useful, as it would offer little guidance for determining what needs to be done to fix the problem.[3]

Of course, the idea that global self-esteem might be carved into more specific "domains" is not new; indeed, self-esteem research has for some time evinced an increasing focus on domain-specificity (Harter, Waters, & Whitesell, 1998). Previous researchers have proposed various numbers of types or dimensions of self-esteem, such as competence or achievement, virtue or morality, power or control, and love-worthiness or acceptance by others (e.g., Coopersmith, 1967; Epstein, 1973). In most cases, multidimensionality has been inferred from factor-analytic results (Harter et al., 1998). An evolutionary perspective, in contrast to this descriptive approach, offers a strong theoretical basis for distinguishing types or dimen-sions of self-esteem in terms of the ways in which they operate to help solve different kinds of adaptive problems. By "carving nature at its joints," this approach is more likely to distinguish types or domains of self-esteem that correspond to real, functional differences in the operation of these mechanisms, thereby offering a more powerful heuristic for guiding empirical research.

Social inclusion

We concur with Leary et al. (1995) and numerous other self-esteem theorists with respect to the assumption that self-esteem is (largely) social in origin and reflects (largely) affect-laden perceptions of how others feel about us.[4] From an evolutionary perspective, however, we expect that several functionally distinct kinds of relationships are important for different reasons, and that domain-specific sociometers might therefore be associated with each. We will not attempt to resolve the question of exactly how many such sociometers there might be, but merely illustrate a few major categories of interpersonal relationships and the kinds of sociometers that might be associated with them.

A crucial problem of social life concerns acceptance in various forms of coalitions and alliances. This includes *macro-level* groups (i.e., one's tribe, village, community, or nation) as well as *micro-level* groups within the larger population. As suggested by Leary et al. (1995), it has always been important for humans to be "socially included" within the local population in order to obtain various benefits of group living, such as access to local resources and defense against outgroups. Self-esteem in this domain, we hypothesize, should be related to feelings of belongingness (Baumeister & Leary, 1995) and a sense of being an accepted member of one's local community or nation. It might also be correlated with such constructs as nationalism or patriotism (Schatz, Staub, & Lavine, 1998).

Within local populations, humans, like chimpanzees (Wrangham & Peterson, 1996), routinely form smaller coalitions and alliances. Inclusion in these micro-level groups affords a variety of benefits, including mutual social support, physical protection, access to external resources (e.g., food, shelter, territory), access to mating opportunities, and coalitional support in negotiating status and dominance hierarchies. Self-esteem in this domain should be reflected in feelings of being loved and/or valued by family, friends, and colleagues, and should be correlated empirically with such constructs as perceived social support, social integration, and (absence of) loneliness.

An evolutionary perspective on group affiliation highlights several types of micro-level groups that should be especially relevant to self-esteem.

Instrumental coalitions.   A special type of group relationship involves instrumental coalitions, which we define as a group of two or more individuals who coordinate their efforts to achieve shared, valued objectives. Participation in instrumental coalitions involves interdependence and subordination of individual interests to shared goals that cannot be achieved alone. Over the course of human evolutionary history, intergroup aggression and hunting of large game animals involved formation of instrumental coalitions. These coalitional activities were crucial both for obtaining animal protein and for obtaining greater sexual access to women (as a recurrent resource that flowed to the victors of war; Chagnon, 1992; Manson &

Wrangham, 1991). Because group-level hunting and warfare are engaged in predominantly (and in most cases exclusively) by men in all human societies (Manson & Wrangham, 1991; Murdock & Provost, 1973), and because of the historical importance of these coalitional activities to male reproductive success, selection can be expected to have shaped men's affiliative psychologies to especially value participation in these kinds of groups. (See especially Tiger's, 1969, book-length treatise on the emotional satisfaction and self-validation achieved by men through participation with other men in instrumental coalitions.) Hence, we hypothesize that perceived inclusion in instrumental coalitions (such as competitive sports teams, secret societies, and gangs) will be an important facet of self-esteem, and that it should on average be more central to men's than to women's overall feelings of self-worth.

Mating relationships. From an evolutionary perspective, no interpersonal relationships are more important than mating relationships. Attracting and retaining mates is a sine qua non of successful reproduction. It follows, therefore, that specialized sociometers should be designed to assess one's success in the "mating game." We expect that separate sociometers monitor success in short-term mating (i.e., success in achieving short-term sexual access to a variety of partners) and long-term mating (i.e., success in forming committed relationships with reliable and nurturant mates). According to sexual strategies theory (Buss & Schmitt, 1993), both short- and long-term mating strategies are components of both women's and men's evolved psychologies, but women and men differ (on average) in the relative weightings they place on short- and long-term strategies.

Because men (much more than women) can increase the number of offspring produced through short-term matings (see Trivers, 1972), selection can be expected to have shaped men's (more than women's) sexual psychology to value short-term matings; hence, we hypothesize that inclusion in short-term sexual relationships will be a more central aspect of male than female self-esteem. Conversely, because women's reproduction is limited more than men's by access to economic and nutritional resources (Clutton-Brock, 1988; Mulder, 1987), and because women in hunting-and-gathering societies depend on men to underwrite their reproduction by providing a substantial amount of the calories consumed by women and their children (Kaplan & Lancaster, 1999), selection can be expected to have shaped women's (more than men's) sexual psychology to value long-term relationships with reliable and investing mates. Hence, we hypothesize that inclusion in long-term mating relationships will be a more central aspect of female than male self-esteem. Consistent with this theorizing, Lalumiere, Seto, and Quinsey (1995) report that number of sexual partners since puberty and in the past year were negatively correlated with self-esteem among women, but positively correlated with self-esteem among men.

Family relationships. Kin-based relationships are of great importance to humans and many other species, though they unfortunately have received scant attention from social psychologists (Daly et al., 1997). Whereas investment in relationships with non-kin is largely based on social exchange (i.e., mutual cooperation and reciprocity), investment in kin-based relationships is often nepotistic. That is, individuals often invest in genetic relatives (even in the absence of reciprocity) because they have a biological interest in their well-being. As specified by inclusive fitness theory (Hamilton, 1964), genes for such *altruistic* behavior can spread

through a population as long as (1) they cause an organism to help close relatives to reproduce, and (2) the cost to the organism's own reproduction is offset by the reproductive
benefit to those relatives (discounted by the probability that the relatives who receive the
benefit have inherited the same genes from a common ancestor). Inclusive fitness theory
gives deeper meaning to the expression "blood runs thicker than water" and leads one to
expect that close kin are the individuals from whom one can most expect reliable support
and assistance (see Buss, 1999, and Daly & Wilson, 1988, for reviews of empirical findings).

Further, inclusive fitness theory predicts that, all else being equal, individuals will allocate
investment toward genetic relatives who are most able to convert that investment into
current and future reproduction. This implies that investment will preferentially be directed
toward younger relatives over older ones. Thus, for example, people tend to leave much more
of their estates to offspring than to siblings (Smith, Kish, & Crawford, 1987), even though
the average genetic relatedness is the same across these two types of relationships. These
considerations lead us to hypothesize that people have specialized psychological mechanisms
for monitoring inclusion in kin-based alliances, and that the functioning of these mechanisms will show predictable patterns of developmental change across the lifespan. For
example, perceived levels of inclusion and support from parents should become less central to
self-esteem as individuals mature from childhood to adolescence to adulthood, making the
transition from being primarily receivers to primarily givers of familial investment.

Between-group competition

Feeling "included" within social groups of various types is only one source of self-esteem
related to group membership, however. Many of the most important benefits of social
inclusion relate to actual or potential competition *between* groups. From an evolutionary
perspective, the value of being included by other people is therefore inextricably linked to the
relative quality and strength of one's own group vis-à-vis other groups. We therefore expand
the definition of "sociometer" to encompass both perceived levels of social inclusion (i.e.,
how much gas is in the tank) and the quality or social value of the people or groups who are
including or excluding us (i.e., the octane of the gas).[5]

A principal adaptive function of inclusion within one's local population concerns defense
against outgroups. Ongoing inter-village warfare and raiding is common between many
hunter-gatherer groups (Ember, 1978; Manson & Wrangham, 1991), and of course our
newspapers are filled today with reports of inter- and intra-national warfare, ethnic cleansing,
and so on. High self-esteem should therefore be associated with beliefs not only about
inclusion in a collective, but also the perceived quality and strength of that collective relative
to competing groups. Luhtanen and Crocker (1992) have developed a measure of *collective*
self-esteem designed to assess this construct, which they interpret to be the most crucial
aspect of self-esteem in social identity theory (Tajfel, 1982; Tajfel & Turner, 1986). Consistent with this, we take great pride in the accomplishments of our country in the Olympic
Games, in warfare, and in other international affairs.

Similarly, coalitions and alliances within populations are frequently competitive with one
another, and the adaptive value of belonging to them is therefore yoked to their relative

strength and quality. Some groups control important resources and confer many benefits on those who belong while other groups do not (e.g., compare being a member of the Notre Dame football team versus belonging to most other football teams). The purpose of instrumental coalitions is often to defeat competing coalitions in a zero-sum game for scarce resources (as in politics, business, and gang wars). Sociometers for monitoring the relative strength of one's coalitions and alliances would have been selected for because inclusion in larger and stronger groups afforded benefits to the individual which translated into survival and reproduction. We take pride in the accomplishments of our school basketball team, our political party, our fraternity or sorority, or the Society for Personality and Social Psychology, because our coalitions' strength is to some extent our own.

Mating relationships are also alliances, of which the principal evolutionary function is successful childrearing (Daly et al., 1997; Kirkpatrick, 1998). Within local populations, married couples are often highly competitive, intent on maintaining the best lawn or Christmas lighting on the block or otherwise "keeping up with the Joneses." Bring groups of parents together in a room and they will often spend much of the time boasting about their respective children's accomplishments in a conversational can-you-top-this game. Bumper stickers proudly announce "My child is an honor roll student at X School," one implication of which is that your child probably is not. Thus, people draw self-esteem not only from having a spouse and a satisfying marital or dating relationship, but also from the accomplishments and quality of their partnership relative to others'.

Finally, the quality and strength of one's kin-based alliances and extended family provide an important source of self-esteem. One takes great pride in being a Capulet or a Montague, a Hatfield or a McCoy, a Rockefeller or a Kennedy. Family ties and nepotism play crucial roles in politics and competition for power and prestige. Royalty, which is invariably defined along family lines, presents a clear example of strong kin-based coalitions that have succeeded at the expense of other family lines, and belonging to a royal family is undoubtedly an important source of self-esteem for those who do. Kin-based coalitions are frequently in direct competition with one another, often violently. (See Daly & Wilson, 1988, for discussion.)

Within-group competition

In addition to tracking the relative strength of one's own group vis-à-vis other groups, self-esteem should also track one's own individual position *within* various groups. As discussed in the next section, knowing where one stands relative to the competition is extremely valuable for guiding behavior in a variety of ways. Indeed, the optimal choice among alternative paths to reproductive success often differs considerably depending on one's standing relative to others. Consequently, we propose that another distinct set of sociometers is designed to assess one's local standing with respect to competition within the kinds of groups discussed above.[6]

Within local populations, interindividual competition within most social species is ongoing with respect to several overlapping dimensions. Numerous researchers have proposed that the self-esteem system in humans is related to dominance hierarchies, suggesting that self-esteem reflects an assessment of one's status, rank, or prestige relative to (mainly intrasexual) local competitors (Barkow, 1989; Gilbert, Price, & Allan, 1995). Whether based on physical size and strength, genetic lineage, quality of territory, or other factors, species ranging from crawfish (Barinaga, 1996) to chimpanzees (de Waal, 1982) display some form of dominance ranking that determines access to resources and/or mates. Human status hierarchies are clearly much more complex than, say, chickens' pecking orders, but there can be little doubt that status-striving is a universal human motive (e.g., Buss, 1999; Daly & Wilson, 1988; Symons, 1979). As discussed in the next section, self-assessments of dominance or status function to guide individuals to either challenge or submit in conflictual situations.

Other researchers have focused specifically on the adaptive problem of attracting mates, and suggested that self-esteem might reflect self-evaluations of the degree to which one is valued as a mate by members of the other sex (e.g., Dawkins, 1982; Kenrick, Groth, Trost, & Sadalla, 1993; Wright, 1994). Self-perceived *mate value* is determined by social feedback concerning one's attractiveness to the opposite sex, such as previous history of success and failure in mating, in combination with appraisals of the extant competition (Gutierres, Kenrick, & Partch, in press). Other indicators might include feedback with respect to intrasexual competition concerning one's abilities, intelligence, and other characteristics indicative of potential mate quality. As discussed in the next section, self-assessments of mate value are important for guiding choices of mates and of mating strategies.

Within-group competition also takes place within otherwise cooperative coalitions and alliances. For example, same-sex friends or members of a group may vie for the same award, the same starting position on a baseball team, the same job opening, or the same potential mate. Likewise, dating and marital partners may compete over issues of investment and power within their relationship. Similarly, different family members often compete for access to familial resources of power and wealth (consider the ugly legal disputes that some-times emerge over the distribution of a deceased family member's estate). And, of course, sibling rivalry over parental investment is well known in a variety of literatures, including countless ethological examples with respect to nonhuman species. As discussed in the next section, choosing the right strategies for negotiating and investing in relationships with other group members, from mates to kin to instrumental coalition partners, is contingent on self-evaluations of relative status within the group.

Global vs. specific, trait vs. state

Most previous researchers who have emphasized the domain-specificity of self-esteem have still retained the construct (and measures) of global self-worth or self-esteem, typically re-garding it as a higher-order construct in a hierarchical model under which specific self-evaluations are nested (e.g., Harter et al., 1998). Our view is not inconsistent with this conceptualization, except insofar as it provides a theoretical basis for identifying the specific domains and the conditions under which each is most relevant. We suspect, however, that it is the domain-specific sociometers that are generally more functionally important in terms of guiding behavior and personality development.

However global self-esteem is sliced, its dimensions or components are invariably intercorre-lated empirically. If, as we have argued, self-esteem comprises numerous domain-specific sociometers, why should this be the case? In fact, our perspective suggests several reasons to expect sociometers will be intercorrelated. First, certain characteristics are valued in the context of many different relationship domains. A man of large stature and physical strength, for example, is potentially valuable both as a mate (i.e., with respect to providing protection to mates and offspring) and as a coalitional partner (e.g., as part of a hunting or war party). Similarly, psychological traits such as kindness and loyalty are highly valued in both friends and mates. To the extent that one evinces such characteristics, then, he or she is likely to be socially accepted across a variety of relationship contexts, and consequently to experience high self-esteem across these domains.

Second, high status or inclusion in certain kinds of relationships often confers benefits with respect to other forms of status or inclusion. High status within the local population, for example, renders one desirable to others as a potential coalition partner or mate. Conversely, ties to a strong coalition (the benefits of which are resources available for social exchange) enhance one's value as a potential mate or friend. In this way success in one domain can lead to success in another, one consequence of which is that self-esteem in those respective domains will be intercorrelated. Moreover, to the extent that such interrelations among characteristics and domains were regular features of ancestral environments, it seems plausible that sociometers may themselves be interconnected within our psychological architecture. For example, to the extent that high status attained through intrasexual or intergroup competition was regularly predictive of enhanced mate value and mating opportunities – a widespread phenomenon throughout the animal world – it seems possible that (especially for men) a status sociometer might be designed to send output directly to a mate-value sociometer.

Although much of our discussion up to this point has focused implicitly on *state* self-esteem, we suggest that *trait* self-esteem is similarly domain-specific. Leary and Baumeister (in press) propose that state self-esteem reflects an (affect-laden) appraisal of one's current level of social inclusion, whereas trait self-esteem reflects an appraisal of one's *potential* or likely future level of inclusion. In other words, state self-esteem gauges current *acceptance*, whereas trait self-esteem gauges *acceptability*. We suggest that this same distinction might be applied within each of the separate self-esteem domains we propose, as will become evident in the next section.

Multiple Functions of Self-esteem

Implicit in the view that the brain/mind comprises a number of domain-specific sociometers is the assumption that these sociometers do a number of different things: sociometers evolved because they are (or were, to our distant ancestors) useful in many ways for solving adaptive problems. The fuel-gauge analogy, as well as the word "socio*meter*" itself, is somewhat misleading on this point, because gauges and meters do nothing more than display measurements.[7] Perhaps a better analogy is an engine-temperature sensor that not only sends output to a dashboard gauge, but also automatically activates an auxiliary cooling fan when a critical temperature is attained. Similarly, many older cars contained a small reserve gas tank that came on line when the primary tank was detected as empty.

In this view, the dashboard gauges can be thought of as affective outputs of different sociometers. We propose that in addition to indicating the presence of specific types of problems in this way, sociometers have a second (and perhaps more important) function: to activate strategies for solving these problems. Just as temperature and fuel-level sensors function to activate different mechanical systems (e.g., cooling fans or reserve fuel tanks), we propose that different sociometers function to activate different psychological systems and processes, both at a broad level (in terms of guiding personality development) and at a more specific level (in terms of guiding day-to-day decision making and behavioral strategies). In this section we outline several of these proposed functions.

Guiding personality development

One of the basic assumptions of an evolutionary psychological perspective is that individuals have evolved to be able to function competently in a variety of different environments. According to conditional adaptation models (e.g., Belsky, Steinberg, & Draper, 1991; Mealey, 1995), what enables this flexibility and adaptation is that, as part of the inherited architecture of the brain, humans possess a repertoire of alternative developmental paths. Which strategy is "chosen" depends both on genotype and on exposure to evolutionarily relevant environmental cues during childhood.

Attachment theorists, for example, emphasize the role of early family relationships and support in the development of subsequent personality. In attachment theory, children's perceptions of inclusion and exclusion by relevant caregivers are conceptualized as their *internal working models* of attachment (Bowlby, 1969/1982). In Belsky et al.'s (1991) theory of the development of reproductive strategies, contextual stressors in early childhood are hypothesized to foster more negative and coercive (or less positive and harmonious) family relationships, which in turn are hypothesized to provoke earlier pubertal and sexual development. A key element of the theory is that the child's perception of support by family members – his or her family sociometer – influences subsequent development of differential reproductive strategies. Consistent with this, Ellis, McFadyen-Ketchum, Dodge, Pettit, and Bates (1999) found that greater warmth and positivity in the parent–child relationship, as observed in the summer prior to kindergarten, predicted later pubertal timing in daughters in the seventh grade (see also Graber, Brooks-Gunn, & Warren, 1995).

Alternative courses of personality development may also derive (in part) from self-assessment of competitive abilities (cf. Tooby & Cosmides's, 1990, discussion of "reactive heritability"). For example, many theorists have suggested that low self-esteem is a contributing factor to delinquency and criminality (e.g., Kaplan, 1980; Rosenberg, Schooler, & Schoenbach, 1989). Mealey (1995) specifically cites a perceived inability to compete for resources and mates according to conventional, socially sanctioned means as a primary causal factor in secondary sociopathy. Similarly, individual differences in self-perceived mate value may influence the development of reproductive strategies (e.g., Gangestad & Simpson, in press; Kenrick et al., 1993). For example, men (but not women) who perceive themselves as relatively low in mate value have been found to pursue a more monogamous mating strategy, including later age of first sexual intercourse, fewer sexual partners, lower frequency of sexual intercourse, and reception of fewer sexual invitations from the opposite sex (Lalumiere et al., 1995). In sum, variations in self-perceived competitive abilities may function to channel individuals toward different life strategies that adaptively mesh with their competitive abilities.

Directly addressing a deficiency

In addition to influencing the development of personality dispositions such as sociopathy and sociosexual orientation, variations in self-esteem should also influence more immediate decision-making and behavioral choices. Leary et al. (1995) discuss only one way in which a warning message from the sociometer might be used to organize or guide behavior: consistent with the fuel-gauge analogy, they suggest that the function of an "E" reading is to alert one to the need to refill the gas tank. That is, the sociometer indicates that one has a deficiency of something (in this case, social inclusion), and the behavioral response is to redouble efforts to obtain that something. For example, a sociometer sensitive to cues that one's current mating relationship is in jeopardy should activate a number of behavioral responses for defending the relationship (or replacing it).

Although a sociometer may sometimes be useful for guiding behavior in this way, simply refilling the tank often is not an available or adaptive strategy. If people have learned from repeated rejections that members of the opposite sex do not find them attractive, then simply increasing efforts to make oneself more attractive are likely to be ineffective. Persistent attempts by a subordinate to be "socially included" by a powerful, dominant competitor could well lead to physical injury or death. Moreover, if self-esteem invariably worked this way, we should expect people with low self-esteem to work harder and persevere longer at tasks than those with high self-esteem; however, precisely the opposite pattern has been demonstrated in empirical research (e.g., Perez, 1973; Shrauger & Sorman, 1977). It is likely, therefore, that sociometers guide decision-making and behavior in other ways as well.

Guiding adaptive relationship choices

All individual have a limited amount of investment – time, energy, resources – to budget toward various activities. Because natural selection favors individuals who make propitious decisions relative to the alternatives available to them in budgeting investment, selection should act against individuals who either (1) invest too heavily in social relationships that are substantially lower in value than they can command on the social marketplace (and thus fail to get a fair return on the value they bring to the relationships), or (2) waste investment pursuing social relationships that are higher in value than what they can realistically obtain in the social marketplace. Accordingly, we hypothesize that an important function of self-esteem is to guide individuals to approach social relationships that are of the highest quality possible, yet defensible given one's own social value (Hoop & Ellis, 1990).

For example, if a job candidate for an academic position is continually rejected by first-tier institutions, the accompanying decrement in professional self-esteem should guide the candidate to recalibrate his or her job search downward toward second- or third-tier institutions. Conversely, a plethora of job interviews and offers from lower tier institutions should boost professional self-esteem, leading the candidate to redirect his or her job search upward. Through gauging the response to his or her job applications, the candidate discovers his or her niche of acceptance and rejection on the job market. We propose that the candidate's feelings of professional self-esteem reflect his or her internal, subjective perception of this niche. These feelings function to guide job search effort toward institutions with which the candidate is well matched. Variation across candidates in feelings of professional self-esteem should make the job search process faster, more efficient, and ultimately more successful by adaptively guiding candidates toward positions that are of relatively high quality within the individual's range of affordability.

Similar self-evaluative processes should also guide approach behavior toward other types of social relationships, such as friendships and mateships (see Kenrick et al., 1993). In the mating domain, self-assessed mate value (relative to the perceived competition) provides important information for guiding partner preferences. One of us (L.K.) finds Helen Hunt particularly desirable as a potential mate, but prudently avoids wasting very much time or effort in trying to win her affections. Conversely, people (as well as close kin and friends concerned about their welfare) are clearly sensitive to the issue of choosing mates of lower value than that permitted by their own "market value." Along these lines, much evidence suggests that people typically wind up mating with partners who are similar to themselves, both in overall attractiveness (Feingold, 1988) and on a wide array of specific characteristics (Buss, 1985). Although a variety of explanations for this effect are available (see Kalick & Hamilton, 1986), several studies point explicitly to the effect of self-evaluations on mate preferences. For example, a classic study by Berscheid, Dion, Walster, and Walster (1971) showed that men's and women's minimal standards for attractiveness of a date were related to their own level of attractiveness. Similarly, Kenrick et al. (1993) and Regan (1998) showed that, at least for women, self-appraisals on mate value and other socially desirable characteristics were predictive of minimal standards acceptable in a potential mate.

Calibrating investment within ongoing relationships

Although processes of self-evaluation should generally guide individuals toward social partners with whom they are reasonably well-matched, people nonetheless sometimes become involved in "mismatched" relationships. As mentioned above, heavy investment in a social relationship that is substantially lower in value than an individual can command on the social marketplace should be selected against; however, relatively low-investment strategies in mismatched relationships may have been favored by natural selection. Consider, for example, a woman who can choose between two husbands, A and B. Her friends consider Husband A to be a "good catch" for her: he is healthy, strong, professionally successful, well-liked, and respected by his peers. Husband B, by contrast, is physically weak, has a floundering career, few friends, and is submissive to others. Even though the woman's friends think that "she could do better" than Husband B, marrying Husband A is not necessarily the best choice. In order to maintain her relationships with Husband A, she may have to devote most of her time, energy, and resources to the marriage. This heavy investment in one domain restricts the amount of investment she can allocate to other domains, such as development of a professional career, pursuit of additional mateships, and maintenance of friendships. In contrast, in order to maintain her relationship with Husband B, she may have to devote relatively little of her time, energy, and resources to the marriage (while monopolizing most of Husband B's investment in return). Meanwhile, she is able to channel most of her investment into other domains. This suggests that mating downward in mate value could be an evolutionarily stable strategy in certain contexts.

Given these kinds of dynamics, natural selection can be expected to have designed psychological mechanisms to evaluate (1) one's own value in social relationships, (2) the value of relationship partners, and (3) the difference between these two evaluations. We hypothesize that these assessments of relative value function to calibrate not only one's own level of investment in ongoing relationships, but also the level of investment expected from partners. Individuals who perceive themselves to be higher in value than their relationship partners can be expected to invest less and expect more in return.

For example, differential levels of parental investment by mate value have been documented in both birds and humans. Burley (1986) showed that after being experimentally manipulated to be more attractive to females, male zebra finches reduced their levels of parental care (and achieved increased success in extra-pair matings) while their mates increased their parental care. Among the Aka pygmies of central Africa, men who hold positions of high status in the tribe (*kombeti*) only hold their infants for an average of 30 minutes per day, whereas men who lack positions of status hold their infants for an average of 70 minutes per day (Hewlett, 1991). *Kombeti*, who are highly desired as husbands, appear to calibrate levels of parental investment downward and then channel extra investment into additional matings (they are usually polygynous, with two or more wives). In contrast, lower-status men with fewer resources, who are fortunate to even have one wife, appear to calibrate levels of parental investment upward (compensating for their weaker position by investing more time in caring for and protecting their children).

Negotiating dominance/status hierarchies

A parallel line of reasoning applies to behavioral choices regarding agonistic or competitive relationships. In most species, very few intrasexual conflicts are resolved by actual fighting; instead, mismatches are typically avoided because competitors are able to quickly gauge who would likely win a fight, and the expected loser defers to the expected winner. Thus, self-assessments of fighting ability or status – in the animal literature, *resource-holding potential*, or *RHP* – lead individuals to back down from agonistic encounters in which they are likely to lose (so as not to risk injury and waste energy) and to initiate such encounters when they are likely to win (so as to take advantage of available resources and opportunities; Gilbert et al., 1995; Parker, 1974). Wenegrat (1984) has argued that RHP may be one element of human self-esteem.

Chimpanzees, along with many other primate and non-primate species including humans, have elaborate, differentiated behavioral patterns for interacting with other individuals of higher versus lower status than themselves (de Waal, 1982). High-status competitors are treated with deference and respect; one behaves in dominant ways toward those below and in submissive ways toward those above (e.g., Maclay & Knipe, 1972). Although now-discredited group-selectionist theories interpreted such behaviors as designed for maintaining the social order for the good of the group or the species (e.g., Wynne-Edwards, 1986), a more defensible interpretation is that different alternative strategies are more adaptive depending on one's status within the local hierarchy. For those near the bottom an adaptive strategy is to bide one's time and hope for a change in the competitive landscape, showing deference and using strategies such as ingratiation to remain in favor with more powerful individuals (Dawkins, 1989; Wrangham & Peterson, 1996).

The ability to accurately gauge one's status within the local hierarchy, and hence the potential adaptive utility of the various behavioral strategies, is crucial for guiding appropriate dominant and submissive behavior. Low RHP, for example, leads weaker, smaller organisms to avoid directly challenging dominant competitors (and likely suffering serious injury or death in the attempt). Price, Sloman, Gardner, Gilbert, and Rhode (1994) conceptualize depression as a yielding mechanism that functions to inhibit aggressive behavior toward rivals and superiors when one's status is low.

Social psychologists have found that people adopt different *self-presentational strategies* as a function of differential self-esteem (Baumeister, Tice, & Hutton, 1989; Wolfe, Lennox, & Cutler, 1986). Those with high self-esteem (reflecting high self-perceived status) can afford to adopt riskier *acquisitive* or *enhancing* strategies in which they call attention to their strengths and abilities and portray themselves as confident and optimistic. In contrast, those with low self-esteem (reflecting low self-perceived status) tend to adopt a more self-protective self-presentational strategy in which they seek to deflect attention from themselves and approach tasks without raising others' expectations about their likelihood of success. Other researchers have shown that men possessing traits that facilitate intrasexual competitive success adopt different strategies than those who do not when competing for a date (e.g., engaging in direct comparison with and derogation of competitors; Simpson, Gangestad, Christensen, & Leck, 1999).

Summary

An evolutionary perspective on self-esteem focuses attention on the adaptive, functional value of self-evaluations – on the ways in which these evaluations are useful (or, more precisely, were useful to our ancestors) in solving adaptive problems. Because different types of interpersonal relationships differ qualitatively with respect to the particular adaptive problems they pose, a number of different sociometers serving a variety of functions – from guiding personality development to initiating submission to dominant competitors – are needed to negotiate these relationships successfully.

Implications for Some Issues in the Self-esteem Literature

We believe that an evolutionary perspective on self-esteem, and particularly the ideas of domain-specificity and adaptive functionality, offer a useful framework for reconceptualizing (and for generating empirically testable hypotheses about) a variety of major issues in the self-esteem literature. In this section we offer some illustrative examples with respect to a small sample of such issues.

Stability and contingency of self-esteem

Recent work by Kernis and his colleagues (Greenier, Kernis, & Waschull, 1995; Kernis, Cornell, Sun, Berry, & Harlow, 1993) suggests that the degree of stability in self-esteem over time, in addition to the average level of self-esteem, is an important individual-difference variable. Although level and stability are not statistically independent (i.e., stability is positively correlated with level), stability has a number of unique correlates. The two general issues on which we have focused in this paper – multiplicity of domains and multiplicity of adaptive functions – each lead to a hypothesis concerning the nature of individual differences in the stability of self-esteem.

The first possibility is that individual differences in the stability of self-esteem reflect the fact that the activity of any given sociometer varies across time. Once one has established satisfactory levels of inclusion in social groups, for example, the corresponding sociometer may go off-line until circumstances change and it is needed again (Leary & Baumeister, in press). Similarly, a mate-value sociometer should be active when one is on the "mating market," but turn off after one commits to a stable pair-bond relationship (Frank, 1988; Kirkpatrick, 1998). We would therefore hypothesize that self-esteem is more stable among people currently involved in satisfying, ongoing relationships than among those who are not. We would also generally expect people in novel social environments (e.g., college freshmen) to display relatively unstable self-esteem until they have determined their position in local status and dominance hierarchies, and have established new friendships and coalitions. This perspective also helps to explain why self-esteem tends to be highly unstable during adolescence (Harter et al., 1998), a period during which we would expect many sociometers to be more or less chronically active.

The second possibility is that stable versus unstable self-esteem reflects activation of two distinct sociometers in different domains. A given sociometer should produce variable output to the extent that feedback about successes and failures is itself variable; such variability might be expected to differ naturally between domains. In competition with respect to status or mate value, for example, success can vary considerably across time: one might be congratulated by one's boss one day but castigated the next, or have a date invitation rejected one day but accepted the next. Inclusion in friendships and coalitions, in contrast, typically does not vary as much from day to day. This perspective could explain why Kernis et al. (1993, Study 2) unexpectedly found that people with relatively unstable (global) self-esteem were more likely than those with stable self-esteem to identify competence and physical attractiveness – but not social acceptance – as important determinants of their self-worth. People whose status-competition sociometers are highly active may be prone to less stable self-esteem, whereas those whose self-esteem hinges more upon social acceptance may evince more stable self-esteem.

Other constructs in the self-esteem literature may also be subject to similar reinterpretations. For example, although it is typically conceptualized in terms of exaggerated or unstable high self-esteem, *narcissism* "may be less a matter of having a firm conviction about one's overall goodness . . . than a matter of being emotionally invested in one's superiority" (Bushman & Baumeister, 1998, p. 220). That is, narcissism might reflect a disproportionately high level of activity of competition-related sociometers (e.g., status and dominance) relative to social-inclusion sociometers. This interpretation is consistent with other observations about narcissists, such as their high levels of hostility and aggressiveness (e.g., Bushman & Baumeister, 1998).

Social comparison and BIRGing

Another closely related issue concerns the degree to which social comparison processes are involved in the determination and maintenance of self-esteem. Since Festinger's (1954) seminal work, an enormous body of research has examined the role of social comparison in social psychological processes (e.g., Suls & Wills, 1991), including self-esteem.

Our view suggests that some sociometers are more inherently social-comparative than others. Mate value and status are by definition competitive, reflecting relative success in a zero-sum game, but inclusion in friendships or coalitions is ordinarily less so. Thus, our view provides a perspective for distinguishing among domains of self-esteem with respect to the degree to which social comparison processes are involved. In addition, it suggests that individual differences in the degree to which people are actively engaged in social comparison thinking are a function of which sociometers (domains) are currently active.

Whereas competitive domains are inherently social-comparative, the construct of *basking in reflected glory* ("BIRGing"; Cialdini et al., 1976; Tesser, Millar, & Moore, 1988) seems more clearly related to cooperative relationships such as friendships and coalitions. An individual's accomplishments indirectly benefit his or her friends and associates; a person's success is his or her partners' success, leading us to take pride in the accomplishments of our family members and coalition partners. In contrast, competitors for mating opportunities are unlikely to BIRG; in zero-sum contests, one person's success is another's failure. We think that theories such as Tesser's model of self-evaluation maintenance (Tesser, 1988; Beach & Tesser, 1995) could be extended and clarified by differentiating qualitatively different kinds of relationships and evaluations in the context of multiple, functionally distinct sociometers.

Self-enhancement

If, as we have argued, sociometers are designed to monitor our current standing with respect to particular domains in the service of guiding us toward adaptive strategic choices, one might expect them to be designed to do so as accurately as possible. However, a vast body of literature suggests that most of us have modestly inflated views of ourselves (e.g., more of us believe that we are above average than is mathematically possible) and display a variety of related "positive illusions" (Taylor & Brown, 1988). Why should a well-designed (from an evolutionary perspective) sociometer evince such a pervasive self-enhancement bias?

We believe that there may well be an inherent positive bias in the calibration of some, if not all, sociometers. As summarized by Alcock (1995; also see Haselton & Buss, 2000), our evolved psychology is designed to be adaptive, not necessarily truthful. Adaptations for information processing are biased to the extent that some kinds of errors are consistently more costly (in inclusive fitness terms) than others. A rabbit is better served by mistaking a harmless rustling of leaves caused by the wind for a predator than the other way around; ancestral rabbits that were accurate rather than paranoid did not become rabbit ancestors. Krebs and Denton (1997) suggest that many familiar social cognitive biases, from positive illusions to ingroup and outgroup biases, reflect adaptive design of these cognitive systems rather than malfunctions. Leary, Haupt, Strausser, and Chokel (1998) suggest that the self-esteem sociometer might indeed be calibrated with a built-in positive bias in this manner – "much like a fuel gauge that indicates that the gas tank is fuller than it really is" (p. 1290).

Although the adaptive advantages of accuracy were one selection pressure that shaped the evolution of sociometers, we suspect that there was another, conflicting pressure as well. Because one's value in interpersonal domains is primarily a function of how one is evaluated by others, one way to raise one's value on that dimension is by deceiving others about one's true value. The effectiveness of impression management strategies is limited by others' well-tuned abilities to detect deception in self-presentation; it is difficult to convince others of our worth if we are not so convinced ourselves. (See Zahavi & Zahavi, 1997, for a discussion of other reasons why dishonest signaling systems in general are unlikely to evolve.) Positive illusions may therefore represent a form of *self*-deception designed to enhance the effectiveness of an ongoing attempt to "induce others to overvalue us" (Krebs & Denton, 1997).

An interesting alternative perspective, offered by Leary and Baumeister (in press), likens self-esteem-enhancement to drug abuse. High self-esteem feels good by virtue of its design and, consequently, we seek out ways to experience that affective high. Much as "a drug such as cocaine may create a euphoric feeling without one's having to actually experience events that normally bring pleasure . . . [C]ognitively inflating one's self-image is a way of fooling the natural sociometer mechanism into thinking that one is a valued relational partner" (p. 24). We would add that one might alternatively fool other sociometers into thinking that one has high status, or is a desirable mate, and so forth.

According to Leary and Downs (1995, p. 129), "most behaviors that have been attributed to the need to maintain self-esteem may be parsimoniously explained in terms of the motive to avoid social exclusion." We concur, but add that many such behaviors might be explained in terms of other self-esteem domains and functions. From our perspective, self-enhancement processes represent just one aspect – and, in some sense, only a peripheral aspect – of the adaptive design of sociometers more generally.

Self-verification and depressive realism

Based on the traditional assumption that seeking high self-esteem is a fundamental motive, one might expect that self-enhancing biases would be particularly evident among people with the lowest levels of social inclusion, status, and other forms of social success; after all, it is they who presumably need it the most. We are inclined to hypothesize exactly the opposite. If sociometers are designed to motivate and organize alternative behavioral strategies as a function of status, mate value, or social inclusion, then individuals who are failing are those for whom a positive bias would be *least* adaptive. If one's social-inclusion sociometer sounds an alarm, particularly in light of its (default) positive bias, it suggests that something is seriously wrong. Fooling oneself into believing otherwise could have disastrous consequences.

Instead, the alert should motivate efforts to reappraise one's situation as accurately as possible, in order to determine if major behavioral changes or alternative strategies are called for. This analysis is consistent with research by Swann (1987) and others demonstrating that persons with low self-appraisals prefer self-verifying (consistency-enhancing) rather than self-enhancing feedback from others. Moreover, whereas self-enhancement processes may occur automatically and effortlessly, self-verification (or consistency) processes are cognitively effortful (Swann, Hixon, Stein-Seroussi, & Gilbert, 1990). Our hypothesis is that sociometers are calibrated by default to be (modestly) upwardly biased, for reasons discussed above, but that additional cognitive processes designed to deactivate these biases and to generate accurate self-appraisals are activated by low readings.

This view is also consistent with much research indicating that depressed people are "sadder but wiser," in that their views of themselves and their worlds are not biased by positive illusions and are in fact more accurate (e.g., Alloy & Abramson, 1979). Although the proximal consequences and correlates of depression appear dysfunctional in many modern circumstances, it is possible that depression involves activation of a behavioral strategy for taking time out to reassess one's situation and/or to wait for better times. If one has repeatedly experienced failure in the competition for mates, for example, an adaptive strategy would be to suspend competitive efforts temporarily and wait for a change in the competitive landscape (e.g., due to competitors weakening, dying, or moving away). The capacity to experience learned helplessness may be an adaptation designed to enable individuals to determine when they are truly helpless – that is, when continuation of one's current behavioral strategy is unlikely to lead to success with respect to a particular domain. Although it is certainly possible that at least some forms of depression are truly maladaptive, and represent some kind of malfunctioning of an otherwise adaptive system, our perspective suggests that it might be fruitful to reexamine depression in terms of a behavioral strategy activated by low self-esteem in one or more domains.

Cross-cultural differences in self-esteem processes

A common misunderstanding about evolutionary psychology is that the posited existence of species-universal psychological mechanisms seems inconsistent with the observation of cross-cultural variability in behavior. A simple illustration shows why this is not true. Human skin is designed with a callus-producing mechanisms that responds to friction by toughening the skin. Although this adaptation is shared by people in all cultures, enormous variability can be observed both between people and between cultures depending on experience and environmental variability: calluses on the feet are common in cultures where people walk barefoot, but not where they typically wear shoes (Buss, 1995).

Several researchers have suggested that the emphasis on achievement, task performance, and other social-comparative dimensions as a primary basis for self-esteem is unique to modern Western cultures – specifically, *individualistic* (versus *collectivist*) cultures (Markus & Kitayama, 1991; Triandis, Bontempo, Villareal, Asai, & Lucca, 1988). In collectivist cultures, it is argued, self-esteem is more closely related to matters concerning one's acceptance within the group or society rather than to interindividual competition. Our perspective suggests a way to conceptualize this difference in terms of the particular sociometers that are regularly activated within the local environment (cf. the callus analogy). In environments in which success depends on integration within the local group, or strong coalitional relationships, coalition-related sociometers are likely to be regularly or chronically activated, whereas a sociometer designed to monitor status and rank might remain quiescent; the reverse is true in cultures in which success in most domains depends on competition rather than cooperation.

Another view is suggested by Leary and Baumeister (in press), who suggest that contemporary Westerners' (especially Americans') obsession with self-esteem may be a consequence of the relative (and evolutionarily novel) instability of social relationships in modern society. When people move away from their families, change jobs, and get divorced at high rates, they repeatedly find themselves in new contexts in which they must reassess or rebuild their relative standing and interpersonal relationships.

Implications for intervention

In recent years, the idea that low self-esteem lies at the heart of a variety of personal and societal problems has become popular among legislators and the general public, and has led to interventions designed to boost the self-esteem of schoolchildren as a prevention strategy (e.g., California Task Force to Promote Self-esteem and Personal and Social Responsibility, 1990). The perspective on self-esteem we have outlined in this chapter suggests at least two ways in which such a strategy could be severely misguided.

Our view (like Leary's) of self-esteem as a functional, dynamic system that monitors one's degree of success in particular domains, rather than as an end in itself, suggests that manipulating self-esteem is like treating symptoms without treating their underlying cause. Interventions designed to manipulate self-esteem directly are akin to counseling drivers to feel better about the fact that their car is overheating, rather than stopping and adding water to the radiator. (See Leary, 1999, for a general discussion of implications of the sociometer model for clinical and counseling psychology.)

Second, our view (unlike Leary's) further suggests that interventions are likely to fail unless they are directed toward the relevant domain of self-esteem. For example, individuals who feel a lack of coalitional inclusion may remain unaffected by attempts to manipulate their feelings of (or actual) accomplishment and competence – and vice versa. Adding water to the radiator will not be very helpful if the gas tank is empty. Our perspective suggests that intervention strategies must first identify the domain of self-esteem in which an individual is at risk, determine the conditions that are leading to negative self-evaluations within this domain, and then target intervention strategies accordingly. Again, however, effective interventions are likely to be those that work toward fixing the underlying causes of the problems, not the gauges that simply monitor them.

Conclusion

Sociometer theory represents a significant advance in self-esteem research, and opens the door to a dynamic view of self-esteem processes based on evolutionary psychology. As Leary and colleagues have argued, self-esteem reflects the operation of adaptation(s) designed to monitor success and failure in negotiating interpersonal relations. We have offered an extension of the model, based on evolutionary psychology, and attempted to illustrate just a few of the ways in which a functional, domain-specific view of sociometers might inform research on long-standing issues in the self-esteem literature.

With respect to the structure of self-esteem, an evolutionary approach offers a way of potentially "carving nature at its joints." That is, it should be possible to identify components or dimensions of self-esteem that parallel the actual design of our species-general cognitive architecture, rather than simply reflecting the conscious self-reflections of contemporary Western college students. We believe this approach offers a promising basis for constructing better self-esteem measures and for generating hypotheses about the antecedents and consequences of varying levels of self-esteem within specific domains.

From an evolutionary perspective, function is inextricably tied to structure. Following Leary et al. (1995), an evolutionary approach shifts attention away from the problem of enhancing, maintaining, and restoring self-esteem per se, and toward the interpersonal relationships and problems that sociometers are designed to monitor. It shifts attention away from the gauges in the dashboard of the car and toward the engine, transmission, and auxiliary components that actually determine automotive functioning. Such an approach is not only theoretically rich and inherently interesting, but has clear implications for practice and intervention.

We wish to emphasize once again that this chapter is intended as no more than a general framework for guiding research and generating testable hypotheses. Future research may well show that there are many more (or at least different) sociometers than we have suggested here. We have no doubt that many more adaptive functions of such sociometers remain to be identified, and that many other current issues in the self-esteem literature can be usefully reexamined from this perspective. We are equally confident that a functional, evolutionary approach has enormous heuristic value for guiding and generating exciting new research on self-esteem in social psychology and the many other disciplines within which the construct of self-esteem plays an important role.

NOTES

1 Even though happy people may on average live slightly longer or suffer fewer medical problems, such effects typically are not evident until well beyond the primary reproductive years.
2 We acknowledge that many researchers might prefer to use a term such as *self-evaluation* rather than *self-esteem* in referring to distinct domains. However, we prefer to follow Leary and Baumeister (in press) in defining self-esteem in terms of affectively laden appraisals of one's own value.
3 Actually, many modern automobiles do in fact come equipped with a kind of general warning light, labeled simply "engine" or something equally cryptic, which is activated by an on-board computer

that internally monitors a variety of specific aspects of engine functioning. The reason for this design, we presume, is that the kinds of engine problems that would activate it are those that drivers would be unable to repair without a mechanic. Although the computer monitors many domains of engine functioning, in this case they all have just one functional solution for the average driver: Bring the car to a mechanic – i.e., someone with the experience and knowledge required to solve the problem. Human infants are designed in a similar manner: they respond to all kinds of discomfort and cues of potential danger with attachment behaviors intended to increase proximity to a primary caregiver (Bowlby, 1969/1982). Adults, however, have much more differentiated strategic and behavioral repertoires, and we suspect that their brains/minds are designed to implement a diverse collection of adaptive strategies for dealing with different problems.

4   Another major source of self-esteem recognized by most theorists involves self-perceived competence and abilities or self-efficacy (Bandura, 1977) – self-evaluations that are not inherently social in nature. Given space limitations, we have chosen to focus our discussion only on interpersonal relationships. We hope it will be evident, however, that the theoretical approach adopted in this chapter could be applied to self-evaluations of skills and competencies in a similar manner. To some extent this analysis would resemble that of Harter (1993), in which the importance of self-perceived competencies derives in large part from their anticipated impact on the evaluations of important others – with different competencies linked to different classes of relationships.

5   We thank Mark Leary for suggesting the analogy of octane versus fuel level. We also note that Leary's own preference is to reserve the term "sociometer" for the latter (personal communication, July 1999). We think, however, that *socio-meter* aptly describes many of the other facets of self-esteem discussed in this paper as well.

6   Leary and Baumeister (in press) argue instead that the role of dominance in self-esteem is in the service of social inclusion; that is, status "is sometimes a criterion for inclusion" and "has implications for one's relational value" (p. 19). We address the interrelatedness of sociometers later in the chapter, but simply note here that status/dominance and inclusion/acceptance are often quite independent. For example, it may be "lonely at the top" because intense status-striving can undermine social inclusion.

7   We thank Don Forsyth for bringing this point to our attention.

REFERENCES

Alcock, J. E. (1995). The belief engine. *Skeptical Inquirer, 19*(3), 14–18.

Alloy, L. B., & Abramson, L. Y. (1979). Judgment of contingency in depressed and nondepressed students: Sadder but wiser? *Journal of Experimental Psychology, 108*, 441–485.

Bandura, A. (1977). Self-efficacy: Toward a unifying theory of behavioral change. *Psychological Review, 84*, 191–215.

Barinaga, M. (1996). Social status sculpts activity of crayfish neurons. *Science, 171*, 290–291.

Barkow, J. H. (1989). *Darwin, sex, and status: Biological approaches to mind and culture.* Toronto: University of Toronto Press.

Baumeister, R. F., & Leary, M. R. (1995). The need to belong: Desire for interpersonal attachments as a fundamental human motivation. *Psychological Bulletin, 117*, 497–529.

Baumeister, R. F., Smart, L., & Boden, J. M. (1996). Relation of threatened egotism to violence and aggression: The dark side of self-esteem. *Psychological Review, 103*, 5–33.

Baumeister, R. F., Tice, D. M., & Hutton, D. G. (1989). Self-presentational motivations and personality differences in self-esteem. *Journal of Personality, 57*, 547–579.

Beach, S. R. H., & Tesser, A. (1995). Self-esteem and the extended self-evaluation maintenance model: The self in social context. In M. H. Kernis (Ed.), *Efficacy, agency, and self-esteem* (pp. 145–170). New York: Plenum.

Belsky, J., Steinberg, L., & Draper, P. (1991). Childhood experience, interpersonal development, and reproductive strategies: An evolutionary theory of socialization. *Child Development, 62*, 647–670.

Berscheid, E., Dion, K., Walster, E., & Walster, G. W. (1971). Physical attractiveness and dating choice: A test of the matching hypothesis. *Journal of Experimental Social Psychology, 1*, 173–189.

Bowlby, J. (1969/1982). *Attachment and loss: Vol. 1. Attachment.* New York: Basic Books. (Original work published 1969).

Burley, N. (1986). Sexual selection for aesthetic traits in species with biparental care. *American Naturalist, 127*, 415–445.

Bushman, B. J., & Baumeister, R. F. (1998). Threatened egotism, narcissism, self-esteem, and direct and displaced aggression: Does self-love or self-hate lead to violence? *Journal of Personality and Social Psychology, 75*, 219–229.

Buss, D. M. (1985). Human mate selection. *American Scientist, 73*, 47–51.

Buss, D. M. (1995). Evolutionary psychology: A new paradigm for psychological science. *Psychological Inquiry, 6*, 1–30.

Buss, D. M. (1999). *Evolutionary psychology: The new science of the mind.* Boston: Allyn & Bacon.

Buss, D. M., & Schmitt, D. P. (1993). Sexual strategies theory: An evolutionary perspective on human mating. *Psychological Review, 100*, 204–232.

California Task Force to Promote Self-esteem and Personal and Social Responsibility (1990). *Toward a state of self-esteem.* Sacramento: California State Department of Education.

Chagnon, N. A. (1992). *Yanomamo: The last days of Eden.* San Diego, CA: Harcourt Brace Jovanovich.

Cialdini, R. B., Borden, R. J., Thorne, A., Walker, M. R., Freeman, S., & Sloan, L. R. (1976). Basking in reflected glory: Three (football) field studies. *Journal of Personality and Social Psychology, 34*, 366–375.

Clutton-Brock, T. H. (Ed.) (1988). *Reproductive success: Studies of selection and adaptation in contrasting breeding systems.* Chicago: University of Chicago Press.

Colvin, C. R., Block, J., & Funder, D. C., (1995). Overly positive self-evaluations and personality: Negative implications for mental health. *Journal of Personality and Social Psychology, 68*, 1152–1162.

Cooley, C. H. (1902). *Human nature and the social order.* New York: Scribner's.

Coopersmith, S. (1967). *The antecedents of self-esteem.* San Francisco: W. H. Freeman.

Daly, M., Salmon, C., & Wilson, M. (1997). Kinship: The conceptual hole in psychological studies of social cognition and close relationships. In J. A. Simpson & D. T. Kenrick (Eds.), *Evolutionary social psychology* (pp. 265–296). Mahwah, NJ: Erlbaum.

Daly, M., & Wilson, M. (1988). *Homicide.* New York: Aldine de Gruyter.

Dawkins, R. (1982). *The extended phenotype.* San Francisco: W. H. Freeman.

Dawkins, R. (1989). *The selfish gene* (new ed.). Oxford: Oxford University Press.

de Waal, F. (1982). *Chimpanzee politics: Power and sex among apes.* Baltimore: Johns Hopkins University Press.

Ellis, B. J., McFadyen-Ketchum, S., Dodge, K. A., Pettit, G. S., & Bates, J. E. (1999). Quality of early family relationships and individual differences in the timing of pubertal maturation in girls: A longitudinal test of an evolutionary model. *Journal of Personality and Social Psychology, 77*, 387–401.

Ember, C. R. (1978). Myths about hunter-gatherers. *Ethnology, 27*, 239–448.

Epstein, S. (1973). The self-concept revisited: Or a theory of a theory. *American Psychologist, 28*, 404–416.

Feingold, A. (1988). Matching for attractiveness in romantic partners and same-sex friends: A meta-analysis and theoretical critique. *Psychological Bulletin, 104*, 226–235.

Festinger, L. (1954). A theory of social-comparison processes. *Human Relations, 7,* 117–140.

Frank, R. H. (1988). *Passions with reason: The strategic role of the emotions.* New York: Norton.

Gangestad, S. W., & Simpson, J. A. (in press). The evolution of human mating: Trade-offs and strategic pluralism. *Behavioral and Brain Sciences.*

Gilbert, P., Price, J., & Allan, S. (1995). Social comparison, social attractiveness, and evolution: How might they be related? *New Ideas in Psychology, 13,* 149–165.

Graber, J. A., Brooks-Gunn, J., & Warren, M. P. (1995). The antecedents of menarcheal age: Heredity, family environment, and stressful life events. *Child Development, 66,* 346–359.

Greenberg, J., Solomon, S., & Pyszczynski, T. (1986). The causes and consequences of a need for self-esteem: A terror management theory. In R. F. Baumeister (Ed.), *Public self and private self* (pp. 189–212). New York: Springer-Verlag.

Greenier, K. D., Kernis, M. H., & Waschull, S. B. (1995). Not all high (or low) self-esteem people are the same: Theory and research on stability of self-esteem. In M. H. Kernis (Ed.), *Efficacy, agency, and self-esteem* (pp. 51–71). New York: Plenum.

Gutierres, S. E., Kenrick, D. T., & Partch, J. J. (in press). Beauty, dominance, and the mating game: Contrast effects in self-assessment reflect gender differences in mate selection. *Personal and Social Psychology Bulletin.*

Hamilton, W. D. (1964). The evolution of social behavior. *Journal of Theoretical Biology, 7,* 1–52.

Harter, S. (1993). Causes and consequences of low self-esteem in children and adolescents. In R. F. Baumeister (Ed.), *Self-esteem: The puzzle of low self-regard* (pp. 87–116). New York: Plenum.

Harter, S., Waters, P., & Whitesell, N. R. (1998). Relational self-worth: Differences in perceived worth as a person across interpersonal contexts among adolescents. *Child Development, 69,* 756–766.

Haselton, M. G., & Buss, D. M. (2000). Biases in cross-sex mindreading: Errors in design or errors by design? *Journal of Personality and Social Psychology,78,* 81–91.

Hewlett, B. S. (1991). *Intimate fathers: The nature and context of Aka pygmy paternal infant care.* Ann Arbor: University of Michigan Press.

Hoop, D. K., & Ellis, B. J. (1990). *An evolutionary approach to cognitive concepts in personality.* Unpublished manuscript, University of Michigan.

Kalick, S. M., & Hamilton, T. E. (1986). The matching hypothesis reexamined. *Journal of Personality and Social Psychology, 51,* 673–682.

Kaplan, H. B. (1980). *Deviant behavior in defense of self.* New York: Academic Press.

Kaplan, H. S., & Lancaster, J. B. (1999, April). The evolution of human life course and male parental investment. In J. B. Lancaster (Chair), *Evolutionary and cross-cultural perspectives on male parental investment.* Symposium conducted at the biennial meeting of the Society for Research in Child Development, Albuquerque, NM.

Kenrick, D. T., Groth, G. E., Trost, M. R., & Sadalla, E. K. (1993). Integrating evolutionary and social exchange perspectives on relationships: Effects of gender, self-appraisal, and involvement level on mate selection criteria. *Journal of Personality and Social Psychology, 64,* 951–969.

Kernis, M. H., Cornell, D. P., Sun, C., Berry, A., & Harlow, T. (1993). There's more to self-esteem than whether it is high or low: The importance of stability of self-esteem. *Journal of Personality and Social Psychology, 65,* 1190–1204.

Kirkpatrick, L. A. (1998). Evolution, pair-bonding, and reproductive strategies: A reconceptualization of adult attachment. In J. A. Simpson & W. S. Rholes (Eds.), *Attachment theory and close relationships* (pp. 353–393). New York: Guilford Press.

Krebs, D. L., & Denton, K. (1997). Social illusions and self-deception: The evolution of biases in person perception. In J. A. Simpson & D. T. Kenrick (Eds.), *Evolutionary social psychology* (pp. 21–47). Mahwah, NJ: Erlbaum.

Lalumiere, M. L., Seto, M. C., & Quinsey, V. L. (1995). *Self-perceived mating success and the mating choices of human males and females.* Unpublished manuscript, Queen's University at Kingston, Ontario, Canada.

Leary, M. R. (1999). The social and psychological importance of self-esteem. In R. M. Kowalski & M. R. Leary (Eds.), *The social psychology of emotional and behavioral problems* (pp. 197–221). Washington, DC: APA Books.

Leary, M. R., & Baumeister, R. F. (in press). The nature and function of self-esteem: Sociometer theory. In M. Zanna (Ed.), *Advances in experimental social psychology.* San Diego, CA: Academic Press.

Leary, M. R., & Downs, D. L. (1995). Interpersonal functions of the self-esteem motive: The self-esteem system as a sociometer. In M. H. Kernis (Ed.), *Efficacy, agency, and self-esteem* (pp. 123–144). New York: Plenum.

Leary, M. R., Haupt, A. L., Strausser, K. S., & Chokel, J. T. (1998). Calibrating the sociometer: The relationship between interpersonal appraisals and state self-esteem. *Journal of Personality and Social Psychology, 74,* 1290–1299.

Leary, M. R., Tambor, E. S., Terdal, S. K., & Downs, D. L. (1995). Self-esteem as an interpersonal monitor: The sociometer hypothesis. *Journal of Personality and Social Psychology, 68,* 518–530.

Luhtanen, R., & Crocker, J. (1992). A collective self-esteem scale: Self-evaluation of one's social identity. *Personality and Social Psychology Bulletin, 18,* 302–318.

Maclay, G., & Knipe, H. (1972). *The dominant man.* New York: Delta.

Manson, J. H., & Wrangham, R. W. (1991). Intergroup aggression in chimpanzees and humans. *Current Anthropology, 32,* 369–390.

Markus, H. R., & Kitayama, S. (1991). Culture and the self: Implications for cognition, emotion, and motivation. *Psychological Review, 98,* 224–253.

Mealey, L. (1995). The sociobiology of sociopathy: An integrated evolutionary model. *Behavioral and Brain Sciences, 18,* 523–599.

Mulder, M. B. (1987). Resources and reproductive success in women with an example from the Kipsigis of Kenya. *Journal of Zoology, London, 213,* 489–505.

Murdock, G. P., & Provost, C. (1973). Factors in the division of labor by sex: A cross-cultural analysis. *Ethnology, 12,* 203–235.

Parker, G. A. (1974). Assessment strategy and the evolution of fighting behavior. *Journal of Theoretical Biology, 47,* 223–243.

Perez, R. C. (1973). The effect of experimentally-induced failure, self-esteem, and sex on cognitive differentiation. *Journal of Abnormal Psychology, 81,* 74–79.

Price, J. S., Sloman, R., Gardner, R., Gilbert, P., & Rhode, P. (1994). The social competition hypothesis of depression. *British Journal of Psychiatry, 164,* 309–315.

Regan, P. C. (1998). Minimum mate selection standards as a function of perceived mate value, relationship context, and gender. *Journal of Psychology & Human Sexuality, 10,* 53–73.

Rosenberg, M. (1979). *Conceiving the self.* New York: Basic Books.

Rosenberg, M., Schooler, C., & Schoenbach, C. (1989). Self-esteem and adolescent problems: Modeling reciprocal effects. *American Sociological Review, 54,* 1004–1018.

Schatz, R. T., Staub, E., & Lavine, H. (1999). On the varieties of national attachment: Blind versus constructive patriotism. *Political Psychology, 20,* 151–174.

Shrauger, J. S., & Sorman, P. B. (1977). Self-evaluations, initial success and failure, and improvement as determinants of persistence. *Journal of Consulting and Clinical Psychology, 45,* 784–795.

Simpson, J. A., Gangestad, S. W., Christensen, P. N., & Leck, K. (1999). Fluctuating asymmetry, sociosexuality, and intrasexual competitive tactics. *Journal of Personality and Social Psychology, 76,* 159–172.

Smith, M. S., Kish, B. J., & Crawford, C. B. (1987). Inheritance of wealth as human kin investment. *Ethology and Sociobiology, 8,* 171–182.

Solomon, S., Greenberg, J., & Pyszczynskki, T. (1991). A terror management theory of social behavior: On the psychological functions of self-esteem and cultural worldviews. In M. P. Zanna (Ed.), *Advances in Experimental Social Psychology* (vol. 24, pp. 93–159). San Diego: Academic Press.

Suls, J., & Wills, T. A. (Eds.). (1991). *Social comparison: Contemporary theory and research*. Hillsdale, NJ: Erlbaum.

Swann, W. B., Hixon, J. G., Stein-Seroussi, A., & Gilbert, D. T. (1990). The fleeting gleam of praise: Cognitive processes underlying behavioral reactions to self-relevant feedback. *Journal of Personality and Social Psychology, 59*, 17–26.

Swann, W. B. (1987). Identity negotiation: Where two roads meet. *Journal of Personality and Social Psychology, 53*, 1038–1051.

Symons, D. (1979). *The evolution of human sexuality*. New York: Oxford University Press.

Symons, D. (1987). If we're all Darwinians, what's all the fuss about. In C. Crawford, D. Krebs, & M. Smith (Eds.), *Sociobiology and psychology* (pp. 121–145). Hillsdale, NJ: Erlbaum.

Symons, D. (1992). On the use and misuse of Darwinism in the study of human behavior. In J. H. Barkow, L. Cosmides, & J. Tooby (Eds.), *The adapted mind* (pp. 137–159). New York: Oxford University Press.

Tajfel, H. (1982). Social psychology of intergroup relations. *Annual Review of Psychology, 33*, 1–39.

Tajfel, H., & Turner, J. C. (1986). The social identity theory of intergroup behavior. In S. Worchel & W. Austin (Eds.), *Psychology of intergroup relations* (2nd ed., pp. 7–24). Chicago: Nelson-Hall.

Taylor, S. E., & Brown, J. D. (1988). Illusion and well-being: A social psychological perspective on mental health. *Psychological Bulletin, 103*, 193–210.

Tennen, H., & Affleck, G. (1995). The puzzles of self-esteem: A clinical perspective. In M. H. Kernis (Ed.), *Efficacy, agency, and self-esteem* (pp. 241–262). New York: Plenum.

Tesser, A. (1988). Toward a self-evaluation maintenance model of social behavior. In L. Berkowitz (Ed.), *Advances in experimental social psychology* (Vol. 21, pp. 181–227). New York: Academic Press. 181–227.

Tesser, A., Millar, M., & Moore, J. (1988). Some affective consequences of social comparison and reflection processes: The pain and pleasure of being close. *Journal of Social and Personality Psychology, 54*, 49–61.

Tiger, L. (1969). *Men in groups*. New York: Random House.

Tooby, J., & Cosmides, L. (1990). On the universality of human nature and the uniqueness of the individual: The role of genetics and adaptation. *Journal of Personality, 58*, 17–67.

Tooby, J., & Cosmides, L. (1992). The psychological foundations of culture. In J. H. Barkow, L. Cosmides, & J. Tooby (Eds.), *The adapted mind* (pp. 19–136). New York: Oxford University Press.

Triandis, H. C., Bontempo, R., Villareal, M. J., Asai, M., & Lucca, N. (1988). Individualism and collectivism: Cross-cultural perspectives on self-ingroup relations. *Journal of Personality and Social Psychology, 54*, 323–338.

Trivers, R. L. (1972). Parental investment and sexual selection. In R. B. Campbell (Ed.), *Sexual selection and the descent of man: 1871–1971* (pp. 136–179). Chicago: Aldine.

Wenegrat, B. (1984). *Sociobiology and mental disorder: A new view*. Menlo Park, CA: Addison-Wesley.

Wolfe, R. N., Lennox, R. D., & Cutler, B. L. (1986). Getting along and getting ahead: Empirical support for a theory of protective and acquisitive self-presentation. *Journal of Personality and Social Psychology, 50*, 356–361.

Wrangham, R., & Peterson, D. (1996). *Demonic males: Apes and the origins of human violence*. Boston: Houghton Mifflin.

Wright, R. (1994). *The moral animal: The new science of evolutionary psychology*. New York: Pantheon.

Wynne-Edwards, V. C. (1986). *Evolution through group selection*. Oxford: Blackwell Scientific.

Zahavi, A., & Zahavi, A. (1997). *The handicap principle*. New York: Oxford University Press.

CHAPTER FOUR

Is Loving the Self Necessary for Loving Another? An Examination of Identity and Intimacy

W. Keith Campbell and Roy F. Baumeister

In this chapter, we examine one important facet of the relation between identity and intimacy. Our review of this broad literature is guided by an effort to assess the popular belief that self-love is necessary for loving another. We begin by addressing some of the possible sources of this belief, including the work of Erikson, Maslow, and Rogers, as well as the influence of what has come to be called the "self-esteem movement." We then address several specific questions: Does self-love result in love for others? Does self-love lead others to love the self? Does loving others result in self-love? Finally, does being loved lead to self-love?

Neither "self-love" nor "loving others" are well defined psychological constructs. Therefore, in our review, we strive to be inclusive rather than exclusive in our use of these terms (although there are certainly variants of both terms that we did not examine or uncover). Our conceptualization of self-love focuses primarily on two constructs, self-esteem and narcissism. We also examine related constructs, such as social dominance and positive self-beliefs, as well as dependency and depression. Our conceptualization of loving others includes a range of relationship variables including love styles, attraction, commitment, and relationship maintenance behaviors.

Why Popular Culture has it that Self-love Is a Prerequisite for Loving Others

The notion that self-love is a necessary precursor to loving others appears to be widely accepted in popular culture. One has only to look on the shelves of any large bookstore or on the Internet to see a large selection of individuals and organizations promoting the importance of achieving self-love. Titles of books and cassette courses include *Learning how to love yourself*, and *How to love yourself: Cherishing the incredible miracle that you are* (Cruse, 1987; Hay, 1992). At the same time, it is difficult to find individuals or organizations promoting the importance of humility for loving others or maintaining relationships. (Certain religious organizations may be an example of the latter, but their messages are arguably drowned out by the groups promoting self-love. In addition, several religious or quasi-religious groups proudly promote the virtue of self-love.)

Where did the belief that self-love is crucial for loving others come from? We review several possibilities. One is that this view stems from a misreading of the work of Erik Erikson. In his theory of psychosocial development, Erikson postulated that a sense of identity had to be established before intimacy with another could be achieved (Erikson, 1950). In Erikson's scheme, the task of establishing identity arose primarily in the teen and early young adult years. These years were spent wrestling with a crisis between achieving a solid sense of self and being trapped in a state of role confusion. If this early identity crisis was resolved appropriately, the young adult years became a time to experience intimacy. (What Erikson had in mind when he used the term *intimacy* was likely heterosexual marriage, although other stable sexual relationships would probably be evidence of similarly successful resolutions to the question of intimacy.) As Erikson put it, the crisis became one of intimacy versus isolation.

In general, some research has supported Erikson's speculations regarding the importance of achieving identity before the establishment of intimacy. Longitudinal data have shown that the establishment of identity in the teen years predicts stable intimate relationships in the young adult years, both in terms of marital status and marital stability (Kahn, Zimmerman, Csikszentmihalyi, & Getzels, 1985). These findings, however, do not unequivocally support the notion that self-love is a necessary precursor to loving others. Although a clear sense of self or identity is associated with a degree of high self-esteem (J. D. Campbell et al., 1996), stable self-views do not necessarily imply self-love. Certainly, a stable view of the self is more central to Erikson's conceptualization of identity than a positively valenced view of the self.

Two other highly influential psychological thinkers, Rogers (1961) and Maslow (1962), may have also inadvertently played a role in focusing society on the importance of self-love. These authors emphasized the importance of living up to one's ideals, even becoming self-actualized. This self-actualization was, of course, presumed to have beneficial effects on interpersonal relationships. Conversely, the positive regard of others was presumed to be a helpful first step toward self-actualization. Indeed, Rogers's model of psychotherapy rested on the therapist's ability to have unconditional positive regard for the client, as well as an accurate, empathic stance toward the client. Furthermore, it is clear that self-actualization and self-love are not the same thing, although people may have interpreted them as such. Self-actualization includes an accurate view of self, and an acceptance of the failings, problems, and shortcomings that the self contains. Self-actualization is more closely related to self-acceptance than self-love, but some of this detail may have been lost in the popularization of Rogers's work.

In addition to sharing many insights into self-actualization with Rogers, Maslow spoke of deficiency or "D" love – that is, love for which the goal is to correct for failings or deficits in the self. This concept clearly indicates that Maslow felt that self-love was not necessary for love of others. Deficit love could be based on precisely a lack of self-love, for example, if someone full of self-doubts and insecurities latched on to someone else to provide support and shore up the sense of self. Alternatively, it is plausible that individuals with inflated self-opinions would engage in loving to overcome deficits in the self. For example, a man with no job, bad looks, and weak interpersonal skills, who, at the same time, thinks he is a winner in the game of life, might seek out relational partners who would confirm his inflated self-views. Maslow also spoke of self-actualized ("B") love. Self-actualized love is evidenced not by self-love but by acceptance of one's own and others' faults, psychological non-defensiveness, spontaneity, and honesty.

Furthermore, the theoretical relationship between loving self and loving others can be inferred from Maslow's (1968) hierarchy of needs, in which he explained that people first address the most urgent, basic needs and only move on to higher needs when the basic ones are satisfied. In Maslow's hierarchy, belongingness needs are more basic to human functioning than self-esteem needs and self-actualization. Thus, in his theory, receiving love is a prerequisite for self-love, rather than the other way around. In sum, it would be a misreading of Maslow's views to propose that self-love leads to loving others.

The final source for the view that self-love may be necessary for the love of others is what is popularly called the "self-esteem movement." This is a general term for a group of movements, efforts, or attempts that stress the importance of self-esteem for success in a host of domains. The most visible emblem of this movement was the California Task Force to Promote Self-esteem and Personal and Social Responsibility. The California Task Force was signed into law by Governor George Deukmejian in 1986, and the driving force behind the legislation was Assemblyman John Vasconcellos. (Not coincidentally, Vasconcellos was strongly influenced by the work of Carl Rogers and had undergone client-centered therapy in the 1960s.) According to the California Task Force, self-esteem is important, perhaps necessary, for staying off welfare, succeeding in school, and resisting the temptations of premarital sex and drugs (Mecca, Smelser, & Vasconcellos, 1989). Indeed, self-esteem improvement has become an integral component of several efforts to cure social ills. Certainly, the ideas of the self-esteem movement have spread far into popular culture. This movement may help account for the belief that self-love is necessary for intimate relationships. (To be fair, the goal of the California Task Force was arguably noble and explicitly *not* designed as a strategy for promoting narcissism. Furthermore, the Task Force did make an effort to garner scientific evidence to support their views. Apparently, some of this has gotten lost in the dissemination and popularization of these ideas.) If feeling good about oneself is good for keeping a job, staying off drugs, and staying in school, it might also be good for staying in relationships.

Today, popular books on self-esteem often appear to consider it a truism that self-love is necessary for loving others. Nathaniel Branden, one of the most prolific promoters of self-esteem, notes that "it is not difficult to see the importance of self-esteem to success in romantic relationships" and makes explicit reference to the phrase "If you do not love yourself, you will be unable to love others" (Branden, 1994, pp. 7–8). Lesser known authors echo this point. As one author notes in a description of his book, *Loving is becoming intimate with your real self*, "You may well have noticed that people who love themselves find it easy to love others and to accept love from others" (Dolan, 1999). In the present chapter we will attempt to examine systematically the link between self-love and the love of others to see if this is actually the case.

Does Loving the Self Promote Loving Others?

We turn now from popular beliefs and theoretical speculations to actual research findings. As any experienced researcher might expect, the empirical links between self-love and loving others are far more complex and dubious than popular wisdom holds.

Self-esteem

The first step in our analysis is to examine the literature on the association between self-esteem and loving others. The popular view would predict that high self-esteem would be related to love for others. This, however, does not always appear to be the case. In an early look at this question, Dion and Dion (1975) found that low self-esteem was associated with more intense experiences of love as well as more unrequited love. (High self-esteem was associated with more frequent love experiences, but only when the favorable views of self were coupled with low defensiveness. There was no main effect of self-esteem on frequency of love.) Hendrick and Hendrick (1986) found that low self-esteem was associated with more manic love, although high self-esteem was associated with greater passionate love. Manic love is evidenced by obsession with the love object and experiencing bouts of both intense joy and intense sorrow in the relationship (Hendrick & Hendrick, 1986, 1990; Lee, 1973). This intense love experience, which in the past has been called "lovesickness" or being "sick of love," has also been reported in the clinical literature as related to low self-esteem (Moss, 1995).

Other studies have likewise linked low rather than high self-esteem to some kinds of love. In one study, women who were self-identified as "loving too much" reported self-esteem that was lower than published norms (Petrie, Giordano, & Roberts, 1992). Meanwhile, research conceptualizing love more broadly as acceptance for others has found little evidence that high self-esteem predicts love. Using a German sample, Schuetz (in press) found no relationship between self-esteem and acceptance for others. Overall, it seems, there is little evidence that self-esteem promotes loving others. Indeed, low self-esteem may be predictive of certain experiences of love.

Self-esteem may play a role in maintaining intimacy, however. Relational fidelity, for example, may be associated with high self-esteem, although evidence for any causal relationship (in either direction) is lacking (Sheppard, Nelson, & Andreoli-Mathie, 1995). Likewise, self-esteem may act as a buffer that partially shields the self from relationship stressors, such as inequity (Longmore & DeMaris, 1997) and childbirth (Terry, 1991). Put another way, romantic relationships may be affected by problems from both inside and outside of the relationship. To the extent that possessing self-esteem helps the individual cope with these negative events, self-esteem will be beneficial to the relationship. Furthermore, low self-esteem may damage romantic relationships in other ways. Low-self-esteem individuals may develop a pattern of emotional neediness in relationships. They find it difficult to fathom that someone could care about them all that much. (Not surprisingly, if you do not like yourself, you tend to assume that others will not like you.) Researchers have found that individuals low in self-esteem (at least when also depressed) constantly seek reassurance from close others (Joiner, Alfano, & Metalsky, 1992). This pattern of behavior, however, may not aid in the longevity of the relationship. On the contrary, it might impair or shorten it.

Still, it is far from clear whether self-esteem has any consistent effect on duration or maintenance of relationships. One study of marital interactions yielded a negative relationship between narcissistic grandiosity (and instability) and positive interactions with the spouse, suggesting that some forms of self-love are detrimental to good relationship maintenance. This effect was especially noticeable when participants discussed ego-threatening topics (Schuetz, 1998). Self-acceptance, however, did predict liking for and positive interactions with the spouse. Self-esteem may also be implicated in violent or aggressive responses to self-esteem threat (Baumeister, Smart, & Boden, 1996). Such threats, for example, may include jealousy stemming from one's partner's desire to leave the romantic relationship. This violence may serve some purpose in maintaining a relationship but may also seriously damage any benefits gained from it. Finally, high self-esteem may be associated with exit behaviors in response to relationship conflict (Rusbult, Morrow, & Johnson, 1987). In other words, people with favorable opinions of themselves are more likely to respond to relationship conflict by doing things that might end the relationship, possibly because they begin looking for alternative partners. This may be good for the self but detrimental to the relationship. Of course, it is possible that leaving a bad relationship may lead to a better future relationship. For example, research has noted that a lack of alternatives often leads individuals to remain in abusive relationships, whereas the presence of alternatives helps them exit (Rusbult & Martz, 1995). Still, these findings confirm that self-love can prove detrimental to relationships, contrary to the simple view that self-love breeds love for others.

Narcissists

We now turn our attention to the classic symbol of self-love in Western culture: Narcissus, the hopelessly attractive character in Greek mythology who refused the romantic offers of others and fell in love with himself. This classic image of self-love has been adapted theoretically to describe a modern personality pattern called *narcissism*. Narcissism is a personality variable that includes highly positive evaluations of self vis-à-vis others. These positive beliefs are maintained by intrapersonal strategies (e.g., fantasies of power [Raskin & Novacek, 1991], self-serving biases [Rhodewalt & Morf, 1998]) as well as interpersonal strategies) (e.g., admiration-seeking [Buss & Chiodo, 1991], social dominance [Bradlee & Emmons, 1992]). Narcissism, as one may guess, has several implications for relational functioning.

If self-love is a prerequisite for intimacy, then narcissists, the true paragons of self-love, ought to have the greatest intimate connections with others. This simple theoretical prediction, however, is contradicted by the data. Narcissists have been noted by both clinicians and social/personality psychologists to be deficient in the domain of intimacy. The formula looks something like this: self-love leads to more self-love, but detracts from other-love – when other-love is defined as caring, concern, empathy, or intimacy. This formula goes back to some of the earliest clinical reports. For example, Nacke noted a paraphilia (which he named after Narcissus) that involved kissing or touching the self (Nacke, 1899; cited in Freud, 1914/1957). Even Freud, in his introductory work on narcissism, noted two types of individuals, those of the "anaclitic" (attachment) type and those of the "narcissistic" type. The anaclitic type directs love outward toward objects (i.e., experiences intimacy). The narcissistic type, on the other hand, directs love inward to the self. For the narcissist, the object of intimacy becomes: "(a) what he himself is (i.e., himself), (b) what he himself was, (c) what he himself would like to be, (d) someone who was once part of himself" (Freud, 1914/1957, p. 90). In a later work, Freud expanded his definition of self-love to include self-sufficiency and self-preservation. Narcissists are concerned with protecting and maintaining the self (Freud, 1931/1950).

These observations are amplified in the social and personality psychology literature on the trait of narcissism. Narcissists (i.e., people who score high on the trait scale of narcissism) have high self-esteem (Raskin, Novacek, & Hogan, 1991a, 1991b) and think about themselves often (Emmons, 1987; Raskin & Shaw, 1988). They see themselves as superior (Gabriel, Critelli, and Ee, 1994) and unique (Emmons, 1984) individuals. Their self-love is associated with less need for intimacy and greater need for power (Carroll, 1987), less agreeableness and greater hostility (Rhodewalt & Morf, 1995), less communion and more agency (Bradlee & Emmons, 1992), reduced empathy and perspective taking (Watson, Grisham, Trotter, & Biderman, 1984), and (when conceptualized as inflated self-views) greater conflict in discussion (Colvin, Block, & Funder, 1995), as compared with other people. Clearly, narcissistic self-love does not seem to improve the capacity to love others; rather, it seems to impair it.

In fact, it appears that narcissists use intimate relationships to bolster or increase their own self-love. Put another way, narcissists use relationships as a forum for self-regulation — specifically, regulating the positivity of the self. This interpersonal self-regulation can take several forms. Narcissists take credit from (and even derogate) fellow group members (Gosling, John, Craik, & Robins, 1998; John & Robins, 1994) and close or similar others (W. K. Campbell, Reeder, Sedikides, & Elliot, in press; Farwell & Wohlwend-Lloyd, 1998; Morf and Rhodewalt, 1993) in achievement settings. Narcissists report that they are smarter and more attractive than other college students (Gabriel et al., 1994) and criticize others who tell them differently (Kernis & Sun, 1994). They show off to others as part of an effort to feel grandiose or important (Buss & Chiodo, 1991; Raskin et al., 1991a, 1991b). When they date, they are attracted to other wonderful people to whom they feel similar and who make them feel important by association (W. K. Campbell, 1999). Indeed, these strategies are evident in narcissists' love styles. Narcissists report being game-playing and pragmatic (but not selfless) in romantic relationships — there is little correlation between narcissism and other love styles (W. K. Campbell & Foster, 1999). (Similar experiences of love have also been reported by individuals who are high in psychological individualism, especially when it contains placing self-interest above other-interest; Dion & Dion, 1991.) Taken together, these interpersonal self-regulatory strategies may temporarily help prop up a narcissist's sense of self-worth, but this effect is likely not to last indefinitely. Narcissists' quest for self-love actually turns off other individuals (Paulhus, 1998). It appears that not only does self-love not increase love for others but it actually decreases others' love for the self. We shall return to this point later in the chapter.

Is there any benefit of narcissism for maintaining romantic relationships? The data available so far have not shown any such benefits. It is conceivable that there are some potential benefits of narcissism to maintaining relationships. Narcissists tend to think they are better than other people (e.g., Gabriel et al., 1994). If this perceived superiority on the part of narcissists extends into their interpersonal relationships, it may increase the longevity of the relationship. Specifically, individuals who believe that their relationships are superior to others' express more commitment (Buunk & van der Eijnden, 1997; Van Lange & Rusbult, 1995), and so if narcissists hold these relationship superiority beliefs, they may also experience increased commitment. On the other hand, narcissists presumably regard themselves as exceptionally attractive to other people in general, and so they may have inflated confidence about their ability to replace a partner who does not fully satisfy them.

Echoes

It appears that self-love as defined by narcissism does not predict intimacy. So what about the opposite of narcissism? If one reflects on the story of Narcissus, there was, at least in some of the tellings, another important character, Echo. Echo was desperately in love with Narcissus, so much so that she repeated every word that he said. Hence, even if narcissism is detrimental to love, maybe "echoism" promotes love. This has intuitive appeal, although the myth tells us otherwise. Echo may have been willing to experience love, but she did not win a healthy relationship with Narcissus. How do modern research findings square with this bit of mythological wisdom?

First, we can look in the clinical literature for an analogue to echoism. One likely candidate is the dependent personality disorder. Individuals diagnosed with dependent personality disorder will go to great lengths to maintain intimate relationships. One of the criteria for the disorder is engaging in unpleasant behaviors for the sake of the relationship, up to and including suffering serious abuse. Dependent individuals will also refrain from expressing disagreement or conflict in the relationship. If the relationship does end, they will quickly seek out another one to take its place (American Psychiatric Association, 1994). In short, these clinically diagnosed "echoes" are likely to maintain relationships at great cost to the self. These relationships, however, may exhibit certain negative characteristics (e.g., abuse) and, although they may not last, they will certainly be replaced quickly.

Is there evidence that being an echo may help maintain a relationship? The answer seems to be a qualified "yes." Several (although not all) of the relationship maintenance mechanisms identified by researchers support this contention. Individuals who are willing to make sacrifices for the sake of their relationship – for example, giving up a favorite hobby or job – are likely to display greater commitment and longer lasting relationships (Van Lange et al., 1997). In fact, accommodation in relationship conflict – for example, not escalating a conflict that one's partner starts – is usually related to commitment and may lead to relationship endurance. Furthermore, as noted earlier, high-self-esteem individuals may be more likely to respond to conflicts with strategies that are detrimental to the relationship (Rusbult et al., 1987).

Summary

We have reviewed several lines of research examining whether loving one's self (as evidenced by self-esteem and narcissism) predicts intimacy or love. The answer to this question is clearly more complicated than popular sentiment would suggest. Self-esteem does not promote love, especially manic love, but a healthy degree of self-esteem may function to maintain ongoing relationships, at least in certain situations (e.g., when problems outside the relationship impact the relationship). Similarly, narcissism does not seem to promote intimacy or love (except when love involves game-playing and pragmatism). Furthermore, narcissism does not appear to bode well for relationship maintenance. The complement to narcissism, which we call echoism, does appear to be related to relationship maintenance. These relationships, however, may not always be healthy or lasting. Taken together, the evidence indicates that loving the self is not a prerequisite for loving others and may even detract from it.

Does Loving the Self Prompt Others to Love the Self?

In this section we address the effect of self-love on the love received from others. Does loving the self lead others to love the self? Put another way: Do people generally tend to love people who love themselves?

There are some obvious reasons to think that self-love is an attractive characteristic in a potential romantic partner. It seems intuitively plausible that individuals who are self-assured and ambitious inspire confidence and may make good leaders. It is difficult, for example, to think of a successful or popular United States president who did not have a strong sense of confidence in his beliefs and his ability to make those beliefs a reality. Reagan's popularity rested in large part on his optimistic forecasts regarding the future of America and the world – a future that could supposedly be realized if his policies were implemented. Similarly, Clinton has been called the "Comeback Kid" for his ability to confidently overcome multiple threats to his presidency.

In the realm of romantic relationships, self-confidence, success, and esteem are arguably desirable traits in a potential partner. The attractive heroines and heroes of popular culture are not, in general, weak of will. Sharon Stone and Harrison Ford are attractive, in part, because the characters they play are strong and self-confident. Few people are romantically attracted to emotionally needy individuals (W. K. Campbell, 1999). Even Freud suggested that narcissism is an attractive quality in a potential romantic partner, although his reasoning behind this statement was somewhat complicated (see discussion of the ego ideal below).

We find additional evidence for this desire to be with confident and assured individuals in the depression literature (see Segrin & Dillard, 1992, for a review). Depression, a component of which is low self-esteem, does not bode well for relationships, romantic or otherwise. Depressed people are not fun to be around, and they drive relationship partners away. Indeed, in situations where the other cannot escape the depressive's cone of gloom, the other may well find himself or herself becoming fed up or worse. College roommates of depressed individuals, for example, are likely to increasingly dislike those depressed individuals over the course of a semester (Joiner, Alfanso, & Metalsky, 1993). Furthermore, the roommates of depressed individuals may themselves become depressed (Joiner et al., 1992). Of course, depressives may love others as much as or more than anyone else (although there is some evidence that depressives experience a reduction in sex-drive). The point is that depressives are not necessarily loved in return.

Can we therefore conclude that people who love themselves are loved by others? The answer may not be as simple as it seems upon first glance. There is a host of research suggesting that self-love may be at best a mixed blessing in a potential leader, romantic partner, or friend. In fact, self-love may be seriously undesirable.

Confidence may be an important quality of leaders, but a good dose of humility may add to a leader's appeal. A popular leader can show humility in several ways. A leader may be well served by having a sense of humor, especially self-deprecating humor. A leader who makes small slip-ups or other minor mistakes may also be popular. For example, a confident leader who garbles her words, and then makes a joke out of it, or a leader who slips on his way out of a famous golfer's house and can laugh about it, may gain in popular appeal. This so called "pratfall effect" (Aronson, Willerman, & Floyd, 1966) may operate in several ways. First, a leader who makes a small mistake now and again may reassure the public that he is just like everyone else, and can thus be trusted to work for the "people." Imagine if Dan Quayle, after his famous mishap over the word "potato," had laughed at himself and said he should have paid more attention to his teachers in school. This incident might have actually have helped him politically, even winning over part of the teachers' vote to the Republicans. Second, the ability to laugh at oneself may imply that the self-confident leader is not rigid and defensive. This implies that the leader will act reasonably and appropriately in response to threats, rather than on the basis of emotional impulses. It is hard to imagine a Mussolini or a Stalin laughing at himself. Clearly, laughing at oneself does not necessarily imply a serious lack of self-love but may imply a healthy dose of humility.

In the realm of romantic relationships, self-love is also not always attractive. When people talk about themselves chronically (as narcissists are prone to do; Raskin & Shaw, 1988), we may get the sense that they are not interested in or concerned about the well-being of anyone but themselves (and this may well be the case). Researchers have tested some of these ideas in the laboratory. In one study, actors were videotaped playing the role of narcissists. When this tape was shown to subjects, the narcissists were not seen as attractive. In fact, they were rated as less attractive than controls (Carroll, Corning, Morgan, & Stevens, 1991). The clinical literature suggests that narcissists themselves may be aware of the negative influence of talking too much about the self. Narcissists, it seems, often use charm or flattery, rather than or in addition to self promotion, to get others romantically attracted to them (Masterson, 1988). To the outside observer the narcissist may look slippery, slimy, or otherwise snake-like, but this strategy often may work.

A second line of research on romantic attraction has argued that social dominance, a personal quality strongly related to self-love (correlations with narcissism range from .76 [Raskin, Novacek, & Hogan, 1991a], to .36 [Raskin & Terry, 1988]), is ultimately not as important as agreeableness in winning the attraction of others (Cunningham, Druen, & Barbee, 1997). We may like self-confident, socially dominant, or narcissistic traits in others, but it is perhaps more important to be nice, kind, and caring.

Summary

Where inconsistency exists, it may be wise to look for a moderator variable. In this case, such a variable may be relationship duration. It is possible that self-love is an important facilitator in the initial stages of a relationship, but may become detrimental as the relationships proceeds (Paulhus, 1998; Tice, Butler, Muraven, & Stillwell, 1995). We may like self-confident leaders or romantic partners to start with, but being in the presence of excessive self-love may be exasperating after a time. One of the authors, for example, spent an amusing evening at a restaurant listening to a young male regale loudly a potential romantic partner with stories of his ice-climbing adventures. A typical statement used by the suitor was: "Ice-climbing is not for everyone: it takes a certain verve." After three minutes, the author was admiring; after thirty minutes he was ready to take a piton to the story-teller. The target of the story-teller's affection, on the other hand, appeared impressed. Still, one wonders how many dinners she could endure where ice-climbing was the only topic of conversation.

Does Loving Others Promote Self-love?

The next step in our effort to identify the link between self-love and other-love is to address the question: Does loving others in a close relationship promote loving the self? Alternatively, does loving others in a close relationship actually lead to a decrease in self-love? An examination of the literature suggests that the answer to both questions may be "yes." Intimacy can promote positive self-views, but it can also temper those positive self-views. This conclusion will likely not come as a surprise to the lay reader. Individuals commonly report that increased self-esteem is a major benefit of entering romantic relationships – and, indeed, a possible outcome of being in love (Aron, Paris, & Aron, 1995) – but also that loss of self-esteem is an important potential cost of romantic involvement (Sedikides, Oliver, & Campbell, 1994; also Baumeister, Wotman, & Stillwell, 1993).

Loving others can help

How might intimacy with close others lead to a more positive identity? We discuss four pathways. First, there seems to be a communication gap between close others that can leave both parties feeling good about themselves. Close partners find it difficult to tell us the truth about ourselves (Felson, 1993). They would rather talk about our positive than negative traits (Blumberg, 1972) even to the point of distortion (Manis, Cornell, & Moore, 1974). They also may refrain from judging us (at least to our face; Goffman, 1959), and may even flatter us (Jones, 1973). Finally, intimate others feel driven to stay mum about the bad news in our lives (Tesser & Rosen, 1975).

Intimate others may also buffer us from the effects of bad news (Cohen & Wills, 1985). Close relationships are often where we turn to cope with life's grimmer aspects. Such social support from close others may help us feel good about our lives and ourselves (Cohen & Hoberman, 1983; Major, Testa, & Bylsma, 1991).

Close relationships can also help us to love ourselves in somewhat less noble ways. One of these involves leaching esteem from a close other who does well (at least in a non-self-relevant domain; Tesser, 1988) or is physically attractive (Sigall & Gould, 1977). If one dates a famous celebrity, for example, one might start to think that one is a pretty impressive person in one's own right. This process has been called identification (A. Freud, 1936; Tajfel

& Turner, 1986), reflection (Tesser, 1988), and, most poetically, basking in reflected glory (Cialdini et al., 1976).

An interesting version of this process of identification was noted by Freud (1922/1959) and further elaborated by Reik (1944). According to Freud, the experience of love, specifically manic or euphoric love, was the result of the lover projecting his or her ideal self ("ego ideal") onto the object of affection. According to Freud, the result of this projection was twofold. First, the target of affection becomes idealized. Second, the lover feels the pleasure of having the psychological tension normally produced by the ideal self alleviated. In other words, the lover feels as if he or she has reached her ideal self simply by perceiving the love object. Freud described this state as the experience of mania. (To understand this experience, one might recall the early stages of an infatuation where the worries and complexities of the working world vanish and consciousness is filled with images of the loved one.) Although this theory is somewhat fanciful, there are several findings that can be seen as supportive. Researchers have noted that individuals in romantic relationships report feeling closer to their ideal selves (i.e., diminished actual/ideal self-discrepancy; W. K. Campbell, Sedikides, & Bosson, 1994). Similarly, the seeking of the ideal self has been implicated in attraction (Karp, Jackson, & Lester, 1970; LaPrelle, Hoyle, Insko, & Bernthal, 1990), and low-self-esteem individuals may report enhanced attraction to targets of affection (Mathes & Moore, 1985). Additionally, idealization of a relationship partner is related to a more satisfying relationship and to enhanced self-views (Murray, Holmes, & Griffin, 1996a, 1996b).

Finally, when we cannot gain esteem from identifying with a close other's success, we can get it from favorable comparisons in the moments when they fail. This is especially true if we are the ones who outperform them. As noted by Tesser (1988), self-evaluation is particularly enhanced when a close other is outdone in a highly self-relevant domain.

Loving others can also hurt

One of the important consequences of intimacy with others is sharing. We share with those we love, and the things we share include resources, successes, positive evaluations, and, indeed, ourselves. One consequence of this sharing is that it can, under certain circumstances, bound or attenuate self-love.

An important aspect of any intimate relationship is sharing resources. This sharing may even occur without explicit or implicit reciprocity (Clark, 1984). When seeking out rewards, relationship partners may engage in a strategy by which they strive to maximize the outcomes for both individuals (Rusbult & Arriaga, 1997). For example, two lovers may share a helping of dessert, rather than one keeping this reward for himself or herself. This strategy is clearly important in maintaining relationships, but will, at least at times, lead to negative individual-level outcomes.

This sharing becomes especially relevant to self-love or self-esteem when the resources shared are highly diagnostic of important self attributes. This can be seen clearly in a study of the self-serving bias as evidenced by close and non-close others (Campbell, Sedikides, Reeder, & Elliot, in press; Sedikides, Campbell, Reeder, & Elliot, 1998). To describe briefly this research: two strangers are brought into the laboratory and asked to perform an interdependent task. In this case, the task is a dyadic test of creativity in which both partners are asked to come up with multiple uses for a brick and a candle. The strangers are then given bogus success or failure feedback at the dyadic level, that is, they are told that they performed well or poorly as a dyad. Each dyad member is then asked to attribute responsibility privately to the self or to the partner for the task outcome. In the case of strangers, what one finds is evidence of the self-serving bias. Individuals take credit for success and blame their partners for failure, thus maintaining positive self beliefs. A rather different picture emerges, however, when the partners are not strangers but close others. In this instance, individuals refrain from showing the self-serving bias. Instead, they share credit with their partners for successes and failures. Put another way, the close relationship acts a buffer that suppresses self-enhancement or self-love.

A similar pattern of findings is evident in research on positive evaluations. The majority of individuals, for example, report that they are better than the average other on a host of positive traits (Alicke, 1985; Dunning & Cohen, 1992). This is a robust self-enhancement effect and can be seen clearly, for example, by asking a classroom of students to report how they compare to the average citizen on the trait of "modesty." Still, the above-average effect, despite its strength, can be reduced. One way of doing this is to ask individuals to compare themselves not to the average citizen, but instead compare themselves to a specific college student or a friend (Alicke, Klotz, Breitenbecher, Yurak, & Vredenburg, 1995). Put another way, the positivity of self-evaluations drops to the extent that the comparison group involves close others. The extension of positive evaluations of the self into the realm of close others has been demonstrated repeatedly (e.g., Brown, 1986; Taylor & Koivumaki, 1976).

The message here is that loving others involves the incorporation of the others by the self. This sharing of self, in many cases, may inhibit opportunities for self-love. This ideais not a new one. Freud (1914/1957) suggested that there was a limited store of lust ("libido") and the lust that was connected to the representation of others ("objects") became unavailable for connection to the self. James (1890) also noted the social nature of the self, and our dependence on close others' successes and failures for our own feelings of self-worth. Finally, Heider (1958) noted that affection for the other ("sentiment relation") can lead to an assumed sharing of attitudes with the other.

More recently, researchers have proposed that the self expands to incorporate the other in love relationships. Furthermore, the extent of the incorporation has important cognitive consequences (for a review, see Aron & Aron, 1997). Relationship closeness may even lead close others to protect each other's self-concepts (Beach & Tesser, 1995). Finally, a similar process can be seen in the groups literature. Individuals feel that the group is an important aspect of the self-concept, therefore group outcomes influence the self and individual outcomes are shared with the group (Turner, Oakes, Haslam, & McGarty, 1994).

It is also essential to consider the common experience of unrequited love, which is to say, loving someone who fails to reciprocate that love. Reports of these experiences agree that unrequited love is generally a blow to self-esteem – sometimes minor and transient, but at other times powerful and lasting (Baumeister et al., 1993). A central reason appears to be that romantic rejection commonly carries a strong implicit message that the rejected person was not good or desirable enough to be a suitable partner for the rejecter, and this negative evaluation is hard for the rejected lover to dismiss.

Summary

It appears that loving others can increase the love of the self. The channels for this process include receiving skewed communications from loved others that protect or enhance the self, associating with idealized close others, and outperforming loved others. Intimacy with another may, however, also constrain self-love. The basic model for this is sharing. People not only share resources in close relationships, but also successful outcomes, positive evaluations, and, more generally, their self-concepts. The issue can be looked at this way: If a person loves someone worse off than him- or herself, he or she may increase in self-love via downward comparison and social support, but lose self-love via identification and sharing. If the person loves someone better off than him- or herself, he or she may decrease in self-love via upward comparisons, but gain self-love via identification, sharing and social support. If the person loves someone equal to him- or herself, he or she may end up with little gain in self-love, except via distorted feedback and social support. In sum, the gain in self-love offered by loving others depends strongly on the extent to which various processes occur.

Does Being Loved Lead to Self-love?

Our final question is whether receiving love boosts self-love The answer of "yes" seems obvious. One of the oldest ideas in study of the self is that self-evaluation flows from the evaluations of others. This idea was put forth memorably by Cooley (1902), who spoke of the "looking glass self." Insofar as self and self-evaluation are shaped by the appraisals of others, one may conclude that if appraisals are positive (i.e., if others love the self) then self-appraisals will become similarly positive (i.e., self-love).

Unfortunately, the evidence for the influence of the appraisals of others on the self is somewhat tempered by several factors. The self, to a large extent, seems to perceive positivity in the appraisals of others – regardless of whether this positivity actually exists (Felson, 1993). In other words, individuals selectively interpret information in a way that makes them feel good. For example, we have all witnessed the young male whose amorous advances are turned down, yet who still manages to feel he is attractive: "She really likes me. She's just playing hard to get, etc. . . ."

At the same time, some individuals have dismal self-opinions that cannot be swayed by the opinions of others. This phenomenon has baffled researchers since at least the time of Freud. Why is it that individuals who have negative self-views simply change those views when reliable others tell them that the negative views are incorrect? Clinical examples include the self-loathing exhibited by depressives and the distorted body images displayed by anorexics. More common, perhaps, is the example of a friend who bemoans being a bad parent or professional. Although he or she may clearly be successful in both domains, we will be unable to convince him otherwise. In fact, this friend may be uncomfortable with the positive feedback and actually want to refrain from discussing the issue again. Researchers have actually found evidence for such phenomena in individuals with very low self-esteem. Such individuals may prefer to associate with people who evaluate them poorly rather than positively (Swann, 1983).

The affection of others, however, may be an especially powerful force in shaping self-evaluation during childhood. This is likely because the immaturity of the self in early stages of development leaves it wide open to outside influence. This process has been noted by object relations theorists (Greenberg & Mitchell, 1983) and well documented by researchers on attachment theory (Ainsworth, Blehar, Waters, & Wall, 1978). To provide a brief summary, individual representations of self and other emerge out of the early interactions with the primary caregiver. Where the primary caregiver provides a constant source of support and a "secure base" for environmental exploration, high self-esteem is likely to result. Where this security is absent, a positive sense of self is less likely to result (Bartholomew & Horowitz, 1991; Griffin & Bartholomew, 1994).

In short, the opinions of others likely do matter. However, these appraisals are shaped strongly by preexisting self-evaluations. For this reason, the strength of outside appraisals in shaping the self is likely to be strongest in infancy and to wane gradually across the lifespan. Still, there may be specific instances in adulthood where the positive appraisals of intimate or loving others play an important role in modifying self-beliefs. We describe several of these below.

One such instance would be the change in self-discrepancy that may occur in the context of romantic relationships. Researchers have noted that, in the context of romantic relationships, individuals often will see themselves as more like, or more similar to, their ideal selves (W. K. Campbell et al., 1994). How does this transition occur? One explanation for the process involves the mechanism of behavioral confirmation. A three-step version of this process, termed the "Michelangelo Phenomenon," has been tested (Drigotas, Rusbult, Wieselquist, & Whitton, 1999). In the first step, the loving other (O) expects the self (P) to act in a manner consistent with P's ideal self. Second, P behaves in a manner consistent with O's expectations, and therefore consistent with P's ideal self. Third, P notes cognitively the reduction in the distance between the actual and ideal self (i.e., feels reduced self-discrepancy). Take the following example. Craig's ideal self is humorous. At the same time, his romantic partner, Kerry, expects him to be humorous and laughs at or otherwise encourages his jokes. The result is that Craig becomes more humorous, perceives himself as more humorous, and therefore feels closer to his ideal self. A similar process has been examined by Ruvolo and Brennan (1997). Although the findings were qualified somewhat by gender, these researchers found that being loved and being supported in romantic relationships is associated with growth toward the ideal self.

The appraisals we do receive from loving others may be more positive than reality may support. People who love us may see us in a light that is more favorable than that in which we may view ourselves. Indeed, Murray, et al. (1996a, 1996b) have found evidence that these idealized appraisals actually lead to better functioning in romantic relationships. Specifically, idealization correlates positively with relationship satisfaction and persistence, and negatively with relationship conflict. Furthermore, these idealized appraisals from others may lead to more positive self-appraisals.

Are there cases where being loved would actually decrease self-love? Some have argued that in highly committed relationships (i.e., marriage) – although not in dating relationships

– individuals actually strive for and receive accurate rather than flattering self-appraisals (Swann, De La Rhonde, Hixon, 1994; Swann, Hixon, & De La Rhonde, 1992). This phenomenon may exemplify a preference on the part of marriage partners for predictability in their lives over self-esteem.

Another special case may involve unrequited feelings of love. That is, the experience of being loved by someone whom you do not love. While these situations are painful for the lover, they can also have consequences for the object of affection. For example, the love object may experience intense feelings of guilt and confusion that may be damaging to self-evaluation (Baumeister et al., 1993). Similarly, being loved may not enhance self-evaluations if the admirer is considered unworthy (W. K. Campbell, 1999). It might feel good to be loved by a "10," but the affections of a "2" may leave us feeling nothing or even a little negative.

Summary

Being loved may often lead to self-love. However, there are certain important qualifications to this seemingly obvious statement. First, the influence of an other's love on the self is strongly influenced by existing levels of self-evaluation. If you hate yourself to begin with, the love of others will have a hard time changing your self-evaluation Being loved is also likely to have a minimal (and possibly negative) effect on self-love when (1) the love from the other is not reciprocated, (2) the other is a loser, or, (3) you have low self-esteem and the other is your spouse.

Summary and Conclusion

Despite popular belief that loving oneself is a prerequisite for loving others, the actual connections between loving self and loving others are complex, inconsistent, and often weak. Although a healthy self-esteem may sometimes be advantageous to preserving relationships, self-esteem is often unrelated to relationship outcomes, and some forms of self-love (especially narcissism) seem largely detrimental. Loving oneself is clearly not a prerequisite and only occasionally helpful for loving others.

By the same token, loving oneself does not necessarily increase one's chances of attracting the love of others. Confidence may be appealing, especially in terms of initial attraction, but self-love in general may be a source of trouble and instability in long-term relationships. Highly egotistical people may have the highest levels of self-love but they are certainly not the most liked and loved by others – indeed, such traits of extreme self-love are often disliked by others.

The processes of giving and receiving love may provide a boost to self-love under favorable circumstances, and these seem to represent the strongest link between loving self and loving others. They reverse the widespread view that self-love comes first: rather, it appears that giving and receiving love contribute to loving the self. Even these relationships break down under unfavorable circumstances, however. In particular, loving someone who fails to reciprocate that love can provide a devastating blow to self-esteem that can last for months or conceivably even years. More generally, love can entail sacrifices to the self, and these too can be damaging to the self and self-love. Loving someone is thus a potentially useful strategy for boosting self-love but one that carries a significant risk of backfiring.

Just as it was wrong to assert that loving oneself leads to loving others, it would be wrong to insist that loving self and loving others are completely unrelated, orthogonal phenomena. Recent empirical findings have demolished the sweeping, positive generalizations and begun to replace them with narrowly focused, specific effects, which may operate independently of each other, either as potentially additive phenomena or confined to separate, non-overlapping situations. Given this present state of knowledge, the relationships between self-love and loving others make a promising topic for creative research and empirically based theoretical advances.

REFERENCES

Ainsworth, M. D. S., Blehar, M. C., Waters, E., & Wall, S. (1978). *Patterns of attachment*. Hillsdale, NJ: Erlbaum.

Alicke, M. D. (1985). Global self-evaluations as determined by the desirability and controllability of trait adjectives. *Journal of Personality and Social Psychology, 49,* 1621–1630.

Alicke, M. D., Klotz, M. L., Breitenbecher, D. L., Yurak, T. J., & Vredenburg, D. S. (1995). Personal contact, individuation, and the better-than-average-effect. *Journal of Personality and Social Psychology. 68,* 804–825.

American Psychiatric Association (1994). *Diagnostic and statistical manual of mental disorders* (4th Ed.). Washington, DC: Author.

Aron, A., & Aron, E. N. (1997). Self-expansion motivation and including other in the self. In S. Duck (Ed.), *Handbook of personal relationships: Theory, research and intervention* (2nd Ed., pp. 251–270). Chichester, England: Wiley.

Aron, A., Paris, M., & Aron, E. N. (1995). Falling in love: Prospective studies in self-concept change. *Journal of Personality and Social Psychology, 69,* 1102–1112.

Aronson, E., Willerman, B., & Floyd, J. (1966). The effect of a pratfall on increasing interpersonal attractiveness. *Psychonomic Science, 4,* 227–228.

Bartholomew, K., & Horowitz, L. M. (1991). Attachment styles among young adults: A test of a four category model. *Journal of Personality and Social Psychology, 61,* 226–244.

Baumeister, R. F., Smart, L., & Boden, J. M. (1996). Relation of threatened egotism to violence and aggression: The dark side of high self-esteem. *Psychological Review, 103,* 5–33.

Baumeister, R. F., Wotman, L., & Stillwell, A. M. (1993). Unrequited love: On heartbreak, anger, guilt, scriptlessness, and humiliations. *Journal of Personality and Social Psychology, 64,* 377–394.

Beach, S. R. H., & Tesser, A. (1995). Self-esteem and the extended self-evaluation maintenance model: The self in social context. In M. Kernis (Ed.), *Efficacy, agency, and self-esteem* (pp. 145–170). New York: Plenum.

Blumberg, H. H. (1972). Communication of interpersonal evaluations. *Journal of Personality and Social Psychology, 23,* 157–162.

Bradlee, P. M., & Emmons, R. A. (1992). Locating narcissism within the interpersonal circumplex and the five-factor model. *Personality and Individual Differences, 13,* 821–830.

Branden, N. (1994). *The six pillars of self-esteem*. New York: Bantam.

Brown, J. D. (1986). Evaluations of self and others: Self-enhancement biases in social judgments. *Social Cognition, 4,* 353–376.

Buss, D. M., & Chiodo, L. M. (1991). Narcissistic acts in everyday life. *Journal of Personality, 59,* 179–215.

Buunk, B. P., & van der Eijnden, R. J. J. M. (1997). Perceived prevalence, perceived superiority, and relationship satisfaction: Most relationships are good, but ours is the best. *Personality and Social Psychology Bulletin, 23,* 219–228.

Campbell, J. D., Trapnell, P. D., Heine, S. J., Katz, I. M., Lavallee, L. F., & Lehman, D. R. (1996). Self-concept clarity: Measurement, personality correlates, and cultural boundaries. *Journal of Personality and Social Psychology, 70,* 141–156.

Campbell, W. K. (1999). *Narcissism and romantic attraction. Journal of Personality and Social Psychology, 77,* 1254–1270.

Campbell, W. K., & Foster, C. A. (1999). *Narcissism and love.* Unpublished manuscript, Case Western Reserve University.

Campbell, W. K., Reeder, G. D., Sedikides, C., & Elliot, A. T. (in press). *Narcissism and comparative self-enhancement strategies. Journal of Research in Personality.*

Campbell, W. K., Sedikides, C., & Bosson, J. (1994). Romantic involvement, self-discrepancy, and psychological well-being: A preliminary investigation. *Personal Relationships, 1,* 399–404.

Campbell, W. K., Sedikides, C., Reeder, G. D., & Elliot, A. J. (in press). Among friends?: An examination of friendship and the self-serving bias. *British Journal of Social Psychology.*

Carroll, L. (1987). A study of narcissism, affiliation, intimacy, and power motives among students in business administration. *Psychological Reports, 61,* 355–358.

Carroll, L., Corning, A. F., Morgan, R. R., & Stevens, D. M. (1991). Perceived acceptance, psychological functioning, and sex role orientation of narcissistic persons. *Journal of Social Behavior and Personality, 6,* 943–954.

Cialdini, R. B., Borden, R. J., Thorne, A., Walker, M. R., Freeman, S., & Sloan, L. R. (1976). Basking in reflected glory: Three (football) field studies. *Journal of Personality and Social Psychology, 34,* 366–375.

Clark, M. S. (1984). Record keeping in two types of relationships. *Journal of Personality and Social Psychology, 47,* 549–557.

Cohen, S., & Hoberman, H. (1983). Positive events and social supports as buffers of life change stress. *Journal of Applied Social Psychology, 13,* 99–125.

Cohen, S., & Wills, T. A. (1985). Stress, social support, and the buffering hypothesis. *Psychological Bulletin, 98,* 310–357.

Colvin, C. R., Block, J., & Funder, D. C. (1995). Overly positive self-evaluations and personality: Negative implications for mental health. *Journal of Personality and Social Psychology, 68,* 1152–1162.

Cooley, C. H. (1902). *Human nature and the social order.* New York: Scribner's.

Cruse, S. W. (1987). *Learning how to love yourself.* New Jersey: Health Communications.

Cunningham, M. R., Druen, P. B., & Barbee, A. P. (1997). Angels, mentors and friends: Trade-offs among evolutionary, social, and individual variables in physical appearance. In J. A. Simpson & D. T. Kendrick (Eds.), *Evolutionary social psychology* (pp. 109–140). Hillsdale, NJ: Erlbaum.

Dion, K. D., & Dion, K. L. (1991). Psychological individualism and romantic love. *Journal of Social Behavior and Personality, 6,* 17–33.

Dion, K. K., & Dion, K. C. (1975). Self-esteem and romantic love. *Journal of Personality, 43,* 39–57.

Dolan, A. (1999). *Loving is becoming intimate with your real self.* New York: First Books.

Drigotas, S. M., Rusbult, C. E., Wieselquest, J., & Whitton, S. W. (1999). Close partner as sculptor of the ideal self: Behavioral affirmation and the Michelangelo phenomenon. *Journal of Personality and Social Psychology, 77,* 293–323.

Dunning, D., & Cohen, G. L. (1992). Egocentric definitions of traits and abilities in social judgment. *Journal of Personality and Social Psychology, 63,* 341–355.

Emmons, R. A. (1984). Factor analysis and construct validity of the Narcissistic Personality Inventory. *Journal of Personality Assessment, 48,* 291–300.

Emmons, R. A. (1987). Narcissism: Theory and measurement. *Journal of Personality and Social Psychology, 52,* 11–17.

Erikson, E. H. (1950). *Childhood and society.* New York: Norton.

Farwell, L., & Wohlwend-Lloyd, R. (1998). Narcissistic processes: Optimistic expectations, favorable self-evaluations, and self-enhancing attributions. *Journal of Personality, 66,* 65–83.

Felson, R. B. (1993). The (somewhat) social self: How others effect self-appraisals. In J. Suls (Ed.), *Psychological perspectives on the self* (Vol. 4, pp. 1–26). Hillsdale, NJ: Erlbaum.

Freud, A. (1936). *The ego and the mechanisms of defense* (Rev. Ed.). In *The Writings of Anna Freud* (Vol. 2). New York: International Universities Press.

Freud, S. (1957). On narcissism: An introduction. In J. Strachey (Ed. and Trans.), *The standard edition of the complete psychological works of Sigmund Freud* (Vol. 14, pp. 67–104). London: Hogarth Press. (Original work published 1914)

Freud, S. (1950). Libidinal types. In J. Strachey (Ed. and Trans.), *The standard edition of the complete psychological works of Sigmund Freud* (Vol. 21, pp. 217–220). London: Hogarth Press. (Original work published 1931)

Freud, S. (1959). *Group psychology and the analysis of the ego* (Trans. J. Strachey). New York: Norton. (Original work published 1922)

Gabriel, M. T., Critelli, J. W., & Ee, J. S. (1994). Narcissistic illusions in self-evaluations of intelligence and attractiveness. *Journal of Personality, 62,* 143–155.

Goffman, E. (1959). *The presentation of self in everyday life.* New York: Doubleday.

Gosling, S. D., John, O. P., Craik, K. H., & Robins, R. W. (1998). Do people know how they behave? Self-reported act frequencies compared with on-line codings by observers. *Journal of Personality and Social Psychology, 74,* 1337–1349.

Greenberg, J. R., & Mitchell, S. A. (1983). *Object relations in psychoanalytic theory.* Cambridge, MA: Harvard University Press.

Griffin, D. W., & Bartholomew, K. (1994). Models of the self and other: Fundamental dimensions underlying measures of adult attachment. *Journal of Personality and Social Psychology, 67,* 430–445.

Hay, L. L. (1992). *How to love yourself: Cherishing the incredible miracle that you are.* Carlsbad, CA: Hay House.

Heider, F. (1958). *The psychology of interpersonal relations.* New York: Wiley.

Hendrick, C., & Hendrick, S. S. (1986). A theory and method of love. *Journal of Personality and Social Psychology, 50,* 392–402.

Hendrick, C., & Hendrick, S. S. (1990). A relationship specific version of the Love Attitudes Scale. *Journal of Social Behavior and Personality, 5,* 239–254.

James, W. (1890). *The principles of psychology* (Vol. 1). New York: Henry Holt.

John, O. P., & Robins, R. W. (1994). Accuracy and bias in self-perception: Individual differences in self-enhancement and the role of narcissism. *Journal of Personality and Social Psychology, 66,* 206–219.

Joiner, T. E., Alfano, M. S., & Metalsky, G. I. (1992). When depression breeds contempt: Reassurance seeking, self-esteem, and rejection of depressed college students by their roommates. *Journal of Abnormal Psychology, 101,* 165–173.

Joiner, T. E., Alfano, M. S., & Metalsky, G. I. (1993). Caught in the crossfire: Self-consistency, self-enhancement and the response of others. *Journal of Social and Clinical Psychology, 12,* 113–134.

Jones, S. C. (1973). Self and interpersonal evaluations: Esteem theories versus consistency theories. *Psychological Bulletin, 79,* 185–199.

Kahn, S., Zimmerman, G., Csikszentmihalyi, M., & Getzels, J. W. (1985). Relations between identity in young adulthood and intimacy at midlife. *Journal of Personality and Social Psychology*, *49*, 1316–1322.

Karp, E. S., Jackson, J. G., & Lester, D. (1970). Ideal-self fulfillment in mate selection. A corollary to the complementary need theory of mate selection. *Journal of Marriage and the Family*, *32*, 269–272.

Kernis, M. H., & Sun, C. (1994). Narcissism and reactions to interpersonal feedback. *Journal of Research in Personality*, *28*, 4–13.

LaPrelle, J., Hoyle, R. H., Insko, C. A., & Bernthal, P. (1990). Interpersonal attraction and descriptions of the traits of others: Ideal similarity, self-similarity, and liking. *Journal of Research in Personality*, *24*, 216–240.

Lee, J. A. (1973). *The colors of love: An exploration of the ways of loving*. Don Mills, Ontario: New Press.

Longmore, M. A., & DeMaris, A. (1997). Perceived inequity and depression in intimate relationships: The moderating effect of self-esteem. *Social Psychology Quarterly*, *60*, 172–184.

Major, B., Testa, M., & Bylsma, W. H. (1991). Response to upward and downward comparisons: The impact of esteem relevance and perceived control. In J. Suls & T. A. Wills (Eds.), *Social comparison: Contemporary theory and research* (pp. 237–260). Hillsdale, NJ: Erlbaum.

Manis, M., Cornell, S. D., & Moore, J. C. (1974). The transmission of attitude-relevant information through a communication chain. *Journal of Personality and Social Psychology*, *30*, 81–94.

Maslow, A. H. (1962). *Toward a psychology of being*. Princeton, NJ: Van Nostrand.

Maslow, A. H. (1968). *Toward a psychology of being* (2nd edn). Princeton, NJ: Van Nostrand.

Masterson, J. F. (1988). *The search for the real self*. New York: Free Press.

Mathes, E., & Moore, C. (1985). Reik's complementary theory of romantic love. *Journal of Social Psychology*, *125*, 321–327.

Mecca, A. M., Smelser, N. J., & Vasconcellos, J. (1989). *The social importance of self-esteem*. Berkeley: University of California Press.

Morf, C. C., & Rhodewalt, F. (1993). Narcissism and self-evaluation maintenance: Explorations in object relations. *Personality and Social Psychology Bulletin*, *19*, 668–676.

Moss, E. (1995). Treating the love-sick patient. *Israel Journal of Psychiatry and Related Sciences*, *32*, 167–173.

Murray, S. L., Holmes, J. G., & Griffin, D. W. (1996a). The benefit of positive illusions: Idealization and the construction of satisfaction in close relationships. *Journal of Personality and Social Psychology*, *70*, 79–98.

Murray, S. L., Holmes, J. G., & Griffin, D. W. (1996b). The self-fulfilling nature of positive illusions in romantic relationships: Love is not blind, but prescient. *Journal of Personality and Social Psychology*, *71*, 1155–1180.

Paulhus, D. L. (1998). Interpersonal and intrapsychic adaptiveness of trait self-enhancement: A mixed blessing? *Journal of Personality and Social Psychology*, *74*, 1197–1208.

Petrie, J., Giordano, J. A., & Roberts, C. S. (1992). Characteristics of women who love too much. *Affilia*, *7*, 7–20.

Raskin, R. N., & Novacek, J. (1991). Narcissism and the use of fantasy. *Journal of Clinical Psychology*, *47*, 490–499.

Raskin, R. N., Novacek, J., & Hogan, R. (1991a). Narcissism, self-esteem, and defensive self-enhancement. *Journal of Personality*, *59*, 19–38.

Raskin, R. N., Novacek, J., & Hogan, R. (1991b). Narcissistic self-esteem management. *Journal of Personality and Social Psychology*, *60*, 911–918.

Raskin, R. N., & Shaw, R. (1988). Narcissism and the use of personal pronouns. *Journal of Personality*, *56*, 393–404.

Raskin, R. N., & Terry, H. (1988). A principal components analysis of the Narcissistic Personality Inventory and further evidence of its construct validity. *Journal of Personality and Social Psychology*, *54*, 890–902.

Reik, T. (1944). *A psychologist looks at love*. New York: Farrar & Rinehart.

Rhodewalt, F., & Morf, C. C. (1995). Self and interpersonal correlates of the narcissistic personality inventory. *Journal of Research in Personality*, *29*, 1–23.

Rhodewalt, F., & Morf, C. C. (1998). On self-aggrandizement and anger: A temporal analysis of narcissism and affective reactions. *Journal of Personality and Social Psychology Bulletin*, *74*, 672–685.

Rogers, C. (1961). *On becoming a person*. Boston: Houghton Mifflin.

Rusbult, C. E., & Arriaga, X. B. (1997). Interdependence theory. In S. Duck (Ed.), *Handbook of personal relationships: Theory, research and intervention* (2nd Ed., pp. 221–250). Chichester, England: Wiley.

Rusbult, C. E., & Martz, J. M. (1995). Remaining in an abusive relationship: An investment model analysis of nonvoluntary commitment. *Personality and Social Psychology Bulletin*, *21*, 558–571.

Rusbult, C. E., Morrow, G. D., & Johnson, D. J. (1987). Self-esteem and problem-solving behaviour in close relationships. *British Journal of Social Psychology*, *26*, 293–303.

Ruvolo, A. P., & Brennan, C. J. (1997). What's love got to do with it? Close relationships and perceived growth. *Personality and Social Psychology Bulletin*, *23*, 814–823.

Schuetz, A. (in press). Self-esteem and interpersonal strategies. In J. P. Forgas, K. D. Williams, & L. Wheeler (Eds.), *The social mind: Cognitive and motivational aspects of interpersonal behavior*. New York: Cambridge University Press.

Schuetz, A., & Tice, D. T. (1997). Associative and competitive indirect self-enhancement in close relationships moderated by trait self-esteem. *European Journal of Social Psychology*, *27*, 257–273.

Sedikides, C., Campbell, W. K., Reeder, G. D., & Elliot, A. J. (1998). The self-serving bias in relational context. *Journal of Personality and Social Psychology*, *74*, 378–386.

Sedikides, C., Oliver, M. B., & Campbell, W. K. (1994). Perceived benefits and costs of romantic relationships for women and men: Implications for exchange theory. *Personal Relationships*, *1*, 5–21.

Segrin, C., & Dillard, J. P. (1992). The interactional theory of depression A meta-analysis of the research literature. *Journal of Social and Clinical Psychology*, *11*, 43–70.

Sheppard, V. J., Nelson, E. S., & Andreoli-Mathie, V. (1995). Dating relationships and infidelity: Attitudes and behavior. *Journal of Sex and Marital Therapy*, *21*, 202–212.

Sigall, H., & Gould, R. (1977). The effects of self-esteem and evaluator demandingness on effort expenditure. *Journal of Personality and Social Psychology*, *35*, 12–20.

Schuetz, A. (in press). Coping with threats to self-esteem: The differing patterns of subjects with high versus low self-esteem in first person accounts. *European Journal of Psychology*, *12*, 169–186.

Swann, W. B., Jr. (1983). Self-verification: Bringing social reality into harmony with the self. In J. Suls & A. G. Greenwald (Eds.), *Psychological perspectives on the self* (Vol. 2, pp. 33–66). Hillsdale, NJ: Erlbaum.

Swann, W. B., De La Rhonde, C., & Hixon, J. G. (1994). Authenticity and positivity strivings in marriage and courtship. *Journal of Personality and Social Psychology*, *66*, 857–869.

Swann, W. B., Hixon, J. G., & De La Rhonde, C. (1992). Embracing the bitter "truth": Negative self-concepts and marital commitment. *Psychological Science*, *3*, 118–121.

Tajfel, H., & Turner, J. C. (1986). The social identity theory of intergroup behavior. In S. Worchel & W. G. Austin (Eds.), *Psychology of Intergroup Relations* (2nd ed., pp. 7–24). Chicago: Nelson-Hall.

Taylor, S. E., & Koivumaki, J. H. (1976). The perception of self and others: Self-enhancement biases in social judgments. *Journal of Personality and Social Psychology*, *33*, 403–408.

Terry, D. J. (1991). Stress, coping, and adaptation to new parenthood. *Journal of Social and Personal Relationships*, *8*, 527–547.

Tesser, A. (1988). Toward a self-evaluation maintenance model of social behavior. In L. Berkowitz (Ed.), *Advances in experimental social psychology* (Vol. 21, pp. 181–227). New York: Academic Press.

Tesser, A., & Rosen, S. (1975). The reluctance to transmit bad news. In L. Berkowitz (Ed.), *Advances in experimental social psychology* (Vol. pp. 193–232). New York: Academic Press.

Tice, D. M. (1993). Self-concept change and self-presentation: The looking glass self is also a magnifying glass. *Journal of Personality and Social Psychology, 63*, 435–451.

Tice, D. M., Butler, J. L., Muraven, M. B., & Stillwell, A. M. (1995). When modesty prevails: Differential favorability of self-presentation to friends and strangers. *Journal of Personality and Social Psychology, 69*, 1120–1138.

Turner, J. C., Oakes, P. J., Haslam, A., & McGarty, C. (1994). Self and collective: Cognition and social context. *Personality and Social Psychology Bulletin, 20*, 454–463.

Van Lange, P. A. M., & Rusbult, C. E. (1995). My relationship is better than – and not as bad as – yours is: The perception of superiority in close relationships. *Personality and Social Psychology Bulletin, 21*, 32–44.

Van Lange, P. A. M., Rusbult, C. E., Drigotas, S. M., Arriaga, X. B., Witcher, B. S., & Cox, C. L. (1997). Willingness to sacrifice in close relationships. *Journal of Personality and Social Psychology, 72*, 32–44.

Watson, P. J., Grisham, S. O., Trotter, M. V., & Biderman, M. D. (1984). Narcissism and empathy: Validity evidence for the narcissistic personality inventory. *Journal of Personality Assessment, 45*, 159–162.

CHAPTER FIVE

Self-expansion Model of Motivation and Cognition in Close Relationships and Beyond

Arthur Aron, Elaine N. Aron,
and Christina Norman

The self-expansion model proposes that a central human motivation is self-expansion and that one way people seek such expansion is through close relationships in which each includes the other in the self (Aron & Aron, 1986, 1996, 1997). In this chapter we first examine the motivational aspect of the model (what is meant by self-expansion motivation) and the research it has generated in the close relationship area. The second section examines the inclusion-of-other-in-the-self aspect of the model and the research it has generated in the close relationship area. A final section considers recent extensions of the inclusion-of-other-in-the-self notion to social psychology topics beyond the direct study of close relationships, including empathy and helping and intergroup relations.

Self-expansion Motivation

The first overarching principle of the self-expansion model is that people seek to expand the self in the sense that they seek to enhance their potential efficacy by increasing the physical and social resources, perspectives, and identities that facilitate achievement of any goal that might arise.[1] (For a recent elaboration of the motivational aspect of the model, see Aron, Norman, & Aron, 1998.) The emphasis here is not on a motivation for the actual achievement of goals, but on a motivation to attain the resources to be able to achieve goals. Probably for humans the most important resource for achieving goals is knowledge.[2] Other kinds of resources are also relevant, such as social status and community, possessions and wealth, and physical strength and health.

The idea for the proposed motivation emerged in part from R. W. White's (1959) classic argument that there is a biologically based fundamental drive for efficacy or competence that is comparable to such drives as hunger and thirst and is centered in the nervous system.

However, White emphasized the satisfaction arising from acting effectively, while we would, as just noted, emphasize the satisfaction arising from knowing that one has the potential to act effectively. The present view was also developed taking into account self-efficacy models of motivation (for a review, see Gecas, 1989). However, our view is somewhat different from Bandura's (1977), the most widely cited self-efficacy theory. Bandura emphasizes the role of self-efficacy expectancy (the perceived likelihood that self will be able to achieve a particular goal) as a mediator of the motivational process of selecting a goal or energizing oneself with regard to a particular goal, rather than our view that something like self-efficacy expectancy (in a general sense) is a goal in its own right. Yet another long-standing motivational view that influenced the development of the self-expansion model is the idea of intrinsic motivation (e.g., Deci & Ryan, 1987), the value associated with the *process* of achieving a goal, as opposed to extrinsic motivation, the value of the goal itself. However, we hold that both intrinsic and extrinsic motives can be directed, ultimately, to self-expansion. Finally, the intrinsic motivation idea is in a sense allied with phenomenological views, such as Maslow's (1970), that the ultimate motivation is to actualize the full potential of the self. However, the self-expansion model lays out the processes involved in a much more precise way, and there are major differences. For example, Maslow argued that self-actualization does not come into play until more "basic" motives like hunger and safety are satisfied, while the self-expansion model posits that self-expansion can play a major role at any point, even, for example, when one is hungry or in danger.

There are also important links with current work in the social psychology of motivation, most of which focuses on the processes involved in attaining goals and the influence of goals on cognitive processes (e.g., Higgins & Sorrentino, 1990). Where social psychology has focused on the selection of goals, it has tended to emphasize how we combine values with expectancies, leaving unspecified the question of what makes something of value. In contrast, the self-expansion model specifically proposes that what makes a potential goal of value is the extent to which it facilitates self-expansion.

There has been some speculation in recent years in mainstream social psychology that is relevant to this issue of what makes something of value, focusing on various self-oriented motives (Sedikides & Strube, 1995). In this context, Taylor, Neter, and Wayment (1995) proposed a self-related motive that they labeled "self-improvement," that is roughly comparable to self-expansion. Taylor et al. conducted a series of studies in which participants reported using quite different sources of information when satisfying self-improvement motives than when satisfying other self-motives such as self-verification (the desire to have confirmed what you believe you are) or self-enhancement (the desire to see yourself in the most positive light).

Our motivational model can also be understood in the context of some of the major current relationship theories. For example, interdependence theory (Kelley & Thibaut, 1978; Rusbult & Arriaga, 1997) focuses on the ways in which expected benefits and costs guide behavior in relationships. What the self-expansion model adds is a specification of what counts as an expected benefit or cost. Similarly, self-expansion motivation is at least in principle intimately linked with attachment models (e.g., Bowlby, 1969; Shaver & Hazan, 1993). The core of attachment theory is a dialectical process in which an infant naturally explores the environment, but regularly monitors and periodically returns to the caregiver as a source of safety. The focus of most attachment work has been on the sense of safety provided by caregivers and relationship partners. The exploration motivation, which is the foundation of the process to begin with, has been largely ignored. We think that self-expansion processes describe this aspect of attachment very well. Indeed, we have argued elsewhere (Aron, Aron, & Allen, 1998) that one can construe attachment styles as arising from early experiences of consistent support in self-expansion (secures), consistent failure to support self-expansion (avoidants), or inconsistent support and failure (anxious/ambivalents).

Research generated by the motivational aspect of the model

Self-expansion from developing a relationship.   One implication of the proposed self-expansion motivation in the relationship area is that developing a relationship expands the self. In this regard, Sedikides (personal communication, October, 1992) collected self-descriptions of participants who were or were not currently in a close relationship. These self-descriptions were analyzed for number of different domains of the self they included. Consistent with this prediction (based on the self-expansion model), he found that the self-descriptions of those in relationships included terms representing significantly more domains of the self.

Following up on this idea, in a longitudinal study, Aron, Paris, and Aron (1995) tested 325 students five times, once every two and a half weeks over a ten-week period. At each testing the participants listed as many self-descriptive words or phrases as came to mind during a three-minute period in response to the question, "Who are you today?" and answered a number of other questions which included items indicating whether the participant had fallen in love since the last testing. As predicted, there was a significantly greater increase in diversity of self-content domains in the self-descriptions from before to after falling in love. (This was found when comparing this increase to the average changes from before to after other testing sessions for those who fell in love, and when comparing this increase to the typical testing-to-testing changes for participants who did not fall in love.) In a sense, there was a literal expansion of self. A second study, with a new sample of 529 participants, administered scales measuring self-efficacy and self-esteem every two and a half weeks. As predicted, there was a significantly greater increase in these variables from before to after falling in love. (Again, this was found when comparing the increase to the average changes from before to after other testing sessions for those who fell in love, and when comparing this increase to the typical testing-to-testing changes for those who did not fall in love.) In both of these studies, the effects on the self were maintained when measures of mood change were controlled statistically.

Self-expansion process as a motivator.   Another key implication of the motivational aspect of the model that has generated a number of studies is based on the idea that the process of rapid expansion is affectively positive, that rapid self-expansion produces strong positive affect (so long as the rate of expansion is not so great as to be stressful). Because this rapid expansion is pleasurable, in addition to a desire to be expanded (to possess high levels of potential efficacy), a key motivator is the desire to experience the process of expanding, to feel oneself increasing rapidly in potential self-efficacy. This notion is similar to Carver and

Scheier's (1990) self-regulatory process in which people monitor the rate at which they are making progress towards goals and experience positive affect when the perceived rate exceeds an acceptable or desired rate. Indeed, they argue further that accelerations in the rate cause feelings of exhilaration. Our notion of being motivated to experience the expanding process is also similar to Pyszczynski, Greenberg, and Solomon's (1997) "Self-expansive" motivational system (one of their three main motivations). Expansive activities are motivating because of the pleasure that "engagement [in them] provides" (p. 6).

Some support for this process-motivation aspect of the model comes from the research on the arousal-attraction effect. As we have detailed elsewhere (e.g., Aron, Norman, & Aron, 1998), this aspect of the self-expansion model suggests what may be an important mechanism driving the arousal-attraction effect, best known from the Dutton and Aron (1974) suspension-bridge study, the basic results of which are now well replicated (for a review, see Foster, Witcher, Campbell, & Green, 1998). The idea is that because arousal often co-occurs with rapid self-expansion, when a potential relationship partner is associated with arousal, the partner is positively valued because of the link with rapid self-expansion.

Other support for this self-expansion process-motivation idea comes from research on unreciprocated love. Based on the self-expansion model, Aron, Aron, and Allen (1998) developed and provided empirical support for a mini-theory of unreciprocated love that proposes three motivational factors: (1) high levels of desirability (the extent to which self believes a relationship with the beloved would expand the self), (2) greater-than-zero levels of probability that a relationship (and hence self-expansion) is possible, and (3) opportunity to experience the expanding process associated with the falling in and being in love (even if it is not reciprocated). Regarding this third factor, falling and being in love may itself be desirable by permitting the individual to experience the process of expanding the self through enacting the culturally scripted role of the lover (and thus experiencing a dramatically different life perspective) and redirecting attention and resources to a single very important goal (and thus experiencing a rapid increase in apparent energy). While in principle these three motivational factors might also have been derived from other theoretical models, the self-expansion model's focus on the benefits of rapid expansion is more likely to bring such ideas to mind – particularly ideas like that of the third factor.

The major line of work developed directly from the principle of the self-expansion process as a motivator and, supporting that view, is a set of studies focusing on a predicted increase in satisfaction in long-term relationships from joint participation in self-expanding activities. This work emerged from a consideration of the well-documented typical decline in relationship satisfaction after the "honeymoon period" in a romantic relationship, a lowered average level which is also maintained over subsequent years (e.g., Tucker & Aron, 1993). When two people first enter a relationship, typically there appears to be an initial, exhilarating period in which the couple spends hours talking, engaging in intense risk-taking and self-disclosure. From the perspective of the self-expansion model, this initial exhilarating period is one in which the partners are expanding their selves at a rapid rate by virtue of the intense exchange in which they are rapidly including in the self perspectives and identities of the other. Once the two know each other fairly well, opportunities for further rapid expansion of this sort inevitably decrease. When rapid expansion occurs there is a high degree of satisfaction; when expansion is slow or nonexistent, there is little emotion, or perhaps boredom. If slow expansion follows a period of rapid expansion, the loss of enjoyable emotion may be disappointing and attributed to the particular relationship. There has been surprisingly little previous theorizing about the reasons for the decline in marital satisfaction, other than fairly general allusions to habituation-type processes (e.g., Huesmann, 1980; Jacobson & Margolin, 1979; Plutchik, 1967). The self-expansion model adds to a simple habituation idea by specifying what about the other and the relationship becomes decreasingly novel (the loss of new information to be included in the self) and, most important from the current perspective, by specifying why habituation leads to dissatisfaction (the decline in the highly desired rapid rate of self-expansion, in this case associated with the relationship). Thus the model provides a more precise and motivationally based explanation for the role of habituation in relationships.

Basically, our notion is that if self-expanding activities create positive affect, then when couples engage in such activities *together*, this positive affect should become associated with both the behaviors involved in that activity and also the behavior of staying near the other and any other behaviors that maintain the relationship. (The point is, the self-expansion model contributes an explanation for why certain kinds of activities would be especially rewarding: they arise as a result of or are associated with the process of expanding the self.) What distinguishes an activity that is self-expanding? We think novelty is the key aspect. Participating in a novel activity expands the self by providing new information and experiences. However, arousal is also relevant. Novelty is arousing (Berlyne, 1960) so that through life experience, arousal is likely to be associated with novelty, and hence with self-expansion. In terms of how self-expanding activities are recognized, we have assumed that the most likely ordinary-language label is "exciting," since this term covers both arousal and novelty (and as noted in the research below, it is precisely novel and/or arousing activities that couples label as exciting).

There is substantial evidence that, in general, time spent together is correlated with marital satisfaction (e.g., L. K. White, 1983) and some evidence from these studies that the correlation is strongest for intense activities. There are also some survey data focusing directly on the link of "exciting" activities and satisfaction. Aron, Norman, Aron, McKenna, and Heyman (2000, Studies 1 & 2), in both a newspaper questionnaire study and a telephone survey, found strong correlations between the two variables, even after partialing out measures of relationship-relevant socially desirable response bias. Additional analyses in these studies suggested that boredom with the relationship is a key mediator of this association.

In a field experiment to test this idea (Reissman, Aron, & Bergen, 1993), volunteer married couples were randomly assigned to spend one and a half hours each week for ten weeks engaging together in either "exciting" or "pleasant" (but not particularly exciting) activities selected from an individually prepared list of activities both spouses had rated above the midpoint on the scale corresponding to their condition. As predicted, change in marital satisfaction was significantly greater for exciting-condition than pleasant-condition couples. (Change in marital satisfaction was intermediate for a third group of couples who had been randomly assigned to a no-activity control condition.)

We have also conducted three experiments in order to establish a laboratory paradigm in which we could test crucial points of the theory under highly controlled conditions (Aron et al., 2000 Studies 3–5). In these experiments couples came to our lab for what they believed was an assessment session involving questionnaires and being videotaped interacting.

Indeed, when they came, that is what happened – they completed some questionnaires, participated together in a task that was videotaped, and then completed some more question-naires. However, from our perspective, the questionnaires before the task served as a pretest, those after as a posttest, and the task itself was experimentally manipulated so that some couples engaged in a self-expanding activity (one that was novel and arousing) and those in the control condition, in a more mundane activity. (In the expanding activity the couple was tied together on one side at the wrists and ankles and then took part in a task in which they crawled together on mats for 12 meters, climbing over a barrier at one point, while pushing a foam cylinder with their heads. This was a timed task such that the couple received a prize if they beat a time limit and the situation was rigged so that they almost make it in the prize-winning time the first two tries and then just barely make it on the third try. In the mundane condition one partner slowly crawled to the middle of the mat and back, then the other partner did the same, then the first partner repeated this, and so on.)

The first study employing this paradigm, in which participants were mainly student dating couples, found, as predicted, a significantly greater increase in relationship satisfaction for the expanding-condition couples. The second study replicated the first experiment's results with married couples recruited from the community. It also included a no-activity condition in which, it turned out, the increase in satisfaction was less than even in the mundane-activity condition. Thus, the difference between the expanding-activity and mundane-activity condi-tions is clearly due to increased satisfaction in the expanding condition and not decreased satisfaction in the mundane condition. A third experiment, also with couples recruited from the community, included a short videotaped discussion of a standardized topic (e.g., plan a trip together), before and after the interaction task. This study again replicated the basic finding of greater increases in satisfaction for the expanding activity group on the usual questionnaire ratings. More importantly, this study found the same effect on measures based on blind coding of the videotaped interactions using standard rating protocols for statements made during the interaction. Specifically, from before to after the activity, couples in the expanding-activity condition, compared to couples in the mundane-activity condition, showed significantly greater increases in positive and supportive statements and decreases in hostile statements. Preliminary results of two additional experiments (Aron, Aron, & Norman, 1999) demonstrated that the effect cannot be accounted for by arousal alone, that the sense of expansion mediates the effect, and that the effect requires that the partner be salient during the expanding activity.

Summary

We described the desire to expand the self as a core motive. The goal is to acquire social and material resources, perspectives, and identities that enhance one's ability to accomplish goals. The basic idea is linked to long-standing models of competence motivation, self-efficacy, intrinsic motivation, and theories of self-actualization. While social cognition approaches have generally focused on how goals lead to behavior rather than on what goals we select, work in the area of self-evaluation is an exception, and within that domain Taylor et al. (1995) have proposed that self-improvement, an idea much like self-expansion, may be an important motive. The self-expansion motive is also, of course, specifically relevant to major relationship theories, in that it specifies one basis for evaluating ultimate benefits and costs in interdependence approaches, and it seems to describe well the exploratory motive that plays an important, though mainly implicit, role in attachment theories. The motivational aspect of the self-expansion model has generated a number of studies in the relationship area. One such line of work has shown that entering a new relationship (operationalized as falling in love) expands the self in the sense that one's spontaneous self-description increases in diversity and in the sense of an increase in perceived self-efficacy. Other studies have focused on the implication of the model that rapid self-expansion creates positive affect and thus people are motivated to experience rapid self-expansion in order to experience this positive affect – an idea consistent with a proposal by Carver and Scheier (1990) that strong positive affect is associated with rapid progress toward goals. This motivation suggests a major mechanism driving the arousal-attraction effect, provides a motivational explanation for the maintenance of unreciprocated love, and offers a way to understand the decline in relationship satisfaction after the early relationship stages as well as a means of minimizing or reversing that decline (by having couples participate together in expanding activities).

Including Other in the Self

Having postulated a general motivation to expand the self, we also proposed that the desire to enter and maintain a particular relationship can be seen as one, especially satisfying, useful, and human, means to this self-expansion – cognitively, the self is expanded through including the other in the self, a process which in a close relationship becomes mutual, so that each person is including the other in his or her self. (For fuller reviews of the inclusion-of-other-in-the-self aspect of the self-expansion model, see Aron & Aron, 1986, 1996.) That is, people seek relationships in order to gain what they anticipate as self-expansion. When faced with a potential relationship, one compares one's self as it is prior to the relationship – lacking the other's perspectives, resources, and identities – to the self as prospectively imagined after it has entered the relationship, a self now with access both to the self's own perspectives and so forth *plus* the other's perspectives and so forth. Metaphorically, I will have the use of all my house plus gain the use of yours. Thus before one enters a relationship, the motive of self-expansion may seem to have a decidedly self-centered air to it. But after entering, the effect of including each other in each other's self is an overlapping of selves. Now I must protect and maintain my house *and* your house, as *both* are "mine" (as both are now "yours"). This post-inclusion, larger self creates (and explains) the sometimes remarkably unselfish nature of close relationships.

The notion that in a relationship each is included in each other's self is consistent with a wide variety of social psychological ideas about relationships. For example, Reis and Shaver (1988) identified intimacy as mainly a process of an escalating reciprocity of self-disclosure in which each individual feels his or her innermost self validated, understood, and cared for by the other. Indeed, perhaps the most prominent idea in social psychology directly related to the present theme is the "unit relation," a fundamental concept in Heider's (1958) cognitive account of interpersonal relations. This idea is also related to Ickes, Tooke, Stinson, Baker, and Bissonnette's (1988) idea of "intersubjectivity" – which Ickes and his colleagues made vivid by citing Merleau-Ponty's (1945) description of a close relationship as a "double being" and Schutz's (1970) reference to two people "living in each other's subjective contexts of meaning" (p. 167).

Several currently active lines of theory-based social psychology research focus on closely related themes. For example, in a series of experimental and correlational studies, Tesser (1988) has shown that a relationship partner's achievement, so long as it is not in a domain that threatens the self by creating a negative social comparison, is "reflected" by the self (i.e., the self feels pride in the achievement as if it were the self's). Another relevant line of work focuses on what is called "fraternal relative deprivation" (Runciman, 1966), in which the relative disadvantage of the group to which the self belongs affects the self as if it were the self's own deprivation. Yet another example is work arising from social identity theory (Tajfel & Turner, 1979) which posits that one's identity is structured from membership in social groups.

In the field of marketing, Belk (1988) has proposed a notion of ownership in which "we regard our possessions as part of ourselves" (p. 139), an idea that has been the subject of considerable theoretical discussion and several studies. For example, Sivadas and Machleit (1994) found that items measuring an object's "incorporation into self" (items such as "helps me achieve my identity" and "is part of who I am") form a separate factor from items assessing the object's importance or relevance to the self. Ahuvia (1993) has attempted to integrate Belk's self-extension approach with the self-expansion model and has proposed that processes hypothesized in the domain of personal relationships also apply to relations to physical objects and experiences. In an interview study, Ahuvia showed that people sometimes describe their "love" of things in much the same way as they describe their love of relationship partners, that they often consider this "real" love, and that they treat these love objects as very much a part of their identity. At the same time, as with human relationships, there is often a sense of autonomous value to the object, even a sense of being controlled by or at the mercy of it. These ideas about including the owned object in the self are also related to the notion of relationship, as each "possessing" the other (e.g., Reik, 1944).

In the relationship domain, Agnew, Van Lange, Rusbult, and Langston (1998) have explicitly linked the inclusion-of-other-in-the-self model with interdependence, describing it as "cognitive interdependence – a mental state characterized by a pluralistic, collective representation of self-in-relationship" (p. 939). Cialdini, Brown, Lewis, Luce, and Neuberg (1997) have linked the model to evolutionary theories of relationships, suggesting that interpersonal closeness, experienced as including other in the self, may be how we recognize those with whom we share genes (a kind of literal, physical self-other inclusion) in the interest of knowing with whom one should share resources to enhance collective fitness. Finally, although there has been no explicit work on the possible link, we think that there may be a close connection between self-other inclusion and communal relationships (e.g., Clark & Mills, 1979, 1993). That is, we see including other in the self as the foundation for spontaneously being concerned with the others' needs (since other's needs are my needs) and thus both directly facilitating communal motivation (attention to and acting on other's needs) and having possibly functioned historically to help create a social norm of communal orientation in close relationships.

The notion of relationship as an overlap of selves has been popular more generally among psychologists and sociologists, starting at least with James (1890/1948). For example, Bakan (1966) wrote about "communion" in the context of his expansion on Buber's (1937) "I–Thou" relationship. Jung (1925/1959) emphasized the role of relationship partners as providing or developing otherwise unavailable aspects of the psyche, so leading to greater wholeness. Maslow took it for granted that "beloved people can be incorporated into the self" (1967, p. 103). And from a symbolic interactionist perspective, McCall (1974) described "attachment" as "incorporation of ... [the other's] actions and reactions ... into the content of one's various conceptions of the self" (p. 219).

Research generated by the inclusion-of-other-in-the-self aspect of the model

One line of relevant research focuses on the extent to which people *view* relationships as connected or overlapping selves. Sedikides, Olsen, and Reis (1993) found that people spontaneously cluster information about other people in terms of their relationships with each other, grouping the people together on recall tasks based on their relationships. This suggests that cognitive representations of other individuals are in a sense overlapped or at least tied together as a function of these others being perceived as being in close relationships with each other. Focusing on the issue of the perceived overlap of one's self with a relationship partner, Aron, Aron, and Smollan (1992) asked participants to describe their closest relationship using the Inclusion of Other in the Self (IOS) Scale (see figure 5.1), which consists of a series of overlapping circles from which one selects the pair that best describes one's relationship with a particular person. The scale appears to have levels of reliability, as well as of discriminant, convergent, and predictive validity, that match or exceed other measures of closeness—measures which are typically more complex and lengthy. (For example, the correlation between a score on this test and whether the participant remained in a romantic relationship three months later was .46.) Further, most measures of closeness seem to fall into one of two

Please circle the picture below which best describes your relationship.

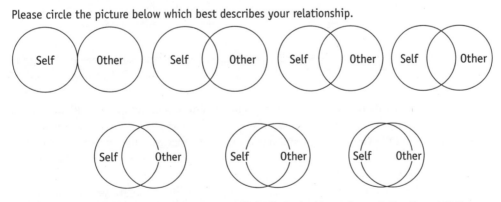

Figure 5.1 The Inclusion of Other in the Self (IOS) Scale (Aron, Aron, & Smollan, 1992). Respondents are instructed to select the picture that best describes their relationship.

factors: they measure either *feelings of closeness* or *behaviors associated with closeness*. The IOS Scale, however, loads, to some extent, on both of these factors. This suggests that the Scale may be tapping the core meaning of closeness and not merely a particular aspect of it. The point of all this is that this measure may be so successful because the metaphor of overlapping circles representing self and other corresponds to the reality of how people process information about relationships.

Agnew et al. (1998), in a study of dating couples, found that scores on the IOS Scale correlated highly with a variety of relationship measures, such as satisfaction, commitment, investment in the relationship, and centrality of the relationship. Most interesting, the IOS Scale correlated moderately with proportion of first-person plural pronouns ("we" and "us") the dating partners used when speaking about their relationship, a finding that Agnew et al. took as an indication of what they called "cognitive interdependence." Cross et al. (1997) found that IOS Scale ratings of close others correlated with what they called "interdependent self-construal" (an example item is "When I feel close to someone, I typically think of their triumphs as if they are my own"). In another study, Loving and Agnew (1998) found that the overall IOS Scale correlated significantly with reported self-partner overlap in specific areas of personal, physical, work, and social lives, with personal and social being most important. The IOS Scale has also been used in a wide variety of relationships studies along with other relationship measures where its performance is generally similar to those other measures. In one example Aron, Melinat, Aron, Vallone, and Bator (1997) found that IOS Scale scores were greater after an experimental task involving gradual self-disclosure and relationship building activities, as compared to a small-talk control group. In another example, Knee (1998) conducted a longitudinal study in which couples with initial high IOS Scale scores were more likely to stay together if the two of them believed in relationship destiny, but couples with low initial IOS Scale scores were more likely to stay together if the partners did not believe in relationship destiny. In the third section of the paper we describe several studies that have used the IOS Scale successfully in areas of social psychology other than close relationships. We should also mention that Tropp and Wright (2000) have developed (and demonstrated the reliability and validity of) a version of the IOS Scale that assesses overlap of self and ingroup; Uleman, Rhee, Bardoliwalla, Semin, & Toyama (in press) have applied the Tropp and Wright version of the IOS Scale successfully in a series of cross-cultural studies; and Perreault and Bourhis (1999) successfully used a similar adaptation of the Scale in their research on ingroup identification.

Finally, regarding the principle behind the IOS Scale, we should note that even before it was developed (and unknown to the IOS Scale authors), Pipp, Shaver, Jennings, Lamborn, and Fischer (1985) had used overlapping-circle diagrams as part of a closeness measure. They had adolescents draw a picture of two circles, one representing the self and one a parent, "in relation to each other as you believe best illustrates your relationship with that parent . . ." (p. 993). Among other findings, Pipp et al. reported that perceived closeness and the amount of overlap of the circles were both strongly related to scale ratings of love and friendship.

Several studies have focused more directly on the underlying cognitive mechanisms of including other in the self. One set of such studies was based on the well-established differences in actor versus observer perspectives in attributional processes (Jones & Nisbett, 1971).

In the context of the self-expansion model, to the extent a particular person is included in the self, the difference between self's and that particular person's perspective should be reduced. Several studies support this conclusion. Nisbett, Caputo, Legant, and Marecek (1973, Study 3) found that the longer people had been in a relationship with a close friend, the less willing they were to make dispositional attributions about the friend. Similarly, Goldberg (1981) found that participants made fewer dispositional attributions for people they have spent more time with, compared to people they have spent less time with. Other research has followed this same theme of examining actor-observer differences in attribution but using different approaches. Prentice (1990) had participants describe each of several persons, describing each such person in each of three different, relatively important specific situations. She found least overlap across situations for descriptions of self, next least for familiar others, and most for unfamiliar others. This finding suggests that people are making situational attributions for self and those close to self but regard less familiar others in terms that are not differentiated by situation. Using yet another approach, Sande, Goethals, and Radloff (1988) found that self, and then liked friends, and then disliked friends, were progressively less likely to be attributed *both* poles of pairs of opposite traits (e.g., "serious-carefree"). The point here is that for self – and those liked by self – behaviors can vary according to the situation, even to the extent of representing opposites. But for those distant from self, a single-sided trait description (i.e., a dispositional attribution) is quite adequate. Aron, Aron, Tudor, and Nelson (1991, introduction to Study 2) replicated Sande et al.'s procedure, but compared different degrees of *closeness* (as opposed to liking vs. disliking). They found choices of both traits were most frequent for self, next for best friend, and least for a friendly acquaintance.

Yet another approach relevant to including the other's perspective in the self is based on an adaptation of a research paradigm developed by Lord (1980, 1987). Lord presented participants with a series of concrete nouns, for each of which they were instructed to form as vivid and interesting a mental image as possible of a target person *interacting* with whatever the noun referred to. The target person was sometimes self and sometimes someone else, such as Johnny Carson. On a free recall task afterwards, Lord found *fewer* nouns were recalled which were imaged with self than which were imaged with the other target person. He interpreted these results in terms of a figure–ground difference between one's experience of self and other when acting in the world. Because self, being ground, is less vivid than other, imaging things interacting with the self is less enhancing to memory than imaging them interacting with someone other than self. In this light, Aron et al. suggested that if the other is included in the self, other should become more like ground and less like figure – that is, more like the self. Based on this reasoning, Aron, Aron, et al. (1991, Experiment 2) replicated Lord's procedures, again using as target persons self and a prominent entertainment personality, but also added a third target, a close other, the participant's mother. Consistent with predictions, recall was greatest for nouns imaged with the entertainment personality and much less for both those imaged with self and those imaged with mother. This result was also replicated in a new sample, substituting friend of mother for the entertainment personality (to deal with the possibility that entertainment personalities are simply especially vivid images). In the replication, participants were also asked to rate their similarity, closeness, and familiarity with their mother. Also, consistent with the model's closeness emphasis, the difference in recall for nouns imaged with mother's friend minus recall for nouns imaged with mother (presumably indicating the degree to which other is included in the self) correlated .56 with ratings of closeness to mother, but only .13 with similarity, and only .16 with familiarity.

Another influential general body of research in social cognition has focused on the unique role of self-representations, going back to the pioneering articles by Markus (1977) and Rogers, Kuiper, and Kirker (1977), and what has become known as the self-reference effect (that information processing and memory is enhanced for information related to the self). If, in a close relationship, each includes other in the self, then any advantage for self-relevant information over other-relevant information should be lessened when other is in a close relationship with self – a pattern supported by several studies (for a review, see Symons & Johnson, 1997). In one such study, Bower and Gilligan (1979) found little difference in incidental memory for trait adjectives which participants had earlier judged for their relevance to their own life or their mother's life. In another study, Keenan and Baillet (1980) had participants indicate whether trait adjectives were true of a particular person. The persons were self, best friend, parent, friend, teacher, favorite TV character, and the US president. They found a clear linear trend from self through president of increasing time to make the decisions and fewer adjectives recognized later. Similarly, Prentice (1990) showed that both the content and organization of self-descriptions and other-descriptions tended to follow a pattern in which familiar others were intermediate between self and unfamiliar others.

Why is there this continuum from self to close others to strangers? We have argued that it is because the knowledge structures of a close other actually share elements (or activation potentials) with the knowledge structures of the self. Thus we hypothesized that self and close-other traits may actually be confused or interfere with each other. To test this idea, Aron, Aron, et al. (1991, Experiment 3) had married participants first rate 90 trait adjectives for their descriptiveness of themselves and their spouse. After a distracting intermediate task, they made a series of "me" – "not-me" reaction time choices to these traits. The prediction was that there would be the most confusion – and thus longer response latencies – for trait words that were different for self and spouse. (The confusion is hypothesized to arise because one is asked here to rate these traits as true or false for *self*; but if other is part of self, when self and other differ on a trait, the difference is a discrepancy between two parts of "self.") The results were as predicted: longer response times when the trait was different between self and spouse. The same pattern was obtained in a follow-up study. Also, in the follow-up study, participants completed the IOS Scale, which correlated significantly with the difference between the average response time to spouse-different words minus the average response time to spouse-similar words. Aron and Fraley (1999) and Smith, Coates, and Walling (1999) independently replicated the significant association of the reaction time measure with the IOS Scale in samples of individuals in romantic relationships; Aron and Fraley also tested for and found significant correlations of the reaction time measure with Sande et al.'s (1988) attribution measure, self-report measures of love and commitment, and change in self-reported closeness over a three-month period.

Finally, Omoto and Gunn (1994) found a self-other confusion effect for episodic memory. In their study, participants paired with friends versus participants paired with strangers were more likely to mix up whether they or their partner had earlier solved particular anagram tasks. Although the focus of their study was on other issues, these data would seem to suggest that in a personal relationship identities are sufficiently intermixed that we can actually confuse biographical memories of self and other.

Summary

A key proposal of the self-expansion model is that participants in a close relationship include each other in their selves in the sense that other's perspectives, resources, and identities are to some extent one's own. This idea is consistent with a number of ideas in social psychology and in psychology more generally, as well as having direct links with some major relationship models including interdependence theory ("cognitive interdependence"), evolutionary psychology (from the perspective of inclusive fitness), and the communal-exchange norm model (communal orientation). One line of research has shown that a Venn-diagram metaphor of self and other as overlapping circles (the IOS Scale) is a remarkably effective measure of emotional and behavioral interpersonal closeness, suggesting that this metaphor may capture how people spontaneously process information about relationships. Various nonobvious cognitive procedures have also been employed to demonstrate the role of inclusion of other in the self. These include studies showing that in a close relationship (vs. a less close relationship) there is less difference in self–other perspectives in attributions and in imaging tasks, differences in response time and memory for material related to self and other are reduced, characteristics of other interfere with self-relevant processing to a greater extent (suggesting that there is overlap in semantically based cognitive structures representing self and other), and there are self–other confusions in episodic memories.

Implications of Including Other in the Self for Other Social Psychology Topics

This final section considers recent extensions of the inclusion-of-other-in-the-self notion to two major social psychology topics beyond the direct study of close relationships – empathy and helping, and intergroup relations.[3]

Empathy and helping

An implication of our including-other-in-the-self notion is that when other is part of the self, helping other is helping self. That is, since whatever is given to other is to some extent given to self, then from the psychological perspective, giving to other is selfish, egoistic. Yet at the same time, there need be no direct benefit to self's welfare whatsoever for the process to work. Thus, from an external observer's perspective, the motivation is entirely unselfish, purely altruistic. Several studies lend support to the basic idea that in a close relationship there is less distinction between own and other's outcomes. Aron, Aron, et al. (1991, Study 1 and first and second replications) found that in a money allocation game, participants distributed money about equally to self and close others but they distributed more to themselves when other was a stranger or acquaintance; further, this result was robust over conditions in which real money was involved and participants believed that the other person would not be able to know one's allocations. MacKay, McFarland, and Buehler (1998) found that false feedback about a relationship partner's performance affected own mood only when the partner was a close relationship partner. Beach et al. (1998) supported an "extended" version of Tesser's self-esteem maintenance model in which, for example, participants' affective reaction to success or failure of their partner outperforming the self was impacted by whether or not the performance was in a domain believed to be important to the partner. (In a parallel fashion, De La Ronde & Swann, 1998, demonstrated an extended version of Swann's self-verification model, such that when married participants were given feedback inconsistent with their view of their partner, they attempted to restore the original view even when it was negative.) Finally, Medvene (in press) found the usual equity effect of greatest satisfaction for those who are neither under- nor overbenefited in a romantic relationship, but this pattern was much weaker for those who scored high on the IOS scale. That is, for couples who reported high levels of including other in the self, over- and underbenefit did not much affect their satisfaction – presumably because if other is included in the self, a benefit to other *is* a benefit to self.

Furthermore, we think that even in relatively transitory relationships people often include others in the self to some slight extent – that inclusion of other in the self is the essence of relationshipness (Aron & Aron, 1993). Indeed, one may be especially likely to include another person in the self if one becomes aware that this person is in need, because this awareness increases the other person's saliency and because recognizing another's need is associated with close relationships (Clark, Mills, & Corcoran, 1989). Finally, a number of studies by Batson and his colleagues have shown that empathy can be a key mediator between perceived need and helping: "the more empathy felt for a person in need, the more altruistic motivation to have that need reduced" (Batson, 1991, p. 87). But what *is* empathy? One interpretation (though not Batson's) is that empathy means feeling spontaneously what the other feels. In our terms, empathy means the other's feelings are my feelings, the other's need is my need. That is, we see empathy as a subset of including other in the self. If becoming aware of a person in need produces empathy, then becoming aware of a person in need produces including other in the self. Thus, Wegner (1980) suggested that empathy may "stem in part from a basic confusion between ourselves and others" (p. 133), which he proposed may arise from an initial lack of differentiation between self and caregiver in infancy (Hoffman, 1976). Davis, Conklin, Smith, and Luce (1996), explicitly linking their thinking with the self-expansion model, emphasized the importance of taking the perspective of the other, in which "the mental processes associated with perspective taking cause an observer's thoughts and feelings about a target to become, in some sense, more 'selflike'" (pp. 713–714).

In a study conducted by Cialdini et al. (1997), participants responded to a variety of scenarios involving a person in need. The finding was that the extent to which a person indicated they would help the other was mediated by measures of both empathic feeling and including other in the self; however, when they included both in the equation, empathic feeling dropped out and the measure of including other in the self turned out to be the key mediator. However, Batson et al. (1997) challenged Cialdini et al.'s conclusions, arguing that self–other overlap may account for some cases of altruism (particularly in close relationships), but altruism can exist independently of this effect (particularly when it is towards strangers). Their study used a standard perspective-taking empathy manipulation – participants attended to a video of a supposed person in need under instructions either to listen objectively or to imagine how the person in need feels – and then provided the participant an opportunity to help the person in need. Results were that differences across conditions in helping remained, even after controlling for measures of including other in the self. This controversy continued in two subsequent commentaries (Batson, 1997; Neuberg, Cialdini, Brown, Luce, & Sagarin, 1997).

Regardless of the precise eventual outcome of this controversy, it would still be consistent with including other in the self being at least one route to enhanced empathy. Davis et al.'s (1996) experiment would seem to be consistent with this view. In two experiments using a standard perspective-taking manipulation, participants in the high-empathy condition were more likely to attribute self-descriptive traits to the empathy target. Addressing the role of including other in the self more directly, Aron, Fraley, and Cialdini (2000) conducted three experiments using standard perspective-taking manipulations, in each case finding (1) a significant effect on the standard empathic feeling measure, and (2) that this effect was partially or totally mediated by the IOS Scale.

In sum, the idea of including other in the self and several supportive studies suggest that in a close relationship other's outcomes are to some extent self's outcomes, possibly explaining the apparently unselfish behavior sometimes found in such relationships. We also suggested that there may even be some degree of including other in the self with strangers, particularly when the stranger is in need so that the person is salient and the context of needs (and hence a communal relationship) is primed. Studies by Cialdini et al. (1997) support this view; however Batson et al. (1997) have challenged whether including other in the self can fully account for empathy with strangers. Other studies focusing just on empathy (a presumed mediator of helping) suggest that it is facilitated by including other in the self.

Extensions to intergroup relations

What does including other in the self have to do with intergroup relations? One possibility is a link with Allport's (1954) "contact hypothesis," the idea that under appropriate conditions (such as equal status), contact with a member of an outgroup can lead to reduced prejudice toward that outgroup. Some recent research (Pettigrew, 1997, 1998), however, suggests that such contact is only effective in reducing prejudice when the other is in a close relationship (such as a friendship) with self. In this light, we have suggested that a key mechanism driving this effect is inclusion in the self of the outgroup member – and hence also of the outgroup member's group membership.

In a questionnaire study conducted by McLaughlin-Volpe, Aron, Wright, and Reis (2000, Study 1), respondents indicated their prejudice towards and relationships with members of each of three different ethnic outgroups. Differences between outgroups in the number of friends one had or the amount of interaction with members of those outgroups did not predict parallel differences in prejudice toward those outgroups. However, differences among outgroups in the extent to which one included in the self a friend in that outgroup did significantly predict parallel differences in prejudice – the greater the inclusion of the outgroup friend in the self, the less prejudice was found for that outgroup. In another series of studies conducted by these authors, instead of ethnic outgroups, they used students at rival US universities as the outgroup – USC for UCLA and vice versa, Texas for Texas A&M. This provided outgroups about which participants would probably be willing to admit to having negative attitudes. The findings were the same as before. *Amount* of outgroup contact was not associated with prejudice. However, as long as the participant had interacted with at least one outgroup member, the degree of inclusion of this outgroup member in the self was associated with less prejudice. In a final study, 100 students kept records over a one-week period of every social interaction lasting ten minutes or longer (this was a version of the Rochester Interaction Record method; Reis & Wheeler, 1991). That is, they carried around little booklets and as soon as possible after each such interaction they would record in the booklet their answers to a short series of questions about the interaction, notably including the initials of the interaction partners and completing the IOS scale for felt closeness during the interaction. At the end of the week, participants were given some prejudice measures towards each of the major ethnic groups at their university and also, based on the initials on each record, indicated the ethnicity of each interaction partner. During the study itself, participants had no way to know the study had anything whatsoever to do with inter-ethnic interaction. The results, quite consistent with everything we have reported before, were that number of interactions with outgroup individuals had little relation to prejudice, but there was a clear association between prejudice and including outgroup interaction partners in the self. In the most important analysis, we found that differences among ethnic groups, in the extent to which one included members of a particular ethnic group in the self, predicted parallel differences in prejudice towards those ethnic groups – of course in the direction of the more inclusion of other in the self, the less prejudice. Two additional results that were found over the three studies are of particular interest. First, structural equation modeling analyses using instrument variables suggested that there were unique causal paths in both directions – that including other in the self led to reduced prejudice and that reduced prejudice also led to including other in the self (though the effect of inclusion on prejudice was bigger and more consistent). Second, in each study there was a significant interaction in predicting prejudice between number of interactions and inclusion of other in the self. When inclusion of other in the self was high, the more interactions, the less prejudice. However, when inclusion of other in the self was low, with more interactions, there was either no relation to prejudice or actually *higher* levels of prejudice.

The self-expansion model has also generated a new theoretical idea that goes beyond the contact hypothesis, taking it one step further. Specifically, we reasoned that under some conditions direct contact with an outgroup member may not be necessary. It may be enough simply to be aware that someone *else* in the ingroup has an outgroup friend. This possible impact of knowledge of an ingroup member's outgroup friendship is what we have labeled the *extended contact hypothesis* (Wright, Aron, McLaughlin- Volpe, & Ropp, 1997). That is, we reasoned as follows. Ordinarily, in self's conception of the world, my ingroup is part of myself and outgroups are not part of myself. Thus, I spontaneously treat ingroup members, to some extent, like myself, including feeling empathy with their troubles, taking pride in their successes, generously sharing resources with them, and so forth. Outgroup members, because they are not part of myself, receive none of these advantages. Literally, I could not care less about them.

However, we argue, this changes when someone who is in the ingroup, and thus part of myself, is known to have an outgroup person as part of that person's self. In this case, the outgroup friend – and hence to some extent the outgroup itself – becomes part of myself. The effect is that, to some extent, I begin to see members of that group as part of myself. Thus my ingroup–outgroup distinctions are directly undermined, as are negative attitudes I may have held toward the outgroup.

This logic rests on two key assumptions. First, it assumes that an ingroup member is part of the self. This idea is supported in studies conducted by Smith and his colleagues (Smith et al., 1999; Smith & Henry, 1996) and by Tropp and Wright (2000), employing a version of the reaction time procedure from one of the relationship studies we described earlier (e.g., Aron, Aron et al., 1991, Experiment 3) in which participants were slower at deciding whether a trait was true or false of themselves when the trait was not equally true or false of a close relationship partner. In these studies, this same pattern was found when the trait was not equally true or false of their ingroup (but the same pattern was not found for whether the trait was not equally true or false for an outgroup). The authors interpret these studies as demonstrating that individuals spontaneously include ingroup members, but not outgroup members, in the self.

Second, our logic assumes that we spontaneously group together persons we perceive as friends. In support of this idea, as noted earlier, Sedikides et al. (1993), using a procedure involving clustering of recall, found that observers treat partners in a close relationship as a single cognitive unit in a manner that Sedikides et al. explicitly associate with self–other overlap. Putting these various findings together leads to the following: In an observed ingroup–outgroup friendship, the ingroup member is part of myself, the outgroup member is part of that ingroup member's self, and hence part of myself. Presuming that the outgroup member's group membership is part of what I have included of that outgroup member in myself, then to some extent the outgroup is part of myself.

Having come up with the extended contact idea and having identified at least one plausible mechanism, the initial question was whether the phenomenon exists. In that regard, Wright et al. (1997) conducted two questionnaire surveys involving prejudice toward actual ethnic outgroups, plus a laboratory-constructed intergroup conflict study modeled after the Sherif Robber's Cave studies, and a minimal-group experiment. In the questionnaire studies part-icipants indicated, for each of three ethnic outgroups, how many people they knew of their own ethnic group who had a friend in that outgroup. Participants were also asked about their own direct friendships with individuals in each of the three ethnic outgroups. As expected from the extended contact hypothesis, knowing ingroup members who have friends in a particular ethnic outgroup was significantly associated with having relatively less pre-judice towards that ethnic outgroup – even after controlling for direct friendships with members of that ethnic outgroup. These studies were important because they show the predicted association in a real-world setting involving actual prejudice towards actual ethnic outgroups. Moreover, that these findings hold up even after controlling for direct outgroup friendships lends support to the hypothesized causal direction of this association from extended contact to reduced prejudice. Nevertheless, an unambiguous case for a causal interpretation of this association required an experimental manipulation of the hypothesized independent variable, knowledge that an ingroup member has an outgroup friend.

Wright et al.'s (1997, Study 3) first study involving such a manipulation utilized a laboratory-constructed intergroup conflict procedure, inspired by Sherif's Robber's Cave studies (Sherif, Harvey, White, Hood, & Sherif, 1961) and the series of similarly constructed experiments with adults from industrial organizations by Blake and Mouton (see Blake, Shepard, & Mouton, 1964, for a review). Wright et al. actually conducted four such studies, each involving the construction of an intergroup conflict, between two interacting seven-person groups. In each day-long experiment, they first introduced activities designed to induce strong intergroup conflict, and then, later in the day, systematically introduced an intervention involving the creation of cross-group friendships (Aron, Melinat, et al., 1997) for a small subset of the group members. The results were clear (and even with only four replications, significant): the first two testings (both preintervention) showed an increase in outgroup prejudice, but the third testing (postintervention) showed a decrease.

These findings are nevertheless limited in that there was no control group that did not get the intervention. (As did Sherif and his colleagues before them, Wright et al. considered it impractically costly to conduct a series of control experiments in which there were no interventions.) Thus, it remained possible that the obtained effects could be due to time-related factors (or factors associated with repeated testing) unrelated to the experimental intervention. Therefore, the next study (Wright et al., 1997, Study 4) was designed to test the causal direction of the extended contact hypothesis, employing a true experimental design. This was accomplished by employing a modified "minimal group procedure" (Turner, 1978). Numerous experiments using this paradigm have demonstrated that mere categorization of participants can lead to discrimination in favor of the ingroup on attitude measures, evaluations, and on the allocation of resources (see Brewer, 1979; Mullen, Brown, & Smith, 1992, for reviews). Following typical procedures in this kind of research, participants were told that they were divided into groups based on their performance on an object estimation task. The researchers then arranged for participants to observe an ingroup and an outgroup member – actually confederates – interacting in the solution of a puzzle task. The behavior of the confederates when they arrived to do the puzzle task suggested that their existing relationship was that of warm friends, unacquainted strangers, or disliked acquaintances. For example, in the friendly condition, when the ingroup and outgroup member met they expressed delight at seeing an old friend and hugged; in the neutral condition they showed no sign of any previous acquaintance; and in the hostile condition they showed signs of displeasure about being paired with this person, implying they had a long-standing hostile relationship. The result was that those who observed what they believed was an ingroup member having a close outgroup friend showed less outgroup bias over several measures, compared to those who observed an ingroup member have either no relationship or a hostile relationship with an outgroup member.

In sum, the self-expansion model predicts that forming a relationship with an outgroup person, or even becoming aware that someone in your ingroup has a friendship with an outgroup person, should reduce prejudice towards that outgroup. The logic is that when one's own friend is of the outgroup, as part of including this friend in the self, one includes the friend's group identity, thus undermining ingroup–outgroup distinctiveness and negative feelings toward the outgroup (if the outgroup is part of me, and I value myself, then it would be inconsistent to devalue the outgroup). This logic is extended to knowledge that an ingroup person has an outgroup friend because when I include ingroup members in the self, I also include to some extent the identities I perceive them to include in their self. Several studies generated by these ideas yielded supportive results.

Summary

In this section we have examined implications of the inclusion-of-other-in-the-self idea for areas of social psychology beyond close relationships, including empathy and helping, and intergroup relations. In addition to the direct importance of this work for these particular areas, this research is also important as an illustration of the potential for advancing know-ledge from work that crosses subarea boundaries within social psychology – in this case between close relationships and prosocial behavior and between close relationships and intergroup relations. As Mackie and Smith (1998) said, "the very exercise of considering the continuities between the topics [of different areas of social psychology] . . . offers some sug-gestion as to the kinds of underlying principles or processes that we think would be central to . . . an integrated theory" (p. 520), noting also that one result of such work is that "wheels invented in one domain need not be reinvented in another" (p. 521).

Conclusions

We understand the self-expansion model as a conceptual framework that sensitizes researchers to variables and patterns that might otherwise be missed. We believe that the various theoret-ical insights and research programs that have been generated by this model (as summarized in this chapter) support the utility of this conceptual framework as a heuristic of this kind. However, we do not see the conceptual framework as a precise theory from which highly specific predictions can be formally derived. We see it, rather, as a stimulus for the devel-opment of precise theories, a platform for viewing relationships and relationship-linked phenomena that turns one in directions that would not otherwise be considered. Further, the developing body of research around this perspective both shapes the overall conceptual framework and provides a set of methods and concepts that we believe offer considerable promise for furthering understanding of cognition and motivation in close relationships, and beyond.

ACKNOWLEDGMENT

The preparation of this paper and several of the studies reported here were supported by grants from the National Science Foundation.

NOTES

1   We have also discussed (Aron & Aron, 1986; Aron, Norman, & Aron, 1998) three other major aspects of the self-expansion model that are of some importance, but we do not discuss them in this chapter (other than in this note) because we are only beginning to conduct systematic studies of them. One of these aspects is that, along with the desire to expand the self, we hypothesize an equally strong desire to integrate expansion experiences and make sense of them, a desire for wholeness or coherence which sometimes preempts the desire for expansion until it is satisfied to some degree. Expansion and integration are seen as two steps in a general pattern of movement toward self-expansion. Second, we have argued that if expansion proceeds at a rate faster than it can be integrated, this will be stressful. That is, too rapid expansion is distressing and thus aversive. A final major angle of the motivational angle of the model that has not yet received much research attention is the suggestion that there are individual specialties or preferences for modes of expansion. Further, these may change over the course of a day or a lifetime. Thus, some individuals at some times may seek expansion through creative work, at other times through relationships, at other times through physical development, and so forth.

2   Sorrentino, Raynor, Zubek, and Short (1990) argue for two basic sources of value in determining goals: information value and affective value. The former is akin to our notion of knowledge.

3   There has also been some preliminary work extending the model to persuasion and attitude change (Steele, 1999; Steele & Aron, 2000) and to the role of relationship cognition in logical processing (Dorrity, 2000). However, in the interest of space, the focus of this section is on the two areas in which the most research has been done.

REFERENCES

Agnew, C. R., Van Lange, P. A. M., Rusbult, C. E., & Langston, C. A. (1998). Cognitive interdependence: Commitment and the mental representation of close relationships. *Journal of Personality and Social Psychology, 74*, 939–954.

Ahuvia, A. (1993). *I love it! Towards a unifying theory of love across diverse love objects.* Unpublished PhD dissertation, Northwestern University.

Allport, G. (1954). *The nature of prejudice.* Reading, MA: Addison-Wesley.

Aron, A., & Aron, E. N. (1986). *Love as the expansion of self: Understanding attraction and satisfaction.* New York: Hemisphere.

Aron, A., & Aron, E. N. (1993). Relationship as a region of the life space. *Personal Relationship Issues, 1*, 22–24.

Aron, A., & Aron, E. N. (1996). Self and self-expansion in relationships. In G. J. O. Fletcher & J. Fitness (Eds.), *Knowledge structures in close relationships: A social psychological approach* (pp. 325–344). Mahwah, NJ: Erlbaum.

Aron, A., & Aron, E. N. (1997). Self-expansion motivation and including other in the self. In W. Ickes (Section Ed.) & S. Duck (Ed.), *Handbook of personal relationships* (2nd Ed., Vol. 1, pp. 251–270). London: Wiley.

Aron, A., Aron, E. N., & Allen, J. (1998). Motivations for unrequited love. *Personality and Social Psychology Bulletin, 24*, 787–796.

Aron, A., Aron, E. N., & Norman, C. (1999, August). Relationship effects of participating together in novel and arousing activities. In A. Aron (Chair), *Making relationships work – new ideas from the social psychology laboratory.* Symposium conducted at the American Psychological Association, Boston.

Aron, A., Aron, E. N., & Smollan, D. (1992). Inclusion of Other in the Self Scale and the structure of interpersonal closeness. *Journal of Personality and Social Psychology, 63*, 596–612.

Aron, A., Aron, E. N., Tudor, M., & Nelson, G. (1991). Close relationships as including other in the self. *Journal of Personality and Social Psychology, 60*, 241–253.

Aron, A., & Fraley, B. (1999). Relationship closeness as including other in the self: Cognitive underpinnings and measures. *Social Cognition, 17*, 140–160.

Aron, A., Fraley, B., & Cialdini, R. (2000). *Empathy as including other in the self.* Manuscript in preparation.

Aron, A., Melinat, E., Aron, E. N., Vallone, R., & Bator, R. (1997). The experimental generation of interpersonal closeness: A procedure and some preliminary findings. *Personality and Social Psychology Bulletin, 23*, 363–377.

Aron, A., Norman, C. C., & Aron, E. N. (1998). The self-expansion model and motivation. *Representative Research in Social Psychology, 22*, 1–13.

Aron, A., Norman, C. C., Aron, E. N., McKenna, C., & Heyman, R. (2000). Couple's shared participation in novel and arousing activities and experienced relationship quality. *Journal of Personality and Social Psychology, 78*, 273–283.

Aron, A., Paris, M., & Aron, E. N. (1995). Falling in love: Prospective studies of self-concept change. *Journal of Personality and Social Psychology, 69*, 1102–1112.

Bakan, D. (1966). *The duality of human existence: Isolation and commitment in Western man.* Boston: Beacon Press.

Bandura, A. (1977). Self-efficacy: Toward a unifying theory of behavioral change. *Psychological Review, 84*, 191–215.

Batson, C. D. (1991). *The altruism question: Toward a social-psychological answer.* Hillsdale, NJ: Erlbaum.

Batson, C. D. (1997). Self–other merging and the empathy-altruism hypothesis: Reply to Neuberg et al. (1997). *Journal of Personality and Social Psychology, 73*, 517–522.

Batson, C. D., Sager, K., Garst, E., Kang, M., Rubchinsky, K., & Dawson, K. (1997). Is empathy-induced helping due to self–other merging? *Journal of Personality and Social Psychology, 73*, 495–509.

Beach, S. R., Tesser, A., Fincham, F. D., Jones, D. J., Johnson, D., & Whitaker, D. J. (1998). Pleasure and pain in doing well, together: An investigation of performance-related affect in close relationships. *Journal of Personality and Social Psychology, 74*, 923–938.

Belk, R. W. (1988). Possessions and the extended self. *Journal of Consumer Research, 15*, 139–168.

Berlyne, D. E. (1960). *Conflict, arousal, and curiosity.* New York: McGraw-Hill.

Blake, R. R., Shepard, H. A., & Mouton, J. S. (1964). *Managing intergroup conflicts in industry.* Houston, TX: Gulf.

Bower, G. H., & Gilligan, S. G. (1979). Remembering information related to one's self. *Journal of Research in Personality, 13*, 420–432.

Bowlby, J. (1969). *Attachment and loss: Vol. 1. Attachment.* New York: Basic Books.

Brewer, M. B. (1979). In-group bias in the minimal intergroup situation: A cognitive-motivational analysis. *Psychological Bulletin, 86*, 307–324.

Buber, M. (1937). *I and thou.* New York: Scribner's.

Carver, C., & Scheier, M. (1990). Principles of self-regulation, action, and emotion. In E. T. Higgins & R. M. Sorrentino (Eds.), *Handbook of motivation and cognition: Foundations of social behavior* (Vol. 2). New York: Guilford Press.

Cialdini, R. B., Brown, S. L., Lewis, B. P., Luce, C., & Neuberg, S. L. (1997). Reinterpreting the empathy-altruism relationships: When one into one equals oneness. *Journal of Personality and Social Psychology, 73*, 481–494.

Clark, M. S., & Mills, J. (1979). Interpersonal attraction in exchange and communal relationships. *Journal of Personality and Social Psychology, 37*, 12–24.

Clark, M. S., & Mills, J. (1993). The difference between communal and exchange relationships: What it is and is not. *Personality and Social Psychology Bulletin, 19*, 684–691.

Clark, M. S., Mills, J., & Corcoran, D. (1989). Keeping track of needs and inputs of friends and strangers. *Personality and Social Psychology Bulletin, 15*, 533–542.

Cross, S. E., Morris, M. L., Brunscheen, S., Frederick, K., McGregor, A., Meyer, G., & Proulx, B. (1997, August). *The interdependent self-construal and descriptions of close relationships*. Paper presented at the American Psychological Association Convention, Chicago.

Davis, M. H., Conklin, L., Smith, A., & Luce, C. (1996). Effect of perspective taking on the cognitive representation of persons: A merging of self and other. *Journal of Personality and Social Psychology, 70*, 713–726.

Deci, E. L., & Ryan, R. (1987). The support of autonomy and the control of behavior. *Journal of Personality and Social Psychology, 53*, 1024–1037.

De La Ronde, C., & Swann, W. B., Jr. (1998). Partner verification: Restoring shattered images of our intimates. *Journal of Personality and Social Psychology, 75*, 374–382.

Dorrity, K. (2000). *Social logic*. Manuscript under review.

Dutton, D. G., & Aron, A. (1974). Some evidence for heightened sexual attraction under conditions of high anxiety. *Journal of Personality and Social Psychology, 30*, 510–517.

Foster, C. A., Witcher, B. S., Campbell, W. K., & Green, J. D. (1998). Arousal and attraction: Evidence for automatic and controlled processes. *Journal of Personality and Social Psychology, 74*, 86–101.

Gecas, V. (1989). Social psychology of self-efficacy. *American Sociological Review, 15*, 291–316.

Goldberg, L. R. (1981). Unconfounding situational attributions from uncertain, neutral, and ambiguous ones: A psychometric analysis of descriptions of oneself and various types of others. *Journal of Personality and Social Psychology, 41*, 517–552.

Heider, F. (1958). *The psychology of interpersonal relations*. New York: Wiley.

Higgins, E. T., & Sorrentino, R. M. (1990). *Handbook of motivation and cognition: Foundations of social behavior*. New York: Guilford Press.

Hoffman, M. L. (1976). Empathy, role taking, guilt, and development of altruistic motives. In T. Lickona (Ed.), *Moral development and behavior*. New York: Holt.

Huesmann, L. R. (1980). Toward a predictive model of romantic behavior. In K. S. Pope et al. (Eds.), On love and loving (pp. 152–171). San Francisco: Jossey-Bass.

Ickes, W., Tooke, W., Stinson, L., Baker, V., & Bissonnette, V. (1988). Naturalistic social cognition: Intersubjectivity in same-sex dyads. *Journal of Nonverbal Behavior, 12*, 58–84.

Jacobson, N. S., & Margolin, G. (1979). *Marital therapy: Strategies based on social learning and behavior exchange principles*. New York: Brunner/Mazel.

James, W. (1948). *Psychology*. Cleveland, OH: Fine Editions Press. (Original work published 1890)

Jones, E. E., & Nisbett, R. (1971). The actor and the observer: Divergent perceptions of the causes of behavior. In E. E. Jones, D. Kanouse, H. Kelley, R. Nisbett, S. Valins, & B. Weiner (Eds.), *Attribution: Perceiving the causes of behavior* (pp. 79–94). Morristown, NJ: General Learning Press.

Jung, C. G. (1959). Marriage as a psychological relationship. In V. S. DeLaszlo (Ed.), *The basic writings of C. G. Jung* (R. F. C. Hull, Trans., pp. 531–544). New York: Modern Library. (Original work published 1925)

Keenan, J. M., & Baillet, S. D. (1980). Memory for personally and socially significant events. In R. S. Nickerson (Ed.), *Attention and performance* (Vol. 8, pp. 652–669). Hillsdale, NJ: Erlbaum.

Kelley, H. H., & Thibaut, J. W. (1978). *Interpersonal relationships: A theory of interdependence*. New York: Wiley.

Knee, C. R. (1998). Implicit theories of relationships: Assessment and prediction of romantic relationship initiation, coping, and longevity. *Journal of Personality and Social Psychology, 74*, 360–370.

Lord, C. G. (1980). Schemas and images as memory aids: Two modes of processing social information. *Journal of Personality and Social Psychology, 38*, 257–269.

Lord, C. G. (1987). Imagining self and others: Reply to Brown, Keenan, and Potts. *Journal of Personality and Social Psychology, 53*, 445–450.

Loving, T. J., & Agnew, C. R. (1998, June). *Examining components of the "self" in self-other inclusion.* Paper presented at the International Conference on Personal Relationships, Saratoga Springs, NY.

MacKay, L., McFarland, C., & Buehler, R. (1998, August). *Affective reactions to performances in close relationships.* Paper presented at the American Psychological Association, San Francisco.

Mackie, D. M., & Smith, E. R. (1998). Intergroup relations: Insights from a theoretically integrative approach. *Psychological Review, 105*, 499–529.

Markus, H. (1977). Self-schemata and processing information about the self. *Journal of Personality and Social Psychology, 35*, 63–78.

Maslow, A. H. (1967). A theory of metamotivation: The biological rooting of the value-life. *Journal of Humanistic Psychology, 7*, 93–127.

Maslow, A. H. (1970). *Motivation and personality.* New York: Harper & Row.

McCall, G. J. (1974). A symbolic interactionist approach to attraction. In T. L. Huston (Ed.), *Foundations of interpersonal attraction* (pp. 217–231). New York: Academic Press.

McLaughlin-Volpe, Aron, A., Wright, S. C., & Reis, H. T. (2000). *Intergroup social interactions and intergroup prejudice: Quantity versus quality.* Manuscript under review.

Medvene, L. (in press). Including the other in self: Implications for judgments of equity and satisfaction in close relationships. *Journal of Social and Clinical Psychology.*

Merleau-Ponty, M. (1945). *Phénoménologie de la perception.* Paris: Gallimard.

Mullen, B., Brown, R., & Smith, C. (1992). Ingroup bias as a function of salience, relevance, and status: An integration. *European Journal of Social Psychology, 22*, 103–122.

Neuberg, S. L., Cialdini, R. B., Brown, S. L., Luce, C., & Sagarin, B. J. (1997). Does empathy lead to anything more than superficial helping? Comment on Batson (1997). *Journal of Personality and Social Psychology, 73*, 510–516.

Nisbett, R. E., Caputo, C., Legant, P., & Marecek, J. (1973). Behavior as seen by the actor and as seen by the observer. *Journal of Personality and Social Psychology, 27*, 154–164.

Omoto, A. M., & Gunn, D. O. (1994, May). *The effect of relationship closeness on encoding and recall for relationship-irrelevant information.* Paper presented at the May Meeting of the International Network on Personal Relationships, Iowa City, IA.

Perreault, S., & Bourhis, R. Y. (1999). Ethnocentrism, social identification, and discrimination. *Personality and Social Psychology Bulletin, 25*, 92–103.

Pettigrew, T. F. (1997). Generalized intergroup effects on prejudice. *Personality and Social Psychology Bulletin, 23*, 173–185.

Pettigrew, T. F. (1998). Intergroup contact theory. *Annual Review of Psychology, 49*, 65–85.

Pipp, S., Shaver, P., Jennings, S., Lamborn, S., & Fischer, K. W. (1985). Adolescents' theories about the development of their relationships with parents. *Journal of Personality and Social Psychology, 48*, 991–1001.

Plutchik, R. (1967). Marriage as dynamic equilibrium: Implications for research. In H. L. Silverman (Ed.), *Marital counseling: Psychology, ideology, science* (pp. 347–367). Springfield, IL: Charles C. Thomas.

Prentice, D. A. (1990). Familiarity and differences in self- and other-representations. *Journal of Personality and Social Psychology, 59*, 369–383.

Pyszczynski, T. A., Greenberg, J., & Solomon, S. (1997). Why do we need what we need? A terror management perspective on the roots of human social motivation. *Psychological Inquiry, 8*, 1–20.

Reik, T. (1944). *A psychologist looks at love.* New York: Farrar & Reinhart.

Reis, H. T., & Shaver, P. (1988). Intimacy as interpersonal process. In S. Duck (Ed.), *Handbook of personal relationships: Theory, research and interventions* (pp. 367–389). Chichester, England: Wiley.

Reis, H. T., & Wheeler, L. (1991). Studying social interaction with the Rochester Interaction Record. In M. P. Zanna (Ed.), *Advances in experimental social psychology* (Vol. 24, pp. 269–318). San Diego, CA: Academic Press.

Reissman, C., Aron, A., & Bergen, M. R. (1993). Shared activities and marital satisfaction: Causal direction and self-expansion versus boredom. *Journal of Social and Personal Relationships, 10,* 243–254.

Rogers, T. B., Kuiper, N. A., & Kirker, W. S. (1977). Self-reference and the encoding of personal information. *Journal of Personality and Social Psychology, 35,* 677–688.

Runciman, W. G. (1966). *Relative deprivation and social justice.* Berkeley: University of California Press.

Rusbult, C., & Arriaga, X. (1997). Interdependence theory. In W. Ickes (Section Ed.) & S. Duck (Ed.), *Handbook of personal relationships* (2nd Ed., Vol. 1, pp. 221–250). London: Wiley.

Sande, G. N., Goethals, G. R., & Radloff, C. E. (1988). Perceiving one's own traits and others': The multifaceted self. *Journal of Personality and Social Psychology, 54,* 13–20.

Schutz, A. (1970). *On phenomenology and social relations.* Chicago: Chicago University Press.

Sedikides, C., Olsen, N., & Reis, H. T. (1993). Relationships as natural categories. *Journal of Personality and Social Psychology, 64,* 71–82.

Sedikides, C., & Strube, M. J. (1995). The multiply motivated self. *Personality and Social Psychology Bulletin, 21,* 1330–1335.

Shaver, P. R., & Hazan, C. (1993). Adult romantic attachment: Theory and evidence. In D. Perlman & W. Jones (Eds.), *Advances in personal relationships* (Vol. 4, pp. 29–70). London: Jessica Kingsley.

Sherif, M., Harvey, O. J., White, B. J., Hood, W. R., & Sherif, C. W. (1961). *Intergroup conflict and cooperation: The Robbers Cave experiment.* Norman, OK: University of Oklahoma Book Exchange.

Sivadas, E., & Machleit, K. A. (1994). A scale to determine the extent of object incorporation in the extended self. *American Marketing Association, 5,* 143–149.

Smith, E., Coats, S., & Walling, D. (1999). Overlapping mental representations of self, in-group, and partner: Further response time evidence and a connectionist model. *Personality and Social Psychology Bulletin, 25,* 873–882.

Smith, E., & Henry, S. (1996). An in-group becomes part of the self: Response time evaluation. *Personality and Social Psychology Bulletin, 22,* 635–642.

Sorrentino, R. M., Raynor, J. O., Zubek, J. M., & Short, J. C. (1990). Personality functioning and change: Informational and affective influences on cognitive, moral, and social development. In E. T. Higgins & R. M. Sorrentino (Eds.), *Handbook of motivation and cognition: Foundations of social behavior* (Vol. 2, pp. 193–228). New York: Guilford Press.

Steele, J. L. (1999). *Cognitive mechanisms of attitude change in close relationships.* Doctoral dissertation, State University of New York at Stony Brook.

Steele, J. L., & Aron, A. (2000). *Do you believe what I believe? Attitude change in close relationships.* Manuscript under review.

Symons, C. S., & Johnson, B. T. (1997). The Self-reference effect in memory: A meta-analysis. *Psychological Bulletin, 121,* 371–394.

Tajfel, H., & Turner, J. C. (1979). An integrative theory of intergroup conflict. In W. G. Austin & S. Worchel (Eds.), *The social psychology of intergroup relations* (pp. 33–47). Monterey, CA: Brooks/ Cole.

Taylor, S. E., Neter, E., & Wayment, H. A. (1995). Self-evaluative processes. *Personality and Social Psychology Bulletin, 21,* 1278–1287.

Tesser, A. (1988). Toward a self-evaluation maintenance model of social behavior. In L. Berkowitz (Ed.), *Advances in experimental social psychology* (Vol. 11, pp. 288–338). San Diego, CA: Academic Press.

Tropp, L. R., & Wright, S. C. (2000). *Ingroup identification as the inclusion of ingroup in the self.* Manuscript under review.

Tucker, P., & Aron, A. (1993). Passionate love and marital satisfaction at key transition points in the family life cycle. *Journal of Social and Clinical Psychology, 12,* 135–147.

Turner, J. C. (1978). Social categorization and social discrimination in the minimal group paradigm. In H. Tajfel (Ed.), *Differentiation between social groups: Studies in the social psychology of intergroup relations* (pp. 101–140). London: Academic Press.

Uleman, J. S., Rhee, E., Bardoliwalla, N., Semin, G., & Togama, M. (in press). The relational self: Closeness to ingroups depends on who they are, culture and types of closeness. *Asian Journal of Social Psychology.*

Wegner, D. M. (1980). The self in prosocial action. In D. M. Wegner & R. R. Vallacher (Eds.), *The self in social psychology* (pp. 131–157). New York: Oxford University Press.

White, L. K. (1983). Determinants of spousal interaction: Marital structure or marital happiness. *Journal of Marriage and the Family, 45,* 511–519.

White, R. W. (1959). Motivation reconsidered: The concept of confidence. *Psychological Review, 66,* 297–333.

Wright, S. C., Aron, A., McLaughlin-Volpe, T., & Ropp, S. A. (1997). The extended contact effect: Knowledge of cross-group friendships and prejudice. *Journal of Personality and Social Psychology, 73,* 73–90.

CHAPTER SIX

Psychological Consequences
of Devalued Identities

Jennifer Crocker and Diane M. Quinn

The person who is stigmatized is a person whose social identity or membership in some social category calls into question his or her full humanity – the person is devalued, spoiled, or flawed in the eyes of others (Goffman, 1963; Jones et al., 1984). The stigmatized are often the targets of negative stereotypes (Jones et al., 1984), and elicit emotional reactions such as pity, anger, anxiety, or disgust (e.g., Katz, 1981; Weiner, Perry, & Magnusson, 1988; Weiner, 1995), but the central feature of social stigma is devaluation and dehumanization by others (Goffman, 1963; Crocker, Major, & Steele, 1998). In nearly every culture, some groups are devalued or stigmatized, although the particular social identities considered to be flawed differ across cultures and historical eras (see Archer, 1985; Becker & Arnold, 1986; Jones et al., 1984; and Solomon, 1986, for reviews).

In this chapter, we contrast the traditional social science assumption that the psychological consequences of social stigma are deeply internalized with an alternative view, that the consequences of social stigma emerge in the situation, as a function of the meaning that situation has for people with valued and devalued identities. Due to space limitations, we focus on the consequences of devalued identities for self-esteem and performance on intellectual tests, two areas in which recent research has led to dramatically new understandings of these phenomena.

> ## The psychological consequences of stigma:
> ## internalized or situationally constructed?

Most discussions of stigma assume that the psychological and behavioral consequences of stigmatization result from internalization of devaluing images and stereotypes, or from other

Preparation of this manuscript was supported by an NIMH predoctoral traineeship to Diane M. Quinn, and by NIMH grant 1 R01 MH58869-01 to Jennifer Crocker.

effects that stigmatization has on the personality, character, and values of the stigmatized. This view was expressed by Allport (1954) when he asked, ". . . what would happen to your personality if you heard it said over and over again that you are lazy and had inferior blood?" (p. 42). Consistent with Allport's view, differences associated with race, gender, and other valued or devalued social identities are typically explained in terms of inherent or internalized characteristics of the stigmatized themselves. Explanations tend to focus on biological differences, differences in access to resources such as good schools or safe neighborhoods, differences in exposure to prejudice and discrimination, or differences in socialization experiences. Each of these explanations suggests that differences between people with valued and devalued social identities reflect deeply internalized and stable characteristics, and that these group differences are exceedingly difficult, if not impossible, to eliminate. For example, research on race differences in performance on tests of intellectual abilities has tended to attribute such differences to genetic differences, or to socialization experiences and differential access to high quality schooling (sec Steele, 1992, 1997, for discussions). Recently, African Americans' poor school achievement has been attributed to an oppositional identity that devalues the importance of school (Ogbu, 1986; Osborne, 1995), or to inferiority feelings that result from internalizing negative stereotypes about the intellectual abilities of African Americans (e.g., S. Steele, 1990). Women's poor math achievement has been linked to poor academic self-concepts and devaluation of mathematics as a consequence of negative stereotypes about women's math ability (Frome & Eccles, 1998; Jacobs & Eccles, 1992), as well as genetic male superiority in mathematical reasoning ability (Benbow & Stanley, 1980). Research on gender differences in vulnerability to a variety of psychological disorders such as depression and eating disorders has often attributed such differences to biological processes that increase the vulnerability of girls and women to these disorders, to personality characteristics that make them vulnerable, or to socialization experiences (e.g., Nolen-Hoeksema, 1987 for a review).

We argue that existing psychological models of group differences place undue emphasis on internalized and relatively immutable differences, and fail to recognize the extent to which differences between those with valued and devalued identities are highly dependent on the social context and features of the immediate situation in which the stigmatized find themselves. Thus, research indicates that the consequences of stigma have a "now you see it, now you don't" quality that is unacknowledged in most analyses.

In its essence, our argument is that to understand why stigmatized and nonstigmatized people behave or feel differently, we must understand both the unique meanings of situations for the stigmatized and the nonstigmatized, and how features of the situation, often very subtle features, can alter those meanings. Although these differences may be stable across similar situations that have the same meaning, and hence may appear to be internalized, it is often possible to alter the features of the situation and attenuate or eliminate those differences. In some respects, this is a very social psychological analysis, recognizing the power of the situation to affect self-esteem, performance on standardized tests, and other psychological experiences and behavior. However, most social psychological analyses of the power of the situation have assumed that a particular situation means the same thing for everyone in it. In contrast, recent research suggests that the same situation can have very different meanings, implications, and consequences for people with different social identities.

Collective Representations and the Meaning of Situations

One strategy for understanding what meanings might be important for particular situations is to examine the collective representations significant to a particular situation or context. Collective representations are shared beliefs, values, ideologies, or systems of meaning. Collective representations that affect the meaning of situations for the stigmatized may take the form of awareness of cultural stereotypes about one's group, understandings of why one's group occupies the position it does in the social hierarchy, and ideologies such as belief in a just world or belief in the Protestant ethic. These collective representations may lead the same situation to have different meanings, and different implications for self-worth, for stigmatized and nonstigmatized people. Thus, to understand the effects of having a devalued identity, we must understand both the collective representations that stigmatized individuals bring to situations, and how features of the situation, often very subtle features, make those collective representations relevant in that situation, or irrelevant.

Cultural values and ideologies

Most often, those who have valued versus devalued identities will have shared collective representations, as a result of living in a society in which those meanings are widely shared, and widely represented in popular culture. Many ideologies, for example, are endorsed broadly both by those who have valued and those who have devalued identities. In highly individualistic cultures, such as North America and many northern European cultures, the values of individualism, including independence, self-reliance, and personal responsibility for one's outcomes in life constitute a core ideology (Kleugel & Smith, 1981, 1986). Although these values are widely shared, they have unique implications for people with devalued identities (Jost & Banaji, 1994; Sidanius & Pratto, 1993). In particular, these ideologies suggest that the negative outcomes of people with devalued identities are under their control, and often deserved. For example, Crandall (1994) found that conservative political values, endorsement of the Protestant ethic, and belief in a just world all were related to the belief that being overweight is under one's control. Overweight and normal-weight Americans are equally likely to endorse this ideology (Crandall, 1994; Quinn & Crocker, 1999), but the ideology has different implications for these two groups. Specifically, belief in the Protestant ethic is associated with low levels of psychological well being in the overweight, but high levels of psychological well being in the normal weight (Quinn & Crocker, 1999, Study 1).

Beliefs about prejudice and discrimination

One collective representation shared by members of many stigmatized groups is the belief that others are prejudiced against them. This belief may affect the meaning that positive and negative events have for the stigmatized and the implications of those events for the self (Crocker & Major, 1989; Major & Crocker, 1994). In general, stigmatized individuals seem to be aware of prejudice against people with their social identity. For example, Rosenberg (1979) found that African Americans past the age of 14 are generally aware that others are prejudiced against their group. Most women believe that women are discriminated against (Crosby, 1982). Mentally retarded persons are aware of the negative consequences of their label (Gibbons, 1981), as are the blind (Scott, 1969), the obese (Harris, Waschull, & Walters, 1990; Jarvie, Lahey, Graziano, & Framer, 1983; Millman, 1980) the mentally ill (Link, 1987), and homosexuals (D'Emilio, 1983). People with different devalued identities differ in their beliefs about prejudice and discrimination against their group. For example, South Asian and Haitian women in Montreal believe that their group is discriminated against more than do Inuit people (Taylor, Wright, & Porter, 1994). Furthermore, individuals who share a devalued social identity differ in their beliefs about discrimination against their group. For example, Taylor et al. (1994) showed that undergraduate women at a university are more likely to believe that women are targets of discrimination than are non-university women.

Although many stigmatized people believe that others are prejudiced against their group, they do not always believe that they personally have experienced prejudice and discrimination. In general, people believe that their group is discriminated against more than they personally are discriminated against (see Taylor et al., 1994, for a review). For example, Crosby (1984) found that employed women tended to believe that women in general are discriminated against, but did not believe that they personally had been discriminated against, a phenomenon she labeled "denial of discrimination." Denial of personal discrimination is not always found in members of stigmatized groups, however (Taylor et al., 1994).

Black students' collective representations include the belief that Blacks are frequently the targets of racial discrimination. Crocker and her colleagues (Crocker, Luhtanen, Blaine, & Broadnax, 1994; Crocker, Luhtanen, Broadnax, & Blaine, 1999) investigated self-esteem and collective representations about prejudice and discrimination in a sample of 91 Black and 96 White college students at a large public university. African American students were more likely to believe that they personally had been discriminated against than were Whites. In results from the same study reported elsewhere (Crocker et al., 1999), they also found that Black students had very different understandings of the plight of Black Americans than did White students: They were higher in system blame (i.e., more likely to believe that problems confronting the Black community are caused by prejudice and discrimination) and more likely to believe that the U.S. government conspires to harm Black Americans, than were Whites. Thus, the collective representations of Black students clearly include the beliefs that Blacks in general, and they personally, are targets of racial prejudice. These beliefs are not widely shared by White students, regarding either their own experiences with racial prejudice, or their understanding of Blacks' experiences with racial prejudice.

Awareness of stereotypes

A related collective representation that the stigmatized may bring to situations is awareness of specific stereotypes about their group. Because these stereotypes are often pervasive in the culture, it may be inevitable that members of stigmatized groups know the content of those stereotypes (Devine, 1989; Gaertner & Dovidio, 1986). That is not to say that stigmatized individuals inevitably accept the validity of these stereotypes, although some do (see Jost & Banaji, 1994, for a discussion). Rather, stigmatized individuals are aware of the accusations against them that are contained in those stereotypes. African Americans, for example, are likely to be well aware that stereotypes accuse them of being intellectually inferior and aggressive; women are well aware that stereotypes accuse them of being emotional, bad at math, and lacking in leadership aptitude; gay men are aware that stereotypes accuse them of being flamboyant, effeminate, and promiscuous; the overweight are aware that stereotypes accuse them of lacking self-control and being inwardly miserable (Allon, 1982; Jones et al., 1984).

Contingencies of self-esteem

Another collective representation that people bring with them to situations is beliefs about what makes a person worthwhile – beliefs that Crocker and Wolfe (1998) have called contingencies of self-esteem. Self scholars have long noted that individuals differ in the value or importance they place on doing well in a particular domain (e.g., Steele, 1992; Tesser, 1988). Of course, domains may be important for a variety of reasons – because they are instrumentally useful for achieving one's goals, because they are important to significant others such as parents or in the larger culture, and of most interest here, because they form the basis of one's self-esteem. When self-esteem is at stake in situations that are relevant to one's contingencies of worth, emotional reactions, thoughts, and behavior are likely to be affected (Baumeister, 1998; Crocker & Wolfe, 1998; Kernis & Waschull, 1995; Steele, 1988).

Typically, research on the importance of various domains focuses on specific arenas of competence, such as school competence, athletic competence, attractiveness, and so on (e.g., Harter, 1986). Crocker and Wolfe (1999) have expanded the focus of this work to include contingencies of self-esteem not directly related to competence. They argue that self-esteem can also be based on such contingencies as having power over others, receiving approval or regard from others, being virtuous or moral, and being loved by God. These contingencies of self-esteem may determine the meaning of particular situations for people. For example, a student whose self-esteem is based on others' approval may be more personally distressed by prejudice directed against her than a student whose self-esteem is based mainly on God's love.

Are contingencies of self-esteem collective, rather than merely personal, representations? Gender scholars have suggested that women and men differ in the basis of their self-esteem. For example, women's self-esteem is more strongly correlated with their perceived physical attractiveness, whereas men's self-esteem is more strongly correlated with their perceived physical effectiveness (Harter, 1986; Lemer, Orlos, & Knapp, 1976). Given the pervasive cultural messages that women are objectified, and evaluated in terms of their physical appearance (Fredrickson & Roberts, 1997), it is not surprising that women's self-esteem would be more strongly linked to their appearance than is men's. Because of differences in the degree to which self-esteem is based on appearance, situations such as speaking in public may have different meanings for men and women.

Josephs, Markus, and Tafarodi (1992) argued that the self-esteem of men "is derived, in part, from fulfilling the goals ascribed to their gender – being independent autonomous, separate, and better than others" (p. 392), whereas the self-esteem of women is derived, at least in part, from "being sensitive to, attuned to, connected to, and generally interdependent with others" (p. 392; see also Cross & Madson, 1997; Markus & Oyserman, 1989; Wood, Christensen, Hebl, & Rothgerber, 1997, for reviews). In a series of studies, Josephs et al. (1992) showed that the tendency to see oneself as superior to others is more strongly associated with self-esteem among men than among women. In a second study, encoding words with reference to close others (a group or one's best friend) facilitated recall for high self-esteem women more than for high self-esteem men, or low self-esteem subjects of either gender. In a third study, women responded with more defense of self-esteem when threatened with failure on a test of "interdependent thinking" than on a test of "independent thinking," whereas men showed the reverse pattern. These results suggest that self-esteem is linked more to interdependence in women and independence in men.

Two studies by Wood and her colleagues (Wood et al., 1997) also suggest that there are gender differences in the standards that people use in evaluating the self, but only for people who aspire to meet society's gender ideals. In one of their studies (Wood et al., Study 2), men and women viewed slides depicting communal relationships or dominant relationships, and imagined themselves in the scene depicted. Participants for whom traditional gender ideals were personally important had more positive affect, and fewer discrepancies between their actual and ideal selves when imagining themselves in the gender congruent relationships (dominant relationships for men and communal relationships for women). Participants for whom traditional gender ideals were of only moderate or low relevance generally did not show these effects.

Evidence of racial or ethnic differences in the bases of self-esteem has also appeared from time to time. For example, White Americans' self-esteem is more strongly correlated with self-efficacy than is the case among African Americans, whereas African Americans' self-esteem is more strongly correlated with religiousness than is the case among White Americans (Blaine & Crocker, 1995; St. George & McNamara, 1984). The self-esteem of African Americans may be based less on approval and regard from others than is the case for European Americans. In a study of collective self-esteem among Black, White, and Asian college students, Crocker et al. (1994) found that feelings of regard for one's racial group were strongly correlated with beliefs about how others regard one's racial group for both White and Asian college students, but were uncorrelated among Black college students, consistent with the idea that Black students' self-esteem is less likely to depend on the approval or regard they receive from others.

Wolfe, Crocker, Coon, and Luhtanen (1999) directly measured the degree to which students base their self-esteem on others' approval. European American students were most likely to base their self-esteem on approval from others, followed by Asian American students, and African American students were least likely to base their self-esteem on approval from others. These group differences in basing self-esteem on others' approval have now been replicated in a number of college student samples (Wolfe et al., 1999). Similar effects were found in a sample of women ranging in age from 18 to 90 recruited at a downtown mall in Buffalo, NY (Kerr, Crocker, & Broadnax, 1995). Again, African American women scored significantly lower on a three-item version of the Wolfe et al. (1999) scale than did the European American women.

These collective representations about what makes a person worthwhile influence the meaning of events for stigmatized and nonstigmatized individuals. For example, for those whose self-esteem is based on God's love rather than others' approval, situations in which others are prejudiced may have very different meaning than they do for people whose self-worth is highly contingent on others' approval. For those whose self-esteem is based on school competency, testing situations may have very different meaning than they do for people whose self-esteem is less contingent on school competency.

Constructing the Consequences of Devalued Identities

How do these various collective representations shape the experience and behavior of the stigmatized in particular situations? In the next sections of this chapter, we consider research on self-esteem, performance on academic tests, and self-objectification, that illustrates that these collective representations interact with subtle features of situations to create, or eliminate, psychological differences between stigmatized and nonstigmatized individuals.

Self-esteem

Self-esteem refers to a global judgment about the worth or value of the self (Rosenberg, 1979). To many people who do not have a negative social identity conferred by a stigma, it can seem obvious, even inevitable, that the stigmatized are low in self-esteem (Jones et al., 1984). This assumption is shared by many psychologists. For example, Cartwright (1950) argued that, "The group to which a person belongs serves as a primary determinant of his self-esteem. To a considerable extent, personal feelings of worth depend on the social evaluation of the group with which a person is identified. Self-hatred and feelings of worthlessness tend to arise from membership in underprivileged or outcast groups" (p. 440).

Yet, empirical research on the consequences of having a devalued identity has been inconsistent. Comparisons of average levels of self-esteem among stigmatized and nonstigmatized groups have yielded conflicting results (Crocker & Major, 1989). For example, studies comparing the self-esteem of African Americans to that of Americans of European descent typically report either no difference, or higher self-esteem in African Americans (Gray-Little & Hafdahl, 2000; Porter & Washington, 1979; Rosenberg, 1965). Studies of gender differences in self-esteem typically find no differences, or very small differences favoring males (Maccoby & Jacklin, 1974; Major, Barr, Zubek, & Babey, 1999). Studies comparing self-esteem in obese and nonobese populations also typically find no differences or very small differences (Friedman & Brownell, 1995; Miller & Downey, 1999).

In almost all of these studies, self-esteem is conceptualized as a stable trait that is consistent across situations, rather than as a psychological state. Consistent with some other self-esteem researchers (e.g., Heatherton & Polivy, 1991; Leary & Downs, 1995), we (Crocker, 1999; Crocker & Quinn, in press; Crocker & Wolfe, 1999) have argued that self-esteem is not a stable characteristic that individuals bring with them to situations, but rather that feelings of self-worth, self-regard, and self-respect are constructed in the situation. People bring a set of beliefs, values, and standards to the situations in which they find themselves. When positive or negative events happen, self-esteem depends on the meaning those events have for the self, which depends, in turn, on the individual's chronically accessible beliefs, attitudes, and values (see Schwarz & Strack, 1999, for a discussion).

Attributions to prejudice and self-esteem.   A study illustrating this situational construction of self-esteem in the stigmatized was conducted by Crocker and her colleagues (Crocker, Voelkl, Testa, & Major, 1991, Study 2). In that study, African American and European American students received information that another student (always European American and the same sex as the participant) either was or was not interested in becoming friends with them. Participants believed that the European American student either was or was not aware of their race, because the blinds on a one-way mirror were either up (other aware of race) or down (other unaware of race). The feedback had little impact on the self-esteem of European American students. For African American students, however, the effect of the feedback on self-esteem depended on whether students believed the other person (the evaluator) was aware of their race or not. When the blinds were down (other unaware of race), the self-esteem of African American students went up following positive feedback and down following negative feedback, as expected. When the blinds were up, however, self-esteem was unaffected by negative feedback, and went down following positive feedback. Examination of the degree to which the students thought the other's reactions to them reflected prejudice and racism suggested why this was the case. The feedback was more likely to be attributed to prejudice when it was negative, and when the blinds were up. Thus, self-esteem was buffered when negative feedback was received, if the blinds were up and the feedback could be attributed to prejudice rather than one's own flaws. The typical boost in self-esteem from positive feedback, however, was reversed when it was attributed to prejudice, rather than one's own qualities.

In the present context, two points can be made about this study. First, it is clear from this and other research that African Americans have collective representations about the prejudice and racism of White Americans, and these beliefs affect the meaning and implications for self-esteem of positive and negative feedback from Whites. Second, a rather subtle variation in the situation (whether the blinds on the mirror were up or down), rendered these beliefs about prejudice relevant (blinds up) or irrelevant (blinds down) for interpreting the meaning of the positive and negative feedback.

Not all researchers have found that attributing negative feedback to an evaluator's prejudice is self-protective. For example, Ruggiero and Taylor (1997) found that women who received a negative evaluation from a man showed higher performance self-esteem, but lower social self-esteem when they attributed the evaluation to his prejudice against women. Again, however, these results are likely dependent on the collective representations that participants bring with them to this situation. For example, many women (and men) endorse gender stereotypes (Swim, 1995), so the women in the Ruggiero and Taylor study may have believed that the man's prejudice was justified. Furthermore, the women likely had self-esteem that was based more on others' approval than did the African American students in Crocker et al.'s study. These explanations for the discrepant results suggest that the collective representations that the stigmatized bring to situations are multidimensional and complex, and predicting the responses of the stigmatized to these situations requires a full understanding of these complexities.

Beliefs about biased tests and self-esteem.   Similar to beliefs about individual prejudice and discrimination are beliefs about institutional bias, such as testing instruments that are biased against Blacks. A series of studies by Major and her colleagues (Major, Spencer, Schmader, Wolfe, & Crocker, 1998) demonstrates the influence of subtle contextual features on self-esteem among African American students taking a test. In one study (Major et al., 1998, Study 2), Black and White students took an intellectual test. For students in one condition of the experiment, race was never mentioned by the experimenter. For the other half of the students, the experimenter mentioned that one purpose of the research was to find out if the test was racially biased. Students then received information that they had done poorly on the test, and their self-esteem was measured. In the condition in which race was never mentioned by the experimenter, Black students' self-esteem following failure was lower than was that of White students. When the possibility that the test could be biased had been mentioned by the experimenter, however, the Black students' self-esteem was higher than was that of White students. Thus, the impact of poor test performance on self-esteem depended on the collective representations about biased tests that Black students brought with them to the testing situation, and features of the situation that made the beliefs salient or not.

Ideology and self-esteem.   Another type of collective representation that may affect the meaning of situations for the stigmatized and nonstigmatized is ideologies, or widely shared cultural values. The values may be so widely shared and unquestioned that people are not even aware that they represent ideologies, or are not shared by people in different cultures. None the less, these ideologies and cultural values provide an important standard against which the self is evaluated, and hence can be a source of high or low self-esteem (Greenberg, Pyszczynski, & Solomon, 1986; Greenberg et al., 1993). The stigmatized are particularly likely to fall short when evaluated in the context of these ideologies and cultural values – indeed, people with particular social identities may be stigmatized *because* they are perceived as not measuring up to these ideologies and shared values (see Crocker et al., 1998, for a discussion).

As noted previously, one of the dominant ideologies in the United States is individualism (Kleugel & Smith, 1981, 1986). Individualism encompasses a variety of beliefs and values, all focused on personal responsibility, freedom, and the power of individuals to work autonomously and achieve their goals. Although this ideology, on the face of it, has nothing to do with body shape or size, endorsement of the Protestant ethic and related notions of personal responsibility are associated with attitudes toward the overweight. Crandall (1994) demonstrated that the belief that being fat results from a lack of willpower is part of a larger system of beliefs about personal responsibility, including conservative political leanings, belief in a just world, and endorsement of the Protestant ethic. This link between individualistic ideology and anti-fat attitudes, especially willpower beliefs, suggests that individualistic ideologies may provide a frame by which the overweight evaluate themselves, and consequently affects their self-esteem. Although endorsement of individualism may be positively related to self-esteem among those who are relatively successful, it may be negatively related to self-esteem in the overweight. Indeed, a study of 257 female undergraduates at the University of Michigan revealed exactly this pattern (Quinn & Crocker, 1999, Study 1).

Although ideologies such as the Protestant ethic may be endorsed by many people in our culture, competing ideologies, such as egalitarianism, are also widely endorsed (e.g., Katz, 1981). Consequently, whether the Protestant ethic is used as a standard against which the stigmatized evaluate themselves may depend on features of the situation that make the Protestant ethic, or competing, more inclusive ideologies salient. We investigated this hypothesis in the context of the stigma of being overweight (Quinn & Crocker, in press, Study 2).

In this study, women who rated themselves as overweight or normal weight in a pretest at the beginning of the semester were recruited for a study of comprehension and mood effects of media messages (Quinn & Crocker, in press, Study 2). The salience of the Protestant ethic was manipulated by having women read a political speech. For half of the women, the speech emphasized the values of the Protestant ethic (e.g., "America is a country where people can stand proud on their accomplishments. Self-reliance and self-discipline are the cornerstones of this country"). For the remaining women, the speech emphasized inclusiveness (e.g., "America is a country in which we strive to combine our differences into unity . . . A country whose divergent but harmonizing communities are a reflection of our deeper community values . . .") which was taken from Ronald Reagan's 1988 State of the Union address. After reading the speech, women rated it on a number of measures included to support the cover story. Then, all women read a "newspaper article" about the negative social experiences of the overweight. This latter message was included to ensure that all women were focused on their weight and the negative consequences of being overweight. Dependent measures included several state measures of psychological well-being, including the Rosenberg (1965) self-esteem inventory modified to reflect momentary feelings about the self. The results showed that in the Protestant ethic condition, overweight women had lower self-esteem than did normal weight women, whereas in the inclusive message condition, the difference between overweight and normal weight women did not approach significance. Taken together, these studies on ideology and the psychological well-being of overweight women indicate that the self-esteem of women who are overweight, or think they are, depends on the collective representations that are salient.

In sum, research on self-esteem in people with devalued identities has tended to assume that self-esteem is a trait that is consistent across situations and social contexts, and that being devalued necessarily results in low self-esteem. In contrast, the very recent studies reviewed here indicate that self-esteem is best conceived as a psychological state, and that self-esteem in the stigmatized depends jointly on the collective representations they bring to situations, and features of the situation that make those collective representations relevant or not. Whether the stigmatized are high or low in self-esteem will depend greatly on the situations in which they find themselves.

Note that in this view some stigmatized people may have consistently low (i.e., traitlike) self-esteem across time, if they have internalized ideologies that devalue their worth, or if they chronically find themselves in situations that devalue them. However, in our view these individuals could experience high self-esteem if alternative, more accepting ideologies were made highly salient, or if they were able to escape the devaluing situation.

Test performance

Members of stigmatized groups, particularly ethnic minorities and women, consistently tend to underperform on tests of at least some types of academic abilities. As noted, differences in test performance have been explained in terms of genetics and socialization, and both of these explanations view testing differences as relatively stable. However, until recently the testing situation itself was rarely seen as differentially affecting stigmatized and nonstigmatized groups. Stereotypes about stigmatized groups remain well known in the culture (Devine, 1989). Even though no overt act of discrimination or stereotyping may take place, those who are devalued bring their collective representations of stereotypes into testing situations with them. Knowledge of the stereotypes – and whether they could be applied to the self – may affect performance when the stereotypes are salient and/or applicable. A testing situation may have very different meanings for the stigmatized and non-stigmatized.

Stereotype threat.   Recently, Claude Steele and his colleagues (Steele, 1997; Steele & Aronson, 1995; Spencer, Steele, & Quinn, 1999) have described a type of situation or "predicament" in which a member of a stereotyped group is in a situation in which he or she could confirm the negative stereotype through personal behavior. They have called this type of situation a "stereotype threat" situation. Stereotype threat theory predicts that although members of stigmatized and nonstigmatized groups may be in the same situation, such as taking a standardized test, the situation has different meaning for the stigmatized and nonstigmatized, and, consequently, different outcomes.

Recent research has examined the consequences of stereotype threat for test performance. Steele and Aronson (1995) gave a standardized test to African American and European American college students. Half of the students were told that the purpose of the test was to gauge verbal ability (diagnostic condition), whereas the other half were told the purpose was simply to better understand problem solving (nondiagnostic condition). When the participants believed the test to be diagnostic, African American students performed worse than European American students – just as is seen on standardized tests such as the SAT and GRE. However, when the same test was described as nondiagnostic, African American and European American students performed equally well on the test. Using similar methods, Quinn and Spencer (1996) altered the perceived diagnosticity of a math test for men and women students with equal math backgrounds. When the test was perceived as diagnostic, women underperformed. When the same test was perceived as nondiagnostic, women and men performed equally. Brown and Josephs (1999) manipulated whether a diagnostic test was described as diagnosing whether a student was exceptionally strong or exceptionally weak at math. Brown and Josephs hypothesized that if women were most concerned with the possibility of confirming the negative stereotype about their math ability, they should perform worse when the test was described as diagnostic of weakness at math, than when it was described as diagnostic of strength. This is exactly what was found. Men, however, showed a reverse pattern of effects. The effects of describing a test to be diagnostic or nondiagnostic of intellectual ability have also been shown to affect those of low socio-economic status in France (Croizet & Claire, 1998).

These studies demonstrate that it is not immutable differences in ability, but rather something about the testing situation, in this case, the threat of one's ability being judged, that affects group differences in performance. In order to show that it is the devalued identity that is interacting with the situation, a variety of studies have manipulated the salience of the stereotyped identity. Steele and Aronson (1995) gave African Americans and European Americans a standardized test, which was described as nondiagnostic for all participants. Immediately before the test, participants answered several demographic questions. For half of the participants, the final demographic question concerned their race, whereas for the other half of the participants this question was omitted. With just this small change in the situation, this subtle reminder of identity, the African Americans performed worse than the European Americans.

Research on women, who are stereotyped to be inferior at math, has shown that gender differences in performance can be eliminated when a test is described as gender-fair—thereby removing the applicability of the stereotype to a particular testing situation (Spencer et al., 1999). Research by Levy (1996) found that when the elderly were primed with a negative stereotype about the elderly they performed worse on a memory test than if primed with a positive stereotype. Shih, Pittinsky, and Ambady (1999) have nicely demonstrated that it is the particular social identity that is salient in a situation that affects test performance. Although most studies have concentrated on the one identity that is devalued, Shih et al. examined participants who had both an identity connected with a positive stereotype about math ability – Asian Americans – and a negative stereotype about math ability – women. Shih et al. had Asian American women take a quantitative test. Before the test participants completed a questionnaire which made their female identity salient, their Asian identity salient, or neither identity salient. Results showed that the women scored the highest on the test when their Asian identity was salient, intermediate when no identity was salient, and the lowest when their female identity was made salient.

These dramatic effects on performance with just small changes in the situation show that the consequences of having a devalued identity are constructed within the situation. The fact that performance differences can so easily be eradicated demonstrates that differences in performance on tests of intellectual ability are not caused by genetic or deeply internalized differences. Instead, it seems that the testing situation has different meanings for those in stigmatized and nonstigmatized groups.

Research on stereotype threat has examined the meaning of the testing situation by assessing some of the cognitions accessible in stereotype threat situations. For example, using the diagnostic paradigm described above, Steele and Aronson (1995) gave participants a word fragment completion task in which fragments could be completed either with words related to the African American stereotype or not. Results showed that African Americans in the diagnostic condition had more stereotypical completions than any other group. Because this was a situation in which they could be judged in the light of a negative stereotype, the meaning of the situation – literally what was on their mind – was quite different for the African American and European American students. Spencer et al. (1999), in a study described previously, found that women felt more anxiety than men in the stereotype threat condition. Stangor, Carr, and Kiang (1998) showed that when women were told that they were about to work on a task in which men performed better than women, earlier positive feedback about their performance was undermined, and their task expectations were lowered. Taken together, these studies suggest that in situations in which a negative stereotype could be used to judge one's performance, members of stigmatized groups experience the situation quite differently than nonstigmatized people – in such a situation, stereotypes about their group can be activated, they may feel more anxious, previous positive experiences in the domain may be undermined, and their performance may suffer.

One might wonder how individual members of groups that are the targets of negative ability stereotypes ever learn to do well on academic tasks, if they are constantly exposed to stereotype threatening testing contexts. However, research on stereotype threat indicates that it takes a toll on performance only under very specific circumstances: When the individual is highly identified with the domain being tested (e.g., Aronson, Lustina, Keough, Steele, & Brown, 1999); when the content of the test is at the very limits of the person's ability, as when college freshmen take the advanced GRE exam in mathematics (e.g., Spencer et al., 1999), and when the negative stereotype is salient (e.g., Steele & Aronson, 1995). Thus, stereotype threat is not likely to be a constant in the lives of stigmatized groups. Rather, it is likely to occur when one moves to a new level of difficulty in some domain, as in the transition from high school to college, or the transition from college to graduate school.

Self-objectification.   In addition to the activation of stereotypes related to ability, women's test performance may be affected by their devalued identity in a different way. One way women are devalued is through sexual objectification. Objectification theory, proposed by Fredrickson and Roberts (1997), argues that in American culture there is a very strong and constant focus on women's bodies. In the media and in face-to-face contact, women are often objectified – that is they are reduced to being just their bodies. Fredrickson and Roberts hypothesize that because of this focus on bodies, girls and women learn to self-objectify, or to view their own bodies from a third-person perspective. That is, women learn to monitor their outward appearance, to be especially concerned with others' perceptions of their appearance, and to be more preoccupied with how their body looks than what it can do. Maintaining this third-person perspective on the body may have a number of negative consequences, including increased body shame, restrained eating, and disrupted attention. If women are distracted by thoughts about how they appear to others, they cannot devote their full attention to the task at hand. Although there are differences at the trait level to the extent that people, both men and women, self-objectify (Fredrickson, Roberts, Noll, Quinn, & Twenge, 1998), some situations may also induce self-objectification. Because the negative consequences of objectification are particularly strong for women, a self-objectifying situation will have very different meanings for men and women, and one consequence of those different meanings may be disrupted performance for women.

Fredrickson et al. (1998) brought men and women into a lab and had them try on either a swimsuit or sweater, in private. While wearing either the swimsuit or the sweater, participants were asked to look at themselves in a full-length mirror and to think about how they would feel about wearing the garment in public. They were also asked to take a math test while wearing the garment. It was hypothesized that all participants in the swimsuits would view themselves in a self-objectifying manner, but that this would have a very different meaning and different consequences for the women compared to men. Results showed that although both men and women described themselves more in terms of their bodies when in the swimsuit compared to the sweater, only the women in the swimsuit felt increased body shame, revulsion, and disgust with themselves. In addition, women in the swimsuit performed worse on the math test than any of the other three groups. Thus, although both men and women were in the same situation – trying on either a swimsuit or a sweater – this situation had very different meanings and consequences for women and men. For women, feeling objectified led to increased feelings of shame about their bodies, and decreased cognitive resources available to devote to the math test, resulting in worse performance.

In order to demonstrate that self-objectification disrupts performance by consuming cognitive resources, Fredrickson and Quinn (1999) conducted a second study in which participants – in this case all women – were again asked to try on a swimsuit or a sweater. Instead of taking a math test, participants performed a modified Stroop task in which they pronounced the color of words that appeared on a computer screen. Their reaction times to pronounce the words were recorded. Results showed that when wearing the swimsuit, as compared to the sweater, participants were slower to pronounce the words – regardless of whether the words were body related or neutral. Based on these results, it seems that for women being in a state of self-objectification leads to having fewer cognitive resources to devote to the task at hand. Thus, in this case, the consequences of having a devalued identity are unrelated to the content of the devalued identity, but none the less are situationally detrimental.

Implications and conclusions

The studies described here were not designed to test the notion that the effects of stigma on self-esteem depend on the collective representations that the stigmatized bring to the situation, and features of the situation that make those collective representations relevant or not. None the less, the pattern of results across these studies seems very consistent with this view. The consequences of social stigma for self-esteem and performance on intellectual tests are not deeply internalized and immutable, but rather depend on features of the situation – sometimes very subtle features – that alter the meaning of that situation. Furthermore, they demonstrate that what appears to be the same situation in an objective sense may be subjectively experienced very differently, and have very different meanings, implications for self-esteem, and consequences for intellectual performance, for people with valued and devalued identities. Some important implications for the study of social stigma follow from this perspective.

First, understanding the experience of the stigmatized requires that we understand the collective representations that the stigmatized bring with them to situations. Research on the experience of the stigmatized should not only document the collective representations that the stigmatized and nonstigmatized bring with them to situations, but should also explore how those collective representations affect the meaning of situations for the stigmatized and nonstigmatized. We cannot assume that the same situation will mean the same thing for stigmatized and nonstigmatized people.

Second, our analysis suggests that the experience of disadvantaged, devalued, or stigmatized groups cannot be understood by creating stigmatized identities or minimal groups in the laboratory. Such studies strip away the shared beliefs and values that the stigmatized bring with them that give situations their meaning. In the present analysis, the effects of stigma are crucially dependent on those collective representations.

Third, this analysis suggests that stigmatization and its consequences do not require the immediate presence of prejudiced individuals. Because collective representations are widely known and shared among the stigmatized, it is not necessary for a prejudiced person to communicate the devaluation of the stigmatized for that devaluation to be felt. The stigmatized bring with them to situations collective representations that may devalue them, as the Protestant ethic devalues the overweight, or deflect devaluation, as awareness of prejudice and system blame may for African American students.

Recursive effects.   We also want to emphasize that there is a recursive aspect to the consequences of stigma that is not captured by the laboratory experiments described here. Specifically, although the consequences of stigma are constructed in the situation as a joint function of the collective representations the stigmatized bring to bear in those situations and features of the situation that make those collective representations relevant or irrelevant, it is also true that experiences the stigmatized have in these situations can affect their collective representations. Thus, there is a loop from collective representations to meaning of situations back to collective representations. For example, when stigmatized individuals attribute a rejection to prejudice against them, this may in turn inform the individual's beliefs about the degree of prejudice against their group among nonstigmatized individuals.

Long-term consequences of stigma.   Our analysis has emphasized the temporary consequences of social stigma that are constructed in the immediate social situation, as a function of the meaning that situation has for the stigmatized person. We believe that this perspective remedies a tendency in the social sciences to assume that the experience of having a devalued identity necessarily leads to internalization of that devaluation and to distortions in the character of the stigmatized. However, it is crucially important to recognize that these transient consequences may ultimately have important long-term consequences. For example, as Steele (1997) has noted, the effects of stereotype threat on performance on intellectual tests may lead talented students to disidentify with school, or with a domain of academic such as mathematics. This disidentification may, in turn, increase the likelihood that these students will drop out of their major, or drop out of school altogether. Thus, to say that these consequences are constructed in the situation in no way suggests that they are trivial.

REFERENCES

Allon, N. (1982). The stigma of overweight in everyday life. In B. Wolman (Ed.), *Psychological aspects of obesity: A handbook* (pp. 130–174). New York: Van Nostrand Reinhold.

Allport, G. (1954). *The nature of prejudice.* New York: Doubleday Anchor Books.

Archer, D. (1985). Social deviance. In G. Lindzey & E. Aronson (Eds.), *Handbook of social psychology* (3rd ed., Vol. 2, pp. 743–804). New York: Random House.

Aronson, J., Lustina, M. J., Keough, K., Steele, C. M., & Brown, J. (1999). When White men can't do math: Necessary and sufficient factors in stereotype threat. *Journal of Experimental Social Psychology*, *35*, 29–46.

Baumeister, R. F. (1998). The self. In D. Gilbert, S. T. Fiske, & G. Lindzey (Eds.), *Handbook of social psychology* (4th ed., Vol. 2, pp. 680–740). Boston, MA: McGraw-Hill.

Becker, G., & Arnold, A. (1986). Stigma as a social and cultural construction. In S. C. Ainlay, G. Becker, & L. Coleman (Eds.), *The dilemma of difference: A multidisciplinary view of stigma* (pp. 39–57). New York: Plenum.

Benbow, C. P., & Stanley, J. C. (1980). Sex differences in mathematical ability: Fact or artifact? *Science*, *210*, 1262–1264.

Blaine, B., & Crocker, J. (1995). Religiousness, race, and psychological well being. Exploring social psychological mediators. *Personality and Social Psychology Bulletin*, *21*, 1031–1041.

Brown, R. P., & Josephs, R. A. (1999). A burden of proof: Stereotype relevance and gender differences in math performance. *Journal of Personality and Social Psychology*, *76*(2), 246–257.

Cartwright, D. (1950). Emotional dimensions of group life. In M. L. Raymert (Ed.), *Feelings and emotions* (pp. 439–447). New York: McGraw-Hill.

Crandall, C. S. (1994). Prejudice against fat people: Ideology and self-interest. *Journal of Personality and Social Psychology*, *66*(5), 882–894.

Crocker, J. (1999). Social stigma and self-esteem: Situational construction of self-worth. *Journal of Experimental Social Psychology*, *35*(1), 89–107.

Crocker, J., Luhtanen, R., Blaine, B., & Broadnax, S. (1994). Collective self-esteem and psychological well being among White, Black, and Asian college students. *Personality and Social Psychology Bulletin*, *20*, 502–513.

Crocker, J., Luhtanen, R., Broadnax, S., & Blaine, B. (1999). Belief in U.S. government conspiracies against Blacks: Powerlessness or system blame. *Personality and Social Psychology Bulletin*, *25*, 941–953.

Crocker, J., & Major, B. (1989). Social stigma and self-esteem: The self-protective properties of stigma. *Psychological Review*, *96*, 608–630.

Crocker, J., Major, B., & Steele, C. (1998). Social stigma. In D. Gilbert, S. T. Fiske, & G. Lindzey (Eds.), *The handbook of social psychology* (4th ed., Vol. 2, pp. 504–553). New York: McGraw Hill.

Crocker, J., & Quinn, D. M. (in press). Social stigma and the self: Meanings, situations, and self-esteem. To appear in T. Heatherton, R. Kleck, & J. Hull (Eds.), *Stigma*. New York: Guilford Press.

Crocker, J., & Wolfe, C. T. (1999). *Contingencies of self-esteem*. Manuscript under review, University of Michigan, Ann Arbor.

Crocker, J., Voelkl, K., Testa, M., & Major, B. (1991). Social stigma: The affective consequences of attributional ambiguity. *Journal of Personality and Social Psychology*, *60*, 218–228.

Croizet, J., & Claire, T. (1998). Extending the concept of stereotype threat to social class: The intellectual underperformance of students from low socioeconomic backgrounds. *Personality and Social Psychology Bulletin*, *24*(6), 588–594.

Crosby, F. (1982). *Relative deprivation and working women*. New York: Oxford University Press.

Crosby, F. (1984). The denial of personal discrimination. *American Behavioral Scientist*, *27*, 371–386.

Cross, S. E., & Madson, L. (1997). Models of the self: Self-construals and gender. *Psychological Bulletin*, *122*(1), 5–37.

D'Emilio, J. (1983). *Sexual politics, sexual communities: The making of a homosexual minority in the United States: 1940–1979*. Chicago, IL: University of Chicago Press.

Devine, P. G. (1989). Stereotypes and prejudice: Their automatic and controlled components. *Journal of Personality and Social Psychology, 56,* 5–18.

Fredrickson, B. L., & Quinn, D. M. (1999). *Sex differences in self-objectification and use of cognitive resources.* Manuscript in preparation. University of Michigan.

Fredrickson, B. L., & Roberts, T. (1997). Objectification theory: Toward understanding women's lived experiences and mental health risks. *Psychology of Women Quarterly, 21,* 173–206.

Fredrickson, B. L., Roberts, T., Noll, S. M., Quinn, D. M., & Twenge, J. M. (1998). That swimsuit becomes you: Sex differences in self-objectification, restrained eating, and math performance. *Journal of Personality and Social Psychology, 75*(1), 269–284.

Friedman, M. A., & Brownell, K. D. (1995). Psychological correlates to obesity: Moving to the next research generation. *Psychological Bulletin, 117*(1), 3–20.

Frome, P. M., & Eccles, J. S. (1998). Parents' influence on children's achievement-related perceptions. *Journal of Personality and Social Psychology, 74*(2), 435–452.

Gaertner, S. L., & Dovidio, J. F. (1986). The aversive form of racism. In J. F. Dovidio & S. L. Gaertner (Eds.), *Prejudice discrimination, and racism* (pp. 61–89). San Diego, CA: Academic Press.

Gibbons, F. X. (1981). The social psychology of mental retardation: What's in a label? In S. S. Brehm, S. M. Kassin, & F. X. Gibbons (Eds.), *Developmental social psychology* (pp. 249–270). New York: Oxford University Press.

Goffman, E. (1963). *Stigma: Notes on the management of spoiled identity.* Englewood Cliffs, NJ: Prentice-Hall.

Gray-Little, B., & Hafdahl, A. R. (2000). Factors influencing racial comparisons of self-esteem: A quantitative review. *Psychological Bulletin, 126,* 26–54.

Greenberg, J., Pyszczynski, T., & Solomon, S. (1986). The causes and consequences of a need for self-esteem: A terror management theory. In R. F. Baumeister (Ed.), *Public self and private self.* New York: Springer-Verlag.

Greenberg, J., Pyszczynski, T., Solomon, S., Pinel, E. et al. (1993). Effects of self-esteem on vulnerability-denying defensive distortions: Further evidence of an anxiety-buffering function of self-esteem. *Journal of Experimental Social Psychology, 29,* 229–251.

Harris, M. B., Waschull, S., & Walters, L. (1990). Feeling fat: Motivations, knowledge, and attitudes of overweight women and men. *Psychological Reports, 67,* 1191–1202.

Harter, S. (1986). Processes underlying the construction, maintenance, and enhancement of the self-concept in children. In J. Suls & A. G. Greenwald (Eds.), *Psychological perspectives on the self* (Vol. 3, pp. 136–182). Hillsdale, NJ: Erlbaum.

Heatherton, T. F., & Polivy, J. (1991). Development and validation of a scale from measuring state self-esteem. *Journal of Personality and Social Psychology, 60,* 895–910.

Jacobs, J. E., & Eccles, J. S. (1992). The impact of mothers' gender-role stereotypic beliefs on mothers' and children's ability perceptions. *Journal of Personality and Social Psychology, 63*(6), 932–944.

Jarvie, G. J., Lahey, B., Graziano, W., & Framer, E. (1983). Childhood obesity and social stigma: What we know and what we don't know. *Developmental Review, 3,* 237–273.

Jones, E. E., Farina, A., Hastorf, A. H., Markus, H., Miller, D. T., & Scott, R. A. (1984). *Social stigma: The psychology of marked relationships.* New York: Freeman.

Josephs, R. A., Markus, H. R., & Tafarodi, R. W. (1992). Gender and self-esteem. *Journal of Personality and Social Psychology, 63,* 391–402.

Jost, J. T., & Banaji, M. R. (1994). The role of stereotyping in system-justification and the production of false consciousness. *British Journal of Social Psychology, 33,* 1–27.

Katz, I. (1981). *Stigma: A social-psychological perspective.* Hillsdale, NJ: Erlbaum.

Kemis, M. H., & Waschull, S. B. (1995). The interactive roles of stability and level of self-esteem: Research and theory. In M. P. Zanna (Ed.), *Advances in experimental social psychology* (Vol. 27, pp. 93–141). San Diego, CA: Academic Press.

Kerr, K., Crocker, J., & Broadnax, S. (1995, August). *Feeling fat and feeling depressed: The stigma of overweight in Black and White women.* Paper presented at the annual meeting of the American Psychological Association, New York.

Kluegel, J. R., & Smith, E. R. (1981). Beliefs about stratification. *Annual Review of Sociology, 7,* 29–56.

Kluegel, J. R., & Smith, E. R. (1986). *Beliefs about inequality: Americans' view of what is and what ought to be.* Hawthorne, NJ: Aldine de Gruyer.

Leary, M. R., & Downs, D. L. (1995). Interpersonal functions of the self-esteem motive: The self-esteem system as sociometer. In M. Kernis (Ed.), *Efficacy, agency, and self-esteem* (pp. 123–144). New York: Plenum.

Lerner, R. M., Orlos, J. B., & Knapp, J. R. (1976). Physical attractiveness, physical effectiveness, and self-concept in late adolescents. *Adolescence, 11*(43), 313–326.

Levy, B. (1996). Improving memory in old age through implicit self-stereotyping. *Journal of Personality and Social Psychology, 71,* 1092–1107.

Link, B. G. (1987). Understanding labeling effects in the area of mental disorders: An assessment of the effects of expectations of rejection. *American Sociological Review, 52,* 96–112.

Maccoby, E. E., & Jacklin, C. N. (1974). *The psychology of sex differences.* Stanford, CA: Stanford University Press.

Major, B., Barr, L., Zubek, J., & Babey, S. H. (1999). Gender and self-esteem: A meta-analysis. In W. B. Swan, J. H. Langlois, & L. A. Gilbert (Eds.), *Sexism and stereotypes in modern society: The gender science of Janet Taylor Spence* (pp. 223–253). Washington, DC: American Psychological Association.

Major, B., & Crocker, J. (1994). Social stigma: The affective consequences of attributional ambiguity. In D. M. Mackie & D. L. Hamilton (Eds.), *Affect, cognition, and stereotyping: Interactive processes in intergroup perception* (pp. 345–370). New York: Academic Press.

Major, B., Spencer, S. J., Schmader, T., Wolfe, C. T., & Crocker, J. (1998). Coping with negative stereotypes about intellectual performance: The role of psychological disengagement. *Personality and Social Psychology Bulletin, 24*(1), 34–50.

Markus, H., & Oyserman, D. (1989). Gender and thought: The role of the self-concept. In M. Crawford & M. Gentry (Eds.), *Gender and thought: Psychological perspectives* (pp. 100–127). New York: Springer-Verlag.

Miller, C., & Downey, K. T. (1999). A meta-analysis of heavyweight and self-esteem. *Personality and Social Psychology Review, 3,* 68–84.

Millman, M. (1980). *Such a pretty face: Being fat in America.* New York: Norton.

Nolen-Hoeksema, S. (1987). Sex differences in unipolar depression: Evidence and theory. *Psychological Bulletin, 101*(2), 259–282.

Ogbu, J. (1986). The consequences of the American caste system. In U. Neisser (Ed.), *The school achievement of minority children: New perspectives.* Hillsdale, NJ: Erlbaum.

Osbourne, J. W. (1995). Academics, self-esteem, and race: A look at the underlying assumptions of the disidentification hypothesis. *Personality and Social Psychology Bulletin, 21,* 449–455.

Porter, J. R., & Washington, R. E. (1979). Black identity and self-esteem: A few of studies of Black self-concept, 1968–1978. *Annual Review of Sociology, 5,* 53–74.

Quinn, D. M., & Crocker, J. (1999). When ideology hurts: Effects of feeling fat and the Protestant ethic on the psychological well being of women. *Journal of Personality and Social Psychology, 77,* 402–414.

Quinn, D. M., & Spencer, S. J. (1996, August). *Stereotype threat and the effect of test diagnosticity on women's math performance.* Paper presented at the annual American Psychological Association conference, Toronto, Canada.

Rosenberg, M. (1965). *Society and the adolescent self-image.* Princeton, NJ: Princeton University Press.

Rosenberg, M. (1979). *Conceiving the self.* New York: Basic Books.

Ruggiero, K. M., & Taylor, D. M. (1997). Why minority group members perceive or do not perceive the discrimination that confronts them: The role of self-esteem and perceived control. *Journal of Personality and Social Psychology*, 72(2), 373–389.

Schwarz, N., & Strack, F. (1999). Reports of subjective well being: Judgmental processes and their methodological implications. In E. D. D. Kahneman & N. Schwarz (Eds.), *Well-being: Foundations of hedonic psychology*. New York: Russell Sage.

Scott, R. A. (1969). *The making of blind men: A study of adult socialization*. New York: Russell Sage Foundation.

Shih, M., Pittinsky, T. L., & Ambady, N. (1999). Stereotype susceptibility: Identity salience and shifts in quantitative performance. *Psychological Science*, 10(1), 80–83.

Sidanius, J., & Pratto, F. (1993). The inevitability of oppression and the dynamics of social dominance. In P. M. Sniderman & P. E. Tetlock (Eds.), *Prejudice, politics, and the American dilemma* (pp. 173–211). Stanford, CA: Stanford University Press.

Solomon, H. M. (1986). Stigma and western culture: A historical approach. In S. C. Ainlay, G. Becker, & L. Coleman (Eds.), *The dilemma of difference: A multidisciplinary view of stigma* (pp. 59–76). New York: Plenum.

Spencer, S. J., Steele, C. M., & Quinn, D. M. (1999). Stereotype threat and women's math performance. *Journal of Experimental Social Psychology*, 35(1), 4–28.

St. George, A., & McNamara, P. H. (1984). Religion, race, and psychological well being. *Journal for the Scientific Study of Religion*, 23, 351–363.

Stangor, C., Carr, C., & Kiang, L. (1998). Activating stereotypes undermines task performance expectations. *Journal of Personality and Social Psychology*, 75(5), 1191–1197.

Steele, C. M. (1988). The psychology of self-affirmation: Sustaining the integrity of the self. In L. Berkowitz (Ed.), *Advances in experimental social psychology* (Vol. 21, pp. 261–302). San Diego, CA: Academic Press.

Steele, C. M. (1992, April). Race and the schooling of Black Americans. *The Atlantic Monthly*.

Steele, C. M. (1997). A threat in the air: How stereotypes shape intellectual identity and performance. *American Psychologist*, 52, 613–629.

Steele, C. M., & Aronson, J. (1995). Stereotype vulnerability and the intellectual test performance of African Americans. *Journal of Personality and Social Psychology*, 69, 797–811.

Steele, S. (1990). *The content of our character*. New York: St. Martin's press.

Swim, J. K., Aikin, K. J., Hall, W. S., & Hunter, B. A. (1995). Sexism and racism: Old-fashioned and modern prejudices. *Journal of Personality and Social Psychology*, 68, 199–214.

Taylor, D. M., Wright, S. C., & Porter, L. E. (1994). Dimensions of perceived discrimination: The personal/group discrimination discrepancy. In M. P. Zanna & J. M. Olson (Eds.), *The psychology of prejudice: The Ontario symposium* (Vol. 7, pp. 233–255). Hillsdale, NJ: Erlbaum.

Tesser, A. (1988). Toward a self-evaluation maintenance model of social behavior. In L. Berkowitz (Ed.), *Advances in experimental social psychology* (Vol. 21, pp. 181–227). San Diego, CA: Academic Press.

Weiner, B. (1995). *Judgments of responsibility: A foundation for a theory of social conduct*. New York: Guilford Press.

Weiner, B., Perry, R. P., & Magnusson, J. (1988). An attributional analysis of reactions to stigmas. *Journal of Personality and Social Psychology*, 55, 738–748.

Wolfe, C. T., Crocker, J., Coon, H., & Luhtanen, R. (1998). Manuscript in preparation, University of Michigan, Ann Arbor.

Wood, W., Christensen, N., Hebl, M. R., & Rothgerber, H. (1997). Conformity to sex-typed norms, affect, and the self-concept. *Journal of Personality and Social Psychology*, 73, 523–535.

Group Identities

Introduction

Analogous to the concept of identity as part of the individual self, *group identity* refers to the representation of a group or social category as a collective. Like social identity, collective identity has a two-sided meaning. On the one hand, it refers to the shared belief among members of a social category that they constitute a meaningful social group (a common in-group). On the other hand, it refers to the shared understanding of the meaning or definition of the group – the shared characteristics, values, or purposes that distinguish the in-group from other groups. In effect, this is the distinction between group identity as identification *with* a collective and group identity as the norms, values, and ideologies which that identification entails.

Group identity influences the self-concept of group members in two ways. First, when a group identity is engaged, the construal of self extends beyond the individual person to a more inclusive social unit. The boundaries between self and other group members are eclipsed by the greater salience of the boundaries between in-group and out-groups (Abrams & Hogg). The fortunes and misfortunes of the group as a whole are incorporated into the self and responded to as personal outcomes. Second, the attributes and behaviors of the individual self are assimilated to the representation of the group as a whole, enhancing those features that make the group distinctive from other social categories and at the same time enhancing uniformity and cohesion within the group.

Both definitions of group identity are necessary to understand the formation of groups and the nature of intragroup and intergroup processes. As an extension of the concept of self to the group level, collective identity motivates conformity to group norms, social attraction to fellow group members, acceptance of group leaders, and mobilization for collective action (Hogg; Reicher). Group identity also has a temporal, developmental aspect, which can be viewed in terms of the dynamic relationship between identity processes at the group level and personal identities of individuals within the group (Worchel & Coutant).

The content of group identity is often defined in contrast to or distinction from that of other groups. Thus, the formation and maintenance of a distinctive in-group identity is a function of the intergroup context in which the group is situated (Turner & Reynolds; Simon, Aufderheide, & Kampmeier). As a consequence, the study of the social psychology of group identity has been closely associated with the study of intergroup relations. As Turner and Reynolds point out, collective identification as an in-group does not necessarily imply antagonism toward or conflict with outgroups. Nonetheless, the preservation of group boundaries and maintenance of a positive in-group identity often plays a significant role in prejudice and hostility toward out-groups. By the same token, an understanding of the processes of social categorization and the need for positive group identity can be applied to the design of programs and policies to reduce prejudice and intergroup conflict (Brewer & Gaertner). Thus, the dynamic relation between intragroup and intergroup processes is a subject of considerable social significance in a pluralistic society.

CHAPTER SEVEN

Collective Identity: Group Membership and Self-conception

Dominic Abrams and Michael A. Hogg

No man is an island, entire of itself,
every man is a small piece of the Continent,
a part of the main.

Devotions, 17. John Donne 1624

William James (1890) distinguished between the "I" and the "Me." The "I" is the self as experienced, the active thinking processor. The "Me" is the stock of empirical information about oneself, which has material, social, and spiritual components. The self is a central concept in social psychology (Ashmore & Jussim, 1997; Baumeister, 1999; Dweck, 1999), reflecting in part the importance of the individual in modern society as a target for social influence and a unit of economic activity. However, much of the research activity only considers the self as an individual, and this misses an important part of James's analysis. James argued that, in principle, one has as many social selves as there are individuals who recognize one. In practice, these selves are determined by the groups of people about whose opinion one cares. James argued that people can change their persona to reflect the social audience. These transformations involve shifts of identity in different contexts, not merely forms of strategic self-presentation. James believed that the "club opinion" is a powerful psychological force. That is, there are times when we see ourselves wholly in terms of our representativeness of a group, and we embody the group's perspective as our own. The psychological connection between the self and social groups is the issue we examine in this chapter.

The small group is an obvious domain in which interpersonal and intragroup relationships interact dynamically with the self-concept (Abrams, 1992a; Hogg, in press c; Hogg & Williams, 2000). However, the physically present face-to-face small group context is by no means the only or the most important forum of social interaction and exchange. As individuals, we are encouraged to concentrate on the personal aspects of our lives in terms of idealized or iconic goals, and are consequently drawn away from the traditional framework of specific social commitments and networks (Elias, 1988). Greater access to communication technologies and transportation mean that cultural, ethnic, and geographic groups are less able to constrain their members or restrict access to alternative social perspectives. The "group," or more particularly the ingroup, is no longer restricted to specific social networks of known others. Groups can become represented in the self-concept through many channels. In the light of these social changes, how can social psychology make sense of the relationship between the social groups and the self, and to what extent is the notion of group relevant to the self-concept?

The present review concentrates mainly on the way social categorizations become a part of the self as social identifications (see Abrams & Hogg, 1990; Hogg & Abrams, 1988; Onorato & Turner, in press). The first section describes the historical divergence of sociological and psychological perspectives on the self. The second section describes the predominant perspective on self as an individual comparative entity and describes some taxonomic accounts of the self that distinguish between individual and collective components. The third section examines the social identity approach, which posits that the self-concept is a product of a self-categorization process. We explore the relationship between process-based flexibility and structural stability in the self, and the relationship between social and self-perception. The fourth and fifth sections consider the problem of individual variation and motivation, particularly the relationship between social identity and self-regulation, self-esteem and uncertainty.

Social Psychological Theory and the Self

How has social psychology regarded the role of groups, collectivities, and categories in psychological life? Some theorists have depicted society as a superordinate structure. For example, Wundt's Völkerpsychologie focused on, "those mental products which are created by a community of human life and are, therefore, inexplicable in terms merely of individual consciousness since they presuppose the reciprocal action of many" (Wundt, 1916, p. 3). Wundt regarded collective phenomena, such as language, religion, customs, and myth as social phenomena that could not be understood in terms of the psychology of the isolated individual (this being the province of experimental psychology). The conceptual distinction between the individual and society was also central to Durkheim's (1898) analysis of "social facts" and collective representations. Durkheim strongly believed that societal forces gave rise to collective meanings that were so powerful that they overrode any individual tendencies. Critically, these meanings were not the same as individual beliefs or perceptions, they had a life and force of their own. This non-reductionist analysis was of course a founding plank in sociology and one that, in the minds of many, continues to distinguish it from social psychology (Farr, 1996).

The power of the group is echoed by themes in Le Bon's (1896) analysis of the psychology of the crowd, but Le Bon as well as Tarde (1901), Trotter (1919), McDougall (1920), and Freud (1922) considered the crowd or group mind to be essentially primitive and uncontrolled. This view was attractive to theorists who wanted to explain the apparent irrationality, extremity, and baseness of collectives. However, the idea that the group could have, or generate, a psychological phenomenon that was not individual was incompatible with the views of psychologists such as Watson (1919) and Allport (1924) who wanted the discipline to adopt a strictly rational and scientific approach that focused on behavior rather than on concepts such as "mind."

The split between psychology and more sociological theories of social processes was accentuated with Floyd Allport's pronouncement that, "There is no psychology of groups which is not essentially and entirely a psychology of individuals" (Allport, 1924, p. 4; see Graumann, 1986). By 1925 sociology and psychology had become discrete disciplines (Manicas, 1987), and this meant that social psychology and the study of groups in psychology became separated from its collectivist past. As a result, different levels of analysis were not well articulated in theory and research (Doise, 1986).

According to Farr (1996), there are two social psychologies. The sociological form owes much to collectivist perspectives, and in an extreme form it regards psychological processes as barely relevant for explaining the impact of social categories and institutions on societal change and development. The psychological form is rooted in the behaviorism and reductionism of Watson and Floyd Allport. At its extreme, social categories, institutions, and roles are treated simply as factual inputs that individuals process, without much regard to the way the meaning of the categories is shaped by societal context (see Hopkins, Reicher, & Levine, 1997, for a contentious critique of the way psychologists treat race as a stimulus variable in social cognition research on prejudice).

The direction taken by social psychology throughout the following six decades suggests that, as far as most were concerned, Allport had won the day. For example, the idea that the group somehow dehumanizes us, stripping us of our identity and individuality, re-emerged in the form of deindividuation theory (Diener, 1980; Zimbardo, 1969). As a result, James's view that the group may be represented in the self (as distinct from simply influencing the self) was neglected in much of the theorizing that followed his writing (see Hogg & Abrams, 1988; Reicher, 1984; Tajfel, 1978). An individualistic meta-theoretical framework also pervaded the enormous arena of group dynamics, which was dominant from the 1940s to the 1960s (e.g., Cartwright & Zander, 1969; Shaw, 1981). Despite its roots in Lewin's potentially collectivist field theory (e.g., Lewin, 1952), group process research has largely been a study of interpersonal interaction in small face-to-face groups, in which "I" reigns supreme, and any reference to "we" is largely descriptive; "we" is simply an arithmetic aggregation (Hogg, 1992).

The symbolic interactionist agenda, focusing on interpersonal relations, came to dominate social psychological theorizing about the self. The uptake of concepts such as self-awareness and the perspective of the specific or generalized other (Cooley, 1902; Blumer, 1937; Mead, 1934) and the importance of role and self-presentation (Goffman, 1959) encouraged psychologists to focus on the small-scale interpersonal dynamics that provide feedback about the self and a basis for impression formation (Farr & Moscovici, 1984). Emerging from this sociological tradition are two major themes in the social psychology of the self. Self-awareness (either phenomenologically or in terms of the imagined perceptions of others) and self-evaluation (either for self-knowledge or self-maintenance; Festinger, 1954). Both themes have focused research on intra- or interpersonal situations, which are believed to provide the basis for individual self-concepts.

The symbolic interactionist framework was not without problems. For example one well-cited review found no strong link between people's self-concept and the way others actually perceived them. However, the association between self-concept and beliefs about others' perceptions of self was reasonably strong (Shrauger & Schoeneman, 1979). Perhaps the difficulty of capturing either the relevant set of "others" or the relevant measures of self-concept has led researchers to focus more on the way specific events or encounters can affect a specific self-evaluation. The social psychological analysis of self has tended to be parceled into different themes and effects (e.g. self-presentation, self-enhancement), quite unlike anything that might have been envisaged by theorists such as Mead. In sociological theory concepts such as role are part of a complexly patterned and highly organized system of social regulation of behavior that is widely shared and has long-term meaning and continuity. In contrast, social psychological operationalizations of the role concept have tended to focus on role enactment in terms of specific individual behaviors (e.g. Crocker & Luhtanen, 1990; Snyder, 1981; Wicklund & Gollwitzer, 1982) or to treat role as a general sense of obligation, duty, or commitment (e.g., Mowday, Steers, & Porter, 1979).

Self as a Comparative Entity

In social psychology, the dominant meta-theory remains one in which the self is a unique, individual entity that is relatively autonomous and independently motivated. For example, Baumeister's (1999) choice of articles in his collection of readings on *The Self in Social Psychology* reflects a ballot mailed to the membership of the International Society for Self and Identity, and includes topics such as self-regulation, self-awareness, self-presentation, self-esteem, self-evaluation, and self-affirmation. None of the articles focuses on group processes, intergroup relations, or social identity. The collection is largely concerned with (a North American view of) the self as an individual psychological entity. Baumeister (1998) argues that selfhood is based in three human experiences: reflexive consciousness, interpersonal being, and executive function.

Many theories of the self emphasize its comparative nature, echoing James's distinction between "I" and "Me." Comparisons may be made with self at different times, self in hypothetical states or with real or imagined people. For example, self-discrepancy theory (Higgins, 1987) posits that people make comparisons between the current state and some alternative reference point, such as an ideal self, or self as judged by significant others. According to Higgins (1987), the ideal and ought selves, from either own or other perspectives, represent "self-guides." Consistent with other self-regulation theories (e.g. Carver & Scheier, 1981; Duval & Wicklund, 1972), Higgins assumes that we are motivated to minimize discrepancies between actual states and self-guides. Different discrepancies produce different emotional reactions.

In a similar vein, self-evaluation maintenance theory (Tesser, 1988) and self-affirmation theory (Steele, 1988) both focus on discrepancies or differences between a self-state and some comparative reference point. Self-affirmation theory holds that people are generally motivated to maintain global conceptions of self-adequacy. As long as a relatively central aspect of the self can be affirmed, threats to less central and more specific aspects of the self lose their impact. The need for self-affirmation reduces when specific threats reduce, and similarly self-affirmation can reduce the impact of specific threats. Self-evaluation maintenance theory also endorses the view that people seek to maintain or increase their self-evaluation. However,

Tesser (1988) links self-evaluation directly to a reflection process and a comparison process. The comparison process involves a contrast between self and other, for example, if one is taking the same exam or performing an identical task and can be evaluated on the same dimension. The reflection process could be seen as a form of common self-categorization with the other person. If a person is linked to, or associated with, oneself, their achievements can reflect on the self. Tesser (1988) proposed that comparison is more likely when the dimension of performance is relevant (e.g., self and other both wish to become respected chess players, and are involved in the same chess competition). Reflection is more likely when the dimension is less relevant to oneself (one can bask in the reflected glory of a friend's achievements). As a result, people are motivated to judge others' performance more positively when the comparison dimension is irrelevant and the person is psychologically close, or the dimension is relevant and the person is distant. An implication of the theory is that we avoid similarity with others on dimensions that are important for our self-evaluation. Therefore we should be more comfortable in situations (and groups) that provide personal distinctiveness on relevant attributes (Cialdini, Borden, Thorne, Walker, Freeman, & Sloan, 1976).

Self-esteem is assumed to be an important characteristic that distinguishes people in terms of their traits or personality (Wylie, 1979) as well as being influenced by different situations. Self-esteem appears to be associated with having greater clarity of self-concept (Campbell, 1990). It provides an important buffer against anxiety (Greenberg, Solomon, Pyszczynski, Rosenblatt, Burling, Lyon, Simon, & Pinel, 1992) and may reflect the extent to which people are socially included or excluded (Leary, Tambor, Terdal, & Downs, 1995). Higher self-esteem also seems to be associated with further self-enhancement (Baumeister, Tice, & Hutton, 1989). Generally, research suggests that, given the option, we seem to prefer to evaluate ourselves through self-enhancement, and rather less so through the acquisition of knowledge about ourselves (Sedikides, 1993). People often engage in self-presentational strategies to shape others' perceptions of them (Baumeister, 1982; Snyder & Swann, 1978; Wicklund & Gollwitzer, 1982). More subtly, even though people feel good when they receive positive feedback, ultimately they take seriously feedback that verifies their self-image (Swann, Griffin, Predmore, & Gaines, 1987).

In much of this social psychological research on the self, the structure and content of self is often left implicit, researchers tending to study particular bits of self-related knowledge on a piecemeal basis. However, theory and research tend to start from the position that the individual is the primary locus of comparative judgments. After all, it is the individual that acts, that reacts, and that is reacted to by others.

Cultural differences in the self

Historical and cross-cultural analyses of the self suggest that we need to be cautious about using the individual person, either as the unit of measurement or as the unit of analysis (e.g., Baumeister, 1987; Logan, 1987). There are considerable differences in the way individuals and relationships are defined in different cultures (Bond & Smith, 1996; Triandis, 1994, 1995). Markus and Kitayama (1991) described how Japanese culture (which is relatively collectivist) is more concerned with interdependence, obligation, and social connectedness, whereas North American culture (which is relatively individualistic) is more concerned with independence and individuality. The different cultures also provide a basis for different self-construals (Singelis, 1994), which in turn are associated with different cognitive, emotional, and motivational features. Self-construals are hypothesized to be organized as regulatory schemas in the self-system (Markus & Wurf, 1987). They affect how we attend to and interpret information in terms of its implications for self. Put another way, the self is linked with different information and objects depending on one's self-construal. In individualistic countries such as North America people are more likely to describe themselves in terms of unique and distinctive traits or attributes, and to have self-related motives that reflect the importance of independence from others. In more collectivist cultures such as Japan, people are more likely to view themselves in terms of their family and other social ties and interdependence with others. Consequently, whereas in a North American context it is quite acceptable to proclaim one's achievements and for these to support self-esteem, in Japanese culture self-aggrandizement is frowned upon, and instead the biases seem to be toward modesty (Markus & Kitayama, 1991; Triandis, 1995). Although group memberships are important in both individualistic and collectivist cultures, it seems that commitments to specific social networks and obligations carry more weight in collectivist cultures, for example in relation to loyalty to organizations (Abrams, Ando, & Hinkle, 1998). This type of cross-cultural comparison reveals that there is a multiplicity of possible self-motives and possible self-construals (Singelis, 1994). Social psychological processes seem able to produce different self-conceptions in different ways, and this suggests that the "self" cannot be restricted to a particular type of structure or content. It seems that a crucial element is the contextual meaning of the relationship between the self and others.

The self and the group

Social psychology has always retained some conceptual links with sociology. A subgroup of researchers (e.g., Milgram & Toch, 1969; Sherif, 1966) explored how the individual and the group might be integrated within a psychological framework. This framework necessarily required the analysis of how individual psychological functioning articulates with social structure and context. Examples include Sherif's (1936) research on how norms emerge from interaction and are internalized to influence behavior, some of Asch's (1952) research on conformity to norms, and more recent research on the emergence of social representations out of social interaction (e.g., Farr & Moscovici, 1984). Newcomb (1950) was deeply impressed by Sherif's work as well as by symbolic interactionism, and argued strongly that:

> One's own self and one's own group are interdependently perceived. The self may be figure against the ground of the group, as when one is evaluating oneself, or when one is "self-conscious." Or the group may be figure against the ground of the self, as when one is feeling proud or critical of one's group. Because one's own self is such a supreme value, then, the group which is indispensable to it also has a value. One may regard the self as a part of the group or the group as a part of the self; in either case they are inseparable, and to the individual both are values. (p. 297)

Social psychology is now re-embracing this kind of view, and there have been some interesting developments along the way, such as the scope of the definition of "group" (Brown, 2000). Theoretical orientations to the self vary in emphasis along a continuum from structure to process (Abrams, 1996; Markova, 1987). At one extreme, theorists are concerned primarily with the organization of self-knowledge in memory, whether dynamically related or simply as components of a personality structure. At the other extreme, theorists focus more on how the self functions. Most theories involve a mixture of both structure and process, but are usually more explicit about one than the other. Both consider ways that group and category memberships can be involved in the self-concept.

The organization of self-related information

Psychological models of self-structure assume that the self is well represented as an entity in memory, for example, as schemas (Markus, 1977). The precise nature of the cognitive representation is a matter of debate (Srull & Wyer, 1993). Keenan (1993) suggests that we make trait inferences about ourselves using autobiographical behavioral exemplars. It follows that our ability to make summary descriptions of ourselves depends on the number of instances of relevant behaviors we can retrieve from memory. Exemplar models have attracted support in accounting for group categorization judgments (Judd & Park, 1988; Smith & Zarate, 1990), trait inferences about others (Kahneman & Miller, 1986), and stereotyping (Rothbart & John, 1985). However, in relation to self-judgments Bellezza (1984, 1993) rejects the exemplar view as being unwieldy, and as involving an infinite regress to ever more restrictive categorizations.

Combined processes (e.g., the dual exemplar/summary view espoused by Kihlstrom & Cantor, 1984) may be able to account for transitions from exemplar to trait representation. Klein and Loftus (1993) suggest that trait representation can be functionally independent of autobiographical behavioral exemplars in judgments of self. Judgments about self, in contrast to judgments about others, are usually made with extensive information, acquired across contexts, and involving long retention intervals. These factors facilitate abstraction to summary traits. However, the question remains as to whether self-information is then partitioned into different types or clusters and what they might be. For example, there is evidence that self-information is more closely related to information about others with whom we share close relationships than with friends or strangers, both when measured implicitly and by FMRI techniques (Aron, Aron, Tudor, & Nelson, 1991; Aron, Mashek, & Lewandowski, 1999).

Assumptions about the structure of self often form the basis for different models of motivation (Heckhausen & Dweck, 1998). The relationship between different components of the self-structure is often used to hypothesize a basis for differing goals (as does psychodynamic theory). For example, Higgins (1987) describes discrepancies between different "self-guides." Markus and Nurius (1986) outline the impact "possible selves," and Cantor (1990) examines how individuals set different life tasks for themselves (see Knowles & Sibicky, 1990, for an overview of different perspectives on the self). Markus and Kitayama (1991) have also described how cross-cultural differences in the content of self-definition relate to different associated motivations, as described earlier.

Several structural models distinguish between the more social and the more personal aspects of self. For example, Fenigstein, Scheier, and Buss (1975) (see also Buss, 1980; Carver & Scheier, 1998; Scheier & Carver, 1981) distinguished between the private and public self. Crocker and Luhtanen (1990) distinguished between a generalized collective self and personal self (cf., Greenwald & Pratkanis, 1984). Breckler and Greenwald (1986) proposed that the public, private, and collective selves emerge in a developmental sequence, each setting different ego tasks. In common with many other theorists (e.g., Cheek & Briggs, 1992), Breckler and Greenwald equate the public self with interpersonally orientated issues, the private self with "internal standards," and the collective self with cognitions about group memberships. The question of whether these aspects of self are structurally independent is open to debate, but the practical value of a taxonomic approach seems to be widely accepted by researchers in areas ranging from self-presentation and self-awareness, to cross-cultural differences (Triandis, 1989).

More recently, Brewer and Gardner (1996) distinguished between three levels of self-representation: the collective, relational, and personal self. Brewer and Silver (in press) draw on social psychological, sociological, and political science ideas to characterize four perspectives on social identity: *person-based social identities* (individual group members' internalization of group properties as part of the self-concept); *relational social identities* (based in interpersonal relationships within groups); *group-based social identities* (category definitions of the self based on shared category memberships); and *collective identities* (that are actively created or maintained through collective action).

Collective versus private selves

Trafimow, Triandis, and Goto (1991) proposed an explicit structural model in which self-cognitions are divided into two distinct components or "baskets." The private self contains knowledge of one's own attitudes, traits, feelings, and behavior. The collective self contains affiliations, group memberships, and connections to collectives of all types. In the two-baskets model the strongest associative connections are horizontal (within private self or within collective self). In Trafimow et al.'s studies, North American and Chinese participants were exposed to a prime and after a short delay were asked to complete a Twenty Statements Test (TST; Kuhn & McPartland, 1954). In the first experiment a prime for private self asked subjects to think about how they were different from their family and friends, whereas a prime for collective self asked them to think about what they had in common with their family and friends. In the second experiment, the primes focused on issues of personal glory and power (private prime), or the glory of the family (collective prime). Subsequent self-descriptions on the TST were classified as reflecting personal self-descriptions (such as traits) or social self-descriptions (such as common fate categories). Chinese participants (from a collectivist culture) and participants in the collective prime condition mentioned a higher proportion of social self-descriptions than other participants. Self-descriptions of each type (social or personal) tended to cluster together at a higher than chance level. These results were taken to illustrate that accessibility of traits within a part of the self is greater than accessibility of traits between different parts. This pattern of findings was replicated recently by Trafimow, Silverman, Fan, and Law (1997) in Hong Kong, and by Trafimow and Smith (1998) with Native Americans.

The Social Identity Approach

The social identity approach (Hogg & Abrams, 1988), or perspective (Turner, 1999), encompasses a large volume of research and theory emanating from Tajfel's (1972, 1974) ambitious drive to develop a non-reductionist social psychological theory. Consistent with the way social identity theory was formulated (Tajfel & Turner, 1979), one branch of research has concentrated on the way cognitive contrast and assimilation affect perceptions of social categories and groups, and ultimately the self. This is most clearly formalized in self-categorization theory (Turner, Hogg, Oakes, Reicher, & Wetherell, 1987). The second branch has concerned the nature of intergroup relations in terms of the relative status of each group and the legitimacy and stability of the status relationship. This second branch has proven important for the prediction of behavior, and for our understanding of wider scale intergroup relationships (see Abrams & Hogg, 1990; Brewer & Brown, 1998; Ellemers, Spears, & Doojse, 1999; Giles & Johnson, 1987; Hogg & Abrams, 1993) and is beyond the scope of this review.

The social identity approach emphasizes that categorization involves differentiation of our self and others into meaningfully distinctive categories. The process is both inductive and deductive – inferences are made on the basis of category-based stereotypes, but those stereotypes depend on the features that maximally distinguish the category from relevant other categories (Oakes, 1996; Oakes, Haslam, & Turner, 1994). The process involves both the application of stereotypes to others, and the depersonalization of self. Depersonalization means that the self-inclusive category becomes self-defining. Social identity is the perception of self in terms of stereotypical ingroup attributes.

Throughout the 1980s social identity researchers (e.g., Turner & Giles, 1981) described social and personal identity broadly as consisting of category memberships and traits, respectively (see Hogg & Abrams, 1988, for a comprehensive review). The social identity/personal identity distinction was depicted as if these were two different parts of identity structure. At first glance, this would appear to be consistent with the Trafimow et al. (1991) approach. However, self-categorization theory (Turner, 1985; Turner et al., 1987) more explicitly developed the analysis of social categorization to define personal and social identifications as being functionally antagonistic. Depersonalized self-categorization means that the self and ingroup are one and the same. For example, Smith and Henry (1996) have shown that when social categorizations are made salient, the ingroup becomes psychologically merged with, or linked to, the self. Depersonalization is also consistent with phenomena such as social projection, which seems to operate more strongly when people make judgments about others who share a categorization with self than when they are categorized as outgroup members (Kreuger, 1998; Kreuger & Clement, 1994). The functional antagonism means that if self-categorization becomes salient at a particular level (e.g., European) self-categorization at the lower level (e.g., British) becomes less salient. Which level of categorization is salient is flexibly influenced by contextually bounded comparisons between potential ingroups and outgroups.

Self-description as a function of context

The McGuires' research on distinctiveness revealed that people are more likely to describe themselves in terms of contextually distinct features (e.g., McGuire, McGuire, & Cheever, 1986). Social identity and self-categorization theory would assume that minority status is one of an array of factors that could make a particular categorization meaningful as a basis for perceiving self and others (Oakes, Haslam, & Turner, 1998; Oakes & Turner, 1986). In fact, the simple presence of outgroup category members (regardless of majority/minority status) can be sufficient to make the ingroup gender category salient in the self-concept (Abrams, Thomas, & Hogg, 1990). It makes sense that when only the ingroup is in mind, we distinguish among ingroup members (including self) either as individuals or as subgroup representatives, but when the outgroup is in mind the salient and meaningful distinction is between the ingroup category and the outgroup category. However, the boundary between self and outgroup is potentially quite variable and context dependent (Simon, 1997). A similar point is made by Brewer (1991), who argues that countervailing needs for distinctiveness and assimilation lead people to align themselves with groups that confer a meaningful identity in contrast to other groups, but with a strong sense of similarity or solidarity with a set of ingroup members. This process appears to operate in a context-relevant way, both in minimal group experiments and when the identity is linked to larger scale social categories and groups (Abrams, 1992b).

Trafimow et al.'s (1991) two-baskets model predicts that only one type of self-cognition is accessed at a time for structural reasons. In contrast, self-categorization theory predicts that self-cognitions are a function of the categorization process: personal and social identities are representations of self at different levels of abstraction relative to one another and to the social frame of reference (e.g. Abrams & Hogg, 1990; Turner et al., 1987). Different collective selves (self-categorizations) do not imply one another (unless framed by a superordinate categorization). Instead, any category should be most strongly associated with the specific attributes that are criterial for that particular categorization (Abrams, 1993, 1996, 1999). For example, when self-categorization in terms of gender is salient, the collective (stereotypical) attributes of the gender ingroup should be more likely to be ascribed to the self. These attributes will appear as traits, behaviors, attitudes, etc. (Abrams, Sparkes, & Hogg, 1985; Hogg & Turner, 1987; Lorenzi-Cioldi, 1991; Oakes, Turner, & Haslam, 1991). The links from the gender category to gender-related features will be much stronger than links between one's gender and other categories. The largest number of associative links will be vertical, from categorizations to category features. This category–attribute linkage is well described in the literature on category-based perception (McGarty, 1999; Rosch, 1978). Self-categorization theory can be characterized as a hierarchical process model (Abrams, 1996), because the process generates the potential for the content of self to be determined by inferential cascades from categories to subcategories and other subordinate features.

A significant feature of the social identity approach is that apparent inconsistencies in individuals' behavior can be interpreted as reflecting activation of different depersonalized self-images or self-images that are at different levels of categorization, and framed by different social comparisons (Turner, Oakes, Haslam, & McGarty, 1994). The self can include and exclude attributes with great flexibility, but at any particular moment, the self is a specific product of a context-dependent comparison (cf., Fiske & Von Hendy, 1992; Markus & Nurius, 1986). Research shows that people consider ingroup category memberships as more self-descriptive when intergroup contrasts raise their salience (e.g., Abrams, Thomas, & Hogg, 1990; Hogg & Turner, 1987; Lorenzi-Cioldi, 1991; Simon, Glassner-Bayerl, & Stratenwerth, 1991; Simon & Hamilton, 1994). In a comparison of self-categorization and the two-baskets models, Abrams, Au, Waterman, Garst, and Mallet (reported in Abrams, 1996, 1999) found that priming a category membership increased the proportion of ingroup stereotype-consistent self-descriptions at the level of traits and that social (category) self-descriptions were associated more strongly with "private" (trait) self-descriptions than with other social self-descriptions. Take together, we think the evidence seems more consistent with self-categorization than with the two-baskets model.

How mutable are self-categories?

In some respects, the theoretical consequences of the self-categorization process do not chime well with people's subjective experience of themselves as relatively continuous and meaningfully coherent. If the self were truly as malleable as the self-categorization approach suggests (e.g., Oakes, Haslam, & Reynolds, 1999; Onorato & Turner, in press) it might become impossible to conduct normal social relationships because nobody would behave in a consistent or predictable way across contexts.

Some sociological models of self explicitly incorporate group memberships and roles. For example, Stryker (1987) discusses Master Statuses (see R. H. Turner, 1987). These differ importantly from the personal and interpersonal aspects of self because they are well defined and stable, and do not depend on specific relationships (though they often encompass them). This approach to identity regards roles and broad group memberships as additional parts of an identity structure but it does not develop a clearly social psychological model of how or when such elements of identity will affect behavior. There is a transition straight from the sociological to the psychological level of analysis (Hogg, Terry, & White, 1995).

Deaux (1992, 1996) and Breakwell (e.g., 1986) have argued that self-images involving both social *and* personal features can be meaningful or salient in a social situation, and that many self-images cannot sensibly be described at a single level of abstraction. The self-structure has a unique meaning for each person and is not restricted to a normative framework. In an extension of Rosenberg's (1988) hierarchical classification approach, Deaux (e.g., Reid & Deaux, 1996) suggested that self-classifications (be they roles or social categories) correspond to social identity while self-descriptions in terms of traits correspond to personal features of identity. The traits and categories are each structured hierarchically and traits and categories are linked but the particular structure is different for each individual. The chronic accessibility of particular self-images (cf., Higgins & King, 1981) reflects their vertical position in the hierarchy. An interesting feature of this model is that meanings of identity can change although the category labels may remain constant. Deaux, Reid, Mizrahi, and Ethier (1995) found five types of social identity among students: personal relationships, vocations/avocations, political affiliations, ethnic/religious groups, and stigmatized groups.

These differed along various descriptive dimensions. Deaux et al. suggest that the inter-changeability of identities may depend on their proximity in terms of defining dimensions. Deaux et al. (1995) contrast the idea from social identity theory that social identifications are "collective and relational" with their evidence that few social identities were relational and only ethnic, religious, some stigmatized, and some political identities were seen as collective. Occupational identities, in contrast, were perceived to be more individualistic.

Self-categorization theory does not address consistent individual differences effectively. For example, it does not offer a compelling account of why, when social identity is salient, not all group members feel or behave alike (Abrams, 1990; Deaux, 1996). Thus, there seems to be evidence both for flexibility and for underlying stability in the self-concept. The question is how a process account of the self can account for both features (Abrams, 1990, 1992a). We believe that, to some degree, subjective structural stability in the self must be based on stability in people's social comparisons and social frames of reference, or more specifically, their social relationships and networks (Abrams, 1992, 1996; Cinnarella, 1998; Simmel, 1922). This general subjective stability (within individuals) may be accompanied by many subtle (and not so subtle) variations that allow people to arrive at different interpretations of the same categorization at different times.

Although categorizations may remain very stable (e.g., one's ethnicity) there can be con-siderable flexibility at the level of attributes so that the meaning and evaluation of ethnicity varies depending on the comparison others and social context (Deaux, 1996). Similarly, role categorizations, such as "parent" can be subjectively defined equally easily as a social category membership (e.g., at a Parent–Teachers Association meeting) or as personal category (e.g., as parent to one's own child). The meaning, level, and content of self-categorizations are not determined by the category label, but by the comparison categories with which they are linked in memory and in the particular context. There is evidence that this is true of ingroup and outgroup perceptions (Abrams & Hogg, 1987; Haslam & Turner, 1992; Haslam, Turner, Oakes, McGarty, & Hayes, 1992; Oakes et al., 1994).

In principle, the distinction between categories and attributes is itself highly mutable (Abrams, 1993, 1996, 1999; McGarty, 1999). As already mentioned, a category at one level of abstraction is an attribute at a superordinate level (Bellezza, 1993; Turner et al., 1987). More importantly, the subjective definition of which features are categorical and which are subsidiary attributes should depend again on the comparative context and the perceiver's goals. For example, the same person could categorize himself as an athlete, one of whose attributes is that he is artistic, or an artist whose attributes include athleticism. The designa-tion of which level is categorical would probably be determined by whether the judgment is made in the context of discussions about other athletes or other artists. Subjectively, how-ever, it is unproblematic, because the self will generally be defined in a consistent way within the context of particular social relationships.

Self-perception as social perception

Self-perception and social perception are interdependent because they both arise from social categorizations made in the same contexts. Both reflect the nature of the relationship between the perceiver and the perceived. If targets of perception are judged primarily in terms of a category such as gender, then self is also perceived in terms of gender. Self-inclusive categories are generally defined in contrast with a self-exclusive category (Abrams, 1999; Simon, 1997). Self-categorization theory proposes that online information is integrated with prior expectancies to establish meaningful and functional perceptions of self and others. From this it could follow that category-based processing does not have any special status vis-à-vis individuated or other types of processing, because categorization can occur at any level and because the attributes associated with categories are flexible. In this respect SCT provides a similar model of social cognitive perception to those offered by connectionist approaches (cf., Smith, 1999).

Parallel constraint satisfaction

According to Kunda and Thagard's (1996) parallel constraint satisfaction (PCS) model, perception depends on the parallel operation of excitatory and inhibitory links in a network. When given only category labels as a basis for judgment, the category activates a stereotype, which activates traits and behaviors in the network. However, category information usually arises in combination with other information, such as an instance of behavior. When this happens, the information becomes integrated and may result in different perceptual outcomes. The same trait can also imply different behaviors when applied to members of different groups. For example, lawyers and construction workers are judged to manifest aggressiveness in quite different ways (Kunda, Sinclair, & Griffin, 1995) because the interpretation of aggressiveness is conditional on other features associated with each category. Indeed, contrary to earlier models (Brewer, 1988; Fiske & Neuberg, 1990), Kunda and Thagard (1996) concluded that stereotype-based processing is not a default option and that stereotypes have no primacy over individuating information. They reported a meta-analytic effect size of .69 for the effects of individuating information against an effect size of .19 for stereotype information across 40 studies that orthogonally manipulated the two types of information. Consistent with our interpretation of the self-categorization approach, the PCS model does not make strong a priori assumptions about whether particular features will serve as categories or as traits: ". . . many attributes that are typically viewed as individuating information appear indistinguishable from stereotypes, both structurally and in terms of reference class" (Kunda & Thagard, 1996, p. 301).

Many questions are left unanswered by the PCS model. For example, the question of what people notice in the first place, is left to ideas about contextual salience (cf., Taylor, 1981), accessibility (Higgins & King, 1981), or perceiver goals (Brewer, 1988; Fiske & Neuberg, 1990). Similarly, it is unclear how or why people seek to make judgments about others, or indeed the role of the immediate social context. The model is entirely cognitive, requiring no reference to comparisons between target persons and any other external frame of reference. One important missing component is the relationships that people are perceived to share (Abrams, 1992a, 1999). By extending the model to include links between perceptions of others and the self, it can begin to take on a more social flavor.

The meta-contrast process in self-categorization theory shares with the parallel constraint satisfaction model the assumption that the underlying psychological process maximizes the fit of the stimuli to an optimally meaningful model. To the extent that targets are assumed to share traits or descriptive features with one subset of others, but not with a different subset, a categorization should become salient (comparative fit). To the extent that behaviors exhibited by category members are also more similar to one another than to those of non-category members, a stereotype will be generated (see Abrams, 1996, 1999; McGarty, 1999 for further discussion).

The PCS model could potentially be extended to include self-perception. Category, trait, or behavioral knowledge about oneself may be well organized as networks of information (i.e., structures), but the way those are linked to other, more contextually fluid information should have significant effects on self-perception (Abrams, 1999; Kunda, Fong, Sanitoso, & Reber, 1993). We do not regard the context as the only, or necessarily the major, influence (cf. Oakes et al., 1999), but fully endorse the idea that the meaning of self can be transformed by its association and contrast with other concepts and information. Self-categorization theory would hold that this crucial "other information" emerges from social comparisons. These comparisons allow people to build links *to* other individuals through shared social categories. In turn people can make new inferences about themselves from these emergent categorizations. Indeed, categorizations provide a framework for future behavior and self-evaluations. For example, establishing one's group membership, or category alignment, can often come prior to adopting the group's values and norms in voting decisions, in pursuing organizational goals, when setting targets for achievement, or when evaluating group members (see Abrams, 1992a, Abrams, Marques, Bown, & Henson, in press; Marques, Abrams, Páez, & Martincz-Taboada, 1998).

The Problem of Individual Variation

We have suggested that self-conception can gain subjective stability and continuity while remaining flexible and dynamic. However, the self-categorization view leaves unresolved the problem of the process by which self becomes stylized, or takes on a personality. What systems or processes enable people to develop character, temperament (Plomin & Caspi, 1999), styles of attribution (Metalsky, Halberstadt, & Abramson, 1987), self-expectancies and efficacy (Bandura, 1982), and strategies for pursuing long-term goals (Brandstadter, Rothermund, & Dillmann, 1998; Heckhausen & Schulz, 1998, Markus & Ruvolo, 1989)? Moreover, self-categorization does not sit easily with a life-span perspective because it does not link the categorization processes to continuity and gradual change over time (Abrams, 1992a). Nor does it provide much insight as to how and why people actively develop or create their own environment within which to develop and complete their sense of self-hood (Wicklund & Gollwitzer, 1982) and in which self-defining goals can persist over a large part of the life span (Gollwitzer & Kirchhof, 1998). These are important issues for future research.

There is good evidence that individual differences affect intergroup behavior. Consistent with research in the interpersonal domain, social identity research has revealed that people engage in strategically self-enhancing or self-protective identification. For example, social identification is stronger when the category is relatively more distinctive (Ellemers, Kortekaas

& Ouwerkerk, 1999; Simon, 1993; Simon & Hamilton, 1994) and threats to distinctiveness result in stronger intergroup differentiation (e.g., Brown & Abrams, 1986), particularly among those who identify most highly with the group (Jetten, Spears, & Manstead, 1998). Across a range of domains, people who identify highly are more likely to respond to threats to distinctiveness or identity with a more competitive orientation than are those who identify less strongly (Ellemers, Spears, & Doosje, 1999). Although much of the focus of most of the relevant research is on responses of ingroup bias (e.g., Doosje, Ellemers, & Spears, 1999; Hinkle & Brown, 1990) the interesting point is that responses to social categorization do vary, and this variation needs to be explained.[1] As examples of some of the issues that need to be understood, this section examines self-regulation, self-esteem, and uncertainty.

Regulation of stereotyping and behavior

Self-categorization theory offers only a single source for perception of and action toward others, namely the prototype associated with a salient self-categorization (Turner et al., 1987). Stereotypical perception and judgment following categorization is regarded as functional because it makes the best sense of the relevant intercategory comparisons by maximizing the differences between, and minimizing differences within, categories. Stereotypes are subjectively "reasonable" expectations about group members, and should not be considered biased or faulty perceptions (Oakes et al., 1994; Oakes et al., 1999). Ingroup stereotypes are often positive, but may also have negative connotations (Branscombe, Ellemers, Spears, & Doosje, 1999; Steele & Aronson, 1995; Tajfel, 1981). Outgroup stereotypes may contain evaluatively neutral (e.g., Italian people eat pizza), or positive (e.g., Italian people are sociable) content. These positive and negative elements make up part of the overall image of social categories and groups. If perceivers were to selectively reject negative content per se this would disrupt category-based judgment as a whole, and it would become difficult to make *any* coherent judgments of targets.

In contrast to the self-categorization account, there is evidence that people are often uncomfortable with, or try to suppress, social stereotypes (Bodenhausen & Macrae, 1998; Monteith, 1996). Even if stereotypes are part of the "cognitive success" of the perceiver, they may imply actions that might be construed as "social failure," because people may be concerned not to appear "unreasonable" or out of line (Abrams & Masser, 1998). A social failure such as inappropriately expressing a stereotypical judgment may be a source of embarrassment, and likely to provoke admonishment from others. Prevalent cultural values and norms shape people's sense of right and wrong (e.g., Lerner & Miller, 1978; Seligman, Olson, & Zanna, 1996; Triandis, 1995). Guilt does seem to be associated with awareness of having made unreasonably negative judgments of others (Devine, Monteith, Zuwerink, & Elliott, 1991; Monteith, 1993; Monteith, Devine, & Zuwerink, 1993). Even people with strong prejudices might feel a need to justify these in some way (e.g., Sears & Kinder, 1971; McConahay, 1983), at least to themselves (cf., Adorno, Frenkel-Brunswik, Levinson, & Sanford, 1950; Billig, 1988; Potter & Wetherell, 1987). However, people may not be vigilant for such judgments unless the context demands that they are so (Monteith, 1996). People may wish to moderate their expressions of prejudice for a variety of reasons, including personal values and social norms (Plant & Devine, 1998). All of this evidence suggests that there is no direct or automatic link between categorization and overt judgment and behavior.

Social self-regulation

The general process by which overt behavior is regulated now seems well documented as a comparison–reference value feedback loop (Powers, 1973). Conscious comparison of one's thoughts, intentions, or actions with a reference standard seems to depend on self-focused attention (Carver & Scheier, 1981, 1998; Gibbons, 1990; Wicklund, 1975). Bodenhausen and Macrae (1998) assume that stereotypes are relatively well learned, slow to change, and insensitive to people's personal experiences of different intergroup relationships. To deal with these unwieldy and poorly fitting impressions, the control system somehow locates a much more flexible personal norm or rule which facilitates or inhibits the stereotype and related behavior. Bodenhausen and Macrae (1998) propose that stereotype suppression is more likely when people are self-aware, because they refer to personal standards to filter the output from relatively automatically activated cultural stereotypes.

There are two problems with the Bodenhausen and Macrae model. First, it does not deal with the functional aspect of stereotyping – its flexibility and contextual fit. If stereotypes work well, why should people wish to suppress them? Second, it treats the self only as an observer. As Newcomb (1950) observed, evaluations of self and group are inextricably linked, one being always viewed from the standpoint of the other. Moreover, "the individual not only perceives that he has a certain position in his group; he also directs his behavior toward maintaining it, defending it, or improving it" (Newcomb, 1950, p. 327). The problem facing researchers is how to combine what we know about social categorization with what we know about behavioral self-regulation (see Abrams & Masser, 1998).

Abrams' (1990, 1994, 1996) social self-regulation (SSR) model offers one approach to the problem. The SSR model distinguishes between identity salience (self-categorization) and attentional focus as distinct elements in behavioral regulation. The categorization process and associated stereotyping are conceived of as generally non-conscious processes that make particular self-categorizations salient. According to the Social Identity model of Deindividuation Effects (SIDE model, Postmes & Spears, 1998), raised salience of group membership and lowered salience of individual identity are sufficient to increase ingroup normative behavior. The SIDE model does not address the role of attentional processes in directing information processing and regulating behavior. The SSR model considers that self-regulation can produce different responses to the same salient categorization, depending on the relevant standard or reference point that is attended to. This assumption is based on the large volume of research into self-awareness and self-regulation (see Carver & Scheier, 1981, 1998).

The SSR model considers four conditions: high versus low identity salience, and high versus low self-attention. When both identity salience and self-attention are low, behavior is likely to be task-focused (e.g., toward a previously activated goal), or routine or inactive. In highly ambiguous situations or when routine is interrupted by an external event or stimulus, people may begin to devote their attention to determining the category memberships of targets, or analyzing their individual features (Abrams, 1990, 1994; Hogg & Abrams, 1993;

Hogg & Mullin, 1999). That is, they may seek to establish a relevant self-categorization. Increased self-attention may also lower attentional capacity for processing information about others (Vallacher, 1978). Therefore, when category memberships are already clear, self-attention may increase the use of heuristics or simple assumptions, reducing differentiation among targets (Fenigstein & Abrams, 1993). This could increase the impact of stereotypical perceptions on behaviors and judgments.

The attentional process generally is oriented with respect to a particular goal. Because particular goals, standards, or motives can differ, so too can the consequences of self-attention. When social identity is salient, self-focused attention can result in increased intergroup discrimination (e.g., Abrams, 1985), perhaps in the service of a motivation to enhance a valued aspect of self. However, if interpersonal norms are used as the reference standard, the combination of salient social identity and self-attention may result in reduced intergroup discrimination and increased socially desirable responses (Abrams & Brown, 1989; Froming & Carver, 1981). In summary the behavioral consequences of self-awareness depend on: (a) the aspect of self which is salient; and (b) the standards being used to guide behavior. When social identity is salient, self- (ingroup-) serving motives and generic and specific social norms may represent different subsets of the potential reference values for responding.

The context, in the sense of the current situation and set of relevant goals, also provides normative structure for judgment and behavior. If the context invites application of a relatively simple and undifferentiated cultural stereotype, self-focus should increase its use as the reference value for behavioral options that could follow. For example, in the presence of consistent normative information from other ingroup members, stereotypes and ingroup favoritism are bolstered (Abrams, 1990; Haslam, Oakes, McGarty, Turner, Reynolds, & Eggins, 1996; Marques et al., 1998; Monteith, Deenan, and Tooman, 1996). However, in many situations, particularly small group contexts, negotiations (Kramer & Tyler, 1995; Stephenson, 1991), or role-based encounters with familiar individuals (e.g., faculty meetings), it is likely that we moderate our behavior tactically and strategically to complete plans or reach longer term goals (Gollwitzer & Kirchhof, 1998). We also respond quite differently to group members that behave in unexpected or unlikable ways, even though we do not doubt that they are ingroup members (Abrams et al., in press; Marques et al., 1998; Moreland & McMinn, 1999).

Social self-regulation retains the position of the self at the center of perception, consistent both with SCT and with research suggesting the relative primacy of self-related material in cognition (e.g., Aron et al., 1999; Baumeister, 1999; Smith, 1999). For example, given the prevalence of motives for self-enhancement and self-protection, increased self-awareness should often result in increased ingroup bias, and self–other differentiation (see also Simon, 1993, 1997). However, the SSR framework also allows learned knowledge about society to provide a source of normative standards in addition to the default perceptual output of categorization. Thus, the self and others can be categorized flexibly, while at the same time cultural conventions or specific social norms remain available to guide action. Individuals with different personal knowledge (e.g., personal stereotypes) can therefore coordinate easily with one another by referring to common social rules (e.g., customs, mores, etc.) or social representations. When situations call for subjective stereotypes to be moderated in some way, self-regulation allows them either to be downplayed or expressed as the context requires. The same applies to behavioral choices such as whether to remain in or leave the group: the cultural or normative context provides rules for action in the light of one's salient identity. Different contexts may imply quite different rules for the same self-categorization (cf., Abrams, Ando, & Hinkle, 1998). In conclusion, identity salience does not have a direct route to behavior. Self-regulatory processes intervene to moderate and direct action.

Social Identity and Motivation

Although collective self-conception is grounded in relatively automatic social categorization processes associated with depersonalization, it is also guided by motivational processes and people's specific goals. One motivation relates to self-enhancement, self-esteem, and the pursuit of positive social identity; another relates to epistemic considerations and the pursuit of meaning and subjective certainty.

Self-esteem hypothesis

Much has been written about the role of self-esteem in intergroup behavior (e.g., Abrams, 1992a, 1996, 1999; Abrams & Hogg, 1988; Hogg & Abrams, 1990; Long & Spears, 1997; Oakes & Turner, 1980; Rubin & Hewstone, 1998; Tajfel & Turner, 1979; Turner, 1975, 1999). Tajfel originally proposed, "the need to preserve the integrity of the self-image is the only motivational assumption we need to make in order to understand the direction that the search for coherence will take" (Tajfel, 1969, p. 92). However, when he developed the idea of social identity, Tajfel proposed that social comparison processes in intergroup settings are designed to attain "positively valued distinctiveness from other groups" (Tajfel, 1972, p. 3), and to "achieve a satisfactory concept or image of the self" (Tajfel, 1974, p. 4). Tajfel and Turner's (1979) formal theoretical statement includes the proposition from social comparison theory that, "individuals strive to maintain or enhance their self-esteem: they strive for a positive self-concept" (Tajfel & Turner, 1979, p. 40). When groups acquiesce to relatively low social status, the "price has been the subordinate group's self-esteem" (Tajfel & Turner, 1979, p. 37). Turner (1981) describes the hypothesis succinctly:

> ... one's self-esteem as a group member depends upon the evaluative outcomes of social comparisons between the in-group and out-group. Since it can be supposed that individuals desire positive self-esteem ... there is a tendency to seek positive distinctiveness for the in-group in comparison with the out-group. Thus (the) hypothesis is that self-evaluative social comparisons directly produce competitive intergroup processes which motivate attitudinal biases and discriminatory actions. (p. 80)

Abrams and Hogg (1988) derived two corollaries of what they termed "the self-esteem hypothesis." Corollary 1 is that: "Successful intergroup discrimination will enhance social identity, and hence self-esteem." Corollary 2 is that: "Low or threatened self-esteem will promote intergroup discrimination because of the 'need' for positive self-esteem." Evidence for these two hypotheses (e.g., Corollary 1: Lemyre & Smith, 1985; Oakes & Turner, 1980;

Corollary 2: Crocker & Schwartz, 1985; Hogg & Sunderland, 1991; Wagner, Lampen, & Syllwasschy, 1986) has been reviewed by Rubin and Hewstone (1998).

Abrams and Hogg (1988; Abrams, 1990, 1992; Hogg & Abrams, 1990) pointed out that tests of these corollaries should examine evaluations of the specific social identity salient in the context in which intergroup behavior occurs, because global self-evaluations may not reflect the particular intergroup comparison under investigation. They also proposed that state, rather than trait, self-esteem should be most relevant. Moreover, since personal and social identities should not be salient simultaneously it should be possible that even someone who regarded themselves as personally fair might have little difficulty in being more "fair" to the ingroup than the outgroup (cf., Insko & Schopler, 1998). However, self-evaluation should be dependent on conformity to distinctive ingroup norms, so that in some situations, where group norms were prosocial and cooperative, social identity would be evaluated more positively if members were more positive toward the outgroup (cf., Jetten, Spears & Manstead, 1998).

Numerous studies and articles have tested the hypotheses directly or indirectly (see Rubin & Hewstone, 1998), explored moderating factors (Ellemers, Spears, & Doosje, 1999), or criticized the hypotheses (Abrams, 1990, 1992; Hogg & Abrams, 1993) even to the point of denying that the corollaries were ever part of social identity theory (Farsides, 1995; Long & Spears, 1997). For example, Turner (1999) claims that, "social identity theory does not actually contain these corollaries. In fact in many respects it specifically rejects them. Although the theory assumes that there is a need for positive self-evaluation, it does not equate this need with an individual level motive" (p. 24). "Self-esteem is an outcome of a social psychological process of self-categorization and social comparison in the context of group values and ideologies, not a fixed universal or biological structure" (p. 25). We have always agreed that self-esteem is a social psychological phenomenon and not a universal or biological structure, but we believe a close reading of social identity articles during the 1970s and 1980s does confirm that self-esteem is specified in social identity theory as an important motivator and outcome of intergroup behavior.

Regardless of hair-splitting about the actual hypotheses, we hold to our view that: "In real group contexts the SEH may merely be one of a great many possibilities concerning the motives for intergroup discrimination" (Abrams & Hogg, 1988 p. 323; also see Abrams, 1992 for a detailed exploration). For example, when differences among groups are institutionalized and ideologically legitimized, it seems likely that groups will accept the status quo without particular consequences for self-esteem, particularly for the higher status group. Intergroup behavior in real settings is often based on factors such as the distribution of wealth or power (Ng, 1982), material resources (Caddick, 1981), the nature of goal relations between groups (Sherif, 1966). Under some circumstances, positive self-evaluation might follow merely from engaging in behavior as a group member, perhaps as a product of a sense of efficacy (Gecas & Schwalbe, 1983).

Research has also tended to support Abrams and Hogg's (1988) prediction that chronic or well-learned self-evaluative tendencies can pervade some aspects of intergroup behavior. For example, individuals with low self-esteem might be psychologically less well equipped to engage in competitive intergroup behavior for both cognitive and motivational reasons (cf., Alloy & Abramson, 1982; Beck, 1967). Conversely, people with very high self-esteem might

well seize opportunities to accrue more positive self-evaluations through intergroup comparison (Crocker, Blaine, & Luhtanen, 1993; Crocker & Major, 1989; Luhtanen & Crocker,
1992). The picture is complicated by evidence that self-esteem at both personal and group
levels may affect intergroup behavior (Long & Spears, 1997). Social categorization may be
threatening to people with low category related self-esteem and for people with high personal
self-esteem. Long and Spears (1997) found that these participants showed the highest levels
of intergroup differentiation. As noted earlier, in some situations people seem to prefer
positive evaluations first, and accurate information second (Sedikides, 1993). It seems likely
that the self-system would function in similar ways regardless of whether self-evaluative
judgments are made from interpersonal or intergroup social comparisons.

Rubin and Hewstone's (1998) review divided self-esteem measures into trait, state, global
(all aspects of self), specific, personal, and social aspects of self. They also distinguished
between competitive discrimination (in which outcomes or status were at stake in the absence
of clear norms, such as in the minimal group paradigm) and normative discrimination (in
which there is an historical or normative basis for discrimination). They expected clearest
support for the SEH for competitive discrimination when measures focused on specific social
state self-esteem. The evidence is at best inconclusive. A higher proportion of studies supported the first than the second corollary, but very few met the criteria for measurement of
self-esteem required to test the corollaries properly. For example, Hogg and Sunderland (1991)
manipulated personal self-esteem before participants awarded points to minimal ingroup and
outgroup members. Those with lowered pregroup self-esteem expressed more ingroup favoritism, but favoritism did not predict postgroup self-esteem.

Gagnon and Bourhis (1996) found that discrimination in minimal groups was associated
with subsequent social state self-esteem, but only when participants identified highly with the
ingroup. Platow, Harley, Hunter, Hanning, Shave, and O'Connel (1997) found that among
participants whose personal self-esteem was high, those with low social self-esteem discriminated more than those with higher social self-esteem. None of the studies reviewed tested both
corollaries using specific state social self-esteem measures. Branscombe and Wann (1984)
found that threat to the (North American) identity of participants resulted in lowered self-
esteem among people who identified highly with the ingroup. Moreover, these participants
showed greater derogation of the outgroup and subsequently reported raised self-esteem.
Rubin and Hewstone (1998) concluded that competitive discrimination enhances self-esteem
but is not motivated by depressed self-esteem. In line with Abrams and Hogg's (1988)
review, there appears to be moderate support for Corollary 1 but little support for Corollary
2. Indeed, meta-analytically, the evidence stacks up to suggest that people with high global
personal trait self-esteem are most likely to engage in discrimination (Aberson, Healy, &
Romero, in press). Long and Spears (1997), together with Branscombe and Wann (1994),
Farsides (1995), and subsequently Turner (1999) have emphasized that self-esteem becomes
more motivating when social identity is threatened, and when the categorization is meaningful and relevant.

One likely reason for the mixed findings in the self-esteem literature is that the processes
of measurement may compromise the relationships among the variables (Abrams, 1992a).
If a person has just evaluated his/her group membership positively it would seem likely that
he/she would want to be consistent in subsequent allocation of rewards to group members.

Alternatively, having already evaluated their group positively he/she may feel no further need to engage in discrimination and ingroup bias (Rubin, 2000). Recent developments in measurement such as the Implicit Association Test (Greenwald & Banaji, 1995) and other implicit measures could provide a useful way to access social identity linked self-esteem in ways that may be less susceptible to demand characteristics or reactivity to repeated presentation of the same measures (Farnham, Greenwald, & Banaji, 1999).

Self-meaning

Psychologists have always believed that people are motivated to render their world subjectively meaningful in order to be able to predict events, plan action, and generally act in an adaptive manner. This assumption has a variety of different emphases on simplification, meaning, certainty, and so forth (see Bartlett, 1932; Festinger, 1950; James, 1890; Reykowski, 1982). Many formulations also emphasize individual differences in the degree of uncertainty that people can tolerate (e.g., Adorno et al., 1950; Rokeach, 1960; Sorrentino & Roney, 2000). A central motivation as a group member could be to establish the meaningfulness of one's identity (Abrams & Hogg, 1988; Hogg & Abrams, 1990).

This is an important theme in Tajfel's earlier (1969, 1972) theorizing. People are likely to be in a position to satisfy higher order needs such as self-enhancement only once they can make subjectively valid comparisons. The first task, therefore, is to understand who one is (Abrams, Wetherell, Cochrane, Hogg, & Turner, 1990). This subjective reference point provides the basis for evaluations and reactions to others (see Abrams et al., in press). In short, clarification of the social world and one's linkage to it is the starting point for other self-related processes. The question, "who am I?" precedes the question, "how good am I?" (Abrams, 1990, 1992a). Intertwined with the answer to the latter question will be the value associated with social identity (Sherman, Hamilton, & Lewis, 1999), and the affect associated with different cognitions about ingroup and outgroup members (Smith, 1999).

Uncertainty reduction hypothesis

The idea that uncertainty reduction is a fundamental motivation has been explored and elaborated as the uncertainty reduction hypothesis (e.g., Hogg, in press a, in press b; Hogg & Abrams, 1993; Hogg & Mullin, 1999). Although people may vary in uncertainty orientation, there is also substantial variation caused by immediate or more enduring contextual factors. According to the uncertainty reduction hypothesis, we all feel uncertain sometimes, and need to reduce this uncertainty. A powerful way to do so is to ground one's self-concept in group membership. Groups are represented as prototypes that describe and prescribe perceptions, attitudes, feelings, and behaviors. Social categorization allows a complex and multifaceted social field to be reconfigured in terms of ingroup and outgroup prototypes. When a social category is self-inclusive, the self becomes depersonalized, and thereby assimilated to the ingroup prototype. This gives direction to self-conception and associated attitudes, feelings, and behavior. Furthermore, collective self-conception provides consensual validation from fellow ingroup members for one's identity and associated attitudes, feelings, and behaviors.

Theoretically, the more uncertain one is the stronger is the motivation to self-categorize. Moreover, the motivation should be stronger if one is uncertain about something that is subjectively important in that context; for example, the self-concept or attitudes related to self-conception. It is also likely that, under uncertainty, people seek to identify with groups that are more effective at reducing uncertainty. Such groups would be expected to have consensual, concise, and clearly focused prototypes that are grounded in distinctive, highly entitative groups. This point can be taken one step further to predict that extreme uncertainty may motivate people to join extremist groups that are orthodox, homogeneous, polarized, hierarchically structured, and have clear rules or norms.

There is now a body of empirical studies that provides support for key predictions of the uncertainty reduction hypothesis, in particular the key idea that people self-categorize in terms of an available self-inclusive category only when they are motivated to do so by uncertainty, and that this effect is amplified where the focus of uncertainty is important and the social category is relevant to self-conceptualization and uncertainty reduction (e.g., Grieve & Hogg, 1999; Hogg & Grieve, 1999; Jetten, Hogg, & Mullin, in press; Mullin & Hogg, 1998, 1999; for overviews see Hogg, in press a; Hogg & Mullin, 1999). Uncertainty reduction follows from the perception of ingroup consensus (e.g., McGarty, Turner, Oakes, & Haslam, 1993). Whether uncertainty reduction or self-esteem motives operate as hierarchical or as parallel processes remains an interesting empirical question (see McGarty, 1999).

Conclusions: The Self is a Social Entity

Mackie and Smith (1997) reviewed the literatures on interpersonal and intergroup processes and concluded that many of the theories and models share common assumptions. There does seem to be a trend toward integrating and sharing insights across different domains in social psychology (Stapel, 2000). There has also been a surge in the proportion of social psychology that is concerned with collective phenomena, defined broadly as ranging from stereotyping to small group interaction and intergroup behavior (Abrams & Hogg, 1998). There are still important debates regarding the underlying level of analysis (e.g., Gaertner & Schopler, 1998; Oakes et al., 1999, Turner, 1999). However, ideas and techniques from branches of research that have traditionally been characterized as being at opposite extremes of the non-reductionist–individualistic continuum (such as social identity and social cognition) are now being shared and used to develop fuller theoretical accounts of important social phenomena (Abrams & Hogg, 1999; Lepore & Brown, 1997; Locke & Walker, 1999; Operario & Fiske, 1999; Vescio, Hewstone, & Crisp, 1999). We believe that this openness can produce better understanding of the way society and psychology are articulated, perhaps especially through the medium of the self.

Our view is that society and the individual are mutually instantiated (Abrams, 1992a; Abrams et al., 2000; Hogg & Williams, 2000), Theologians and poets have understood this point for centuries and some sociologically inclined psychologists reached similar conclusions half a century ago (e.g., Newcomb, 1950; Sherif, 1936). We believe that this conclusion is gradually being reflected not just in a corner of the discipline, but as change in the meta-theoretical framework (Doise, 1986; Operario & Fiske, 1999). The combination of a social identity perspective with models of social cognitive, interpersonal, and intergroup processes offers hope for achieving a better understanding of the truly social nature of the self.

NOTE

1   One way that self-conception may gain stability is when particular social comparisons are made relatively frequently and with richness of meaning and because people have enduring relationships within social networks (Simmel, 1922). For cognitive and affective reasons, this would increase the relative accessibility of the relevant self-categorizations. However, this reasoning begins to imply the presence of structural stability, which in turn leads to a "personality" explanation for intergroup behavior, which is anathema to many social identity theorists (e.g., Turner, 1999).

REFERENCES

Aberson, C. L., Healy, M., & Romero, V. (in press). Ingroup bias and self-esteem. *Personality and Social Psychology Review*.

Abrams, D. (1985). Focus of attention in minimal intergroup discrimination. *British Journal of Social Psychology*, *24*, 65–74.

Abrams, D. (1990). How do group members regulate their behavior? An integration of social identity and self-awareness theories. In D. Abrams & M. A. Hogg (Eds.), *Social identity theory: Constructive and critical advances* (pp. 89–112). London and New York: Harvester Wheatsheaf and Springer-Verlag.

Abrams, D. (1992a). Processes of social identification. In G. Breakwell (Ed.), *Social psychology of identity and the self-concept* (pp. 57–99) San Diego, CA: Academic Press.

Abrams, D. (1992b). *Optimal Distinctiveness Theory with bells on: Music sub-culture identification among 16–20 year olds*. Paper presented at the European Association of Experimental Social Psychology Small Group Meeting on Social Cognition. Bristol, April.

Abrams, D. (1993). *From social identity to action*. "British Invited Speaker" presentation, British Psychological Society, Social Psychology Section Conference, Oxford, September.

Abrams, D. (1994). Social self-regulation. *Personality and Social Psychology Bulletin*, *20*, 273–283.

Abrams, D. (1996). Social identity, self as structure, and self as process. In W. P. Robinson (Ed.), *Social groups and identities: Developing the legacy of Henri Tajfel* (pp. 143–168). Oxford, UK: Butterworth Heinemann.

Abrams, D. (1999). Social identity, social cognition, and the self: The flexibility and stability of self-categorization. In D. Abrams & M. A. Hogg (Eds.), *Social identity and social cognition* (pp. 197–229). Oxford, UK: Blackwell.

Abrams, D., Ando, K., & Hinkle, S. W. (1998). Psychological attachment to the group: Cross-cultural differences in organizational identification and subjective norms as predictors of workers' turnover intentions. *Personality and Social Psychology Bulletin*, *24*, 1027–1039.

Abrams, D., & Brown, R. J. (1989). Self-consciousness and social identity: Self-regulation as a group member. *Social Psychology Quarterly*, *52*, 311–318.

Abrams, D., & Hogg, M. A. (1987). Language attitudes, frames of reference and social identity: A Scottish dimension. *Journal of Language and Social Psychology*, *6*, 201–213.

Abrams, D., & Hogg, M. A. (1988). Comments on the motivational status of self-esteem in social identity and intergroup discrimination. *European Journal of Social Psychology*, *18*, 317–334.

Abrams, D., & Hogg, M. A. (1990). An introduction to the social identity approach. In D. Abrams & M. A. Hogg (Eds.), *Social identity theory: Constructive and critical advances* (pp. 1–9). London and New York: Harvester Wheatsheaf and Springer-Verlag.

Abrams, D., & Hogg, M. A. (1998). Prospects for research in group processes and intergroup relations. *Group Processes and Intergroup Relations, 1*, 7–20.

Abrams, D., & Masser, B. (1998). Context and the social self-regulation of stereotyping: Perception, judgment, and behavior. In R. S. Wyer (Ed.), *Advances in social cognition* (Vol. 11, pp. 53–67). Hillsdale, NJ: Erlbaum.

Abrams, D., Marques, J. M., Bown, N., & Henson, M. (in press). Pro-norm and anti-norm deviance within and between groups. *Journal of Personality and Social Psychology.*

Abrams, D., Sparkes, K., & Hogg, M. A. (1985). Gender salience and social identity: The impact of sex of siblings on educational and occupational aspirations. *British Journal of Educational Psychology, 55*, 224–232.

Abrams, D., Thomas, J., & Hogg, M. A. (1990). Numerical distinctiveness, social identity and gender salience. *British Journal of Social Psychology, 29*, 87–92.

Abrams, D., Wetherell, M., Cochrane, S., Hogg, M. A., & Turner, J. C. (1990). Knowing what to think by knowing who you are: Self-categorization and the nature of norm formation, conformity and group polarization. *British Journal of Social Psychology, 29*, 91–119.

Adorno, T. W., Frenkel-Brunswik, E., Levinson, D. J., & Sanford, R. N. (1950). *The authoritarian personality.* New York: Harper.

Alloy, L. B., & Abramson, L. Y. (1982). Learned helplessness, depression, and the illusion of control. *Journal of Personality and Social Psychology, 42*, 1114–1126.

Allport, F. H. (1924). *Social psychology.* New York: Houghton Mifflin.

Aron, A., Aron, E. N., Tudor, M., & Nelson, G. (1991). Close relationships as including other in the self. *Journal of Personality and Social Psychology, 60*, 241–253.

Aron, A., Mashek, D., & Lewandowski, G. (1999). *The relational brain: Spatial and temporal cortical mapping of self and close others.* Society of Experimental Social Psychology Annual Conference, St. Louis, MO. October.

Asch, S. E. (1952). *Social psychology.* Englewood Cliffs, NJ: Prentice-Hall.

Ashmore, R. D., & Jussim, L. (1997). Toward a second century of the scientific analysis of self and identity. In R. D. Ashmore & L. Jussim (Eds.), *Self and identity: Fundamental issues* (Vol. 1, pp. 3–19). New York: Oxford University Press.

Bandura, A. (1982). Self-efficacy mechanisms in human agency. *American Psychologist, 37*, 122–147.

Bartlett, F. C. (1932). *Remembering.* Cambridge, UK: Cambridge University Press.

Baumeister, R. F. (1982). A self-presentational view of social phenomena. *Psychological Bulletin, 91*, 3–26.

Baumeister, R. F. (1987). How the self became a problem: A psychological review of historical research. *Journal of Personality and Social Psychology, 52*, 163–176.

Baumeister, R. F. (1998). The self. In D. T. Gilbert, S. T. Fiske, & G. Lindzey (Eds.), *Handbook of social psychology* (4th Ed., pp. 680–740). New York: McGraw-Hill.

Baumeister, R. F. (1999). The nature and structure of the self: An overview. In R. F. Baumeister (Ed.), *The self in social psychology* (pp. 1–20). Philadelphia, PA: Psychology Press.

Baumeister, R. F., Tice, D. M., & Hutton, D. G. (1989). Self-presentational motivations and personality differences in self-esteem. *Journal of Personality, 57*, 547–579.

Beck, A. T. (1967). *Depression: Clinical, experimental, and theoretical aspects.* New York: Harper and Row.

Bellezza, F. S. (1984). The self as a mnemonic device: The role of internal cues. *Journal of Personality and Social Psychology, 47*, 506–516.

Bellezza, F. S. (1993). Does "perplexing" describe the self-reference effect? Yes! In T. K. Srull & R. S. Wyer, Jr. (Eds.), *The mental representation of trait and autobiographical knowledge about the self: Advances in social cognition.* (Vol. V, pp. 51–60). Hillsdale, NJ: Erlbaum.

Billig, M. (1988). The notion of "prejudice": Some rhetorical and ideological aspects. *Text, 8,* 91–111.

Blumer, H. (1937). Social psychology. In E. P. Schmidt (Ed.), *Man and society* (pp. 144–198). New York: Prentice-Hall.

Bodenhausen, G., & Macrae, C. N. (1998). Stereotype activation and inhibition. In R. S. Wyer (Ed.), *Advances in social cognition* (Vol. 11, pp. 1–52). Hillsdale, NJ: Erlbaum.

Bond, R., & Smith, P. B. (1996). Culture and conformity: A meta-analysis of studies using Asch's (152b, 1956) line judgment task. *Psychological Bulletin, 119,* 111–137.

Brandstadter, H., Rothermund, K., & Dillmann, U. (1998). Maintaining self-integrity and efficacy through adulthood and later life: The adaptive functions of assimilative persistence and accommodative flexibility. In J. Heckhausen & C. S. Dweck (Eds.), *Motivation and self-regulation across the life span* (pp. 365–388). Cambridge, UK: Cambridge University Press.

Branscombe, N., & Wann, D. L. (1984). Collective self-esteem consequences of outgroup derogation when a valued social identity is on trial. *European Journal of Social Psychology, 24,* 641–657.

Branscombe, N., Ellemers, N., Spears, R., & Doosje, B. (1999). The context and content of social identity threat. In N. Ellemers, R. Spears, & B. Doosje (Eds.), *Social identity* (pp. 35–58). Oxford UK: Blackwell.

Breakwell, G. (1986). *Coping with threatened identities.* London: Methuen.

Breckler, S., & Greenwald, A. (1986). Motivational facets of the self. In R. Sorrentino & T. Higgins (Eds.), *Handbook of motivation and cognition* (pp. 145–164). New York: Guilford Press.

Brewer, M. B. (1988). A dual process model of impression formation. In T. K. Srull & R. S. Wyer (Eds.), *Advances in social cognition* (pp. 1–36). Hillsdale, NJ: Erlbaum.

Brewer, M. B. (1991). The social self: On being the same and different at the same time. *Personality and Social Psychology Bulletin, 17,* 475–482.

Brewer, M. B., & Brown, R. J. (1998). Intergroup relations. In D. T. Gilbert, S. T. Fiske, & G. Lindzey (Eds.), *The handbook of social psychology* (4th Ed., pp. 554–594). New York: McGraw-Hill.

Brewer, M. B., & Gardner, W. (1996). Who is this "We"? Levels of collective identity and self-representations. *Journal of Personality and Social Psychology, 71,* 83–93.

Brewer, M. B., & Silver, M. D. (in press). Group distinctiveness, social identification, and collective mobilization. In S. Stryker, T. Owens, & R. White (Eds.), *Self, identity, and social movements.*

Brown, R. J. (2000). *Group processes* (2nd Ed.). Oxford, UK: Blackwell.

Brown, R. J., & Abrams, D. (1986). The effects of intergroup similarity and goal interdependence on intergroup attitudes and task performance. *Journal of Experimental Social Psychology, 22,* 78–92.

Buss, A. H. (1980). *Self-consciousness and social anxiety.* Glencoe, IL: Free Press.

Caddick, B. (1981). Equity theory, social identity and intergroup relations. In L. Wheeler (Ed.), *Review of personality and social psychology* (Vol. 2, pp. 219–245). London: Sage.

Campbell, J. D. (1990). Self-esteem and clarity of the self-concept. *Journal of Personality and Social Psychology, 59,* 538–549.

Cantor, N. (1990). From thought to behavior: "Having" and "doing" in the study of personality and cognition. *American Psychologist, 45,* 735–750.

Cartwright, D., & Zander, A. (Eds.) (1969). *Group dynamics: Research and theory* (3rd Ed.). New York: Harper & Row.

Carver, C. S., & Scheier, M. F. (1981). *Attention and self-regulation: A control theory approach to human behavior.* New York: Springer-Verlag.

Carver, C. S., & Scheier, M. F. (1998). *On the self-regulation of behavior.* Cambridge, UK: Cambridge University Press.

Cheek, J. M., & Briggs, S. R. (1982). Self-consciousness and aspects of identity. *Journal of Research in Personality, 16*, 401–408.

Cialdini, R. B., Borden, R. J., Thorne, A., Walker, M. R., Freeman, S., & Sloan, L. R. (1976). Basking in reflected glory: Three (football) field studies. *Journal of Personality and Social Psychology, 34*, 366–374.

Cinnarella, M. (1998). Exploring temporal aspects of social identity: the concept of possible social identities. *European Journal of Social Psychology, 28*, 227–248.

Cooley, C. H. (1902). *Human nature and the social order.* New York: Scribners.

Crocker, J., Blaine, B., & Luhtanen, R. (1993). Self-esteem: Cognitive and motivational consequences for prejudice and intergroup behavior. In D. Abrams & M. A. Hogg (Eds.), *Group motivation: Social psychological perspectives* (pp. 52–67). Hemel Hempstead, UK: Harvester Wheatsheaf.

Crocker, J., & Luhtanen, R. (1990). Collective self-esteem and ingroup bias. *Journal of Personality and Social Psychology, 58*, 60–67.

Crocker, J., & Major, B. (1989). Social stigma and self-esteem: The self-protective properties of stigma. *Psychological Review, 96*, 608–630.

Crocker, J., & Schwartz, I. (1985). Prejudice and ingroup favoritism in a minimal intergroup situation: Effects of self-esteem. *Personality and Social Psychology Bulletin, 11*, 379–386.

Deaux, K. (1992). Personalizing identity and socializing self. In G. Breakwell (Ed.), *Social psychology of identity and the self-concept* (pp. 9–33). London: Academic Press.

Deaux, K. (1996). Social identification. In E. T. Higgins & A. W. Kruglanski (Eds.), *Social psychology: Handbook of basic principles* (pp. 777–798). New York: Guilford Press.

Deaux, K., Reid, A., Mizrahi, K., & Ethier, K. A. (1995). Parameters of social identity. *Journal of Personality and Social Psychology, 68*, 280–291.

Devine, P. G., Monteith, M. J., Zuwerink, J. R., & Elliot, A. J. (1991). Prejudice with and without compunction. *Journal of Personality and Social Psychology, 60*, 817–830.

Diener, E. (1980). Deindividuation: The absence of self-awareness and self-regulation in group members. In P. B. Paulus (Ed.), *The psychology of group influence.* Hilldsale, NJ: Erlbaum.

Doise, W. (1986). *Levels of explanation in social psychology.* Cambridge, UK: Cambridge University Press.

Doosje, B., Ellemers, N., & Spears, R. (1999). Commitment and intergroup behaviour. In N. Ellemers, R. Spears, & B. Doosje (Eds.), *Social identity* (pp. 84–106). Oxford, UK: Blackwell.

Durkheim, E. (1898). Représentations individuelles et représentations collectives. *Revue de Metaphysique et de Morale, 6*, 273–302.

Duval, S., & Wicklund, R. A. (1972). *A theory of objective self-awareness.* New York: Academic Press.

Dweck, C. (1999). *Self-theories: Their role in motivation, personality, and development.* Philadelphia, PA: Psychology Press.

Elias, N. (1988). *Die Gesellschaft der individuen* (The society of individuals). Frankfurt: Suhrkamp.

Ellemers, N., Kortekaas, P., & Ouwerkerk, J. W. (1999). Self-categorization, commitment to the group and group self-esteem as related but distinct aspects of social identity. *European Journal of Social Psychology, 29*, 371–390.

Ellemers, N., Spears, R., & Doosje, B. (Eds.) (1999). *Social identity.* Oxford, UK: Blackwell.

Farnham, S. D., Greenwald, A. G., & Banaji, M. R. (1999). Implicit self-esteem. In D. Abrams & M. A. Hogg (Eds.), *Social identity and social cognition* (pp. 230–248). Oxford, UK: Blackwell.

Farr, R. M. (1996). *The roots of modern social psychology: 1872–1954.* Oxford, UK: Blackwell.

Farr, R. M., & Moscovici, S. (Eds.) (1984). *Social representations.* Cambridge, UK: Cambridge University Press.

Farsides, T. (1995, September). *Why social identity theory's self-esteem hypothesis has never been tested – and how to test it.* Paper presented at the British Psychological Society Social Psychology Section Annual Conference, York, UK.

Fenigstein, A., & Abrams, D. (1993). Self-attention and the egocentric assumption of shared perspectives. *Journal of Experimental Social Psychology, 29*, 287–303.

Fenigstein, A., Scheier, M. F., & Buss, A. H. (1975). Public and private self-consciousness: Assessment
and theory. *Journal of Consulting and Clinical Psychology, 43*, 522–527.

Festinger, L. (1950). Informal social communication. *Psychological Review, 57*, 272–282.

Festinger, L. (1954). A theory of social comparison processes. *Human Relations, 7*, 117–140.

Fiske, S. T., & Neuberg, S. L. (1990). A continuum of impression formation, from category-based to
individuating processes: Influences of information and motivation on attention and interpretation.
In M. P. Zanna (Ed.), *Advances in experimental social psychology* (Vol. 23, pp. 1–74). New York:
Academic Press.

Fiske, S. T., & Von Hendy, H. M. (1992). Personality feedback and situational norms can control
stereotyping processes. *Journal of Personality and Social Psychology, 62*, 577–596.

Freud, S. (1922). *Group psychology and the analysis of the ego.* London: Hogarth Press.

Froming, W. J., & Carver, C. S. (1981). Divergent influences of private and public self-consciousness
in a compliance paradigm. *Journal of Research in Personality, 15*, 159–171.

Gaertner, L., & Schopler, J. (1998). Perceived ingroup entitativity and intergroup bias: An intercon-
nection of self and others. *European Journal of Social Psychology, 28*, 963–980.

Gagnon, A., & Bourhis, R. Y. (1996). Discrimination in the minimal group paradigm: Social identity
or self-interest. *Personality and Social Psychology Bulletin, 22*, 1289–1303.

Gecas, V., & Schwalbe, M. L. (1983). Beyond the looking-glass self: Social structure and efficacy-based
self-esteem. *Social Psychology Quarterly, 46*, 77–88.

Gibbons, F. X. (1990). Self-attention and behavior: A review and theoretical update. *Advances in
Experimental Social Psychology, 23*, 249–303.

Giles, H., & Johnson, P. (1987). Ethnolinguistic identity theory: A social psychological approach to
language maintenance. *International Journal of the Sociology of Language, 68*, 256–269.

Goffman, E. (1959). *The presentation of self in everyday life.* Garden City, NY: Doubleday Anchor.

Gollwitzer, P. M., & Kirchhof, O. (1998). The willful pursuit of identity. In J. Heckhausen & C. S.
Dweck (Eds.), *Motivation and self-regulation across the life span* (pp. 389–423). Cambridge, UK:
Cambridge University Press.

Graumann, C. F. (1986). The individualization of the social and the desocialization of the individual:
Floyd H. Allport's contribution to social psychology. In C. F. Graumann & S. Moscovici (Eds.),
Changing conceptions of crowd mind and behavior (pp. 97–116). New York: Springer-Verlag.

Greenberg, J., Solomon, S., Pyscczczynski, T., Rosenblatt, A., Burling, J., Lyon, D., Simon, L., & Pinel,
E. (1992). Why do people need self-esteem? Converging evidence that self-esteem serves an anxiety-
buffering function. *Journal of Personality and Social Psychology, 63*, 913–922.

Greenwald, A. G., & Banaji, M. R. (1995). Implicit social cognition: Attitudes, self-esteem, and
stereotypes. *Psychological Review, 102*, 4–27.

Greenwald, A. G., & Pratkanis, A. R. (1984). The self. In R. S. Wyer & T. K. Srull (Eds.), *Handbook
of social cognition* (Vol. 3, pp. 129–178). Hillsdale, NJ: Erlbaum.

Grieve, P. G., & Hogg, M. A. (1999). Subjective uncertainty and intergroup discrimination in the
minimal group situation. *Personality and Social Psychology Bulletin, 25*, 926–940.

Haslam, S. A., Oakes, P. J., McGarty, C., Turner, J. C., Reynolds, K. J., & Eggins, R. A. (1996).
Stereotyping and social influence: The mediation of stereotype applicability and sharedness
by the views of ingroup and outgroup members. *British Journal of Social Psychology, 35*, 369–
397.

Haslam, S. A., & Turner, J. C. (1992). Context-dependent variation in social stereotyping 2: The
relationship between frame of reference, self-categorisation and accentuation. *European Journal of
Social Psychology, 22*, 251–277.

Haslam, S. A., Turner, J. C., Oakes, P. J., McGarty, C., & Hayes, B. K. (1992). Context-dependent variation in social stereotyping 1: The effects of intergroup relations as mediated by social change and frame of reference. *European Journal of Social Psychology*, *22*, 3–20.

Heckhausen, J., & Dweck, C. S. (Eds.) (1998). *Motivation and self-regulation across the life span*. Cambridge, UK: Cambridge University Press.

Heckhausen, J., & Schulz, R. (1998). Developmental regulation in adulthood: Selection and compensa-. tion via primary and secondary control. In J. Heckhausen & C. S. Dweck (Eds.), *Motivation and self-regulation across the life span* (pp. 50–77). Cambridge, UK: Cambridge University Press.

Higgins, E. T. (1987). Self-discrepancy: A theory relating self and affect. *Psychological Review*, *94*, 319–340.

Higgins, E. T., & King G. A. (1981). Accessibility of social constructs: Information processing consequences of individual and contextual variability. In N. Cantor & J. F. Kihlstrom (Eds.), *Personality cognition, and social interaction* (pp. 69–122). Hillsdale, NJ: Erlbaum.

Hinkle, S. W., & Brown, R. J. (1990). Intergroup comparisons and social identity: Some links and lacunae. In D. Abrams & M. A. Hogg (Eds.), *Social identity theory: Constructive and critical advances* (pp. 48–70). Hemel Hempstead, UK: Harvester Wheatsheaf.

Hogg, M. A. (1992). *The social psychology of group cohesiveness* Hemel Hempstead, UK: Harvester Wheatsheaf.

Hogg, M. A. (in press a). Subjective uncertainty reduction through self-categorization: A motivational theory of social identity processes. *European Review of Social Psychology*.

Hogg, M. A. (in press b). Self-categorization and subjective uncertainty resolution: Cognitive and motivational facets of social identity and group membership. In J. P. Forgas, K. D. Williams, & L. Wheeler (Eds.), *The social mind: Cognitive and motivational aspects of interpersonal behavior*. New York: Cambridge University Press.

Hogg, M. A. (in press c). Social identity and the sovereignty of the group: A psychology of belonging. In C. Sedikides & M. B. Brewer (Eds.), *Individual self, relational self, and collective self: Partners, opponents, or strangers*. Philadelphia, PA: Psychology Press.

Hogg, M. A., & Abrams, D. (1988). *Social identifications: A social psychology of intergroup relations and group processes*. London: Routledge.

Hogg, M. A., & Abrams, D. (1990). Social motivation, self-esteem and social identity. In D. Abrams & M. A. Hogg (Eds.), *Social identity theory: Constructive and critical advances* (pp. 28–47). Hemel Hempstead, UK: Harvester Wheatsheaf.

Hogg, M. A., & Abrams, D. (1993). Towards a single-process uncertainty-reduction model of social motivation in groups. In M. A. Hogg & D. Abrams (Eds.), *Group motivation: Social psychological perspectives* (pp. 173–190). London: Harvester Wheatsheaf.

Hogg, M. A., & Grieve, P. (1999). Social identity theory and the crisis of confidence in social psychology: A commentary, and some research on uncertainty reduction. *Asian Journal of Social Psychology*, *2*, 43–57.

Hogg, M. A., & Mullin, B. A. (1999). Joining groups to reduce uncertainty: Subjective uncertainty reduction and group identification. In D. Abrams & M. A. Hogg (Eds.), *Social identity and social cognition* (pp. 249–79). Oxford, UK: Blackwell.

Hogg, M. A., & Sunderland, J. (1991). Self-esteem and intergroup discrimination in the minimal group paradigm. *Journal of Social Psychology*, *30*, 61–62.

Hogg, M. A., Terry, D., & White, K. (1995). A tale of two theories: A critical comparison of identity theory with social identity theory. *Social Psychology Quarterly*, *58*, 255–269.

Hogg, M. A., & Turner, J. C. (1987). Intergroup behaviour, self-stereotyping and the salience of social categories. *British Journal of Social Psychology*, *26*, 325–340.

Hogg, M. A., & Williams, K. D. (2000). From I to we: Social identity and the collective self. *Group Dynamics: Theory, Research, and Practice*, *4*, 81–97.

Hopkins, N., Reicher, S. D., & Levine, M. (1997). On the parallels between social cognition and the "new racism." *British Journal of Social Psychology, 36,* 305–330.

Insko, C. A., & Schopler, J. (1998). Differential distrust of groups and individuals. In C. Sedikides, J. Schopler, & C. A. Insko (Eds.), *Intergroup cognition and intergroup behavior* (pp. 75–108). Mawah, NJ: Erlbaum.

James, W. (1890). *Principles of psychology.* New York: Holt Rinehart & Winston.

Jetten, J., Hogg, M. A., & Mullin, B.-A. (2000). Ingroup variability and motivation to reduce subjective uncertainty. *Group Dynamics: Theory, Research, and Practice, 4,* 184–198.

Jetten, J., Spears, R., & Manstead, A. S. R. (1998). Defining dimensions of distinctiveness: Group variability makes a difference to differentiation. *Journal of Personality and Social Psychology, 74,* 1481–1492.

Judd, C. M., & Park, B. (1988). Outgroup homogeneity: Judgments of variability at the individual and group levels. *Journal of Personality and Social Psychology, 54,* 778–788.

Kahneman, D., & Miller, D. T. (1986). Norm theory: Comparing reality to its alternatives. *Psychological Review, 93,* 136–153.

Keenan, J. M. (1993). An exemplar model can explain Klein and Loftus's results. In T. K. Srull & R. S. Wyer, Jr. (Eds.), *The mental representation of trait and autobiographical knowledge about the self: Advances in social cognition* (Vol. V, pp. 69–78). Hillsdale, NJ: Erlbaum.

Kihlstrom, J. F., & Cantor, N. (1984). Mental representation of the self. In L. Berkowitz (Ed.), *Advances in experimental social psychology* (Vol. 17, pp. 145–177). New York: Academic Press.

Klein, S. B., & Loftus, J. (1993). The mental representation of trait and autobiographical knowledge about the self. In T. K. Srull & R. S. Wyer, Jr. (Eds.), *The mental representation of trait and autobiographical knowledge about the self: Advances in social cognition* (Vol. V, pp. 1–50). Hillsdale, NJ: Erlbaum.

Knowles, E. S., & Sibicky, M. E. (1990). Continuity and diversity in the stream of selves: Metaphorical resolutions of William James's one-in-many-selves paradox. *Personality and Social Psychology Bulletin, 16,* 676–687.

Kramer, R. M., & Tyler, T. R. (1995). *Trust in organizations.* Thousand Oaks, CA: Sage.

Kreuger, J. (1998). On the perception of social consensus. In M. P. Zanna (Ed.), *Advances in experimental social psychology* (Vol. 30). San Diego, CA: Academic Press.

Krueger, J., & Clement, R. W. (1994). The truly false consensus effect: An ineradicable and egocentric bias in social perception. *Journal of Personality and Social Psychology, 67,* 596–610.

Kuhn, M. H., & McPartland, T. S. (1954). An empirical investigation of self-attitudes. *American Sociological Review, 19,* 68–76.

Kunda, Z., Fong, G. T., Sanitoso, R., & Reber, E. (1993). Directional questions direct self-conceptions. *Journal of Experimental Social Psychology, 29,* 63–86.

Kunda, Z., Sinclair, L., & Griffin, D. (1997). Equal ratings but separate meanings: Stereotypes and the construal of traits. *Journal of Personality and Social Psychology, 72,* 720–734.

Kunda, Z., & Thagard, P. (1996). Forming impressions from stereotypes, traits, and behaviors: A parallel-constraint-satisfaction theory. *Psychological Review, 103,* 284–308.

Le Bon (1896). *The crowd: A study of the popular mind.* London: T. Fisher Unwin.

Leary, M. R., Tambor, E. S., Terdal, S. K., & Downs, D. L. (1995). Self-esteem as an interpersonal monitor: The sociometer hypothesis. *Journal of Personality and Social Psychology, 68,* 518–530.

Lemyre, L., & Smith, P. (1985). Intergroup discrimination and self-esteem in the minimal group paradigm. *Journal of Personality and Social Psychology, 49,* 660–670.

Lepore, L., & Brown, R. J. (1997). Automatic stereotype activation: Is prejudice inevitable? *Journal of Personality and Social Psychology, 72,* 275–287.

Lerner, M. J., & Miller, D. T. (1978). Just-world research and the attribution process: Looking back and ahead. *Psychological Bulletin, 85,* 1030–1051.

Lewin, J. (1952). *Field theory in social science*. New York: Harper & Row.

Locke, V., & Walker, I. (1999). Stereotyping, processing goals and social identity: Inveterate and fugacious characteristics of stereotypes. In D. Abrams & M. A. Hogg (Eds.), *Social identity and social cognition* (pp. 164–182). Oxford, UK: Blackwell.

Logan, R. D. (1987). Historical change in prevailing sense of self. In K. Yardley & T. Honess (Eds.), *Self and identity: Psycho-social perspectives* (pp. 13–26). Chichester, UK: Wiley.

Long, K., & Spears, R. (1997). The self-esteem hypothesis revisited: Opposing effects of personal and collective levels of esteem on intergroup differentiation. In R. Spears, P. J. Oakes, N. Ellemers, & S. A. Haslam (Eds.), *The social psychology of stereotyping and group live* (pp. 296–317). Oxford, UK: Blackwell.

Lorenzi-Cioldi, F. (1991). Self-stereotyping and self-enhancement in gender groups. *European Journal of Social Psychology, 21*, 403–417.

Luhtanen, R., & Crocker, J. (1992). A collective self-esteem scale: self-evaluation of one's social identity. *Personality and Social Psychology Bulletin, 18*, 302–318.

Mackie, D. M., & Smith, E. R. (1997). Intergroup relations: Insights from a theoretically integrative approach. *Psychological Review, 105*, 499–529.

Manicas, P. T. (1987). *A history and philosophy of the social sciences*. Oxford, UK: Blackwell.

Markova, I. (1987). Knowledge of the self through interaction. In K. Yardley & T. Honess (Eds.), *Self and identity: Psycho-social perspectives* (pp. 65–80). Chichester, UK: Wiley.

Markus, H. (1977). Self-schemata and processing information about the self. *Journal of Personality and Social Psychology, 35*, 63–78.

Markus, H., & Kitayama, S. (1991). Culture and the self: Implications for cognition, emotion, and motivation. *Psychological Bulletin, 98*, 224–253.

Markus, H., & Nurius, P. (1996). Possible selves. *American Psychologist, 41*, 954–969.

Markus, H., & Ruvolo, A. (1989). Possible selves: Personalized representations of goals. In L. A. Pervin (Ed.), *Goal concepts in personality and social psychology* (pp. 211–241). Hillsdale, NJ: Erlbaum.

Markus, H., & Wurf, E. (1987). The dynamic self-concept: A social psychological perspective. *Annual Review of Psychology, 38*, 299–337.

Marques, J. M., Abrams, D., Páez, D., & Martinez-Taboada, C. M. (1998). The role of categorization and ingroup norms in judgments of groups and their members. *Journal of Personality and Social Psychology, 75*, 976–988.

McConahay, J. B. (1983). Modern racism and modern discrimination: The effects of race, racial attitudes and context on simulated hiring decisions. *Personality and Social Psychology Bulletin, 9*, 551–558.

McDougall, W. (1920). *The group mind*. Cambridge, UK: Cambridge University Press.

McGarty, C. (1999). *Categorization in social psychology*. London: Sage.

McGarty, C., Turner, J. C., Oakes, P. J., & Haslam, A. (1993). The creation of uncertainty in the influence process: The roles of stimulus information and disagreement with similar others. *European Journal of Social Psychology, 23*, 17–38.

McGuire, W. J., McGuire, C. V., & Cheever, J. (1986). The self in society: Effects of social contexts on the sense of self. *British Journal of Social Psychology, 25*, 259–270.

Mead, G. H. (1934). *Mind, self, and society*. Chicago, IL: University of Chicago Press.

Metalsky, G., Halberstadt, L. J., & Abramson, L. Y. (1987). Vulnerability to depressive mood reaction: Towards a more powerful test of the diathesis-stress and causal mediation component of the reformulated theory of depression. *Journal of Personality and Social Psychology, 52*, 386–393.

Milgram, S., & Toch, H. (1969). Collective behavior: Crowds and social movements. In G. Lindzey & E. Aronson (Eds.), *Handbook of social psychology* (2nd Ed., Vol. 4, pp. 507–610). Reading, MA: Addison-Wesley.

Monteith, M. J. (1993). Self-regulation of prejudiced responses: Implications for progress in prejudice-reduction efforts, *Journal of Personality and Social Psychology Bulletin, 65*(3), 469–485.

Monteith, M. J. (1996). Affective reactions to prejudice-related discrepant responses: The impact of standard salience, *Personality and Social Psychology Bulletin, 22*(1), 48–59.

Monteith, M. J., Deenan, N. E., & Tooman, G. D. (1996). The effect of social norm activation on the expression of opinion concerning gay men and blacks. *Basic and Applied Social Psychology, 18*, 267–288.

Monteith, M. J., Devine, P. G., & Zuwerink, J. R. (1993). Self-directed versus other directed affect as a consequence of prejudice-related discrepancies. *Journal of Personality and Social Psychology, 64*(2), 198–210.

Moreland, R. L., & McMinn, J. G. (1999). Gone but not forgotten: Loyalty and betrayal among ex-members of small groups. *Personality and Social Psychology Bulletin, 25*, 1484–1494.

Mowday, R. T., Steers, R., & Porter, L. W. (1979). The measurement of organizational commitment. *Journal of Vocational Behavior, 14*, 224–247.

Mullin, B.-A., & Hogg, M. A. (1998). Dimensions of subjective uncertainty in social identification and minimal intergroup discrimination. *British Journal of Social Psychology, 37*, 345–365.

Mullin, B.-A., & Hogg, M. A. (1999). Motivations for group membership: The role of subjective importance and uncertainty reduction. *Basic and Applied Social Psychology, 21*, 91–102.

Newcomb, T. D. (1950). *Social psychology*. New York: Dryden Press.

Ng, S. H. (1982). Power and appeasement in intergroup discrimination. *Australian Journal of Psychology, 34*, 37–44.

Oakes, P. J. (1996). The categorization process: Cognition and the group in the social psychology of stereotyping. In W. P. Robinson (Ed.), *Social groups and identity: Developing the legacy of Henri Tajfel* (pp. 95–120). Oxford, UK: Butterworth-Heinemann.

Oakes, P. J., Haslam, S. A., & Reynolds, K. J. (1999). Social categorization and social context: Is stereotype change a matter of information or of meaning? In D. Abrams & M. A. Hogg (Eds.), *Social identity and social cognition* (pp. 55–79). Oxford, UK: Blackwell.

Oakes, P. J., Haslam, S. A., & Turner, J. C. (1994). *Stereotyping and social reality*. Oxford, UK: Blackwell.

Oakes, P. J., Haslam, S. A., & Turner, J. C. (1998). The role of prototypicality in group influence and cohesion: Contextual variation in the graded structure of social categories. In S. Worchel, J. F. Morales, D. Páez, & J. C. Deschamps (Eds.), *Social identity: International perspectives* (pp. 75–92). London: Sage.

Oakes, P. J., & Turner, J. C. (1980). Social categorization and intergroup behavior: Does minimal intergroup discrimination make social identity more positive? *European Journal of Social Psychology, 10*, 295–302.

Oakes, P. J., & Turner, J. C. (1986). Distinctiveness and the salience of social category memberships: Is there an automatic perceptual bias towards novelty? *European Journal of Social Psychology, 16*, 325–344.

Oakes, P. J., Turner, J. C., & Haslam, S. A. (1991). Perceiving people as group members: The role of fit in the salience of social categorisations. *British Journal of Social Psychology, 30*, 125–144.

Onorato, R. S., & Turner, J. C. (in press). The "I," the "me," and the "us": The psychological group and self-concept maintenance and change. In C. Sedikides & M. B. Brewer (Eds.), *Individual self, relational self, and collective self: Partners, opponents, or strangers*. Philadelphia, PA: Psychology Press.

Operario, D., & Fiske, S. T. (1999). Integrating social identity and social cognition: A framework for bridging diverse perspectives. In D. Abrams & M. A. Hogg (Eds.), *Social identity and social cognition* (pp. 26–55). Oxford, UK: Blackwell.

Plant, E. A., & Devine, P. G. (1998). Internal and external motivation to respond without prejudice. *Journal of Personality and Social Psychology, 75*, 811–832.

Platow, M. J., Harley, K., Hunter, J. A., Hanning, P., Shave, S., & O'Connell, A. (1997). Intepreting in-group favouring allocations in the minimal group paradigm. *British Journal of Social Psychology, 36*, 107–117.

Plomin, R., & Caspi, A. (1999). Behavioral genetics and personality. In L. A. Pervin & O. John (Eds.), *Handbook of personality: Theory and research* (2nd Ed., pp. 251–276). New York: Guilford Press.

Postmes, T., & Spears, R. (1998). Deindividuation and antinormative behavior: A meta-analysis. *Psychological Bulletin, 123*, 238–259.

Potter, J., & Wetherell, M. (1987). *Discourse and social psychology: Beyond attitudes and behaviour*. London: Sage.

Powers, W. T. (1973). *Behavior: The control of perception*. Chicago, IL: Aldine.

Pratto, F., Sidanius, J., Stallworth, L. M., & Malle, B. F. (1994). Social dominance orientation: A personality variable predicting social and political attitudes. *Journal of Personality and Social Psychology, 67*, 741–763.

Reicher, S. D. (1984). Social influence in the crowd: Attitudinal and behavioural effects of deindividuation in conditions of high and low group salience. *British Journal of Social Psychology, 23*, 341–350.

Reid, A., & Deaux, K. (1996). Relationship between social and personal identities: Segregation or integration. *Journal of Personality and Social Psychology, 71*, 1084–1091.

Reykowski, J. (1982). Social motivation. *Annual Review of Psychology, 33*, 123–154.

Rokeach, M. (Ed.) (1960). *The open and closed mind*. New York: Basic Books.

Rosch, E. E. (1978). Principles of categorization. In E. E. Rosch & B. B. Lloyd (Eds.), *Cognition and categorization*. Hillsdale, NJ: Erlbaum.

Rosenberg, S. (1988). Self and others: Studies in social personality and autobiography. In L. Berkowitz (Ed.), *Advances in experimental social psychology* (Vol. 21, pp. 57–95). New York: Academic Press.

Rothbart, M., & John, O. P. (1985). Social categorization and behavioral episodes: A cognitive analysis of the effects of intergroup contact. *Journal of Social Issues, 41*, 81–104.

Rubin, J. M. (2000). *In-group favouritism and out-group homogeneity: Explanations in terms of social identity theory, self-categorisation theory and self-anchoring theory*. Unpublished Ph.D. Thesis. University of Cardiff, Wales.

Rubin, J. M., & Hewstone, M. (1998). Social identity theory's self-esteem hypothesis: A review and some suggestions for clarification. *Personality and Social Psychology Review, 2*, 40–62.

Scheier, M. F., & Carver, C. S. (1981). Private and public aspects of self. In L. Wheeler (Ed.), *Review of personality and social psychology* (Vol. 2). London: Sage.

Sears, D. O., & Kinder, D. R. (1971). Racial tensions and voting in Los Angeles. In W. Z. Hirsch (Ed.), *Los Angeles: Viability and prospects for metropolitan leadership* (pp. 51–88). New York: Praeger.

Sedikides, C. (1993). Assessment, enhancement, and verification determinants of the self-evaluation process. *Journal of Personality and Social Psychology, 65*, 317–338.

Seligman, C., Olson, J. M., & Zanna, M. P. (Eds.), (1996). *The psychology of values. The Ontario symposium* (Vol. 8). Mahwah, NJ: Erlbaum.

Shaw, M. E. (1981). *Group dynamics: The psychology of small group behavior* (2nd Ed.). New York: McGraw-Hill.

Sherif, M. (1936). *The psychology of social norms*. New York: Harper and Row.

Sherif, M. (1966). *In common predicament*. Boston, MA: Houghton Mifflin.

Sherman, S. J., Hamilton, D. L., & Lewis, A. (1999). Perceived entitativity and the social identity value of group memberships. In D. Abrams & M. A. Hogg (Eds.), *Social identity and social cognition* (pp. 80–110). Oxford, UK: Blackwell.

Shrauger, J. S., & Schoeneman, T. J. (1979). Symbolic interactionist view of self-concept: Through the looking glass darkly. *Psychological Bulletin, 86*, 549–573.

Simmel, G. (1922/1955). *Conflict and the web of group affiliations*. New York: Free Press.

Simon, B. (1993). On the asymmetry in the cognitive construal of ingroup and outgroup: A model of egocentric social categorisation. *European Journal of Social Psychology, 23*, 131–147.

Simon, B. (1997). Self and group in modern society: Ten theses on the individual self and the collective self. In R. Spears, P. J. Oakes, N. Ellemers, & S. A. Haslam (Eds.), *The social psychology of stereotyping and group life*. Oxford, UK: Blackwell.

Simon, B., Glassner-Bayerl, B., & Statenwerth, I. (1991). Stereotyping and self-stereotyping in a natural intergroup context: The case of heterosexual and homosexual men. *Social Psychology Quarterly, 54*, 252–266.

Simon, B., & Hamilton, D. L. (1994). Self-stereotyping and social context: The effects of relative in-group size and in-group status. *Journal of Personality and Social Psychology, 66*, 699–711.

Singelis, T. M. (1994). The measurement of independent and interdependent self-construals. *Personality and Social Psychology Bulletin, 20*, 580–591.

Smith, E. R. (1999). Affective and cognitive implications of a group becoming part of the self: New models of prejudice and of the self-concept. In D. Abrams & M. A. Hogg (Eds.), *Social identity and social cognition* (pp. 183–196). Oxford, UK: Blackwell.

Smith, E. R., & Henry, S. (1996). An in-group becomes part of the self: Response time evidence. *Personality and Social Psychology Bulletin, 22*, 635–642.

Smith, E. R., & Zarate, M. A. (1990). Exemplar and prototype use in social categorization. *Social Cognition, 8*, 243–262.

Snyder, M. (1981). On the self-perpetuating nature of social stereotypes. In. D. L. Hamilton (Ed.), *Cognitive processes in stereotyping and intergroup behavior* (pp. 183–191) New York: Erlbaum.

Snyder, M., & Swann, W. B. (1978). Hypothesis-testing processes in social interaction. *Journal of Personality and Social Psychology, 36*, 1202–1212.

Sorrentino, R. M., & Roney, C. J. R. (2000). *The uncertain mind: Individual differences in facing the unknown*. Philadelphia, PA: Psychology Press.

Srull, T. K., & Wyer, Jr., R. S. (Eds.) (1993). *The mental representation of trait and autobiographical knowledge about the self: Advances in social cognition* (Vol. V). Hillsdale, NJ: Erlbaum.

Stapel, D. A. (2000). Moving from fads and fashions to integration: Illustrations from knowledge accessibility research. *European Bulletin of Social Psychology, 12*, 4–27.

Steele, C. M. (1988). The psychology of self-affirmation: Sustaining the integrity of the self. In L. Berkowitz (Ed.), *Advances in experimental social psychology* (Vol. 21, pp. 261–302). New York: Academic Press.

Steele, C. M., & Aronson, J. (1995). Stereotype threat and the intellectual test performance of African Americans. *Journal of Personality and Social Psychology, 69*, 797–811.

Stephenson, G. M. (1981). Intergroup bargaining and negotiation. In J. C. Turner & H. Giles (Eds.), *Intergroup behaviour* (pp. 168–198). Oxford, UK: Blackwell.

Stryker, S. (1987). Identity theory: Developments and extensions. In K. Yardley & T. Honess (Eds.), *Self and identity: Psychosocial perspectives* (pp. 83–103). Chichester, UK: Wiley.

Swann, W. B., Griffin, J. J., Predmore, S. C., & Gaines, B. (1987). The cognitive-affective crossfire: When self-consistency confronts self-enhancement. *Journal of Personality and Social Psychology, 52*, 881–889.

Tajfel, H. (1969). Cognitive aspects of prejudice. *Journal of Social Issues, 25*, 79–97.

Tajfel, H. (1972). Experiments in a vacuum. In J. Israel & H. C. Tajfel (Eds.), *The context of social psychology*. London: Academic Press.

Tajfel, H. (1974). Social identity and intergroup behavior. *Social Sciences Information, 13*, 65–93.

Tajfel, H. (Ed.) (1978). *Differentiation between social groups: Studies in the social psychology of intergroup relations*. London: Academic Press.

Tajfel, H. (1981). Social stereotypes and social groups. In J. Turner & H. Ciles (Eds.), *Intergroup behaviour* (pp. 144–167). Oxford, UK: Blackwell.

Tajfel, H., & Turner, J. C. (1979). An integrative theory of intergroup conflict. In W. G. Austin & S. Worchel (Eds.), *The social psychology of intergroup relations*. Monterey, CA: Brooks-Cole.

Tarde, G. (1901). *L'Opinion et la foule*. Paris: Libraire Félix Alcan.

Taylor, S. E. (1981). A categorization approach to stereotyping. In D. L. Hamilton (Ed.), *Cognitive processes in stereotyping and intergroup behavior* (pp. 88–114). Hillsdale, NJ: Erlbaum.

Tesser, A. (1988). Toward a self-evaluation maintenance model of social behavior. In L. Berkowitz (Ed.), *Advances in experimental social psychology* (Vol. 21, pp. 181–227). San Diego, CA: Academic Press.

Trafimow, D., Silverman, E. S., Fan, R. M., & Law, J. S. F. (1997). The effects of language and priming on the relative accessibility of the private self and the collective self. *Journal of Cross-Cultural Psychology, 28*, 107–123.

Trafimow, D., & Smith, M. D. (1998). An extension of the "two baskets" theory to Native Americans. *European Journal of Social Psychology, 28*, 1015–1019.

Trafimow, D., Triandis, H. C., & Goto, S. G. (1991). Some tests of the distinction between the private self and the collective self. *Journal of Personality and Social Psychology, 60*, 649–655.

Triandis, H. C. (1989). The self and social behavior in differing cultural contexts. *Psychological Review, 96*, 506–520.

Triandis, H. C. (1994). *Culture and social behavior*. New York: McGraw-Hill.

Triandis, H. C. (1995). *Individualism and collectivism*. Boulder, CO: Westview Press.

Trotter, W. (1919). *Instincts of the herd in peace and war*. London: Oxford University Press.

Turner, J. C. (1975). Social comparison and social identity: Some prospects for intergroup behaviour. *European Journal of Social Psychology, 5*, 5–34.

Turner, J. C. (1981). The experimental social psychology of intergroup behavior. In J. C. Turner & H. Ciles (Eds.), *Intergroup behaviour* (pp. 66–101). Oxford, UK: Blackwell.

Turner, J. C. (1985). Social categorization and the self-concept: A social cognitive theory of group behavior. In J. Lawler (Ed.), *Advances in group processes* (Vol. 2). Greenwich, CT: JAI Press.

Turner, J. C. (1992). *Social influence*. Milton Keynes, UK: Open University Press.

Turner, J. C. (1999). Some current issues in research on social identity and self-categorization theories. In N. Ellemers, R. Spears, & B. Doosje (Eds.), *Social identity* (pp. 6–34). Oxford, UK: Blackwell.

Turner, J. C., & Giles, H. (Eds.) (1981). *Intergroup behaviour*. Oxford, UK: Blackwell.

Turner, J. C., Hogg, M. A., Oakes, P. J., Reicher, S. D., & Wetherell, M. (1987). *Rediscovering the social group: A self-categorization theory*. Oxford, UK: Blackwell.

Turner, J. C., Oakes, P. J., Haslam, S. A., & McGarty, C. (1994). Self and collective: Cognition and social context. *Personality and Social Psychology Bulletin, 20*, 454–463.

Turner, R. H. (1987). Articulating self and social structure. In K. Yardley & T. Honess (Eds.), *Self and identity: Psychosocial perspectives* (pp. 119–132). Chichester, UK: Wiley.

Vallacher, R. R. (1978). Objective self-awareness and the perception of others. *Personality and Social Psychology Bulletin, 4*, 63–67.

Vescio, T., Hewstone, M., & Crisp, R. (1999). Perceiving and responding to multiply categorizable individuals: Cognitive processes and affective ingroup bias. In D. Abrams & M. A. Hogg (Eds.), *Social identity and social cognition* (pp. 111–140). Oxford, UK: Blackwell.

Wagner, U., Lampen, L., & Syllwasschy, J. (1986). Ingroup inferiority, social identity and outgroup devaluation in a modified minimal group study. *British Journal of Social Psychology, 25*, 15–23.

Watson, J. B. (1919). *Psychology from the standpoint of a behaviorist*. Philadelphia, PA: Lippincott.

Wicklund, R. A. (1975). Objective self-awareness. In L. Berkowitz (Ed.), *Advances in experimental social psychology* (Vol. 8, pp. 233–275). New York: Academic Press.

Wicklund, R. A., & Gollwitzer, P. M. (1982). *Symbolic self-completion.* Hillsdale, NJ: Erlbaum.

Wicklund, R. A., & Gollwitzer, P. M. (1987). The fallacy of the private-public self-focus distinction. Journal of Personality, 55, 491–523.

Wundt, W. (1916). *Elements of folk psychology: Outlines of a psychological history of the development of mankind.* London: Allen and Unwin.

Wylie, R. C. (1979). *The self-concept* (2nd Ed.). Lincoln, NB: University of Nebraska Press.

Zimbardo, P. (1969). The human choice: Individuation, reason, and order versus deindividuation, impulse, and chaos. In W. J. Arnold & D. Levine (Eds.), *Nebraska symposium on motivation* (Vol. 17, pp. 237–307). Lincoln, NB: University of Nebraska Press.

CHAPTER EIGHT

It Takes Two to Tango: Relating Group Identity to Individual Identity within the Framework of Group Development

Stephen Worchel and Dawna Coutant

A favorite childhood story is Hans Christian Andersen's tale of the Ugly Duckling. For those whose memories have faded, the story recounts the perils of an ugly fowl whose characteristics set him apart from his siblings. This unsightly bird just did not fit in with the flock. He was criticized, rejected, and mistreated. However, as time passed and the ducklings matured, the ugly duckling grew into a beautiful swan, becoming the envy of all his peers.

In many respects, this has been the fate of "the group" in social psychology. With its focus on the individual, social psychology has had a difficult time accepting the group as a true member of the flock. Although the group has been a part of social psychology since the field's beginning (Triplett, 1898), it has occupied a rather tenuous position. Social psychologists have scoffed at the notion of a "group mind" (Le Bon, 1895/1960). Allport (1924) observed that nobody ever tripped over a group, an insult questioning the very existence of the group. The rejection of the group became so complete that Steiner (1974) entitled an article, "What ever happened to the group in social psychology?" For a time, the group was banished to the foreign lands of organizational psychology and sociology.

But the group could not stay a stranger for long. It wormed its way back into the fold, but its rebirth had a unique twist. Early definitions of the group described it as a unit consisting of several individuals who interacted with each other and occupied "real" space (Shaw, 1981). However, the born-again group was accepted into the domain of social psychology only as a cognitive representation, a figment of the mind. Instead of the individual being in the group, the group was now within the individual; Hogg and Abrams (1988) stated that "the group is thus within the individual . . ." (p. 19).

The cognitive flavoring applied to group research had profound effects on the methodology and theoretical approaches to the study of group dynamics (Abrams & Hogg, 1998; Moreland, Hogg, & Hains, 1994). Rather than examining the individual's behavior in the group context, much of the newer research investigated how individuals perceived the group, formed impressions about group members, and, most importantly, incorporated the group into the representation of the self (Hogg & Abrams, 1999; Turner, 1982). Although there is ample reason to lament the de-emphasis of behavior, the cognitive focus opened some exciting new vistas for study. Henri Tajfel and his associates (Tajfel & Turner, 1979; Hogg & Abrams, 1988) gave "the group" a starring role in the drama of the formation of the individual's identity. They argued that there are two foundations on which this identity is built. One is personal identity, which includes the unique personal characteristics of the single individual. The other is social identity, the memberships the individual claims in various groups. Individuals, it was argued, strive to maintain a positive social identity. Much of this striving occurs through the process of social comparison (Festinger, 1954). Comparisons involving social identity motivate individuals to enhance the position of their ingroup relative to outgroups.

Social identity theory (SIT) gave rise to a rich and broad tradition of research (see Rubin & Hewstone, 1998; Worchel, Morales, Páez, & Deschamps, 1998). Attention was focused on how individuals categorize their social world into ingroups and outgroups (Doise, 1998; Tajfel & Turner, 1979). Other research examined the nature and process of intergroup discrimination, delving into the conditions that lead to the elevation of the ingroup, discrimination against the outgroup, or both (Brewer & Miller, 1984). SIT became the springboard for new approaches to understanding stereotyping (Haslam, Turner, Oakes, McGarty, & Hays, 1992; Ng, 1989; Spears, Oakes, Ellemers, & Haslam, 1997), prejudice (Bagby & Rector, 1992), ethnic violence (Worchel, 1999) and other forms of intergroup relations. The perspective was applied to a host of traditional social psychological issues such as interpersonal perception (Park & Rothbart, 1982), minority influence (Clark & Maass, 1988), and group productivity and social loafing (Worchel, Rothgerber, Day, Hart, & Buttemeyer, 1998).

From Inside the Head to Inside the Group

There can be little argument against the position that individuals develop and hold mental representations of groups and that groups play an important role in the individual's identity, However, groups are not merely entities within the file drawer of the mind. Groups are physical realities that dot the social landscape like trees in a dense forest. Groups have form (social and physical boundaries) and structure (roles and norms) and they have a history. Indeed, groups often survive long after the original members have turned to dust. Our recent work on ethnic identity found that many people spend considerable energy searching for the physical markers that demonstrate the roots of their ethnic groups (Worchel, 1999). The very soil from which the ethnic group sprang becomes sacred ground that is often the source of violent and protracted human conflict. The history of the group is often the justification used to legitimize the group's existence and its behavior (Bar-Tal, 1990). Groups often go to considerable lengths to construct their histories. Indeed, it is the group's history that often forms its identity, and, consequently, the identities of the members of the group. Just as the group is within the individual (Hogg & Abrams, 1988), the individual is within the group, occupying both physical and social space.

The acceptance of the group as a structure that embraces the individual has important implications for personal identity, group perceptions, and intergroup relations. These implications complement rather than compete with the positions taken by social identity theory and self-categorization theory. Indeed, we will argue that viewing groups as dynamic units and studying the interpersonal behavior that occurs within and between groups will lead to a better understanding of, and more accurate predictions about, individual identity.

Expanding the Foundation of Personal Identity

Social identity theory presents individual identity as a point along a continuum ranging from personal identity on one end to social identity on the other end. One's identity at a specific time is represented by a single point on the continuum. A multitude of variables affect whether personal identity or social identity will be most salient, and which of the many group memberships will be most prominent on the social identity side of the equation. The conceptualization of social identity as being composed of group membership leads to the hypothesis that people discriminate in order to enhance the position of their ingroups relative to that of outgroups. The motivation behind this action is to create a positive social identity (Tajfel, 1978), reduce threats to self-esteem (Hogg & Abrams, 1990; Long & Spears, 1997), or reduce uncertainty (Hogg, 2000; Hogg & Abrams, 1993).

We (Worchel, Iuzzini, Coutant, & Ivaldi, 2000) recently offered an expanded model of individual identity. We suggested that there are actually four, rather than two, components that form identity. One component is *personal identity*, agreeing with the SIT model that this dimension includes an individual's specific physical and personality characteristics. A second component, which we labeled *group membership*, encompasses the social identity end of the continuum offered by SIT. Group membership includes the representation (categorization) of the social world into groups and information about membership in these groups (ingroup and outgroup). To this dimension, we added the suggestion that one's social identity is as much about the groups to which one does not belong (outgroups) as the group to which one does belong (ingroup). The third component in our model is *intragroup identity*. This factor recognizes that individuals reside within groups and occupy positions within those groups. The data that comprise intragroup identity include the status and role one has within a group and the relationship one has with ingroup members. This component is similar to, but broader than, the concept of "member esteem" (person's perception of his or her performance in the group) proposed by Luhtanen and Crocker (1992).

The final dimension, *group identity*, recognizes the need of the group to develop an identity of its own. The identity includes the group's boundaries, its beliefs and values, its history, and its reputation within the wider domain of groups. For example, a group's reputation may be conservative, aggressive, supportive, or rigid. This reputation is often portrayed in the symbols the group uses to represent itself. Once formed, groups strive to maintain this collective identity, often pressuring individual members to support and represent this identity. Several investigators have flirted with the existence of a group identity. Bar-Tal (1990) evokes the concept of "group belief" in suggesting that a common belief or attitude can reside within the group. Luhtanen and Crocker (1992) propose a "public collective self-esteem" (regard for the group held by non-members) that clothes a group like a large shroud. Suggesting that the group pressures individuals to uphold a group identity is a departure from the SIT position that views individuals as manipulating groups to serve their individual identities.

We suggested that rather than a single continuum running from personal identity to social identity, individual identity operates at all levels simultaneously. That is, each of the four dimensions has its own continuum ranging from high to low salience. Salience, in this case, refers to the degree of prominence or awareness accorded to a particular dimension at a specific time. The degree of salience of any one dimension is orthogonal to the salience of any other dimension. Therefore, the individual's identity at any single point of time is made up of contributions from each of these dimensions. For example, a Japanese student visiting an American university commented on the difficulty of dealing with the facts that: (1) she was physically distinct from others (personal identity); (2) she was Japanese (group membership); (3) she came from a wealthy Japanese family which implied that her performance should be superior to other Japanese students (intragroup identity); and (4) at the particular time, Japan was very concerned about presenting itself as a country concerned with women's rights (group identity). The student was always aware of each of these dimensions and her behavior was influenced by all of them. However, the student stated that her intragroup and group identities were most salient when she was with her Japanese friends. When she was in a mixed group of American and Japanese students, all of the dimensions were very prominent for her. Worchel et al. (2000) suggested that there may be times when all four dimensions are highly salient, only some dimensions are highly salient, or none of the dimensions are salient. In the latter case, the individual's behavior will be most strongly affected by variables outside the identity, such as environmental conditions. However, when one or more identity dimension is salient, behavior will be influenced by internal (identity) factors.

Our approach gives the group a clear role outside the cognitive structure of the individual. Although we do not deny that individuals hold mental representations of groups and that these representations can and do exert influence, we also argue that groups are entities that exist outside the person and exert real pressure. We suggest that group dynamics has interpersonal and intergroup components that cannot be ignored in the study of the relationship between individual and group. Although group activities have an impact on the identity of the individual member, the group must be examined within a true social paradigm.

One further point is worth mentioning here. Although SIT builds its base within the mind of the individual, it is largely concerned with intergroup relations. In this sense it is largely, although not exclusively, unidirectional. It argues that the well-spring of intergroup behavior lies deep within the individual's concern with individual identity. This, however, may not always be the case. Our model suggests that in addition to this pathway, intergroup behavior may result from a group's concern with its own identity, thereby bypassing direct influence from members' concerns with their own identities. In other words, individuals may react against an outgroup solely to protect their ingroup, without concern for the self. Indeed, it is not difficult to find examples where groups encourage (demand) members to put aside personal identity concerns in order to serve group goals. One is reminded of President John F. Kennedy's famous request, "Ask not what your country can do for you; instead ask what you can do for your country."

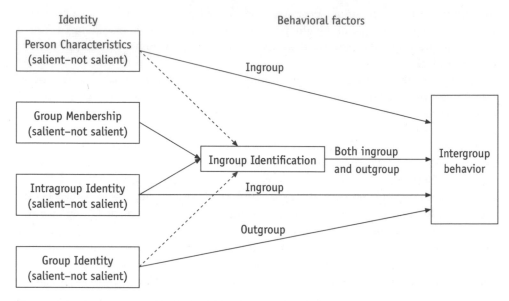

Figure 8.1 Components of individual identity and their influence on intergroup behavior.

Worchel et al. (2000) used the four-dimension model of identity to address the perplexing issue about the route that group discrimination will take (Brewer, 1979; Hinkle & Brown, 1990; Mullen, Brown, & Smith, 1990). The relative position of the ingroup can be enhanced by: (1) directly favoring the ingroup; (2) depreciating the outgroup; or (3) employing both behaviors. Determining exactly which route will be chosen has been the topic of considerable research. Worchel et al. (2000) suggested that one of the factors that determines the nature of intergroup discrimination will be the dimension(s) of identity that are salient at the time of behaving. As seen in Figure 8.1, discrimination will involve enhancing the ingroup position when Person Characteristics are most salient. On the other hand, increasing the salience of the Group Identity dimension will motivate responses aimed at depriving the outgroup. And when Group Membership is highly salient, discrimination will involve behavior directed at both the ingroup and the outgroup, and the level of identification with the ingroup will moderate the intensity of these actions. Evidence for these effects comes from studies designed to have individuals focus on various aspects of their identity before responding in an intergroup situation.

With these points in mind, it is important to explore the factors that influence the salience of each dimension of identity. We can begin this exploration by examining a factor that affects both individual identity and intergroup behavior: group development.

The Pattern of Group Development

Even while accepting the dynamic nature of groups, traditional social psychology has often presented groups as a fixed stage on which individual behavior grabs the spotlight. Individuals act while the group supplies the context. Groups, like loving parents watching their children in the playground, sit passively by without response or change.

This representation of groups has been periodically questioned by investigators over the last 50 or so years. A coordinated challenge arose from the t-group movement that was initiated by Kurt Lewin. The students of t-groups viewed the group as the star of the show, carrying along individual members like flotsam in a raging river. Groups, they argued, develop and change in predictable ways as if following a predetermined script. Tuckman (1965; Tuckman & Jensen, 1977) identified five stages of group development (forming, storming, norming, performing, and adjourning) and described the members' behaviors associated with each stage. Several other investigators (LaCoursiere, 1980; Mullen et al., 1992) have offered models of group development, each suggesting that groups are dynamic entities that follow a developmental pathway, even as group members enter and leave the group. Moreland and Levine (1982) took this dynamic approach a step further by pointing out that individual membership within a group undergoes a series of transitions. Hence, both members and groups follow scripts, albeit separate scripts. These models argue that groups are more than cognitive representations carried by individuals. In fact, they suggest that groups can move along their path of appointed destiny quite independent of the development process of individual group members.

Using this work as a starting point, we (Worchel, 1996; Worchel, 1998; Worchel, Coutant-Sassic, & Grossman, 1992; Worchel, Coutant-Sassic, & Wong, 1993) studied a wide variety of groups ranging from small laboratory groups to large social movements. We, too, observed predictable patterns in group development, but we found that these patterns were often repeated during the life of the group. Group development, we observed, occurs through a series of repeated cycles, rather than by the linear track proposed by other models. Our model has been discussed in detail in several previous publications, so only a brief review is now in order. Our observations suggested that once group members have been selected, groups begin a stage of *group identification*. The goal of this stage is to establish an identity *for the group*. The group focuses on establishing clear boundaries, often seeking competition with other groups (Worchel et al., 1993). The group avoids accepting new members. There are strong pressures for conformity and members often adopt a group uniform. Groupthink (Janis, 1982) is common. Dissenters are punished and/or rejected. The norm of equality is adopted and little distinction is made between members. In fact, deviants are rejected and minorities have little influence (Worchel, Grossman, & Coutant, 1992). There is a high state of emotional excitement and information processing tends to be peripheral (Petty & Cacioppo, 1986).

Once group identity has been established, the focus turns to *group productivity*. During this stage, the group's attention centers on defining goals and developing plans to reach those goals. Groups are often most productive during this stage (Worchel et al., 1992). Distinctions between group members are made on the basis of task-related skills and experiences. Group members become more analytical in their approach to issues and central processing of information predominates (Petty & Cacioppo, 1986). New members are invited into the group, but membership is based on their task-related skills; these workers often hold a more marginal status than older members do. The group is less likely to seek competition with outgroups, but social comparison between groups takes place.

The *individuation* stage that follows is characterized by a decided shift in focus within the group. During the group productivity phase, the group often accumulates resources. Now, members direct attention toward how these resources should be divided. Individuals attempt to establish their own unique identity within the group. Comparison between group members is prevalent, and individual members make their claims on the group resources. The norm of equity rather than equality is emphasized. Differences between group members become salient. Individuals begin to explore membership opportunities in outgroups, and they use these opportunities to establish their "worth" within their group. Leadership becomes fragmented and decentralized. Social loafing is common and individuals demand direct compensation for contributions to the group.

The disintegration of the group continues into the stage of *decay*. At this point, members may defect from the group. Scapegoating takes place and leaders are often blamed for group ills. The individual focus is accelerated, and the need for the group is questioned.

In some cases, the decay destroys the group and it ceases to exist. However, in many other cases, the group, albeit with a different set of members, begins the process of rebuilding. A distinct incident or threat may ignite the rebirth, or the rebuilding may be initiated by the collective actions of a subset of the members. Whatever the reason, the group enters again into the *group identification* stage, and the cycle of group development begins anew.

We have identified several triggers that propel the group from one stage to the next (Worchel, 1996). One such trigger appears to be success in reaching the goal of the stage. For example, when group members feel that they have clearly established the identity and independence of their group, the group moves from the *group identification* phase to the *group productivity* phase. Likewise, the accumulation of resources during the *group productivity* phase invites the *individuation* stage. Interestingly, a second trigger seems to be the failure to reach a goal. Groups that fail to establish consensus on group identity may turn attention toward productivity issues. And the failure to reach productivity goals may excite members to individuate themselves, taking what they can from the group and seeking a safe haven. Although moving the group to a new phase, failure in one stage generally presages difficulties in the next phase. A third motivator for change may be simply the weight of time. In several of the groups that we examined, there seemed to be a collective decision that "we have spent enough time on this issue," and it is time to move on to another issue. Finally, threat plays an interesting role on group development (Rothgerber, 1997). A threat to the group as a whole tends to move the group into the *group identification* stage, regardless of when this threat occurs. Indeed, wily leaders often use the impending danger of an outside group to ignite ingroup concerns with identity. However, if the threat is directed toward individual members, *individuation* may occur. This is especially likely when the threat arises from within the group. For example, an individual who feels that his or her membership within the group is responsible for a personal hardship may seek redress and personal recognition from the ingroup.

Although the model identifies discrete stages, the boundaries between the stages are often fuzzy, characterized more by an emphasis of concern than by a focus on only one issue. These fuzzy boundaries are especially prevalent when the group is moving from one stage to another. Further, the impact of threat demonstrates that the order of progression from one stage to the next is not necessarily fixed. Events may occur that propel the group to leap over stages, either forwards or backwards. There is, however, a most likely course that will be followed.

Earlier publications offered support for the model and the impact of group development on productivity (Worchel et al., 1992; Worchel et al., 2000), intergroup relations (Worchel et al., 1993), leadership (Worchel, Jenner, & Hebl, 1998), and stereotyping (Worchel & Rothgerber, 1997). Therefore, let us examine how group development relates to group and individual identity as well as targets for social comparison. The central theme of this discussion will be that group development has a profound influence on both the formation of identity and on social comparison. And although both are cognitive processes, they are molded and shaped by the dynamic social aspects of groups.

Group Development and the Standard for Social Comparison

One of the most universal of all social behaviors involves comparing oneself with others. Whether the mirror is on the wall or within the social environment, humans spend time and energy searching for their reflection. Charles Horton Cooley (1902) referred to this tendency in coining the term "looking glass self." And Festinger (1954) placed the process center stage in his social comparison theory. In its original form, social comparison theory was elegantly concise and straightforward. Festinger argued that there are many aspects of the self that are not reflected in the mirror on the wall. In many cases, information about the self is reflected in social reality, which can only be defined by comparing with other people. Comparisons, however, are not conducted in a random fashion. We tend to compare with others who are similar to us on relevant dimensions. There have been numerous efforts to improve and refine the theory (Tesser, 1988), but the basic positions have remained and received considerable support (Suls & Wills, 1991).

Although social comparison theory has been invited into many domains of social psychology, one of its most important roles has been in social identity theory (Hogg, in press). Tajfel and Turner (1986) argued that people desire to hold the most positive social identity possible. One step toward this goal is to elevate the relative position (status) of one's ingroup relative to that of outgroups. At the foundation of this jockeying for superiority is the process of social comparison. Individuals compare (and manipulate) the position of their ingroup with that of the outgroup. The result of this process is played out in the intergroup arena, the heart of SIT.

If we compare the treatment of social comparison in Festinger's presentation of the theory and Tajfel's use of it in SIT, an interesting paradox seems to emerge. Festinger argues that we seek similar others with whom to compare. Who should be more similar to a group member than other members of his or her ingroup? Turner and his colleagues (Turner, Hogg, Oakes, Reicher, & Wetherell, 1987) state that the self-categorization process involves carefully placing similar others in the ingroup category, and relegating those who are viewed as dissimilar on important dimensions to the outgroup. This suggests that comparisons should be focused within the group, creating competition and a struggle for relative advantage between group members. However, social identity theory implies that social comparison takes place between individuals in different groups, leading to intergroup competition and conflict.

The situation seems to demand a duel between the two theories to determine which is correct. We suggest that no duel is, in fact, necessary. Indeed, both theories are correct.

Worchel et al. (2000) argue that individuals engage in simultaneous comparisons with ingroup and outgroup members, and that several factors influence which comparison is most salient. We propose that one of the most influential factors that determines the target of social comparison is *group development*. The developmental stage of the group influences whether individuals will be most interested in comparing with outgroup members or with fellow ingroup members.

As the earlier discussion of the group development model indicated, the *group identification* stage is characterized by efforts to create a group identity. Equality between members is stressed, as is conformity. The group is concerned with establishing clear boundaries between the group and outgroups. This is the phase where members are likely to adopt a common group uniform, symbol, or mannerism. Each of these activities should discourage comparisons with and distinctions between ingroup members, and encourage comparisons with outgroup members. Therefore, we would predict that the intergroup comparisons offered by social identity theory should be most evident during the *group identification* stage of development.

On the other hand, the focus of the group during the *individuation* stage turns inward, within the ingroup. At this point, members are concerned with establishing their unique position within the group. They desire to make their claim for group resources and/or group recognition. Equity is the predominant group norm. The demand for equity requires that group members distinguish themselves from other ingroup members. Therefore, the most important comparisons are those that occur within the ingroup. It should also be expected that the search for similar ingroup members to use as standards will be especially salient. In other words, individuals will not only look within the group for standards of social comparison, but also they will focus on comparing themselves to members who have equal tenure, comparable skills, and who have made similar contributions to the group.

At this point, the support for these hypotheses is admittedly incomplete, but it is intriguing. In a longitudinal study of ongoing laboratory groups, Worchel et al. (1993) asked group members several questions about the relationship they preferred to have with ingroup and outgroup members. As Figure 8.2 shows, during the early phase of the group, members desired competition with the outgroup and cooperation within the ingroup. However, toward the end of the group's existence preferences had changed dramatically to show that members wanted competition within the ingroup and cooperation with the outgroup. Several investigators (Festinger, 1954; Goethals & Darley, 1987) have pointed out that competition offers opportunities to make social comparisons. Competition often clearly delineates a winner and a loser and invites a comparison of skills between the opponents. Social comparisons within a cooperative interaction are more difficult to make. In these cases, individuals generally combine efforts, often contributing to the final product in very different ways. Cooperation blurs the boundaries between the participants while competition sharpens these boundaries.

In another study (Worchel et al., 2000), students in a class setting were asked whether they preferred to see the distribution of test scores for their own class or for other classes taking the same test. Overall, there was a strong tendency for students to request the distribution of their own class, suggesting a desire for comparisons within the group. However, the preference for ingroup distributions was greater for tests given late in the semester than on early tests. Although these data did not deal explicitly with the social comparison process,

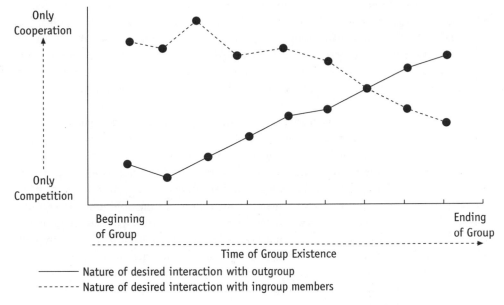

Figure 8.2 Impact of group development on desired relationship with the ingroup and outgroup.

they are consistent with the position that group members desired information that would allow outgroup comparisons during the early class periods and ingroup comparisons later in the group's life.

Relevant to our position is the observation that social identity and self-categorization theories focus considerable attention on the formation of new groups, albeit often in the form of cognitive categories, and behaviors that follow the formation of these groups. For example, research (Bourhis, Sachdev, & Gagnon, 1994; Tajfel, 1970) employing the minimal group paradigm (MPG) often examines participants' behaviors immediately after new groups (or categories) are created and participants have had no opportunity to interact (Tajfel & Turner, 1986). Our developmental model of groups suggests that this early group stage should focus on group identification, and that comparisons should be made between groups rather than within the group. Therefore, we argue, it is not surprising to find social comparisons and intergroup behavior concerned with the outgroup. On the other hand, research aimed at testing hypotheses derived directly from social comparison theory takes place in a different arena. Although much of the research is interpersonal rather than group or intergroup (Goethals & Darley, 1987; Suls & Wills, 1990), those studies that adopt a group focus often deal with long-standing groups or categories. For example, Tesser (1988) examined preferences for comparisons between close friends (ingroup members) versus strangers. Zanna, Goethals, and Hill (1975) studied comparison between same-sex and opposite-sex groups. The distinction between these categories is well established. It is possible, then, that differences in the preferred standard for comparison found by these two bodies of research may be influenced by conditions of the groups which are involved in each paradigm.

An exhaustive examination of the research in the social comparison and social identity areas is beyond the scope of this chapter (see Hogg, in press). Our aim at this point is to simply raise the possibility that group development can influence the social comparison process. To this end, we suggest that a threat to one's ingroup not only instigates groups to move from one stage to another, but it also influences the target for social comparison. Research on group development indicates that a threat to the group moves the group into the *group identification* stage. For example, Rothgerber and Worchel (1997) reported that disadvantaged groups became increasingly concerned about their identity when they perceived that another disadvantaged group was performing better than their group. Worchel and Coutant (1997) suggested that a similar process occurs in the relationship between nations. A threat by one nation to the identity or existence of another nation gives rise to heightened nationalism and an increase in the number of incidents of patriotism within the threatened nation. One further effect of these threats seems to be the diminution of comparisons within the nation and the increase of comparisons with the threatening nation. Finally, Sheeran, Abrams, and Orbell (1995) found that selfesteem was related to intergroup comparisons, but that a temporary threat (unemployment) to personal well-being instigated intrapersonal comparisons. Taken together, these findings appear consistent with the position that the outside threat leads groups to focus on group identity, which, in turn, invites comparisons with the outgroup.

Group Development and Group and Individual Identity

Relating social comparison to group development allows us to introduce the temporal factor to the broader issue of identity in general. We suggest that the quest for identity takes place at two levels, the group and the individual. Moreland and Levine (1982, 1984) also stressed the importance of time in their model of group membership. They argued that individuals go through a series of stages ranging from prospective member to ex-member in their relationship to the group. Each stage is characterized by a specific set of predominant behaviors and by changes in the commitment to the group. Each stage can also be viewed as affecting the way members view themselves, but the exact nature of this relationship has not been fully explored.

Our approach to identity is similar, but decidedly distinct, from that taken by Moreland and Levine. In their model, the group is presented as the context or the field through which the individual member passes. Although they accept that the group may respond differently to the individual as he or she goes through the stages of membership, they do not address the possibility that the group, too, undergoes changes that affect the individual's role and identity. In a sense, their approach casts the group in the role of a spectator watching a butterfly develop through the stages from cocoon to caterpillar to butterfly. The spectator may marvel and be attracted to or repelled by the butterfly at various stages, but the responses are orchestrated by the butterfly. We are proposing that the group is more than an interested spectator in this process. The group, we argue, undergoes a series of predetermined changes, and each of these changes affects the role, behavior, and identity of the individual. The influence of the individual on the group has been aptly represented in research and theory on such topics as leadership (Fiedler, 1978, 1981) and minority influence (Moscovici & Nemeth, 1974). We stress the other side of the coin, the group's influence on the individual. The spectator (the group), we suggest, strongly influences the form taken by the butterfly (the individual).

To understand how the group helps sculpt the individual identity, we refer back to the notion of reflected appraisal (Cooley, 1902). Using Cooley's analogy of the mirror into which individuals gaze to find their identities, we argue that the stages of group development change the nature of the identity mirror. Each stage creates a mirror that emphasizes a different component of the individual's identity. With this picture in mind, let us make specific links between group development stages and the components of individual identity. Recall that we have suggested that there are actually four components to the individual's identity: personal identity, intragroup identity, social membership, and group identity. All of these components exist at any period of time, but the individual's identity is the result of the unique combination of these components and the salience of each.

The initial stage (*group identification*) of group development is concerned with the identity of the group as an entity. There are strong pressures on individual members to focus their attention on building the group's identity and ensuring its independence. During this stage of group development, the individual's attention is guided toward concerns about the group as a whole and its relationship to the outgroup. The individual is the group and the group's identity is the individual's. As a result, the *group identity* and *group membership* components are the most salient parts of the identity puzzle. Individual members view themselves as embodying the group. Further, the identities of the individual members will be very similar within the group, reflecting the group identity itself.

As the group moves into the *group productivity* phase, attention shifts toward identifying and attaining group goals. Group unity is still important, but individual members become important to the extent that they can help the group achieve its goals. Their contribution toward group identity becomes less critical. As a result, the group encourages individuals to focus on different components of their identity. At this stage, *group membership* and *intragroup identity* are emphasized by the individual. Self-identity is most strongly determined by the group to which they belong and by the position or role they have within the group. The identity of group members begins to diverge, but the divergence is built around the positions they occupy within the group.

During the *individuation* stage, the nature of personal identity again changes. As Figure 8.3 indicates, events in the group at this point encourage individuals to emphasize *intragroup identity* and *personal identity*. The intragroup identity focus allows members to negotiate their role in the group and a salient personal identity component sets the stage for a possible withdrawal from the group.

During the *decay* phase, we suggest that *personal identity* becomes most salient. As the group disintegrates, it becomes every man, woman, and child for themselves. The group disavows the individual members and the individuals, in turn, seek to distance themselves from the group. The individual's survival is dependent on his or her personal characteristics that are the currency that can be used to buy membership in other groups or gain favor in the existing group. The group condition encourages an egocentric focus, but the focus is on uniquely individual features as opposed to group-based or social features.

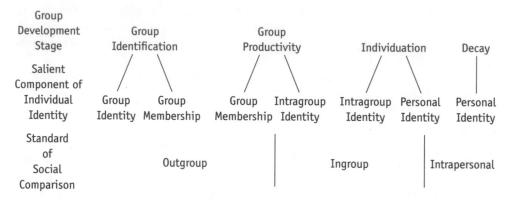

Figure 8.3   Change in the salience of components of individual identity and standard of social comparison as a function of group development stage.

Figure 8.3 presents the hypothesized relationship between group development, salience of domains of identity, and social comparison. As can he seen, we suggest that during the initial phase of development, Group Identity and Group Membership are most salient, and social comparisons tend to be made with outgroup members. However, by the *individuation* phase, Intragroup Identity and Personal Identity have become the focus of the individual's attention, and social comparisons are made with ingroup members. Finally, as the group begins to disintegrate, the focus is on the self: Personal Identity is salient and the individual compares his or her present state with both past conditions and desired personal outcomes.

At present, the basis of support for the proposed relationship between group development and individual identity comes from observations of ongoing work groups. Free discussion within these groups has been examined with an eye toward how individuals talk about and present themselves at various stages of group life. These observations showed that individuals do present themselves differently at the various stages and the presentations approximate the relationship we have outlined. If future research upholds this relationship, it has quite dramatic implications for interactions both within groups and between groups. For example, division of resources should show decided ingroup favoritism during early stages of group development. However, during the latter stages, the division of resources should be aimed at favoring the individual, often to the disadvantage of the ingroup. Further, individuals should view themselves as the prototype of the group during the early stages, but see themselves as unique and separate from other group members later in the group.

From Group-to-Individual Identity to Group-to-Group Identity

Up to this point, we have been concerned with how the group influences the identities of its individual members. The focus on individuals maintains our membership in the psychology camp. However, in closing we would like to spend some of our idiosyncrasy credits and expand our focus. We have argued that groups, like individuals, are concerned with establishing their identity. Groups, like individuals, strive for the most positive identity. This identity is critical for attracting and retaining group members, and, therefore, is crucial for the survival of the group (LaCoursiere, 1980). Just as individuals craft their identities from internal (personal) components and social (interpersonal/intergroup) components, we suggest that group identity springs from two sources. One aspect of group identity, like the personal component of individual identity, is internal. This component involves the composition of the group (its members) and its physical attributes (the territory it occupies, its size, its resources, and so on), Groups, therefore, have a strong interest in attracting the most coveted individuals to the group and ensuring that these members reach their potential. The group can bask in the glory of the achievement of individual members. The advances of individual members reflect on the group itself. However, the motivation to maintain group harmony competes with the group's desire to support individual accomplishments. Too great a difference between the achievements and attributes of individual members within the group will create intragroup conflict and jealousy between group members. As a result, groups must deal with the constant internal tension between developing and advancing the position of individual members and maintaining a harmony that results from internal homogeneity.

It should be noted that we are suggesting that the dilemma facing groups regarding how to treat members is similar to the dilemma faced by members contemplating their relationship with the group. Brewer (1993) suggests that individuals are torn between the desire for interdependence and security which drives them to join groups (and become the prototypical member) and the desire for distinctiveness/uniqueness which pushes them to avoid groups and/or be unique within the group. It is interesting to speculate that this ambivalence may be the source of energy that moves members through the various stages of group membership postulated by Moreland and Levine. We argue that groups, too, are faced with a dilemma. On the one hand, they want to give members the freedom to develop their potential and become unique. On the other hand, the group wants to treat members equally and minimize their distinctiveness (Figure 8.4).

The tension from dealing with these two opposing goals is not only vital for the group's identity, but it also is the source of energy that propels groups through developmental stages and works against stagnation. It is this tension that is responsible for the dynamic nature of groups. Although we wish to avoid becoming too Freudian in our approach, the struggle by the group to achieve a balance between member individuation and interdependence offers fertile grounds for future research.

In addition to this internal struggle, groups also live within a social community populated by other groups. Unfortunately, traditional social psychological approaches to the social community of groups present a rather impoverished picture. With few exceptions (Hartstone & Augoustinos, 1995; Huddy & Virtanen, 1995), investigators of intergroup relations have presented a two-group social field, the ingroup and the outgroup. Although, there may be many situations that involve only two groups, in many other situations, groups inhabit a crowded social world involving many groups (the ingroup and multiple outgroups). And groups must establish their identity within this field.

In a series of studies aimed at examining disadvantaged groups, Rothgerber and Worchel (1997) created a social field involving three groups: a disadvantaged ingroup, a disadvantaged outgroup, and an advantaged outgroup. The general design placed the participant in a disadvantaged group that worked on a series of tasks. Participants were led to believe that

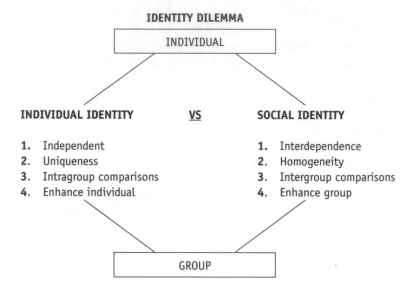

Figure 8.4 Group and individual identity dilemmas: Stressing individual identity or social identity.

two other groups, one disadvantaged and one advantaged, were working on the same tasks. The participants received feedback about the performance of their group and the other groups. They were then given the opportunity to respond to their group and the outgroups.

A number of general patterns in the results are interesting. First, participants differentiated between the two outgroups and they responded differently to each outgroup. This finding is important because it shows that individuals do not necessarily divide their world into an ingroup and an outgroup. They do recognize the social environment as containing several distinct outgroups. A second interesting finding was that the response to an outgroup was influenced by the outgroup's characteristics and behavior *and* the behavior of the other outgroup. For example, the advantaged outgroup that performed at a constantly high level was harmed more when subjects were told that the disadvantaged outgroup performed poorly as compared to when it performed equal or better than the subject's disadvantaged group (Figure 8.5). These data argue that it is important to consider the broad context when examining intergroup relations. Finally, and more important to the present discussion, the results of the studies suggested that the ingroup chose to compare itself with the other similar outgroup (disadvantaged outgroup), and that these comparisons influenced the responses to the outgroup and the perceptions (identity) of the ingroup. When the disadvantaged outgroup (similar outgroup) performed better than the ingroup, that outgroup became a target for harm and the ingroup image suffered. In this case, individual members attempted to distance themselves from the ingroup by presenting themselves as dissimilar to other members and disavowing responsibility for the ingroup's performance. However, strong performance by the dissimilar outgroup (advantaged outgroup) did not elicit harm or affect perceptions of the ingroup.

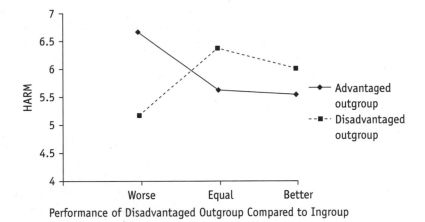

Figure 8.5 Level of harm delivered to outgroups as a function of disadvantaged outgroup's performance compared to ingroup.

This latter pattern of results suggests that the process of establishing a group identity is very similar to that involved in establishing an individual's social identity (Tajfel, 1982). Groups compare themselves with outgroups and these comparisons affect the group's identity. However, when multiple outgroups populate the field the comparisons at the group level conform to social comparison theory predictions in that similar outgroups are chosen as the standard for comparisons. We would, therefore, argue that just as individuals are concerned with their individual identities, so, too, are groups concerned with establishing their identities. However, groups are often torn between the internal concern of allowing individual members to develop their unique identities and the external concern of developing the group identity.

Once again, we can apply the developmental framework to predict the outcome of this internal–external tension. Our group development model proposes that the *group identification* phase is characterized by efforts to establish group identity and group independence. Therefore, this phase should be characterized by concerns with social comparisons between groups and relatively little tolerance for individual concerns with identity. At this point, groups should show a strong sensitivity toward recognizing the various outgroups and distinguishing between these different groups. During the latter phases, *individuation* and *decay*, the emphasis is on individual identity. At this time, groups' focus should be turned within the group. Individual differences should be recognized and tolerated, and relatively little effort should be devoted toward distinguishing between outgroups.

Conclusion

Looking back over the territory we have covered, we hope that by complicating the issue of identity we have ultimately painted a clearer picture. In many respects, the previous research and theory on both social identity and group development has been elegantly simple and admirably focused. However, this laudable foundation has exacted a price. Research on social identity has often yielded conflicting results (Hinkle & Brown, 1990) and required expansion, refinement, and alteration of the basic theory (Mullen, Brown, & Smith, 1992). At the same time, group development models have spawned surprisingly little research and the studies that have used this framework have been narrowly focused on group phases, thereby avoiding the mainstream of social psychology.

Our aim has been to address these issues by explicitly linking the two areas. We have argued that both individuals and groups are engaged in a quest to establish their respective identities. The identities of the two entities are intertwined like the tight embrace of new lovers. The individual's identity is the result of a combination of personal, intragroup, and intergroup characteristics. The group's identity is composed of the fusion of the identities of individual members (internal) and the group's relation to other groups (external). Social comparison is one of the central processes underlying the formation of each of these identities. However, the focus of the comparison is both dynamic and changing in its attention.

Groups, we suggest, take an active role in focusing the comparison process and in shaping individual identity. Groups move through stages like the seasons of the year. The change from stage to stage may be gradual or abrupt, and the course may he altered by outside events. However, there is a dynamic to group change that lumbers along in a rather predictable fashion. These changes play a significant role in orchestrating both the content and process of individual and group identity. The inclusion of group development in the study of identity allows for more precise predictions and a deeper understanding of identity. The group development context removes some of the randomness often associated with changes in personal identity and it offers a framework from which to predict the path of discrimination (advantaging the ingroup as opposed to disadvantaging the outgroup).

Obviously, more data are necessary before the present approach can be embraced. However, it does seem clear that the group is an active participant in the quest for identity. The social world is not simply a willing handmaiden, waiting to be ordered and organized by the individual's cognitive powers. The give-and-take relationship between the individual and the group presents individual identity as a dynamic process rather than a stable endpoint, and it helps explain why groups are forever in a constant state of flux. Both of these objectives should point the way toward new research.

Finally, we would like to leave the reader with one parting thought to contemplate. There is a seductive allure to the conclusion that individuals love and value their ingroup and loathe the outgroups. However, our examination of the complexity of individual identity and the social comparison that occurs within and between groups paints a different picture. Individuals, we argue, are locked in an ambivalent (love–hate) relationship with both their ingroup and the outgroups. They are both attracted and repelled by their ingroup. The attraction to the ingroup is based on the important position it occupies in the self-identity and the security individuals gain from membership. On the other hand, the insidious nature of social comparison with ingroup members and the motivation to remain independent incites resentment against the ingroup. Likewise, individuals are attracted and repelled by outgroups. The attraction has several bases. One is that social comparisons with outgroup members are less ego threatening than ingroup comparisons because of the implied dissimilarity between the individual and outgroup members. The comparison affords the opportunity to learn about the outgroup without personal threat. Second, the outgroup represents an alternative for the individual should he or she exit the ingroup. And in a perverse sense, the outgroup is seen as the agent keeping the ingroup in cheek, thereby preventing it from taking the individual's membership for granted. Indeed, several investigators (Allport, 1954; Fiske, 1999) have remarked on the irony that stereotypes of outgroups are often laced with very positive traits. This dual ambivalence should be at the base of all intergroup behaviors, and its existence may help explain why an individual's responses to the ingroup and outgroup vary so dramatically over time.

REFERENCES

Abrams, D., & Hogg, M. A. (1998). Prospects for research in group processes and intergroup relations. *Group Processes and Intergroup Relations, 1*, 7–20.

Allport, F. H. (1924). *Social psychology*. Cambridge, MA: Riverside Press.

Allport, G. W. (1954). *The nature of prejudice*. Cambridge, MA: Addison-Wesley.

Bagby, R. M., & Rector, N. A. (1992). Prejudice in a simulated legal context: A further application of social identity theory. *European Journal of Social Psychology, 22*, 397–406.

Bar-Tal, D. (1990). *Group beliefs*. New York: Springer-Verlag.

Bourhis, R. Y., Sachdev, I., & Gagnon, A. (1994). Intergroup research with the Tajfel matrices: Methodological notes. In M. Zanna & J. Olson (Eds.), *The social psychology of prejudice: The Ontario symposium* (Vol. 7, pp. 209–232). Hillsdale, NJ: Erlbaum.

Brewer, M. (1979). The role of ethnocentrism in intergroup conflict. In W. G. Austin & S. Worchel (Eds.), *The social psychology of intergroup relations* (pp. 33–47). Monterey; CA: Brooks/Cole.

Brewer, M. B. (1993). Social identity, distinctiveness, and ingroup homogeneity. *Social Cognition, 11*, 150–164.

Brewer, M. B., & Miller, N. (1984). Beyond the contact hypothesis: theoretical perspectives on desegregation. In N. Miller & M. Brewer (Eds.), *Groups in contact: The psychology of desegregation* (pp. 281–302). New York: Academic Press.

Clark, R., & Maass, A. (1988). Social categorization in minority influence: The case of homosexuality. *European Journal of Social Psychology, 18*, 347–364.

Cooley, C. H. (1902). *Human order and social order*. New York: Scribner.

Doise, W. (1998). Social representations in personal identity. In S. Worchel, J. Morales, D. Páez, & J.-C. Deschamps (Eds.), *Social identity: International perspectives*. London: Sage.

Festinger, L. (1954). A theory of social comparison processes. *Human Relations, 7*, 117–140.

Fiedler, F. E. (1978). Recent developments in research on the contingency model. In L. Berkowitz (Ed.), *Group processes* (pp. 209–225). New York: Academic Press.

Fiske, S. (1999). *(Dis)respecting versus (dis)liking: Ambivalent stereotypes*. Paper presented at New England Social Psychology Association, Dartmouth, NH: October.

Goethals, G. R., & Darley, J. M. (1987). Social comparison theory: Self-evaluation and group life. In B. Mullen & G. R. Goethals (Eds.), *Theories of group behavior*. New York: Springer-Verlag.

Hartstone, M., & Augoustinos, M. (1995). The minimal group paradigm: Categorization into two versus three groups. *European Journal of Social Psychology, 25*, 179–193.

Huddy, L., & Virtanen, S. (1995). Subgroup differentiation and subgroup bias among Latinos as a function of familiarity and positive distinctiveness. *Journal of Personality and Social Psychology, 68*, 97–108.

Haslam, S. A., Turner, J. C., Oakes, P. J., McGarty, C., & Hayes, B. K. (1992). Context dependent variation in social stereotyping: The effects of intergroup relations as mediated by social change and frame of reference. *European Journal of Social Psychology, 22*, 3–20.

Hinkle, S., & Brown, R. J. (1990). Intergroup comparisons and social identity: Some links and lacunae. In D. Abrams & M. A. Hogg (Eds.), *Social identity theory: Constructive and critical advances* (pp. 48–70). New York: Springer-Verlag.

Hogg, M. A. (2000). Subjective uncertainty reduction through self-categorization: A motivational theory of social identity processes. *European Review of Social Psychology, 12*.

Hogg, M. A. (in press). Social identity and social comparison. In J. Suls & L. Wheeler (Eds.), *Handbook of social comparison: Theory and research*. New York: Plenum.

Hogg, M. A., & Abrams, D. (1988). *Social identifications: A social psychology of intergroup relations and group processes*. London: Routledge.

Hogg, M. A., & Abrams, D. (1990). Social motivation, self-esteem, and social identity. In D. Abrams & M. Hogg (Eds.), *Social identity theory: Constructive and critical advances* (pp. 28–47). New York: Springer-Verlag.

Hogg, M. A., & Abrams, D. (1993). Toward a single process-uncertainty reduction model of social motivation in groups. In M. Hogg & D. Abrams (Eds.), *Group motivation: Social psychological perspectives* (pp. 173–190). New York: Springer-Verlag.

Hogg, M. A., & Abrams, D. (1999). Social identity and social cognition: Historical background and current trends. In D. Abrams & M. Hogg (Eds.), *Social identity and social cognition* (pp. 1–25). Oxford, UK: Blackwell.

Janis, I. (1982). *Groupthink* (2nd Ed.). Boston, MA: Houghton Mifflin.

LaCoursiere, R. B. (1980). *The life cycle of groups*. New York: Human Sciences Press.

Le Bon, G. (1895/1960). *The crowd* (translation of *Psychologie des foules*). New York: The Viking Press.

Long, M. K., & Spears, R. (1997). The self-esteem hypothesis revisited: Differentiation and the disaffected. In R. Spears, P. Oakes, N. Ellemers, & S. Haslam (Eds.), *The social psychology of stereotyping and group life* (pp. 296–317). Oxford, UK: Blackwell.

Luhtanen, R., & Crocker, J. (1992). A collective self-esteem scale: Self-evaluation of one's social identity. *Personality and Social Psychology Bulletin, 18*, 302–318.

Moreland, R. L., Hogg, M., & Hains, S. (1994). Back to the future: Social psychological research on groups. *Journal of Experimental Social Psychology, 30*, 527–555.

Moreland, R. L., & Levine, J. M. (1982). Socialization in small groups: Temporal changes in individual group relations. In L. Berkowitz (Ed.), *Advances in experimental social psychology* (Vol. 15). New York: Academic Press.

Moreland, R. L., & Levine, J. M. (1984). Role transitions in small groups. In V. L. Allen & E. van de Vliert (Eds.), *Role transitions: Explorations and explanations* (pp. 181–195). New York: Plenum.

Moscovici, S., & Nemeth, C. (1974). Social influence II: Minority influence. In C. Nemeth (Ed.), *Social psychology, Classic and contemporary integrations*. Chicago, IL: Rand-McNally.

Mullen, B. (1987). Self-attention theory: The effects of group composition on the individual. In B. Mullen & G. R. Goethals (Eds.), *Theories of group behavior* (pp. 125–146). New York: Springer-Verlag.

Mullen, B., Brown, R., & Smith, C. (1992). Ingroup bias as a function of salience, relevance, and status: An integration. *European Journal of social Psychology, 22*, 103–122.

Ng, S. H. (1989). Intergroup behaviour and the self. *New Zealand Journal of Psychology, 18*, 1–12.

Park, B., & Rothbart, M. (1982). Perception of outgroup homogeneity and levels of social categorization: Memory for the subordinate attributes of ingroup and outgroup members. *Journal of Personality and Social Psychology, 42*(6), 1051–1068.

Petty, R. E., & Cacioppo, J. T. (1986). The elaboration likelihood model of persuasion. In L. Berkowitz (Ed.), *Advances in experimental social psychology* (Vol. 19, pp. 123–205). New York: Academic Press.

Rothgerber, H. (1997). External intergroup threat as an antecedent to perceptions of ingroup and outgroup homogeneity. *Journal of Personality and Social Psychology, 73*, 1206–1221.

Rothgerber, H., & Worchel, S. (1997). The view from below: Intergroup relations from the perspective of the disadvantaged group. *Journal of Personality and Social Psychology, 73*, 1191–1203.

Rubin, M., & Hewstone, M. (1998). Social identity theory's self-esteem hypothesis: A review and some suggestions for clarification. *Personality and Social Psychology Review, 2*, 40–62.

Shaw, M. E. (1981). *Group dynamics: The psychology of small group behavior.* New York: McGraw-Hill.

Sheeran, P., Abrams, D., & Orbell, S. (1995). Unemployment, self-esteem, and depression: A social comparison theory approach. *Basic and Applied Social Psychology, 17*, 65–82.

Spears, R., Oakes, P., Ellemers, N., & Haslam, S. (Eds.) (1997). *The social psychology of stereotyping and group life.* Oxford, UK: Blackwell.

Steiner, I. D. (1974). Whatever happened to the group in social psychology? *Journal of Experimental Social Psychology, 10*, 94–108.

Suls, J., & Wills, T. A. (Eds.) (1990). *Social comparison: Contemporary theory and research.* Hillsdale, NJ: Erlbaum.

Tajfel, H. (1970). Experiments in intergroup discrimination. *Scientific American, 223*, 96–102.

Tajfel, H. (1978). Interindividual behaviors and intergroup behavior. In H. Tajfel (Ed.), *Differentiation between small groups: Studies in the social psychology of intergroup relations* (pp. 27–60). New York: Academic Press.

Tajfel, H. (1982). *Social identity and intergroup relations.* Cambridge, UK: Cambridge University Press.

Tajfel, H., & Turner, J. C. (1979). An integrative theory of intergroup conflict. In W. G. Austin & S. Worchel (Eds.), *The social psychology of intergroup relations* (pp. 33–47). Monterey, CA: Brooks/Cole.

Tajfel, H., & Turner, J. C. (1986). The social identity theory of intergroup behavior. In S. Worchel & W. G. Austin (Eds.), *The psychology of intergroup relations* (pp. 7–24). Chicago, IL: Nelson-Hall.

Tesser, A. (1988). Toward a self-evaluation maintenance model of social behavior. In L. Berkowitz (Ed.), *Advances in experimental social psychology* (Vol. 21, pp. 181–227). New York: Academic Press.

Tuckman, B. W. (1965). Developmental sequences in small groups. *Psychological Bulletin, 63*, 384–399.

Tuckman, B. W., & Jensen, M. A. C. (1977). Stages of small-group development revisited. *Group and Organization Studies, 2*, 419–427.

Triplett, H. C. (1898). The dynamogenic factors in pacemaking and competition. *American Journal of Psychology, 9*, 507–533.

Turner, J. C. (1982). Toward a cognitive redefinition of the social group. In H. Tajfel (Ed.), *Social identity and intergroup relations.* Cambridge, UK: Cambridge University Press.

Turner, J. C., Hogg, M. A., Oakes, P. J., Reicher, S. D., & Wetherell, M. S. (Eds.) (1987). *Rediscovering the social group: A self-categorization theory.* Oxford, UK: Blackwell.

Worchel, S. (1996). Emphasizing the social nature of groups in a developmental framework. In J. L. Nye & A. M. Brower (Eds.), *What's social about social cognition?* (pp. 261–282) Thousand Oaks, CA: Sage.

Worchel, S. (1998). A developmental view of the search for group identity. In S. Warchel, J. Morales, D. Páez, & J. Deschamps (Eds.), *International perspectives on social identity.* London: Sage.

Worchel, S. (1999). *Written in blood: Ethnic identity and the struggle for human harmony.* New York: Worth.

Worchel, S., & Courant, D. (1997). The tangled web of loyalty: Nationalism, patriotism, and ethno-centrism. In D. Bar-Tal & E. Staub (Eds.), *Patriotism in the life of individuals and nations* (pp. 190–210). Chicago, IL: Nelson-Hall.

Worchel, S., Coutant-Sassic, D., & Grossman, M. (1992). A developmental approach to group dynamics: A model and illustrative research. In S. Worchel, W. Wood, & J. Simpson (Eds.), *Group process and productivity* (pp. 181–202). Newbury Park, CA: Sage.

Worchel, S., Coutant-Sassic, D., & Wong, F. (1993). Toward a more balanced view of conflict: There is a positive side. In S. Worchel & J. A. Simpson (Eds.), *Conflict between people and groups*. Chicago, IL: Nelson-Hall.

Worchel, S., Grossman, M., & Courant, D. (1994). Minority influence in the group context: How group factors affect when the minority will be influential. In S. Moscovici, A. Mucchi-Faina, & A. Maass (Eds.), *Minority influence* (pp. 97–114). Chicago, IL: Nelson-Hall.

Worchel, S., Iuzzini, J., Courant, D., & Ivaldi, M. (2000). A multidimensional model of identity: Relating individual and group identity to intergroup behavior. In R. Brown & D. Capozza (Eds.), *Social identity processes: Trends in theory and research*. London: Sage.

Worchel, S., Jenner, S., & Hebl, M. (1998). Changing of the guard: How origin of the new leader and disposition of the ex-leader affect group performance. *Small Group Research, 29*, 436–451.

Worchel, S., Morales, J. F., Páez, D., & Deschamps, J.-C. (Eds.) (1998). *Social identity: international perspectives*. London: Sage.

Worchel, S., & Rothgerber, H. (1997). Changing the stereotype of the stereotype. In R. Spears, P. Oakes, N. Ellemers, & S. Haslam (Eds.), *The social psychology of stereotyping and group life: Emphasizing the side of group perceptions* (pp. 72–93). London: Sage.

Worchel, S., Rothgerber, H., Day, E., Hart, D., & Buttemeyer, J. (1998). Social identity and indi-vidual productivity within groups. *British Journal of social Psychology, 37*, 389–413.

Zanna, M., Goethals, G. R., & Hill, J. (1975). Evaluating a sex-rated ability: Social comparison with similar others and standard setters. *Journal of Experimental Social Psychology, 11*, 86–93.

CHAPTER NINE

Social Categorization, Depersonalization, and Group Behavior

Michael A. Hogg

Groups exist by virtue of there being outgroups. For a collection of people to be a group there must, logically, be other people who are not in the group (a diffuse non-ingroup, e.g., academics vs. non-academics) or people who are in a specific outgroup (e.g., academics vs. politicians). In this sense, social groups are categories of people; and just like other categories, a social category acquires its meaning by contrast with other categories. The social world is patterned by social discontinuities that mark the boundaries of social groups in terms of perceived and/or actual differences in what people think, feel, and do. Clearly, any analysis of group behavior should, to some extent, rest upon an analysis of categories and of social categorization processes, and of the social relations between categories (intergroup relations). More explicitly, a full analysis of processes within groups invites an integration, or, to use Doise's (1986; Lorenzi-Cioldi & Doise, 1990) terminology, an "articulation," of different levels of explanation – in this case, social categorization, interindividual interaction, and intergroup relations.

Social psychologists have, however, tended to find such an integration problematic. The traditional area of group dynamics which was central to social psychology from the 1940s into the 1960s, largely focused on interpersonal interaction in small task-oriented face-to-face groups, such as military units, teams, and discussion groups (see Cartwright & Zander, 1968; Shaw, 1981). In this context the relevant self-concept was, to use Brewer and Gardner's (1996) terminology, the "relational self." Although this approach provided a rich analysis of, for example, friendship patterns (e.g., Festinger, Schachter, & Back, 1950) and communication networks in groups (e.g., Bavelas, 1968), it did not conceptualize groups as categories, and did not explore the role of social categorization or the wider intergroup context of group behavior (see Hogg, 1992, 1993). Indeed, one issue was precisely how to differentiate groups from categories, and thus identify the "proper" focus for the study of group processes. Researchers in the small-group dynamics tradition have tended to define groups as being, for example, small (e.g., Shaw, 1981) and interactive (e.g., Arrow, McGrath, & Berdahl, 2000; Wilder & Simon, 1998) – a definition which can render problematic the study of, for example, racial prejudice and discrimination as a group process.

The small-group dynamics tradition lost popularity, largely to attribution, social cognition, and intergroup relations research, during the late 1960s and early 1970s – a turn of events famously documented by a series of laments by Steiner (e.g., Steiner, 1974, 1986). Currently, the study of group processes remains more popular outside the social psychological mainstream; in management schools and industrial and organizational psychology departments (Levine & Moreland, 1990, 1995; McGrath, 1997; Sanna & Parks, 1997), and in the fields of education, health care, and international relations (Tindale & Anderson, 1998). However, since the late 1980s there has been a revival of a new and different form of group processes research within social psychology, that articulates with developments in social cognition and the study of intergroup relations and social identity (see Abrams & Hogg, 1998; Hogg & Abrams, 1999; Moreland, Hogg, & Hains, 1994).

While traditional group dynamics failed to explore the social categorization process associated with groups, the social cognition tradition (e.g., Devine, Hamilton, & Ostrom, 1994; Fiske & Taylor, 1991) did the opposite – it explored in great detail the nature of social categories and the categorization process, but failed to explore group processes or intergroup relations. Social cognition was about cognition and perception, not groups. For traditional social cognition, the relevant self-concept was, again to use Brewer and Gardner's (1996) terminology, the "individual self." In recent years there has been gradual convergence of social cognition research, and social identity research into intergroup and group behavior (e.g., Abrams & Hogg, 1999; Leyens, Yzerbyt, & Schadron, 1994; cf. Brown, 2000).

Both group dynamics and social cognition have generally not focused on large-scale intergroup relations and the collective self. The analysis of large-scale social categories, their relations to one another, and the collective self has a long and illustrious history in social psychology, stretching back, in different forms, to Wundt, Le Bon, McDougall, James, and Mead (see Farr, 1996; Hogg & Williams, 2000). However, with the ascendancy of Floyd Allport's (1924) behaviorist vision for social psychology this emphasis has been less prominent for most of what Farr (1996) calls the modern era of social psychology. Social identity theory is a marked exception to this trend (Tajfel, 1972; Tajfel & Turner, 1979; Turner, 1982; see Hogg & Abrams, 1988). Framed by the development of a post-war European approach to social psychology that emphasized societal and intergroup aspects of social behavior (e.g., Tajfel, 1984), and drawing on Tajfel's early work on social perception and prejudice (e.g., Tajfel, 1969), social identity theory integrates a consideration of the categorization process (e.g., Tajfel, 1972), social comparison processes (see Hogg, 2000; Turner, 1975), self-enhancement motivation (see Abrams & Hogg, 1988), and people's beliefs about relations between groups (see Tajfel & Turner, 1979), in order to explain intergroup behavior and the collective self/social identity (see Hogg, in press a). More recently the categorization process has been more fully elaborated (self-categorization theory: Turner, Hogg, Oakes, Reicher, & Wetherell, 1987) as has the motivational role of uncertainty reduction (e.g., Hogg, in press b; Hogg & Mullin, 1999).

Social identity theory and self-categorization theory can be considered to be different but compatible emphases within a general social identity approach (e.g., Hogg, 1996a; Hogg & Abrams, 1988, 1999; Hogg & McGarty, 1990; Turner, 1999). This approach has generated a very large literature (e.g., Abrams & Hogg, 1990a, 1999; Ellemers, Spears, & Doosje, 1999; Hogg & Abrams, 1988; Robinson, 1996; Turner et al., 1987; Worchel, Morales, Páez, & Deschamps, 1998) which has made a significant impact on social psychology, and has helped re-energize interest in groups (e.g., Abrams & Hogg, 1998; Hogg & Abrams, 1999; Hogg & Moreland, 1995; Moreland, Hogg, & Hains, 1994). However, this work has largely not explored intragroup processes and the traditional topics of small group dynamics, except as a byproduct of the main focus on intergroup behavior. In recent years this lacuna has begun to be addressed by, for example, research on social attraction (e.g., Hogg, 1992, 1993), socialization (e.g., Levine & Moreland, 1994), deviance (e.g., Marques & Páez, 1994), leadership (e.g., Hogg, 1996a), and subgroup structure (e.g., Hornsey & Hogg, in press a) – also see Hogg (1996a, 1996b; Hogg & Terry, 2000).

What we are left with, then, is (a) the traditional study of dynamic processes within groups which is restricted to small interactive groups, and does not explicate social categorization processes, large-scale social categories, or the role of intergroup relations; (b) traditional social cognition which has much to say about social categories and social categorization, but little to say about group and intergroup processes; and (c) social identity theory which focuses on social categories, the categorization process and intergroup behavior, but has paid less explicit attention to processes within groups. The aim of this chapter is to fill in some of these gaps; to show how social categorization, contextualized by intergroup relations, influences social processes and structures within groups through processes related to collective self and social identity (also see Hogg, 1996a, 1996b; Hogg & Terry, 2000).

Social Categorization and Social Categories

Categorization

Categorization is probably the most basic and essential of all cognitive processes (e.g., Bruner, 1957; Doise, 1978; Eiser & Stroebe, 1972). It focuses attention on contextually relevant and meaningful aspects of the world – highlighting important distinctions and de-emphasizing unimportant ones. It renders a multifaceted and infinitely varying perceptual field, James's (1892) "blooming, buzzing confusion," contextually meaningful by segmenting it into a smaller number of categories. This is highly adaptive because instead of having to treat each of an infinite variety of stimuli as unique and thus unpredictable, we are able quickly to assign stimuli to pre-existing categories and thus are able to predict what is likely to happen. Categorization renders the world more predictable and thus allows us to plan effective action. For example, if we did not categorize, then an encounter with a large four-legged tan-colored creature with shaggy mane and huge yellow teeth would leave us puzzled as to what might happen and what we should do. The category label "lion" would instantly render the situation meaningful and would provide a very clear prescription of what might happen and what action should be taken.

Social categorization

Categorization operates on non-social and social stimuli alike. However, there are some critical differences. These stem from the fact that social categorization implicates self and thus revolves around comparisons among people, including self. Early research by Tajfel (e.g., Tajfel, 1959; Tajfel & Wilkes, 1963; also see Doise, 1978; Eiser & Stroebe, 1972) identified an accentuation effect of social categorization: categorization accentuates perceived differences between categories and similarities within categories on dimensions believed to be associated with the categorization (i.e., stereotypical dimensions), and the effect is amplified when either or both the categorization and the associated dimension are subjectively important. The process of categorizing people exaggerates perceived similarities among people in the same group (rendering them less easily identifiable – e.g., Taylor, Fiske, Etcoff, & Ruderman, 1978) and differences between people in different groups, and the effect is stronger if it is important to distinguish between the groups (e.g., you belong to one of the groups) and if the perceptual dimension is important (e.g., a strongly evaluative dimension like "nice–nasty" or "honest–dishonest").

According to this research, categorization perceptually homogenizes ingroups and outgroups. Further research suggests there is an asymmetry to this process – a relative homogeneity effect in which outgroups are perceptually homogenized more than are ingroups, especially on group-defining dimensions, and when groups are in competition (e.g., Judd & Park, 1988; Mullen & Hu, 1989; Quattrone & Jones, 1980). There is also some evidence that social minorities perceive the *ingroup* to be more homogenous than the outgroup (Simon & Brown, 1987; also Simon, 1992) presumably because ingroup solidarity may he strategically important for a minority.

Another line of research on categorization processes has identified an illusory correlation effect which is based on paired distinctiveness or on associative meaning (Chapman, 1967; Hamilton, 1979; Hamilton & Gifford, 1976; Hamilton & Sherman, 1989; Mullen & Johnson, 1990). People tend to exaggerate the degree of association between stimuli that are distinctive (i.e., share some unusual feature) or that people believe should go together. These processes, which are more prevalent where people process information from memory than on-line (McConnell, Sherman, & Hamilton, 1994), are implicated in stereotyping of group members. The notion that stereotypical attributes are tightly associated with categories is also supported by research on automaticity, which generally shows that unconscious category-primes automatically produce stereotypical perceptions of category members (e.g., Bargh, 1994; Devine, 1989; cf. Lepore & Brown, 1997, 1999).

What motivates social categorization? The general assumption, elaborating on the description above, is that people categorize others in order to render the social world a meaningful and predictable place in which we can act efficaciously. This suggests that the reduction of subjective uncertainty may be a core motivation for social categorization, and that therefore the more uncertain we are (generally, or in specific contexts) the more likely we are to categorize people (e.g., Hogg, in press b; Hogg & Mullin, 1999). Another motivation is self-enhancement or self-esteem (e.g., Abrams & Hogg, 1988; Turner, 1982). Social categorization almost always involves placing oneself in one of the categories, and thus acquiring the evaluative attributes of that category. It follows, then, that in particular contexts we might categorize people, or categorize people in particular ways, because by so doing there are favorable self-evaluative consequences. I explore this point in more detail below.

Social categories

Social categorization places people in categories. Although categories can be represented in terms of a limited set of necessary attributes, research suggests that this may be restricted to formal scientific taxonomies. In real life, and particularly for social categories, we tend to represent categories as fuzzy sets of attributes where members have a "family resemblance" (e.g., Cantor & Mischel, 1979; Mervis & Rosch, 1981). The fuzzy properties of such a category are embodied by the category prototype, which, because it is an abstraction of properties, no real member may embody – rather, category members vary in the degree to which they match the prototype. Categories can also be represented in terms of specific instances one has encountered – exemplars (Smith & Zárate, 1992). The precise relationship between prototype and exemplar representations of social categories remains to be fully explored (e.g., Fiske & Neuberg, 1990).

Although the category prototype may effectively represent the average group member, this does not necessarily have to be the case (Chaplin, John, & Goldberg, 1988). Prototypes can sometimes be extreme. Indeed, the representation of social categories is influenced not only by properties of the category itself, but also by the wider social comparative context within which the category exists, as well as by people's motivational and strategic goals. Of particular relevance here is the principle of meta-contrast which is thought to govern the context-dependent representation of groups as prototypes (e.g., Turner et al., 1987; also see Oakes, Haslam, & Reynolds, 1999). A critical feature of prototypes is that they maximize similarities within and differences between groups, and thus define groups as distinct entities and elevate their entitativity (Campbell, 1958; also see Brewer & Harasty, 1996; Hamilton & Sherman, 1996; Hamilton, Sherman, & Lickel, 1998; Sherman, Hamilton, & Lewis, 1999). Prototypes form according to the principle of metacontrast; maximization of the ratio of intergroup differences to intragroup differences. Because prototypes capture not only similarities within groups but also differences between groups, prototypes can often be extreme or polarized relative to the central tendency of a specific group. The way we perceive or represent a social group can therefore change as a function of what group or groups it is compared against in a specific context. Transient changes in comparative context produce situation-specific changes in prototypes; enduring changes in comparative context lead to enduring change in prototypes.

Although group prototypes reside in the social comparative context, people have a tendency to attribute these prototypical properties to underlying and immutable psychological properties of the group and its members – they see the group as having a psychological "essence" that is reflected in properties of the prototype (e.g., Medin & Ortony, 1989; Miller & Prentice, 1999). Essentialism, which may to some extent be a group level manifestation of the fundamental attribution error (Ross, 1977) or correspondence bias (Gilbert & Jones, 1986; also see Gilbert & Malone, 1995; Trope & Liberman, 1993), can be seen in the tendency to view racial and gender differences in terms of personality, bio-logy, and genetics.

Self-categorization and Social Identity

Putting together the notions of prototype and of categorization based accentuation, we can see that social categorization perceptually assimilates people to the relevant ingroup or outgroup prototype. A social field comprising multifaceted and unique individuals is perceptually transformed into a social field containing people who to varying degrees match the relevant group prototype – a process called "depersonalization" because the basis of perception is group prototypicality rather than personal idiosyncrasy or interpersonal relationships. Since prototypes capture any and all features that define category membership (i.e., attitudes, feelings, and behaviors) depersonalization makes people in groups appear attitudinally, affectively, and behaviorally relatively homogenous – an effect which closely mirrors stereo-typing. Because prototypes are generally widely shared, the stereotyping process is very much a group not an individual process (Tajfel, 1981; also see Oakes, Haslam, & Turner, 1964).

Thus far we have focused largely on how social categorization affects social perception. However, the critical contribution of self-categorization and social identity theory to the study of group processes is that they link social categorization to self-conception and psycho-logical group membership. The core idea is that we categorize ourselves just as we categorize others, and thus we depersonalize ourselves (e.g., Turner et al., 1987). Prototype-based depersonalization of self is the process that makes group behavior possible. It transforms self-conception so that we conceive of ourselves prototypically (prototypes define and evalu-ate the attributes of group membership), and our behavior assimilates or conforms to the relevant ingroup prototype in terms of attitudes, feelings, and actions. Self-conception in terms of an ingroup prototype is a representation and evaluation of self in collective terms – a representation of self in terms of qualities shared with others. In this sense the collective self is best considered a textured repertoire of relatively distinct social identities tied to all the groups to which we feel we belong. The collective self, or rather collective selves, is tightly tied to group membership.

Social categorization has profound effects on self-conception, social perception, and behavior – it generates characteristically "groupy" effects. A critical question is when do people self-categorize – when does prototypicality become the psychologically salient basis for self-conception, perception, and behavior? Theory and research suggests an interaction between category accessibility and category fit (e.g., Oakes et al., 1994; Oakes & Turner, 1990) that operates within the motivational framework provided by self-esteem and uncertainty reduc-tion (see Hogg, 1996a; Hogg & Terry, 2000). People, influenced by self-enhancement and uncertainty reduction motives, categorize the social context in terms of categories that are chronically accessible in memory (e.g., because they are valued, important, and frequently employed aspects of the self-concept) and/or rendered accessible by the immediate context. That categorization becomes salient which best accounts for relevant similarities and differ-ences among people in the context (structural/comparative fit), which best accords with the social meaning of the context (normative fit), and which best satisfies self-enhancement and self-evaluative concerns. Once fully activated on the basis of optimal fit, category specifications organize themselves as contextually relevant prototypes and are used as a basis for the perceptual accentuation of intragroup similarities and intergroup differences; thereby maximizing separateness and clarity. Self-categorization in terms of the activated ingroup category then depersonalizes behavior in terms of the ingroup prototype.

The construction and nature of social categories, and the specific form that group and intergroup behavior takes is not a mechanical expression of social categorization processes. Because ingroup prototypes define and evaluate social identity, and therefore self, people strive for ingroup prototypes that are evaluatively positive. They pursue evaluatively positive distinctiveness for their own group relative to relevant other groups, because this furnishes positive social identity and positive self-esteem (Turner, 1982; also see Abrams & Hogg, 1988). In an intergroup context, people can adopt a range of strategies to do this (Tajfel & Turner, 1979; also see Ellemers, 1993; Hogg & Abrams, 1988): They can subtly or assertively compete for more favorable dimensions of intergroup comparison, or a more favorable status relationship; they can compare themselves with less favorable outgroups; or they can attempt to categorize themselves and be categorized by others as members of the more favorable outgroup. The choice of strategy rests on people's pragmatic, though not necessarily accurate, beliefs about the nature of intergroup relations in terms of the stability, legitimacy, and permeability of intergroup boundaries, and the probability of success of a particular strategy.

Social identity theory does a relatively good job of tying together social categorization, the self-concept, and intergroup relations. Traditionally, however, the main emphasis has been on large-scale intergroup phenomena such as prejudice, stereotyping, intergroup conflict, and discrimination (e.g., Hogg & Abrams, 1988; Oakes et al., 1994). In the last decade or so there has, however, been an increasing emphasis on small group and intragroup phenomena. The remainder of this chapter is a discussion of some effects of social categorization processes within groups.

Social Categorization Effects Within Groups

Social categorization affects intragroup behavior via self-categorization and prototypebased depersonalization. It produces ingroup identification, a sense of belonging, self-definition in group terms, and ingroup loyalty and favoritism. It also causes conformity to group standards and normative behaviors among members, as well as mutual positive regard and cohesion. Prototypicality becomes the critical and highly salient yardstick of group life such that those who are prototypically deviant are heavily censured, while those who are prototypically central become highly influential. Variation in perceived prototypicality within groups can produce intragroup structural differentiation.

It is important, however, to keep clearly in mind that processes within groups are dynamically interdependent with intergroup processes – one mutually affects the other. A change in the intergroup comparative context can dramatically change the ingroup prototype, and groups themselves have some control over intergroup relations and the representation of outgroups and of intergroup relations. The discussion, below, of social categorization and depersonalization effects on processes within groups is wide ranging, covering conformity, normative behavior, crowd behavior, group polarization, the behavioral expression of attitudes, cohesion and liking, deviance, leadership and power, roles, status, diversity, subgroups, assimilation and pluralism, and organizational mergers and acquisitions.

Conformity and Normative Behavior

One of the most obvious ways in which social categorization affects intragroup behavior is through conformity and normative behavior. Self-categorization depersonalizes attitudes, feelings, and behavior in terms of the ingroup prototype. Effectively, this causes people to conform to the prototype and to behave normatively. To the extent that people within a group agree on the prototype, there is attitudinal consensus and normative homogeneity. The social process associated with conformity through prototype-based depersonalization is referent informational influence (e.g., Hogg & Turner, 1987; Turner, 1982, 1985) – people in a salient ingroup are motivated to learn about the prototype and thus pay close attention to the behavior of ingroup members, particularly those who are prototypical. Although non-ingroup members (e.g., outgroup members, the media) can be informative about ingroup norms, there is little doubt that prototypical ingroup members are the most direct and immediate source of reliable information.

Crowd behavior

Indeed, Reicher (1982, 1984) has used this latter idea to elaborate a social identity explanation of crowd behavior. In contrast to traditional de-individuation type explanations of crowds (e.g., Zimbardo, 1970), Reicher argues that crowd events are generally situations in which social identity is highly salient and thus behavior is carefully regulated by well-established ingroup norms. However, these norms may not prescribe the precise behaviors that are appropriate in what may be, for most people, the rather unusual circumstances of a crowd event. In these circumstances the established group's norms provide the limits for behavior, but members need to pay close attention to the identity-consistent behavior of fellow ingroup members, particularly those who are highly prototypical, in order to learn the precise situation-specific and identity-consistent behaviors to engage in.

Group polarization

The self-categorization analysis of conformity has reasonably good empirical support (see Abrams & Hogg, 1990b; Hogg & Turner, 1987; Turner, 1991; Turner & Oakes, 1989). For example, Abrams, Wetherell, Cochrane, Hogg, and Turner (1990) found support for this analysis across three classic influence paradigms – Sherif's autokinetic paradigm, Asch's conformity paradigm, and the group polarization paradigm. Group polarization (e.g., Moscovici & Zavalloni, 1969) is a particularly interesting case. Social psychologists have tended to view conformity as an averaging process where people in a group converge on an average position.

Against this backdrop, the discovery that small groups could reach a group decision that was more extreme than the average of individual members' pre-discussion positions was quite remarkable. Polarization, which seemed to occur when the pre-discussion mean was already displaced from the midpoint of the relevant attitudescale, seemed not to be a conformity phenomenon at all. Many explanations have been proposed for group polarization, of which the two best established are persuasive arguments and social comparison/cultural values (see Burnstein & Vinokur, 1977; Isenberg, 1986; Sanders & Baron, 1977).

These explanations have tended to separate polarization from conformity; viewing them as quite different phenomena. In contrast, social identity theory treats polarization as a conformity phenomenon. Under conditions of social identification and Self-categorization people conform to a group prototype which can represent the central tendency of the group or which can be polarized away from a relevant outgroup – polasization is conformity to a polarized ingroup prototype or norm (e.g., Wetherell, 1987). This analysis has reasonably good support from empirical studies that experimentally manipulate the salience of group identification and, via the intergroup comparative frame of reference, the position of the ingroup prototype relative to the mean ingroup position – polarization emerges where people identify with a group that has a polarized prototype (e.g., Hogg, Turner, & Davidson, 1990; Mackie, 1986; Mackie & Cooper, 1984; Turner, Wetherell, & Hogg, 1989).

Attitudes and behavior

Group norms that prescribe ingroup attributes may also have a special role in integrating people's attitudes with their behavior. The relationship between attitudes and behavior has long been problematic for social psychology, because attitudes often seem to have a very weak relationship to behavior (see Eagly & Chaiken, 1993). Recently, some researchers have tried to see whether ingroup norms may play an important role in the attitude–behavior relationship (see Terry & Hogg, 2000).

For example, Terry and Hogg (1996) argue that the attitude–behavior relationship is stronger when people self-categorize in terms of a salient group membership for which the attitude is normative/prototypical, particularly if the attitude prescribes the behavior. This idea has been supported in a series of experiments involving attitude issues such as voluntary student unionism, career choice in psychology, computer hacking, and students' responsibility for campus litter (e.g., Terry, Hogg, & McKimmie, in press; Wellen, Hogg, & Terry, 1998; also see Terry, Hogg, & White, 2000). The increased attitude–behavior correspondence is automatically assured by the depersonalization process.

However, the correspondence may also occur for more deliberate, strategic reasons. Specifically, people may enact ingroup-prototypical behavior in order to validate their group membership to themselves. Research suggests that publicly performed behavior can lead to more enduring internal attitudinal and self-representational change (e.g., Brauer, Judd, & Gliner, 1995; Schlenker, Dlugolecki, & Doherty, 1994; Tice, 1992). People may also want to communicate their group membership to fellow members by publicly exhibiting behavior that confirms membership – there is a communicative or self-presentation function to the behavior (Baumeister, 1982; Schlenker, 1980; Tice & Faber, in press). This communicative aspect of behavior has been explored from a more strictly social identity perspective by Abrams (1990, 1994), Emler (1990; Emler & Reicher, 1995), and Reicher and his colleagues (Reicher, Spears, & Postmes, 1995). The core idea is that the depersonalization based link between attitudes and behavior is moderated by strategic considerations revolving around social identity management – people may want to proclaim their identity through behavior, or they may want to conceal it. Ingroups provide an arena in which people, particularly marginal members who aspire to core membership, are more likely to want to proclaim their membership through behavior (including derogation of outgroups) and thus manage their reputations as core members (Noel, Wann, & Branscombe, 1995; Reicher, Levine, & Gordijn, 1998).

Group Cohesiveness and Social Attraction

For the early study of group dynamics, group cohesiveness was both the process of group formation and the index of group solidarity. Although initially defined scientifically by Festinger, Schachter, and Back (1950) in terms of attraction to the group and its goals and members, commentators (e.g., Evans & Jarvis, 1980; Hogg, 1992, 1993; Mudrack, 1989) have observed that most conceptual and operational definitions have tended to refer to the development of bonds of interpersonal liking among members of small interactive groups. In this way there is nothing special about groups; they are a "nominal fallacy" – merely an aggregate of people who like one another.

In contrast, the social identity analysis of categorization processes suggests that group cohesion or solidarity is not only attraction among group members, but also attitudinal and behavioral consensus, ethnocentrism, ingroup favoritism and intergroup differentiation, and so forth – the entire range of effects of categorization-based depersonalization. Self-categorization and depersonalization are the processes of group formation and group solidarity; cohesiveness is a consequence. The relationship between depersonalization and interindividual attraction has been captured by the social attraction hypothesis – group solidarity and cohesion are a reflection of depersonalized prototype-based interindividual attitudes (Hogg, 1992, 1993). A distinction is drawn between interindividual evaluations, attitudes, and feelings that are based on and generated by being members of the same group or members of different groups (depersonalized social attraction), and those that are based on and generated by personal predilections and by the idiosyncrasies and complementaries of close and enduring interpersonal relationships (personal attraction).

Depersonalization may produce ingroup liking in a number of ways: For example, it imbues ingroup members with attributes of the generally evaluatively positive ingroup prototype, and thus renders them prototypically attractive; it accentuates prototype-based similarity between self and fellow members and thus produces similarity-based liking (e.g., Hogg, Hardie, & Reynolds, 1995); and it extends positive self-regard to fellow members who are prototypically closely linked to self (see Cadinu & Rothbart, 1996; Simon, 1997; Simon & Hastedt, 1999; Smith & Henry, 1996).

When a group is salient, ingroup members are liked more if they embody the ingroup prototype – thus, prototypical members are liked more than marginal members. Where the prototype is consensual certain people are consensually liked, and where all members are highly prototypical there is a tight network of social attraction. Of course, outgroup members are liked less than ingroup members. When a group is not salient, liking is based on personal relationships and idiosyncratic preferences. The prediction is that patterns of liking in an aggregate, and the bases of that liking, can change dramatically when an aggregate becomes a salient group (for example when uncertainty or entitativity are high, or when the group is under threat or is engaged in intergroup competition over a valued scarce resource). Social and personal attraction are not isomorphic (see Mullen & Copper, 1994). These predictions have been supported repeatedly by a program of research with laboratory, quasi-naturalistic, sports, and organizational groups (Hogg, Cooper-Shaw, & Holzworth, 1993; Hogg & Hains, 1996; Hogg & Hardie, 1991, 1992, 1997; Hogg, Hardie, & Reynolds, 1995). One application of the social attraction hypothesis is to the explanation of groupthink: Suboptimal decision-making procedures in highly cohesive groups, leading to poor decisions with potentially damaging consequences (e.g., Janis, 1982). There is now evidence that the critical component of cohesiveness associated with groupthink is social attraction not interpersonal attraction (Hogg & Hains, 1998; see Turner, Pratkanis, Probasco, & Leve, 1992).

Differentiation Within Groups

Social categorization perspectives have tended to focus on differentiation between groups, and placed less emphasis on differentiation within groups. However, the social attraction idea explicitly acknowledges that groups are internally differentiated on the basis of prototypicality – an intragroup prototypicality gradient exists. Some people are, or are perceived to be, more prototypical than others (see Hogg, 1996a, 1996b). The notion of a prototypicality gradient has direct implications for the study of deviance and leadership as intragroup processes, and implications for the study of structural differentiation within groups.

Deviance

Within almost all groups there are fringe, marginal, or peripheral members who are perceived only weakly to match the defining or prototypical properties of the group. The social attraction hypothesis explains how such people, particularly in cohesive groups, are consensually unpopular relative to more prototypical members. They can even be cast into a deviant role within the group because they threaten the prototypical integrity of the group relative to outgroups. Marques and his colleagues have pursued this idea through research into what they call the "black-sheep" effect (e.g., Marques, 1990; Marques & Páez, 1994; Marques, Páez, & Abrams, 1998; Marques & Yzerbyt, 1988; Marques, Yzerbyt, & Leyens, 1988). They have shown that a person behaving in a particular way is more strongly rejected if that same person is defined as a non-prototypical member of a salient ingroup than a non-prototypical member of a salient outgroup. Furthermore, these effects are contingent on social categorization processes and are stronger among people who identify strongly with their group.

The notion that ingroup deviants may attract particularly negative reactions from fellow ingroupers because such deviants threaten the integrity and distinctiveness of the ingroup has also been well supported by recent social categorization research (e.g., Branscombe, Wann, Noel, & Coleman, 1993; Jetten, Spears, Hogg, & Manstead, 2000; Jetten, Spears, & Manstead, 1996, 1998). This research also shows that peripheral members may try to reestablish their membership credentials by acting in a markedly derogatory manner toward an outgroup, particularly when this behavior is publicly observable by an ingroup audience (Noel, Wann, & Branscombe, 1995) – see earlier discussion of strategic self-presentational aspects of group behavior. Core members only act in this way when the group's position as a whole is under threat (Jetten, Spears, & Manstead, 1997).

The process of evaluative marginalization of deviants may not only target peripheral individuals, but may also target groups of peripheral members. Under these circumstances an intergroup dynamic may come into play between the dominant majority subgroup and the deviant minority, with the minority perhaps adopting minority influence tactics to reinstate itself or to convert the majority to its own position (Mugny, 1982). Generally speaking, deviance processes within groups should not be viewed as only a mechanical reflection of prototypicality. Deviants also serve an important strategic function for groups – they act as scapegoats for group deficiencies and failures, and their very non-protorypicality can serve to clarify what *is* prototypical.

Thus far, I have restricted discussion to negative deviants – people whose behavior muddies intergroup boundaries because they diverge from the ingroup prototype toward the outgroup prototype. What about "positive" deviants – group members who are a-prototypical but in evaluatively favorable ways; for example, over-achievers or high flyers? On the one hand over-achievers should be socially unattractive because they are a-prototypical, but on the other hand they should be socially attractive because the group can bask in their reflected glory (cf. Burger, 1985; Cialdini, Borden, Thorne, Walker, Freeman, & Sloan, 1976; Cialdini & de Nicholas, 1989; Sigelman, 1986; Wann, Hamlet, Wilson, & Hodges, 1995). There is some evidence that people are evaluatively particularly harsh on over-achievers who suffer a setback or experience a fall (e.g., Feather, 1994), but this research does not differentiate between over-achievers who are members of a salient ingroup and those who are not.

From a social categorization perspective we could predict that the immediate and intergroup social context of over-achievement determines the evaluation of positive ingroup deviants (Hogg & Terry, 2000). There are two dimensions to the model: (a) A functional dimension. Where solidarity and consensual prototypicality are important to the group, perhaps due to uncertainty concerns, positive deviants are dysfunctional for the group; they will be evaluatively downgraded, much like negative deviants. Where solidarity is less critical and prototypicality less consensual, but self-enhancement is important, positive deviants are functional for the group; they will be upgraded as they contribute to a favorable redefinition of ingroup identity. (b) A social attribution dimension. Where positively deviant behavior can be "owned" by the group, the deviant will be favorably evaluated; this would be likely if the deviant modestly attributed the behavior to the support of the group rather than to personal ability, and where the deviant had little personal history of over-achievement (i.e., was a "new" deviant). Where positively deviant behavior cannot readily be "owned" by the group, the deviant will be unfavorably evaluated; this would be likely where the deviant took full personal credit for the behavior without acknowledging the group's support (i.e., "boasted"), and where the deviant had a long personal history of over-achievement (i.e., was an enduring deviant).

A common aspect of deviance is that groups tend to pathologize deviance. People who simply differ, or deviate, from the rest of the group are often viewed in pathological terms as having dysfunctional and deviant personalities – the demonization of deviants is clearly strategic, as described above, but it may also reflect the logic of essentialism and the fundamental attribution error or correspondence bias (see Gilbert & Malone, 1995; Medin & Ortony, 1989; Trope & Liberman, 1993). An example of this process at the societal level is the overemphasis on delinquency as a clinical problem. Although delinquent behavior may reflect pathological problems, it is also behavior that deviates from societal norms of acceptable behavior for adolescents and young adults. Emler (1990; Emler & Reicher, 1995) has suggested that an important aspect of delinquency is reputation management. Delinquent behavior provides a distinctive social identity for young (mainly male) adults, who engage in delinquent acts publicly in order to build a reputation for themselves among their delinquent peers – a reputation that acknowledges and affirms their social identity and group membership. This analysis is relatively consistent with earlier sociological work on labeling theory and deviant careers (e.g., Becker, 1963).

Leadership and power

Whereas prototypical marginality is about deviance, prototypical centrality is about leadership. One way in which social categorization is implicated in leadership is described by leader categorization theory (e.g., Lord, Foti, & DeVader, 1984; Nye & Forsyth, 1991; Nye & Simonetta, 1996; Rush & Russell, 1988). People have preconceptions about how leaders should behave in general and in specific leadership situations. These preconceptions are cognitive schemas of types of leader (i.e., categories of leader that are represented as person-schemas) which operate in the same way as other schemas (see Fiske & Taylor, 1991). When someone is categorized on the basis of their behavior as a leader, the relevant leadership schema comes into play to generate further assumptions about behavior. Leadership schemas vary in situational inclusiveness. Subordinate schemas apply only to specific situations, whereas superordinate schemas apply to a wide range of situations and embody quite general personality characteristics. Good leaders are people who have the attributes of the category of leader that fit situational requirements, This perspective is soundly based in contemporary social cognition. It treats leader categories as nominal categories; that is, cognitive groupings of instances that share attributes but do not have any psychological existence as a real human group. Leadership is viewed as a product of individual information processing, not as a structural property of real groups or as an intrinsic or emergent property of psychological ingroup membership.

An alternative social categorization perspective is framed by social identity theory (Hogg, 1996a, 1999, in press c). Self-categorization constructs a gradient of actual or perceived prototypicality within the group, such that some people are more prototypical than others and act as a focus for attitudinal and behavioral depersonalization. Prototypical members appear to exercise influence, because others behave as they do. Furthermore, such people are also consensually socially liked, which furnishes them with the capacity to actively gain compliance with their requests – people tend to agree and comply with people they like. This empowers the leader, and publicly confirms his or her ability to exercise influence. Furthermore, prototypical leaders are likely to identify strongly with the group and thus exercise influence in empathic and collectively beneficial ways; thus strengthening their perceived prototypicality and consensual social attractiveness. Consensual attractiveness also confirms differential popularity and public endorsement of the leader, imbues the leader with prestige and status, and instantiates an intragroup status differential between leader(s) and followers.

There is also an attribution process that tends to over- or mis-attribute the leader's behavior to stable, internal personality attributes – the fundamental attribution error (Ross, 1977) or correspondence bias (Gilbert & Jones, 1986). Because the behavior being attributed, particularly over an enduring period, includes the appearance or actuality of being influential over others' attitudes and behaviors, being consensually socially attractive, and gaining compliance and agreement from others, the attribution process constructs a charismatic leadership personality for the leader. A number of factors accentuate this attribution process. Because prototypicality is the yardstick of group life it attracts attention and renders highly prototypical members figural against the background of the group; thus enhancing the fundamental attribution error (Taylor & Fiske, 1978). The emerging status-based structural differentiation between leader(s) and followers further enhances the distinctiveness of the leader(s) against the background of the rest of the group. Furthermore, to redress their own perceived lack of power and control, followers seek individualizing information about the leader because they believe that such information is most predictive of how the leader will behave in many situations (Fiske, 1993; Fiske & Dépret, 1996).

Together, these processes transform prototypical group members into leaders who are able to be proactive and innovative in exercising influence. This also equips leaders to maintain their tenure. They can simply exercise power (more of this below), but they can also manipulate circumstances to enhance their perceived prototypicality; they can exercise self-serving ideological control over the content of the prototype, they can pillory ingroup deviants who threaten the self-serving prototype, they can demonize outgroups that clearly highlight the self-serving ingroup prototype, and they can elevate uncertainty to ensure that members are motivated to identify strongly with a group that is defined as the leader wishes (uncertainty can be managed as a resource by people in power, e.g., Marris, 1996).

Direct tests of the social identity theory of leadership have focused on the fundamental core prediction that as a group becomes more salient emergent leadership processes and leadership effectiveness perceptions become less dependent on general leader schemas and more dependent on group prototypicality. There is support for this idea from laboratory experiments (e.g., Duck & Fielding, 1999; Hains, Hogg, & Duck, 1997; Hogg, Hains, & Mason, 1998; Platow & van Knippenberg, 1999) and a naturalistic field study (Fielding & Hogg, 1997). There is also indirect support from a range of studies of leadership that are in the social identity tradition (de Cremer & van Vugt, in press; Foddy & Hogg, 1999; Haslam, McGarty, Brown, Eggins, Morrison, & Reynolds, 1998; Platow, Reid, & Andrew, 1998; van Vugt & de Cremer, 1999). There is also support for the idea that prototype-based depersonalized social attraction may facilitate leadership. There is some direct evidence from the studies by Fielding and Hogg (1997) and de Cremer and van Vugt (in press), whereas in other studies social attraction is a component of the leadership evaluation measure (e.g., Hains, Hogg, & Duck, 1997; Hogg, Hains, & Mason, 1998). The attribution and associated structural differentiation components of the theory have indirect support (e.g., Fiske, 1993; Fiske & Dépret, 1996), but remain to be directly tested.

Definitions of leadership usually distinguish leadership from power. Leadership is a process of influence that enlists and mobilizes the aid of others in the attainment of collective goals; it is not a coercive process in which power is exercised over others. The social identity theory of leadership is consistent with this type of definition. Prototypical leaders do not need to exercise power in order to have influence; they are influential by virtue of their position and the depersonalization process that assimilates members' behavior to the prototype. They and their suggestions are intrinsically persuasive because they embody the norms of the group. In addition to not "needing" to exercise power, it is possible that prototypical leaders may be "unable" to exercise power. High prototypicality is associated with strong ingroup identification; self and group are tightly fused prototypically and thus any form of negative behavior directed against fellow members is effectively directed against self. There may exist an empathic bond between leader and followers that protects against any desire to exercise power over others let alone destructive use of power or the abuse of power.

However, leaders sometimes do exercise power in harmful ways. Why does this happen? How can it be curbed? One possibility is that increasing status-based differentiation between leader and followers effectively instantiates an intergroup relationship. The leader is now no longer prototypical for the followers, and the empathic ingroup bond that protects against abuse of power is severed. Leadership through ingroup prototype-based influence is no longer effective, so the leader now needs to, and can, gain influence by exercising power over other members of the group, "as if" they were outgroup members. Such a relationship is competitive and potentially exploitative; far removed from prototype-based leadership.

The progression from benign influence to destructive wielding of power can be curbed by anything that inhibits the process of structural differentiation, and that re-grounds leadership in prototypicality External threat from an outgroup might be particularly effective – it enhances identification and depersonalization, and increases solidarity and social attraction. Power may, paradoxically, also be curbed by quite the opposite circumstances. If a group becomes less cohesive, more diverse, and less consensual about its prototype, it is less likely that followers will endorse the same person as the leader. Thus, the leader's power base will fragment, and numerous new "contenders" may emerge. Although this limits the leader's ability to abuse power, it also undermines prototype-based leadership. It should also be noted that leaders who have become accustomed to exercise power may vigorously resist any threats to their ability to exercise power.

This analysis of leadership and power is explored fully elaborated by Hogg and Reid (in press). It suggests that leaders only exercise power when the self-categorization contingent processes of social attraction and prototypical attribution structurally differentiate the leader from the rest of the group, and thus change the leader–group relationship from an intragroup relationship into some form of unequal status intergroup relationship. The exercise of power now becomes associated with other intergroup behaviors (e.g., stereotyping, intergroup discrimination, social "dislike") that inevitably widen the gulf between leaders and followers.

Structural differentiation within groups

We have seen how social categorization affects intragroup processes via prototypicality gradients. However, social categorization can also affect intragroup processes by creating subgroups that may have competitive intergroup relations within the superordinate group. I have already discussed two instances of this – deviant subgroups and leader/follower groups.

Another way in which groups can encompass social categories is through roles. Although roles are distinct from one another, they are promotively interdependent in the life of the group. Roles can be very specific in circumscribing behaviors; for example pilot, navigator, and cabin crew in an airplane. Other roles can be somewhat more generic. For example, Moreland and Levine have analyzed group socialization in terms of people's movement through distinct membership roles – newcomer, full member, old-timer, marginal member (e.g., Levine & Moreland, 1994; Moreland & Levine, 1982; Moreland, Levine, & Cini, 1993). Identification with and commitment to the group as a whole is influenced by generic role position (different roles prescribe different prototypes for the same group), and by role transition processes (e.g., initiation rites) that vary in terms of the strength of commitment to the group that they elicit.

Roles are rarely of equal status. For instance, in a restaurant, although chef and washerup are both essential to the group, there is a sharp status differential between these roles. The analysis of status-differentiated roles in groups has been most thoroughly presented by expectation states theory, or status characteristics theory (e.g., Berger, Fisek, Norman, & Zelditch, 1977; Berger, Wagner, & Zelditch, 1985; de Gilder & Wilke, 1994). Influence in groups is governed by the extent to which members have qualities and skills that are very specifically related to the group's purpose – called specific status characteristics. However, general social status outside the group (diffuse status characteristics) creates favorable expectations that the person is also valuable to the group, when in fact diffuse status may have little relevance to the group. This analysis of category differentiation within groups is useful for understanding the dynamics of power and influence within groups, in a way that incorporates a consideration of power and influence in the wider society within which small groups are located.

Another way to approach category structure within groups is in terms of analyses of socio-demographic diversity. This approach recognizes that almost all groups have a membership that is diverse in terms of socio-demographic category memberships such as race, ethnicity, gender, (dis)ability, and so forth. Groups are an arena in which are played out wider intergroup relations that are often evaluatively polarized and emotionally charged; conflict, disadvantage, marginalization, and minority victimization can arise. Research suggests that intragroup socio-demographic relations are likely to be salient and to recreate discriminatory societal relations, when, within the group, role classification is correlated with minority status demographic categorization (Brewer, 1996; Brewer, von Hippel, & Gooden, 1999) – for instance, if there are relatively few female employees in an organization and they are all employed in secretarial or clerical positions. This problem can be ameliorated where demographic categorization and role assignment are cross-cut or uncorrelated within the group (see Vescio, Hewstone, Crisp, & Rubin, 1999). For example, Marcus-Newhall, Miller, Holtz, and Brewer (1993) found that when category membership and role assignment were not convergent (i.e., they were cross-cut), category members were less likely to favor their own category on post-test ratings, and they were less likely to differentiate between the categories than in a convergent role structure.

The general issue here is of how subgroups relate to one another when they are nested within or cross-cut with a superordinate group. Social identity theory, and more general social categorization perspectives, make predictions about the nature of relations between subgroups as a function of the nature of their relationship to the superordinate group (see Hornsey & Hogg, in press a). Much of this work is framed by the "contact hypothesis" to investigate the conditions under which contact between members of different groups might improve enduring relations between the groups (e.g., Brown, 1996; Gaertner, Dovidio, Anastasio, Bachman, & Rust, 1993; Gaertner, Dovidio, & Bachman, 1996; Gaertner, Rust, Dovidio, Bachman, & Anastasio, 1995; Hewstone, 1994, 1996; Pettigrew, 1998).

Subgroups often resist attempts by a superordinate group to dissolve subgroup boundaries and merge them into one large group. This can be quite marked where the superordinate group is very large, amorphous, and impersonal. Thus, assimilationist strategies within nations, or organizations, can produce fierce subgroup loyalty and inter-subgroup competition. Subgroup members derive social identity from their groups and thus view externally imposed assimilation as an identity threat. The threat may be stronger in large superordinate groups due to optimal distinctiveness considerations (Brewer, 1991, 1993). People strive for a balance between conflicting motives for inclusion/sameness (satisfied by group membership) and for distinctiveness/uniqueness (satisfied by individuality). So, in very large organizations, people feel over-included and strive for distinctiveness, often by identifying with distinctive subunits or departments.

Some research suggests that an effective strategy for managing inter-subgroup relations within a larger group is to make subgroup and superordinate group identity simultaneously salient. For example, Hornsey and Hogg (1999, 2000, in press) conducted a series of experiments in which inter-subgroup relations were found to be more harmonious when the subgroups were salient within the context of a salient superordinate group, than when the superordinate group alone or the subgroups alone were salient. This arrangement reduces subgroup distinctiveness and identity threat, at the same time as it reconfigures inter-subgroup relations so that they resemble promotively interdependent role relations rather than competitively interdependent intergroup relations (Hornsey & Hogg, in press a). It is a social arrangement which may capture the policy of multi-culturalism adopted by some countries to manage ethnic diversity at a national level (cf. Prentice & Miller, 1999).

A specific case of subgroup structure is provided by mergers and take-overs in the world of organizations. The post-merger organization contains within it the pre-merger organizations and their intergroup relations. Since these relations are often competitive and sometimes bitter and antagonistic, it is not surprising that mergers often fail (e.g., Blake & Mouton, 1985; Buono & Bowditch, 1989; Haunschild, Moreland, & Murrell, 1994). If a failed merger is defined as one where competitive and hostile intergroup relations prevail within the new organization, then we can predict that this is likely to happen where old loyalties persist in an overly assimilationist environment that threatens a valued and self-definitionally important pre-merger organizational identity (e.g., Hornsey & Hogg, in press a). At the inter-organizational level an organization that believes its lower status position is legitimate and stable and that it is possible for members to pass psychologically into the more prestigious organization (i.e., acquire a social identity as a member of the prestigious organization) will be unlikely to show organizational solidarity or engage in inter-organizational competition. Instead, members attempt as individuals to dis-identify and gain psychological entry to the new organization. This would increase their support for the merger, and their commitment to and identification with the new merged organization. In contrast, an organization which believes its lower status position is illegitimate and unstable, that passing is not viable, and that a different interorganizational status relation is achievable, will show marked solidarity, engage in direct inter-organizational competition, and actively attempt to undermine the success of the merger. Although members of low-status organizations are likely to respond favorably to conditions of high permeability, an opposite effect is likely for employees of the higher status pre-merger organization. Permeable boundaries pose a threat to the status they enjoy as members of a higher status pre-merger organization, and so they are likely to respond negatively to permeable intergroup boundaries. This analysis has support from studies of an airline merger (Terry, Carey, & Callan, in press), and a bank merger (Anastasio, Bachman, Gaertner, & Dovidio, 1997; Gaertner, Dovidio, & Bachman, 1996).

Concluding Comments

The aim of this chapter has been to explore the effects of social categorization on intragroup phenomena. In order to do this I have adopted a social identity perspective, because, by theorizing how social categorization in a wider intergroup social context produces prototype based depersonalization of self and others, it provides probably the best basis for understanding group membership based social categorization effects within groups. Although, social identity theory focuses on social categories, the categorization process and intergroup behavior, it has paid less explicit attention to processes within groups. However, it provides a more promising start, I feel, than the traditional study of dynamic processes within groups, which is restricted to small interactive groups, and does not explicate social categorization processes, large-scale social categories, or the role of intergroup relations; and traditional social cognition, which has much to say about social categories and social categorization, but little to say about group and intergroup processes.

The core premise is that human groups are social categories; but, of course, categories that vary enormously in size, structure, purpose, diversity, longevity, degree of social interaction, and so forth. Social categorization transforms perception, thought, feeling, and action so that self and others are assimilated to the prescriptions of a contextually relevant ingroup or outgroup prototype – a process of prototype-based depersonalization. This very basic social-cognitive process interacts with representations grounded in social experience, to produce the general form and the specific content of group behaviors and collective self-conceptualization.

I showed how this analysis helps us to understand a wide array of intragroup phenomena. We discussed conformity and normative behavior – with a particular emphasis on crowd behavior, group polarization, and the behavioral expression of normative attitudes in group contexts. We saw how consensual social attraction emerged within groups, and how this related to the general solidarity and cohesion of groups, and the social popularity of highly prototypical group members. We saw how categorization-based variability in group pro-totypicality among group members might produce deviant individuals or minority sub-groups, and how even positive deviants might attract negative ingroup reactions. In contrast, highly prototypical group members may become group leaders. We discussed role differen-tiation within groups and how identification with the group as a whole may be influenced by the roles that people occupy within the group. Because roles vary in status, role occupants acquire status within the group through the roles they occupy. However, status within the group is also strongly influenced by socio-demographic status outside the group. This led into a discussion of socio-demographic diversity within groups and the management of subgroup relations within a group.

The extension of social categorization, and more specific social identity, analyses to the study of processes within groups is gathering momentum and providing an exciting new synthesis of the traditional social psychological study of group dynamics and the more contemporary study of social cognition, intergroup relations, and self and identity. One particularly promising arena for this research direction is the study of organizations. Organ-izations are complex groups that contain nested and cross-cut subgroups – they are large impersonal categories as well as small interactive groups, they exist in a matrix of intergroup relations, they provide the context for a host of small group processes, they influence people's attitudes and behaviors, and they contribute significantly to self-definition, social identity, and the self-concept. Organizational psychologists have increasingly adopted some social identity concepts to help understand aspects of organizational processes – since Ashforth and Mael (1989) first introduced the ideas to an organizational readership. This trend has strength-ened (e.g., Pratt, 1998), with the recent involvement of social identity researchers and a developing dialogue between social and organizational psychologists around this theme (see Hogg & Terry, 2000, in press).

REFERENCES

Abrams, D. (1990). How do group members regulate their behaviour? An integration of social identity and self-awareness theories. In D. Abrams & M. A. Hogg (Eds.), *Social identity theory: Constructive and critical advances* (pp. 89–112). London: Harvester Wheatsheaf.

Abrams, D. (1994). Social self-regulation. *Personality and Social Psychology Bulletin, 20,* 473–483.

Abrams, D., & Hogg, M. A. (1988). Comments on the motivational status of self-esteem in social identity and intergroup discrimination. *European Journal of Social Psychology, 18,* 317–334.

Abrams, D., & Hogg, M. A. (Eds.). (1990a). *Social identity theory: Constructive and critical advances.* London: Harvester Wheatsheaf, and New York: Springer-Verlag.

Abrams, D., & Hogg, M. A. (1990b). Social identification, self-categorization and social influence. *European Review of Social Psychology, 1,* 195–228.

Abrams, D., & Hogg, M. A. (1998). Prospects for research in group processes and intergroup relations. *Group Processes and Intergroup Relations, 1,* 7–20.

Abrams, D., & Hogg, M. A. (Eds.). (1999). *Social identity and social cognition.* Oxford, UK: Blackwell.

Abrams, D., Wetherell, M. S., Cochrane, S., Hogg, M. A., & Turner, J. C. (1990). Knowing what to think by knowing who you are: Self-categorization and the nature of norm formation, conformity, and group polarization. *British Journal of Social Psychology, 29,* 97–119.

Allport, F. H. (1924). *Social psychology.* Boston, MA: Houghton-Mifflin.

Anastasio, P. A., Bachman, B. A., Gaertner, S. L., & Dovidio, J. F. (1997). Categorization, recategorization, and common. ingroup identity. In R. Spears, P. J. Oakes, N. Ellemers, & S. A. Haslam (Eds.), The social psychology of stereotyping and group life (pp. 236–256). Oxford, UK: Blackwell.

Arrow, H., McGrath, J. E., & Berdahl, J. L. (2000). A theory of groups as complex systems. Thousand Oaks, CA: Sage.

Ashforth, B. E., & Mael, F. A. (1989). Social identity theory and the organization. Academy of Management Review, 14, 20–39.

Bargh, J. A. (1994). The four horsemen of automaticity: Awareness, intention, efficiency, and control in social cognition. In R. S. Wyer, Jr. & T. K. Srull (Eds.), Handbook of social cognition (2nd Ed., Vol. 1, pp. 1–40). Hillsdale, NJ: Erlbaum.

Baumeister, R. F. (1982). A self-presentational view of social phenomena. Psychological Bulletin, 91, 3–26.

Bavelas, A. (1968). Communication patterns in task-oriented groups. In D. Cartwright & A. Zander (Eds.), Group dynamics: Research and theory (3rd Ed., pp. 503–511). London: Tavistock.

Becker, H. S. (1963). Outsiders. New York: Free Press.

Berger, J., Fisek, M. H., Norman, R. Z., & Zelditch, M., Jr. (1977). Status characteristics and social interaction. New York: Elsevier.

Berger, J., Wagner, D., & Zelditch, M., Jr. (1985). Expectation states theory: Review and assessment. In J. Berger & M. Zelditch, Jr. (Eds.), Status, rewards, and influence (pp. 1–72). San Francisco, CA: Jossey-Bass.

Blake, R. R., & Mouton, J. S. (1985). How to achieve integration on the human side of the merger. Organizational Dynamics, 13, 41–56.

Branscombe, N. R., Wann, D. L., Noel, J. G., & Coleman, J. (1993). Ingroup or outgroup extremity: Importance of the threatened social identity. Personality and Social Psychology Bulletin, 19, 381–388.

Brauer, M., Judd, C. M., & Gliner, M. D. (1995). The effects of repeated expressions on attitude polarization during group discussion. Journal of Personality and Social Psychology, 68, 1014–1029.

Brewer, M. B. (1991). The social self: On being the same and different at the same time. Personality and Social Psychology Bulletin, 17, 475–482.

Brewer, M. B. (1993). The role of distinctiveness in social identity and group behaviour. In M. A. Hogg & D. Abrams (Eds.), Group motivation: Social psychological perspectives (pp. 1–16). London: Harvester Wheatsheaf.

Brewer, M. B. (1996). Managing diversity: The role of social identities. In S. Jackson & M. Ruderman (Eds.), Diversity in work teams (pp. 47–68). Washington, DC: American Psychological Association.

Brewer, M. B., & Gardner, W. (1996). Who is this "we"? Levels of collective identity and self-representations. Journal of Personality and Social Psychology, 71, 83–93.

Brewer, M. B., & Harasty, A. S. (1996). Seeing groups as entities: The role of perceiver motivation. In E. T. Higgins & R. M. Sorrentino (Eds.), Handbook of motivation and cognition, Vol. 3: The interpersonal context (pp. 347–370). New York: Guilford Press.

Brewer, M. B., von Hippel, W., & Gooden, M. P. (1999). Diversity and organizational identity: The problem of entrée after entry. In D. A. Prentice & D. T. Miller (Eds.), Cultural divides: Understanding and overcoming group conflict (pp. 337–363). New York: Russell Sage Foundation.

Brown, R. J. (1996). Tajfel's contribution to the reduction of intergroup conflict. In W. P. Robinson (Ed.), Social groups and identities: Developing the legacy of Henri Tajfel (pp. 169–189). Oxford, UK: Butterworth-Heinemann.

Brown, R. J. (2000). Group processes (2nd Ed.). Oxford, UK: Blackwell.

Bruner, J. S. (1957). On perceptual readiness. Psychological Review, 64, 123–152.

Buono, A. E., & Bowditch, J. L. (1989). *The human side of mergers and acquisitions: Managing collisions between people, cultures, and organizations.* San Francisco, CA: Jossey-Bass.

Burger, J. M. (1985). Temporal effects on attributions for academic performances and reflectedglory basking. *Social Psychology Quarterly, 48,* 330–336.

Burnstein, E., & Vinokur, A. (1977). Persuasive argumentation and social comparison as determinants of attitude polarization. *Journal of Experimental Social Psychology, 13,* 315–332.

Cadinu, M. R., & Rothbart, M. (1996). Self-anchoring and differentiation processes in the minimal group setting. *Journal of Personality and Social Psychology, 70,* 661–677.

Campbell, D. T. (1958). Common fate, similarity, and other indices of the status of aggregates of persons as social entities. *Behavioral Science, 3,* 14–25.

Cantor, N., & Mischel, W. (1979). Prototypes in person perception. In L. Berkowitz (Ed.), *Advances in experimental social psychology* (Vol. 12, pp. 3–52). New York: Academic Press.

Cartwright, D., & Zander, A. (Eds.). (1968). *Group dynamics: Research and theory* (3rd Ed.). London: Tavistock.

Chaplin, W. F., John, O. P., & Goldberg, L. R. (1988). Conceptions of states and traits: Dimensional attributes with ideals as prototypes. *Journal of Personality and Social Psychology, 54,* 541–557.

Chapman, L. J. (1967). Illusory correlation in observational report. *Journal of Verbal Learning and Verbal Behavior, 6,* 151–155.

Cialdini, R. B., Borden, R. J., Thorne, A., Walker, M. R., Freeman, S., & Sloan, L. R. (1976). Basking in reflected glory: Three (football) field studies. *Journal of Personality and Social Psychology, 34,* 366–375.

Cialdini, R. B., & de Nicholas, M. E. (1989). Self-presentation by association. *Journal of Personality and Social Psychology, 57,* 626–631.

de Cremer, D., & van Vugt, M. (in press). Why do people cooperate with leaders in managing social dilemmas? Instrumental and relational aspects of structural cooperation. *Journal of Experimental Social Psychology.*

de Gilder, D., & Wilke, H. A. M. (1994). Expectation states theory and the motivational determinants of social influence. *European Review of Social Psychology, 5,* 243–269.

Devine, P. G. (1989). Stereotypes and prejudice: Their automatic and controlled components. *Journal of Personality and Social Psychology, 56,* 5–18.

Devine, P. G., Hamilton, D. L., & Ostrom, T. M. (Eds.). (1994). *Social cognition: Impact on social psychology.* San Diego, CA: Academic Press.

Doise, W. (1978). *Groups and individuals: Explanations in social psychology.* Cambridge, UK: Cambridge University Press.

Doise, W. (1986). *Levels of explanation in social psychology.* Cambridge, UK: Cambridge University Press.

Duck, J. M., & Fielding, K. S. (1999). Leaders and sub-groups: One of us or one of them? *Group Processes and Intergroup Relations, 2,* 203–230.

Eagly, A. H., & Chaiken, S. (1993). *The psychology of attitudes.* San Diego, CA: Harcourt Brace Joyanovich.

Eiser, J. R., & Stroebe, W. (1972). *Categorization and social judgement.* London: Academic Press.

Ellemers, N. (1993). The influence of socio-structural variables on identity management strategies. *European Review of Social Psychology, 4,* 27–57.

Ellemers, N., Spears, R., & Doosje, B. (Eds.). (1999). *Social identity.* Oxford, UK: Blackwell.

Emler, N. (1990). A social psychology of reputation. *European Review of Social Psychology, 1,* 171–193.

Emler, N., & Reicher, S. D. (1995). *Adolescence and delinquency: The collective management of reputation.* Oxford, UK: Blackwell.

Evans, N. J., & Jarvis, P. A. (1980). Group cohesion: A review and re-evaluation. *Small Group Behavior, 11,* 359–370.

Farr, R. M. (1996). *The roots of modern social psychology: 1872–1954.* Oxford, UK: Blackwell.

Feather, N. T. (1994). Attitudes toward high achievers and reactions to their fall: Theory and research concerning tall poppies. *Advances in Experimental Social Psychology, 26,* 1–73.

Festinger, L., Schachter, S., & Back, K. (1950). *Social pressures in informal groups: A study of human factors in housing.* New York: Harper.

Fielding, K. S., & Hogg, M. A. (1997). Social identity, self-categorization, and leadership: A field study of small interactive groups. *Group Dynamics: Theory, Research, and Practice, 1,* 39–51.

Fiske, S. T. (1993). Controlling other people: The impact of power on stereotyping. *American Psychologist, 48,* 621–628.

Fiske, S. T., & Dépret, E. (1996). Control, interdependence and power: Understanding social cognition in its social context. *European Review of Social Psychology, 7,* 31–61.

Fiske, S. T., & Neuberg, S. L. (1990). A continuum of impression formation, from category-based to individuating processes: Influences of information and motivation on attention and interpretation. In L. Berkowitz (Ed.), *Advances in experimental social psychology* (Vol. 23, pp. 1–74). New York: Academic Press.

Fiske, S. T., & Taylor, S. E. (1991). *Social cognition* (2nd Ed.). New York: McGraw-Hill.

Foddy, M., & Hogg, M. A. (1999). Impact of leaders on resource consumption in social dilemmas: The intergroup context. In M. Foddy, M. Smithson, S. Schneider, & M. A. Hogg (Eds.), *Resolving social dilemmas: Dynamic, structural, and intergroup aspects* (pp. 309–330). Philadelphia, PA: Psychology Press.

Gaertner, S. L., Dovidio, J. F., Anastasio, P. A., Bachman, B. A., & Rust, M. C. (1993). Reducing intergroup bias: The common ingroup identity model. *European Review of Social Psychology, 4,* 1–26.

Gaertner, S. L., Dovidio, J. F., & Bachman, B. A. (1996). Revisiting the contact hypothesis: The induction of a common ingroup identity. *International Journal of Intercultural Relations, 20,* 271–290.

Gaertner, S. L., Rust, M. C., Dovidio, J. F., Bachman, B. A., & Anastasio, P. A. (1995). The contact hypothesis: The role of a common ingroup identity in reducing intergroup bias among majority and minority group members. In J. L. Nye & A. Brower (Eds.), *What's social about social cognition* (pp. 230–260). Newbury Park, CA: Sage.

Gilbert, D. T., & Jones, E. E. (1986). Perceiver-induced constraint: Interpretations of self-generated reality. *Journal of Personality and Social Psychology, 50,* 269–280.

Gilbert, D. T., & Malone, P. S. (1995). The correspondence bias. *Psychological Bulletin, 117,* 21–38.

Hains, S. C., Hogg, M. A., & Duck, J. M. (1997). Self-categorization and leadership: Effects of group prototypicality and leader stereotypicality. *Personality and Social Psychology Bulletin, 23,* 1087–1100.

Hamilton, D. L. (1979). A cognitive attributional analysis of stereotyping. In L. Berkowitz (Ed.), *Advances in experimental social psychology* (Vol. 12, pp. 53–84). New York: Academic Press.

Hamilton, D. L., & Gifford, R. K. (1976). Illusory correlation in interpersonal personal perception: A cognitive basis of stereotypic judgments. *Journal of Experimental Social Psychology, 12,* 392–407.

Hamilton, D. L., & Sherman, J. W. (1989). Illusory correlations: Implications for stereotype theory and research. In D. Bar-Tal, C. F. Graumann, A. W. Kruglanski, & W. Stroebe (Eds.), *Stereotyping and prejudice: Changing conceptions* (pp. 59–82). New York: Springer.

Hamilton, D. L., & Sherman, S. J. (1996). Perceiving persons and groups. *Psychological Review, 103,* 336–355.

Hamilton, D. L., Sherman, S. J., & Lickel, B. (1998). Perceiving social groups: The importance of the entitativity continuum. In C. Sedikides, J. Schopler, & C. A. Insko (Eds.), *Intergroup cognition and intergroup behavior* (pp. 47–74). Mahwah, NJ: Erlbaum.

Haslam, S. A., McGarty, C., Brown, P. M., Eggins, R. A., Morrison, B. E., & Reynolds, K. J. (1998). Inspecting the emperor's clothes: Evidence that random selection of leaders can enhance group performance. *Group Dynamics: Theory, Research. and Practice*, 2, 168–184.

Haunschild, P. R., Moreland, R. L., & Murrell, A. J. (1994). Sources of resistance to mergers between groups. *Journal of Applied Social Psychology*, 24, 1150–1178.

Hewstone, M. R. C. (1994). Revision and change of stereotypic beliefs: In search of the illusive subtyping model. *European Review of Social Psychology*, 5, 69–109.

Hewstone, M. R. C. (1996). Contact and categorization: Social psychological interventions to change intergroup relations. In C. N. Macrae, C. Stangor, & M. R. C. Hewstone (Eds.), *Stereotypes and stereotyping* (pp. 323–368). London: Guilford Press.

Hogg, M. A. (1992). *The social psychology of group cohesiveness: From attraction to social identity.* London: Harvester Wheatsheaf.

Hogg, M. A. (1993). Group cohesiveness: A critical review and some new directions. *European Review of Social Psychology*, 4, 85–111.

Hogg, M. A. (1996a). Intragroup processes, group structure, and social identity. In W. P. Robinson (Ed.), *Social groups and identities: Developing the legacy of Henri Tajfel* (pp. 65–93). Oxford, UK: Butterworth-Heinemann.

Hogg, M. A. (1996b). Social identity, self-categorization, and the small group. In E. H. Witte & J. H. Davis (Eds.), *Understanding group behavior (Vol. 2): Small group processes and interpersonal relations* (pp. 227–253). Mahwah, NJ: Erlbaum.

Hogg, M. A. (1999). *A social identity theory of leadership.* Manuscript submitted for publication, University of Queensland.

Hogg, M. A. (2000). Social identity and social comparison. In J. Suls & L. Wheeler (Eds.), *Handbook of social comparison: Theory and research* (pp. 401–421). New York: Plenum.

Hogg, M. A. (in press a). Social identity and the sovereignty of the group: A psychology of belonging. In C. Sedikides & M. B. Brewer (Eds.), *Individual self, relational self, and collective self: Partners, opponents, or strangers.* Philadelphia, PA: Psychology Press.

Hogg, M. A. (in press b). Subjective uncertainty reduction through self-categorization: A motivational theory of social identity processes. *European Review of Social Psychology.*

Hogg, M. A. (in press c). From prototypicality to power: A social identity analysis of leadership. In E. Lawler, M. Macy, & H. Walker (Eds.), *Advances in group processes* (Vol. 18). Stamford, CT: JAI Press.

Hogg, M. A., & Abrams, D. (1988). *Social identifications: A social psychology of intergroup relations and group processes.* London: Routledge.

Hogg, M. A., & Abrams, D. (1999). Social identity and social cognition: Historical background and current trends. In D. Abrams & M. A. Hogg (Eds.), *Social identity and social cognition* (pp. 1–25). Oxford, UK: Blackwell.

Hogg, M. A., Cooper-Shaw, L., & Holzworth, D. W. (1993). Group prototypicality and depersonalized attraction in small interactive groups. *Personality and Social Psychology Bulletin*, 19, 452–465.

Hogg, M. A., & Hains, S. C. (1996). Intergroup relations and group solidarity: Effects of group identification and social beliefs on depersonalized attraction. *Journal of Personality and Social Psychology*, 70, 295–309,

Hogg, M. A., & Hains, S. C. (1998). Friendship and group identification: A new look at the role of cohesiveness in groupthink. *European Journal of Social Psychology*, 28, 323–341.

Hogg, M. A., Hains, S. C., & Mason, I. (1998). Identification and leadership in small groups: Salience, frame of reference, and leader stereotypicality effects on leader evaluations. *Journal of Personality and Social Psychology*, 75, 1248–1263.

Hogg, M. A., & Hardie, E. A. (1991). Social attraction, personal attraction, and self-categorization: A field study. *Personality and Social Psychology Bulletin*, 17, 175–180.

Hogg, M. A., & Hardie, E. A. (1992). Prototypicality. conformity and depersonalized attraction: A self-categorization analysis of group cohesiveness. *British Journal of Social Psychology, 31,* 41–56.

Hogg, M. A., & Hardie, E. A. (1997). Self-prototypicality, group identification and depersonalized attraction: A polarization study. In K. Leung, U. Kim, S. Yamaguchi, & Y. Kashima (Eds.), *Progress in Asian social psychology* (Vol. 1, pp. 119–137). Singapore: Wiley.

Hogg, M. A., Hardie, E. A., & Reynolds, K. (1995). Prototypical similarity, self-categorization, and depersonalized attraction: A perspective on group cohesiveness. *European Journal of Social Psychology, 25,* 159–177.

Hogg, M. A., & McGarty, C. (1990). Self-categorization and social identity. In D. Abrams & M. A. Hogg (Eds.), *Social identity theory. Constructive and critical advances* (pp. 10–27). London: Harvester Wheatsheaf, and New York: Springer-Verlag.

Hogg, M. A., & Moreland, R. L. (1995, October). *European and American influences on small group research.* Invited paper presented at the Small Groups Preconference of the joint meeting of the European Association of Experimental Social Psychology and the Society for Experimental Social Psychology, Washington, DC.

Hogg, M. A., & Mullin, B.-A. (1999). Joining groups to reduce uncertainty: Subjective uncertainty reduction and group identification. In D. Abrams & M. A. Hogg (Eds.), *Social identity and social cognition* (pp. 249–279). Oxford, UK: Blackwell.

Hogg, M. A., & Reid, S. (in press). Social identity, leadership, and power. In A. Lee-Chai & J. Bargh (Eds.), *The use and abuse of power: Multiple perspectives on the causes of corruption.* Philadelphia, PA: Psychology Press.

Hogg, M. A., & Terry, D. J. (2000). Social identity and self-categorization processes in organizational contexts. *Academy of Management Review, 25,* 121–140.

Hogg, M. A., & Terry, D. J. (Eds.). (in press). *Social identity processes in organizational contexts.* Philadelphia, PA: Psychology Press.

Hogg, M. A., & Turner, J. C. (1987). Social identity and conformity: A theory of referent informational influence. In W. Doise & S. Moscovici (Eds.), *Current issues in European social psychology* (Vol. 2, pp. 139–182). Cambridge, UK: Cambridge University Press.

Hogg, M. A., Turner, J. C., & Davidson, B. (1990). Polarized norms and social frames of reference: A test of the self-categorization theory of group polarization. *Basic and Applied Social Psychology, 11,* 77–100.

Hogg, M. A., & Williams, K. D. (2000). From I to we: Social identity and the collective self. *Group Dynamics: Theory, Research, and Practice, 4,* 81–97.

Hornsey, M. J., & Hogg, M. A. (1999). Subgroup differentiation as a response to an overly inclusive group: A test of optimal distinctiveness theory. *European Journal of Social Psychology, 29,* 543–550.

Hornsey, M. J., & Hogg, M. A. (2000). Subgroup relations: A comparison of mutual intergroup differentiation and common ingroup identity models of prejudice reduction. *Personality and Social Psychology Bulletin, 26,* 242–256.

Hornsey, M. J., & Hogg, M. A. (in press a). Assimilation and diversity: An integrative model of subgroup relations. *Personality and Social Psychology Review.*

Hornsey, M. J., & Hogg, M. A. (in press b). Intergroup similarity and subgroup relations: Some implications for assimilation. *Personality and Social Psychology Bulletin.*

Isenberg, D. J. (1986). Group polarization: A critical review. *Journal of Personality and Social Psychology, 50,* 1141–1151.

James, W. (1892). *Psychology.* London: Macmillan.

Janis, I. L. (1982). *Groupthink: Psychological studies of policy decisions and fiascoes* (2nd Ed.). Boston, MA: Houghton-Mifflin.

Jetten, J., Spears, R., Hogg, M. A., & Manstead, A. S. R. (2000). Discrimination constrained and justified: The variable effects of group variability and ingroup identification. *Journal of Experimental Social Psychology, 36,* 329–356.

Jetten, J., Spears, R., & Manstead, A. S. R. (1996). Intergroup norms and intergroup discrimination: Distinctive self-categorization and social identity effects. *Journal of Personality and Social Psychology, 71,* 1222–1233.

Jetten, J., Spears, R., & Manstead, A. S. R. (1997). Identity threat and prototypicality: Combined effects on intergroup discrimination and collective self-esteem. *European Journal of Social Psychology, 27,* 635–657.

Jetten, J., Spears, R., & Manstead, A. S. R. (1998). Intergroup similarity and group variability: The effects of group distinctiveness on the expression of ingroup bias. *Journal of Personality and Social Psychology, 74,* 1481–1492.

Judd, C. M., & Park, B. (1988). Outgroup homogeneity: Judgments of variability at the individual and group levels. *Journal of Personality and Social Psychology, 54,* 778–788.

Lepore, L., & Brown, R. (1997). Category and stereotype activation: Is prejudice inevitable. *Journal of Personality and Social Psychology, 72,* 275–287.

Lepore, L., & Brown, R. (1999). Exploring automatic stereotype activation: A challenge to the inevitability of prejudice. In D. Abrams, & M. A. Hogg (Eds.), *Social identity and social cognition* (pp. 141–163). Oxford, UK: Blackwell.

Levine, J. M., & Moreland, R. L. (1990). Progress in small group research. *Annual Review of Psychology, 41,* 585–634.

Levine, J. M., & Moreland, R. L. (1994). Group socialization: Theory and research. *European Review of Social Psychology, 5,* 305–336.

Levine, J. M., & Moreland, R. L. (1995). Group processes. In A. Tesser (Ed.), *Advanced social psychology* (pp. 419–465). New York: McGraw-Hill.

Leyens, J.-P., Yzerbyt, V., & Schadron, G. (1994). *Stereotypes and social cognition.* London: Sage.

Lord, R. G., Foti, R. J., & DeVader, C. L. (1984). A test of leadership categorization theory: Internal structure, information processing, and leadership perceptions. *Organizational Behavior and Human Performance, 34,* 343–378.

Lorenzi-Cioldi, F., & Doise, W. (1990). Levels of analysis and social identity. In D. Abrams & M. A. Hogg (Eds.), *Social identity theory: Constructive and critical advances* (pp. 71–88). London: Harvester Wheatsheaf.

Mackie, D. M. (1986). Social identification effects in group polarization. *Journal of Personality and Social Psychology, 50,* 720–728.

Mackie, D. M., & Cooper, J. (1984). Attitude polarization: The effects of group membership. *Journal of Personality and Social Psychology, 46,* 575–585.

Marcus-Newhall, A., Miller, N., Holtz, R., & Brewer, M. B. (1993). Cross-cutting category membership with role assignment: A means of reducing intergroup bias. *British Journal of Social Psychology, 32,* 124–146.

Marques, J. M. (1990). The black-sheep effect: Outgroup homogeneity in social comparison settings. In D. Abrams & M. A. Hogg (Eds.), *Social identity theory: Constructive and critical advances* (pp. 131–151). London: Harvester Wheatsheaf, and New York: Springer-Verlag.

Marques, J. M., & Páez, D. (1994). The "black sheep effect": Social categorization, rejection of ingroup deviates and perception of group variability. *European Review of Social Psychology, 5,* 37–68.

Marques, J. M., Páez, D., & Abrams, D. (1998). Social identity and intragroup differentiation as subjective social control. In S. Worchel, J. F. Morales, D. Páez, & J.-C. Deschamps (Eds.), *Social identity: International perspectives* (pp. 124–141). London: Sage.

Marques, J. M., & Yzerbyt, V. Y. (1988). The black-sheep effect: Judgmental extremity towards ingroup members in inter- and intra-group situations. *European Journal of Social Psychology, 18*, 287–292.

Marques, J. M., Yzerbyt, V. Y., & Leyens, J.-P. (1988). The black-sheep effect: Extremity of judgements towards in-group members as a function of group identification. *European Journal of Social Psychology, 18*, 1–16.

Marris, P. (1996). *The Politics of uncertainty: Attachment in private and public life.* London: Routledge.

McConnell, A. R., Sherman, S. J., & Hamilton, D. L. (1994). The on-line and memory-bases aspects of individual and group target judgments. *Journal of Personality and Social Psychology, 67*, 173–185.

McGrath, J. (1997). Small group research, that once and future field: An interpretation of the past with an eye to the future. *Group Dynamics: Theory, Research, and Practice, 1*, 7–27.

Medin, D. L., & Ortony, A. (1989). Psychological essentialism. In S. Vosnaidou & A. Ortony (Eds.), *Similarity and analogical reasoning* (pp. 179–195). Cambridge, UK: Cambridge University Press.

Mervis, C. B., & Rosch, E. (1981). Categorization of natural objects. *Annual Review of Psychology, 32*, 89–115.

Miller, D. T., & Prentice, D. A. (1999). Some consequences of a belief in group essence: The category divide hypothesis. In D. A. Prentice & D. T. Miller (Eds.), *Cultural divides: Understanding and overcoming group conflict* (pp. 213–238). New York: Russell Sage Foundation.

Moreland, R. L., Hogg, M. A., & Hains, S. C. (1994). Back to the future: Social psychological research on groups. *Journal of Experimental Social Psychology, 30*(6), 527–555.

Moreland, R. L., & Levine, J. M. (1982). Socialization in small groups: Temporal changes in individual-group relations. In L. Berkowitz (Ed.), *Advances in experimental social psychology.* (Vol. 15, pp. 137–192). New York: Academic Press.

Moreland, R. L., Levine, J. M., & Cini, M. (1993). Group socialization: The role of commitment. In M. A. Hogg & D. Abrams (Eds.), *Group motivation: Social psychological perspectives* (pp. 105–129). London: Harvester Wheatsheaf.

Moscovici, S., & Zavalloni, M. (1969). The group as a polarizer of attitudes. *Journal of Personality and Social Psychology, 12*, 125–135.

Mudrack, P. E. (1989). Defining group cohesiveness: A legacy of confusion. *Small Group Behavior, 20*, 37–49.

Mugny, G. (1982). *The power of minorities.* London: Academic Press.

Mullen, B., & Copper, C. (1994). The relation between group cohesiveness and performance: An integration. *Psychological Bulletin, 115*, 210–227.

Mullen, B., & Hu, L. (1989). Perceptions of ingroup and outgroup variability: A meta-analytic integration. *Basic and Applied Social Psychology, 10*, 233–252.

Mullen, B., & Johnson, C. (1990). Distinctiveness-based illusory correlations and stereotyping: A meta-analytic integration. *British Journal of Social Psychology, 29*, 11–28.

Noel, J. G., Wann, D. L., & Branscombe, N. R. (1995). Peripheral ingroup membership status and public negativity toward out-group. *Journal of Personality and Social Psychology, 68*, 127–137.

Nye, J. L., & Forsyth, D. R. (1991). The effects of prototype-based biases on leadership appraisals: A test of leadership categorization theory. *Small Group Research, 22*, 360–379.

Nye, J. L., & Simonetta, L. G. (1996). Followers' perceptions of group leaders: The impact of recognition-based and inference-based processes. In J. L. Nye & A. M. Bower (Eds.), *What's social about social cognition: Research on socially shared cognition in small groups* (pp. 124–153). Thousand Oaks, CA: Sage.

Oakes, P. J., Haslam, S. A., & Reynolds, K. J. (1999). Social categorization and social context: Is stereotype change a matter of information or of meaning? In D. Abrams & M. A. Hogg (Eds.), *Social identity and social cognition* (pp. 5 5–79). Oxford, UK: Blackwell.

Oakes, P. J., Haslam, S. A., & Turner, J. C. (1994). *Stereotyping and social reality*. Oxford, UK: Blackwell.

Oakes, P. J., & Turner, J. C. (1990). Is limited information processing the cause of social stereotyping. *European Review of Social Psychology, 1*, 111–135.

Pettigrew, T. F. (1998). Intergroup contact theory. *Annual Review of Psychology, 49*, 65–85.

Platow, M. J., Reid, S., & Andrew, S. (1998). Leadership endorsement: The role of distributive and procedural behavior in interpersonal and intergroup contexts. *Group Processes and Intergroup Relations, 1*, 35–47.

Platow, M. J., & van Knippenberg, D. (1999, July). *The impact of leaders' ingroup prototypicality and normative fairness on leadership endorsements in an intergroup context.* Paper given at the XII General Meeting of the European Association of Experimental Social Psychology, Oxford, UK.

Pratt, M. G. (1998). To be or not to be? Central questions in organizational identification. In D. Whetten & P. Godfrey (Eds.), *Identity in organizations: Developing theory through conversations* (pp. 171–207). Thousand Oaks, CA: Sage.

Prentice, D. A., & Miller, D. T. (Eds.). (1999). *Cultural divides: Understanding and overcoming group conflict*. New York: Russell Sage Foundation.

Quattrone, G. A., & Jones, E. E. (1980). The perception of variability within ingroups and outgroups: Implications for the law of small numbers. *Journal of Personality and Social Psychology, 38*, 141–152.

Reicher, S. D. (1982). The determination of collective behaviour. In H. Tajfel (Ed.), *Social identity and intergroup relations* (pp. 41–83). Cambridge, UK: Cambridge University Press.

Reicher, S. D. (1984). The St Paul's riot: An explanation of the limits of crowd action in terms of a social identity model. *European Journal of Social Psychology, 14*, 1–21.

Reicher, S. D., Levine, M., & Gordijn, E. (1998). More on deindividuation, power relations between groups and the expression of social identity: Three studies on the effects of visibility to the ingroup. *British Journal of Social Psychology, 37*, 15–40.

Reicher, S. D., Spears, R., & Postmes, T. (1995). A social identity model of deindividuation phenomena. *European Review of Social Psychology, 6*, 161–198.

Robinson, W. P. (Ed.). (1996). *Social groups and identities: Developing the legacy of Henri Tajfel*. Oxford, UK: Butterworth-Heinemann.

Ross, L. (1977). The intuitive psychologist and his shortcomings. *Advances in Experimental Social Psychology, 10*, 174–220.

Rush, M. C., & Russell, J. E. A. (1988). Leader prototypes and prototype-contingent consensus in leader behavior descriptions. *Journal of Experimental Social Psychology, 24*, 88–104.

Sanders, G. S., & Baron, R. S. (1977). Is social comparison relevant for producing choice shifts? *Journal of Experimental Social Psychology, 13*, 303–314.

Sauna, L. J., & Parks, C. D. (1997). Group research trends in social and organizational psychology: Whatever happened to intragroup research? *Psychological Science, 8*, 261–267.

Schlenker, B. R. (1980). *Impression management*. Monterey, CA: Brooks-Cole.

Schlenker, B. R., Dlugolecki, D. W., & Doherty, K. (1994). The impact of self-presentations on self-appraisals and behavior: The roles of commitment and biased scanning. *Personality and Social Psychology Bulletin, 20*, 20–33.

Shaw, M. E. (1981). *Group dynamics: The psychology of small group behavior* (2nd Ed.). New York: McGraw-Hill.

Sherman, S. J., Hamilton, D. L., & Lewis, A. C. (1999). Perceived entitativity and the social identity value of group memberships. In D. Abrams & M. A. Hogg (Eds.), *Social identity and social cognition* (pp. 80–110). Oxford, UK: Blackwell.

Sigelman, L. (1986). Basking in reflected glory revisited: An attempt at replication. *Social Psychology Quarterly, 49*, 90–92.

Simon, B. (1992). The perception of ingroup and outgroup homogeneity: Reintroducing the intergroup context. *European Review of Social Psychology, 3,* 1–30.

Simon, B. (1997). Self and group in modern society: Ten theses on the individual self and the collective self. In R. Spears, P. J. Oakes, N. Ellemers, & S. A. Haslam (Eds.), *The Social psychology of stereotyping and group life* (pp. 318–335). Oxford, UK: Blackwell.

Simon, B., & Brown, R. J. (1987). Perceived intragroup homogeneity in minority–majority contexts. *Journal of Personality and Social Psychology, 53,* 703–711.

Simon, B., & Hastedt, C. (1999). Self-aspects as social categories: The role of personal importance and valence. *European Journal of Social Psychology, 29,* 479–487.

Smith, E. R., & Henry, S. (1996). An in-group becomes part of the self: Response time evidence. *Personality and Social Psychology Bulletin, 22,* 635–642.

Smith, E. R., & Zárate, M. A. (1992). Exemplar-based model of social judgment. *Psychological Review, 99,* 3–21.

Steiner, I. D. (1974). Whatever happened to the group in social psychology? *Journal of Experimental Social Psychology, 10,* 94–108.

Steiner, I. D. (1986). Paradigms and groups. *Advances in Experimental Social Psychology, 19,* 251–289.

Tajfel, H. (1959). Quantitative judgement in social perception. *British Journal of Psychology, 50,* 16–29.

Tajfel, H. (1969). Cognitive aspects of prejudice. *Journal of Social Issues, 25,* 79–97.

Tajfel, H. (1972). Social categorization. English manuscript of "La catégorisation sociale." In S. Moscovici (Ed.), *Introduction à la psychologie sociale* (Vol. 1, pp. 272–302). Paris: Larousse.

Tajfel, H. (1981). Social stereotypes and social groups. In J. C. Turner & H. Giles (Eds.), *Intergroup behaviour* (pp. 144–167). Oxford, UK: Blackwell.

Tajfel, H. (Ed.). (1984). *The social dimension: European developments in social psychology.* Cambridge, UK: Cambridge University Press.

Tajfel, H., & Turner, J. C. (1979). An integrative theory of intergroup conflict. In W. G. Austin & S. Worchel (Eds.), *The social psychology of intergroup relations* (pp. 33–47). Monterey, CA: Brooks/Cole.

Tajfel, H., & Wilkes, A. L. (1963). Classification and quantitative judgement. *British Journal of Psychology, 54,* 101–114.

Taylor, S. E., & Fiske, S. T. (1978). Salience, attention, and attribution: Top of the head phenomena. *Advances in Experimental Social Psychology, 11,* 249–288.

Taylor, S. E., Fiske, S. T., Etcoff, N. L., & Ruderman, A. J. (1978). Categorical and contextual bases of person memory and stereotyping. *Journal of Personality and Social Psychology, 36,* 778–793.

Terry, D. J., Carey, C. J., & Callan, V. J. (in press). Employee adjustment to an organizational merger: An intergroup perspective. *Personality and Social Psychology Bulletin.*

Terry, D. J., & Hogg, M. A. (1996). Group norms and the attitude-behavior relationship: A role for group identification. *Personality and Social Psychology Bulletin, 22,* 776–793.

Terry, D. J., & Hogg, M. A. (Eds.). (2000). *Attitudes, behavior and social context: The role of norms and group membership.* Mahwah, NJ: Erlbaum.

Terry, D. J., Hogg, M. A., & McKimmie, B. M. (in press). Group salience, norm congruency, and mode of behavioral decision-making: The effect of group norms on attitude–behavior relations. *British Journal of Social Psychology.*

Terry, D. J., Hogg, M. A., & White, K. M. (2000). Attitude–behavior relations: Social identity and group membership. In D. J. Terry & M. A. Hogg (Eds.), *Attitudes, behavior, and social context: The role of norms and group membership* (pp. 67–93). Mahwah, NJ: Erlbaum.

Tice, D. M. (1992). Self-presentation and self-concept change: The looking-glass self as magnifying glass. *Journal of Personality and Social Psychology, 63,* 435–451.

Tice, D. M., & Faber, J. (in press). Cognitive and motivational processes in self-presentation. In J. P. Forgas, K. D. Williams, & L. Wheeler (Eds.), *The social mind: Cognitive and motivational aspects of interpersonal behavior.* New York: Cambridge University Press.

Tindale, R. S., & Anderson, E. M. (1998). Small group research and applied social psychology: An introduction. In R. S. Tindale, L. Heath, J. Edwards, E. J. Posavac, F. B. Bryant, Y. Suarez-Balcazar, E. Henderson-King, & J. Myer (Eds.), *Social psychological applications to social issues: Theory and research on small groups* (Vol. 4, pp. 1–8). New York: Plenum Press.

Trope, Y., & Liberman, A. (1993). The use of trait conceptions to identify other people's behavior and to draw inferences about their personalities. *Personality and Social Psychology Bulletin, 19,* 553–562.

Turner, J. C. (1975). Social comparison and social identity: Some prospects for intergroup behaviour. *European Journal of Social Psychology, 5,* 5–34.

Turner, J. C. (1982). Towards a cognitive redefinition of the social group. In H. Tajfel (Ed.), *Social identity and intergroup relations* (pp. 15–40). Cambridge, UK: Cambridge University Press.

Turner, J. C. (1985). Social categorization and the self-concept: A social cognitive theory of group behavior. In E. J. Lawler (Ed.), *Advances in group processes: Theory and research* (Vol. 2, pp. 77–122). Greenwich, CT: JAI Press.

Turner, J. C. (1991). *Social influence.* Milton Keynes, UK: Open University Press.

Turner, J. C. (1999). Some current issues in research on social identity and self-categorization theories. In N. Ellemers, R. Spears, & B. Doosje (Eds.), *Social identity* (pp. 6–34). Oxford, UK: Blackwell.

Turner, J. C., Hogg, M. A., Oakes, P. J., Reicher, S. D., & Wetherell, M. S. (1987). *Rediscovering the social group: A self-categorization theory.* Oxford, UK: Blackwell.

Turner, J. C., & Oakes, P. J. (1986). The significance of the social identity concept for social psychology with reference to individualism, interactionism and social influence. *British Journal of Social Psychology, 25,* 237–239.

Turner, J. C., Wetherell, M. S., & Hogg, M. A. (1989). Referent informational influence and group polarization. *British Journal of Social Psychology, 28,* 135–147.

Turner, M. E., Pratkanis, A. R., Probasco, P., & Leve, C. (1992). Threat, cohesion, and group effectiveness: Testing a social identity maintenance perspective on groupthink. *Journal of Personality and Social Psychology, 63,* 781–796.

van Vugt, M., & de Cremer, D. (1999). Leadership in social dilemmas: The effects of group identification on collective actions to provide public goods. *Journal of Personality and Social Psychology, 76,* 587–599.

Vescio, T. K., Hewstone, M., Crisp, R. J., & Rubin, M. J. (1999). Perceiving and responding to multiply categorizable individuals: Cognitive processes and affective intergroup bias. In D. Abrams & M. A. Hogg (Eds.), *Social identity and social cognition* (pp. 111–140). Oxford, UK: Blackwell.

Wann, D. L., Hamlet, M. A., Wilson, T. M., & Hodges, J. A. (1995). Basking in reflected glory, cutting off reflected failure, and cutting off future failure: The importance of group identification. *Social Behavior and Personality, 23,* 377–388.

Wellen, J. M., Hogg, M. A., & Terry, D. J. (1998). Group norms and attitude–behavior consistency: The role of group salience and mood. *Group Dynamics: Theory, Research, and Practice, 2,* 48–56.

Wetherell, M. S. (1987). Social identity and group polarization. In J. C. Turner, M. A. Hogg, P. J. Oakes, S. D. Reicher, & M. S. Wetherell, *Rediscovering the social group: A self-categorization theory* (pp. 142–170). Oxford, UK: Blackwell.

Wilder, D., & Simon, A. F. (1998). Categorical and dynamic groups. Implications for social perception and intergroup behavior. In C. Sedikides, J. Schopler, & C. A. Insko (Eds.), *Intergroup cognition and intergroup behavior* (pp. 27–44). Mahwah, NJ: Erlbaum.

Worchel, S., Morales, J. E., Páez, D., & Deschamps, J.-C. (Eds.). (1998). *Social identity: International perspectives.* London: Sage.

Zimbardo, P. G. (1970). The human choice: Individuation, reason, and order versus deindividuation, impulse, and chaos. In W. J. Arnold & D. Levine (Eds.), *Nebraska symposium on motivation 1969* (Vol. 17, pp. 237–307). Lincoln, NE: University of Nebraska Press.

CHAPTER TEN

The Psychology of Crowd Dynamics

Stephen Reicher

1 The Challenge of Crowd Psychology

Crowds are the elephant man of the social sciences. They are viewed as something strange, something pathological, something monstrous. At the same time they are viewed with awe and with fascination. However, above all, they are considered to be something apart. We may choose to go and view them occasionally as a distraction from the business of everyday life, but they are separate from that business and tell us little or nothing about normal social and psychological realities. Such an attitude is reflected in the remarkable paucity of psychological research on crowd processes and the fact that it is all but ignored by the dominant paradigms in social psychology. The second edition of *The Handbook of Social Cognition* (Wyer & Srull, 1994) has no entry in the index under "crowd." Indeed, within a discipline that often views literature from a previous decade as hopelessly outdated, the little reference that is made to such research still tends to focus on Gustave Le Bon's work from a previous century (Le Bon, 1895). As we shall shortly see, it is most clearly reflected in the content of Le Bon's research and that of his followers. It was Le Bon, in terms of his theories if not his practices, who divorced crowds from their social context. His theory assumed that crowd participation extinguishes our normal psychological capacities and reveals a primal nature, which is usually well hidden from view. It was he who, with typical Victorian gusto, consigned crowds to the realms of a social scientific theatre of curiosities (cf. Reicher, 1996a; Reicher & Potter, 1985).

The aim of this chapter above all else is to free crowd psychology from being imprisoned at the margins and to restore it to its rightful place at the center of social scientific inquiry and, more specifically, of social psychological thought. As I have previously argued (Reicher, 1982, 1987) one of the more remarkable features of traditional crowd psychology is that it has tended to constitute a theory without a referent. Rather than starting from a set of phenomena in need of explanation, a set of explanations was elaborated in order to underpin certain ideological presuppositions about the crowd – or at least the suppositions of gentleman observers who viewed the masses with alarm from the outside. To them, crowds seemed anonymous, their actions inherently destructive and random, their reasons unfathomable. However, these hostile and external observers never took care to investigate the patterns of crowd action and the conceptions of crowd members to see if their suppositions were warranted. If one did – and there is a growing literature by historians and social scientists that does (e.g. Feagin & Hahn, 1973; Krantz, 1988; Rude, 1964; Williams, 1986) – then two things would become immediately apparent. The first is that crowd action is patterned in such a way as to reflect existing cultures and societies. Perhaps the classic example of this remains E. P. Thompson's study of 18th-century food riots in England (Thompson, 1971, 1991).

Of all examples of crowd action, one might at first think of food riots as a domain in which social analysis has least to offer. Surely starving people are simply motivated by a biological need to eat, to grab – by force if necessary – whatever food is available, and to make off with it. And yet, as Thompson notes, people are often passive in the face of starvation and protests are comparatively rare. When they do occur, food riots are far from inchoate explosions. In an analysis of several hundred such riots in England around the turn of the 19th century, Thompson shows how riots had a characteristic pattern both in terms of how they started and how people behaved within them. Moreover, these patterns reflected collective belief systems. Thus the riots occurred in the context of a shift from feudal to market-based economies. These were matched by different "moral economies." For the one, produce was meant to be sold locally and, for the other, produce was legitimately sold where it fetched the highest price. Riots generally started when grain was being transported to a distant market and the populace attempted to enforce their moral economy against that of the merchants. Events then unfolded in a way that reflected localist beliefs: Grain was sold at a popular price and the money – sometimes even the grain sacks – were handed back to the merchants. In short, and in complete contrast to prevalent visions of anarchy, the food riot demonstrates how crowd action is shaped by ideology and social structure.

The second obvious feature of crowd phenomena is that they are not only shaped by society but also that they in turn bring about social change. Indeed the changes wrought by crowds exist at three levels. There is change in the ways that crowd members see themselves as social actors. Autobiographies and studies of activists (e.g. Biko, 1988; Burns, 1990; Cluster, 1979; Haley, 1980; Teske, 1997) repeatedly show that people do not enter collective movements with fully fledged movement ideologies but that they develop their understanding of society and who they are within it as a consequence of participation. Crowds and collective action also lead to changes in the collective ideologies themselves. Indeed, as Eyerman and Jamison (1991) argue, the actions of social movements "are bearers of new ideas, and have often been the sources of scientific theories and of whole scientific fields, as well as new political and social identities" (p. 3). To take but one example, the rise of environmental Science, of "green" sensibilities and "green" identities cannot be understood outside the actions of anti-nuclear activists, roads protestors, and other collective acts of opposition. Finally, crowd action can bring about the entire restructuring of society. Just over a decade ago, such a point may have required more justification when the role of the sans-culottes in the French Revolution of 1789 (Rude, 1959) or of the July day crowds in the Bolshevik Revolution of 1917 were only historical memories. However, since the transformations in Eastern Europe – whether through the peaceful mass demonstrations of

Czechoslovakia's "velvet revolution," the confrontational demonstrations in East Germany, or the violent clashes between Romanian crowds and state forces in Timisoara and elsewhere (cf. De Rudder, 1989/90; Garton Ash, 1990), the claim hardly needs to be labored.

Putting the two features together, it should be clear that, in simultaneously encompassing social determination and social change, crowd action reflects what is possibly the central paradox of human action. Characteristically, even when this paradox constitutes the focus of inquiry, these twin facets of the human condition are studied in relation to different phenomena. However, both come together in the crowd. It follows both that the crowd provides a privileged arena in which to study social (psychological) processes and also that any adequate explanation of the crowd must take us a long way toward understanding the general bases of human social behavior.

As well as delineating the extent of the challenge, even such a brief account as that provided above suggests the nature of the tools that are necessary to meet it. Thompson's analysis suggests that the impact of structural and ideological factors upon action is achieved through actors' collective understanding of their position as social subjects. Conversely, the work on social change indicates that it is as social subjects that people act collectively in ways that bring about transformations – including the way they understand their own position. In other words, the psychological processes that relate society to crowd action are those of identity. If we are to understand the nature of crowd action we therefore need a model of identity which explains both how society structures identity and how identity organizes action. Failure to do the former will lead to a desocialized crowd psychology, while failure to do the latter will lead to an abstracted social theory. In either case, it will be impossible to complete the cycle of crowd dynamics whereby social factors affect identity which organizes action which then reflects back upon society – and so on.

When one measures the actual performance of traditional crowd psychology against the size of this challenge the results are sorry indeed. The failure has not been to explain either social change or social determination at the expense of the other but to ignore – no, *to deny* – both. The theoretical underpinning of this denial, which has unfortunately been bequeathed to much of social psychology in general, is a theoretical model of the self which writes society out of the picture and which therefore cannot address how it either shapes or is shaped by actors and their actions. This neglect is hardly accidental. It reflects the concerns which led crowds to become a focus of explanation. In order to understand the deficits of classical crowd theory and how to transcend them it is necessary to start by considering the context in which crowd psychology was born.

2   Classic Models of the Crowd

2.1   Mass society and the birth of crowd theory

The rise of industrialization and the growth of cities in Europe and North America during the 19th century posed social as well as technological questions. Most notably, the birth of mass society put the question of social control at the very top of the political and intellectual agenda. How would those who hitherto had been bound into the immediate hierarchies of village life continue to respect the existing social order once they were separated from their overlords as part of the urban masses? Mass society theory (cf. Giner, 1976), which theorized this dilemma, was ideological both in its diagnosis and its cure.

The diagnosis centered on the loss of traditional hierarchies – the church, the family, the army. This, it was proposed, led to a level of rootlessness and mindlessness, which made the mass prey to anarchic impulses, to passing fads, and to unscrupulous agitators. At the core of this argument is an ideological sleight of hand. Opposition to a particular social order from the perspective of alternative forms of social order is rendered as opposition to any social order from the perspective of no social order. Existing social relations are rendered inviolate by pathologizing the alternatives. The cure for those dangers posed by the mass was therefore to reimpose existing hierarchies rather than to acknowledge the problems which nourished alternative visions (Giner, 1976; Nye, 1975).

If the mass was a potential threat to "society," then the crowd was that potential made actual. The crowd was the instrument through which anarchy would replace order. Nowhere did that threat seem more real than in the French Third Republic, the birthplace of crowd psychology. If the bourgeoisie of other industrializing countries feared for what masses and crowds might bring about, France had seen a brief but bloody victory of mass action against the state in the form of the Paris Commune. The republic which grew on the ashes of the Commune was weak and buffeted by forms of popular opposition on all sides: Clericalism, the populism of General Boulanger and, most particularly the rise of syndicalism, anarchism, and socialism. When the founders of crowd science wrote about crowds it was primarily such working-class action they had in mind. These founders were outsiders to the crowd, their presiding sentiment was that of fear and their principal purpose was less to understand than to repress the crowd. The first debate in crowd psychology was actually between two criminologists, Scipio Sighele and Gabriel Tarde, concerning how to determine criminal responsibility in the crowd and hence who to arrest (Sighele, 1892; Tarde, 1890, 1892, 1901).

Yet it would be one-sided to suggest that crowds incited only fear amongst the scholars who studied them and the class they represented. Crowds were also figures of fascination. Nye (1995) points out, in the late 19th century the French in particular and Europeans in general were obsessed with the notion that industrialization and urban life were draining off human energy; were leading to the fatigue of civilization and were thereby threatening the very survival of society. In this *fin de siècle* context the savage energy of crowds appeared as promise as well as threat. The failure of early crowd psychology was that it bemoaned the threat without being able to harness the promise. It was, perhaps, because he dealt with both sides of popular concern that the work of Gustave le Bon stood out from that of his contemporaries and that, of all of them, his work alone continues to have influence.

2.2 Gustave Le Bon and the group mind tradition

Le Bon's book on the crowd was first published in 1895. Moscovici (1981) has argued that it has not simply served as an explanation of crowd phenomena but has served to create the mass politics of the 20th century. Certainly, Le Bon influenced a plethora of dictators and demagogues, most notoriously, Goebbels, Hitler, and Mussolini. This influence was not in spite of but rather an expression of Le Bon's intentions. He repeatedly urged contemporary establishment figures to employ his principles in order to use the power of the crowd for, rather than against, the state. His perspective matched the concerns of the age in their entirety: Fear and fascination in equal measure; denigration of the collective intellect, harnessing of collective energy. Both are equally represented in the core concept of submergence which, for Le Bon, marked the transition from individual psychology to crowd psychology. Simply by being part of the crowd; individuals lose all sense of self and all sense of responsibility. Yet, at the same time, they gain a sentiment of invincible power due to their numbers.

Once individual identity and the capability to control behavior disappears, crowd members become subject to contagion. That is, they are unable to resist any passing idea or, more particularly and because the intellect is all but obliterated, any passing emotion. This may even lead crowd members to sacrifice their personal interests – a further sign of irrationality. Contagion, however, is but an effect of suggestibility. That is, the ideas and emotions, which sweep unhindered through the crowd, derive primarily from the "racial unconscious" – an atavistic substrate which underlies our conscious personality and which is revealed when the conscious personality is swept away. Hence the primitivism of that unconscious is reflected in the character of crowd behavior. Crowd members, Le Bon asserts, have descended several rungs on the ladder of civilization. They are barbarians. But even here, where he seems at his most negative, the two-sidedness of Le Bon's perspective still comes through. For, as he then clarifies, this barbarian "possesses the spontaneity, the violence, the ferocity and also the enthusiasm of primitive beings" (p. 32). The majority of his crowd text is, in fact, essentially a primer on how to take advantage of the crowd mentality, how to manipulate crowds, and how to recruit their enthusiasms to one's own ends. In brief, Le Bon exhorts the would-be demagogue to direct the primitive mass by simplifying ideas, substituting affirmation and exaggeration for proof, and by repeating points over and again. It is important to acknowledge this stress on the power and the potential of crowds as a strength in Le Bon's work which has often been overlooked – and this is an issue that will recur several times in this chapter. None the less there are fundamental criticisms that can be made of his ideas on three different levels.

On a descriptive level, Le Bon's work is thoroughly decontextualized. The crowd is lifted both from the distal and the proximal settings in which it arises and acts. If Le Bon's concern was with the working-class crowds of late 19th-century France, no sense is given of the grievances and social conflicts which led angry demonstrators to assemble. Perhaps more strikingly still, Le Bon writes of crowd events as if crowds were acting in isolation, as if the police or army or company guards whom they confronted were absent, and as if the violent actions directed from one party to another were the random gyrations of the crowd alone. Such decontextualization leads to reification, to generalization and to pathologization. Behaviors that relate to context are seen as inherent attributes of the crowd, they are therefore assumed to arise everywhere irrespective of setting and, by obscuring the social bases of behavior, crowd action is rendered mindless and meaningless.

On a theoretical level, this divorce between crowds and social context is mirrored and underpinned by a desocialized conception of identity. That is, the self is conceptualized as a unique and sovereign construct which is the sole basis of controlled and rational action. Social context plays no part in determining the content of identity but merely serves to moderate its operation. Specifically, crowd contexts serve as the "off switch" for identity. Thus Le Bon's crowd psychology breaks the link both between society and the self and also between the self and behavior. The former rupture means that no action, including crowd action, can either shape or be shaped by society. The latter rupture means that crowd action can have no shape at all, either social or otherwise. If the self is sole basis of control, then loss of self in the crowd means loss of control and emergent psychopathology.

On an ideological level, Le Bon's ideas serve several functions. First, they act as a denial of voice. If crowds articulate grievances and alternative visions of society – if, in Martin Luther King's resonant phrase, crowds are the voice of the oppressed – then Le Bonian psychology silences that voice by suggesting that there is nothing to hear. Crowd action by definition is pathological, it carries no meaning and has no sense. Secondly, this psychology serves as a denial of responsibility. One does not need to ask about the role of social injustices in leading crowds to gather or the role of state forces in creating conflict. Being outside the picture they are not even available for questioning. Violence, after all, lies in the very nature of the crowd. Thirdly, Le Bon's model legitimates repression. Crowds, having no reason, cannot be reasoned with. The mob only responds to harsh words and harsh treatment. Like the mass society perspective from which it sprang, but with more elaboration and hence with more ideological precision, the Le Bonian position defends the status quo by dismissing any protests against it as instances of pathology (cf. Reicher, 1996b; Reicher & Potter, 1985).

McPhail (1991) points to such a political stance as the root of contemporary dissatisfaction with Le Bon. However, even if Le Bon's name has fallen into some disrepute, his intellectual tradition continues to have a strong presence in contemporary psychology where, since the ideology is more implicit, the ideas can still exert their baleful influence. Most directly, the concept of submergence has explicitly been acknowledged as the root of contemporary theories of deindividuation (Cannavale, Scarr, & Pepitone, 1970) – although, as will be argued, deindividuation is a partial appropriation of submergence. The first study in this tradition, by Festinger, Pepitone, and Newcomb (1952) showed that the more anonymous male subjects felt the more they were prepared to express hostility toward their parents. This led to a number of studies which suggested that anonymity, particularly anonymity within a group, enhanced anti-social behavior (Cannavale et al., 1970; Singer, Brush, & Lublin, 1965). The first comprehensive attempt to theorize this relationship was made by Zimbardo (1969).

If Zimbardo echoes the extravagance of Le Bonian language in the title of his theoretical exposition – individuation reason and order versus deindividuation, impulse, and chaos – the exposition itself is rather more prosaic. A series of antecedent variables, notably anonymity, lead to the lowering of self-observation and self-evaluation and hence to the weakening of controls based on guilt, shame, fear, and commitment. The result of these mediating processes is lowered thresholds for exhibiting anti-social behavior. Under conditions of deindividuation, people are liable to act in violent, vandalistic, and destructive ways. Quite quickly, however, it became clear that the model has both conceptual and empirical weaknesses. Conceptually, the model remains rather vague about the psychological mediators which lie between antecedents and behavioral outcomes. Certainly, little attempt was made to explore or provide evidence for these mediators. Empirically, it rapidly became clear that, if deindividuation produced behavioral changes it didn't necessarily lead to anti-social behavior. Indeed at times people may become more generous and more affectionate to others under deindividuated conditions (Diener, 1979; Gergen, Gergen, & Barton, 1973; Johnson & Downing, 1979). These twin issues led Diener (1977, 1980) to revise Zimbardo's model.

Diener employs Duval and Wicklund's notion of "objective self awareness" (Duval & Wicklund, 1972) as the psychological core of deindividuation. Once again a number of antecedents, most particularly perceptual immersion in a group, provide the first stage of the model. The consequence of these factors is to overload the information-processing capacities of the individual and hence to block the possibility of self-directed attention. This equates to a state of lowered objective self-awareness. The consequence of such a state is that individuals, being unable to retrieve internal or internalized standards, become increasingly influenced by environmental stimuli. They show little foresight, they lack inhibitions based on future punishment, their behavior changes with the stimuli to which they are exposed being alternatively prosocial or antisocial as a function of whether the stimuli are pro- or antisocial.

Prentice-Dunn and Rogers (1989) have added one further twist to the tale of deindividuation theory. They borrow a distinction between public self-awareness, which has to do with individuals' concerns about how others evaluate them, and private self-awareness, which approximates to the concept of objective self-awareness and has to do with monitoring the extent to which one's behavior matches one's internal standards (cf. Carver & Scheier, 1981; Fenigstein, Scheier, & Buss, 1975). When public self-awareness is blocked people ignore what others think and hence exhibit antinormative behaviors. When private self-awareness is blocked people lose access to their own internal standards and fall under external control. In effect, then, the model is a hybrid in which loss of public self-awareness approximates to Zimbardo's position and loss of private self-awareness approximates to Diener's. However, Prentice-Dunn and Rogers argue that being in a large group strips away both: Crowds leave us unrestrained either by social or personal standards.

Despite their differences, these models share three things in common. First of all, they consider that individuals have a single and personal identity or set of standards which is the condition for rational and controlled behavior. Secondly, they consider that any loss of access to these standards will lead to disinhibited or at least uncontrolled behavior. Thirdly, they propose that being part of a group – especially large and undifferentiated groups such as crowds – will lead to the occlusion of personal standards and hence to antisocial or asocial behavior. In these respects, deindividuation theory faithfully replicates the notions of loss of identity and loss of control which contribute to Le Bon's concept of submergence. However, as has been stressed, the concept of submergence is not just about loss of identity but also about the gain of a sense of power. It is by ignoring the latter that deindividuation theory becomes only a partial appropriation of the submergence concept. Indeed it could be argued that deindividuation theory discards the strengths and retains the weaknesses of Le Bon's argument.

By ignoring the issue of power, deindividuation models also ignore the potential of crowds and their transformatory possibilities. By retaining an individualistic notion of identity and of its loss in the crowd, deindividuation theory perpetuates the notion of collective action as generically incoherent and socially meaningful. This renders the approach incapable of accounting for the social patterning of those collective events for which the studies and the theory supposedly account. However, it also leads to a neglect of the social patterning which occurs within the studies themselves. A recent meta-analysis of the deindividuation literature (Postmes & Spears, 1998) demonstrates that, overall, participants are more likely to adhere to collective norms when they are supposedly deindividuated. All in all, the continued rupture between society self and action leads deindividuation theory to lack both internal and external validity.

2.3   Floyd Allport and the individualistic tradition

Sometimes influence is better measured by the way one provokes disagreement than through those who express direct agreement. Group mind theory may retain a presence in social psychology, however, it is undoubtedly a minority presence. Le Bon's more enduring impact has to do with Floyd Allport's rejection of the idea of a group mind and then with Allport's subsequent influence. If this seems paradoxical, the important thing to bear in mind is that, in being drawn into debate with Le Bon's position, Allport accepted the terms of that debate and hence these terms were allowed to predominate.

Such acceptance is easily obscured by the ferocity with which Allport condemned any notion of a group mind. He considered any reference to a mind that was separate from the psyche of individuals as a meaningless abstraction or even as "a babble of tongues" (Allport, 1933) and, in his seminal text on social psychology (Allport, 1924) he asserted that: "there is no psychology of groups which is not essentially and entirely a psychology of individuals" (p. 4). When it came to collective action, Allport declared, still more famously: "The individual in the crowd behaves just as he would behave alone only more so" (p. 295). This phrase has launched numerous theories and countless studies in group and crowd psychology. Ironically, however, while it fairly represents Allport's views on group processes in general, it is seriously misleading when it comes to his account of what happens in crowds themselves.

Allport's approach was based upon a combination of instinct and learning theory. He saw individuals as behaving on the basis of enduring response tendencies deriving from their conditioning histories. Conditioning, in turn, was built upon six fundamental prepotent reflexes – including withdrawing from danger, the need for nutrition and for love. When energy is applied to the system, say through the stimulation provoked by others being present, there is an accentuation of the pre-existing tendencies. This is the concept of social facilitation. In general, then, collective behavior arises where there is a coming together of individuals who "owing to similarities of constitution, training, and common situations, are possessed of a similar character" (1924, p. 6). However, excitation is in geometric relation to the number of people present. So, as the group becomes a mass, so there comes a point at which the collective "boils over." At this point, learnt responses simply break down leaving the underlying instinctual apparatus. In particular, masses (or crowds) are governed by the instinct of struggle – which is the tendency to destroy anything that stands in the way of the satisfaction of other instincts.

When one outlines what Allport actually wrote about crowd psychology as opposed to what has been assumed from a single quotation, the similarities with Le Bon are obvious. Crowd members lose their unique and idiosyncratic identities and behave in terms of a primitive animal substrate – the difference being that Allport's substrate is more biological and less mystical. Like Le Bon, Allport's crowd psychology ruptures both the link between society and identity and that between identity and action. His more general group psychology may restore the latter link, but it still rejects the former. That is to say, groups might accentuate identity but it is an asocial identity. The shape of crowd action is determined by character structures not by culture or by ideology. It therefore remains impossible to understand the social shape of collective action let alone the way it shapes society. Therefore, the tradition which derives from Allport may (unwittingly) break with his (and Le Bon's) ideas of identity loss. However, it still retains a desocialized conception of identity which blocks the possibility of understanding the psychological mediation between society and collective action.

In talking of the Allportian tradition one is referring to a more diffuse sense of influences than in the case of Le Bon. Rather than a single model with its roots explicitly acknowledged, there are a number of approaches whose lineage from Allport is a matter of explaining collective action in terms of pre-existing individual tendencies. The most obvious application of such an individualistic meta-theory to crowds is to argue that action is explicable in terms of the individual traits and attributes of participants. Crowd members who take part in violent action or action against the social order might be expected to have violent or antisocial personalities – or, at the very least, to be undersocialized or marginal to society. As the official U.S. Riot Commission report of 1968 acknowledged, the most prevalent view was that "rioters were criminal types, overactive social deviants, or riff-raff – recent migrants, members of an uneducated underclass – alienated from responsible Negroes and without broad social or political concerns" (pp. 125–126).

The evidence disconfirms such a view. To start with, riots are less likely where populations are more marginal or more transient. Indeed, in total contrast to the fears of mass society theorists, an analysis of European cities during the 19th century shows that greater growth and social disorganization were related to lower levels of riot (C. Tilly, 1969, R. Tilly, 1970; Tilly, Tilly, & Tilly, 1975). Riots tended to happen in towns and in areas that were stable and had well-established social networks. Feagin and Hahn (1973) provide similar evidence for the American urban revolts of the 1960s.

Next, there are considerable data that show migrants were under-represented and long-standing residents were over-represented in riot events (Caplan & Paige, 1968; C. Tilly, 1968). This resonates with what, by now, is a copious literature on crowd participants which, whether in the case of Roman mobs (Brunt, 1966), the Sacheverell rioters of 1710 (Holmes, 1976), the Gordon rioters of 1780 (Rude, 1970; Stephenson, 1979), the Wilkite mobs (Rude, 1970), the crowds of the French Revolution (Rude, 1959), the Luddites (Hobsbawm, 1968), the "Captain Swing" rioters (Hobsbawm & Rude, 1969), and many more besides, including the American rioters of the 1960s (Caplan & Paige, 1968; Marx, 1967), shows that rioters were typically members of cohesive groups from the more "respectable" strata of society. The 1968 U.S. Riot Commission draws an explicit portrait of the typical ghetto rioter: "He was born in the state and was a life-long resident of the city in which the riot took place . . . he was somewhat better educated than the average inner-city

Negro . . . he is substantially better informed about politics than Negroes who were not involved in the riots" (pp. 128–129).

Finally, while there is ample evidence, especially from the American revolts of the 1960s, that participants differed from non-participants in terms of ideology and identification – they associated more in terms of Black pride and Black power and accepted an ideology of resistance to oppression (Caplan, 1970; Caplan & Paige, 1968; Forward & Williams, 1970; Marx, 1967; Tomlinson, 1970) – there has been precious little success in finding any individual attributes which reliably predict riot participation (Foster & Long, 1970; Stark, 1972; Turner & Killian, 1987). McPhail (1971) surveyed 288 attempts to associate such attributes with measures of participation in riots between 1965 and 1969, and in only two cases was there a strong relationship. The riff-raff view, whatever guise it takes, is manifestly unsupported.

A rather different attempt to explain crowds in individualistic terms can be found in the form of game theory. The classic statement of this approach is to be found in Olson's (1965) text, *The Logic of Collective Action*. He argued that crowd members act as classic utility maximizers, seeking, as normal, to increase benefits over costs to the individual self but under conditions of altered contingencies. The most consistent champion of this approach has been Richard Berk (1972a, 1972b, 1974a, 1974b). His "rational calculus" model of crowd action involved five steps. First crowd members seek information, secondly they use this information to predict possible events, thirdly they list their behavioral options, fourthly they establish a preference order for the probable outcomes of alternative actions, and fifthly they then decide on a course of action which will minimize costs and maximize rewards. In sum, the probability of an act is a joint function of payoff and perceived probability of support (Berk, 1974b). So, where one perceives mass support, one will be more likely to pursue valued ends which one previously eschewed for fear of resistance or punishment by an outgroup (see also Brown, 1985). The effect of the crowd, therefore, is to transform behavior while maintaining the individual standards and tendencies on which behavior is based.

Berk himself recognizes that both his causal concepts, anticipated payoff and anticipated support, are fraught with problems. Being almost impossible to specify in advance: "analyses of their impact risk circularity" (1974b, p. 365). As a result of this, game theoretical approaches to crowd behavior have generated little research and the area has fallen into disuse. While Berk himself did provide some detailed studies of crowd events (1972b, 1974a), as McPhail (1991) notes, their subtlety serves to expose the limitations and not to reveal the power of game theory. These limitations can be traced directly to the concept of self-embodied in the core notion of human beings as "utility maximizers."

This idea is individualistic in two senses. On the one hand it is presupposed that the subject of utility is the individual actor. The idea that people might seek to accrue benefits for collective units – one's country, one's comrades, even one's family – is not considered. On the other hand the criterion of utility lies in the set priorities of the individual actor – or else it is presupposed that certain things, notably monetary reward, count as utilities for everyone. The possibility that social values and norms might determine utilities, or that the values and norms on which people act, and hence what counts as a utility, might change in collective contexts, is equally ruled out of court. Hence we are back firmly with the problem with which we began. Any model which links behavior to fixed individual tendencies must suppose a commonality of tendencies among crowd members (a proposition which is confounded by the evidence) and must deny the social character of crowd action. These errors of commission and omission are insuperable. More generally still, the view of self which isolates the psychological mechanisms of behavioral control from societal structuration – a view shared by Le Bon and by Allport and by the descendants of both – remains as much of a barrier to the understanding of crowd action as it did a century ago.

3   Models of Crowd Sociality

3.1   Emergent norm theory

Given the divorce between individual and society in psychological social psychology it is unsurprising that sociology began to develop its own social psychology and that perhaps the best-known approach within this tradition is symbolic interactionism, which is concerned with the creation of meaning within social interactions. It is equally unsurprising that the first attempt to explain the social shape of crowd action should involve the application of the approach by sociologists. Emergent norm theory (Turner & Killian, 1987) is an attempt to combine symbolic interactionism with psychological research on the formation of group norms (Asch, 1952; Sherif, 1936; Sherif & Harvey, 1952) in order to account for the social coherence of collective action. The approach seeks to reconcile the claim that crowd action is normal rather than pathological or irrational with the observation that it is not guided by traditional norms but rather tends to transcend, bypass, or even subvert established institutional patterns. As the name of the theory suggests, this reconciliation is effected through the idea that collective behavior takes place under the governance of emergent norms. Understanding collective behavior therefore depends upon explicating the process of norm formation.

For Turner and Killian, collective behavior often takes place in situations that are unusual such that "redefining the situation, making sense of confusion, is a central activity" (1987, p. 26). They draw on Sherif (Sherif, 1936; Sherif & Harvey, 1952) to argue that uncertainty precipitates a search for norms and upon Asch (1952) to argue that the perception of unanimity is central to the validation of norms. Norms are effective to the extent that they are seen as a property of the group rather than a position taken by particular individuals within the group. However, their distinctive contribution concerns the gap in between: How do new norms emerge and gain assent?

Turner and Killian argue that it is an illusion to suppose that crowds are homogenous. Rather, crowds are characterized: "by differential expression, with some people expressing what they are feeling while others do not" (1987, p. 26). Before crowd action takes place there is characteristically an extended period of "milling" during which people engage with others, proffering their own accounts of reality and listening to those of others. Certain individuals are more prominent than others in this process. These so-called "keynoters" help to resolve the ambivalence of the majority by proposing definite action tersely, forcibly, and with no uncertainty. As more people resolve or suppress their ambivalence in favor of the stance of a given keynoter so that proposal is expressed more widely to the exclusion of other proposals. In this way the illusion of unanimity grows and the illusion becomes a self-fulfilling prophecy.

From close to, this provides a compelling picture of crowd action. As is demonstrated by the studies which Turner and Killian cite, and by subsequent studies alike (e.g. Reicher, 1984a; Reicher, 1996b; Stott & Reicher, 1998), the violent and dramatic moments of crowd events may attract all the attention but they almost always occur after a prolonged period of "hanging around" during which crowd members seek to make sense of what is happening. To remove the final moments from the extended temporal context is as serious an act of decontextualization as to remove crowd action from the extended intergroup context. Equally, the notion of crowd members debating how to make sense of novel social situations and then acting upon the resultant collective understandings fits with empirical studies of crowd events (Caplan & Paige, 1968; Fogelson, 1971; Oberschall, 1968; Reddy, 1977; Reicher, 1984a; Smith, 1980; Thompson, 1971).

In these regards, emergent norm theory marks a crucial break with classic crowd psychology and an important step toward understanding the sociality of crowd action. It restores the link between the self-understandings of the subject and actions in the crowd. It also emphasizes the inherent sociality of these understandings. However, this sociality relates almost exclusively to the micro-social interactions among individual crowd members. It comes at the expense of understanding the links between what goes on between crowd members and broader aspects of social reality. This divorce between micro and macro levels of analysis underlies two important limitations to the theory.

First of all, such is that stress on the deliberative process that it becomes very difficult to explain how crowd unity can be achieved without a prolonged period of milling and therefore how crowds could remain united but still shift rapidly in relation to changing circumstances – a problem acknowledged even by adherents to emergent norm theory (e.g. Wright, 1978). It is as if norms must be constructed from scratch through laborious interindividual interactions each time a decision is needed. The lack of any scaffolding to the process of norm creation also makes it hard to explain how crowd norms and crowd behavior reflect broad cultural and ideological understandings – this is the second limitation. When explaining why the suggestions of particular keynoters should prevail over others, Turner and Killian invoke such factors as the status of speakers, their primacy in speaking, their terseness of expression, and the existence of latent support for their position. Without specification, the last suggestion is in danger of slipping into tautology. What is left is a series of factors relating to the attributes of the keynoter. Taken to its extreme, this results in a position whereby crowds act in terms of group norms but these group norms are a function of the individual leaders. Hence emergent norm theory becomes an elitist form of the individualist tradition.

This is certainly not what Turner and Killian intend. However, these problems are inevitable unless a way is found to relate the processes of sense-making in the immediate social context to the broader ideological context. To put it otherwise, emergent norm theory extends the analysis of the processes that shape crowd action from an intraindividual to an interindividual level. However, the subject remains isolated from societal definition and hence the relations of determination between larger-scale social factors and the actions which take place within and between groups remain opaque.

3.2   A social identity model of crowd action

For the purposes of explaining crowd action, perhaps the most significant aspect of social identity theory and its development through self-categorization theory (Tajfel, 1978, 1981; Tajfel & Turner, 1986; Turner, Hogg, Oakes, Reicher, & Wetherell, 1987; Turner, Oakes, Haslam, & McGarty, 1994) is the concept of social identity itself. To start with, the social identity tradition assumes identity to be multiple and to constitute a complex system rather than being unitary. Most notably, a distinction has been made between personal identity, which refers to the unique characteristics of the individual, and social identity, which refers to an individual's self-understanding as a member of a social category (Tajfel, 1978; Turner & Giles, 1981). However, these terms may be misleading and it is important to stress that all identities are social in the sense of defining the person in terms of social relations. It is just that these relations are defined at different levels of abstraction. Personal identity defines how I, as an individual, am unique compared to other individuals while social identity defines how we, as members of one social category are unique compared to members of other social categories (Turner, 1991, 1999; Turner et al., 1987). However, the definition of social categories is inescapably bound up with ideological traditions. What it means to be a Catholic, a socialist, a Scot, or whatever cannot be understood outside of such traditions.

It is equally important to stress that all identities are personal in the sense that they define the individual and are deeply important to the individual. Social identities at times may be even more important than individual survival. It is almost a truism to note that people will not only kill but die for their various faiths – national and political as well as religious. They may even glory in so doing: *dulce et decorum est pro patria mori*. The most important point, however, is to stress how social identity brings the individual and the societal together. It defines individual category members in ideological terms. It thereby provides a good starting point for understanding how the patterns of collective action may be ideologically coherent. It remains to specify in more detail how socio-ideological factors relate to the micro-processes of influence and interaction in the crowd through the mediation of social identity.

According to Turner (1982, 1991; Turner et al., 1987) self-categorization constitutes the psychological basis for group behavior. On defining ourselves as category members we participate in a process of self-stereotyping. That is, we seek to determine the relevance of category identity for action in context and we conform accordingly. We expect fellow group members to do likewise and therefore we also expect to agree with them on matters pertaining to our mutual social identity. How then do we determine what our category implies for how we should act in any given situation? In most of our social lives our actions will be routinized and norms will be clearly specified. Where they are not, there may be mechanisms of debate or else hierarchies of command through which norms may be specified. Such deliberative processes whereby appropriate behavior is derived from consideration of general category identity corresponds to what has been termed the deductive aspect of categorization (Turner, 1982). However, crowd situations are typically exceptional rather than routine and they offer little possibility of deliberation. Crowds are usually unstructured groups with no formal lines of command and the practical possibility of sitting down to agree on norms in the midst of a riot is rather limited. In this situation, the inductive aspect of categorization may take precedence. That is, group norms are inferred from the comments and actions of those seen as typical group members (Reicher, 1982).

In one sense, this account is similar to that of emergent norm theory: Crowd members are faced with the task of making sense of ambiguous situations and look to noteworthy others in order to do so. However, the key difference is that, from a social identity perspective, crowd members approach that task as members of a specific category. Being part of a psychological crowd (as opposed to a set of people who simply happen to be co-present) does not entail a loss of identity but a shift to the relevant social identity. Correspondingly it entails neither a loss of control nor a simple accentuation of pre-potent tendencies, but rather a shift to categorical bases of behavioral control. So, crowd members do not simply ask "what is appropriate for us in this context?" but "what is appropriate for us *as members of this category* in this context?" They won't follow anything but only those suggestions that can be seen as appropriate in terms of category identity. They won't follow anyone but only those seen as category members. More generally, crowd members seek to construe a contextual identity by reference to and within the limits set by the superordinate categorical identity. This relationship, and the fact that identity can be inferred from the acts of ingroup members, explains the rapidity with which consensus can arise. Insofar as social identities are ideologically defined, this (unlike emergent norm theory) also explains how the broad limits of crowd action make sense in terms of societal ideologies (Reicher, 1982, 1987).

Evidence to support the social identity model of crowd action comes from both experimental and field studies. The experimental studies address the deindividuation paradigm. Reicher (1984a) demonstrated that when individuals are already in a group then anonymity in the sense of loss of individuating cues accentuates the predominance of cues to group membership and hence of category salience. This leads to an accentuation of group normative behavior. Conversely, where people start off isolated from each other as individuals, then anonymity accentuates that isolation, weakens group salience, and weakens normative behavior. These findings have been replicated and extended in a number of different settings with a variety of groups and using different manipulations of anonymity (Lea & Spears, 1991; Postmes, Spears & Lea, 1998, 1999; Reicher & Levine, 1994a, b; Reicher, Levine & Cordijn, 1998; Reicher, Spears & Postmes, 1995; Spears & Lea, 1992, 1994; Spears, Lea & Lee, 1990). What is more, as I have already noted, a recent meta-analysis of all the major studies over the last 30 years (Postmes & Spears, 1998) indicates that, when supposedly "deindividuated," subjects tend to act in terms of the norms that are appropriate to the specific groups that were involved.

The first of the field studies dealt with the St. Paul's "riot" of April 1980 – the precursor to a wave of "inner city riots" which affected most major British cities during the 1980s. The events stemmed from a police raid on a Black-owned café in the St. Paul's area of Bristol and led to five hours of sustained conflict followed by attacks against property. Despite the dominance of irrationalist accounts by politicians and in the media (Reicher, 1984a; Reicher & Potter, 1985), a systematic analysis of the events revealed three elements that went together to make up a very different picture. First of all, there were clear limits to crowd action. In the earlier phase of conflict, only the police constituted targets of attacks. In the later phase, after the police had left, only financial institutions and shops owned by outsiders were subjected to collective attack and looting. There were also geographical limits to the action. The rioters chased the police to the boundaries and then stayed put, lighting symbolic bonfires at the limits and directing traffic back in.

Secondly, participants described themselves and others in terms of social identities. On the one hand, they stressed their collective identity as members of a St. Paul's community. Likewise, they described their relations to others on a categorical level: whether people were fellow St. Paul's inhabitants, whether they were outsiders, or whether they were members of categories specifically seen as antagonistic to St. Paul's. They also stressed that part of the pleasure of the events was that people recognized each other and were recognized as from St. Paul's. That is, they may have been anonymous to the police outgroup but they were certainly not anonymous to fellow ingroup members.

Thirdly, there was a clear match between crowd action and the self-definition of crowd members. While only a minority of crowd members were Black, St. Paul's identity was defined in terms of Black experience: To be from St. Paul's was to be oppressed by institutions such as the police, to be exploited by financial institutions, and to be in poverty within an affluent society. Accordingly, those people who were attacked were predominantly members of the police. It was the financial institutions that were physically attacked and the symbols of luxury that were destroyed. Moreover, the geographical character of the identity is reflected in the geographical limits to all the attacks.

This relationship between identity and collective action was apparent not only in terms of outcome but also in terms of process. That is, the actions of individuals in the crowd were extremely varied, however, the importance of social identity was displayed in the ways in which individual actions did or did not generalize. When a stone was thrown at the police it led to a hail of stones. When a stone was thrown at a bus crowd members not only failed to join in but actively dissuaded the perpetrator. Hence it was through the limits of what became collective that the operation of social identity was apparent. No doubt, under the cover of crowd action, individuals did enter St. Paul's to loot for personal gain. Hence the simple record of damage and theft reveals a muddied pattern. But considering events in progress and looking at how consensus emerges and shifts, then the pattern is much clearer.

Such evidence, and further evidence concerning a number of different crowd events in different contexts (Drury & Reicher, 1999, in press; Reicher, 1996b; Stott, 1996; Stott & Drury, 1999; Stott & Reicher, 1998) serves as powerful support for a social identity perspective and, more particularly, for the notion that crowd members act in terms of social identity (as opposed to losing identity) which then guides influence processes among crowd members (as opposed to influence being unguided and unlimited). However, even within the St. Paul's study, the evidence does more than suggest that crowds are simply like other groups in that social identity forms the basis for collective action. Firstly, it indicates that crowds give rise to a sense of power which allows members to express their identity even in the face of outgroup opposition. Indeed it suggests that crowds may be unique in allowing people to give full expression to their identities.

This claim gains further backing from more recent studies in the deindividuation paradigm which show that, when people in groups are anonymous to outgroup members and identifiable to fellow ingroup members (such that they are able to coordinate and to express mutual support) they are more likely to express those aspects of ingroup identity that are punishable by the outgroup (Reicher & Levine, 1994a, b; Reicher, Levine, & Gordijn, 1998;

Reicher, Spears, & Postmes, 1995). Such analyses reintroduce the concept of power to crowd psychology. However, in contrast to the Le Bonian tradition, power is not regarded as a result of identity loss and is not seen as leading to mayhem in crowd events. Rather, power operates in relation to the expression of identity and therefore lends a clearer social form to crowd action.

Thus far, the social identity model fares relatively well in explaining crowd action. It provides a means of linking society to identity and identity to action in such a way as to explain the patterning of crowd events. It acknowledges that people in crowds have the potential to undertake and carry through actions in ways that would normally be impossible. The energy of the crowd invests it with a transformatory potential. However, the evidence points to a second type of transformation with which the model copes less well. That is, in St. Paul's as elsewhere, events did not simply allow crowds to enact repressed aspects of an existing identity. They also led to a change of identity. After the "riots," those who had been involved expressed a new-found confidence in resisting and making claims of the police and of other authorities. They expressed a new sense of pride in themselves and a new sense of their potential. In a model where the emphasis is on the way in which crowd action is a consequence of social identity, how can crowd action lead to social and psychological change? In more general terms, the social identity model may account for the social determination of crowd action, but it is less successful in explaining social and psychological change. In order to overcome this impasse it is necessary to address the relationship between social categorization and social reality.

This is a central issue for self-categorization theorists. In contrast to those who assert that social categorization and group-level perception are a form of functional error by which a human cognitive system of limited processing capacity seeks to simplify an overly complex social world, self-categorization theorists assert that categorization and stereotyping reflect the nature of social reality: We see people in terms of group memberships to the extent that people are organized in terms of group memberships in the world (Oakes, Haslam, & Turner, 1994) even though this may increase the load on our cognitive systems (Nolan, Haslam, Spears, & Oakes, 1999; Spears & Haslam, 1997; Spears, Haslam, & Jansen, 1999). However, while self-categorization theory raises the question of how psychological categories relate to the organization of the social world, it is important to see this as a two-way relationship. To date, the stress has been on the way in which social context defines social categories and hence social action. It is equally important to examine how social categorization can be used to organize collective action and hence affect social context. This aspect of the relationship is important in itself if we are to understand crowd phenomena – particularly the mobilization and direction of mass action. However, it is also important as a precursor to understanding the interplay between determination and change and hence how crowd events unfold. In the next two sections, these issues will be dealt with in turn.

3.3   Categorization and mass mobilization

In technical terms, self-categorization theory proposes that the way we group people in the world (category salience) is a function of accessibility and perceiver readiness. Perceiver readiness has to do with the extent to which certain categories are available within our cognitive system and the extent to which we are accustomed to using them (Turner et al., 1994). Most work, however, has focused on "fit," which has to do with the extent to which the categories fit the distribution of stimuli in the real world. On the one hand those categories are chosen which minimize the ratio of intragroup differences to intergroup differences – comparative fit. On the other hand, categories are chosen such that the nature of differences between stimuli matches normative expectations about group differences – normative fit (Oakes et al., 1994; Oakes & Turner, 1986; Oakes, Turner, & Haslam, 1991). The fit principle, specifically that of comparative fit, is also used to explain the content of category identities. That is, the prototypical group position toward which group members will converge is that position which minimizes intragroup differences compared to intergroup differences. It will therefore vary as a function of which outgroup is present in the specific comparative context (Haslam & Turner, 1992, 1995; Haslam, Turner, Oakes, McGarty, & Hayes, 1992).

While the fit principle assures the link between reality and group process, it should not be thought that this means that social perception and action are purely the result of intrapsychic cognitive computations. In recent formulations (Haslam, 1997; Haslam, Turner, Oakes, McGarty, & Reynolds, 1998) it has been stressed that the adoption of a common category membership frames a process of discussion and debate. The importance of categorization is that it leads group members to expect agreement around the ingroup stereotype and hence to engage in an active search for consensus. None the less, even if a degree of debate is allowed, there is a danger that the emphasis on fit may lead to the impression that in any specific situation, the categories will also be specified and that there will be an irresistible impetus toward a single and consensual definition of the category stereotype. As indicated above, the model may be seen as providing a one-sided relationship between context and self, whereby the context is taken as given and as determining the self – and hence social action. If stasis derives from a rigid notion of context as fixed external reality, balance depends upon problematizing this notion.

Reicher and Hopkins (1996a, 1996b) have argued that, while experimenters may be able to impose a particular frame upon subjects, to specify the positions of those within the frame and to do so in advance of any action, these conditions are far from universal outside the laboratory. Frequently in our social worlds, especially those worlds inhabited by crowds and social movements, the nature of context is not clear and may provide a focus of controversy. So, while categories may indeed be linked to context, one cannot always presuppose the context and read off the categories. It is also true that people may contest the nature of context and therefore dispute the nature of categories. Within a specific situation people may differ over what categories are relevant, over the content of categorical stereotypes and even over who is prototypical of the groups (Herrera & Reicher, 1998; Reicher & Hopkins, 1996a, 1996b; Reicher & Sani, 1998; Sani & Reicher, 1998, 1999).

Taking the argument a stage further, these arguments about categorization are not simply attempts to *understand* context, but an attempt to *create* context. That is, if self-categorization theory is right in suggesting that the character of collective action depends upon the nature of self-categories, then it is through defining these categories that one is able to shape social behavior at any scale from the small group right up to societal mobilizations.

This being the case, then one might expect those concerned with mass mobilization – such as politicians and social movement activists – to be "entrepreneurs of identity" (cf. Besson, 1990). A number of studies have supported this supposition, showing that speakers seek, firstly, to define the boundaries of social categories such that all those they seek to mobilize fall within a common category; secondly, to define the content of category stereotypes such that the position advocated by the speaker is consonant with ingroup identity; and, thirdly, to define the category prototype such that they themselves or the organization they represent exemplifies the category and is therefore able to outline appropriate situational norms (Hopkins & Reicher, 1997a, 1997b; Reicher & Hopkins, 1996a, 1996b; Reicher, Hopkins, & Condor, 1997a, 1997b).

In more familiar terms, this is a model of mass leadership (or, in the terms of emergent norm theory, of keynoter effectiveness). Successful leaders are those who are able to define themselves in the terms of the category definition and who define their proposals as the enactment of the relevant social identity. In one sense, this is consistent with recent studies which show that, when categories are salient, leadership effectiveness is higher for those who match the category prototype (Hains, Hogg, & Duck, 1997; Hogg, 1996) and that, as comparative context changes and with it the category prototype, so different leaders come to the fore (Haslam, 1999). However, in line with the broader meta-theory, these studies tend to presuppose the definition of identity and leadership is something conferred by objective coincidence between personal and group positions. This portrays the leader as essentially passive and helpless in the face of circumstance. The argument being advanced here rejects the notion of identity as given, it makes the leaders much more active in construing both the nature of group identity and their own natures or else their proposals so as to achieve a consonance between the two. It also demands that we give independent weight to the discursive ploys through which speakers seek to make their constructions seem factual and self-evident (cf. Edwards, 1997; Potter, 1996). All in all, leadership is not simply a reflection of existing social realities, but also a matter of creating future realities through the ways in which self-categories are constructed and people are mobilized.

We now have a path from self-categorization to social context which can be added to that from context to categorization. However, this statement needs elaboration or else it threatens to be seriously misleading. If self-categorization is seen as a direct determinant of social reality, then there would be no limits upon the effectiveness of leaders in recreating the world as they wish beyond their ingenuity in offering appropriate constructions (what Billig, 1987, terms "witcraft"). That would be simply to use the one path to supplant the other rather than advancing our understanding of the two-way relationship between categorization and social reality in such a way as to account for the way in which collective action embodies both social determination *and* social change.

However self-categorization does not create reality directly. Rather it organizes collective action which is aimed at creating particular forms of reality. But, of course, such actions may not proceed unhindered, particularly in crowd contexts. As was stressed earlier, crowd events are typically intergroup encounters, and the actions of one group may be resisted by the actions of the other. If identity is about the organization of action, then one might expect that such outgroup resistance to ingroup actions will frame the effectiveness of different identity constructions. Indeed, one can go further and argue that, in the case of crowd events, the outgroup does not just provide resistance to action, but provides the very ground on which it occurs. That is, the physical context within which crowd members act and which they seek to change, is constituted by the presence and actions of the other. The relationship between self-categorization and context is therefore formed out of the intentions for future action by one group and the outcomes of past action by the other group. This relationship, and hence the balance between social determination and social change, is to be understood by analyzing the unfolding dynamics between groups. The elaborated social identity model of crowds is designed to enable just such an analysis.

3.4   An elaborated social identity model (ESIM) of crowds

In order to address the dynamic interplay between groups that constitutes crowd events, ESIM involves a reappraisal of some of the basic terms of the social identity tradition. The first (as already indicated) is the notion of context, which needs to be understood as constituted for one group by the actions of the other (and vice versa). The second is the notion of identity itself. Whereas self-categorization theory, through the concept of comparative fit, proposes that the process of identity definition depends upon the relationship between categories in context, the content of social identity is generally conceptualized (or at least operationalized) in terms of trait lists (e.g. Haslam & Turner, 1992, 1995; Oakes, 1987; Oakes & Turner, 1990).

By contrast ESIM regards social identity as a model of self in social relations, along with the actions that are proper and possible given such a social position. Thus, to be British is to define oneself in a world of nations or to be working class is to define a world in terms of class relations, and class "characteristics" flow from the possibilities that flow from occupying a disempowered position within this world. Such a conception is buttressed by two types of empirical evidence. The first is that when people talk of their identity they tend to do so in the terms of this definition (Reicher, 1984a, 1987). The second is that use of traits without reference to the relational context in which they gain meaning may be highly misleading (Hopkins & Reicher, 1997a, 1997b). To describe the English as "freedom loving" has entirely different connotations as a function of whether it is used in the context of fighting the Nazis or opposing a Pakistani family moving in next door (cf. Schwarz, 1982).

This conception of social identity leads to the question of how we can change identity by acting on identity to be reposed in the following terms: How can action in terms of one's understanding of one's social position lead to a change in that social position and hence a change in one's self-understanding? Social psychology in general, and the social identity tradition in particular, often presuppose that outcomes flow directly from intentions and therefore overlooks any disjunction between the two. However, by invoking the intergroup character of crowd events once more, this disjunction becomes not only explicable but also even mundane. As Shotter (1989) notes, once action is placed in an interactional context, it is always liable to result in unintended consequences. In crowd events, people may act on the basis of one set of understandings but their acts may be interpreted in very different ways by the outgroup. Where the outgroup has the power to privilege its interpretations this may lead actors into unimagined positions.

In a number of studies involving different types of crowd event, including football matches (Stott & Reicher, 1998), student demonstrations (Reicher, 1996), tax protests (Drury & Reicher, 1999), and environmental protests (Drury & Reicher, in press), a common dynamic has been found to underlie processes of change. Each of these events had different psychological crowds with different identities and different intentions coexisting within the physical crowd (or aggregate). Such change as occurred was among "moderate" elements of the crowd who understood themselves as "responsible citizens" acting in socially legitimate ways and who understood those policing them as neutral guarantors of the social order. However, in coming together within a single aggregate, these actors were seen by police as an indistinguishable part of an illegitimate crowd which constituted a danger to the social order. Moreover, given their technological and communicational resources, the police were able to impose this understanding upon the crowd by stopping all of them from continuing in their activities – whether they were marching to a football match, lobbying parliament about student funding, registering opposition to a new tax, or registering opposition to the destruction of green areas in order to construct a road.

As a consequence of being impeded in carrying out such "legitimate" activities and in response to being treated as dangerous and oppositional by the police, "moderate" crowd members in turn came to see the police as an illegitimate opposition. Furthermore, having experienced a common fate at the hands of the police, previously disparate crowd members came to see themselves as part of a common category even with more radical elements from whom they had previously felt distanced. This extension of the ingroup category, along with the solidarity that was both expected and obtained among ingroup members, led to a sense of empowerment and a willingness to challenge the police. Such challenges confirmed the initial police perception and, in turn, led them to increase the level of constraint they sought to impose on crowd members. In this way a process of escalation was initiated and sustained.

These interactions led, both during and subsequent to the actual events, to a series of changes: In subjects' sense of themselves (from "moderate" to "oppositional"), to a change in their sense of identification with others (including other oppositional groups within a common identity), to a change in their sense of empowerment and potential (as a function of being part of a larger movement), and even to a change in their very reasons for collective action (from the specific aim of the original protest to the need to challenge illegitimate authority and hence the intrinsic value of sustaining protest).

On a theoretical level, these examples show clearly how categorization and context interrelate within intergroup dynamics. The category definitions deployed by the police led to their physical deployment against the crowd and constituted the context in which the crowd acted. This led to recategorizations by the crowd and common action against the police – thus constituting a new context within which the police in their turn reacted. Not only does categorization for the one group shape the actions which become the context for the other, but in the process the very categories and the relations between them are altered. It can also be seen that the process of change results from certain crowd members acting on one understanding of social relations and this leading to them being placed in a new set of social relations as a consequence of the way their presence and their actions were understood and reacted to by an outgroup. Hence, in line with the reconceptualizations offered above, it can be seen how acting on identity led to a change of identity due to the dynamics that ensued from a mismatch between how certain crowd members saw their social location and how the police (re)located them.

It should be stressed that this model is not meant to suggest that change is a feature of all crowds or even of all within particular crowds. Indeed the particular conditions which initiate the process of change – where there is an asymmetry between the understandings of different parties and where one group has the power to enact its understanding over the other – may be relatively rare. Many events may be relatively routinized and the understandings which each has of the other will match. What is more, where change does occur it needn't always be in the direction of radicalization and empowerment. It could be that one's view of an outgroup and of one's social position is moderated when they facilitate actions when they were expected to impede them.

Clearly, the particular evidence of change obtained in the studies mentioned above results from the particular configuration of social relations between groups which obtained within them. ESIM is not intended to substitute for such situated social analysis, but rather to provide a psychological model which operates within ideological and structural settings. The aim is to explain what aspects of these settings are crucial and how they articulate with crowd psychology in order to produce different outcomes. The role of crowds in affirming and consolidating a social order due to the symmetry of understandings between the different parties to an event is every bit as important and requires just as much study as the processes of conflict and change that may be initiated by asymmetric perspectives.

4   Conclusion

At the outset, the aim of this chapter was defined as seeking to re-place crowd psychology at the center of social scientific and sociological thought. The grounds for doing so were that crowd events encompass both social determination and social change and therefore an adequate crowd psychology must necessarily address the full complexity of human sociality and the inherently two-sided nature of the relationship between the individual and society. Throughout the chapter, attempts both to ignore such questions and also to answer them have been documented – attempts which have revolved around two interrelated themes: The decontextualization or contextualization of crowd action; the use of desocialized or socialized conceptions of self and identity.

Having reached the end of the chapter, it would clearly be both presumptuous to suggest that we now have a comprehensive understanding of crowd phenomena. Indeed certain key phenomena are all but missing from the contemporary literature. Most obviously, the attempt to combat dominant irrationalist accounts has led to a focus on crowd cognitions and understandings while emotions and the phenomenology of crowd participation has been largely ignored. It is time to revisit these aspects of the crowd, but in doing so, we should not repeat the classic mistake of counterposing intellect and emotion and seeing the latter as usurping the former. Just as it was argued that empowerment operates in relation to identity, so progress depends on investigating how emotion relates to the self-understandings of crowd members. There may be joy in being part of a crowd, in being fully recognized as a group member, and being able fully to express one's identity; there may be anger at outgroup attempts to impede such expression; however, what counts as expression and its denial is a function of the precise definition of identity at any moment in time. While we may not understand the crowd in full, we do at least have a framework within which to address both the well-visited and the neglected corners of the field.

This framework involves reconceptualizing core concepts such as "context," "social identity," and "intentionality." Above all, it requires us to look at collective phenomena as interactive and as developing over time. If such a framework is necessary to the understanding of crowds, it may also have more general applicability to the field of social psychology. Indeed, in the course of analysis, we have encountered many of the central phenomena of social psychology and seen how they develop through the course of events. These include stereotypes, attitudes, social influence, minority influence, and polarization to name but a few. The changes that did (or did not) occur would have been inexplicable by restricting the analysis to a cognitive plane alone, without addressing the active construction of social categories and, most crucially, without studying ingroup understanding in relation to unfolding intergroup dynamics.

Crowd psychology points to the necessity of developing a historical and interactive set of methods and of concepts if we are to understand social understanding and social action. A historical and interactive psychology which focuses on the way in which our understandings shape and are shaped in practice, which looks at our cognitions in relation to the constraints on our action, and which recognizes how constraint in turn derives from the cognitions of others, is the only way of avoiding the bugbear of reification. Because of their transparent historical and interactive nature, crowd events provide an ideal location from which to generate an understanding of our dynamic psychological nature. It is also an ideal location within which to study that nature. There is much to be gained by restoring crowd psychology to the position of prominence it had at the birth of our discipline, but with the ambition of embracing crowd dynamism rather than repressing it.

REFERENCES

Allport, F. (1924). *Social psychology*. Boston, MA: Houghton Mifflin.
Allport, F. H. (1933). *Institutional behavior*. Chapel Hill: University of North Carolina Press.
Asch, S. (1952). *Social psychology*. Englewood Cliffs, NJ: Prentice-Hall.
Berk, R. (1972a). The controversy surrounding analyses of collective violence: Some methodological notes. In J. Short & M. Wolfgang (Eds.), *Collective violence*. Chicago, IL: Aldine.
Berk, R. (1972b). The emergence of muted violence in crowd behavior: A case study of an almost race riot. In J. Short & M. Wolfgang (Eds.), *Collective violence*. Chicago, IL: Aldine.
Berk, R. (1974a). A gaming approach to crowd behavior. *American Sociological Review, 39*, 355–373.
Berk, R. (1974b). *Collective behavior*. Dubuque, IA: Brown.
Besson, Y. (1990). *Identités et conflits au Proche-Orient*. Paris: L'Harmattan.
Biko, S. (1988). *I write what I like*. Harmondsworth, UK: Penguin.
Billig, M. (1987). *Arguing and thinking*. Cambridge, UK: Cambridge University Press.
Brunt, P. (1968). The Roman mob. *Past and Present, 35*, 3–27.
Burns, S. (1990). *Social movements of the 1960s*. Boston, MA: Twayne.
Cannavale, F., Scarr, H., & Pepitone, A. (1970). De-individuation in the small group: Further evidence. *Journal of Personality and Social Psychology, 16*, 141–147.

Caplan, N. (1970). The new ghetto man: A review of recent empirical studies. *Journal of Social Issues*, *26*, 59–73.

Caplan, N., & Paige, J. (1968). A study of ghetto rioters. *Scientific American*, *219*, 15–21.

Carver, C. S., & Scheier, M. F. (1981). *Attention and self-regulation: A control theory approach to human behavior*. New York: Springer-Verlag.

Cluster, D. (1979). *They should have served that cup of coffee*. Boston, MA: South End Press.

De Rudder (1989/90). Le Walesa de Timisoara. *Le Nouvel Observateur*. December 28, 1989–January 3, *1990*, 46–47.

Diener, E. (1977). Deindividuation: Causes and consequences. *Social Behaviour and Personality*, *5*, 143–155.

Diener, E. (1979). Deindividuation, self-awareness and disinhibition. *Journal of Personality and Social Psychology*, *37*, 1160–1171.

Diener, E. (1980). Deindividuation: The absence of self-awareness and self-regulation in group members. In P. Paulus (Ed.), *The psychology of group influence*. Hillsdale, NJ: Erlbaum.

Drury, J., & Reicher, S. (1999). The intergroup dynamics of collective empowerment: Substantiating the social identity model of crowd behavior. *Group Processes and Intergroup Relations*, *2*, 381–402.

Drury, J., & Reicher, S. (in press). Collective action and psychological change: The emergence of new social identities. *British Journal of Social Psychology*.

Duval, S., & Wicklund, R. (1972). *A theory of objective self-awareness*. New York: Academic Press.

Edwards, D. (1997). *Discourse and cognition*. London: Sage.

Eyerman, R., & Jamison, A. (1991). *Social movements: A cognitive approach*. Cambridge, UK: Polity.

Feagin, J., & Hahn, H. (1973). *Ghetto revolts*. New York: Macmillan.

Fenigstein, A., Scheier, M. F., & Buss, A. H. (1975). Public and private self-consciousness: Assessment and theory. *Journal of Consulting and Clinical Psychology*, *43*, 522–527.

Festinger, L., Pepitone, A., & Newcomb, T. (1952). Some consequences of deindividuation in a group. *Journal of Abnormal and Social Psychology*, *47*, 382–389.

Fogelson, R. (1971). *Violence in protest*. New York: Doubleday.

Forward, J., & Williams, J. (1970). Internal-external control and Black militancy. *Journal of Social Issues*, *26*, 75–92.

Foster, J., & Long, D. (1970). *Protest! Student activism in America*. New York: Morrow.

Garton Ash, T. (1990). *We the people: The revolution of 89*. London: Granta.

Gergen, K., Gergen, M., & Barton, W. (1973). Deviance in the dark. *Psychology Today*, *7*, 129–130.

Giner, S. (1976). *Mass society*. London: Martin Robertson.

Hains, S., Hogg, M., & Duck, J. (1997). Self-categorization and leadership: Effects of group prototypicality and leader stereotypicality. *Personality and Social Psychology Bulletin*, *23*, 1087–1099.

Haley, A. (1980). *The autobiography of Malcolm X*. Harmondsworth, UK: Penguin.

Haslam, A. (1999). *Psychology in organizations: The social identity approach*. London: Sage.

Haslam, A., & Turner, J. (1992). Context-dependent variation in social stereotyping 2: The relationship between frame of reference, self-categorization and accentuation. *European Journal of Social Psychology*, *22*, 251–277.

Haslam, A., & Turner, J. (1995). Context-dependent variation in social stereotyping 3: Extremism as a self-categorical basis for polarized judgement. *European Journal of Social Psychology*, *25*, 341–371.

Haslam, A., Turner, J., Oakes, P., McGarty, C., & Hayes, B. (1992). Context dependent variation in social stereotyping I: The effects of intergroup relations as mediated by social change and frame of reference. *European Journal of Social Psychology*, *22*, 3–20.

Haslam, A., Turner, J., Oakes, P., McGarty, C., & Reynolds, K. (1998). The group as a basis for emergent stereotype consensus. *European Review of Social Psychology*, *8*, 203–239.

Herrera, M., & Reicher, S. (1998). Making sides and taking sides: An analysis of salient images and category constructions for pro- and anti-Gulf war respondents. *European Journal of Social Psychology*, *28*, 981–993.

Hobsbawm, E. (1968). *Labouring man.* London: Weidenfeld & Nicolson.

Hobsbawm, E., & Rude, G. (1969). *Captain Swing.* London: Lawrence & Wishart.

Hogg, M. (1996). Intragroup processes, group structure, and social identity. In W. Robinson (Ed.), *Social groups and identities: Developing the legacy of Henri Tajfel.* London: Butterworth.

Holmes, G. (1976). The Sacheverell riots. *Past and Present*, *72*, 55–85.

Hopkins, N., & Reicher, S. (1997a). Constructing the nation and collective mobilisation: A case study of politicians' arguments about the meaning of Scottishness. In G. Barfoot (Ed.), *Ethnic stereotypes and national purity.* DQR Studies in Literature.

Hopkins, N., & Reicher, S. (1997b). The construction of social categories and processes of social change. In G. Breakwell & E. Lyons (Eds.), *Changing European identities.* London: Butterworth.

Johnson, R., & Downing, L. (1979). Deindividuation and violence of cues: Effects on prosocial and antisocial behavior. *Journal of Personality and Social Psychology*, *37*, 1532–1538.

Krantz, F. (1988). *History from below.* Oxford, UK: Blackwell.

Lea, M., & Spears, R. (1991). Computer-mediated communication, de-individuation, and group decision making. *International Journal of Man-Machine Studies, Special Issue on CSCW and Groupware*, *39*, 283–301. Reprinted in S. Greenberg (Ed.), *Computer-supported co-operative work and groupware.* London: Academic Press.

Le Bon, G. (1895, trans. 1947). *The crowd: A study of the popular mind.* London: Ernest Benn.

Marx, G. (1967). *Protest and prejudice: A study of belief in the Black community.* New York: Harper & Row.

McPhail, C. (1971). Civil disorder participation. *American Sociological Review*, *38*, 1058–1073.

McPhail, C. (1991). *The myth of the madding crowd.* New York: Aldine de Gruyter.

Moscovici, S. (1981). *L'age des foules.* Paris: Fayard.

Nolan, M., Haslam, S., Spears, R., & Oakes, P. (1999). An examination of resource-based and fit-based theories of stereotyping under cognitive load. *European Journal of Social Psychology*, *29*, 641–663.

Nye, R. (1975). *The origins of crowd psychology.* London: Sage.

Nye, R. (1995). Savage crowds, modernism, and modern politics. In E. Barkan & R. Bush (Eds.), *Prehistories of the future: The primitivist project and the culture of modernism.* Stanford, CA: Stanford University Press.

Oakes, P. (1987). The salience of social categories. In J. Turner, M. Hogg, P. Oakes, S. Reicher, & M. Wetherell (Eds.), *Rediscovering the social group: A self-categorization theory.* Oxford, UK: Blackwell.

Oakes, P., Haslam, A., & Turner, J. (1994). *Stereotyping and social reality.* Oxford, UK: Blackwell.

Oakes, P., & Turner, J. (1986). Distinctiveness and the salience of social category memberships: Is there an automatic bias towards novelty? *European Journal of Social Psychology*, *16*, 325–344.

Oakes, P., & Turner, J. (1990). Is limited information-processing capacity the cause of social stereotyping? *European Review of Social Psychology*, *1*, 111–135.

Oakes, P., Turner, J., & Haslam, A. (1991). Perceiving people as group members: The role of fit in the salience of social categorizations. *British Journal of Social Psychology*, *30*, 125–144.

Oberschall, A. (1968). The Los Angeles riot of August 1965. *Social Problems*, *15*, 322–341.

Olson, M. (1965). *The logic of collective action.* Cambridge, MA: Harvard University Press.

Postmes, T., & Spears, R. (1998). Deindividuation and antinormative behavior: A meta-analysis. *Psychological Bulletin*, *123*, 238–259.

Postmes, T., Spears, R., & Lea, M. (1998). Breaching or building social boundaries? SIDE-effects of computer-mediated communication. *Communication Research*, *25*, 689–715.

Postmes, T., Spears, R., & Lea, M. (1999). Social identity, normative content, and "deindividuation" in computer-mediated groups. In N. Ellemers, R. Spears, & B. Doosje (Eds.), *Social identity*. Oxford, UK: Blackwell.

Potter, J. (1996). *Representing reality*. London: Sage.

Prentice-Dunn, S., & Rogers, R. W. (1989). Deindividuation and the self-regulation of behavior. In P. Paulus (Ed.), *The psychology of group influence*. Hillsdale, NJ: Erlbaum.

Reddy, W. (1977). The textile trade and the language of the crowd at Rouen, 1752–1871. *Past and Present*, *74*, 62–89.

Reicher, S. (1982). The determination of collective behaviour. In H. Tajfel (Ed.), *Social identity and intergroup relations*. Cambridge, UK: Cambridge University Press, and Paris: Maison des Sciences de l'Homme.

Reicher, S. (1984a). The St Paul's "riot": An explanation of the limits of crowd action in terms of a social identity model. *European Journal of Social Psychology*, *14*, 1–21.

Reicher, S. (1984b). Social influence in the crowd: Attitudinal and behavioural effects of deindividuation in conditions of high and low group salience. *British Journal of Social Psychology*, *23*, 341–50.

Reicher, S. (1987). Crowd behaviour as social action. In J. Turner, M. Hogg, P. Oakes, S. Reicher, & M. Wetherell, *Rediscovering the social group: A self-categorization theory*. Oxford, UK: Blackwell.

Reicher, S. (1996a). The crowd century: Reconciling theoretical failure with practical success. *British Journal of Social Psychology*, *35*, 535–553.

Reicher, S. (1996b). The battle of Westminster: Developing the social identity model of crowd behaviour in order to deal with the initiation and development of collective conflict. *European Journal of Social Psychology*, *26*, 115–134.

Reicher, S., & Hopkins, N. (1996a). Constructing categories and mobilising masses: An analysis of Thatcher's and Kinnock's speeches on the British miners' strike 1984–5. *European Journal of Social Psychology*, *26*, 353–371.

Reicher, S., & Hopkins, N. (1996b). Seeking influence through characterising self-categories: An analysis of anti-abortionist rhetoric. *British Journal of Social Psychology*, *35*, 297–312.

Reicher, S., Hopkins, N., & Condor, S. (1997a). Stereotype construction as a strategy of influence. In R. Spears, P. Oakes, A. Haslam, & N. Ellemers (Eds.), *Stereotyping and social identity*. Oxford, UK: Blackwell.

Reicher, S., Hopkins, N., & Condor, S. (1997b). The lost nation of psychology. In G. Barfoot (Ed.), *Ethnic stereotypes and national purity*. DQR Studies in Literature.

Reicher, S., & Levine, M. (1994a). Deindividuation, power relations between groups and the expression of social identity: The effects of visibility to the outgroup. *British Journal of Social Psychology*, *33*, 145–163.

Reicher, S., & Levine, M. (1994b). On the consequences of deindividuation manipulations for the strategic communication of self: Identifiability and the presentation of social identity. *European Journal of Social Psychology*, *24*, 511–524.

Reicher, S., Levine, M., & Gordijn, E. (1998). More on deindividuation, power relations between groups and the expression of social identity: Three studies on the effects of visibility to the ingroup. *British Journal of Social Psychology*, *37*, 15–40.

Reicher, S., & Potter, J. (1985). Psychological theory as intergroup perspective: A comparative analysis of "scientific" and "lay" accounts of crowd events. *Human Relations*, *38*, 167–189.

Reicher, S., & Sani, F. (1998). Introducing SAGA: The structural analysis of group arguments. *Group Dynamics*, *2*, 267–285.

Reicher, S., Spears, R., & Postmes, T. (1995). A social identity model of deindividuation phenomena. *European Review of Social Psychology*, *6*, 161–198.

Rude, G. (1959). *The crowd in the French revolution.* Oxford, UK: Oxford University Press.

Rude, G. (1964). *The crowd in history.* New York: Wiley.

Rude, G. (1970). *Paris and London in the eighteenth century.* London: Collins.

Sani, F., & Reicher, S. (1998). When consensus fails: An analysis of the schism within the Italian Communist Party. *European Journal of Social Psychology, 28,* 623–645.

Sani, F., & Reicher, S. (1999). Identity, argument, and schism: Two longitudinal studies of the split in the Church of England over the ordination of women. *Group Processes and Intergroup Relations, 2,* 279–300.

Schwarz, W. (1982). "The People" in history: The Communist Party historians group 1946–56. In R. Johnson (Ed.), *Making histories: Studies in history writing and politics.* London: Hutchinson.

Sherif, M. (1936). *The psychology of social norms.* New York: Harper.

Sherif, M., & Harvey, O. (1952). A study in ego-functioning: Elimination of stable anchorages in individual and group situations. *Sociometry, 15,* 272–305.

Shotter, J. (1989). Social accountability and the social construction of "you." In J. Shotter & K. Gergen (Eds.), *Texts of identity.* London: Sage.

Sighele, S. (1892). *La foule criminelle: Essai de psychologie collective.* Paris: Felix Alcan.

Singer, J., Brush, C., & Lublin, S. (1965). Some aspects of deindividuation: Identification and conformity. *Journal of Experimental Social Psychology, 1,* 356–378.

Smith, D. (1980). Tonypandy 1910: Definitions of community. *Past and Present, 87,* 158–184.

Spears, R., & Haslam, A. (1997). Stereotyping and the burden of cognitive load. In R. Spears, P. J. Oakes, N. Ellemers, & A. Haslam (Eds.), *The social psychology of stereotyping and group life.* Oxford, UK: Blackwell.

Spears, R., Haslam, A., & Jansen, R. (1999). The effect of cognitive load on social categorization in the category confusion paradigm. *European Journal of Social Psychology, 29,* 621–639.

Spears, R., & Lea, M. (1992). Social influence and the influence of the "social" in computer-mediated communication. In M. Lea (Ed.), *Contexts of computer-mediated communication* (pp. 30–65). Hemel Hempstead, UK: Harvester-Wheatsheaf.

Spears, R., & Lea, M. (1994). Panacea or panopticon? The hidden power in computer-mediated communication. *Communication Research, 21,* 427–459.

Spears, R., Lea, M., & Lee, S. (1990). De-individuation and group polarization in computer-mediated communication. *British Journal of Social Psychology, 29,* 121–134.

Stark, R. (1972). *Police riots: Collective violence and law enforcement.* Belmont, CA: Wadsworth.

Stephenson, J. (1979). *Popular disturbances in England, 1700–1870.* London: Longman.

Stott, C. (1996). *The intergroup dynamics of crowd behaviour.* Unpublished Ph.D. thesis. University of Exeter, UK.

Stott, C., & Drury, J. (1999). The intergroup dynamics of empowerment: A social identity model. In P. Bagguley & J. Hearn (Eds.), *Transforming politics: power and resistance.* London: Macmillan.

Stott, C., & Reicher, S. (1998). Crowd action as intergroup process: Introducing the police perspective. *European Journal of Social Psychology, 26,* 509–529.

Tajfel, H. (1978). *Differentiation between social groups.* London: Academic Press.

Tajfel, H. (1982). *Social identity and intergroup relations.* Cambridge, UK: Cambridge University Press and Paris: Maison des Sciences de l'Homme.

Tajfel, H., & Turner, J. (1986). The social identity theory of intergroup behavior. In S. Worchel & W. G. Austin (Eds.), *Psychology of intergroup relations.* Chicago, IL: Nelson-Hall.

Tarde, G. (1890). *La philosophie pénale.* Lyon, France: Storck.

Tarde, G. (1892). Les crimes des foules. *Archives de l'Anthropologie Criminelle, 7,* 353–386.

Tarde, G. (1901). *L'opinion et la foule.* Paris: Felix Alcan.

Teske, N. (1997). *Political activists in America.* Cambridge, UK: Cambridge University Press.

Thompson, E. P. (1971). The moral economy of the English crowd in the eighteenth century. *Past and Present, 50,* 76–136.

Thompson, E. P. (1991). *Customs in common.* Harmondsworth, UK: Penguin.

Tilly, C. (1968). Race and migration to an American city, In T. Wilson (Ed.), *The metropolitan enigma.* Cambridge, MA: Harvard University Press.

Tilly, C. (1969). Collective violence in European perspective. In H. Graham & T. Gurr (Eds.), *Violence in America.* New York: Signet.

Tilly, C., Tilly, L., & Tilly, R. (1975). *The rebellious century: 1830–1930.* London: Dent.

Tilly, R. (1970). Popular disorders in Germany in the nineteenth century: A preliminary survey. *Journal of Social History, 4,* 1–41.

Tomlinson, T. (1970). Ideological foundations for Negro action: A comparative analysis of militant and non-militant views of the Los Angeles riot. *Journal of Social Issues, 25,* 93–119.

Turner, J. (1982). Towards a cognitive redefinition of the social group. In H. Tajfel (Ed.), *Social identity and intergroup relations.* Cambridge, UK: Cambridge University Press.

Turner, J. (1991). *Social influence.* Milton Keynes, UK: Open University Press.

Turner, J. (1999). Social identity theory: Where are we now? In B. Doosje, N. Ellemers, & R. Spears (Eds.), *Social identity.* Oxford, UK: Blackwell.

Turner, J., & Giles, H. (1981). *Intergroup behaviour.* Oxford, UK: Blackwell.

Turner, J., Hogg, M., Oakes, P., Reicher, S., & Wetherell, M. (1987). *Rediscovering the social group: A self-categorization theory.* Oxford, UK: Blackwell.

Turner, J., Oakes, P., Haslam, S., & McGarty; C. (1994). Self and collective: Cognition and social context. *Personality and Social Psychology Bulletin, 20,* 454–463.

Turner, R., & Killian, L. (1987). *Collective behavior* (3rd Ed.). Englewood Cliffs, NJ: Prentice-Hall.

U.S. Riot Commission (1968). *Report of the national advisory commission on civil disorders.* New York: Bantam.

Williams, D. (1986). *The Rebecca riots.* Cardiff: University of Wales Press.

Wright, S. (1978). *Crowds and riots.* London: Sage.

Wyer, R., & Srull, T. (1994). *The handbook of social cognition* (2 Vols.). Hillsdale, NJ: Erlbaum.

Zimbardo, P. G. (1969). The human choice: Individuation, reason, and order versus deindividuation, impulse, and chaos. In W. J. Arnold & D. Levine (Eds.), *Nebraska symposium on motivation.* Lincoln, NE: University of Nebraska Press.

CHAPTER ELEVEN

The Social Identity Perspective in Intergroup Relations: Theories, Themes, and Controversies

John C. Turner and Katherine J. Reynolds

Introduction

There has been a steady growth of research on intergroup relations in the last 30 years and the social identity perspective, comprising social identity theory (SIT; Tajfel & Turner, 1979) and self-categorization theory (SCT; Turner, Hogg, Oakes, Reicher, & Wetherell, 1987), has played a leading role in this development. In fact, research in this tradition is being pursued more vigorously now than ever before (e.g., Abrams & Hogg, 1999; Ellemers, Spears, & Doosje, 1999; Haslam, in press; Mummendey & Wenzel, 1999; Oakes, Haslam, & Turner, 1994; Spears, Oakes, Ellemers, & Haslam, 1997; Tyler, Kramer, & John, 1999; Worchel, Morales, Paez, & Deschamps, 1998). Its basic ideas about the role of social categorization and social identities in group processes are now widely accepted throughout the field (e.g., Brewer & Brown, 1998; Fiske, 1998). These ideas are moreover finding their way into new areas (Abrams & Hogg, 1999; Haslam, in press; Turner & Haslam, in press; Turner & Onorato, 1999).

This chapter will provide an overview of the social identity perspective by discussing key ideas and addressing important misunderstandings. The latter are worth discussing to identify themes in current research and directions for the future. It will be argued that there has been a failure to take seriously the metatheory behind the perspective. The tendency has been to divorce psychological processes from the social forces that structure their functioning. SIT and SCT emphasize that intergroup relations cannot be reduced to individual psychology but emerge from an interaction between psychology and society (Tajfel, 1972a, 1979; Turner, 1996).

Note: This research was supported by a Large Australian Research Council grant to John Turner, Kate Reynolds, and Alex Haslam.

The first section summarizes the basic ideas of SIT and SCT while highlighting the similarities and differences between them. In the second section a series of questions, which raise key themes and controversies within social identity research, are addressed. The final section attempts to identify and examine the necessary features of a comprehensive social psychological analysis of social conflict between groups. It is concluded that the social identity perspective, although not intended as a "sovereign" approach to intergroup conflict, has made a significant contribution toward understanding intergroup relations, and that future progress depends on the metatheoretical ideas within which SIT and SCT developed being fully understood and embraced.

The Theories: Similarities and Differences

Many researchers tend to confuse SIT and SCT. Some use the term "social identity theory" to refer to ideas from both theories indiscriminately. Others, in distinguishing the theories, misattribute ideas from one to the other. For these reasons it is useful to highlight the main points of similarity and difference between SIT and SCT. Space is not available for detailed summaries of the theories but these are widely available (e.g., Turner, 1999).

SIT attempts to make sense of intergroup relations in real societal contexts (Tajfel, 1978; Tajfel & Turner, 1979). It provides a comprehensive theory of intergroup relations and social change in socially stratified societies (the term social identity theory was first employed by Turner & Brown, 1978, to describe this complex analysis of intergroup relations) and addressed ingroup bias, social conflict, intergroup relations: "Why do people in groups discriminate against each other?", "Why are they ethnocentric?". Its response to these questions was the idea that people have a need for positive social identity which requires them to establish a positively valued distinctiveness for their own group compared to other groups.

The theory has *three* indispensable elements (or "legs of a conceptual tripod," as Tajfel, 1979, put it). As well as (1) an analysis of aspects of collective psychology (i.e., the need for a positive social identity), the theory delineated how this motivation interacted with (2) specific intergroup status differences in society and (3) the tendency to deal with one's identity problems as either an "individual" or as a "group" (defined as movement along a continuum from interpersonal to intergroup behavior).

SIT was used to explore the psychological consequences for members of the relative status position of their group (high or low status) and the perceived nature of intergroup status differences (secure vs. insecure, i.e., legitimate or stable vs. illegitimate or unstable), and to elaborate the different ways in which group members could and would react to the challenges posed to their social identities by their different locations in the social structure and their shared beliefs about the nature of the social structure (the main strategies identified being "individual mobility," "social creativity," and "social competition").

Tajfel developed the idea of the "interpersonal–intergroup continuum" (the extent to which one acted as an individual in terms of interpersonal relationships or as a group member in terms of intergroup relationships) to explain when social identity processes were likely to come into operation and how social interaction differed qualitatively between these extremes (Tajfel, 1974, 1978). He argued that as behavior became more intergroup, attitudes to the outgroup within the ingroup tended to become more consensual and that outgroup members tended to be seen as homogeneous and undifferentiated members of their social category.

Shift along the continuum was a function of an interaction between psychological and social factors. He emphasized the degree to which group members shared an ideology of "individual mobility" or "social change" and saw the social system as characterized by rigid and intense social stratification. He suggested that the perceived impermeability of group boundaries tended to be associated with an ideology of "social change," characterized by a belief that people cannot resolve their identity problems through individual action and mobility but are only able to change their social situation by acting collectively in terms of their shared group membership.

Contrary to many reviews the basic psychological idea of SIT was not the distinction between personal and social identity. As Tajfel stated on numerous occasions, it was the notion that social comparisons between groups were focused on the establishment of positive ingroup distinctiveness. Social identity was distinguished from the rest of the self-concept but not from personal identity. The interpersonal–intergroup continuum in SIT was not related to personal versus social identity but to "acting in terms of self" versus "acting in terms of group" (Tajfel, 1974).

The distinction between personal and social identity was the beginning of SCT and was not made until the end of the 1970s. SCT began with the insight that Tajfel's distinction between interpersonal and intergroup behavior could be explained by a parallel and under-lying distinction between *personal* and *social identity* (Turner, 1978, 1982). SCT was not concerned with ethnocentrism or discrimination but with psychological group membership: "What is a psychological group?", "How are people able to act psychologically in a collective way as group members?". It tried to explain how people became a group and the psychological basis of group processes.

The basic idea was that self-perception or self-conception varies between personal and social identity and that as one moves from defining self as an individual person to defining self in terms of a social identity, group behavior becomes possible and emerges. In other words, when a shared social identity is psychologically operative or salient there is a depersonalization of self-perception such that people's perceptions of their mutual and collective similarities are enhanced. Subsequently the distinction between personal and social identity was related to the more general hypothesis that there are different levels of self-categorization, but this was a reconceptualization of the founding notion, that personal and social identity can be distinguished and that group behavior is simply people acting more in terms of social than personal identity.

A fundamental point of SCT which has been central to the analysis of stereotyping and other group phenomena is that when we perceive ourselves as "we" and "us" as opposed to "I" and "me," this is ordinary and normal self-experience in which the self is defined in terms of others who exist outside of the individual perceiver and is therefore not purely personal. It is a shared cognitive representation of a collective entity which exists reflexively in the minds of individual group members and is structured by the realities of group life in a particular social system. Social identity is a collective self, not a "looking-glass" self – it is not an "I" as perceived by the group, but a "we" who are the group and who define ourselves for ourselves (Turner, Oakes, Haslam, & MacGarty, 1994; Turner & Onorato, 1999).

Just as SIT provides a new way of approaching intergroup relations, so SCT provides a new way of thinking about social groups. It has provided new analyses of group formation and cohesion, social cooperation, social influence (conformity, polarization, minority influence, and leadership), crowd behavior, "de-individuation," the contact hypothesis, social stereotyping, the self-concept, and personality. Current work on the theory has in fact gone far beyond traditional group issues (Turner, 1999).

Attributing the distinction between personal and social identity (and the hypothesis that the shift from personal to social identity transforms individual into group behavior) to SIT acts therefore to strip SCT of its core idea. The result is that the theory loses its force as an explanation of group psychology. It tends to be reduced to a purely cognitive analysis of categorization processes, an application of Tajfel's (1969) accentuation theory to self-perception but with a more developed analysis of the contextual factors determining the "salience" of social categorizations. SCT is then described as "social-cognitive" (Abrams & Hogg, 1999), as a turn away from the more "social" and "motivational" SIT to less social and more individual-cognitive ideas. It is assumed to ignore or reject the role of self-esteem in social identity processes, and to have been developed to replace SIT (Operario & Fiske, 1999). SIT in turn is reduced to a "self-esteem" theory, one which explains intergroup relations in terms of the need for positive self-esteem and has little interest in cognitive analysis. The failure of its supposed self-esteem predictions then leads it to be dismissed as a "macro-social" metatheory (Operario & Fiske, 1999), a polite way of saying that it has been empirically falsified.

In fact, both SIT and SCT are "cognitive" in the classic social psychological sense that they assume that to explain and predict behavior we need to understand how people perceive, define, and make sense of the world and themselves. Both are in the Gestalt (as opposed to behaviorist) tradition which derives from Sherif, Asch, Lewin, Heider, Festinger, and others. Both are also part of the cognitive tradition which goes back to Bruner's "New Look" in perception through Tajfel's (1957) analysis of categorization and values (other "cognitive" influences on SCT include Rosch, Medin, and Barsalou and colleagues). Neither is an individual-level cognitive theory of the form that dominated social cognition research in the 1980s. Further, despite assertions to the contrary, SCT assumes explicitly that "self-categories tend to be evaluated positively and that there are motivational pressures to maintain this state of affairs" (Turner et al., 1987, p. 57). SCT provides a specific analysis of self-esteem, seeing it as an expression of the degree to which self at any level is perceived as relatively prototypical of a higher-order, valued self-category. SCT does not discuss self-esteem in the same terms as SIT for the simple reason that SIT had already done the job and SCT was not seen as a replacement for SIT but as complementary to it (see Turner & Oakes, 1989, for a summary of how SCT emerged from social identity work).

Themes and Controversies

Are social groups the same as categories?

Rabbie, Schot, and Visser (1989) contrast social groups, which they define as "dynamic wholes," social systems characterized by perceived interdependence among members, with social categories, which they define as collections of individuals who share at least one attribute in common. They suggest that the social identity perspective assumes that groups are the same as categories.

Social groups are, of course, not the same as cognitive categories and the social identity perspective does not suggest that they are. In answering this charge, Tajfel (1982) criticized Rabbie and Horwitz for confusing two types of categories. The term "category" can mean an objective collection of people as defined by an outsider in terms of some common characteristic – a sociological category, for example, such as single-parent families. Such a group exists objectively, but it is a "membership" group (Turner, 1991). It need have no psychological or subjective significance for its members. It is not a "reference" group in classic terms.

The social identity perspective is explicitly and specifically addressed to reference groups. It uses the term "category," not in the sense of sociological categories, but in the sense of self-categories. Such "categories" are psychological representations in the mind; they are cognitive structures which people use *to define themselves* and to change their behavior. The point of SCT is to explain how a sociological group becomes a psychological group, how a membership group becomes a reference group. The idea is that people create cognitive categories to represent themselves as a higher-order entity and that, insofar as they represent themselves in terms of such categories, in terms of psychological concepts which become part of their mental functioning, they are able to transform their relationships to each other. As one moves from the "I" to the "we," we transform our behavioral and psychological relationships to each other so that we can now act in terms of a higher-order, emergent entity called a psychological group.

Rabbie and others confuse sociological categories (objective collections) with self-categories (psychological concepts). A social group, on the other hand, is a body of real people that acts in the world; it is a social system. The members interact, behave, and have relationships with each other. They share an identity, have goals, are interdependent, and they have social structures. A group has a social as well as a psychological reality. Such groups cannot be confused with either type of category above, but nevertheless their existence requires explanation. As psychologists, we assume that part of the explanation has to do with the psychology of their members. And part of their psychology is the way in which they create higher-order social categorical representations of themselves to transform their relations to each other and themselves. This does not mean that a group is only psychological, or that it is explained solely by social psychology. But self-categorization theorists are entitled to point to the psychological processes involved in group formation as a contribution to their explanation.

Rabbie et al. also suggest that the social identity perspective rejects the role of goal interdependence in group formation and that the "minimal group" studies which inspired the development of SIT and SCT were misinterpreted by Tajfel and Turner. They claim that minimal intergroup behavior is motivated by personal self-interest and hence does not provide evidence that self-categorization is alone sufficient for psychological group formation. Their points have been answered in detail by Turner and Bourhis (1996) but it is important to note that relevant studies demonstrate that ingroup bias is influenced by participants' degree of identification with minimal ingroups rather than by the degree to which they stand to gain financially from ingroup favoritism (e.g., Bourhis, Turner, & Gagnon, 1997).

Does SIT predict a positive correlation between ingroup identification and ingroup bias?

Hinkle and Brown (1990) propose that one of the basic propositions of SIT is that there should be a direct causal link between ingroup identification and ingroup bias. This translates into the hypothesis that positive correlations should be obtained between individual differences in identification with some ingroup and individual differences in the degree to which that group is favored over the outgroups in the setting. In fact, such correlations are not uniformly positive but often tend to be weak and quite variable (Brown, Hinkle, Ely, Fox-Cardamone, Maras, & Taylor, 1992; Hinkle & Brown, 1990). These findings are then cited as evidence against the theory and are used to justify attempts at major revision (Brown et al., 1992). The lack of simple positive relationships between ingroup identification and bias is probably the single most frequently cited empirical "disconfirmation" of SIT. We suggest that such an inference is unjustified (see also Turner, 1999).

The proposition is a version of SIT's basic idea that positive social identity requires positive ingroup distinctiveness, but SIT did not equate this idea with a direct causal connection between ingroup identification and ingroup bias. On the contrary, the causal relationship was always assumed to be mediated by a number of complicating factors and "ingroup bias" ("social competition") is only one of several individual and group strategies which can be pursued to achieve positive distinctiveness (others being "individual mobility" and "social creativity").

SIT assumed that whether or not ingroup bias was observed was a function, inter alia, of the specific intergroup comparison being made and the interaction between the relative status position of the ingroup, the perceived impermeability of group boundaries, and the nature of the perceived status differences on the relevant dimension. Turner and Brown (1978), for example, showed early on just how complex the relationship between ingroup bias and different intergroup status differences could be. Low status groups tended to be discriminatory when their position was unstable and illegitimate but not when it was secure; high status groups tended to be particularly discriminatory when their position was legitimate but unstable but not when it was both illegitimate and unstable. In this light the variable relationship between measures of ingroup identification and ingroup bias is in line with the theory and only to be expected. Nothing in the summary of the theory above implies simple positive correlations.

Another issue is that identification in the relevant studies is often not experimentally manipulated but is an individual difference variable. The use of individual difference methodology is inconsistent with the SCT hypothesis that there is a psychological discontinuity between people acting as individuals and people acting as group members (e.g., Turner & Onorato, 1999). The role of social identity salience is fundamental to this point. If one obtains intergroup attitudes from subjects responding in terms of their personal differences from others, in terms of their personal identities, then the attitudes obtained are not likely to remain unchanged when the subjects' social identities become salient. SCT predicts directly that depersonalizing participants enhances intragroup homogeneity and thus will modify correlations between the intergroup responses and a prior individual difference score (Haslam & Wilson, 2000; Reynolds, Turner, Haslam, & Ryan, 1999; Verkuyten & Hagendoorn, 1998).

These and related issues are elaborated elsewhere (Turner, 1999). An important point to be made here is that differences in ingroup identification, conceptualized appropriately, are of central interest to the social identity perspective (see Ellemers et al., 1999). What we need to avoid is the idea that identification expresses some kind of fixed and stable self-structure or personality trait which is chronically salient across situations and directly expressed in just one collective strategy independently of the social meaning of the intergroup relationship. From a self-categorization viewpoint, measures of identification may be a way of getting at the individual's readiness to self-categorize in terms of some identity, reflecting the psychological resources a person will tend to bring to the task of understanding self and constructing self-categories in some setting. They will reflect the centrality of some group membership in a person's understanding of their place in the social order and their relationships to others and also their commitment to that identity as a consequence of that understanding and their social values.

Does SIT actually contain the so-called "self-esteem hypothesis"?

The "self-esteem hypothesis" in this context refers to two supposed corollaries of SIT advanced by Hogg and Abrams (1990): that (1) successful intergroup discrimination elevates self-esteem and (2) depressed or threatened self-esteem promotes intergroup discrimination. The predictions which tend to be made and which receive mixed support are that ingroup bias should enhance or be correlated with (individual) self-esteem and that low (individual) self-esteem or ingroup status should enhance or be correlated with ingroup bias. The lack of support for these predictions is another widely cited "disconfirmation" of SIT.

Some of the problems with these corollaries have been discussed by Farsides (1995), Long and Spears (1997), Rubin and Hewstone (1998), and Turner (1999). The first point to note is that they are not actually contained in SIT. In fact, the theory can be seen as inconsistent with them. The theory assumes that there is a need for positive self-evaluation, but it does not equate this need with an individual-level motive. On the contrary, it is concerned with positively valued social identity, not individual-level self-esteem, and it does not even predict main effects of low group status or depressed social identity on ingroup bias, let alone such effects as a function of low personal self-esteem. Under conditions where social identity is salient, it is *insecure* (unstable and/or illegitimate) *social identity* in *interaction with low or high* status that prompts the need for positive distinctiveness and the search for positive distinctiveness *can take a variety of forms.* Social identity processes are only expected to come into play where social identity is salient and under such conditions people act in terms of their shared social identity, not in terms of their individual-level self-esteem.

For example, a low status group whose inferiority is stable and legitimate on the status dimension and which sees group boundaries as impermeable may seek positive distinctiveness on alternative dimensions (social creativity) but it is not likely to discriminate on the status dimension. A high status group with positive social identity which perceives its superiority as legitimate but unstable and under threat may be highly discriminatory. The personal self-esteem of group members is of no relevance to these predictions, and not even does positive or negative social identity in isolation lead to any consistent outcome. What matters is status position in interaction with the perceived nature of status differences and group boundaries.

Where discrimination takes place and successfully achieves positive distinctiveness, this might be reflected in a relevant status-related measure of collective self-esteem (but perhaps not for a high status group protecting what it has), but there is no reason why it should necessarily be reflected in a measure of personal self-esteem. If positive distinctiveness is achieved through some strategy other than social competition on the status dimension, then collective self-esteem could increase or be maintained without any basis in intergroup discrimination. To determine whether ingroup bias or some other intergroup strategy enhances positive social identity, one has to measure the self-evaluative aspects of the specific social not personal identity in relation to the specific situational dimension of comparison, what Rubin and Hewstone (1998) refer to as "social," "specific," and "state" self-esteem, not "personal," "global," and "trait" self-esteem. Why would a more positive social identity affect personal, global, and trait self-esteem? Perhaps where there is no other outlet, the participants may sometimes employ whatever measure is available to express the situationally relevant intergroup comparison, but this cannot be taken for granted.

The social identity perspective provides a different way of thinking about self-esteem from the traditional view that it is an individual psychological property which drives and motivates behavior independently of the social context. It makes a core assumption of a psychological discontinuity between individual and group behavior, personal and social identity and therefore personal and social categorical self-esteem (Branscombe & Ellemers, 1998; Brewer & Weber, 1994; Crocker & Luhtanen, 1990; Turner, 1982; Turner et al., 1987, pp. 57–65). The need for a positive social identity is not driven by some fixed "inner" motive but arises from the interaction of social identities, social comparison, and social values in specific intergroup relationships (Tajfel, 1972b; Turner, 1975). There are different levels of self-esteem just as there are different levels of self-categorization (e.g., Brewer & Weber, 1994) and self-esteem at any level is a function of judgments of self in relation to higher-level identity-based norms and values through relevant self-other comparisons on specific dimensions.

Are ingroup bias and therefore prejudice universal and inevitable features of relations between human social groups?

Two widespread misconceptions are that the social identity perspective sees ethnocentrism as a universal feature of relations between human social groups and that ingroup bias can be directly equated with social conflict and prejudice between groups. For example, using minimal groups, Mummendey and colleagues (e.g., Mummendey & Otten, 1998) have systematically demonstrated positive–negative asymmetry in social discrimination. Although the ingroup is favored on positively evaluated dimensions, there is a tendency toward fairness or outgroup favoritism on negative dimensions. It is only when the positive distinctiveness of the ingroup is threatened (e.g., through minority or insecure low status) that ingroup favoritism in the negative domain arises. Because ingroup bias in the minimal group paradigm is assumed by many to be the same as prejudice and because it is not found on negative dimensions (which is equated with overt hostility or aggression), the claim is then made that SIT has proved itself unable to deal with aggression and hostility in the full-blown sense, because it can only deal with bias on positive dimensions. The same kind of idea is found in more general assertions that SIT is an argument for the universality of prejudice.

In fact, SIT never equated ingroup bias with social hostility. It conceptualized it as a strategy for comparative, positively valued ingroup distinctiveness. Ingroup bias expressed evaluative (social) competition, evaluative differentiations between groups. It was never identified directly with aggression or hostility. It was of interest because of the processes to which it pointed in intergroup relations, processes which had hitherto been largely ignored. The value of SIT was that it identified these processes explicitly and used them to create an analysis of socially structured intergroup relations. On the basis of this novel theoretical analysis one could then derive hypotheses about the generation of social conflict and aggression.

There are several ways that one can get from SIT to a prediction of aggression, but they are all theoretical rather than merely an empirical assertion that ethnocentrism and social conflict are the same thing. Social conflict cannot be equated with the outcome of just one psychological process but must be understood in terms of the interplay of many as they are shaped by the historical, social, economic, and political structure of society. In Tajfel and Turner (1979), for example, it is hypothesized that one of the ways in which intergroup conflict develops is where insecure identities and a socially competitive need for positively valued distinctiveness are correlated with a salient division into groups and a realistic conflict of interests. SIT linked realistic conflict and insecure identity processes to explain the specific conditions under which aggression might develop.

In relation to ethnocentrism, there are suggestions that the theory is refuted by evidence that groups sometimes show outgroup favoritism. But the theory never claimed that ingroup favoritism was a universal feature of intergroup relations. For example, if members of low status groups define their inferiority as legitimate and stable, then they will see their group as consensually inferior on that dimension. There are many consensual status systems in which groups agree with each other about their respective inferiorities and superiorities. SIT did not assert that groups never see themselves as inferior, it argued that such self-perceived inferiority will have psychological consequences and motivate a range of responses.

Part of the issue is that the term "ingroup bias" has come to be used as a synonym for ingroup favoritism, implying that the latter always reflects an irrational, indiscriminate, reality-distorting psychological bias. It is assumed that ingroup favoritism (being a "bias") always accompanies ingroup–outgroup categorization, regardless of the specific nature of the intergroup relationship. But for a researcher to define ingroup favoritism as a bias is to make a value judgment from the perspective of an outside observer. Such a judgment often reflects no more than the fact that the relevant groups disagree with each other (both asserting that they are superior to each other). Groups may disagree with each other without irrationality being involved (Mummendey & Wenzel, 1999; Reynolds, Turner, & Haslam, 2000; Turner & Oakes, 1997). Diversity in opinion between individuals does not necessarily indicate bias or irrationality and the same is true for group-based disagreement. Group differences of opinion arise from the natural relativity of perception in which meaningful and veridical representations of reality are constructed from each group's singular perspective and from attempts to (in)validate certain views over others (Turner & Oakes, 1997).

Where there is consensual inferiority and superiority between groups in a particular social system then there is agreement about the nature of social reality. Groups share a similar interpretation of their respective strengths and weaknesses and if members are asked to evaluate their own and other groups on dimensions characteristic of each group, their responses will reflect both ingroup and outgroup favoritism. Conversely, with some (insecure) group relations there is less agreement regarding the extent to which attributes characterize one group compared to another. Expressions of ingroup favoritism are most likely when the same valued dimension is claimed as characteristic of both groups and are part of the process of social competition and potential group conflict. In these terms ingroup favoritism is not indiscriminate ethnocentrism or a psychological bias but rather depends on self-categorization as an ingroup member and the extent to which the relationship to the outgroup is secure or insecure and the comparative dimension important and relevant to the group comparing itself. In SIT so-called ingroup biases are expressions of the fact that the social reality of intergroup relations is being contested rather than that it is being perceptually distorted.

These considerations have implications for the explanation of positive–negative asymmetry in minimal groups (Reynolds et al., 2000). SIT and SCT maintain that in order to behave in terms of a particular group membership, self-definition in terms of the social category *must be psychologically salient*. SCT argues that the extent to which perceivers can meaningfully categorize themselves in terms of more (or less) inclusive categories depends on the interaction between context-specific judgments of similarity and difference (comparative and normative fit) and the perceivers' expectations, motives, and goals (perceiver readiness). Perceivers seek meaningful self-definition in terms of the comparative and normative features of the stimulus information available. It is possible that, where groups are minimal, it is less meaningful for perceivers to categorize and define themselves on the basis of negative than positive dimensions. It may be difficult for ingroup members to discriminate on negative dimensions because they provide a less appropriate, less fitting basis for self-definition.

To display ingroup favoritism in the negative domain ingroup members have to indicate that they are "less bad than the outgroup" on particular dimensions. This means that in order to discriminate, ingroup members have to accept, or at least countenance, a negative self-definition. Because participants may not believe that they are defined by particular negative dimensions they may be unwilling to define themselves and act in these terms. Negative dimensions may not fit participants' normative beliefs about themselves as well as positive dimensions and consequently, identification and intergroup discrimination will be minimized.

An implication is that it should be possible to find ingroup favoritism on both positive and negative dimensions when both provide a meaningful and relevant basis for self-definition in ingroup–outgroup terms. Recent empirical work supports this analysis (Reynolds et al., 2000). In one study, ingroup members evaluated the ingroup and the outgroup on positive and negative dimensions that were typical of the ingroup, typical of the outgroup, typical of both groups, and typical of neither group. There was no evidence of positive–negative asymmetry and ingroup favoritism was found on certain negative traits. Responses were ingroup-favouring on (a) positive traits that were typical of the ingroup and (b) negative traits that were typical of the outgroup, and outgroup-favouring on (a) positive traits that were typical of the outgroup and (b) negative traits that were typical of the ingroup.

A different pattern of results characterized responses on traits typical of both groups. In line with such evaluations being less consensual (the traits are fitting for both groups) ingroup favoritism was evident on both positive and negative traits. With traits typical of neither group, the pattern of discrimination was either fairness or outgroup favoritism. Such non-fitting dimensions (as with evaluations of minimal groups on negative dimensions) are not relevant to self and are therefore of little consequence for group-based status concerns.

This analysis and evidence indicate that ingroup favoritism is not the result of a generic drive or bias for ethnocentrism triggered automatically by being in a group. Nor is it the equivalent of outgroup hostility and aggression. These judgments (and the degree to which social hostility is involved) are constrained by social realities, varying with the degree to which the relevant social identity provides a meaningful fit between the perceiver and the situation and the degree to which the social structure of intergroup status differences is secure and consensual or insecure, contestable, and open to dispute (e.g., Ellemers, 1993; Ellemers, van Rijswijk, Roef, & Simons, 1997; Tajfel & Turner, 1979; Turner, 1996).

Social Identity: Implications and Future Directions

SIT and SCT are grounded in the metatheory of social psychological interactionism (Tajfel, 1972a, 1979; Turner & Oakes, 1997), which holds that social psychological processes emerge from a functional interaction between mind and society. The theories deal with psychological processes which are socially structured and which are qualitatively transformed by their interaction with social life and social processes. The interactionist perspective leads to a very different analysis of prejudice and intergroup relations from that currently dominant.

An alternative to the "prejudice" model of intergroup relations and human social conflict

As implied above, researchers sometimes appear to believe that SIT holds that ethnocentrism and prejudice are inevitable and irrational. The analysis goes as follows: People form groups; inherent in group formation is the need for superiority, which in turn is motivated by the drive for positive self-esteem; hence once one is in a group, one displays ethnocentrism, and ethnocentrism is the same as prejudice. The need for positive social identity is thus used to argue for the hypothesis that ethnocentrism is inevitable, an automatic and therefore irrational product of group formation. Intergroup attitudes are seen as products of irrational psychological biases, implying that unjustifiable prejudice is inherent in group life.

The social identity perspective is actually an argument against this view. It not only provides a specific theory of intergroup relations, it also resurrects the intergroup approach to social conflict pioneered in social psychology by Sherif (e.g., 1967) and his colleagues. Although Sherif was a realistic group conflict theorist, pointing to the role of conflicts of interests between groups in social antagonism, he stressed as fundamental the idea that intergroup relations rather than individual and interpersonal processes determined intergroup attitudes. SIT and SCT are intergroup theories in exactly the same sense. They argue that intergroup attitudes are always the product of an interaction between people's collective psychology as group members and the perceived social structure of intergroup relationships. The interaction between collective psychology and social reality is assumed to be mediated by group members' socially shared and socially mediated understanding of their intergroup relations (i.e., their collective beliefs, theories, and ideologies about the nature of the social system and the nature of the status differences between groups).

In this respect, as has been argued elsewhere (Turner, 1996), the social identity perspective provides a way of going beyond the "prejudice" model of social conflict which has dominated the field since the 1920s. The implicit orthodoxy in intergroup relations research is that social antagonism in its various forms is a product of prejudice, that is, of defect, irrationality, and pathology at the level of individual psychology. Negative outgroup attitudes are assumed to be inherently pathological, irrational, invalid, and unjustifiable.

This notion is summarized by three main ideas that pervade much research: That specific dysfunctional individual-difference or personality factors more or less directly predispose people to more or less hostility against outgroups; that there are individual-level cognitive and/or motivational processes which directly produce negative outgroup attitudes and which are socially irrational since they are purely psychologically caused; and that intergroup attitudes are inherently mindless, meaningless, and devoid of rational content. Personality, cognitive limitations, and ignorance become possible explanations of intergroup relations precisely because they ignore issues of social structure, but, in our view, this oversight also renders these explanations limited and incoherent.

The social identity perspective rejects each of these ideas. It emphasizes that we need to understand social conflict as psychologically meaningful, as an expression of how people define themselves socially, and of their understanding of the reality of their intergroup relationships. Social conflict can be a rational reaction to people's historically evolved understanding of themselves in interaction with their theories of the social world and the reality of social structure. We do not need to posit defective personality types, individual-level psychological processes which directly cause outgroup hostility as a result of some single variable, factor, or state (social categorization, ingroup identification, frustration, low self-esteem, low social status, positive or negative mood, etc.), or inherent defects in human cognition, motivation, or emotions (e.g., the supposed oversimplification and over-generalization of stereotyping) to explain social antagonism. It is a result of ordinary, adaptive, and functional psychological processes in interplay with the realities of social life. This is an important and radically different approach to social conflict from the traditional emphasis on "prejudice."

One example of the difference in approach is provided by research on stereotyping. Much SCT work has been done over the last decade to argue for its rationality and validity (Oakes et al., 1994). An aspect of the "prejudice" model is the social cognition view that stereotyping is due to limited attentional resources and shortcuts in information processing. Such impressions are interpreted as less valid and accurate than individuated judgments which reflect a person's true personal characteristics (Fiske, 1998). This view is not surprising if the influence of group realities and social structure is denied in theory and research. If groups do not exist and there are only individuals, then any judgment of people as a group must be invalid, must be erroneous. If there is not an analysis of collective psychology and social structure that can be used to explain stereotypes and stereotyping then the explanation must be sought in individual psychology. The end point is a view that stereotypes and intergroup perceptions are a function of individual psychology (and pathology).

The alternative view is that stereotypes and intergroup attitudes are expressions of collective cognition, of people's attempt to make sense of the world, to create a meaningful but collectively shaped representation of group realities. Stereotypes are not just held by individuals perceiving individuals, they describe people's group attributes and are shared within groups; they are products of group interaction and anchored in group memberships. They serve group purposes and are products of social influence and communication as much as they are products of an individual cognitive process. They also have an ideological content related to people's theories, beliefs, ideologies about the nature of the intergroup relationship.

This view does not see stereotyping as psychologically defective, invalid, or unjustifiable, but rather as an outcome of an adaptive, rational, and reality-oriented psychological process. This does not mean that every specific stereotype is valid but that the same reasonable psychological process is behind everybody's stereotypes (both those with which we agree and those with which we disagree). Validity is not purely a psychological question. It is also a social and a political question and we are entitled to argue about stereotypes, to accept some and reject some, to try, as a society, to put right those we think are wrong. The fact that we engage in social and political debate over differing stereotypes is not proof that they are psychologically defective. Rather it speaks to the functional aspects of human collective psychology, to the fact that we seek to produce higher-order collective truths from the relativities of lower-level group judgments (see Oakes et al., 1994, chapter 8; Turner & Oakes, 1997).

It is paradoxical in light of these points that the social identity perspective is sometimes reduced to a "prejudice" theory. Arguments that SIT predicts that social categorization automatically and inevitably leads to ingroup bias, that intergroup relations should be characterized by universal ethnocentrism, that ingroup bias is inherent in group formation, that low status groups should always be more biased than high status groups, that intergroup discrimination is driven by an individual need for self-esteem and should directly enhance individual self-esteem, and so on, interpret it in this way. They imply that the theory is simply the assertion of a universal, irrational drive for ethnocentrism, unconstrained by social realities or the social meaning of intergroup attitudes and that some simple, single factor which triggers or relates to this drive should be positively correlated with intergroup discrimination virtually independent of social context or the perceived nature of intergroup relations. As we have seen, this is a misconception.

What do we need to explain human social conflict?

Is the social identity perspective a "sovereign" theory of intergroup conflict? Were social identity processes ever meant to provide exclusive or comprehensive explanations of human social conflict? The point is sometimes made that the social identity perspective does not provide a complete account of intergroup relations, as if it had ever been claimed that it did. Suffice it to say, Tajfel and Turner both stated that social identity processes were not the only factor in intergroup relations, that realistic group interests, for example, were important. The social identity perspective never rejected the insights of Sherif's realistic conflict analysis. It did reconceptualize the relationship between realistic group interests, psychological group formation, and intergroup relations (Turner & Bourhis, 1996), but it never denied the empirical importance of conflicting group interests in intergroup conflict. Indeed Tajfel and Turner were also clear that one cannot explain human social conflict through social psychology alone. Social psychology *in toto* is only a part of the story, let alone any particular theory of intergroup processes.

What does one need to explain human intergroup conflict and how does the social identity analysis fit into the picture? There are, of course, different views on this matter, but the elements of an "intergroup" view consistent with the spirit of the social identity perspective can be found in Sherif's work, in Tajfel's writings, in the self-categorization analysis of stereotyping, and in the preceding discussion of the relative role of "prejudice" or "intergroup relations" in intergroup attitudes.

SIT and SCT assume that intergroup attitudes are always an outcome of an interaction between people's collective psychology as group members and the social structure of intergroup relationships. They further assume that this interaction is mediated by people's collective beliefs, theories, and ideologies about intergroup relationships and the wider social system, by socially structured cognition. Thus human social conflict is not a matter of psychological irrationality, pathology, or error. It must be seen as an outcome of the social, psychological, and historical processes which have shaped people's collective understandings of themselves, their ingroups and outgroups, and their relationships with other groups. It is an outcome of the collective theories and ideologies which they have developed to make sense of, explain, and justify intergroup relationships, of the ways in which people are influenced by these ideas, and of the particular kinds of social psychological processes that are relevant to predicting how their shared understandings of intergroup relationships will translate into attitudes and actions.

From this perspective, restricting ourselves to social psychology, there are four general requirements for an account of intergroup conflict:

1 An analysis of the *psychological group*; one must know when and why people form groups and what groups are psychologically and be able to answer the question of when people will behave individually or collectively.
2 An idea of the *processes* that come into play in *intergroup relations*; one must know what processes shape how people behave toward ingroups and outgroups as a function of intergroup relationships.
3 A *theory of social influence*; one must know how group identities, goals, and beliefs become consensual, shared, and normative, how they are validated, spread, changed, and anchored in group interaction and how collective beliefs about intergroup relationships, how stereotypes about one's own and other groups, are disseminated and/or changed. It is also necessary to confront the facts of political and other forms of leadership and the role of moderates and extremists in shaping group ideology.

4 An ability to analyze the *content of group beliefs* relevant to intergroup relations and the wider society; one must know how groups understand themselves, their relationships with other groups and who they see as outgroups. What are the collective theories and ideologies which they have developed to make sense of, explain, justify, and rationalize their intergroup relationships and how are we to describe and explain the development of these collective social theories?

In terms of these components social psychology has made good progress in understanding social conflict. We have much work relevant to the main elements of the picture and the social identity perspective is central to it. SCT is a theory of the psychological group. In terms of intergroup processes, we have realistic conflict theory, which looks at the role of group goals and collective group interests, SIT, which looks at the interaction between identity, social values, and intergroup comparisons, and we have (fraternal) relative deprivation theory, which is relevant to social comparisons between groups and the collective emotions of anger, resentment, and frustration. SCT also provides a detailed and systematic analysis of social influence that has been applied to conformity, crowd behavior, group polarization, leadership, minority influence, and even political rhetoric (Haslam, in press; Reicher & Hopkins, 1996; Turner, 1991, 1999; Turner & Haslam, in press). We also know to some degree (or can speculate) on the basis of existing theory how these processes interact with each other. For example, SCT shows how identity processes and self-categorization are relevant to perceived interdependence, cooperation, and competition between groups. We know how conflicts of interests are relevant to the salience of social categorizations. We know that shared ideologies are relevant to the identities and stereotypes one forms (Brown, P. & Turner, in press) and play a role in mutual influence (Reicher, 1987). We know that social identities are social comparative and provide a basis for the experience of collective emotions (E. Smith, 1993).

What is it that we do not have? There are two definite weaknesses. Despite the theoretical insights into how psychological group membership, intergroup processes, social influence, and collective beliefs are likely to affect each other, relatively little systematic research into these interrelationships has been conducted (although there are honorable exceptions). We have, for example, not much tried to integrate what we know from SCT and social identity processes with what we know about realistic conflict and relative deprivation, although it is evident that relative deprivation is intimately linked to realistic conflict and social identity processes. In addition, we still know very little about how groups create the content of their collective beliefs. How and why do groups develop specific ideologies? How do certain ideologies win out over others? How are they spread? Researchers have noted this neglect for years but little real progress seems to have been made in terms of testable social psychological theory.

The social identity perspective contributes to our general understanding in several ways, in relation to the group, intergroup processes, and social influence, and is relevant to the role of ideology. It helps also to clarify where future research needs to be directed for integrative progress, at the synthesis of all the main elements of the picture, at the links between the intergroup processes, and at the development of a social psychological approach to the content of group beliefs.

Conclusion

The social identity perspective emphasizes that we need to understand intergroup relations as psychologically meaningful, as an expression of how people define their social identities, and an interaction between their collective psychology as group members and the perceived social structure of intergroup relations. Social antagonism can be a (psychologically) rational reaction to people's collective understanding of themselves in interaction with their theories of the social world and social structural realities. We do not need to posit sick or defective personality types, individual-level psychological processes operating in a social vacuum, or intergroup perceptions as inherently distorting of social reality to explain stereotypes, "prejudice," and social conflict.

Part of the reason for the prevalence of traditional views has to do with metatheory. Social psychology is still dominated by "the individualistic thesis" (Asch, 1952). The social identity perspective also tends willy-nilly to be assimilated to this thesis (and reduced to a prejudice analysis). It tends to be divorced from the interactionist metatheory within which it developed. In reality, SIT and SCT take for granted that it is not possible to develop adequate social psychological theories, which do not distort the phenomena under consideration, unless one accepts that the relevant psychology is socially structured, emergent, and always functions in a social context. Social psychology is not biology, nor sociology, nor general (i.e., individual) psychology; its focus is on the socially systematic regularities of psychological functioning and human conduct. Its processes must take such an interaction between the psychological and the collective for granted and be explanatory of and consistent with its effects.

To fail to appreciate that SIT and SCT were intended to unravel aspects of the mind–society interaction and to divorce the psychological processes they posit from the social processes with which they were assumed to interact, is to individualize them and misconstrue their psychological ideas. Misinterpretations of SIT and SCT are not an accident and neither are they wilful; they represent the intellectual influence of individualism, an influence which is felt whenever social identity ideas are divorced from their proper metatheoretical home. Understanding the metatheory of social identity is not a luxury; it is a crucial part of its legacy and a prerequisite for the full development of social psychology's analysis of intergroup relations and human social conflict.

REFERENCES

Abrams, D., & Hogg, M. A. (1999). *Social identity and social cognition.* Oxford, UK. Blackwell.

Asch, S. E. (1952). *Social psychology.* Englewood Cliffs, NJ: Prentice-Hall.

Bourhis, R. Y., Turner, J. C., & Gagnon, A. (1997). Interdependence, social identity, and discrimination: Some empirical considerations. In R. Spears, P. J. Oakes, N. Ellemers, & S. A. Haslam (Eds.), *The social psychology of stereotyping and group life.* Oxford, UK: Blackwell.

Branscombe, N. R., & Ellemers, N. (1998). Coping with group-based discrimination: Individualistic versus group-level strategies. In J. K. Swim & C. Stangor (Eds.), *Prejudice: The target's perspective* (pp. 243–266). New York: Academic Press.

Brewer, M. B., & Brown, R. J. (1998). Intergroup relations. In D. T. Gilbert, S. T. Fiske, & L. Gardner (Eds.), *The handbook of social psychology* (4th ed., Vol. 2. pp. 554–594). Boston, MA: McGraw-Hill.

Brewer, M. B., & Weber, J. G. (1994). Self-evaluation effects of interpersonal versus intergroup social comparison. *Journal of Personality and Social Psychology, 66*, 268–275.

Brown, P. M., & Turner, J. C. (in press). The role of theories in the formation of stereotype content. In C. McGarty, V. Y Yzerbyt, & R. Spears (Eds.), *Stereotypes as explanations: The formation of meaningful beliefs about social groups.* Cambridge, UK: Cambridge University Press.

Brown, R. J., Hinkle, S., Ely, P. G., Fox-Cardamone, L., Maras, P., & Taylor, L. A. (1992). Recognizing group diversity: Individualist-collectivist and autonomous-relational social orientations and their implications for intergroup processes. *British Journal of Social Psychology, 31*, 327–342.

Crocker, J., & Luhtanen, R. (1990). Collective self-esteem and ingroup bias. *Journal of Personality and Social Psychology, 58*, 60–67.

Ellemers, N. (1993). The influence of socio-structural variables on identity-enhancement strategies. *European Review of Social Psychology, 4*, 27–57.

Ellemers, N., Spears, R., & Doosje, B. (1999). *Social identity: Context, commitment, content.* Oxford, UK: Blackwell.

Ellemers, N., van Rijswijk, W., Roefs, M., & Simons, C. (1997). Bias in intergroup perceptions: Balancing group identity with social reality. *Personality and Social Psychology Bulletin, 23*, 186–198.

Farsides, T. (1995). *Why social identity theory's self-esteem hypothesis has never been tested – and how to test it.* Paper presented to BPS Social Psychology Section Conference, York, UK, September.

Fiske, S.-T. (1998). Stereotyping, prejudice, and discrimination. In D. T. Gilbert, S. T. Fiske, & L. Gardner (Eds.), *The handbook of social psychology* (4th ed., Vol. 2, pp. 357–411). Boston, MA: McGraw-Hill.

Haslam, S. A. (in press). *The psychology of organizations: A social identity approach.* London: Sage.

Haslam, S. A., & Wilson, A. (2000). In what sense are prejudicial beliefs *personal?* The importance of an ingroup's shared stereotypes. *British Journal of Social Psychology, 39*, 45–63.

Hinkle, S., & Brown, R. J. (1990). Intergroup comparisons and social identity: Some links and lacunae. In D. Abrams & M. A. Hogg (Eds.), *Social identity theory. Constructive and critical advances* (pp. 48–70). London: Harvester Wheatsheaf.

Hogg, M. A., & Abrams, D. (1990). Social motivation, self-esteem, and social identity. In D. Abrams & M. A. Hogg (Eds.), *Social identity theory. Constructive and critical advances* (pp. 28–47). London: Harvester Wheatsheaf.

Long, K., & Spears, R. (1997). The self-esteem hypothesis revisited: Differentiation and the disaffected. In R. Spears, P. J. Oakes, N. Ellemers, & S. A. Haslam (Eds.), *The social psychology of stereotyping and group life* (pp. 296–317). Oxford, UK: Blackwell.

Mummendey, A., & Otten, S. (1998). Positive–negative asymmetry in social discrimination. In W. Stroebe, & M. Hewstone (Eds.), *European review of social psychology* (Vol. 9, pp. 107–143). Chichester, UK: Wiley.

Mummendey, A., & Wenzel, M. (1999). Social discrimination and tolerance in intergroup relations: Reactions to intergroup difference. *Personality and Social Psychology Review, 3*, 158–174.

Oakes, P. J., Haslam, S. A., & Turner, J. C. (1994). *Stereotyping and social reality.* Oxford, UK: Blackwell.

Operario, D., & Fiske, S. (1999) Integrating social identity and social cognition: A framework for bridging diverse perspectives. In D. Abrams & M. A. Hogg (Eds.), *Social identity and social cognition* (pp. 26–54). Oxford, UK: Blackwell.

Rabbie, J. M., Schot, J. C., & Visser, L. (1989). Social identity theory: A conceptual and empirical critique from the perspective of a Behavioural Interaction Model. *European Journal of Social Psychology, 19*, 171–202.

Reicher, S. (1987). Crowd behaviour as social action. In J. C. Turner, M. A. Hogg, P. J. Oakes, S. D. Reicher, & M. S. Wetherell, *Rediscovering the social group: A self-categorization theory* (pp. 171–202). Oxford, UK: Blackwell.

Reicher, S., & Hopkins, N. (1996). Self-category constructions in political rhetoric: An analysis of Thatcher's and Kinnock's speeches concerning the British Miners' Strike (1984–5). *European Journal of Social Psychology, 26*, 353–372.

Reynolds, K. J., Turner, J. C., Haslam, S. A., & Ryan, M. K. (1999). *The role of personality and group factors in explaining prejudice.* Manuscript submitted for publication.

Reynolds, K. J., Turner, J. C., & Haslam, S. A. (2000). When are we better than them and they worse than us? A closer look at social discrimination in positive and negative domains. *Journal of Personality & Social Psychology, 78*, 64–80.

Rubin, M., & Hewstone, M. (1998). Social identity theory's self-esteem hypothesis: A review and some suggestions for clarification. *Personality and Social Psychology Review, 2*, 40–62.

Sherif, M. (1967). *Group conflict and co-operation: Their social psychology.* London: Routledge and Kegan Paul.

Smith, E. R. (1993). Social identity and social emotions: Toward new conceptualizations of prejudice. In D. M. Mackie & D. L. Hamilton (Eds.), *Affect, cognition, and stereotyping: Individualistic processes in group perception* (pp. 297–315). San Diego, CA: Academic Press.

Spears, R., Oakes, P. J., Ellemers, N., & Haslam, S. A. (Eds.), (1997). *The social psychology of stereotyping and group life.* Oxford, UK: Blackwell.

Tajfel, H. (1957). Value and the perceptual judgment of magnitude. *Psychological Review, 64*, 192–204.

Tajfel, H. (1969). Cognitive aspects of prejudice. *Journal of Social Issues, 25*, 79–97.

Tajfel, H. (1972a). Experiments in a vacuum. In J. Israel & H. Tajfel (Eds.), *The context of social psychology.* London: Academic Press.

Tajfel, H. (1972b). La catégorisation sociale (Social categorization). In S. Moscovici (Ed.), *Introduction à la psychologie sociale* (pp. 272–302). Paris: Larousse.

Tajfel, H. (1974). Social identity and intergroup behaviour. *Social Science Information, 13*, 65–93.

Tajfel, H. (1978). (Ed.). *Differentiation between social groups: Studies in the social psychology of intergroup relations.* London: Academic Press.

Tajfel, H. (1979). Individuals and groups in social psychology. *British Journal of Social and Clinical Psychology, 18*, 183–190.

Tajfel, H. (1982). (Ed.). *Social identity and intergroup relations.* Cambridge, UK: Cambridge University Press.

Tajfel, H., & Turner, J. C. (1979). An integrative theory of intergroup conflict. In W. G. Austin & S. Worchel (Eds.), *The social psychology of intergroup relations* (pp. 33–47). Monterey, CA: Brooks/Cole.

Turner, J. C. (1975). Social comparison and social identity: Some prospects for intergroup behaviour. *European Journal of Social Psychology, 5*, 5–34.

Turner, J. C. (1978). *Towards a cognitive redefinition of the social group.* Paper presented to the Research Conference on Social Identity, European Laboratory of Social Psychology (L.E.P.S.), Université de Haute Bretagne (Rennes II), Rennes, France.

Turner, J. C. (1982). Towards a cognitive redefinition of the social group. In H. Tajfel (Ed.), *Social identity and intergroup relations* (pp. 15–40). Cambridge, UK: Cambridge University Press and Paris: Editions de la Maison des Sciences de l'Homme.

Turner, J. C. (1991). *Social influence*. Milton Keynes, UK: Open University Press.

Turner, J. C. (1996). *Social identity theory and the concept of prejudice*. Invited Keynote Lecture, 40th Kongress der Deutschen Gesellschaft für Psychologie (40th Congress of the German Psychological Society), Ludwig-Maximilians-Universität, Munich, Germany, September 22–26.

Turner, J. C. (1999). Some current issues in research on social identity and self-categorization theories. In N. Ellemers, R. Spears, & B. Doosje (Eds.), *Social identity: Context, commitment, content* (pp. 6–34). Oxford, UK: Blackwell.

Turner, J. C., & Brown, R. J. (1978). Social status, cognitive alternatives, and intergroup relations. In H. Tajfel (Ed.), *Differentiation between social groups* (pp. 201–234). London: Academic Press.

Turner, J. C., & Bourhis, R. Y. (1996). Social identity, interdependence, and the social group: A reply to Rabbie et al. In W. P. Robinson (Ed.), *Social groups and identities: Developing the legacy of Henri Tajfel* (pp. 25–63). Oxford, UK: Butterworth-Heinemann.

Turner, J. C., & Haslam, S. A. (in press). Social identity, organizations, and leadership. To appear in M. E. Turner (Ed.), *Groups at work. Advances in theory and research*. Hillsdale, NJ: Erlbaum.

Turner, J. C., Hogg, M. A., Oakes, P. J., Reicher, S. D., & Wetherell, M. S. (1987). *Rediscovering the social group: A self-categorization theory*. Oxford, UK: Basil Blackwell.

Turner, J. C., & Oakes, P. J. (1989). Self-categorization theory and social influence. In P. B. Paulus (Ed.), *The psychology of group influence* (2nd ed., pp. 233–275). Hillsdale, NJ: Erlbaum.

Turner, J. C., & Oakes, P. J. (1997). The socially structured mind. In C. McGarty & S. A. Haslam (Eds.), *The message of Social psychology* (pp. 355–373). Oxford, UK: Blackwell.

Turner, J. C., Oakes, P. J., Haslam, S. A., & McGarty, C. (1994). Self and collective: Cognition and social context. *Personality and Social Psychology Bulletin, 20*, 454–463.

Turner, J. G., & Onorato, R. (1999). Social identity, personality; and the self-concept: A self-categorization perspective. In T. R. Tyler, R. Kramer, & O. John (Eds.), *The psychology of the social self* (pp. 11–46). Hillsdale, NJ: Erlbaum.

Tyler, T. R., Kramer, R., & John, O. (Eds.), (1999). *The psychology of the social self*. Hillsdale, NJ: Erlbaum.

Verkuyten, M., & Hagendoorn, L. (1998). Prejudice and self-categorization. The variable role of authoritarianism and ingroup stereotypes. *Personality and Social Psychology Bulletin, 24*, 99–110.

Worchel, S., Morales, J. F., Paez, D., & Deschamps, J.-C. (Eds.), (1998). *Social identity: International perspectives*. London, UK & Newbury Park, CA: Sage.

CHAPTER TWELVE

The Social Psychology of Minority–Majority Relations

Bernd Simon, Birgit Aufderheide, and Claudia Kampmeier

Groups are a fact and a medium of social life. The evolution of humankind as well as the development of each single individual took and still takes place within social groups. Physical as well as social existence critically depends on, and is shaped by, coordinated human action within and between social groups. In turn, groups are embedded in a structured context of intergroup relations characterized by a number of parameters such as goal interdependence, relative power, size, status, prestige, etc. An adequate analysis of human perception and behavior must therefore take into account social group memberships as well as the wider intergroup context.

The focus in this chapter is on the effect of group membership in the context of minority–majority relations. Many, if not most, real-life intergroup contexts consist of groups that hold either a minority or majority position vis-à-vis each other (Farley, 1982; Tajfel, 1981). A common definition of minority or majority group membership rests on numbers. Groups with fewer members are then defined as minorities and numerically larger groups as majorities (e.g., Brewer, 1991; Moscovici & Paicheler, 1978; Simon, 1992). In addition, relative power or social status is sometimes used as a criterion for defining minority and majority group membership (e.g., Tajfel, 1981). That definition assigns oppressed groups a minority position and dominant groups a majority position even when the numerical relation is balanced or reversed. For instance, in most societies, women would then be considered a (social) minority and men a (social) majority. Similarly, during apartheid in South Africa, Whites would have been considered a majority and Blacks a minority, even though the former group was numerically smaller than the latter (Tajfel, 1978). In this chapter, however, we start from a numerical definition of minority and majority group membership. This approach is in line with the bulk of research on minority–majority relations conducted by

Our own research reported in this chapter was supported by grants from the Deutsche Forschungsgemeinschaft (Si 428/2–1,2,3).

experimental social psychologists (e.g., Brewer, 1991, 1998; Mullen, 1991; Simon, 1992, 1998a). Also, in real life, numerical asymmetries often, though not necessarily, co-vary with power or status asymmetries such that the numerical minority is also a low-status or oppressed minority, and the numerical majority a high-status or dominant majority. This appears to be the case especially in Western democratic societies with their ideological emphasis on majority rule (Sachdev & Bourhis, 1984; Sherif, 1966). However, this correlation also implies that the effects of relative group size and status or power are often confounded in real life. Consequently, although relative group size constitutes the central independent variable in the research discussed in this chapter, power and status dimensions are not ignored in our analysis. In particular, we also try to disentangle the effects of relative group size and status.

In line with our basic premise that group memberships and the corresponding intergroup relations have a profound influence on social life, we examine a wide spectrum of possible consequences, or in other words, dependent variables. These fall into four broad classes, namely, (1) self-definition, (2) information processing, (3) well-being, and (4) behavior. This classification is not meant to suggest a mutual independence of the underlying psychological processes, nor is it intended as a conceptually exhaustive list. Rather, it is viewed as a helpful ordering scheme for reviewing the pertinent literature and structuring this chapter. More specifically, we examine whether membership in a minority group and membership in a majority group each constitute a distinct social psychological situation for the particular group member which elicits distinct reactions from her or him related to each of these four classes of dependent variables. In the next four major sections of this chapter, we therefore deal in turn with each class and discuss, in an exemplary, non-exhaustive fashion, typical minority–majority differences. In the final section, we then attempt to integrate these four parts and present a first outline of a more comprehensive theory of the social psychology of minority–majority relations.

Self-definition in Minority–Majority Contexts

There is wide agreement among social psychologists that our perception of other people is strongly influenced by our knowledge of their group memberships. For example, we readily perceive outgroup members as relatively similar to one another and attribute rather extreme and negative characteristics to them (e.g., Messick & Mackie, 1989; Tajfel, 1982). However, it is not just other people who are group members. We ourselves also belong to social groups or categories which may influence how we see ourselves. Self-categorization theorists have therefore suggested distinguishing between two basic forms of self-definition, namely between the individual self (or personal identity) and the collective self (or social identity) (Turner, Hogg, Oakes, Reicher, & Wetherell, 1987). Following self-categorization theory, the individual self stands for self-definition as a unique individual ("me") and the collective self for self-definition as an interchangeable group member ("we"). Relative to the individual self, the collective self is a cognitive representation of oneself at a higher level of abstraction or inclusiveness that implies depersonalization of individual self-perception.

Elaborating on the distinction between the individual self and the collective self, Simon (1997, 1998a) has proposed a self-aspect model (SAM) which should be particularly helpful in understanding minority–majority differences in self-definition. According to that model, the collective self emerges when self-definition centers on a single self-aspect that the person shares with other, but not all other people in the relevant social context (e.g., "First and foremost, I am a Christian."). The individual self, on the other hand, emerges when self-definition is based on a more comprehensive set or configuration of different, nonredundant self-aspects (e.g., "I am female, Christian, musical, a lawyer, have brown hair, like French cuisine, etc.").

Numerical distinctiveness

According to the self-aspect model, the collective self is predicated on focused self-definition. It follows that factors which facilitate this focusing or concentration process should also facilitate the collective self. One factor that could play such a facilitating role is the numerical distinctiveness of a social-categorical self-aspect. This may be so because novel or rare features generally tend to move in the perceptual foreground and thus become particularly salient (Fiske & Taylor, 1991; Mullen, 1991). By virtue of its numerical distinctiveness membership in a (numerical) minority should thus facilitate the collective self. There is indeed a growing body of evidence indicating that minority group membership may possess a particular "attention-grabbing power" so that it figures prominently in self-definition. For example, McGuire and McGuire (1988) found that children tended to think of themselves in terms of their gender and ethnicity to the extent that their respective group membership (e.g., being a boy or a girl) held a minority position in their usual social milieu. Laboratory research conducted in more controlled social environments points in the same direction. Simon and Hamilton (1994, Experiment 1) found that members of laboratory-created minority groups self-stereotyped more strongly than members of laboratory-created majority groups. In self-descriptions, minority members more strongly endorsed positive and negative ingroup attributes and more strongly rejected negative outgroup attributes. They also indicated more perceived similarity between themselves and their ingroup as well as more perceived homogeneity of the ingroup as a whole. Similarly, Brewer and Weber (1994) showed that minority members aligned their self-perceptions more strongly with a portrait of another ingroup member than did majority members. And again in line with Simon and Hamilton (1994, Experiment 1), this minority–majority difference was observed even when it implied the incorporation of negative ingroup characteristics into one's self-definition on the part of minority members (see also Ellemers, Kortekaas, & Ouwerkerk, 1999).

Meaningful social categorization

Oakes and colleagues (Oakes, 1987; Oakes & Turner, 1986) questioned that it is numerical distinctiveness per se that facilitates the collective self and instead emphasized the role of meaningful social categorization. Thus, being one of two men in an otherwise all-female psychology class should not matter with regard to self-definition unless the discussion shifts to relevant topics such as abortion or affirmative action policies. That is, any potential salience advantage of numerically distinct self-aspects may not translate into increased collective self-definition until possession or nonpossession of the critical self-aspect (e.g., being male) can systematically be related to the current social context (e.g., a discussion about affirmative action policies). Given such a relationship, however, social categorization into ingroup and outgroup based on the particular self-aspect becomes meaningful because it now fits the current social context. Then, minority group membership should indeed "benefit" from its salience advantage. Direct evidence for the hypothesized role of meaningful social categorization in minority–majority contexts was obtained by Simon, Hastedt, and Aufderheide (1997). In addition to relative ingroup size (minority vs. majority), we manipulated meaningfulness of the underlying social categorization (low vs. high) as a second independent variable by either weakening or strengthening the perceived correlation between group membership and performance on the alleged experimental task. As expected, the two independent variables had an interactive effect on several indicators of the collective self (e.g., self-ascribed typicality relative to self-ascribed individual uniqueness). The collective self was significantly stronger for minority members than for majority members, but only when the social categorization was meaningful. Otherwise, minority and majority members did not differ from each other. Moreover, the minority–majority difference in the high-meaningfulness condition was mainly due to an increase in the collective self among minority members. A second experiment replicated these findings and showed that a stronger meaningfulness manipulation led to an even stronger effect on minority members, but remained ineffectual with regard to majority members.

Note that in real-life minority–majority contexts the role of meaningfulness typically remains implicit. That is, people tend to focus mostly on minority–majority categorizations for which they have seemingly "good" reasons to presume the necessary social contextual fit or meaningfulness. They may do so either on the basis of actually observed correlations between minority–majority membership and important dimensions of the social context (e.g., actual correlations between ethnicity and religious practices) or on the basis of collectively shared belief systems (e.g., racist ideologies or myths). However, even in experimental research the role of meaningfulness often remains implicit because, in the attempt to construct a credible cover story, research participants are typically also provided with a meaningful link between social categorization and the current social context. In the Simon and Hamilton (1994) research, for example, participants were told that group membership was correlated with the introversion–extroversion dimension of personality. As all ratings relating to self-definition had to be made with reference to that personality dimension, social categorization was indeed highly meaningful in that research context. As a consequence, meaningfulness is often taken for granted as a given constant, and its critical role is overlooked. To progress in our understanding of minority–majority differences, we have to avoid this "taken-for-granted fallacy," however. In the Simon et al. (1997) research, we did so by explicitly increasing or decreasing the meaningfulness of social categorization in minority–majority contexts. Therefore, the major contribution of that research was to have made explicit the role of meaningful social categorization in minority–majority contexts thereby guarding against an overestimation of the role of numerical distinctiveness.

Relative group status

Another complication regarding the interpretation of minority–majority differences in self-definition concerns the role of status or power.[1] As indicated in the introduction, a numerical asymmetry may often co-vary with a status or power asymmetry such that the numerical minority is also a low-status or oppressed group and the numerical majority also a high-status or dominant group. However, the existence of many high-status, powerful numerical minorities or elites (e.g., the aristocracy in England, Brahmins in India, or – at least for many decades – Whites in South Africa) proves that this is not necessarily so. Simon and Hamilton (1994, Experiment 2) experimentally disentangled relative ingroup size (minority vs. majority) and ingroup status (low vs. high) by creating low- and high-status minority and majority groups in the laboratory. It was predicted that collective self-definition would be a direct function of the attractiveness of the respective ingroup (Tajfel & Turner, 1986). Ingroup attractiveness in turn was expected to vary according to the "scarcity principle" (Ditto & Jemmott, 1989) which postulates that the attractiveness of positively valenced and negatively valenced characteristics (i.e., high- and low-status group member-ship) is more polarized when the perceived frequency of these characteristics is low rather than high (i.e., when the ingroup is a minority rather than a majority) (Ellemers, Doosje, Van Knippenberg, & Wilke, 1992). The results were in line with these predictions. Overall, minority members were more willing to see themselves in terms of their collective self when ingroup status was high as opposed to low, whereas ingroup status was mostly ineffectual for majority members.

It should be noted, however, that these interactive effects are also compatible with a somewhat different perspective. The self-aspect model suggests that, given a meaningful social categorization (such as in Simon & Hamilton's research), numerical minority mem-bers' self-definition is much more centered or focused on group membership than numerical majority members' self-definition. Consequently, ingroup status is much more likely to "hit the heart" of minority members' self-definition. It should thus have a much more powerful impact on minority members' than on majority members' self-definition.

Although it is impossible at this point to draw any definite conclusions as to whether the original *scarcity account* or the latter *centrality account* (or some combination of both) pro-vides a superior explanation, there is some indirect evidence that supports the centrality account. For example, Simon, Aufderheide, and Hastedt (2000) found that, when ques-tioned immediately after the experimental manipulation of relative ingroup size, members of numerical minorities seemed to pay less attention to alternative self-aspects as they produced significantly less complex self-descriptions than members of numerical majorities. (But this effect disappeared when self-complexity was measured toward the end of the experimental session [see also Simon, 1998a, pp. 12–14].) Another potentially relevant pattern of results was observed in a real-life minority–majority context (Simon, Glässner-Bayerl, & Stratenwerth, 1991). In that field study, we found that members of a low-status, oppressed minority (gay men) showed greater awareness of their group membership than did members of the corr-esponding high-status, dominant majority (heterosexual men). At the same time, however, minority members also tended to be less glad to belong to their ingroup than were majority members. In line with our self-aspect model, this pattern thus points to an interesting ambivalence of members of low-status minorities toward their group membership. On the one hand, group membership appears to take a central and therefore particularly salient position in the cognitive self-definitions of members of low-status minority groups, while on the other hand, its negative value connotations make it an unattractive self-aspect. We will return to this cognitive-affective crossfire later in this chapter.

Information Processing in Minority–Majority Contexts[2]

Several social psychological approaches to social perception distinguish between two major levels or types of information processing, namely between individual-level or person-based processing, on the one hand, and group-level or category-based processing, on the other hand (Brewer, 1988, 1998; Fiske & Neuberg, 1990; Turner et al., 1987). Group-level processing is characterized, among other things, by the accentuation of perceived interchangeability of all members belonging to the same group, whereas accentuation of interpersonal differences is characteristic of individual-level processing. Following self-categorization theory (Turner et al., 1987), self-definition and information processing are closely interrelated such that the individual self underlies, and is itself reinforced by, individual-level processing, whereas the collective self underlies, and is reinforced by, group-level processing. Consequently, it can be assumed that the level of information processing is determined by variables similar to those that influence the level of self-definition. In light of the minority–majority differences in self-definition discussed in the preceding section, we should therefore also expect minority–majority differences in information processing.

Perception of ingroup and outgroup homogeneity

Taking perceived ingroup and outgroup homogeneity as an indicator of group-level information processing, it appears that there are indeed interesting minority–majority differences. Whereas members of (numerical) majorities tend to perceive more homogeneity in the outgroup than in the ingroup, members of (numerical) minorities often show the opposite tendency (Simon, 1992). Thus majority members seem to engage in group-level processing primarily regarding information about outgroup members, whereas minority members may engage in group-level processing also regarding information about ingroup members, and perhaps even more so than regarding information about outgroup members.

These differences nicely correspond to the minority–majority differences in self-definition discussed in the preceding section. However, this correspondence might not be too surprising given that measures of perceived group homogeneity tend to overlap with measures of self-definition as both are often based on ratings of perceived similarities and differences within the ingroup (e.g., Simon & Hamilton, 1994). It is therefore also necessary to review research which employed alternative methodologies to gauge information processing.

Recognition errors

A more sophisticated experimental paradigm which examines group-level relative to individual-level information processing is the recognition confusion task developed by Taylor and her colleagues, in which research participants have to remember who of a number of alleged ingroup and outgroup members made which statement (Taylor, Fiske, Etcoff, & Ruderman, 1978; Brewer, 1998; Lorenzi-Cioldi, 1998; Simon, 1998a; for a critical review, see Klauer & Wegener, 1998). In a first presentation stage, participants are typically presented with a number of statements each of which is identified as being made by either an ingroup member or an outgroup member. Statements are carefully pretested to avoid confounding variables (e.g., differential attractiveness of ingroup and outgroup statements), and their total number usually varies between 6 and 16 across studies. Statements are presented on audio or videotape or simply as written sentences on a computer screen, and each alleged speaker is identified by photographs or written information. In a second (recognition) stage, participants are presented with each statement once again. But this time, information as to who was the speaker is left out. Instead, participants are provided with lists of the names or photographs of all former speakers and are instructed to remember "who said what" and to match statements and faces or names accordingly. Three types of confusion errors can be distinguished: (1) within-ingroup errors resulting from attributing a statement allegedly made by a particular ingroup member erroneously to another ingroup member; (2) within-outgroup errors resulting from attributing a statement allegedly made by a particular outgroup member erroneously to another outgroup member; (3) intergroup errors resulting from attributing a statement allegedly made by an ingroup member erroneously to an outgroup member and vice versa. To anticipate a general result, the latter error type appears to be rather insensitive to experimental variations of relative ingroup size so that the following discussion focuses on intragroup errors (i.e., within-ingroup errors and within-outgroup errors). High numbers of such errors indicate the degree to which group members are seen or remembered as interchangeable exemplars of their respective groups or, in other words, the degree to which the perceiver engages in group-level as opposed to individual-level information processing.

Research on minority–majority differences in information processing using the recognition confusion task yielded mixed results. Thus Brewer, Weber, and Carini (1995, Experiment 3) found no minority–majority differences in the processing of information about outgroup members, but observed that, relative to majority members, minority members tended toward *less* group-level processing, or at least additional individual-level processing, when information about ingroup members was concerned. The latter finding is particularly surprising in light of the preceding discussions of minority–majority differences in self-definition and perceived group homogeneity which seemed to suggest that minority members should be particularly likely to engage in group-level, but not individual-level, processing of ingroup information. One obvious way to reconcile this apparent contradiction is to look for possible moderator variables. Recent research by Simon et al. (2000) indeed points to the existence of such variables. As a first step, we experimentally designed a standard minority–majority context in which group membership was highlighted at the expense of participants' individuality. The recognition confusion task was administered, and confusion errors served as the main dependent variable. As expected, minority members showed more group-level information processing than majority members. This standard minority–majority context was then contrasted with another minority–majority context which differed from the first in only one aspect. In this new context, we administered an individualizing self-description task before measuring the dependent variables. We predicted and found that this individualization process undermined the minority–majority difference in group-level information processing. It should be noted that, as in the Brewer et al. research (1995, Experiment 3), effects were observed only for within-ingroup errors, whereas within-outgroup errors were again insensitive to the experimental manipulations. However, the critical interaction effect was replicated in a second experiment with different measures of information processing (e.g., participants' use of abstract vs. concrete information), and this time the effect was obtained for processing of both ingroup and outgroup information (although the effect was somewhat weaker for the latter). More importantly, in this second experiment, the interaction effect involved a significant reversal. When individualization was fostered, group-level information processing decreased for minority members, but increased for majority members so that minority members showed less group-level information processing than majority members. Our tentative explanation was that individualization is compatible with majority group membership because, unlike minorities, majorities are typically construed as consisting of unique individuals (Mullen, 1991). In a seemingly paradoxical fashion, individualized self-perception may thus reinforce majority members' group membership and their group-level perspective. Although the pattern of results obtained in our individualized minority–majority context closely resembles that observed by Brewer et al. (1995, Experiment 3), it remains an open question at this point whether or exactly how such a moderator variable may have been operating in those authors' experiment. One possibility is that individualization processes were inadvertently fostered through the assignment of individual ID numbers, even though that assignment was apparently arbitrary. It is a well-established social psychological phenomenon that arbitrary category labels foster group formation processes (Tajfel, 1982). By the same token, even arbitrary ID numbers may foster individualization processes.

Relative group status

So far, we have focused in this section on minority and majority groups that were defined in purely numerical terms. But what about intergroup contexts in which ingroup and outgroup differ not only in size, but also in status? There is some research that addresses this issue as well. Lorenzi-Cioldi (1998, Study 7) manipulated relative group size and group status as orthogonal experimental factors and examined their effects on information processing using the recognition confusion task. He found that relative ingroup size did not influence information processing. Instead, there was only a general effect of group status. Participants showed more group-level information processing (i.e., more withingroup errors) regarding low-status groups than regarding high-status groups, irrespective of whether these groups were minority or majority ingroups or minority or majority outgroups. The author interpreted these processing differences in terms of socially shared, stable, and generalized conceptions about low-status and high-status groups which, for various cognitive (e.g., attributional) and social (e.g., normative and ideological) reasons, should involve more differentiated mental representations of high-status groups relative to low-status groups (see also Sedikides, 1997).

However, such a static view may underestimate the role of motivated and strategic cognition in information processing (Fiske & Taylor, 1991; Kunda, 1990). For example, research by Doosje, Ellemers, and Spears (1995) as well as by Simon and Hastedt (1997, Experiment 1) suggests that members of low-status or otherwise unattractive groups prefer group-level information processing as part of a group-level strategy to cope with their collective predicament, whereas they tend more toward individual-level information processing when individual escape seems possible or acceptable. Simon and Hastedt (1997, Experiment 2) examined this motivational or strategic approach also in a minority–majority context. In addition to relative ingroup size, we manipulated two other independent variables. As an analogue of ingroup status, we varied ingroup attractiveness by highlighting either positive or negative ingroup characteristics. Although this manipulation differs from the standard manipulation of ingroup status (e.g., Simon & Hamilton, 1994; Lorenzi-Cioldi, 1998), it still captures the central social psychological component of the concept of ingroup status, namely its (positive or negative) implications for group members' self-evaluations (Tajfel & Turner, 1986). Individualization of the self was manipulated as a third independent variable as it was directly relevant to testing the role of motivated and strategic cognition in information processing. Whereas half of the participants worked on the dependent measures immediately after the manipulation of relative ingroup size and ingroup attractiveness, the remaining participants were additionally administered an individualizing self-description task between the manipulation of the two other independent variables and the measurement of the dependent variables. Within-ingroup errors derived from the recognition confusion task served again as the main dependent variable. (There were no effects on within-outgroup errors in this experiment.) It was predicted and found that our third independent variable served as an important moderator of the combined influence of relative ingroup size and ingroup attractiveness. When individualization of the self was difficult (i.e., in a standard intergroup context without an individualizing self-description task), ingroup attractiveness had opposite effects on minority and majority members: Minority members showed more group-level information processing when the ingroup was attractive as opposed to unattractive, whereas majority members showed more group-level information processing when the ingroup was unattractive. However, when individualization of the self was facilitated by way of a self-description task, ingroup attractiveness had identical effects on minority and majority members: Irrespective of relative ingroup size, group-level information processing was stronger when the ingroup was attractive as opposed to unattractive.

Taken together, these results suggest that high status of the minority ingroup motivates group-level information processing, and low status of the minority ingroup motivates individual-level information processing. Most likely, this is so because, depending on whether ingroup status is high or low, either group-level or individual-level perspectives are most conducive to the achievement or maintenance of positive self-evaluations (Tajfel & Turner, 1986). For majority members, however, the relationship between ingroup status and information processing seems to depend on an additional strategic consideration. As indicated above, group-level information processing can be part of a group-level strategy to cope collectively with a shared predicament such as low ingroup status (Doosje et al., 1995; Simon, 1998b). Moreover, large ingroup size can be an important resource in the collective struggle for social change (Klandermans, 1997). In light of their numerical superiority, members of low-status majority groups may therefore consider a group-level strategy including group-level information processing a viable option, but only as long as there is no easier individual way out of the predicament such as distancing oneself from the ingroup through individualization (see also Lalonde & Silverman, 1994; Wright, Taylor, & Moghaddam, 1990). Conversely, for minority members, who do not have such a resource at their disposal, a group-level strategy to cope with low ingroup status would generally be too risky.

Well-being in Minority–Majority Contexts

Our group memberships do not only influence how we define ourselves and how we process social information, they should also have an influence on our emotions or feelings (Turner et al., 1987). In this section, we examine whether there are systematic differences in minority and majority members' well-being. Because neither the quantity nor the quality of the research available for this purpose allows a more fine-grained differentiation, we look at well-being in a rather broad sense including a variety of temporary emotional states or moods (e.g., happiness, anxiety, depression) as well as more stable positive or negative feelings about oneself and one's situation (e.g., self-respect, self-acceptance, self-esteem).

"There is safety in numbers?"

From a theoretical point of view, there is some reason to assume that membership in a minority group, even when defined in purely numerical terms, may be associated with less positive feelings or well-being than membership in a majority group. For example, based on Festinger's (1954) theory of social comparison processes, it could be argued that members of relatively small groups are at a disadvantage, compared with members of larger groups, when it comes to soliciting consensual validation from many similar others. As a consequence, members of (numerical) minorities may feel less secure than members of (numerical) majorities. This minority–majority difference may be further accentuated for two reasons. First, because group membership tends to be a more central self-aspect for minority members than for majority members (McGuire & McGuire, 1988), consensual validation concerning characteristics related to one's group membership should be a more salient task for minority members than for majority members. Second, at least in Western cultures with their ideological emphasis on majority rule, numerical inferiority is likely to be associated with error, deviance, and weakness (Sherif, 1966, p. 111: "There is safety in numbers"; see also Sachdev & Bourhis, 1984, pp. 37–39). Unfortunately, empirical evidence on differences in (numerical) minority and majority members' well-being is sparse. In fact, we know of only one experiment in which the researchers looked at group members' well-being in purely numerically defined minority–majority contexts. Using a mood adjective checklist, Bettencourt, Charlton, and Kernahan (1997, Study 1) found no overall differences between minority and majority members, although separate analyses of each item indicated that minority members felt indeed less relaxed than majority members.

Relative group status and power

A few researchers have looked at aspects of minority and majority members' well-being in laboratory contexts in which, in addition to relative ingroup size, ingroup status and/or ingroup power were manipulated as well. Sachdev and Bourhis (1991) found that well-being was influenced by relative ingroup size irrespective of ingroup status and ingroup power. In keeping with our theoretical analysis, minority members felt less comfortable, less satisfied and less happy about their group membership than majority members. However, this minority–majority difference was not replicated by Ellemers et al. (1992). They found that relative ingroup size and ingroup status interacted such that members of high-status minority groups felt most pride, while members of low-status minority and low- and high-status majority groups did not differ from each other.

Another category of research focused on real-life minority–majority contexts in which numerical asymmetries were confounded with status and/or power asymmetries. Typically, that research examined whether members of low-status (oppressed or stigmatized) minority groups had lower self-esteem than members of high-status (dominant) majority groups. In light of our preceding theoretical discussion of the well-being implications of membership in a numerical minority as well as several other theoretical perspectives that predict lower self-esteem among members of low-status groups (Crocker & Major, 1989), one would expect that members of low-status minority groups should suffer from deficient self-esteem compared with members of high-status majority groups. Yet, after reviewing relevant research conducted over a time span of more than 20 years, Crocker and Major (1989) had to conclude that such self-esteem deficits seemed rather rare. That review spurred many efforts to account for this discrepancy between theory and data. Thus subsequent research provided valuable insights into several psychological mechanisms by which members of low-status minority groups may protect their self-esteem (e.g., attributional externalization, selective social comparisons), but it also identified possible harmful effects of such self-protective mechanisms (Crocker & Quinn, this volume, chapter 12; Major & Crocker, 1993; see also Branscombe, Schmitt, & Harvey, 1999).

However, there is also new evidence which confirms that, at least under some conditions, members of low-status minority groups differ in well-being from members of high-status majority groups as originally expected. Thus Hewstone, Islam, and Judd (1993, Experiment 2) found lower self-esteem for members of a low-status minority group (Hindus in Bangladesh) than for members of a high-status majority group (Muslims in Bangladesh). Research conducted by Islam and Hewstone (1993) in a similar context further indicates that in direct intergroup encounters members of low-status minority groups may suffer from increased intergroup anxiety. In addition, Frable, Platt, & Hoey (1998) found that members of low-status minority groups whose group membership or stigma was concealable as opposed to visible experienced lower self-esteem and more negative affect than members of high-status majority groups. Frable et al.'s (1998) observation that the well-being of members of low-status minority groups was negatively affected only when their stigma was concealable is in line with other research which points to the positive or compensatory role of intragroup support and collective identification in the well-being of members of low-status minority groups (Branscombe et al., 1999; Phinney, 1990; Verkuyten, 1995). For these compensatory resources should be less easily available when it is not immediately clear (i.e., visible!) who is one of "us." Similarly, Simon et al. (1991) observed that members of a low-status minority group with a concealable stigma (gay men) tended to be less happy with their group membership than members of the corresponding high-status majority group (heterosexual men).

Intergroup Behavior in Minority–Majority Contexts

The socially undesirable phenomenon of intergroup discrimination is widely regarded as the paradigmatic case of intergroup behavior (Sumner, 1906; Allport, 1954; Tajfel, 1982). Our discussion of minority–majority differences in intergroup behavior therefore focuses primarily on minority–majority differences in intergroup discrimination. Currently the most prominent social psychological explanation of intergroup discrimination is provided by social identity theory (Tajfel & Turner, 1986). It holds that, from a social psychological perspective, intergroup discrimination can be understood as an attempt to establish a positively valued distinctiveness for one's ingroup in order to achieve or maintain a positive social identity or, in other words, a positive collective self. Although there are still many open questions concerning this phenomenon and its adequate explanation, there is nevertheless wide consensus among social psychologists that social identity theory provides a very helpful framework for a better understanding of intergroup discrimination in general (Smith & Mackie, 1995) and in minority–majority contexts in particular (e.g., Mullen, Brown, & Smith, 1992).

Salience or threat?

Most researchers who examined the effect of relative ingroup size on intergroup discrimination started with the expectation that members of (numerical) minorities would show stronger intergroup discrimination than members of (numerical) majorities (but see also Moscovici & Paicheler, 1978, for a notable exception). There are two typical arguments as to why this should be the case. For one, it is argued that, due to its numerical distinctiveness or salience, minority group membership engenders a "heightened sense of kindredness" (Gerard & Hoyt, 1974) or, in other words, is more "identifying" than majority group membership (also Mullen et al., 1992). As a consequence, minority group membership arouses stronger social identity concerns (i.e., a stronger motivation to achieve or maintain a positive social identity or collective self) which then translate into more discriminatory behavior. Note that this argument corresponds directly to the centrality account derived from our self-aspect model (Simon, 1997; 1998a) which we discussed in the section on self-definition. The second argument centers on possible threatening implications of being in the numerically smaller group. As reviewed in the preceding section on well-being, there is good theoretical reason to assume that members of (numerical) minorities feel more insecure than members of (numerical) majorities. To compensate for this insecurity, minority members should therefore strive to strengthen their positive social identity by discriminating against the majority outgroup, when given the opportunity (e.g., Sachdev & Bourhis, 1984). As both the salience argument as well as the threat argument predict stronger intergroup discrimination on the part of minority members, we will first review the relevant research and then examine which of them provides a better account of the empirical evidence.

In a meta-analysis of research findings secured over a time span of 15 years, Mullen et al. (1992) found that their index of intergroup discrimination decreased as a function of the proportionate size of the ingroup (i.e., the size of the ingroup divided by the sum of the size of the ingroup and the size of the outgroup). However, their index of intergroup discrimination was derived primarily from ingroup and outgroup ratings on evaluative attribute dimensions which are rather indirect or remote indicators of actual intergroup behavior. Fortunately, other research has employed more direct measures of intergroup behavior. Following Tajfel, Billig, Bundy, & Flament (1971), researchers have used various types of resource-allocation tasks in which research participants are requested to distribute meaningful resources (e.g., money, course credit) between ingroup and outgroup, members. Using such a task with laboratory-created (numerical) minorities and majorities, Sachdev and Bourhis (1984) obtained a complex pattern of results. They found some evidence that, unlike majority members, minority members were more concerned with their ingroup's absolute outcome than with intergroup fairness. But majority members also showed discriminatory tendencies. Although they did not appear particularly interested in maximizing their ingroup's absolute outcome, majority members seemed concerned about maintaining or establishing outcome differentials between the ingroup and the outgroup in favor of the ingroup. More recent experimental research by Bettencourt et al. (1997) yielded results more in line with the expected minority–majority difference in intergroup discrimination. In the context of forced intergroup cooperation, they found that when participants' attention was not experimentally focused on particular aspects of the cooperative setting (control condition), members of (numerical) minorities showed more intergroup discrimination against the outgroup than members of (numerical) majorities. The latter even tended toward reversed discrimination in favor of the minority outgroup. In two additional experimental conditions, participants were instructed by the experimenter to focus their attention either on interpersonal aspects of the cooperation (individual-focus condition) or on each group's contribution to the overall task (task-focus condition). While the interpersonal focus did not eliminate the minority–majority difference in intergroup discrimination, the task focus did. In fact, there was even a slight reversal in the task-focus condition such that majority members now seemed to show more intergroup discrimination than minority members. Note that Bettencourt et al.'s (1997) results do not support a salience account of increased intergroup discrimination on the part of minority members compared with majority members, because such a minority–majority difference was observed even when minority members' attention was experimentally redirected away from their group memberships to interpersonal aspects. On the other hand, the reversal toward more intergroup discrimination on the part of majority members in the task-focus condition supports a *threat account* of intergroup discrimination. As suggested by Bettencourt et al. (1997, p. 653), the task-focus instructions which requested all participants to acknowledge each group's contributions to the cooperative endeavor might have strengthened especially the minority group who would have received less recognition otherwise. Thus rendered on more equal footing with majority members, minority members should feel less threatened and therefore less motivated to discriminate against the majority outgroup. In contrast, for majority members, this equal footing might have lessened their otherwise perceived superiority and might thus have strengthened their motivation to discriminate against the minority outgroup.

Relative group status and power

Other research has examined intergroup discrimination in laboratory contexts in which, in addition to relative ingroup size, ingroup status and/or ingroup power were manipulated as well. For example, Mummendey, Simon, Dietze, Grünert, Haeger, Kessler, Lettgen, and Schäferhoff (1992, Experiment 2) varied both relative ingroup size and ingroup status and found main effects of both variables, but no interaction effect.[3] That is, members of (numerical) minorities showed more intergroup discrimination than members of (numerical) majorities, and members of low-status groups showed more intergroup discrimination than members of high-status groups (see Otten, Mummendey, & Blanz, 1996, for similar findings). As a result of the compound effects of relative ingroup size and ingroup status, members of low-status minority groups were most discriminatory (see also Espinoza & Garza, 1985).

Sachdev and Bourhis (1991) also manipulated relative ingroup size and ingroup status and even added ingroup power as a third independent variable. Unfortunately, they used the same criterion (i.e., creativity) for both the status manipulation and the resource-allocation task. This confound renders the status effects inconclusive because it is impossible to decide whether allocation decisions in favor of a high-status ingroup are to be considered a true effect (i.e., intergroup discrimination) or simply a manipulation check (i.e., a reproduction of the experimentally created status differential). We therefore limit our discussion here to the effects of relative ingroup size and ingroup power including their interactive effects. Sachdev and Bourhis (1991) again found a complex pattern of results. More specifically, their results indicated that members of (numerical) minorities were generally less fair than members of (numerical) majorities, although the latter also appeared to be concerned about maintaining or establishing some intergroup differentials in favor of the ingroup (see Sachdev & Bourhis, 1984). Moreover, members of powerful minorities tended to be more discriminatory than members of powerful majorities, while the opposite tendency was observed for members of powerless minorities and majorities. This interactive effect of relative ingroup size and ingroup power points to an interesting explanation as to why the evidence of increased intergroup discrimination on the part of minority members compared with majority members is often weak or inconsistent. Due to their numerical inferiority, minority members may often suffer from insufficient self-confidence or insufficient trust in their collective efficacy which then prevents them from engaging in assertive intergroup behavior.

Thus threat may play a dual, and perhaps contradictory, role in minority–majority relations (see also Ng & Cram, 1988). On the one hand, the threatening implications of the numerical inferiority of one's ingroup may lead to feelings of insecurity and an increased need for a positive social identity which in turn increases the willingness to discriminate against outgroups. On the other hand, however, numerical inferiority may threaten minority members' self-confidence and feelings of collective efficacy which are necessary preconditions of assertive intergroup behavior (Klandermans, 1997; Moscovici & Paicheler, 1978). In other words, minority members may often feel the need for discriminatory behavior in favor of the ingroup, but at the same time they may lack the necessary confidence to put this desire into action.

Integration and Conclusions

Thus far we have reviewed research on four important aspects of social life in intergroup contexts, namely self-definition, information processing, well-being, and intergroup discrimination. The particular focus was on the effect of minority and majority group membership on each of these four aspects. The empirical findings reveal a high degree of complexity both between and within these aspects, and this complexity is further magnified when, in addition to the size asymmetry, status and power asymmetries between ingroup and outgroup are taken into account as well. Nevertheless, there are also common themes in the observed minority–majority differences which provide a starting point for an integrative perspective. In the remainder of this chapter we will try to pull these themes together in an attempt to form the first building blocks of a more comprehensive theory of the social psychology of minority–majority relations. Though informed by the research findings reviewed in this chapter, these building blocks should not be taken as proven empirical generalizations, but as informed conjectures or hypotheses which can be, and should be, tested empirically.

The cognitive-affective crossfire

Our basic premise it that membership in a minority group and membership in a majority group each constitute a distinct social psychological situation for the particular group member which elicits distinct cognitive, affective, and behavioral reactions. Most importantly, it appears that, unlike majority members, minority members typically find themselves in a *cognitive-affective crossfire*. On the one hand, being a small figure against a large background, it is very likely that their group membership is particularly salient to others as well as to themselves. It is therefore very difficult for minority members to forget or ignore their group membership. There are always many more other people who do not forget minority members' group membership and continually remind them of it by word and deed. In this way, their respective group membership becomes a much more central self-aspect for minority members than for majority members. On the other hand, minority membership entails specific risks and stressful experiences which may be largely unknown to majority members. These risks range from insecurizing deficits in consensual validation to personal persecution and extermination because of one's alleged deviance from the norm. These risks and the negative affective consequences are further exacerbated when numerical inferiority is also associated with status and/or power inferiority. In other words, compared with majority members, there are stronger cognitive forces pushing minority members toward their group (or keeping them in it), while at the same time there are also stronger affective forces pulling them away from it (or keeping them out of it). As a consequence, minority members should develop strategies to escape from, or at least cope with, this cognitive-affective crossfire. Depending on the perceived affordances or opportunity structure of the social context (e.g., the permeability of group boundaries), they may opt for individualistic strategies involving psychological dis-identification or actual exit from their group or for collective strategies involving assertive intergroup behavior, or for a combination of both (Simon, 1998b; Simon, Loewy, Stürmer, Weber, Freytag, Habig, Kampmeier, & Spahlinger, 1998; Tajfel & Turner, 1986).

Mindful minorities and mindless majorities

It also appears that, relative to majority members, minority members are more likely to be *mindful of the intergroup dimension* of their life space (Azzi, 1992; Frable, Blackstone, & Scherbaum, 1990). Whatever strategy minority members opt for in order to escape from, or cope with, the cognitive-affective crossfire discussed above, it is difficult for them to ignore the intergroup dimension. Assertive intergroup behavior directed against the majority group as well as assimilation attempts to become one of "them" presuppose an intergroup perspective with the majority group as a point of reference (Moscovici & Paicheler, 1978). In particular, minority members need to be mindful of the intergroup differences and intragroup similarities, be it in order to overcome them individually by assimilation or mimicry or in order to restructure them and the associated value hierarchy by collective action. Conversely, majority members can be more mindless in this respect, at least as long as they don't feel threatened by an assertive minority. As there are, by definition, more majority members than minority members, majority members are likely to interact most of the time with their own kind so that for them interpersonal similarities and differences are more relevant behavioral guidelines than intergroup differences and intragroup similarities. To illustrate this differential mindfulness in minority–majority contexts, the relationship between proponents of minority positions and adherents of majority or mainstream positions in science can serve as an instructive example. In order to be recognized in the scientific community (e.g., get their work published), proponents of minority positions need to be very knowledgeable about the mainstream, its strengths and weaknesses, as well as about the differences between the minority and the mainstream positions and how these differences could be bridged. Conversely, adherents of the mainstream, whose rules typically rule the community, do not need to pay too much attention to the minority. They can ignore it much longer and garnish this ignorance with occasional displays of "*se montrer bon prince*" (Moscovici & Paicheler, 1978, p. 253).

Assertive and defensive intergroup behavior

As indicated above, majority members usually tend toward an interpersonal perspective because the status quo is typically structured in such a way that this perspective works for them and in favor of them (Apfelbaum, 1979; Tajfel, 1978). If, under such conditions, they perceive group members at all, and not just "people," it is outgroup members, not ingroup members they perceive. At best, they then adopt a quasi-intergroup perspective in that they construe "them," the minority, as an odd group that differs from ordinary people (Simon, 1993). However, truly intergroup situations with both minority and majority members adopting an intergroup perspective can arise as well. This is most likely to be the case when minority members show assertive intergroup behavior in order to escape from or cope with the cognitive-affective crossfire (or worse) because such assertiveness may incite defensive intergroup behavior on the part of majority members. Then, "the empire strikes back." Note that, on the surface, assertive and defensive intergroup behavior may take the same form such as intergroup discrimination. From a theoretical point of view, however, the underlying meaning is different because such phenotypically similar behavior serves different purposes for minority and majority members. The *assertive-defensive distinction* could thus be another important building block for a better understanding of minority–majority relations (Moscovici & Paicheler, 1978).

NOTES

1   Given the limited scope of this chapter, we do not attempt to systematically disentangle the effects of status and power, although we acknowledge the importance of such an endeavor (e.g., Sachdev & Bourhis, 1991).

2   In addition to the work discussed in this section, other research has also investigated effects of relative group size on information processing (e.g., Biernat & Vescio, 1993; Taylor et al., 1978; Van Twuyver & Van Knippenberg, 1999). However, that research focused on the effects of the relative sizes of the stimulus groups about which research participants had to process information, whereas the relative size of the participants' ingroup was not systematically varied. That research is therefore not included in this review.

3   Unlike most prior work, Mummendey et al. (1992) requested participants to distribute negative, rather than positive, outcomes between ingroup and outgroup (i.e., negative auditory stimulation and meaningless syllables to memorize). In this context, intergroup discrimination therefore means allocating less negative outcomes to the ingroup.

REFERENCES

Allport, G. W. (1954). *The nature of prejudice*. Cambridge, MA: Addison-Wesley.

Apfelbaum, E. (1979). Relations of domination and movements for liberation: An analysis of power between groups. In W. G. Austin & S. Worchel (Eds.), *The social psychology of intergroup relations* (pp. 188–204). Monterey, CA: Brooks/Cole.

Azzi, A. E. (1992). Procedural justice and the allocation of power in intergroup relations: Studies in the United States and South Africa. *Personality and Social Psychology Bulletin, 18*, 736–747.

Bettencourt, B. A., Charlton, K., & Kernahan, C. (1997). Numerical representation of groups in cooperative settings: Social orientation effects on ingroup bias. *Journal of Experimental Social Psychology, 33*, 630–659.

Biernat, M., & Vescio, T. K. (1993). Categorization and stereotyping: Effects of group context on memory and social judgment. *Journal of Experimental Social Psychology, 29*, 166–202.

Branscombe, N. R., Schmitt, M. T., & Harvey, R. D. (1999). Perceiving pervasive discrimination among African Americans: Implications for group identification and well-being. *Journal of Personality and Social Psychology, 77*(1), 135–149.

Brewer, M. B. (1988). A dual process model of impression formation. In T. Srull & R. Wyer (Eds.), *Advances in social cognition* (Vol. 1, pp. 1–36). Hillsdale, NJ: Erlbaum.

Brewer, M. B. (1991). The social self: On being the same and different at the same time. *Personality and Social Psychology Bulletin, 17*, 475–482.

Brewer, M. B. (1998). Category-based vs. person-based perception in intergroup contexts. In W. Stroebe & M. Hewstone (Eds.), *European review of social psychology* (Vol. 9, pp. 77–106). Chichester, UK: Wiley.

Brewer, M. B., & Weber, J. G. (1994). Self-evaluation effects of interpersonal versus intergroup social comparison. *Journal of Personality and Social Psychology, 66*, 268–275.

Brewer, M. B., Weber, J. G., & Carini, B. (1995). Person memory in intergroup contexts: Categorization versus individuation. *Journal of Personality and Social Psychology, 69*, 29–40.

Crocker, J., & Major, B. (1989). Social stigma and self-esteem: The self-protective properties of stigma. *Psychological Review, 96*, 608–630.

Ditto, P. H., & Jemmott, J. B. I. (1989). From rarity to evaluative extremity: Effects of prevalence information on evaluations of positive and negative characteristics. *Journal of Personality and Social Psychology, 57*, 16–26.

Doosje, B., Ellemers, N., & Spears, R. (1995). Perceived intragroup variability as a function of group status and identification. *Journal of Experimental Social Psychology, 31*, 410–436.

Ellemers, N., Kortekaas, P., & Ouwerkerk, J. W. (1999). Self-categorization, commitment to the group and group self-esteem as related but distinct aspects of social identity. *European Journal of Social Psychology, 29*, 371–389.

Ellemers, N., Doosje, B., Van Knippenberg, A., & Wilke, H. (1992). Status protection in high status minority groups. *European Journal of Social Psychology, 22*, 123–140.

Espinoza, J. A., & Garza, R. T. (1985). Social group salience and interethnic cooperation. *Journal of Experimental Social Psychology, 21*, 380–392.

Farley, J. (1982). *Majority–minority relations.* Englewood, NJ: Prentice-Hall.

Festinger, L. (1954). A theory of social comparison processes. *Human Relations, 7*, 117–140.

Fiske, S. T., & Neuberg, S. L. (1990). A continuum of impression formation, from category-based to individuating processes: Influences of information and motivation on attention and interpretation. In M. P. Zanna (Ed.), *Advances in experimental social psychology* (Vol. 23, pp. 1–74). New York: Random House.

Fiske, S. T., & Taylor, S. E. (1991). *Social cognition* (2nd ed.). New York: McGraw-Hill.

Frable, D. E. S., Blackstone, T., & Scherbaum, C. (1990). Marginal and mindful: Deviants in social interactions. *Journal of Personality and Social Psychology, 59*, 140–149.

Frable, D. E. S., Platt, C., & Hoey, S. (1998). Concealable stigmas and positive self-perceptions: Feeling better around similar others. *Journal of Personality and Social Psychology, 74*, 909–922.

Gerard, H., & Hoyt, M. F. (1974). Distinctiveness of social categorization and attitude toward ingroup members. *Journal of Personality and Social Psychology, 29*, 836–842.

Hewstone, M., Islam, M. R., & Judd, C. M. (1993). Models of crossed categorization and intergroup relations. *Journal of Personality and Social Psychology, 64*, 779–793.

Islam, M. R., & Hewstone, M. (1993). Dimensions of contact as predictors of intergroup anxiety, perceived outgroup variability, and outgroup attitude: An integrative model. *Personality and Social Psychology Bulletin, 19*, 700–710.

Klandermans, B. (1997). *The social psychology of protest.* Oxford, UK: Blackwell.

Klauer, K. C., & Wegener, I. (1998). Unraveling social categorization in the "Who said what?" paradigm. *Journal of Personality and Social Psychology, 75,* 1155–1178.

Kunda, Z. (1990). The case for motivated reasoning. *Psychological Bulletin, 108,* 480–498.

Lalonde, R. N., & Silverman, R. A. (1994). Behavioral preferences in response to social injustice: The effects of permeability and social identity salience. *Journal of Personality and Social Psychology, 66,* 78–85.

Lorenzi-Cioldi, F. (1998). Group status and perceptions of homogeneity. In W. Stroebe & M. Hewstone (Eds.), *European review of social psychology* (Vol. 9, pp. 31–75). Chichester, UK: Wiley.

Major, B., & Crocker, J. (1993). Social stigma: The consequences of attributional ambiguity. In D. M. Mackie & D. L. Hamilton (Eds.), *Affect, cognition, and stereotyping: Interactive processes in group perception* (pp. 345–370). San Diego, CA: Academic Press.

McGuire, W. J., & McGuire, C. V. (1988). Content and process in the experience of self. In L. Berkowitz (Ed.), *Advances in experimental social psychology* (Vol. 21, pp. 97–144). New York: Academic Press.

Messick, D. M., & Mackie, D. M. (1989). Intergroup relations. *Annual Review of Psychology, 40,* 45–81.

Moscovici, S., & Paicheler, C. (1978). Social comparison and social recognition: Two complementary processes of identification. In H. Tajfel (Ed.), *Differentiation between social groups* (pp. 251–266). London: Academic Press.

Mullen, B. (1991). Group composition, salience, and cognitive representations: The phenomenology of being in a group. *Journal of Experimental Social Psychology, 27,* 297–323.

Mullen, B., Brown, R., & Smith, C. (1992). Ingroup bias as a function of salience, relevance, and status: An integration. *European Journal of Social Psychology, 22,* 103–122.

Mummendey, A., Simon, B., Dietze, C., Grünert, M., Haeger, G., Kessler, S., Lettgen, S., & Schäferhoff, S. (1992). Categorization is not enough: Intergroup discrimination in negative outcome allocation. *Journal of Experimental Social Psychology, 28,* 125–144.

Ng, S. H., & Cram, F. (1988). Intergroup bias by defensive and offensive groups in majority and minority conditions. *Journal of Personality and Social Psychology, 55,* 749–757.

Oakes, P. J. (1987). The salience of social categories. In J. C. Turner, M. A. Hogg, P. J. Oakes, S. D. Reicher, & M. S. Wetherell (Eds.), *Rediscovering the social group. A self-categorization theory* (pp. 117–141). Oxford, UK: Basil Blackwell.

Oakes, P. J., & Turner, J. C. (1986). Distinctiveness and the salience of social category memberships: Is there a perceptual bias towards novelty? *European Journal of Social Psychology, 16,* 325–344.

Otten, S., Mummendey, A., & Blanz, M. (1996). Intergroup discrimination in positive and negative outcome allocations: Impact of stimulus valence, relative group status, and relative group size. *Personality and Social Psychology Bulletin, 22,* 568–581.

Phinney, J. S. (1990). Ethnic identity in adolescents and adults: Review of research. *Psychological Bulletin, 108,* 499–514.

Sachdev, I., & Bourhis, R. Y. (1984). Minimal majorities and minorities. *European Journal of Social Psychology, 14,* 35–52.

Sachdev, I., & Bourhis, R. Y. (1991). Power and status differentials in minority and majority group relations. *European Journal of Social Psychology, 21,* 1–24.

Sedikides, C. (1997). Differential processing of ingroup and outgroup information: The role of relative group status in permeable boundary groups. *European Journal of Social Psychology, 27,* 121–144.

Sherif, M. (1966). *The psychology of Social norms.* New York: Harper Torchbook.

Simon, B. (1992). The perception of ingroup and outgroup homogeneity: Re-introducing the intergroup context. In W. Stroebe & M. Hewstone (Eds.), *European review of social psychology* (Vol. 3, pp. 1–30). Chichester, UK: Wiley.

Simon, B. (1993). On the asymmetry in the cognitive construal of ingroup and outgroup: A model of egocentric social categorization. *European Journal of Social Psychology, 23,* 131–147.

Simon, B. (1997). Self and group in modern society: Ten theses on the individual self and the collective self. In R. Spears, P. J. Oakes, N. Ellemers, & S. A. Haslam (Eds.), *The social psychology of stereotyping and group life* (pp. 318–335). Oxford, UK: Blackwell.

Simon, B. (1998a). The self in minority–majority contexts. In W. Stroebe & M. Hewstone (Eds.), *European review of social psychology* (Vol. 9, pp. 1–31). Chichester, UK: Wiley.

Simon, B. (1998b). Individuals, groups, and social change: On the relationship between individual and collective self-interpretations and collective action. In C. Sedikides, J. Schopler, & C. Insko (Eds.), *Intergroup cognition and intergroup behavior* (pp. 257–282). Mahwah, NJ: Lawrence Erlbaum.

Simon, B., Aufderheide, B., & Hastedt, C. (2000). The double negative effect: The (almost) paradoxical role of the individual self in minority and majority members' information processing. *British Journal of Social Psychology, 39,* 73–93.

Simon, B., Glässner-Bayerl, B., & Stratenwerth, I. (1991). Stereotyping and self-stereotyping in a natural intergroup context: The case of heterosexual and homosexual men. *Social Psychology Quarterly, 54,* 252–266.

Simon, B., & Hamilton, D. L. (1994). Self-stereotyping and social context: The effects of relative ingroup size and ingroup status. *Journal of Personality and Social Psychology, 66,* 699–711.

Simon, B., & Hastedt, C. (1997). When misery loves categorical company: Accessibility of the individual self as a moderator in category-based representation of attractive and unattractive ingroups. *Personality and Social Psychology Bulletin, 23,* 1254–1264.

Simon, B., Hastedt, C., & Aufderheide, B. (1997). When self-categorization makes sense: The role of meaningful social categorization in minority and majority members' self-perception. *Journal of Personality and Social Psychology, 73,* 310–320.

Simon, B., Loewy, M., Stürmer, S., Weber, U., Freytag, P., Habig, C., Kampmeier, C., & Spahlinger, P. (1998). Collective identification and social movement participation. *Journal of Personality and Social Psychology, 74,* 646–658.

Smith, E. R., & Mackie, D. M. (1995). *Social psychology.* New York: Worth.

Sumner, W. C. (1906). *Folkways.* Boston, MA: Ginn.

Tajfel, H. (1978). *The Social psychology of minorities.* London: Minority Rights Group (No. 7).

Tajfel, H. (1981). *Human groups and social categories: Studies in social psychology.* Cambridge, UK: Cambridge University Press.

Tajfel, H. (1982). Social psychology of intergroup relations. *Annual Review of Psychology, 33,* 1–39.

Tajfel, H., & Turner, J. C. (1986). The social identity theory of intergroup behavior. In S. Worchel & W. G. Austin (Eds.), *Psychology of intergroup relations* (pp. 7–24). Chicago, IL: Nelson-Hall.

Tajfel, H., Billig, M. G., Bundy, R. P., & Flament, C. (1971). Social categorization and intergroup behaviour. *European Journal of Social Psychology, 1,* 149–178.

Taylor, S. E., Fiske, S. T., Etcoff, N. L., & Ruderman, A. J. (1978). Categorical and contextual bases of person memory and stereotyping. *Journal of Personality and Social Psychology, 36,* 778–793.

Turner, J. C., Hogg, M. A., Oakes, P. J., Reicher, S. D., & Wetherell, M. S. (1987). *Rediscovering the social group. A self-categorization theory.* Oxford, UK: Basil Blackwell.

Van Twuyver, M., & Van Knippenberg, A. (1999). Social categorization as a function of relative group size. *British Journal of Social Psychology, 38*(2), 135–156.

Verkuyten, M. (1995). Self-esteem, self-concept stability, and aspects of ethnic identity among minority and majority youth in the Netherlands. *Journal of Youth and Adolescence, 24,* 155–173.

Wright, S. C., Taylor, D. M., & Moghaddam, F. M. (1990). Responding to membership in a disadvantaged group: From acceptance to collective protest. *Journal of Personality and Social Psychology, 58,* 994–1003.

CHAPTER THIRTEEN

Toward Reduction of Prejudice: Intergroup Contact and Social Categorization

Marilynn B. Brewer and Samuel L. Gaertner

The purpose of this chapter is to summarize the history and current status of social psychology's unique contributions to the reduction of prejudice and social discrimination. The type of prejudice and discrimination that we address in this chapter can exist as either differential positive evaluation and treatment favoring the ingroup or as differential negative evaluation and treatment intended to disadvantage the outgroup, or both (see Brewer, 1999; Gaertner et al., 1997; Mummendey & Wenzel, 1999). Our focus here is on reducing discriminatory behavior in intergroup settings, and as such this chapter is complementary to other chapters in this volume that deal with intrapersonal prejudice, stereotyping, and stereotype change.

Both theoretically and empirically, social psychology's contributions to prejudice reduction embody two major research traditions – contact hypothesis and social categorization/social identity theory. We begin by tracing the development of the contact hypothesis. Then we discuss the importance of the social categorization approach for understanding the etiology of prejudice and discrimination as well as the implications of this perspective for understanding the processes by which the contact hypothesis may operate. Three different models for category-based prejudice reduction – decategorization, recategorization, and mutual differentiation – are reviewed and compared. Finally, we present an integration of these approaches that suggests that these models may represent complementary, rather than competing, processes underlying prejudice reduction.

The Contact Hypothesis

The "contact hypothesis" is a general set of ideas about reducing intergroup prejudice and discrimination that developed among social scientists in the 1940s in the context of

Preparation of this chapter was supported by NSF Grant No. SBR 95-14398 (to the first author) and NIMH Grant MH 48721 (to the second author).

interracial relations in the United States (Allport, 1954; Watson, 1947; Williams, 1947). The basic idea behind the hypothesis is that hostility between groups is fed by unfamiliarity and separation and that *under the right conditions*, contact among members of different groups will reduce hostility and promote more positive intergroup attitudes.

Classic studies

According to Allport (1954), the four most important of these qualifying conditions were (a) integration has the support of authority, fostering *social norms* that favor intergroup acceptance, (b) the situation has high "acquaintance potential," promoting *intimate contact* among members of both groups, (c) the contact situation promotes *equal status* interactions among members of the social groups, and (d) the situation creates conditions of *cooperative interdependence* among members of both groups. Each of these conditions was derived from results of early research on racial desegregation and intergroup contact in the United States, on which the hypothesis was initially based.

Social and institutional support. Unambiguous institutional support was assumed to create a climate for emergence of social norms of tolerance and acceptance. Two early studies of racially integrated housing projects in the United States (Deutsch & Collins, 1951; Wilner, Walkley, & Cook, 1955) documented the close relationship between institutional endorsement and changes in prevailing social norms. Compared to White residents of segregated housing projects, residents in the integrated projects expressed significantly more favorable attitudes toward interracial interaction, particularly when they believed that such interactions were expected and normative.

Acquaintance potential. Two basic reasons were expressed for why intimate, personalized contact should have more positive impact than brief, casual, or formal contact. One reason is that the development of close relationships is in itself rewarding – positive affect that would potentially generalize to the outgroup as a whole (Cook, 1962). Second is the potential to acquire new, more accurate information about outgroup members that would disconfirm negative stereotypes (Cook, 1978) and increase perceived intergroup similarity (Pettigrew, 1971; Stephan & Stephan, 1984).

The early housing project studies found that the relative proximity between Black and White families was an important correlate of positive attitude change. Greater proximity was associated with more frequent and more intimate contact between groups, and those with the most interactive contact with their Black neighbors developed the most favorable racial attitudes (Wilner et al., 1955).

Equal status. Segregated groups are often unequal in status, with associated negative stereotypes about the lower status group members' competence and abilities. The framers of the contact hypothesis were aware that contact situations that perpetuate status differentials would reinforce rather than disconfirm such negative expectations and hence emphasized the importance of equal-status participation within the contact situation. Residential integration most often provides opportunity for contact under equal-status conditions, but contact in work or school settings may not. When contact with members of a disadvantaged group places the outgroup member in a subordinate role, stereotypic expectations are strengthened rather than weakened (Cohen, 1984). Most field studies confirm the importance of equal-status contact as a necessary if not sufficient condition for positive attitude change (Amir, 1976).

Cooperative interaction.   The condition of contact that has received the most attention and research since the 1950s is the stipulation regarding cooperative interdependence between members of the different social groups in the contact situation. This focus is due in large part to the influence of the now classic field experiment conducted by Muzafer Sherif and his colleagues in the summer of 1954 in a boys' camp in Robbers Cave, Oklahoma (Sherif, Harvey, White, Hood, & Sherif, 1961).

The researchers divided 22 eleven-year-old boys into two separate groups prior to their arrival at summer camp and initially kept these groups apart to develop their group identities. Then, in accord with Sherif et al.'s (1961) functional theory of intergroup relations, the introduction of group-oriented, competitive activities (e.g., tug-of-war, football, baseball) instigated intergroup hostility, including hostile verbal exchanges and actual fighting between members of the two groups. Subsequent intergroup contact under neutral, noncompetitive conditions, however, did not calm the ferocity of these exchanges. Only after the research team introduced a series of superordinate goals, ones that could not be achieved without the full cooperation of both groups, did the relations between the two groups become more harmonious. Supportive of Sherif's theoretical perspective, the descriptive record and systematic measures provide rich documentation of the effectiveness of cooperative interaction in reducing conflict and promoting cross-group friendships.

From Robbers Cave onward, many field studies of intergroup contact have confirmed that intergroup cooperation leads to more friendliness and less ingroup bias than situations that do not promote or require cooperative interaction. Probably the most extensive application of the contact hypothesis has been the implementation of cooperative learning programs in desegregated school classrooms. There is a sizable body of evidence that demonstrates the effectiveness of cooperative learning groups for increasing attraction and interaction between members of different social categories (Aronson, Blaney, Stephan, Sikes, & Sanpp, 1978; Johnson & Johnson, 1975; Slavin, 1983). Meta-analyses of studies in ethnically mixed classrooms confirm the superiority of cooperative learning methods over individualistic or competitive learning in promoting cross-ethnic friendships and reduced prejudice (Johnson, Johnson, & Maruyama, 1984).

Laboratory experiments: Defining the limits

The elements of the Robbers Cave experiment provided a prototype for subsequent laboratory experiments on the contact hypothesis and its moderating conditions. The basic laboratory paradigm is essentially a scaled-down version of the summer camp model.

A brief review of these laboratory experiments identifies a number of factors that either inhibit or facilitate the effectiveness of contact to reduce ingroup–outgroup biases and promote positive attitudes toward outgroup members. Among the moderating variables confirmed by experimental studies are the frequency and duration of intergroup interaction (Worchel, Andreoli, & Folger, 1977; Wilder & Thompson, 1980), the presence of intergroup anxiety (Stephan & Stephan, 1985; Wilder & Shapiro, 1989), the structure of cooperative tasks (Bettencourt, Brewer, Croak, & Miller, 1992; Deschamps & Brown, 1983; Gaertner, Dovidio, Rust et al., 1999; Marcus-Newhall, Miller, Holtz, & Brewer, 1993), the outcome of co-operation (Worchel et al., 1977), and status equalization (Cohen, 1984). In general, results of laboratory experiments confirm the premises of the contact hypothesis but also indicate the complexity – and potential fragility – of effects of intergroup contact even under highly controlled conditions.

The issues of generalization

Despite the wealth of experimental evidence documenting the potential for prejudice reduction following cooperative intergroup contact, a number of issues regarding the validity of the contact hypothesis remain. One concern is whether findings obtained under the relatively benign conditions of intergroup relations between experimentally created groups in the laboratory can be generalized to real-world social groups with a history of conflict and hostility, inequalities of status and power, and political struggle. With established groups, resistance to contact and cooperative interdependence may be strong enough to make questions of the conditions of contact moot (Brewer, 2000a), and the history of outcomes of forced desegregation and contact is mixed at best (e.g., Cook, 1985; Gerard & Miller, 1975; Stephan, 1986).

Another issue is whether any positive effects of contact, when they do occur, are generalized from the immediate contact experience to attitudes toward the outgroup as a whole. A majority of laboratory experiments on contact effects are limited in that they assess only attitudes toward ingroup and outgroup participants within the contact setting. Presumably, however, the ultimate goal of contact interventions is reduction of prejudice toward whole social groups, not simply creation of positive attitudes toward specific group members. Evidence regarding the effectiveness of contact in this generalized sense is more sparse.

In what is probably the most comprehensive laboratory test of interracial contact effects, Cook (1971, 1984) conducted a series of experiments in which highly prejudiced White subjects worked with a Black confederate in an ideal contact situation (equal status, co-operative interdependence, with high acquaintance potential and equalitarian social norms) over an extended period of time. Perceptions of the Black co-worker were measured at the completion of the contact experience, and general racial attitudes were assessed before, immediately after, and up to three years following the experimental sessions. Across all variations of this experiment, White participants displayed predominantly positive behaviors toward their Black co-worker and expressed highly favorable evaluations in the post-experimental questionnaires. Whether liking for this individual member of the outgroup resulted in changed attitudes toward Blacks and race-related issues, however, varied across the experiments and for different attitude measures.

One major reason why generalization fails is that the newly positively valued outgroup member is regarded as an exception and not typical or representative of the outgroup in general (Allport, 1954; Rothbart & John, 1985; Wilder, 1984). In Cook's studies, significant differences in post-contact attitude change among those who participated in the contact experience compared to control subjects were obtained only in an initial experiment in which what Cook (1984) referred to as a "cognitive booster" was introduced during the course of the experiment. This added element was a guided conversation (led by a research confeder-ate) in which the negative effects of discriminatory policies and practices were directly connected to the now-liked Black co-worker. This booster served to make salient the co-worker's category membership and to establish a link between feelings toward this individual and members of the group as a whole. In a later, conceptually related experiment, Van Oudenhoven, Groenewoud, & Hewstone (1996) found that Dutch students' evaluations of Turkish people in general were more positive after an episode of cooperative interaction with an individual Turkish person when his ethnicity was explicitly mentioned during the cooperative session than when ethnicity remained implicit only. Again, the explicit linkage appears to be a necessary mechanism for generalized contact effects.

Contact: The theoretical challenge

The basic idea behind the original contact hypothesis was elegantly simple: If separation and unfamiliarity breed stereotypes and intergroup prejudice (negative attitudes, hostility), then these effects should be reversible by promoting contact and increased familiarity between members of different groups or social categories. The underlying theoretical assumptions were that contact under cooperative interactive conditions provides opportunity for positive experiences with outgroup members that disconfirm or undermine previous negative attitudes and ultimately change attitudes toward and beliefs about the group as a whole.

Outside of the laboratory, research on the effects of contact during the 1960s and 70s took place almost entirely in these highly politicized field contexts (i.e., schools, public housing, the military) where a multitude of variables determined the social and psychological condi-tions of contact and the success or failure of the contact experiences (cf. Amir, 1969; Cook, 1985). Even laboratory experiments have unveiled a plethora of moderating variables that further qualify the basic assumptions regarding contact effects. As a consequence, the contact hypothesis itself accumulated a growing list of qualifiers and modifications (beyond the initial list of equal-status, intimate, cooperative contact) based primarily on experience rather than underlying theory. By the late 1970s (as one social psychologist put it), the elegant hypothesis had become more like a "bag lady, encumbered with excess baggage" (Stephan, 1987).

In his review of the current status of contact research, Pettigrew (1998) suggested that the challenge is to distinguish between factors that are *essential* to the processes underlying positive contact experiences and their generalization, and those that merely *facilitate* (or inhibit) the operation of these processes. To make this distinction, contact researchers needed a more elaborated theory of what the underlying processes are and how they mediate the effects of intergroup contact under different conditions. During the 1980s, research on the contact hypothesis was enriched by one such theoretical perspective that arose from European re-search on social categorization and social identity.

Social Categorization/Social Identity Theory

Social identity theory, as articulated by Tajfel (1978) and Turner (1975, 1985), represents the convergence of two traditions in the study of intergroup attitudes and behavior – social categorization, as represented in the work by Doise (1978), Tajfel (1969), and Wilder (1986), and social comparison, as exemplified by Lemaine (1974) and Vanneman and Pettigrew (1972). The theoretical perspective rests on two basic premises:

1. Individuals organize their understanding of the social world on the basis of categorical distinctions that transform continuous variables into discrete classes; categorization has the effect of minimizing perceived differences *within* categories and accentuating intercategory differences.
2. Since individual persons are themselves members of some social categories and not others, social categorization carries with it implicit *ingroup–outgroup* (we–they) distinctions; because of the self-relevance of social categories, the ingroup–outgroup classification is a superimposed category distinction with affective and emotional significance.

These two premises provide a framework for conceptualizing any social situation in which a particular ingroup–outgroup categorization is made salient. In effect, the theory posits a basic *intergroup schema* with the following characteristic features:

1. assimilation within category boundaries and contrast between categories such that all members of the ingroup are perceived to be more similar to the self than members of the outgroup (the *intergroup accentuation* principle);
2. positive affect (trust, liking) selectively generalized to fellow ingroup members but not outgroup members (the *ingroup favoritism* principle);
3. intergroup social comparison associated with perceived negative interdependence between ingroup and outgroup (the *social competition* principle).

The affective and behavioral consequences of this schema lead to intergroup situations characterized by preferential treatment of ingroup members, mutual distrust between ingroup and outgroup, and intergroup competition. According to this theoretical perspective, the starting point for intergroup discrimination and prejudice is a cognitive representation of the social situation in which a particular categorical distinction is highly salient. The role of category salience in intergroup bias has been well documented in experimental research using the minimal intergroup paradigm (Brewer, 1979; Diehl, 1990; Tajfel, Billig, Bundy, & Flament, 1971; Turner, 1981). Given a salient ingroup–outgroup distinction, preferential treatment of the ingroup is fueled by motivational factors including the need for self-esteem and positive distinctiveness (Turner, 1975), reduction of uncertainty (Hogg & Abrams, 1993), and the needs for belonging and differentiation (Brewer, 1991).

Because of the affective ties between self and ingroup, the primary process underlying intergroup discrimination is *ingroup favoritism*, or preferential attitudes and behavior toward the ingroup and its members relative to the outgroup. Whether ingroup bias also extends to derogation and negative treatment of the outgroup is more uncertain (Brewer, 1979,

1999; Mummendey & Wenzel, 1999), depending on whether the structural relations between groups and associated social norms foster and justify hostility or contempt. But ingroup differentiation and associated biases lay the groundwork for all forms of social discrimination and prejudice. In essence, social identity theory provides a perspective on intergroup relations as a complex interplay between cognitive and motivational processes within individuals and structural features of the social environment that make group distinctions salient and meaningful.

> ## Combining Contact and Categorization Theories: Alternative Models for Reducing Ingroup Bias and Intergroup Discrimination

One advance toward a more integrative theory of intergroup relations was achieved when contact research was combined with concepts of social categorization and social identity theory to provide a theoretical framework for understanding the cognitive mechanisms by which cooperative contact is presumed to work (see Brewer & Miller, 1984; Gaertner, Mann, Murrell, & Dovidio, 1989; Hewstone, 1996; Hewstone & Brown, 1986; Wilder, 1986). From the social categorization perspective, the issue to be addressed is how intergroup contact and cooperation can be structured so as to alter cognitive representations in ways that would eliminate one or more of the basic features of the negative intergroup schema. Based on the premises of social identity theory, three alternative models for contact effects have been developed and tested in experimental and field settings, namely: Decategorization, recategorization, and mutual differentiation. Each of these models can be described in terms of (a) the structural representation of the contact situation that is recommended, (b) the psychological processes that promote attitude change within the contact setting, and (c) the mechanisms by which contact experiences are generalized to changed attitudes toward the outgroup as a whole.

Decategorization: The personalization model

The first model is essentially a formalization and elaboration of the assumptions implicit in the contact hypothesis itself (Brewer & Miller, 1984). A primary consequence of salient ingroup–outgroup categorization is the deindividuation of members of the outgroup. Social behavior in category-based interactions is characterized by a tendency to treat individual members of the outgroup as undifferentiated representatives of a unified social category, ignoring individual differences within the group. The personalization perspective on the contact situation implies that intergroup interactions should be structured so as to reduce the salience of category distinctions and promote opportunities to get to know outgroup members as individual persons.

The conditional specifications of the contact hypothesis (equal status, intimate, cooperative interaction) can be interpreted as features of the situation that reduce category salience and promote more differentiated and personalized representations of the participants in the contact setting. Attending to personal characteristics of group members not only provides the opportunity to disconfirm category stereotypes, it also breaks down the monolithic perception of the outgroup as a homogeneous unit (Wilder, 1978). In this scheme, the contact situation encourages attention to information at the individual level that replaces category identity as the most useful basis for classifying participants.

Repeated personalized contacts with a variety of outgroup members should, over time, undermine the value and meaningfulness of the social category stereotype as a source of information about members of that group. This is the process by which contact experiences are expected to generalize – via reducing the salience and meaning of social categorization in the long run (Brewer & Miller, 1988).

A number of experimental studies provide evidence supporting this perspective on contact effects (Bettencourt et al., 1992; Marcus-Newhall et al., 1993). Miller, Brewer, and Edwards (1985), for instance, demonstrated that a cooperative task that required personalized interaction with members of the outgroup resulted not only in more positive attitudes toward outgroup members; in the cooperative setting but also toward other outgroup members shown on a videotape, compared to cooperative contact that was task-focused rather than person-focused.

The personalization model is also supported by the early empirical evidence for the effects of extended, intimate contact on racial attitudes, reviewed above. More recently, extensive data on effects of intergroup friendships have been derived from surveys in Western Europe regarding attitudes toward minority immigrant groups (Hamberger & Hewstone, 1997; Pettigrew, 1997; Pettigrew & Meertens, 1995). Across samples in France, Great Britain, the Netherlands, and Germany, Europeans with outgroup friends scored significantly lower on measures of prejudice, particularly affective prejudice (Pettigrew, 1998). This positive relationship did not hold for other types of contact (work or residential) that did not involve formation of close personal relationships with members of the outgroup. Although there is clearly a bi-directional relationship between positive attitudes and extent of personal contact, path analyses indicate that the path from friendship to reduction in prejudice is stronger than the other way around (Pettigrew, 1998).

Other recent research also reveals two interesting extensions of the personalized contact effect. One is evidence (again from European survey data) that personal friendships with members of one outgroup may lead to tolerance toward outgroups in general and reduced nationalistic pride – a process that Pettigrew (1997) refers to as "deprovincialization." A second extension is represented by evidence that contact effects may operate indirectly or vicariously. Although interpersonal friendship across group lines leads to reduced prejudice, even knowledge that an ingroup member befriended an outgroup member has potential to reduce bias (Wright et al., 1997). Also, interpersonal processes involving the arousal of empathic feelings for an outgroup member, can increase positive attitudes toward members of that group more widely (Batson et al., 1997).

Recategorization: The common ingroup identity model

The second social categorization model of intergroup contact and prejudice reduction is also based on the premise that reducing the salience of ingroup–outgroup category distinctions is key to positive effects. In contrast to the decategorization approaches described above, recategorization is not designed to reduce or eliminate categorization but rather to structure a definition of group categorization at a higher level of category inclusiveness in ways that reduce intergroup bias and conflict (Allport, 1954, p. 43). Specifically, the common ingroup identity model (Caertner & Dovidio, 2000; Gaertner, Dovidio, Anastasio, Bachman, & Rust, 1993; Gaertner, Dovidio, Nier, Ward, & Banker, 1999) proposes that intergroup bias and conflict can be reduced by factors that transform participants' representations of memberships from two groups to one, more inclusive group. With common ingroup identity, the cognitive and motivational processes that initially produced ingroup favoritism are redirected to benefit the former outgroup members. Among the antecedent factors proposed by the common ingroup identity model are the features of contact situations (Allport, 1954) that are necessary for intergroup contact to be successful (e.g., interdependence between groups, equal status, equalitarian norms). From this perspective, cooperative interaction, for example, enhances positive evaluations of outgroup members, at least in part, because cooperation transforms members' representations of the memberships from "Us" and "Them" to a more inclusive "We."

To test this hypothesis directly, Gaertner, Mann, Dovidio, Murrell, and Pomare (1990) conducted a laboratory experiment that brought two three-person laboratory groups together under conditions designed to vary independently the members' representations of the aggregate as one group or two groups (by varying factors such as seating arrangement) and the presence or absence of intergroup cooperative interaction. Supportive of the hypothesis concerning how cooperation reduces bias, among participants induced to feel like two groups, the introduction of cooperative interaction increased their perceptions of one group and also reduced their bias in evaluative ratings relative to those who did not cooperate during the contact period. Also supportive of the common ingroup identity model, reduced bias associated with introducing cooperation was due to enhanced favorable evaluations of outgroup members. In further support for the common ingroup identity model, this effect of cooperation was mediated by the extent to which members of both groups perceived themselves as one group.

Three survey studies conducted in natural settings across very different intergroup contexts offered converging support for the proposal that the features specified by the contact hypothesis can increase intergroup harmony in part by transforming members' representations of the memberships from separate groups to one more inclusive group. Participants in these studies included students attending a multi-ethnic high school (Gaertner, Rust, Dovidio, Bachman, & Anastasio, 1994), banking executives from a wide variety of institutions across the United States who had experienced a corporate merger (Bachman, 1993), and college students who were members of blended families whose households wre composed of two formerly separate families trying to unite into one (Banker & Gaertner, 1998).

To provide a conceptual replication of the laboratory studies of cooperation, the surveys included items (specifically designed for each context) to measure participants' perceptions of the conditions of contact, their representations of the aggregate (i.e., one group, two subgroups within one group, two separate groups and separate individuals), and a measure of intergroup harmony or bias. Across these three studies, conditions of contact reliably predicted the measures of intergroup harmony and bias. Also, as expected, the conditions of contact systematically influenced participants' representations of the aggregate. Supportive of the hypothesized mediating process, the relationships between the conditions of contact and bias in affective reactions among high school students, intergroup anxiety among corporate executives, and stepfamily harmony were reliably weaker after the mediating role of group representations was taken into account. The more the aggregate felt like one group, the lower the bias in affective reactions in the high school, the less the intergroup anxiety for the bankers, and the greater the amount of stepfamily harmony (Gaertner, Dovidio, & Bachman, 1996).

Challenges to the decategorization/recategorization models

Although the structural representations of the contact situation advocated by the decategorization (personalization) and recategorization (common ingroup identity) models are different, the two approaches share common assumptions about the need to reduce category differentiation and associated processes. Because both models rely on reducing or eliminating the salience of intergroup differentiation, they involve structuring contact in a way that will challenge or threaten existing social identities. Both cognitive and motivational factors conspire to create resistance to the dissolution of category boundaries or to re-establish category distinctions across time. Although the salience of a common superordinate identity or personalized representations may be enhanced in the short run, these may be difficult to maintain across time and social situations.

Brewer's (1991) optimal distinctiveness theory of the motives underlying group identification provides one explanation for why category distinctions are difficult to change. The theory postulates that social identity is driven by two opposing social motives – the need for inclusion and the need for differentiation. Human beings strive to belong to groups that transcend their own personal identity, but at the same time they need to feel special and distinct from others. In order to satisfy both of these motives simultaneously, individuals seek inclusion in distinctive social groups where the boundaries between those who are members of the ingroup category and those who are excluded can be clearly drawn. Highly inclusive superordinate categories do not satisfy distinctiveness needs, while high degrees of individuation fail to meet needs for belonging and for cognitive simplicity and uncertainty reduction (Hogg & Abrams, 1993). These motives are likely to make either personalization or common ingroup identity temporally unstable solutions to intergroup discrimination and prejudice.

Pre-existing social-structural relationships between groups may also create strong forces of resistance to changes in category boundaries. Cognitive restructuring may be close to impossible (at least as a first step) for groups already engaged in deadly hostilities. Even in the absence of overt conflict, asymmetries between social groups in size, power, or status create additional sources of resistance. When one group is substantially numerically smaller than the other in the contact situation, the minority category is especially salient and minority group members may be particularly reluctant to accept a superordinate category identity that is dominated by the other group. Another major challenge is created by pre-existing status differences between groups, where members of both high- and low-status groups may be threatened by contact and assimilation (Mottola, 1996).

The mutual differentiation model

These challenges to processes of decategorization/recategorization led Hewstone and Brown (1986) to recommend an alternative approach to intergroup contact wherein cooperative interactions between groups arc introduced without degrading the original ingroup–outgroup categorization. More specifically, this model favors encouraging groups working together to perceive complementarity by recognizing and valuing mutual superiorities and inferiorities within the context of an interdependent cooperative task or common, superordinate goals. This strategy allows group members to maintain their social identities and positive distinctiveness while avoiding insidious intergroup comparisons. Thus, the mutual differentiation model does not seek to change the basic category structure of the intergroup contact situation, but to change the intergroup affect from negative to positive interdependence and evaluation.

In order to promote positive intergroup experience, Hewstone and Brown recommend that the contact situation be structured so that members of the respective groups have distinct but complementary roles to contribute toward common goals. In this way, both groups can maintain positive distinctiveness within a cooperative framework. Evidence in support of this approach comes from the results of an experiment by Brown and Wade (1987) in which work teams composed of students from two different faculties engaged in a cooperative effort to produce a two-page magazine article. When the representatives of the two groups were assigned separate roles in the team task (one group working on figures and layout, the other working on text), the contact experience had a more positive effect on intergroup attitudes than when the two groups were not provided with distinctive roles (see also Deschamps & Brown, 1983; Dovidio, Gaertner, & Validzic, 1998).

Hewstone and Brown (1986) argue that generalization of positive contact experiences is more likely when the contact situation is defined as an *intergroup* situation rather than an interpersonal interaction. Generalization in this case is direct rather than requiring additional cognitive links between positive affect toward individuals and representations of the group as a whole. This position is supported by evidence, reviewed above, that cooperative contact with a member of an outgroup leads to more favorable generalized attitudes toward the group as a whole when category membership is made salient during contact (e.g., Van Oudenhoven, Groenewoud, & Hewstone, 1996; Brown, Vivian, & Hewstone, 1999).

Although ingroup–outgroup category salience is usually associated with ingroup bias and the negative side of intergroup attitudes, cooperative interdependence is assumed to override the negative intergroup schema, particularly if the two groups have differentiated, complementary roles to play. Because it capitalizes on needs for distinctive social identities, the mutual differentiation model provides a solution that is highly stable in terms of the cognitive-structural aspects of the intergroup situation. The affective component of the model, however, is likely to be more unstable. Salient intergroup boundaries are associated with mutual distrust (Insko & Schopler, 1987) which undermines the potential for cooperative interdependence and mutual liking over any length of time. By reinforcing perceptions of group differences, the differentiation model risks reinforcing negative beliefs about the outgroup. In the long run, intergroup anxiety (Greenland & Brown, 1999; Islam & Hewstone, 1993), and the potential for fission and conflict along group lines remains high.

Hybrid Models: An Integration of Approaches

As reviewed above, each of the cognitive-structural models of intergroup contact and prejudice reduction has its weaknesses and limitations, particularly when one seeks to generalize beyond small group interactions in laboratory settings. These criticisms have led a number of writers to suggest that some combination of all three models may be necessary to create conditions for long-term attitude change (e.g., Brewer, 1996; Gaertner et al., 1996; Hewstone, 1996; Pettigrew, 1998). In this final section, we discuss some of these hybrid approaches and their implications for the reduction of prejudice and discrimination in pluralistic societies.

Multiple social identities

Individuals are members of multiple social groups which imply different social identities and ingroup loyalties. Yet social identities have been treated as if they were mutually exclusive, with only one social categorization (ingroup–outgroup differentiation) salient at any one time. New research has begun to challenge this assumption of exclusivity and to explore the implications of holding multiple group identities, or identities at different levels of inclusiveness, simultaneously.

Hierarchical dual identities. In recent work regarding the development of a common ingroup identity, it has been proposed that embracing a more inclusive superordinate identity does not necessarily require each group to forsake its original group identity completely (Gaertner et al., 1990, 1994). In many contexts this may be impossible or undesirable. In some intergroup contexts, however, when members simultaneously perceive themselves as members of different groups but also as part of the same team or superordinate entity, intergroup relations between these subgroups are more positive than if members only considered themselves as separate groups (Brewer & Schneider, 1990). For example, minority students in the multi-ethnic high school who identified themselves using both a minority subgroup and an American superordinate identity had lower intergroup bias than those students who identified themselves using only their minority group identity (Gaertner et al., 1994). Also, the greater the extent to which majority and minority students perceived the study body as ". . . different groups . . . all playing on the same team" (the dual identity item), the lower their degree of intergroup bias. By contrast, the more they conceived of the student body as "belonging to different groups" the higher the intergroup bias.

Moreover, a dual identity compared to a revised more inclusive purely one group identity may facilitate the generalization of the benefits of contact to members of the outgroup not specifically included within the recategorized representation. With a dual identity the associative link to others beyond the contact situation remains intact (see also Hewstone, 1996; Hewstone & Brown, 1986).

Other research also supports the value of a dual identity for reducing bias and improving intergroup relations. Two studies further suggest that the intergroup benefits of a strong superordinate identity remain relatively stable even when the strength of the subordinate identity becomes equivalently high (Huo, Smith, Tyler, & Lind, 1996; Smith & Tyler, 1996). This suggests that identification with a more inclusive social group does not require individuals to deny their ethnic identity. In addition, a dual identity can also lead to even more positive outgroup attitudes than those associated with a superordinate identity alone (Hornsey & Hogg, 2000). In terms of promoting more harmonious intergroup interactions, a dual identity capitalizes on the benefits of common ingroup membership as well as those accrued from mutual differentiation between the groups.

Crosscutting identities.   Embedded categories at different levels of inclusiveness represent only one form of multiple ingroup identities. Individuals may also be members of social categories that overlap only partially, if at all. Many bases of social category differentiation – gender, age, religion, ethnicity, occupation – represent crosscutting cleavages. From the standpoint of a particular person, other individuals may be fellow ingroup members on one dimension of category differentiation but outgroup members on another. (For instance, for a woman business executive, a male colleague is an ingroup member with respect to occupation but an outgrouper with respect to her gender identification.) It is possible that such orthogonal social identities are kept isolated from each other so that only one ingroup–outgroup distinction is activated in a particular social context. But there are reasons to expect that simultaneous activation of multiple ingroup identities both is possible and has potential for reducing prejudice and discrimination based on any one category distinction.

Evidence from both anthropology (e.g., Gluckman, 1955) and political sociology (e.g., Coser, 1956) has long suggested that societies characterized by crosscutting loyalty structures are less prone to schism and internal intergroup conflict than societies characterized by a single hierarchical loyalty structure. More recently, social psychologists have also begun to consider the implications of such multiple crosscutting social identities for reduction of ingroup bias at the individual level (Brown & Turner, 1979; Deschamps & Doise, 1978; Marcus-Newhall et al., 1993; Vanbeselaere, 1991). A number of mechanisms have been proposed for why crosscutting group memberships would decrease ingroup bias and intergroup discrimination. For one thing, the increased complexity of a multiple social categorization reduces the salience or degree of differentiation associated with any one ingroup–outgroup distinction. Beyond the cognitive effects of category complexity, motivational factors also enter in to reduce the likelihood of intense ingroup–outgroup discrimination. First, the presence of multiple group loyalties potentially reduces the importance or significance of any one social identity for self-definition or belonging. Further, cross-category connections and consistency (balance) motives militate against negative attitudes toward outgroups that contain members who are fellow ingroupers on some other category dimension. Finally, crosscutting category memberships increase the degree of interpersonal interaction and contact across any particular category boundaries (Brewer, 2000b).

Experimental studies with both natural and artificial categories have demonstrated that adding a crosscutting category distinction reduces ingroup bias and increases positive attitudes toward crossed category members compared to simple ingroup–outgroup differentiation

(Vanbeselaere, 1991) or compared to situations in which category distinctions are convergent or superimposed (Bettencourt & Dorr, 1998; Marcus-Newhall et al., 1993; Rust, 1996). In these studies, cooperative interaction in the context of crosscutting social identities and roles increases intracategory differentiation and reduces perceived intercategory differences, resulting in less category-based evaluations of individual group members. Further, the benefits of cross-categorization may be enhanced when both category distinctions are embedded in a common superordinate group identity (Gaertner, Dovidio, Nier et al., 1999; Rust, 1996). Thus, crossed categorization and recategorization may work together to produce enhanced inclusiveness and reduced intergroup discrimination.

Limitations of dual identification. The effectiveness of dual identities for increasing harmony between groups may vary across intergroup domains. For example, maintaining strong identification with the earlier subgroup identities following a corporate merger may threaten the primary goal of the merger. Similarly, in stepfamilies, the salience of the former family identities, even with the simultaneous recognition of a more inclusive family identity, may violate members' expectations about what their ideal family should be like. Whereas in the survey studies of executives who experienced a corporate merger (Bachman, 1993) and of stepfamily members (Banker & Gaertner, 1998) the perception of a one-group identity was positively related to favorable conditions of contact and to better outcomes (e.g., reduced bias and family harmony) the dual identity representations seemed to be diagnostic of serious problems. As these "dual identities" become stronger in the merger and stepfamily contexts the conditions of contact were more unfavorable and negative outcomes increased. In contrast, in the multi-ethnic high school study (Gaertner et al., 1994), the strength of the dual identity was related to positive conditions of contact and to reduced intergroup bias. Here, the salience of the subgroup identities, within the context of a superordinate entity that provides connection between the subgroups, may signal the prospects for good intergroup relations without undermining the goals of the school or those of the different ethnic or racial groups.

Crosscutting category memberships, also, do not always result in reduced category salience and greater intergroup acceptance (Vanbeselaere, 1991). If one category distinction is more socially meaningful or functionally important than others, intergroup discrimination based on that categorization may be unaffected by the existence of crosscutting memberships in other, less important groups. More important, multiple group identities may be combined into a single ingroup (e.g., categorization based on shared ethnicity *and* gender) which is more exclusive than either category membership considered separately (Brewer, 2000b). Whether multiple social identities can contribute to the reduction of prejudice and discrimination ultimately depends on whether individuals can be made aware of their multiple category memberships under conditions that promote inclusiveness rather than differentiation (Urban & Miller, 1998).

Reciprocal process models

The utility of each of the categorization-based strategies for reducing intergroup bias – that is, decategorization, recategorization, and mutual differentiation – has received empirical support. But the question remains as to how these alternatives that seem so different, even opposite, relate to one another? Should the three models be conceptualized as competitors, that is, as independent processes that reduce bias through different pathways? Or, are they different processes that are complementary and which can reciprocally facilitate each other?

Pettigrew (1998) has proposed that the essential conditions of intergroup contact reduce prejudice over time by initiating a sequence of strategies for reducing bias. He suggests that the sequence unfolds beginning with decategorization, followed in turn by mutual differentiation and recategorization. Pettigrew's reformulated contact theory (1998) proposes that this combination, over time, can maximally reduce prejudice toward outgroup members, and also generalize across situations, to different outgroup members, and even to different outgroups (see Pettigrew, 1997).

The order in which these category-based processes unfold, however, probably depends upon specific features of the contact situation, such as whether contact emphasizes group-on-group interaction (as at Robbers Cave) or interaction among individuals from different groups (as among neighbors). Nevertheless, the cogency of Pettigrew's general perspective receives converging support from a re-analysis of Sherif et al.'s detailed descriptions of Robbers Cave (Gaertner, Dovidio, Banker et al., 2000), and from recent laboratory studies that were designed to examine the possible interplay between decategorization, recategorization, and mutual differentiation (e.g., Dovidio et al., 1997).

Gaertner et al.'s (2000) analysis of the Robbers Cave study revealed that introducing superordinate goals instigated a sequence of social processes that alternated between recategorization, decategorization, mutual differentiation (when groups were respectful to one another), as well as categorization (when intergroup relations were conflictual). Indeed, Sherif and his colleagues (Sherif et al., 1961) emphasized that intergroup harmony was achieved gradually, only after the groups cooperated on a series of superordinate goals. A close analysis of their detailed description of events during the summer camp experiment reveals that an alternation pattern among the different categorization processes was evident throughout the gradual transition from conflicted to harmonious relations between the groups. In one instance, after the groups cooperated to move a stalled truck carrying their food, the boys immediately rejoiced, chanting repeatedly, "We won the tug-of-war against the truck." The inclusive pronoun "we" signals the momentary recategorization of these groups that was followed by the boys intermingling across group lines with friendlier, more interpersonal interactions. Over time, mutual differentiation began to replace the original categorized representation until finally, as camp concluded, recategorization and friendlier interpersonal relations across group lines characterized the boys' interactions.

The sequence which proceeded from recategorization to friendlier interpersonal relations observed at Robbers Cave was replicated in a laboratory experiment (Dovidio et al., 1997) in which the members of two groups were induced to conceive of themselves as one group or two groups and then given the opportunity to self-disclose or to offer assistance to an ingroup or outgroup member. As expected, the degrees of self-disclosure and prosocial behavior toward outgroup members were together *generally* greater among participants in the one-group relative to the two-group condition. Self-disclosure and prosocial behaviors are particularly interesting because they elicit reciprocity which can further accelerate the intensity of positive interpersonal interactions across group lines even when the initial recategorization process lasts only temporarily. In terms of a longitudinal analysis, these increasingly positive interpersonal relations can fuel the progression to a next stage in the sequence, for example, mutual differentiation or the formation of a more permanent recategorized bond between the memberships. This possibility is illustrated in a laboratory study in which personalized, self-disclosing interactions among the members of two groups meeting group-on-group transformed their perceptions of the aggregate from two groups to one group (Gaertner, Rust, & Dovidio, 1997).

Within an alternating sequence of categorization processes, mutual differentiation may emerge frequently to neutralize threats to original group identities posed by the recategorization and decategorization processes. As suggested by a recent laboratory experiment (Dovidio, Gaertner, & Validzic, 1998), however, mutual differentiation can facilitate recategorization among equal status groups which may otherwise experience threats to the distinctiveness of their group identities. Groups with equal status that earlier were instructed to approach their common problem from different perspectives more strongly perceived themselves as one group and had lower intergroup levels of bias compared to groups that earlier were assigned the same task perspective, or groups that were unequal in status regardless of whether they earlier shared the different task perspectives. Thus, recategorization, decategorization, and mutual differentiation processes seem to share the capacity to facilitate each other, supporting the view that when viewed over time, these processes are complementary and reciprocal.

Conclusions: Implications for Multicultural Societies

The contact hypothesis, with its conceptual and empirical elaborations, is a prescription for promoting positive intergroup relations within a context where groups must live together interdependently. The same basic principles apply whether we are considering two nuclear families joining into a common household, departments or companies combined within an organization, diverse ethnic or religious groups within a nation, or nation-states within an international community. In any of these contexts, the goals of contact and cooperation compete with natural tendencies toward ingroup–outgroup differentiation, separation, and exclusion. Personalization across category boundaries and formation of common superordinate identities – processes that reduce the social meaning of category boundaries – are in tension with pluralistic values that seek to maintain cultural variation and distinct social identities.

The tension between differentiation and integration must be recognized and acknowledged in any complex social system. Exclusive focus on either assimilation or separation as the solution to intergroup discrimination and conflict is neither desirable nor realistic. Proponents of multiculturalism assert that alternatives to these extremes are possible, that groups can maintain distinct identities at the same time as their members participate in a shared, superordinate group structure. Berry (1984), for instance, has argued that there are four different forms of interethnic relations possible in a pluralistic society, depending on how members of the diverse ethnic groups relate to their own ethnic identity and to their role in the society at large. In Berry's classification system, integration is the form of intercultural relations in which identification with ethnic subgroups and identification with the larger society are both engaged. We believe that the reciprocal relations among processes of personalization, recategorization, and mutual differentiation discussed above are compatible with this view of social integration and constitute the necessary underpinnings for an equalitarian multicultural society.

REFERENCES

Allport, G. W. (1954). *The nature of prejudice.* Cambridge, MA: Addison-Wesley.

Amir, Y. (1969). Contact hypothesis in ethnic relations. *Psychological Bulletin, 71,* 319–342.

Amir, Y. (1976). The role of intergroup contact in change of prejudice and ethnic relations. In P. Katz (Ed.), *Towards the elimination of racism* (pp. 245–308). New York: Pergamon.

Aronson, E., Blaney, N., Stephan, C., Sikes, J., & Sanpp, M. (1978). *The jigsaw classroom.* London: Sage.

Bachman, B. A. (1993). *An intergroup model of organizational mergers.* Unpublished Ph.D. dissertation, University of Delaware, Newark, DE.

Banker, B. S., & Gaertner, S. L. (1998). Achieving stepfamily harmony: An intergroup relations approach. *Journal of Family Psycholgy, 12,* 310–325.

Batson, C. D., Polycarpou, M., Harmon-Jones, E., Imhoff, H., Mitchener, E., Bednar, L., Klein, T., & Highberger, L. (1997). Empathy and attitudes: Can feeling for a member of a stigmatized group improve feelings toward that group? *Journal of Personality and Social Psychology, 72,* 105–118.

Berry, J. W. (1984). Cultural relations in plural societies: Alternatives to segregation and their sociopsychological implications. In N. Miller & M. Brewer (Eds.), *Groups in contact: The psychology of desegregation* (pp. 11–27). New York: Academic Press.

Bettencourt, B. A., Brewer, M. B., Croak, M. R., & Miller, N. (1992). Cooperation and reduction of intergroup bias: The role of reward structure and social orientation. *Journal of Experimental Social Psychology, 28,* 301–319.

Bettencourt, B. A., & Dorr, N. (1998). Cooperative interaction and intergroup bias: Effects of numerical representation and crosscut role assignment. *Personality and Social Psychology Bulletin, 24,* 1276–1293.

Brewer, M. B. (1979). In-group bias in the minimal intergroup situation: A cognitive-motivational analysis. *Psychological Bulletin, 86,* 307–324.

Brewer, M. B. (1991). The social self: On being the same and different at the same time. *Personality and Social Psychology Bulletin, 17,* 475–482.

Brewer, M. B. (1999). The nature of prejudice: Ingroup love or outgroup hate? *Journal of Social Issues, 55,* 429–444.

Brewer, M. B. (2000a). Superordinate goals versus superordinate identity as bases of intergroup cooperation. In D. Capozza & R. Brown (Eds.), *Social identity processes* (pp. 117–132). New York: Sage.

Brewer, M. B. (2000b). Reducing prejudice through cross-categorization: Effects of multiple social identities. In S. Oskamp (Ed.), *Reducing prejudice and discrimination* (pp. 165–183). Mahwah, NJ: Erlbaum.

Brewer, M. B., & Miller, N. (1984). Beyond the contact hypothesis: Theoretical perspectives on desegregation. In N. Miller & M. Brewer (Eds.), *Groups in contact: The psychology of desegregation* (pp. 281–302). New York: Academic Press.

Brewer, M. B., & Miller, N. (1988). Contact and cooperation: When do they work? In P. Katz & D. Taylor (Eds.), *Eliminating racism: Means and controversies* (pp. 315–326). New York: Plenum.

Brewer, M. B., & Schneider, S. K. (1990). Social identity and social dilemmas: A double-edged sword. In D. Abrams & M. Hogg (Eds.), *Social identity theory: Constructive and critical advances* (pp. 169–184). London: Harvester Wheatsheaf.

Brown, R. J., & Turner, J. C. (1979). The criss-cross categorization effect in intergroup discrimination. *British Journal of Social and Clinical Psychology, 18*, 371–383.

Brown, R. J., Vivian, J., & Hewstone, M. (in press). Changing attitudes through intergroup contact: The effects of group membership salience. *European Journal of Social Psychology, 29*.

Brown, R. J., & Wade, G. (1987). Superordinate goals and intergroup behaviour: The effect of role ambiguity and status on intergroup attitudes and task performance. *European Journal of Social Psychology, 17*, 131–142.

Cohen, E. G. (1984). The desegregated school: Problems in status power and interethnic climate. In N. Miller & M. Brewer (Eds.), *Groups in contact: The psychology of desegregation* (pp. 77–96). New York: Academic Press.

Cook, S. W. (1962). The systematic analysis of socially significant events. *Journal of Social Issues, 18*, 66–84.

Cook, S. W. (1971). *The effect of unintended interracial contact upon racial interaction and attitude change.* (Final report, Project No. 5–1320). Washington, DC: U.S. Department of Health, Education, and Welfare, Office of Education.

Cook, S. W. (1978). Interpersonal and attitudinal outcomes in cooperating interracial groups. *Journal of Research and Development in Education, 12*, 97–113.

Cook, S. W. (1984). Cooperative interaction in multiethnic contexts. In N. Miller & M. Brewer (Eds.), *Groups in contact: The psychology of desegregation* (pp. 155–185). New York: Academic Press.

Cook, S. W. (1985). Experimenting on social issues: The case of school desegregation. *American Psychologist, 40*, 452–460.

Coser, L. A. (1956). *The functions of social conflict.* New York: Free Press.

Deschamps, J.-C., & Brown, R. J. (1983). Superordinate goals and intergoup conflict. *British Journal of Social Psychology, 22*, 189–195.

Deschamps, J.-C., & Doise, W. (1978). Crossed category memberships in intergroup relations. In H. Tajfel (Ed.), *Differentiation between social groups* (pp. 141–158). Cambridge, UK: Cambridge University Press.

Deutsch, M., & Collins, M. E. (1951). *Interracial housing: A psychological evaluation of a social experiment.* Minneapolis, MN: University of Minnesota Press.

Diehl, M. (1990). The minimal group paradigm: Theoretical explanations and empirical findings. In W. Stroebe & M. Hewstone (Eds.), *European review of social psychology* (Vol. 1, pp. 263–292). Chichester, UK: Wiley.

Doise, W. (1978). *Groups and individuals: Explanations in social psychology.* Cambridge, UK: Cambridge University Press.

Dovidio, J. F., Gaertner, S. L., & Validzic, A. (1998). Intergroup bias: Status differentiation and a common ingroup identity. *Journal of Personality and Social Psychology, 75*, 109–120.

Dovidio, J. F., Gaertner, S. L., Validzic, A., Matoka, K., Johnson, B., & Frazier, S. (1997). Extending the benefits of re-categorization: Evaluations, self-disclosure, and helping. *Journal of Experimental Social Psychology, 33*, 401–420.

Gaertner, S. L., & Dovidio, J. F. (2000). *Reducing intergroup bias: The common ingroup identity model.* Philadelphia: Psychology Press.

Gaertner, S. L., Dovidio, J. F., Anastasio, P. A., Bachman, B. A., & Rust, M. C. (1993). The common ingroup identity model: Recategorization and the reduction of intergroup bias. In W. Stroebe & M. Hewstone (Eds.), *European review of social psychology* (Vol. 4, pp. 1–26). London: Wiley.

Gaertner, S. L., Dovidio, J. F., & Bachman, B. A. (1996). Revisiting the contact hypothesis: The induction of a common ingroup identity. *International Journal of Intercultural Relations, 20*, 271–290.

Gaertner, S. L., Dovidio, J. F., Banker, B., Houlette, M. Johnson, K. M., & McGlynn, E. A. (2000). Reducing intergroup conflict: From superordinate goals to decategorization, recategorization, and mutual differentiation. *Group Dynamics, 4,* 98–114.

Gaertner, S. L., Dovidio, J. F., Banker, B., Rust, M. C., Nier, J., & Ward, C. M. (1997). Does pro-Whiteness necessarily mean anti-Blackness? In M. Fine, L. Powell, L. Weis, & M. Wong (Eds.), *Off White* (pp. 167–178). New York: Routledge.

Gaertner, S. L., Dovidio, J. F., Nier, J. A., Ward, C. M., & Banker, B. S. (1999). Across cultural divides: The value of a superordinate identity. In D. Prentice & D. Miller (Eds.), *Cultural divides: Understanding and overcoming group conflict* (pp. 173–212). New York: Russell Sage Foundation.

Gaertner, S. L., Dovidio, J. F., Rust, M. C., Nier, J. A., Banker, B., Ward, C. M., Mottola, G. R., & Houlette, M. (1999). Reducing intergroup bias: Elements of intergroup cooperation. *Journal of Personality and Social Psychology, 76,* 388–402.

Gaertner, S. L., Mann, J. A., Dovidio, J. F., Murrell, A. J., & Pomare, M. (1990). How does cooperation reduce intergroup bias? *Journal of Personality and Social Psychology, 59,* 692–704.

Gaertner, S. L., Mann, J. A., Murrell, A. J., & Dovidio, J. F. (1989). Reduction of intergroup bias: The benefits of recategorization. *Journal of Personality and Social Psychology, 57,* 239–249.

Gaertner, S. L., Rust, M. C., & Dovidio, J. F. (1997). *The value of a superordinate identity for reducing intergroup bias.* Unpublished manuscript, University of Delaware, Newark, DE.

Gaertner, S. L., Rust, M. C., Dovidio, J. F., Bachman, B. A., & Anastasio, A. (1994). The contact hypothesis: The role of a common ingroup identity on reducing intergroup bias. *Small Groups Research, 25,* 224–290.

Gerard, H. B., & Miller, N. (1975). *School desegregation: A long-term study.* New York: Plenum.

Greenland, K., & Brown, R. J. (1999). Categorization and intergroup anxiety in contact between British and Japanese nationals. *European Journal of Social Psychology, 29,* 503–521.

Gluckman, H. M. (1955). *Custom and conflict in Africa.* London: Blackwell.

Hamberger, J., & Hewstone, M. (1997). Inter-ethnic contact as a predictor of prejudice: Tests of a model in four West European nations. *British Journal of Social Psychology, 36,* 173–190.

Hewstone, M. (1996). Contact and categorization: Social psychology interventions to change intergroup relations. In C. N. Macrae, C. Stangor, & M. Hewstone (Eds.), *Stereotypes and stereotyping* (pp. 323–368). New York: Guilford Press.

Hewstone, M., & Brown, R. J. (1986). Contact is not enough: An intergroup perspective on the "contact hypothesis." In M. Hewstone & R. Brown (Eds.), *Contact and conflict in intergroup encounters* (pp. 1–44). Oxford, UK: Blackwell.

Hogg, M. A., & Abrams, D. (1993). Towards a single-process uncertainty-reduction model of social motivation in groups. In M. Hogg & D. Abrams (Eds.), *Group motivation: Social psychological perspectives* (pp. 173–190). London: Harvester Wheatsheaf.

Hornsey, M. J., & Hogg, M. A. (2000). Subgroup relations: A comparison of the mutual intergroup differentiation and common ingroup identity models of prejudice reduction. *Personality and Social Psychology Bulletin, 26,* 242–256.

Huo, Y., Smith, H., Tyler, T. R., & Lind, E. A. (1996). Superordinate identification, subgroup identification, and justice concerns: Is separatism the problem; is assimilation the answer? *Psychological Science, 7,* 40–45.

Insko, C. A., & Schopler, J. (1987). Categorization, competition, and collectivity. In C. Hendrick (Ed.), *Group processes. Review of personality and social psychology* (Vol. 8, pp. 213–251). Beverly Hills, CA: Sage.

Islam, M. R., & Hewstone, M. (1993). Dimensions of contact as predictors of intergroup anxiety, perceived outgroup variability, and outgroup attitude: An integrative account. *Personality and Social Psychology Bulletin, 19,* 700–710.

Johnson, D. W., & Johnson, R. T. (1975). *Learning together and alone.* Englewood Cliffs, NJ: Prentice-Hall.

Johnson, D. W., Johnson, R. T., & Maruyama, G. (1984). Goal interdependence and interpersonal attraction in heterogeneous classrooms: A meta-analysis. In N. Miller & M. Brewer (Eds.), *Groups in contact: The psychology of desegregation* (pp. 187–212). New York: Academic Press.

Lemaine, G. (1974). Social differentiation and social originality. *European Journal of Social Psychology, 4,* 17–52.

Marcus-Newhall, A., Miller, N., Holtz, R., & Brewer, M. B. (1993). Crosscutting category membership with role assignment: A means of reducing intergroup bias. *British Journal of Social Psychology, 32,* 125–146.

Miller, N., Brewer, M. B., & Edwards, K. (1985). Cooperative interaction in desegregated settings: A laboratory analogue. *Journal of Social Issues, 41*(3), 63–79.

Mottola, G. (1996). *The effects of relative group status on expectations of merger success.* Ph.D dissertation. University of Delaware. Newark, DE.

Mummendey, A., & Wenzel, M. (1999). Social discrimination and tolerance in intergroup relations: Reactions to intergroup differences. *Personality and Social Psychology Review, 3,* 158–175.

Pettigrew, T. F. (1971). *Racially separate or together?* New York: McGraw-Hill.

Pettigrew, T. E. (1997). Generalized intergroup contact effects on prejudice. *Personality and Social Psychology Bulletin, 23,* 173–185.

Pettigrew, T. E. (1998). Intergroup contact theory. *Annual Review of Psychology, 49,* 65–85.

Pettigrew, T. F., & Meertens, R. W. (1995). Subtle and blatant prejudice in Western Europe. *European Journal of Social Psychology, 25,* 57–75.

Rothbart, M., & John, O. P. (1985). Social categorization and behavioral episodes: A cognitive analysis of the effects of intergroup contact. *Journal of Social Issues, 41*(3), 81–104.

Rust, M. C. (1996). *Social identity and social categorization.* Unpublished doctoral dissertation. University of Delaware.

Sherif, M., Harvey, O. J., White, B. J., Hood, W. R., & Sherif, C. W. (1961). *Intergroup conflict and cooperation: The Robbers Cave experiment.* Norman, OK: University of Oklahoma Book Exchange.

Slavin, R. E. (1983). *Co-operative learning.* New York: Longman.

Smith, H. J., & Tyler, T. R. (1996). Justice and power: When will justice concerns encourage the advantaged to support policies which redistribute economic resources and the disadvantaged to willingly obey the law? *European Journal of Social Psychology, 26,* 171–200.

Stephan, W. G. (1986). The effects of school desegregation: An evaluation 30 years after *Brown.* In M. Saks & L. Saxe (Eds.), *Advances in applied social psychology* (Vol. 3, pp. 181–206). Hillside, NJ: Erlbaum.

Stephan, W. G. (1987). The contact hypothesis in intergroup relations. In C. Hendrick (Ed.), *Group processes and intergroup relations: Review of personality and social psychology* (Vol. 9, pp. 13–40). Beverly Hills, CA: Sage.

Stephan, W. G., & Stephan, C. W. (1984). The role of ignorance in intergroup relations. In N. Miller & M. Brewer (Eds.), *Groups in contact: The psychology of desegregation* (pp. 229–255). New York: Academic Press.

Stephan, W. G., & Stephan, C. W. (1985). Intergroup anxiety. *Journal of Social Issues, 41*(3), 157–175.

Tajfel, H. (1969). Cognitive aspects of prejudice. *Journal of Social Issues, 25,* 79–97.

Tajfel, H. (1978). Social categorization, social identity, and social comparison. In H. Tajfel (Ed.), *Differentiation between social groups* (pp. 61–76). London: Academic Press.

Tajfel, H., Billig, M., Bundy, R., & Flament, C. (1971). Social categorization and intergroup behaviour. *European Journal of Social Psychology, 1,* 149–178.

Turner, J. C. (1975). Social comparison and social identity: Some prospects for intergroup behaviour. *European Journal of Social Psychology*, 5, 5–34.

Turner, J. C. (1981). The experimental social psychology of intergroup behaviour. In J. Turner & H. Giles (Eds.), *Intergroup behaviour* (pp. 66–101). Oxford, UK: Blackwell.

Turner, J. C. (1985). Social categorization and the self-concept: A social cognitive theory of group behavior. In E. Lawler (Ed.), *Advances in group processes* (Vol. 2, pp. 77–122). Greenwich, CT: JAI Press.

Urban, L. M., & Miller, N. (1998). A theoretical analysis of crossed categorization effects: A metaanalysis. *Journal of Personality and Social Psychology*, 74, 894–908.

Vanbeselaere, N. (1991). The different effects of simple and crossed categorizations: A result of the category differentiation process or of differential category salience? In W. Stroebe & M. Hewstone (Eds.), *European review of social psychology* (Vol. 2, pp. 247–278). Chichester UN: Wiley.

Van Oudenhoven, J. P., Groenewoud, J. T., & Hewstone, M. (1996). Cooperation, ethnic salience, and generalization of interethnic attitudes. *European Journal of Social Psychology*, 26, 649–661.

Vanneman, R. D., & Pettigrew, T. F. (1972). Race and relative deprivation in the urban United States. *Race*, 13, 461–486.

Watson, G. (1947). *Action for unity.* New York: Harper.

Wilder, D. A. (1978). Reduction of intergroup discrimination through individuation of the outgroup. *Journal of Personality and Social Psychology*, 36, 1361–1374.

Wilder, D. A. (1984). Intergroup contact: The typical member and the exception to the rule. *Journal of Experimental Social Psychology*, 20, 177–194.

Wilder, D. A. (1986). Social categorization: Implications for creation and reduction of intergoup bias. In L. Berkowitz (Ed.), *Advances in experimental social psychology* (Vol. 19, pp. 291–355). New York: Academic Press.

Wilder, D. A., & Shapiro, P. N. (1989). Role of competition-induced anxiety in limiting the beneficial impact of positive behavior by an out-group member. *Journal of Personality and Social Psychology*, 56, 60–69.

Wilder, D. A., & Thompson, J. E. (1980). Intergroup contact with independent manipulations of in-group and out-group interaction. *Journal of Personality and Social Psychology*, 38, 589–603.

Williams, R. M., Jr. (1947). *The reduction of intergroup tensions.* New York: Social Science Research Council.

Wilner, D. M., Walkley, R. P., & Cook, S. W. (1955). *Human relations in interracial housing.* Minneapolis, MN: University of Minnesota Press.

Worchel, S., Andreoli, V., & Folger, R. (1977). Intergroup cooperation and intergroup attraction: The effect of previous interaction and outcome of combined effort. *Journal of Experimental Social Psychology*, 13, 131–140.

Wright, S. C., Aron, A., McLaughlin-Volpe, T., & Ropp, S. A. (1997). The extended contact effect: Knowledge of cross-group friendships and prejudice. *Journal of Personality and Social Psychology*, 73, 73–90.

Author Index

Subject Index